PERSPECTIVES ON RADIO AND TELEVISION

PERSPECTIVES ON RADIO AND TELEVISION

Telecommunication in the United States

Third Edition

F. LESLIE SMITH

University of Florida

HARPER & ROW, PUBLISHERS, New York
Grand Rapids, Philadelphia, St. Louis, San Francisco,
London, Singapore, Sydney, Tokyo

1817

Sponsoring Editor: Jane Kinney
Project Editor: David Nickol
Art Direction: Lucy Krikorian
Text Design: Edward Smith Design, Inc.
Cover Coordinator: Heather A. Ziegler
Cover Design: M'NO Production Services, Inc.
Photo Research: Mira Schachne
Production: Paula Roppolo

PERSPECTIVES ON RADIO AND TELEVISION: Telecommunication in the United States,
Third Edition

Library of Congress Cataloging-in-Publication Data
Smith, F. Leslie, 1939-
  Perspectives on radio and television : telecommunication in the
United States / F. Leslie Smith. -- 3rd ed.
    p. cm.
  ISBN 0-06-046301-5
  1. Broadcasting--United States. I. Title.
HE8689.8.S63 1990   89-26812
384.54'0973--dc20   CIP

90 91 92 93 9 8 7 6 5 4 3 2 1

For Cynthia Margaret Ann Canning Smith:
I, too, Red Barber; I, too.

CONTENTS

PART TWO

CREATIVE/INFORMATIONAL PERSPECTIVE   120

6   Production, Programs, and Performance   123

PART THREE

PHYSICAL PERSPECTIVE   232

PART FOUR

LEGAL/ETHICAL PERSPECTIVE   306

19 Local Outlets 424

20 Networks 456

PART SIX

COMPARATIVE PERSPECTIVE 492

PREFACE

The two previous editions of this book set forth these objectives— (1) to describe the field of radio-TV in the United States comprehensively, (2) in a manner the reader could grasp and enjoy, and (3) in a form the classroom teacher could use. Judging by your warm response, these were objectives successfully accomplished. My sincerest thanks to the critics, radio-TV executives, teachers, and students (especially the students!) who made the previous editions of *Perspectives* such a success; because of your kind endorsement, I have aimed this third edition at those same three goals.

THE FIRST GOAL: BREADTH

In working toward the first goal, I found that the scope of *Perspectives* must be broad. After all, "radio and television" is a field that covers subjects ranging from *A&P Gypsies* to Zworykin, Vladimir K., and encompasses areas as diverse as churn and charlatans, static and statistics. For the reader to get a complete picture of the field, it seemed to me that the book would have to include not only the usual material but also new information on subjects such as ethics, careers, and rivals to U.S. commercial radio and television.

THE SECOND GOAL: TO THE STUDENT

You will find *Perspectives* easy to understand at first reading—whether you are a beginning radio-TV major or a nonmajor elective student. Terms are defined as they occur in the narrative. In-text notes refer to sections that contain explanatory information. Boldface type indicates words and concepts that are especially important. And a short, selective list of books for further reading follows every chapter.

THE THIRD GOAL: TO THE INSTRUCTOR

Perspectives was written to adapt to *your* teaching situation. The book is divided into logical chapter divisions by subject matter, and you assign them in the order appropriate for your course and your students. Each chapter stands by itself. If you feel that the technical aspects should come first in the course, then teach it that way; make Chapters 10, 11, and 12 the initial reading assignments. Want to start with career opportunities? Put Chapter 21 first on your syllabus.

Perspectives is also an integrated whole and can be used straight through, as written.

Whether or not you are experienced in teaching the survey course, please read Chapter 1. That is where the rationale and plan of the book is laid out; it "sets up" the remaining 25 chapters.

ACKNOWLEDGMENTS

The following persons supplied information or illustrative material, without which the revision would be incomplete: Harrie Bos, Nederlandse Omroep Stichting; Ann K. Bowman, American Advertising Federation; James Conway, Independent Broadcasting

Authority; Claudia G. Copquin, UNIVISION; Paula Darte, National Public Radio; Jill Davidson, Cable Rep Advertising; Richard Dunn, BBC; Laurence Frerk, Nielsen Media Research; Richard Grefé, Corporation for Public Broadcasting; Robert D. Haslach, Royal Netherlands Embassy; Dewitt F. Helm, Jr., Association of National Advertisers; James R. Hood, United Press International; Mark Hopkinson, British Information Services; Al Hulsen, then of American Public Radio; J. Janku, International Radio and Television Organization; Dolores Jenkins, University of Florida library; B. K. Khurana, Doordarshan; Rick Lehner and James Morgese, WUFT; Karin Lindfors, Nordvision; Al Mangum, North Carolina News Network; Miriam Q. Murphy, Statistical Research, Inc.; Nan B. Myers, Arbitron Ratings Co.; Tommie Nichols, Turner Broadcasting System, Inc.; Keshav P. Pande, All India Radio; Renee Smith, Birch Radio; Michael Type, European Broadcasting Union; Priscilla West, Neuharth Reading Room, University of Florida; Robert N. Wold, Wold Communications; Karen Wolfstead and Jimmy Cromwell, WCJB. Other organizations that provided material include COMSAT, Electronic Media Rating Council, International Telecommunication Union, and National Cable Television Association.

The publisher, Harper & Row, deserves credit for taking a chance on the first edition and for marketing successfully both editions. Special thanks go to David Nickol, the first-rate project editor who got the manuscript into the form you now read.

Most academic authors do *not* thank their administrators. But then, many authors do not work under leadership that is enlightened, effective, and equitable. I do. And I deeply appreciate the encouragement and support of Paul Smeyak and Ralph Lowenstein, who head the Department of Telecommunication and the College of Journalism and Communications, respectively.

I took advantage of two of the college's support programs in revising this edition of *Perspectives*—the Professional Summer and the Research Summer. I spent the 1986 Professional Summer at WESH (TV), the NBC affiliate in Orlando/Daytona Beach. Special thanks go to two extra-special people—John Evans, who made the arrangements for Channel 2 to hire me, and Ken Smith, who supervised my working/learning experiences in the program department.

Two persons helped greatly in my application and award of the 1987 Research Summer. James L. Terhune, associate dean of the college, guided me through the intricacies of dealing with the university administration and fiscal policies. Mary Ann Ferguson, research director of the college, also encouraged me to apply, and she heads the college research committee that made the award.

Harper & Row submitted the manuscript to the following readers who provided helpful comments and suggestions: Susan Tyler Eastman, Indiana University, Bloomington; John Fraser, Long Island University; Val Limburg, Washington State University; Alfred Owens, Youngstown State University; and Susan Zahn, Cleveland State University. Bill F. Chamberlin, Joseph L. Brechner Eminent Scholar of Journalism here at Florida, provided significant help in revising Part Four, Legal/Ethical Perspective. He generously shared resources developed in working on *The Law of Public Communication*, the fine volume of which he is coauthor, and he critiqued the regulatory sections of *Perspectives*.

The individuals who teach the survey of telecommunication course here at the University of Florida use *Perspectives* as the required text. Kay Ford, David Ostroff, and John Wright have provided continuing and valuable feedback for improving the third edition. Dave, John, and Cindy Smith also made substantive contributions to the actual process of revision. Dave did much of the research and rewriting that strengthened and added new sections to the chapter on foreign national and international radio and television. John updated the chapters in Part Seven, as he had done for the second edition. Cindy Smith did research, proofread copy, and made suggestions for rewriting. Without her help and encouragement, you would not be holding this volume in your hand today. Finally, I thank my wonderful daughter Hallie, whose expenses at college made it absolutely necessary that I finish this revision and get it on the market.

KEEP THOSE CARDS AND LETTERS COMING . . .

I started requesting direct reader response in the first edition. The suggestions I received proved invaluable in revising and improving the text. Once again I would like to solicit comment from you, the reader—student, instructor, radio-TV employee or executive, interested member of the public. Contact me directly (BITNET: lessmith@uffsc) or through the publisher and describe what you like or do not like about the book, what you think is strong and weak about it, any errors you may find, what you had trouble understanding, and—most important—what you think could be done to improve future editions. This is a complete revision and, as you will see, I took previous comments and recommendations to heart.

F. Leslie Smith

CHAPTER 1

Preview

The first edition of this book, published in 1979, opened with the question, "Why study broadcasting?" The next few paragraphs then cited some of the broadcast trade's always impressive statistics—figures on audience, advertising expenditures, and influence—to demonstrate the necessity to study broadcasting. Today, the responses to that question are just as valid; in fact, the figures have grown even more impressive. The question itself, however, has had to be broadened.

1.1 CHANGES

Since 1979, we have experienced one of the most exciting periods in the short history of electronic media. As consumers of media, we have enjoyed a rapid expansion of options. For the first time ever, many can choose from a number of programming alternatives—not simply additional situation comedies, but true alternatives. As students of media, we have watched as the very structure of radio and television has begun to change. New technology and fresh thinking have challenged the "givens"—concepts that once seemed cast in bronze and sunk in cement, concepts as basic as broadcast stations, advertising support of programming, and public ownership of the airwaves.

Technology has ignited much of the change. By 1979, some new technology had already appeared; still, broadcast radio and television were the primary electronic media. Today, some of what were "new media" in 1979 have grown, expanded, and diversified—cable television, cable networks, pay cable, wireless cable, videocassette recorders, video games, corporate video, home computers. Others, not yet widely available, seem about to grow and expand—interactive cable, direct broadcast satellite, various forms of electronic text. Yet other technology has emerged *since* 1979—the low-power television service, *C*-band direct, high-definition television, digital audio and video, stereophonic television sound, video graphics generators and animators, the charge-coupled device (in effect, a tubeless video pickup tube), continuing developments in solid-state electronics, particularly miniaturization.

1.2 BROADCASTING

The movers and shakers seemed convinced; these new media would stay, spread, and compete. Naturally, they would compete at the expense of broadcasting, particularly the broadcast television networks.

Some early returns from the marketplace

indicated that such predictions were not all "blue sky." Cable networks captured some programming that would previously have run on the broadcast networks, particularly sports. By 1988, cable had spread to over 50 percent of U.S. television homes. VCR penetration had reached that level the year before. National advertisers invested increasing amounts in cable networks—a quarter-billion dollars by the mid-1980s—most of which would otherwise have been spent on the broadcast networks. In 1978, the total percentage of the television audience that all three commercial networks drew was 93. By 1990, it had dropped by more than 20 points. Advertising agency personnel projected that this trend would continue, and the percentages would bottom, according to some predictions, in the 50s. The broadcast trade no longer had a monopoly in radio and television.

Commercial broadcasting is not quite ready to lie down quietly and wait for the undertaker. It is still the dominant form of radio and television, and the broadcast trade is still viable. But other media, other delivery systems, other means of economic support challenge that dominance.

1.3 RADIO AND TELEVISION

Thus, the question "Why study broadcasting?" must be broadened—not because broadcasting is dead (far from it!) but because the field of radio and television has expanded. This expansion has taken us far beyond commercial network broadcasting, that which we had called "the norm" since 1930. As consumers and students of radio and television, we must study these new uses of radio and television, as well as the old. The more appropriate (and inclusive) question is, "Why study radio and television?"

Like the last edition of *Perspectives on Radio and Television*, this edition takes advantage of the generic terms in its title. Its framework for analysis is radio and television, of which broadcasting is but one use. On the other hand, because it is by far the most popular and widespread form of radio and television, broadcasting—particularly commercial broadcasting—receives the lengthiest, most detailed coverage.

Academics and others have adopted the term *telecommunication* to refer to this framework. Most devices and practices included under telecommunication are actually new or supplementary uses to which the technologies of radio and (particularly) television have been put. To consumers, TV is TV, and it does not matter where the programming comes from or how it is delivered. Even for media such as video games, computer software, and teletext, the display vehicle is often the screen of a TV receiver. So this volume retains "radio and television" in the main title and "telecommunication" in the subtitle.

And why study radio and television? In exploring the phrasing of that question, we have also answered it. The facts and figures cited above demonstrate that radio and television are a major factor in our lives, our society, and our economy. Their size, nature, pervasiveness, and ubiquity all indicate the necessity to study radio and television. The important question then is, "What are radio and television?" That is what we will answer in this book.

1.4 FORMAT

What are radio and television? The question is not only important but also complex, even for a book with 26 chapters and 600 pages. Thus, this question—What are radio and television?—has been broken down into a number of smaller questions.

How did radio and television come about?

What are the messages of radio and

television, and how are these messages formed?

How are the messages sent?

Within what kind of legal and ethical framework do radio and television operate?

How do they generate the revenues that allow them to exist?

What are some of the alternatives to the profit-driven, U.S. model of radio and television?

What relationships exist among radio and television, the individual, the group, and the society?

Each of these smaller questions represents a different way of looking at, or a different perspective on, radio and television.

This book is written to answer these questions, and thus the title, *Perspectives on Radio and Television.* Each of the seven main sections reflects a different perspective—historical, creative/informational, physical, legal/ethical, economic, comparative, and sociopsychological. Each perspective is further broken down into a number of different major topics, which are the chapters within each section. Especially important names, words, phrases, and other information are printed in **boldface** type. When you come across a new or unfamiliar word, you will find either an explanation in context or a reference to another section that contains the explanation.

You will find the writing style in the following pages informal, its function being primarily to describe and explain the concepts as completely and simply as possible. The subject of radio and television is intrinsically interesting; the aim of the writing is to let it emerge that way from the pages of this book.

FURTHER READING

These are some principal sources, although others exist. Your reference librarian can help you find various periodicals and books on specific media.

Bower, Robert. *The Changing Television Audience in America.* New York: Columbia UP, 1985. Compares the audience of 1980 with those of 1970 and 1960.

Broadcasting. Weekly. The single most important periodical for the trade aspects of broadcasting. It treats other uses of radio and television (such as cable), particularly as they relate to the broadcasting trade. Two companion publications were introduced in 1989: *Broadcasting Abroad* (monthly) and *Broadcasting Cable* (biweekly).

Broadcasting/Cablecasting Yearbook. Washington: Broadcasting, annual. From the publisher of *Broadcasting* magazine. This one-volume compilation contains much information about broadcasting and cable, including a short history and status report, important FCC rules, state-by-state listings of outlets with descriptions, and many other directories of various people and organizations involved in radio and television.

Cablevision. Weekly. Fulfills somewhat the same role for cable television and radio that *Broadcasting* does for broadcast television and radio.

Channels of Communication. Monthly. Commentary on various aspects of electronic media.

Meyrowitz, Joshua. *No Sense of Place: The Impact of Electronic Media on Social Behavior.* New York: Oxford UP, 1985. How TV has changed American culture.

The Roper Organization. *America's Watching: 30th Anniversary 1959–1989.* New York: TIO, 1989. Based on a survey; compares findings from past years.

Television Digest. Weekly. Summary of the week's developments in electronic mass and consumer media.

Television Factbook. Washington: Television Digest, annual. This two-volume compendium is similar to *Broadcasting Yearbook* but focuses on television and contains additional data.

Television/Radio Age. Weekly. Contains longer and more explanatory articles and has a somewhat longer-range view than some other weekly publications.

ONE

HISTORICAL PERSPECTIVE

To understand radio and television as they are today, we have to look back to see the chain of events that got us from Heinrich Hertz to Home Box Office, from Sarnoff to satellites. Our perspective in this section is historical, and the four chapters answer the question, "How did it all happen?"

In Chapter 2, we look at the technical and industrial origins of radio and television. We start before the middle of the nineteenth century and, as we travel forward in time, meet the devices and the companies on which modern electronic mass media were founded. In Chapter 3, beginning in 1929 we focus on the development of radio broadcasting. In Chapter 4, we pick up in 1942 and survey the history of television broadcasting. In Chapter 5, we begin in 1950 and trace the rise of cable and other radio-TV technologies.

CHAPTER 2

Origins of Radio and Television: From 1842

In the United States, the ends of mass marketing provide the economic rationale—the reason to exist—for profit-driven radio and television. Broadcasting, the oldest form of radio and television, provided the model for other electronic media. Cable, pay cable, and even home video represent outgrowths from and variations on the for-profit pattern established by advertising-supported broadcasting. For this reason, it is easy to forget that broadcasting was not originally developed to meet the needs of a consumer audience. No corporate marketing expert sat down one day to design the concept of broadcasting as an arm of marketing. The appropriate model for the initial development of broadcasting is not Athena, who sprang full grown from the head of Zeus, but Topsy, who just "grow'd."

At least, that was the case for *radio* broadcasting. *Television* broadcasting, on the other hand, was more the result of purposeful corporate planning. The mass-audience/mass-marketing aspect of broadcasting was already in place. Moneyed organizations saw television's potential to generate revenue and took on the task of its technological development.

In this chapter, we study the origins of commercial broadcasting. First, we look at radio and the beginning of the broadcasting trade. Then we look at television, nurtured and introduced primarily by that trade.

2.1 RADIO AND THE BROADCASTING TRADE

The prehistory and history of American commercial radio unfolded in at least seven stages: radiotelephonic communication, industrial firms with an interest in communications, broadcast stations, the audience, advertising as financial support, the networks, and comprehensive federal regulation. All developed over a period of time through trial and error, sometimes by sheer coincidence.

2.1.1 Stage 1: Radiotelephonic Communication

The first stage in the development of broadcasting was the achievement of **radiotelephony**—transmission and reception of sound via radio waves. Like broadcasting itself, radiotelephony is not one unique device, but rather the combination of a series of discoveries and inventions—electricity, telegraphy, telephony, and wireless telegraphy.

Scientific interest and research in **electricity** began in earnest during the Renaissance and reached its peak in the eighteenth and early nineteenth centuries. In the 1880s, **Thomas Edison** began to wire New York City, the first step in what would become the electrification of America.

The idea behind **telegraphy**—relaying messages from one point to another—had been around for centuries. The ancient Greeks employed beacon fires and torches to convey information over distances. Various forms of visual signaling devices had been used down through the years. But these were cumbersome, time-consuming, and subject to problems due to bad weather and human error. In the nineteenth century, several persons worked on a totally different idea—the development of an *electrical telegraph.* An American, **Samuel F. B. Morse,** was credited as first to succeed. Morse had worked on his electromagnetic telegraph system for more than a decade when he finally patented it in 1842. A simple device, the Morse telegraph used electrical wire with electromagnetically equipped clicking keys at both ends and two electrical signals: current on and current off. The length of these two signals was varied to produce either dot clicks or dash clicks, and combinations of these dots and dashes represented letters of the alphabet. Even today, this is called the Morse code.

Congress appropriated $30,000 for Morse to build an experimental electrical telegraph line between Washington, D.C., and Baltimore. In May 1844, the words "What hath God wrought!" were transmitted as the first message. The experiment was successful; a message had been sent over wire via electricity.

Thirty-two years later, electricity was used to send voice communication by wire. **Alexander Graham Bell** (Figure 2.1) filed a formal application to patent his telephone on March 7, 1876. Three days later, Bell operated his telephone successfully for the first time.

In the meantime, a group of scientific discoveries had begun that eventually led to **wireless telegraphy.** Beginning in 1864, **James Clerk Maxwell** wrote a series of theoretical papers showing that energy passed through space as waves traveling at the speed of light. He said that light waves were electromagnetic, but there were probably other electromagnetic waves, too, invisible because they differed in length from light waves. In other words, Clerk Maxwell predicted the existence of something that could not be seen, felt, heard, or smelled, something that we now call **radio waves.**

In 1887, the German scientist **Heinrich Hertz** demonstrated the existence of radio waves. He constructed a device (Figure 2.2) that included two coils or hoops of wire, one of which was an oscillator (a device that produced radio waves). He found that the oscillating coil excited electrical current in the other coil. When he moved the two coils farther and farther apart, the results were the same. This was the first transmission and reception of radio waves. Hertz had proved Clerk Maxwell correct. Others started experimenting with **Hertzian waves,** as they came to be called.

Scientists had predicted **wireless telegraphy** for years, and in the 1880s American and English scientists developed some crude devices to that end. Most, however, were based on electrical induction* and therefore were limited in range. Interestingly, no one

---

*When a conductor (a substance capable of carrying current, such as a copper wire) carries a voltage (current), a magnetic field is built up around it. A second conductor has a voltage induced in it when it is moved through this field. This process is known as "induction."

(a)   (b)

Figure 2.1 Invention of the telephone. (a) Bell's device, the 1876 liquid telephone. (b) Alexander Graham Bell in 1876, the year the telephone was invented. Sulfuric acid was used as part of the transmission apparatus; the receiver was a tuned reed. Supposedly, on the night of March 10, 1876, Bell spilled acid on his clothes and uttered the first articulate sentence ever spoken over an electric telephone, ''Mr. Watson, come here; I want you!'' (Photograph courtesy of AT&T Archives. Used by permission.)

had thought of using Hertzian waves to carry information. Transmission and reception of these waves remained a laboratory stunt, pure science. It took a nonscientist to bring all the elements together. **Guglielmo Marconi** (Figure 2.3), a young Italian, put together Hertz's oscillating coil, a Morse telegraph key, a coherer (a radio wave detection

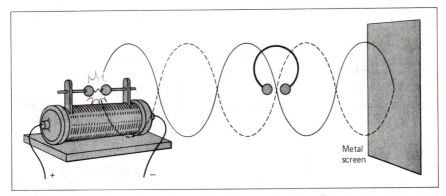

Figure 2.2 Hertz's device. The wires led to a power source. The power source caused electrical sparks to oscillate between two metal balls. These sparks sent out waves of high-frequency alternating current. The waves hit a metal screen that reflected them. When properly positioned between the spark gap and the metal screen, an open copper wire loop would spark in resonance with the metal balls.

Figure 2.3 Guglielmo Marconi.   Marconi and his apparatus for "telegraphy without wires" shortly after his arrival in England in 1896. (Photograph courtesy of GEC-Marconi. Used by permission.)

device), and grounded transmitting and receiving antennas of his own design. In 1895, at the age of 21, Marconi succeeded in sending a message over a distance of $1\frac{1}{4}$ miles using electricity *without wires.*

The final step, of course was to combine wireless transmission and reception with voice. **Reginald Fessenden,** an electrical engineering professor at the University of Pittsburgh, felt that a high-frequency generator was needed to transmit speech. He contracted with General Electric (GE) to have one built. GE shipped the great 50,000-cycle machine to Fessenden's wireless station at Brant Rock on the Massachusetts coast. Combining the generator with a telephone and his recently patented high-frequency arc, Fessenden made the first wireless voice transmission on Christmas Eve, 1906.

Momentous as Fessenden's achievement was, his *technology* was eclipsed just one week later. On December 31, 1906, another American scientist transmitted and received code via radio waves from one side of his laboratory to the other. The scientist was Dr. **Lee De Forest** (Figure 2.4), and his method of reception was based on his invention, the **Audion** (Figure 2.5)—the immediate forerunner of the triode vacuum tube and ancestor of the transistor and the "chip," the integrated circuit.

The Audion's origin dated from 1879, when Edison invented the electric light bulb. Four years later, Edison noted that when a metallic plate was put in a bulb along with the light filament, current flowed from the filament to the plate. No immediate practical application was seen for this "Edison effect,"

Figure 2.4 Lee De Forest. In 1922, De Forest became interested in film and produced a system for film sound called "Phonofilm." It had little success, primarily because the film trade felt it had no use for sound at the time. Ultimately, however, film sound succeeded because of a De Forest invention, the Audion. Here, De Forest holds an early vacuum tube used in a film camera, about 1926. (Photograph courtesy of AT&T Archives. Used by permission.)

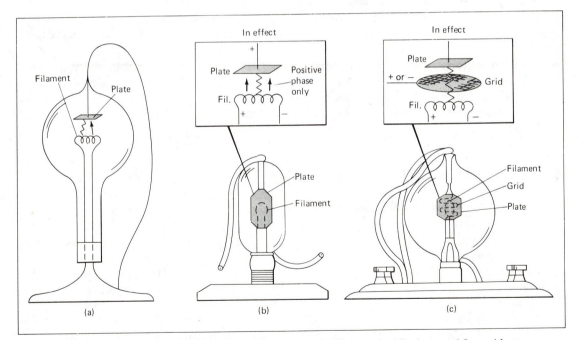

Figure 2.5 Development of the Audion. (a) In 1883, Edison noted that current flowed from the hot filament to a plate inside the bulb. (b) Fleming connected the plate to an antenna, and the incoming waves made the plate alternate rapidly from positive to negative. Thus it alternately attracted and repelled current from the filament and reproduced the incoming radio signals as DC current in the earphones. (c) De Forest introduced a grid between the plate and the filament. The weak current from the antenna went to the grid and controlled the higher voltage that passed from the filament to the plate.

although later James A. Fleming, a fellow worker of Marconi, used it to develop the two-element Fleming valve (tube) in improving wireless communication. What De Forest did was to insert in the bulb, between the filament and the plate, a third element, a tiny grid of fine wire. The grid carried a weak electric current. By varying the minute charge on the grid, he also varied the higher-voltage current that flowed through it from the filament, or negative element, to the plate, or positive element. In other words, the Audion could take a weak electric signal and magnify it. Put multiple Audions in tandem, and you got increased amplification.

The invention of the Audion launched the electronic age, the second industrial revolution. Thus the full implication of the Audion extends far beyond the realm of wireless transmission. But for our purposes, in one stroke De Forest had developed a device that would eventually perform all four **basic operations of radiotelephony—generation, modulation, detection, and amplification.** There would be further refinements in equipment and circuitry for transmission and reception, but all the basic devices necessary for broadcasting had now been developed.

2.1.2 Stage 2: Industrial Developments

Important not only as new technology, the devices and discoveries described above led to the formation of certain corporate entities. American Telephone and Telegraph, General Electric, Westinghouse Electric and Manufacturing Company, Marconi Telegraph Company of America, Radio Corporation of America—these were the companies that would play significant roles in the development of broadcasting.

In July 1877, Alexander Graham Bell and six close associates formed the Bell Telephone Company. By the turn of the century, the company had passed into other hands

and had purchased a manufacturing rival, Western Electric Company. In 1900, the telephone company changed its name to the **American Telephone and Telegraph Company** (AT&T).

In October 1878, Thomas A. Edison was well on his way to development of the incandescent light. He persuaded a syndicate of financiers to underwrite his research. They formed the Edison Electric Light Company. Edison later sold his interest, but from this beginning emerged the **General Electric Company** (GE). GE did wireless transmission research and development work for the United States and the Allies during World War I.

In 1869, George Westinghouse received the first of many patents on a railway air brake. His interests eventually led him to the problem of electrical power. In 1886, he founded the forerunner of the **Westinghouse Electric and Manufacturing Company,** which he left in 1911. The company retained his name and got involved in radio early in World War I, when it accepted a contract from the British government to do research in wireless transmission. After the United States entered the war, the Westinghouse Company manufactured wireless equipment for the armed forces.

Guglielmo Marconi offered the wireless telegraph to the government of his native Italy. Italy refused it, so in 1896 Marconi went to England and patented his device. In 1897, a company was formed to promote the Marconi wireless apparatus. Later, the **Marconi Wireless Telegraph Company of America** (also called **American Marconi**) was formed to further Marconi interests in the United States. The British Marconi firm owned a controlling interest in American Marconi.

2.1.2.1 Patent Problems After De Forest developed the Audion and tested its wireless transmission capabilities successfully in the laboratory, he formed the De Forest Radio Telephone Company. De Forest ran more tests over wider distances—he equipped a fleet of 24 U.S. Navy ships for a cruise around the world; he transmitted phonograph records of music from the Eiffel Tower in Paris that were heard all over Europe; and he transmitted performances from the stage of the Metropolitan Opera.

Meanwhile, AT&T had come to the conclusion that coast-to-coast long-distance telephone would not be possible without a "repeater"—telephone terminology for an amplifier. Repeaters used three-element tubes. Irving Langmuir, a GE scientist, had greatly improved the Audion by expelling all gases from the bulb, creating the **vacuum tube.** Harold D. Arnold of AT&T had also made improvements. However, De Forest's patent—the first to involve the third element—was essential.

De Forest was fighting a court battle. He had been arrested in 1912, charged with using the mails to defraud by selling stock in his company. He was acquitted in 1913. However, needing money, he had sold his patent rights on the Audion to AT&T for $50,000. With this patent, the telephone company was able to stretch its long-distance reach to the West Coast in 1914 and, soon after, overseas.

At this point, a number of different companies owned a number of different patents that collectively were vital to the further development of wireless transmission, but individually these companies were blocking that development. Almost any attempt to build or use equipment for commercial purposes infringed on several patents. For example, suppose a vacuum tube was used. The vacuum tube involved patents on devices and improvements developed by Fleming for Marconi; by De Forest, but now owned by AT&T; by Arnold for AT&T; by Langmuir for GE; and by others. The United Wireless Company, for a time the most ex-

tensive American company in wireless telegraphy, was caught in the patent bind. Found guilty in the courts of infringing on Marconi patents, United was so weakened that American Marconi was able to absorb United and thereby attain a monopoly on radio communications in the United States.

When the United States entered World War I, the government closed all civilian wireless stations and ordered that patents be pooled. This goverment-enforced **patent pool** allowed war contractors—including Westinghouse, GE, and AT&T's Western Electric—to manufacture tubes and circuits for military radios without regard to patent infringement. As a result, wireless equipment developed, improved, and became standardized. But when the war ended, so did the patent pool. No one company could manufacture and market the improved equipment because it would infringe on the patents of others.

The end of war contracts caused other problems. Westinghouse, for example, had made great progress in the development of wireless transmitters and receivers and had geared up for their production to supply military needs. Now there was no stable market for this equipment. GE had turned out expensive equipment such as the Alexanderson alternator.* Without government contracts, GE would be obliged to dismiss many skilled employees.

The end of World War I in 1918 left the U.S. government still in control of the nation's wireless communications facilities. The Alexander Bill, introduced in Congress in November, would have perpetuated a government monopoly of radio. The U.S. Navy favored the bill, but it was bitterly opposed

---

*Ernst F. W. Alexanderson, a Swedish emigrant and electrical engineer at GE, had worked with Fessenden on the development of the alternator and then later perfected it, "working along different lines from Fessenden" (Sterling and Kittross, 1978, p. 28; see chapter bibliography).

by civilian wireless interests and was voted down in committee, reaffirming the principle of private ownership of electronic communication facilities.*

2.1.2.2 Radio Corporation of America At about this time, British Marconi tried to buy exclusive rights to the Alexanderson alternator from GE. Supposedly, the firm's offer touched off two trains of thought in the administration of President Woodrow Wilson. First, if British Marconi possessed the alternator, Great Britain would be able to establish a worldwide monopoly in wireless communications. Second, national security demanded that no foreign-controlled corporation be permitted to dominate U.S. wireless communications. Therefore, two U.S. Navy officers visited GE and requested that the company not sell its alternator patents to British Marconi. It was also suggested that GE sponsor the establishment of a powerful American wireless communications organization.

Owen D. Young (Figure 2.6), general counsel of GE, proceeded to set up the new firm, **Radio Corporation of America** (RCA). American Marconi stock was purchased from the British firm, and, in November 1919 all the assets, patents, and goodwill of American Marconi were transferred to RCA. Individuals who held stock in American Marconi received shares of RCA. Young chaired the board of directors; Edward J. Nally of American Marconi became president.

The actual formation of RCA was only part of the plan. The major corporations holding patents on wireless devices entered into a series of agreements, with RCA serving as the enabling vehicle (Table 2.1). Some of these agreements involved cross-licensing

Figure 2.6 Owen D. Young. Young set up the Radio Corporation of America in 1919. (Photograph courtesy of General Electric Co. Used by permission.)

or patent pooling. GE, RCA, AT&T, and Western Electric pooled their various wireless patents. In return, GE and AT&T received stock in RCA. Later, Westinghouse acquired critical patents; these were put into the pool, and Westinghouse received RCA stock. The United Fruit Company* group, including the Wireless Specialty Apparatus Company and the Tropical Radio Telegraph Company, put their wireless assets in the pool, for which United Fruit received RCA stock.

These agreements were not limited to patents alone. Under the provisions of the agreements, GE and Westinghouse had exclusive rights to use the pooled patents to manufacture receivers, and RCA would sell large percentages of them. AT&T was to control all toll radiotelephonic communication, including exclusive rights to manufacture

---

*This was at least the second time the government had refused a monopoly on some form of electromagnetic communication. Morse wanted to sell the telegraph to the government, but Congress took no action on the matter.

*United Fruit Company used ships to get products from its Latin American plantations to its North American markets. The company used radio to direct the movements of these ships.

Table 2.1 OUTSTANDING OR AUTHORIZED STOCK OF RCA—SPRING 1921

Shareholders	Preferred stock		Common stock		Total stock	
	Shares	(%)	Shares	(%)	Shares	(%)
General Electric	620,800	15.7	2,364,826	41.3	2,985,626	30.8
Westinghouse and The International Radio Telegraph Company	1,000,000[a]	25.3	1,000,000	17.5	2,000,000	20.1
American Telephone & Telegraph Co.	500,000	12.7	500,000	8.7	1,000,000	10.3
United Fruit Company	200,000	5.1	200,000	3.5	400,000	4.1
Others	1,635,174	41.3	1,667,174	29.1	3,302,348	34.1
Totals	3,955,974	100.0[b]	5,732,000	100.0[b]	9,687,974	100.0[b]

[a]To be issued.
[b]Totals may not add up to exactly 100.0 percent because the figures are rounded out.
Source: Gleason L. Archer, *Big Business and Radio* (New York: American Historical Co., 1939), p. 8.

radio transmitters for sale or lease to others. Also, AT&T and Western Electric could now use the pooled patents in telephone equipment. GE and Westinghouse could make transmitters for themselves, but not for others.

This series of agreements linked the corporations into two groups—the **Telephone Group** (AT&T and Western Electric) and the **Radio Group** (all other parties). They had pooled their patents and divided the communications world among themselves. All eventualities had been foreseen and provided for—except one. It arose even as the agreements were being drawn up, and it rendered them all but worthless. It was called "broadcasting."

2.1.3 Stage 3: Stations

Frank Conrad (Figure 2.7) worked as a chief technician at the Westinghouse plant in East Pittsburgh. Conrad was also an amateur radio enthusiast and had a receiver and a transmitter licensed as **8XK** in the garage of his Wilkinsburg, Pennsylvania, home. In spring 1920, Conrad played phonograph records while transmitting. He soon received mail requests to play specific records at specific times.

Conrad tried to comply with the requests, but the mail became so heavy that he finally announced he would transmit music for two hours each Wednesday and Saturday evening at 7:30. His two sons added live vocal

(a)

(b)

Figure 2.7 Conrad and 8XK. (a) Frank Conrad in his laboratory a few years after KDKA went on the air. (b) Conrad's transmitter for 8XK. (Photographs courtesy of Westinghouse Electric Corp. Used by permission.)

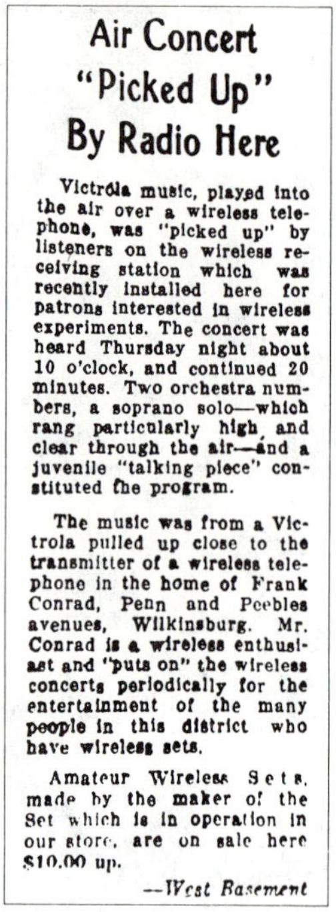

Air Concert "Picked Up" By Radio Here

Victrola music, played into the air over a wireless telephone, was "picked up" by listeners on the wireless receiving station which was recently installed here for patrons interested in wireless experiments. The concert was heard Thursday night about 10 o'clock, and continued 20 minutes. Two orchestra numbers, a soprano solo—which rang particularly high and clear through the air—and a juvenile "talking piece" constituted the program.

The music was from a Victrola pulled up close to the transmitter of a wireless telephone in the home of Frank Conrad, Penn and Peebles avenues, Wilkinsburg. Mr. Conrad is a wireless enthusiast and "puts on" the wireless concerts periodically for the entertainment of the many people in this district who have wireless sets.

Amateur Wireless Sets, made by the maker of the Set which is in operation in our store, are on sale here $10.00 up.

--*West Basement*

Figure 2.8 The inspiration for KDKA.

and instrumental talent. As the summer wore on, the Conrads began transmitting every evening, and the popularity of their concerts continued to grow. Several local newspaper articles mentioned the concerts. On September 29, 1920, the *Pittsburgh Sun* carried an advertisement for a local department store (Figure 2.8), noting that receiving sets for those who wished to listen to the Conrad radio concerts were available for purchase in the store's west basement.

This advertisement came to the attention of Harry P. Davis, a Westinghouse vice-president. The audience for Conrad's transmissions had been people who had the technical knowledge to put together their own receivers. But, reasoned Davis, the concerts would probably be popular with almost everyone if there were simple-to-operate receivers, complete in one suit. Westinghouse had developed and manufactured just such receivers during the war. The company could probably develop a civilian market for these re-

ceivers, concluded Davis, if it were to operate a radio station that would supply programs on a regular schedule announced in advance.

The next day Davis called in Conrad and a few others, told them his idea, and said he wanted a Westinghouse radio station ready for the November 2, 1920, presidential election. That was just 33 days away.

Conrad and his crew installed a transmitter in a shack on top of the East Pittsburgh Westinghouse plant. They strung a wire antenna between a steel pole on the roof and a nearby smokestack. The U.S. Department of Commerce licensed* the station to operate on 360 meters (833.3 kHz[†]) and awarded it the call letters **KDKA**. On the night of the election (Figure 2.9), returns were telephoned to the station from the offices of the *Pittsburgh Post*. A recruit from the plant's public information office read them over the air. Between returns, the microphone was pushed up to the horn of a hand-wound phonograph. Conrad was in his garage in Wilkinsburg, ready to assume transmission duties with 8XK in case of problems with the hastily installed KDKA transmitter. But KDKA stayed on the air. Warren G. Harding won the election over James M. Cox, and broadcasting was on its way.

2.1.4 Stage 4: Audience—Who Invented Broadcasting?

KDKA was not necessarily the first broadcasting station. KCBS, San Francisco (formerly KQW, San Jose, California); WHA, Madison, Wisconsin; WWJ, Detroit; and

---

*The Westinghouse transmitter was licensed as a "limited commercial station." This referred to its use by a private firm, not to permission to sell advertising time. Broadcast advertising would not develop until 1922. The Commerce Department did not license the Westinghouse operation as a broadcast station because there was no such category; the department started licensing broadcast stations as such in 1921.

[†]The letters *kHz* are an abbreviation for *kilohertz*, meaning a thousand cycles per second; *MHz*, for *megahertz*, means a million cycles per second.

Figure 2.9 KDKA and its opening-day staff. (Photograph courtesy of Westinghouse Electric Corp. Used by permission.)

probably others—all have some claim to being the first. However KDKA was assuredly *one* of the first. Its story typifies what happened elsewhere around the country— technically minded tinkerers built transmitters and found themselves programming on a regular basis.

To whom were they programming? Certainly, their audience consisted in part of others like themselves—people engaged in amateur radio transmission. But another type of **radio hobbyist** was also in the audience. This hobbyist, spiritual ancestor of today's shortwave listener, was interested in **reception**—how many stations could be received, from how far away they could be received, and how clearly they could be received.

For the most part, the "listen-in" hobbyists had to be content with receiving the conversations of others, usually in Morse code. Naturally, these early listeners responded enthusiastically when Conrad and others transmitted voice and music. The content seemed aimed at the listeners, elevating their status from eavesdroppers to audience. As mail came in from listeners, the pioneer radio

station operators responded by setting up regular schedules of transmissions, programming for a general audience. They evolved from radio station operators into radio broadcasters. It was at this point that radio ceased to be just point-to-point communication and *broadcasting* was born.

Who invented broadcasting? As much as anyone could be said to have "invented" it, the **audience** did.

As the months passed, the early stations experimented with program types. They broadcast the first play-by-play sports, the first radio dramas, the first religious services, and so on.

The number of broadcast stations increased. The Department of Commerce had issued 30 licenses by the end of 1920. In 1921 the department issued 28 more licenses. But in 1922 the rush began, and by the end of July, 430 more licenses were issued. On the other hand, a high percentage of these stations were short-lived. They had no means of self-support, and they often consisted primarily of junklike collections of wires and tubes.

2.1.5 Stage 5: Advertising—Who Invented Commercial Broadcasting?

The more successful stations improved their facilities. They increased transmitter power. They added studios—rooms for performers, separate from the transmitter. These studios usually had heavy drapes on ceilings and walls to cut down reverberation. They were sometimes furnished in the style of middle-class hotel lobbies or living rooms of the day, complete with potted palms, pianos, and bird cages.

Announcers and performers were often employees from other departments of the company that operated the station. The programs were primarily musical, with some recitations, some talks for children, and a sprinkling of "remotes" from church services, sports events, and ballrooms where dance bands played. Occasionally, a star from another medium, anxious to experience the novelty of broadcasting, would perform gratis before the microphone of a station. Much of the programming still came from phonograph records. Programs, as such, were rare.

But then the novelty began to wear off, and fewer people volunteered to perform. Some stations even paid performers. This created a problem. The stations cost money to operate but did not bring in direct revenue. They were serious financial drains on their owners—primarily radio manufacturers and dealers, newspapers, educational institutions, and department stores. Various methods were suggested to pay for broadcasting—wealthy individuals should endow stations; cities and states should operate stations out of tax revenues; a common fund should be established to receive contributions that would be distributed to the stations; receivers or tubes should be taxed or licensed. However, none of these was the answer.

In 1922, AT&T opened radio station

WEAF in New York based on a novel concept—**toll broadcasting.** AT&T saw WEAF's service as parallel to telephone service. The company would provide no programs, only facilities. Whoever wished to address a message to the radio audience would pay a toll or fee to use the station. It was to be a **telephone booth of the air.** Of course, the telephone company soon found that it had to provide programming on a **sustaining** (unsponsored) basis when there were no messages. A regular schedule of programming was needed to create and hold an audience if people were expected to pay tolls to broadcast messages.

On August 28, 1922, at 5:00 p.m., WEAF aired its first toll broadcast. A Mr. Blackwell spoke for ten minutes on the Queensboro Corporation's Hawthorne Court, a condominium in the Jackson Heights section of Long Island, New York. The toll was $50. The first commercial had been broadcast.

Shortly thereafter, WEAF did away with talks such as the one for Hawthorne Court. Radio came into people's homes, and the station felt the public would not accept the intrusion of direct advertising. Instead, the advertiser was allowed to buy or sponsor a program, elements of which would reflect that sponsorship. For example Browning King, Inc., sponsored a program but could not mention that the firm sold clothing. Instead, the program featured the "Browning King Orchestra" (Figure 2.10a), which was frequently mentioned.

Similar programs included the *Eveready Hour* (battery company), the *Cliquot Club Eskimos* (ginger ale) (Figure 2.10b), the *Ipana Troubadours* (toothpaste), the *Gold Dust Twins* (cleanser), the *Silvertown Cord Orchestra* and its "Silver Masked Tenor" (Goodrich tires) (Figure 2.10c), the *Lucky Strike Orchestra* (tobacco company), the *A&P Gypsies* (food store chain), and the *Happiness Boys* (candy store chain) (Figure 2.10d). Most were musical programs, primitive and corny by to-

(a)

(b)

(c)   (d)

Figure 2.10 Radio performers of the 1920s. (a) Browning King Orchestra. (b) Cliquot Club Eskimos. (c) Joseph M. White, the "Silver Masked Tenor." (d) Billy Jones and Ernie Hare, the Happiness Boys. (Used by permission of the National Broadcasting Co.)

day's standards. Nonetheless, they were significant: first, they were **programs,** individually presented units of the broadcast schedule, complete in themselves, and second, they were deemed **suitable for sponsoring** by advertisers.

The *Eveready Hour* was one of the best. The sponsor's advertising agency took an active hand in production. Scripted and rehearsed—rarities in those days—the *Eveready Hour* went on one of AT&T's ad hoc network hookups in 1924, making it one of the first successful network series.

As the 1920s wore on, direct advertising messages—commercials—crept back into programming, but with restrictions. For example, in 1923, WEAF decreed that a commercial must mention only sponsor and product and must avoid direct selling and mention of price. Although a few stations continued to refuse local advertising until the early 1930s, for the most part, radio was commercial by the end of the 1920s. In 1929, the first code of the National Association of Broadcasters contained provisions for the airing of advertising but banned it during the period 7 to 11 p.m.—business was for daylight hours only! Mass advertising had also grown into an institution during the 1920s, and, in the process, worries about intrusions into the home were forgotten.

2.1.6 Stage 6: Networks

Under the intraindustry cross-licensing agreements, AT&T had been granted all rights for toll radiotelephonic communication. In AT&T's opinion, toll broadcasting was just another form of toll radiotelephonic communication, and only AT&T-licensed stations could charge tolls or fees for announcements by advertisers. Committed to toll broadcasting, AT&T sold its stock in RCA and removed its directors from the RCA board in 1923.

Westinghouse had put WJZ on the air in 1921. Licensed to Newark, New Jersey, WJZ had studios in New York City. RCA bought WJZ in mid-1923 and made it the main rival of AT&T's WEAF. WJZ epitomized the broadcasting philosophy of the Radio Group—**operation of a station by one company** to stimulate sales. WEAF epitomized the philosophy of the Telephone Group—operation of a station as **a service paid for by many different companies** that wished to present messages designed to stimulate sales.

WJZ was prohibited from toll broadcasting by AT&T's interpretation of the cross-licensing agreements. Unable to sell advertising, it began to persuade other companies to share the cost of programming expenses in exchange for free time and publicity. Still, WJZ lost money. In addition, by having other companies underwrite programs, WJZ was giving away that which WEAF was trying to sell. Naturally, this upset AT&T.

2.1.6.1 The AT&T "Network" AT&T's master plan for toll broadcasting included live interconnection of stations. A small number of transmitters across the country would be leased to local corporations. These local stations could sell advertising and run local programs, but they would also be tied into AT&T's long lines for occasional live interconnection when an advertiser wished to reach a multicity audience.

AT&T ran the **first permanent network line** from New York to WMAF, South Dartmouth, Massachusetts, in June 1923. Stations had been linked previously for simultaneous broadcasts, but no permanent hookups had been made. The special line for WMAF ran through Providence, Rhode Island, so that by late summer, WJAR in Providence became the third station on the network. Network technology and programming improved. At the end of 1923, six stations were on the chain. By the end of 1924, the number was 26, and the AT&T network reached from coast to coast.

Denied use of AT&T telephone lines, General Electric and RCA attempted to put together a network fed by WJZ and connected by telegraph lines. Even though the telegraph wires were technically unsuited for broadcast-quality voice transmission, the WJZ network built up to some 14 stations by the end of 1925.

In line with the telephone company's plan for toll broadcasting, and in spite of many requests for transmitters, AT&T restricted sale and lease of their transmitters. But stations signed on the air with transmitters from other sources—building them, importing them, and so on. AT&T entered suit against one such station in 1924. The station settled out of court, and AT&T decided to license all stations that applied, regardless of the origins of their transmitters. An AT&T license would also allow a station to charge fees for use of its time. Hundreds of stations paid the license fees.

AT&T also wanted to market radio receivers. The Radio Group argued that this would violate the cross-licensing agreements. A referee appointed by the two sides to hear the dispute agreed with the Radio Group. Then AT&T produced an influential, convincing legal opinion that said the agreements were probably unlawful in the first place, a violation of the antitrust laws. It was time to renegotiate.

2.1.6.2 David Sarnoff and the National Broadcasting Company Owen Young, RCA board chairman, opened negotiations with AT&T. But key discussions involved RCA's vice-president and resident expert on broadcasting, David Sarnoff. Sarnoff, born in Czarist Russia, had emigrated to the United States in 1900 at age 9. At 15, he went to work for American Marconi; at 17 the company made him a wireless telegraphy operator. In 1912, at 21, Sarnoff made headlines

as the operator in contact with the sinking S.S. *Titanic*, not leaving his station for 72 hours. He began to rise in company ranks.

In 1916, Sarnoff wrote a memo to his superior suggesting the development of what he called a **radio music box,** describing in essence the system of broadcasting that would not develop for another five years. American Marconi seems to have ignored the idea. When RCA was formed, Sarnoff moved to the new company as commercial manager and renewed his radio music box idea, passing it on to Owen Young. The idea was almost ignored again, but by this time KDKA had made its debut, and RCA radio receivers began moving into stores. Sarnoff's star was ascending. He became RCA general manager in 1921.

In 1922, Sarnoff wrote a letter to an RCA board member, suggesting the formation of an RCA-controlled company to specialize in broadcasting. RCA took no immediate action, but once negotiations with AT&T were under way, his idea began to seem attractive. In January 1926, it was decided that a new company would be formed, owned by RCA, GE, and Westinghouse—a company that would specialize in broadcasting. Nine months later this company went into business as the **National Broadcasting Company** (NBC).

After intricate negotiation, representatives from the telephone and radio groups reached an agreement. AT&T would get out of broadcasting entirely. RCA would carry on all commercial networking activity, using AT&T long lines. AT&T and Western Electric would not market receivers. AT&T would not manufacture and market transmitters, but Western Electric and RCA could. AT&T sold its broadcasting activities, including WEAF, to RCA.

On September 9, 1926, NBC was formed, and shortly thereafter it voted to buy out RCA's broadcasting assets. The word "toll" was quietly dropped, but the idea of radio advertising as a means of support was retained.

NBC inaugurated network service on November 15, 1926 (Figure 2.11), with a $4\frac{1}{2}$-hour special program aired coast to coast on 25 stations. On January 1, 1927, NBC set up two separate national networks. The **red network,** derived primarily from the Telephone Group hookups, had 25 stations based on WEAF. The weaker **blue network,** derived from the Radio Group, had six stations based on WJZ. The colors, according to one story, came from the red and blue pencils used by engineers to draw in the stations and connections of the two networks on their maps. Also in 1927, NBC adopted a three-tone chime that became familiar to nearly every American as the network's audio identification signal. On December 23, 1928, NBC began regular coast-to-coast service with 58 affiliates. In 1943, NBC would have to sell one of its networks; it chose to divest the

blue network, which later became the **American Broadcasting Company** (ABC).

2.1.6.3 Columbia Broadcasting System Even before NBC had gotten well under way, a rival network was developing. **George A. Coats** and **Arthur Judson** formed the Judson Radio Program Corporation in September 1926 as an organization to provide programming for radio. They asked David Sarnoff for help, and when he refused, Judson swore that he and Coats would set up their own network. They formed the United Independent Broadcasters network in January 1927 and signed 12 stations as affiliates, beginning with WCAU, Philadelphia. However, they found that station compensation* and AT&T line charges would cost so much

---

*A network pays an affiliated station for carrying network programming containing advertising; this payment is compensation for the network's use of the station's time.

Figure 2.11 NBC goes on the air. NBC's chief engineer gives the signal to put on the air the network's first show, November 15, 1926. (Photograph courtesy of the National Broadcasting Company, Inc. Used by permission.)

that they would need greater financial resources. Judson and Coats convinced the Columbia Phonograph Company to invest in the venture. The network now became the Columbia Phonograph Broadcasting System.

On September 19, 1927, the Columbia Phonograph Broadcasting System aired its first program, *The King's Henchman,* performed by artists from the Metropolitan Opera. The Columbia Phonograph Company, losing heavily in the new network, withdrew from the venture. Oddly, the infant chain was allowed to keep "Columbia" in its name. Coats and Judson persuaded some Philadelphia residents to invest in the network. In the process the name was changed to the **Columbia Broadcasting System** (CBS). But the money continued to drain away with no sign of any return, and soon the new stockholders also wanted out.

Meanwhile, **William S. Paley,** who at age 27 was production and advertising director for his family's Congress Cigar Company in Philadelphia, had sponsored a program on the new network and had been impressed with the results. When he learned that CBS was for sale, he persuaded his family to join him in buying a controlling interest and took over the network in September 1928. Paley purchased a station in New York and brought Paramount Pictures in as a partner. The network lost over one-third million dollars in 1928 but showed a profit thereafter. Within a few years, CBS became a serious rival of NBC.

We have now seen the origins of three major networks—ABC, CBS, and NBC. While they had been developing, the whole legal structure of broadcasting was changing.

2.1.7 Stage 7: Regulation

Congress passed the **Wireless Ship Act** in 1910. This law required certain classes of ocean vessels to carry wireless apparatus and an operator. Two years later, as a direct result of the *Titanic* disaster, Congress passed the **Radio Act of 1912,** spelling out exactly how and why radio would be used on ships. It specified that the secretary of commerce and labor would assign wavelengths and issue licenses and that it was illegal to operate without a license. These laws all pertained, of course, to radio as *point-to-point* communication.

Then *broadcasting* was born. Unlike point-to-point stations, which operated only intermittently and for brief periods of time, broadcasting stations operated continuously, thereby enormously increasing the potential for interference. At first, the Commerce Department assigned all broadcasting stations to one wavelength. As the number of stations increased, a second channel was opened. But more and more broadcasting stations signed on.

The transmitters in use then were often unstable and drifted off assigned wavelengths. The result was **interference,** and the Commerce Department seemed unable to solve the problem. Some broadcasters took matters in their own hands. If station A's signal interfered with that of station B, B changed frequency, time of operation, power, or even location to overcome the interference, without consent of the Commerce Department. Inevitably, the result was that B now interfered with stations C, D, and E, which then proceeded to take the same action that B had taken. The result was interference raised to intolerable levels. Finally, the Commerce Department opened a whole band of wavelengths, 545 to 299 meters (550 to 1500 kHz), the basis of today's AM radio band.

Despite the increased number of wavelengths, interference problems continued. Both the public and the broadcasters complained. Commerce Secretary **Herbert Hoover** (Figure 2.12) called four **radio conferences,** one each in 1922, 1923, 1924, and 1925, attended by leaders of the radio industry. Conferees recommended that Congress

Figure 2.12 Herbert Hoover. In 1926, Commerce Secretary Hoover found that the Radio Act of 1912 did not grant him the legal power to regulate broadcasting. The next year, the comprehensive Radio Act was passed, and Hoover took part in the first public demonstration of intercity (Washington, D.C., to New York) television. The box at the extreme left was the camera; a telephone provided the sound. (Photograph courtesy of AT&T Archives. Used by permission.)

pass legislation to regulate broadcasting and that Hoover take interim action to straighten out the problems. But Congress would not act, and Hoover found that he could not act.

The Radio Act of 1912, enacted some eight years before KDKA signed on the air, had been written with no provision for discretionary action to enforce it. In a series of legal decisions—*Hoover* v. *Intercity Radio Co.* (1923),[1] *United States* v. *Zenith Radio* (1926),[2] and an Attorney General's Opinion in 1926[3]—the Commerce secretary found that under existing law he *had* to issue a license when application was made, he *had* to assign a frequency to a station, and he could make *no* regulations or restrictions on the operation of broadcast stations. In other words, Hoover had no power to straighten out the mess.

To complicate matters further, there were

characters and charlatans on radio. "Doctor" John Brinkley used KFKB, Milford, Kansas, to peddle patent medicines and to advertise his sexual rejuvenation operations. Norman Baker used KTNT, Muscatine, Iowa, to attack what he called the "radio trust" (network broadcasting) and later to advertise a cancer clinic. Reverend Robert "Fighting Bob" Shuler used KGEF, Los Angeles, California, to muckrake and battle corruption in Los Angeles officialdom. Evangelist Aimee Semple McPherson used KSFG, also Los Angeles, to propagate her brand of the gospel. Her station constantly deviated from its assigned frequency, causing interference. When Commerce Secretary Hoover ordered an inspector to close down KFSG, she wired Hoover to call off his "minions of Satan" because he should not "expect the Almighty to abide by your wavelength nonsense." She said she had to "fit into His wave reception" when she prayed. There were other such broadcasters.

With the Radio Act of 1912 useless for broadcast regulation and with the public clamoring over the interference problem, Congress finally acted. It passed the **Radio Act of 1927,** creating a five-member **Federal Radio Commission** (FRC) and giving it appropriate discretionary powers to carry out its duties. The FRC was to regulate all radio, including point-to-point, but a large part of its time was spent straightening out broadcasting. The FRC first got the interference under control and then turned its attention to programming—the Brinkleys, the Shulers, and all the rest.

Seven years later, Congress passed the **Communications Act of 1934.** This superseded the 1927 law but included most of the same provisions. The Communications Act increased the commission to seven members (reduced again to five in 1983), renamed it the **Federal Communications Commission** (FCC), and gave it interstate wire communication to regulate, along with radio.

2.1.8 Radio on the Verge

In just eight years, broadcasting had begun and had passed successfully though a critical formative stage. What was the status of broadcasting in 1928? How close had it come to what we now call "American commercial broadcasting"?

Mass communication scholar John W. Spalding asserts that radio had met all the requirements to serve national advertisers by 1928. Development of networks and regulation and reception meant that broadcasts could be transmitted dependably and received in the home with reasonable fidelity. The first comprehensive audience research on radio was being completed; it would show that radio had an audience of consid-

erable size. Radio had accepted advertising as a means of underwriting program production. And radio had started dividing its time into *programs*—programs that were not yet in the formats that would eventually become popular in radio and would be passed on to television, but nonetheless programs that advertisers would sponsor.

The foundations of the broadcasting trade were laid; radio was about to start building. We pick up its story, beginning in 1929, in Chapter 3. But what about television?

2.2 TELEVISION

The crucial technical process on which modern television is founded is **scansion.** Scansion is the systematic and continuous translation of minute parts of an image into specific electrical charges suitable for transmission and retranslation into a series of pictures that gives the illusion of motion. In 1884, **Paul Nipkow,** a German, developed a device that would scan a picture (Box 2.1).

Nipkow's **scanning disk** set off a whole line of research based on **mechanical scansion**—television systems that required spinning discs. Among the researchers were E. E. Fournier, C. F. Jenkins, and John Baird. Fournier, a French scientist, experimented in the early 1900s. Jenkins, an American, transmitted motion pictures via radio waves in June 1925. In England, Baird demonstrated the first true live television picture on January 26, 1926 (Box 2.2). Jenkins and Baird began broadcasting in 1929. The British Broadcasting Corporation (BBC) took over Baird's transmissions three years later and began regularly scheduled telecasts in 1936.

But the future of television lay in **electronic scansion,** not mechanical scansion. Dr. **Vladimir K. Zworykin** (Figure 2.13), a Russian-born American, was a research scientist for Westinghouse in Pittsburgh. In 1923, Zworykin demonstrated a crude but

Box 2.1 The Nipkow Scanning Disk

The Nipkow pickup device (''camera'') consisted of a flat spinning disc (a) with a ring of small holes at increasing distances from the edge. When the disc was spun, each hole allowed, in its turn, a separate bit of picture information—light reflected from a part of the physical scene being scanned—to reach a phototube. This phototube generated a current that varied with the amount of light falling on it. Thus each bit of picture information was translated by the element into a specific electrical charge. These charges could be fed by wire to another scanning disc (b) that acted as a viewer. The electrical charges illuminated the viewer glow lamp or discharge lamp and the viewer disc spun in synchronization with that of the pickup device. Someone facing the viewer scanning disc at eye level with the glow lamp would then see a rough image of the scene being scanned. The photograph (c) shows an early research apparatus based on the scanning disc. The viewing disc is at the right; the pickup at the left. (Photograph courtesy of AT&T Archives. Used by permission.)

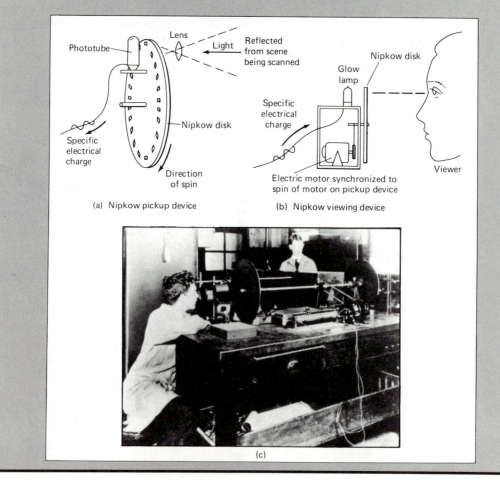

(a) Nipkow pickup device

(b) Nipkow viewing device

(c)

Box 2.2 John Baird's Television System

The strange-looking device with the bicycle chain (a) is the 1926 version of Baird's receiving apparatus. Baird developed an intermediate film scanner television process (b). A film camera shot the scene. The film was not wound on a spool in the camera. Instead, it moved out of the camera immediately and directly into a film processor. As soon as it was developed, the film exited the processor and went into a video pickup—the primitive equivalent of today's telecine unit (Section 12.2.5). (*Source:* Sydney A. Moseley and H. J. Barton Chapple, *Television To-day and To-morrow* (*sic*). New York: Pitman, 1940.)

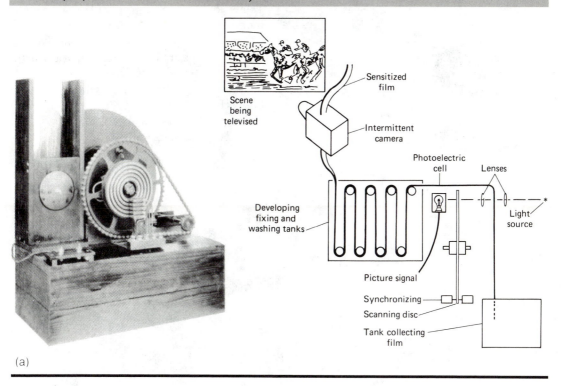

(a)

working all-electronic television system based on a camera tube that he named the **iconoscope.** Three years later, he developed a television receiver using a form of cathode ray tube that he called a **kinescope.**

Television was still technically primitive by today's standards. The resolution (amount of picture information) was only 30 horizontal lines, compared with today's 525 lines. The picture was not sharp (Figure 2.14). In 1930, the television research activities of Westinghouse, GE, and RCA were consolidated in **RCA's Electronic Research Laboratory,** Camden, New Jersey. This brought Zworykin together with some 40 other engineers. Work proceeded at a quick pace on the iconoscope, the cathode ray receiver, resolution, and other problems of electronic television. In 1936, RCA signed on experimental television station W2XF, New

Figure 2.13 Dr. Vladimir K. Zworykin. Dr. Zworykin holds an early model of his iconoscope. (Photograph courtesy of RCA Corp. Used by permission of General Electric Co.)

York, and continued developmental work. By 1939, RCA achieved a 441-line resolution, and in that year the company inaugurated a limited but regular schedule of programming, including a live telecast of President Franklin D. Roosevelt opening the New York World's Fair.

Meanwhile, others had been active in television development—AT&T, CBS, Allen B. DuMont Laboratories, and Philco Radio and Television Corporation. By 1937, 17 experimental television stations were operating.

One individual who played a major role in television research was **Philo Farnsworth.** He had outlined a system of all-electronic television as early as 1922, when he was a high school student, had filed a patent application for his system in 1927, had demonstrated a working model of his **image-**

Figure 2.14 1928 Television picture. In 1928, RCA-NBC cameras ran experimental transmissions in mid-Manhattan, including this 60-line version of Felix the Cat. (Photograph courtesy of RCA Corp. Used by permission of General Electric Co.)

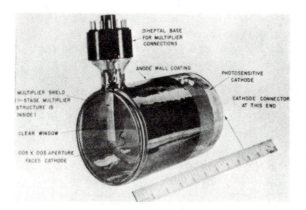

Figure 2.15 Farnsworth's all-electronic television system. This diagram shows an image dissector. (*Source:* William C. Eddy, *Television: The Eyes of Tomorrow.* New York: Prentice, 1945. Used by permission.)

dissector camera (Figure 2.15) to financial backers in 1928, and by 1932 had built up a strong patent structure in electronic television. Farnsworth did so much important basic research in the field that he was able to force RCA to break its tradition of never paying royalties. After Farnsworth refused to sell his patents outright, RCA, in 1939, entered into a licensing agreement for their use.

The development of television transmission standards was a controversial issue. In 1938, the Radio Manufacturers Association (RMA) recommended a set of standards to the FCC. The FCC soon found that the broadcasting trade was really divided on the matter. In 1940, the FCC cooperated with the RMA to form the **National Television System Committee** (NTSC) composed of engineers from across the industry. The NTSC drew up standards for television, and the FCC adopted them in April 1941.

The NTSC standards called for 18 channels located between 50 and 295 MHz in the very high frequency (VHF) band. Five years later the commission reduced the number of channels to 13, and then reduced the number to 12 in 1948 by deleting channel 1. Except for the number of channels, those 1941 standards are still in force: each channel 6 MHz wide, amplitude modulation of video and frequency modulation of audio, 525 horizon-

tal lines of resolution, and 30 frames (complete pictures) per second. In 1945, the FCC adopted its first table of assignments, distributing television channels among 140 cities for a total of 500 stations.

With the adoption of the NTSC standards in 1941, television was ready to be discovered by the public. We now leave television temporarily, but we shall resume its story in Chapter 4, beginning in 1941. Now, let us check radio's progress.

NOTES

1. 286 F. 1003 (1923).
2. 12 F.2d 614 (1926).
3. 35 Ops. Att'y Gen. 126 (1926).

FURTHER READING

Abramson, Albert. *The History of Television, 1880 to 1941.* Jefferson: McFarland, 1987. Focuses on technology.

Aitken, Hugh G. H. *The Continuous Wave: Technology and American Radio 1900–1932.* Princeton: Princeton UP, 1985.

Banning, William P. *Commercial Broadcast Pioneer: The WEAF Experiment 1922–1926.* Cambridge: Harvard UP, 1946.

Barnouw, Erik. *A Tower in Babel.* New York: Oxford UP, 1966. First of three-volume *A History of Broadcasting in the United States.*

Baudino, Joseph E., and John M. Kittross. "Broadcasting's Oldest Station: An Examination of Four Claimants." *Journal of Broadcasting* 21 (1977): 61–83. KDKA wins.

Bilby, Kenneth. *The General: David Sarnoff and the Rise of the Communications Industry.* New York: Harper, 1986.

Carson, Gerald. *The Roguish World of Dr. Brinkley.* New York: Holt, 1960.

De Forest, Lee. *Father of Radio: The Autobiography of Lee De Forest.* Chicago: Wilcox, 1950.

Douglas, Susan J. *Inventing American Broadcasting: 1899–1922.* Baltimore: Johns Hopkins UP, 1987.

Everson, George. *The Story of Television: The Life of Philo T. Farnsworth.* New York: Norton, 1949. New York: Arno, 1974.

Fessenden, Helen. *Fessenden: Builder of Tomorrow.* New York: Coward, 1940. New York: Arno, 1974. The author was Reginald's wife.

Hoffer, Thomas W. "TNT Baker: Radio Quack." *American Broadcasting: A Source Book on the History of Radio and Television.* Edited by Lawrence W. Lichty and Malachi C. Topping. New York: Hastings, 1975. 568–78.

Jolly, W. P. *Marconi.* New York: Stein, 1972.

Maclaurin, W. Rupert. *Invention and Innovation in the Radio Industry.* New York: Macmillan, 1949. New York: Arno, 1971. Industrial and technological development of broadcasting.

Orbison, Charley. "'Fighting Bob' Shuler: Early Radio Crusader." *Journal of Broadcasting* 21 (1977): 460–72.

Spalding, John W. "1928: Radio Becomes a Mass Advertising Medium." *Journal of Broadcasting* 8 (1964): 31–44.

Sterling, Christopher H., and John M. Kittross. *Stay Tuned: A Concise History of American Broadcasting.* Belmont: Wadsworth, 1978.

CHAPTER 3

Radio: From 1929

By 1929, radio and the broadcasting trade were ready to grow. And grow they did. Radio *was* the broadcasting trade until the 1950s. During that decade, television spread and grew into the dominant glamour medium. Radio, in turn, underwent a radical and sometimes painful transition. In the 1960s, FM radio emerged as a competitive medium. Throughout the 1970s, unused FM frequencies were activated, more AM stations signed on the air, and in the 1980s, competition intensified. This, then, is the story of radio.

3.1 GROWTH AND DOMINANCE

During the great economic depression of the 1930s, many businesses suffered, lost money, and even dissolved. One exception was broadcasting. Although profits dropped and a few stations gave up licenses, generally speaking, broadcasting emerged from the 1930s strong and stable. The 1940s were pure profit, up to a point.

3.1.1 Audience

In 1925, only 10 percent of U.S. homes had radio receivers. Still, radio was leaving the hobby stage (Figure 3.1). Radio receivers were undergoing changes for the better—manufactured sets were available for those who did not wish to build their own, loudspeakers replaced earphones, superheterodyne circuitry improved the audio signal, and alternating-current (AC) operation made it possible to plug in to home electric outlets and eliminate messy, short-lived batteries. Just five years later, 46 percent of all homes had radios.

The stock market crashed in 1929, and the economic depression set in. Most families had little money, and what they had went for food, clothing, and shelter. But radio, after an initial investment for the receiver, brought hours of entertainment at little cost. People saved pennies to buy radios and keep them in good repair.

Receiver prices dropped (Figure 3.2). Production of radios fell in 1930, 1931, and 1932. In 1933, sales increased, especially sales of small, inexpensive table models. By 1935, radio penetration reached 67 percent. People also began to put radios in their cars.

As the economy recovered, ominous events took place in Europe, events that would lead to World War II. Radio reported these events, often with on-the-spot coverage. The public listened to and relied on radio for the latest news, and the percentage of radio-equipped homes continued to climb.

(a)   (b)

Figure 3.1 Development of RCA radio receivers.   (a) Radios in the early 1920s, such as this one-tube Aeriola Senior, were usually powered by messy wet-cell batteries that leaked acid and required earphones. (b) By the late 1930s, radio receivers were quite sophisticated. This RCA Model 813-K received both broadcast and shortwave bands, had an easy-to-tune dial plus eight push buttons, featured a "magic eye" to help with precision tuning, and pumped 20 watts of amplifier power through a 12-inch speaker. RCA even offered remote control as an option for the Model 813-K! (Photographs courtesy of RCA Corp. Used by permission of General Electric Co.)

War production priorities halted manufacture of civilian radios, but after the war, the public went on a buying spree. By 1950, 95 percent of all homes in the United States had at least one working radio receiver.

3.1.2 Stations

At first the U.S. Department of Commerce had managed to keep the number of broadcast stations down (Figure 3.3). In 1926, the department found it had almost no power to regulate broadcasting (Section 2.1.7), and the number of stations rose from 528 to 733, an increase of 39 percent in one year. The Federal Radio Commission (FRC) took over, and the number of stations dropped to 618 in 1929, showing a slight decline during the depths of the economic depression. After 1934 the number grew steadily, leveled off somewhat during World War II, and reached 956 by the end of 1945.

Stations grew in other ways (Box 3.1). Most increased transmitter power and coverage. WLW, Cincinnati, received special authorization from the Federal Communications Commission (FCC) to use "superpower"—500,000 watts—during the period 1934–1939. The number of stations having

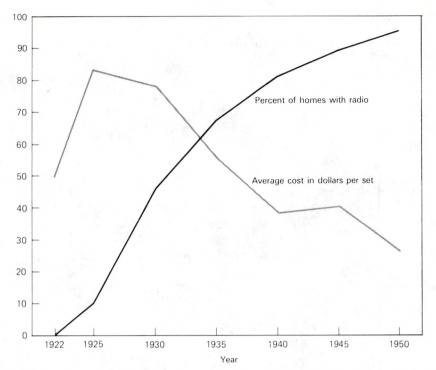

Figure 3.2 Radio set penetration and cost per set: 1922–1950. Generally, as prices dropped, more and more people bought radios. (*Sources:* U.S. Department of Commerce and *Broadcasting Yearbook 1977*. Washington: Broadcasting, 1977.).

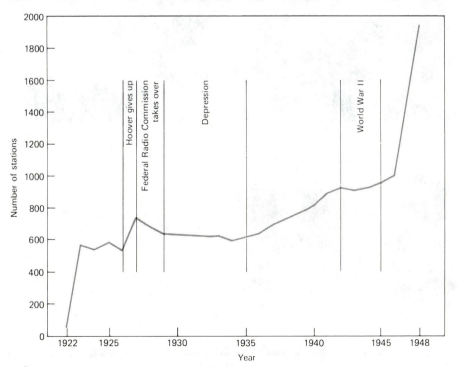

Figure 3.3 Total AM stations authorized: 1922–1948. (*Sources:* Federal Radio Commission, Federal Communications Commission, U.S. Department of Commerce.)

Box 3.1 From Shack to Tent to "Live Wall"

When KDKA started, the shack on the right (a), on the roof of the East Pittsburgh Westinghouse plant, housed the entire station. Photograph (b) shows the interior. After about six months, the station decided to broadcast large musical groups. The first band and orchestra programs originated from the plant auditorium, but its acoustics were more than the primitive microphones of the day could handle. So the station pitched the tent seen here and originated its musical programs from the tent. Since there were no walls or other hard surfaces off which the sound could bounce, music broadcasts had more clarity. In the fall, a wind blew the tent down. The tent had worked so well, that when the station built its first permanent studio, its walls were draped with hangings (b); in effect, a tent inside the studio! As years passed, both microphones and studio design became more sophisticated. By the late 1930s, many studios had a "live wall"—one without acoustical deadening (c)— in order to enhance the sound of programming. (Photographs a and b used by permission of the National Broadcasting Company, Inc. Photograph c from John S. Carlile, *Production and Direction of Radio Programs.* New York: Prentice-Hall, 1939.)

(a)

(b)

(c)

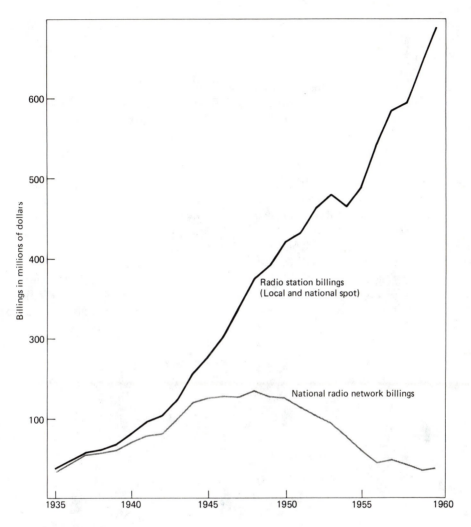

Figure 3.4 Radio station and network gross advertising revenues: 1935–1960. Both station and network revenues grew at a healthy rate until 1945. At that point, network billings leveled off, and in 1949 they began a long decline. Station revenues continued to climb except for one dip in 1954. (*Source:* Federal Communications Commission.)

to share time on a single frequency decreased.

Broadcasting started to earn money during the 1930s (Figure 3.4). By the end of the 1920s, nine out of ten stations sold commercial time; most did not make enough to meet expenses. Then radio listenership shot up. More advertisers put more money into the new medium. From 1935 to 1940, radio advertising billings jumped 96 percent. While half was in network advertising, local and national spot advertising (national advertising placed with individual stations) accounted for increasing shares. Still, about one-third of all stations operated at a loss.

Then came World War II. Raw materials

and assembly lines were diverted to the war effort. Many manufacturers ceased production of consumer goods and had little or nothing to sell to the public. They did have defense contracts, did earn profits, and did have plans to return to the manufacture and marketing of consumer goods after the war. The federal excess profits tax took a huge bite out of corporate earnings, but the tax could be reduced by deducting for legitimate business expenditures, such as advertising. Institutional advertising would keep the names of these companies before the public. The war caused a shortage of paper, so the amount of advertising these companies could place in newspapers and magazines was limited. They turned to broadcasting. From 1940 through 1945, radio advertising billings increased by 99.4 percent. At the same time, the number of stations increased by only 17.4 percent. A few more stations shared a lot more money, and over 95 percent earned a profit.

3.1.3 Networks

The networks took a large share of this prosperity. They earned profits even during the economic depression, dipping to their lowest point in 1933 but recovering well thereafter. The National Broadcasting Company (NBC) had a slight head start on the Columbia Broadcasting System (CBS), had two networks (which meant two affiliates in many cities), and enjoyed the corporate backing of the Radio Corporation of America (RCA). NBC got the largest audiences, the best programs, and the established performers. Yet the shrewd management of **William Paley** (Figure 3.5), CBS president and majority stockholder, usually earned CBS a healthy profit too.

Figure 3.5 Opening of the CBS building, 1929. The young network's young president, Bill Paley, is in the center, to the right of the man holding the hat. (Photograph courtesy of CBS. Used by permission.)

Paley developed the **network option.** An **affiliate** (a station that contracted to carry the network's programs) could carry any or all network sustaining (unsponsored) programs free (NBC charged for sustaining programs), in return for which the affiliate gave CBS an option on (advance permission to use) all nonnetwork time during its broadcast day. When a new sponsored program series started, CBS could order the affiliate to **clear** time for it—that is, cancel local programming and broadcast the network series. The network paid the affiliate to carry the series. Under the option plan, written into each affiliation contract between network and station, the station received revenue and programming with no effort, while the network could guarantee station clearance to an advertiser.

With the option in place, CBS added affiliates. From 16 in 1927, CBS went to 112 in 1940, versus 53 for NBC Red and 60 for NBC Blue. In 1935, NBC adopted its own version of the option.

Paley made another shrewd move in 1948. A number of popular programs and stars incorporated themselves and moved to CBS—*Amos 'n' Andy*, Jack Benny, Edgar Bergen, Red Skelton, and others. At NBC, the comedians had been highly paid employees and so had to pay taxes at the personal income rate. At CBS, as incorporated entities, they paid taxes at the lower capital-gains rate. CBS had suggested the idea to Music Corporation of America, agent for many of the comedians, and the exodus became known as Paley's **talent raid.** The move quickly paid off, putting CBS solidly ahead of NBC in the critical 7–8 p.m. time period as early as January 1949. This gave CBS a programming lead that it kept, took into television, and never really lost for years.

The networks had expanded in other ways. Both formed **artist management bureaus** and **concert booking companies.** This guaranteed a ready reserve of perform-

Figure 3.6 David Sarnoff, 1930. (Photograph courtesy of RCA Corp. Used by permission of General Electric Co.)

ers for their programs and income from the personal appearance tours of the talent they represented. Both networks were affiliated with **phonograph record companies.** RCA had bought the Victor Talking Machine Company in 1929, and CBS purchased its former owner, Columbia Records, in 1938. NBC and CBS each owned and operated profitable **broadcast stations** in a number of large cities.

David Sarnoff (Figure 3.6) became president of RCA in 1930 and continued to build that company's communications empire. In 1933, NBC moved into its Radio City home in New York's Rockefeller Center. The next year, Sarnoff assumed the chair of the NBC board. General Electric (GE) and Westinghouse had withdrawn from ownership of both RCA and NBC in 1932 after the threat of an antitrust suit, leaving RCA a separate corporate entity and NBC its wholly owned subsidiary (GE would buy RCA outright 53 years later). Also in 1932, William Paley had bought out Paramount's 49 percent share of CBS.

The **Mutual Broadcasting System** (MBS) started in 1934. It was to be mutual in practice as well as name. Member stations were to pool resources, each contributing program material. This would eliminate the expense of a network program department. The network would own no stations.

Initially, Mutual consisted of four cooperating stations—WOR, Newark; WGN, Chicago; WLW, Cincinnati; and WXYZ, Detroit. MBS eventually did acquire a staff to coordinate the cooperative programming activities of member stations. Most powerful, large-city stations had already affiliated with CBS or one of the NBC networks, so Mutual became the network of small-town and lower-powered stations. MBS attempted to make up in numbers of network stations the coverage it lacked from its affiliates' low power. By 1940, MBS had 140 affiliates; in 1945, 384.

The **American Broadcasting Company** (ABC) grew out of NBC Blue. NBC had made the red network the stronger of its two chains. The blue network had less popular programs, smaller audiences, and fewer sponsors. In 1943, when NBC was forced to divest one of its two chains, the blue network was formed as a separate corporation and sold. The buyer was Edward J. Noble, Lifesavers candy manufacturer. Upon its sale, the network became the third strongest, since its affiliates had more power than Mutual's. In 1945, the network became ABC.

3.1.4 Programming

During the 1930s, radio presented reformers and rogues, messiahs and maniacs, saints and sinners. In 1932, the United States inaugurated a president who promised a "new deal" to a citizenry burdened with economic depression. Franklin D. Roosevelt used radio to talk directly to the American people. Two other entirely different American political leaders used radio effectively as well—Huey Long and Father Charles Coughlin, each with his own idea of how to save the nation. Dr. Brinkley was still peddling patent medicines by radio, now from Mexico. A whole

breed of "outlaw" stations developed in the Southwest, especially Texas and Oklahoma. These stations operated without licenses because their owners said they transmitted intrastate only and so were not liable to FRC jurisdiction.

But when most people speak of "old-time radio," they mean the mainstream network entertainment programs. Radio developed its program formats in the 1930s. They stayed popular through the 1940s and into the 1950s. Most program types transferred successfully to television.

Radio played somewhat the same role for the American public that television did later. Radio ran a full schedule of entertainment programs. Most were live. Many were performed before studio audiences. Millions listened. The years 1930 through about 1953 have been called **radio's golden age.** That may overstate the average quality of programming. Nonetheless, the programming was unique, and it did achieve a high degree of development as popular culture.

Radio could also report news. The foundations for broadcast news were laid in the 1930s. After a few false starts, the networks assembled personnel and techniques that would be needed to report the biggest story yet, World War II.

3.1.4.1 Programs and Performers   National advertisers began using radio heavily in the 1930s. Both advertising and radio were developing into big business. In 1931, for example, American Tobacco Company spent 19 million depression dollars to advertise Lucky Strike cigarettes. A sponsor of a program series paid up to $500,000 per year for production costs alone; air time might cost another $4,000 per week. The sponsor controlled programming. The sponsor's advertising agency produced the program; the network was all but a common carrier, merely renting facilities and selling air time.

One program type that developed in the

early 1930s was **comedy-variety.** A comedian acted as master of ceremonies to introduce and bridge the various acts and guests on the program. Often the comedian had come out of vaudeville. This program type initiated the radio careers of Eddie Cantor, Al Jolson, George Burns and Gracie Allen, Ed Wynn, Fred Allen, and Jack Benny—all performers who earned near-legendary status in radio (Figure 3.7).

Drama became popular. During the 1920s, some efforts had been made to broad-

(a)

(b)

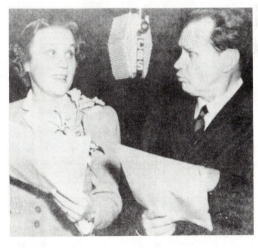
(c)

(d)

Figure 3.7 Husband-wife radio comedy teams. (a) George Burns and Gracie Allen. (b) Jack Benny and Mary Livingston. (c) Jim and Marion Jordan ("Fibber McGee and Mollie"). (d) Fred Allen and Portland Hoffa. (Photographs a and c courtesy of CBS; photographs b and d courtesy of the National Broadcasting Company, Inc. Used by permission.)

Figure 3.8 Radio sound effects technician and equipment.   (Photograph courtesy of the National Broadcasting Company, Inc. Used by permission.)

cast drama by putting microphones on the stage of Broadway plays. There had also been attempts to write and perform drama especially for radio. However, the birth of true radio drama came in the 1930s, when writers and performers learned to create for the ear, for a **"blind" audience.** Radio drama's **sound effects** staff came into its own (Figure 3.8). Technicians used odds and ends that—when rubbed, tinkled, opened, closed, crumpled, or clopped near a microphone— sounded like what the script called for. Dramatic dialogue usually provided verbal definition of the sound effect—"Listen to that rain!" "Wasn't that a shot?" "Here come two men on horses!" Through sound effects and dialogue, the listener's imagination created settings and characters. It was a **theater of the mind.**

Radio drama comprised several program types. These included continuing series, anthology series, mystery and adventure series (often using characters developed in comics or film), and experimental dramatic series. Writers and directors on the experimental series raised the level of radio drama to an art form. Orson Welles' experimental *Mercury Theater of the Air* (Figure 3.9) produced the scariest radio drama of all, the Halloween 1938 production of H. G. Wells' *War of the Worlds.* Thousands panicked, believing Martians had invaded Earth.

Some of the longest-lived dramas were serialized into 15-minute segments presented each day, Monday through Friday. Aimed at housewives and often sponsored by soap companies, this dramatic genre acquired the name **soap opera.** The first soap opera was broadcast on NBC in 1932. By the end of 1938, 38 sponsored daytime soap operas were broadcast daily, and the number was growing. They appealed to millions. Social scientists investigated the relationship between these slow-moving, emotionally charged, humorless dramas and their loyal audience.

In the early 1930s, radio brought together a mixture of drama and news. News events from the preceding week were put into script form and reenacted before network microphones. The result was the *March of Time*. First broadcast in 1931, it changed networks several times and went off the air in 1945. The *March of Time* spawned several imitators.

Radio broadcast many other program types: contests and games; children's shows; public interest programs; classical, light classical, Western, and popular music. There were programs for people with special interests, for example, in gardening, cooking, and march music. There were sports broadcasts, religious programs, country music programs, disk jockey programs, and every kind of dramatic and music program you could think of.

Program ratings were developed. Based on audience surveys, these ratings showed that the public preferred comedy. During the 1930s, the favorite evening programs were *Amos 'n' Andy*, Eddie Cantor, Rudy Vallee (musical variety), *Maxwell House Showboat* (variety), Burns and Allen, Fred Allen, Major Bowes' *Original Amateur Hour*, and Bing Crosby (musical variety). In 1950, preferences had not changed much. Comedians were still the favorites—Jack Benny, Edgar Bergen, Bob Hope, Burns and Allen. Bing Crosby hosted the favorite variety hour. Arthur Godfrey had replaced Major Bowes as the best-liked amateur-hour host. *Lux Radio Theater* was the favorite dramatic series. *Amos 'n' Andy* was still among the top ten rated programs.

Many radio series were long lived. In 1950, the networks were running 108 series

Figure 3.9 Mercury Theater of the Air.   Orson Welles directs. (Photograph courtesy of CBS. Used by permission.)

that had been on the air ten years or more, 12 of them for twenty years.

3.1.4.2 News

News reporting was part of broadcasting from the birth of radio. KDKA's first transmission reported the results of the Harding-Cox election. Individual stations broadcast news reports on a daily basis in the early 1920s.

H. V. Kaltenborn (see Figure 3.11), one of radio's first commentators, went on the air in 1923 at WEAF. Later, he worked for CBS and then NBC. Other well-known commentators of the early 1930s included Boake Carter, Gabriel Heatter, Edwin C. Hill, Floyd Gibbons, and **Lowell Thomas** (Figure 3.10). Thomas stayed with network news for 46 years, retiring from his CBS Radio commentary program in 1976.

Radio established a reputation for on-the-spot coverage. One example was the famous report of the ***Hindenburg*** disaster by Herbert Morrison of WLS, Chicago. On May 7, 1937, Morrison was in Lakehurst, New Jersey, recording a description of the arrival of the passenger dirigible *Hindenburg.* Suddenly the ship burst into flames. Morrison, horrified, described the scene as his engineer continued to record. That night, NBC broke

Figure 3.11 Paul White and H. V. Kaltenborn. (Photograph courtesy of CBS. Used by permission.)

its rule barring broadcast of recordings to use Morrison's description.

3.1.4.3 Radio Covers the War

As the 1930s wore on, the world groaned closer to war. Worldwide interest focused on Europe. The radio networks increased news activities. Correspondents reported and tried to make sense of the senseless. Listeners heard the voices of Hitler, Mussolini, Chamberlain, and other European political leaders.

Paul White (Figure 3.11), head of CBS news, organized a team of correspondents that would become the model for broadcast reportage. Each member combined objective reporting with compassion and an eye for the telling detail. Their names became legendary in broadcast news—William L. Shirer, Eric Sevareid, Larry Lesueur, Howard K. Smith, Charles Collingwood, Robert Trout, Richard C. Hottelet, Bill Downs, Winston Burdett, Ned Calmer, Cecil Brown, John Daly. The other networks also fielded teams of outstanding reporters, individuals who risked and sometimes lost their lives to keep the American public informed.

Perhaps more than anyone else, it was **Edward R. Murrow** (Figure 3.12) on whom the public relied to explain the whys and

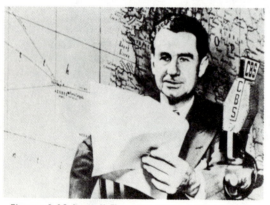

Figure 3.10 Lowell Thomas: news and commentary. (Photograph courtesy of CBS. Used by permission.)

Figure 3.12 Edward R. Murrow in London. (Photograph courtesy of CBS. Used by permission.)

hows of a distant and ominous war. CBS had sent Ed Murrow to Europe in 1937 to arrange for broadcasts of special events and to report the news. But as Hitler began marching, Murrow devoted all efforts toward news reporting. At 8:00 p.m. eastern standard time on March 3, 1938, he broadcast his first report from Vienna as that beautiful, historic city awaited Hitler's arrival. The same broadcast included reports from correspondents in London, Paris, Berlin, Rome, and New York. This was radio's first world news roundup. Later, based in England, Murrow opened broadcasts with the words "This—is London," and Americans heard him report from a rooftop while bombs fell in that blacked-out city, from an Air Corps C-47 headed toward Holland, from London streets smashed by German bombs in the Battle of Britain, from the North African front.

On December 7, 1941, radio reported that the Japanese had attacked Pearl Harbor, Hawaii. The next day, 79 percent of all U.S. homes listened to radio as President Roosevelt asked Congress for a declaration of war. Radio stepped up its already heavy reporting activities, and news was reported every hour.

As U.S. industries were mobilized for the war effort, so was radio. Unlike the situation in World War I, operation of radio stations was left in civilian hands. The government formed an **Office of War Information** (OWI) to coordinate propaganda and information services. The advertising industry organized the **War Advertising Council** and worked with OWI to create and schedule war-related public service campaigns—war bond purchase appeals, "careless talk costs lives," forest fire prevention, promotion of victory gardens, and many others.

One spectacular success in war bond appeals involved the radio singer Kate Smith. In a marathon drive in February 1944, she urged listeners to buy bonds. They did—$108 million worth.

Entertainment programming continued more or less unchanged. Most programs promoted the win-the-war theme in some way. A number of government-created propaganda and meet-your-armed-services programs were broadcast. Some programs originated from armed forces bases and hospitals; Bob Hope, well-known radio and film comedian, was a leader in this area. Care was taken that broadcasts did not contain information the enemy could use, such as weather reports.

Overseas, **Tokyo Rose** used Japanese government transmitters to broadcast popular music, propaganda, and sweet talk to American soldiers in the Pacific. **Axis Sally** was her German counterpart.

Inspired by an unauthorized station built and operated by service personnel in Alaska, the War Department created the **Armed Forces Radio Service** (AFRS). AFRS grew to a network of stations in the Pacific and European war theaters that provided entertainment and information for American troops.

Commercial radio's greatest achievements during World War II were in news and public affairs. Reporters began to use voice-recording machines to record actual events for later broadcast. Special radio series combined journalism and drama—the first step toward the development of the radio documentary. Eyewitness accounts were broadcast as events occurred—Murrow's description of the London air raids, the Japanese attack on Manila, the Allied invasion of Normandy on D day, American troop landings on Japanese-held Pacific islands, the surrender of Germany, and the Japanese signing of surrender documents aboard the U.S.S. *Missouri* in Tokyo Bay.

3.1.5 Problems

The golden age of radio was not without occasional spots of tarnish. Some of these involved newspaper publishers, music, editorials, networks, and public service.

3.1.5.1 Press-Radio War Before radio, newspapers had a monopoly on news, using their various editions to get out fast-breaking stories. Now, radio could air a story immediately, beating the next newspaper edition by hours. The *extra*, a special newspaper edition that rushed important news to the public, had been doomed by 1929. Publishers, seeing readers and advertisers turn to radio,

decided to act. In 1933 the major news services—Associated Press (AP), United Press (UP), and International News Service (INS)—announced that they would no longer provide news to networks.

The networks had no formal news-gathering operations. Now, if they wished to continue to broadcast news, they would have to gather their own. NBC's effort was small, based on the long-distance telephoning efforts of A. A. Schechter. Each day Schechter managed to gather enough news for the Lowell Thomas program. CBS organized a full-fledged news department headed by Paul W. White. White established correspondents around the country and exchange arrangements with overseas news agencies. The **press-radio war** had begun.

The publishers forced a showdown. In December 1933, they met with representatives of CBS and NBC at New York's Hotel Biltmore. The two sides agreed to the creation of a **Press-Radio Bureau.** Beginning on March 1, 1934, the Press-Radio Bureau would provide a restricted diet of news to broadcasters for restricted use on the air. As a result, radio would not be able to report news before the newspapers. CBS was to disband its news service; NBC was not to build one.

There were ways around the restrictions. Radio could offer all the "comment" and "interpretation" it wanted, so radio's newscasters became "commentators" or "analysts." Most radio *stations* did not even join the Press-Radio Bureau and did not feel bound by the Biltmore agreements.

By mid-1935, the restrictions were falling apart. First, rival news services were formed to provide news to radio stations. Then UP and INS offered news to stations. By the end of the decade, even AP provided news to stations. In 1940, the Press-Radio Bureau went out of business, and radio went on to report World War II.

3.1.5.2 Music Problems with music had started early. Under the 1909 copyright law, copyrighted music could not be performed in public for profit without permission of the copyright holder. The **American Society of Composers, Authors and Publishers** (ASCAP) organized to grant permission to music users and to collect and pay royalty fees to copyright-holder members.

In 1922, ASCAP demanded that station owners pay royalties. Broadcasters were outraged. A test suit was brought against WOR, Newark, and the court ruled[1] that since a large department store ran WOR for publicity (stations did not run advertising yet), the station's use of music was "for profit." Stations had to pay ASCAP annual fees starting at $250. Broadcasters, still angry, formed an anti-ASCAP organization that eventually became the trade group, the National Association of Broadcasters (NAB). By 1936, the license fee was $2\frac{1}{3}$ percent of a station's advertising income.

In 1937, ASCAP announced a sharp increase to take effect in the early 1940s. Broadcasters resolved to fight. They contributed funds to form a rival music licensing organization, **Broadcast Music, Incorporated** (BMI). Finally, the showdown came. ASCAP raised its rates; broadcasters refused to pay and relied on music from BMI and the public domain (music on which there was no copyright or the copyright had expired). This period in 1941 became known as the **era of "Jeannie with the Light Brown Hair,"** since that song, no longer under copyright, was used on the air so often.

The broadcasters won the battle when ASCAP reduced its demands. Then **musicians stopped making records.** James C. Petrillo, president of the American Federation of Musicians (AFM), said that sound films, juke boxes, and the use of records on radio stations had put musicians out of work. At its 1942 convention, AFM decided to stop making recordings. The major record companies met AFM demands in 1943 and 1944.

3.1.5.3 Broadcaster Editorials The license of WAAB, Boston, was up for renewal. Mayflower Broadcasting Corporation filed an application with the FCC to build a new station in Boston to operate on WAAB's frequency. The FCC held hearings on the matter in 1939. Mayflower's application was denied; WAAB's license was renewed.[2] But during the proceedings it was revealed that WAAB had editorialized during 1937 and 1938. In its decision the FCC said "the broadcaster cannot be an advocate." This **Mayflower doctrine** effectively discouraged broadcast editorials until the FCC reversed itself in 1949.[3] Leaders in the radio trade denounced the doctrine; to most stations it made little difference, since they had no desire to air editorials.

3.1.5.4 The Network Case CBS and NBC affiliation contracts deprived affiliated stations of control over their own programming. Under the option clause, for example, both networks could require that affiliates broadcast sponsored network shows even if local programming had to be canceled. The FCC launched an investigation in 1938.

Three years later, the commission issued its findings as the *Report on Chain Broadcasting*. At the same time, the FCC adopted regulations to deal with matters described in the report. The report said that, through affiliation contracts, NBC and CBS controlled the programming of their affiliated stations, stations that accounted for 85 percent of the total nighttime broadcast transmitter power of all stations in the country. Network control violated federal law, which put responsibility for programming on the station licensee. Such control also smacked of monopoly.

The new regulations aimed at breaking

this illegal control. CBS would have to eliminate the network option plan and NBC relinquish one of its networks. The regulations limited the term of affiliate contracts to three years, gave affiliates the right to reject programs, gave networks the right to offer rejected programs to nonaffiliated stations, limited network station ownership to one per city, and prohibited networks from controlling affiliate advertising rates. The report also mentioned the networks' artist bureaus: How could a network artist bureau represent the best economic interests of both performers, as their agent, and the network, as their employer?

CBS and NBC got rid of their artist bureaus immediately. But they contended that the other regulations would end network broadcasting, even commercial broadcasting itself. The networks and other broadcasters mounted a full-scale attack on the FCC. A committee of the U.S. House of Representatives investigated the commission.

NBC and CBS both challenged the regulations in court. The case wound its way up the judicial ladder to the U.S. Supreme Court. On May 10, 1943, the High Court announced its ruling in *NBC* v. *U.S.*,[4] **affirming the constitutional validity of the chain broadcasting regulations.** NBC sold the blue network, and CBS modified its network option requirements.

3.1.5.5 The Blue Book Released in 1945, this publication's official title was *Public Service Responsibility of Broadcast Licensees*. It had a blue cover, hence "the Blue Book."

The Blue Book reported on programming by a group of licensees. These licensees had broadcast excessive numbers of commercials, had not carried local public interest programs, had not aired network public affairs programs, and generally had not fulfilled the promises they made on their license renewal applications. Quoting statements by broad-

casting business leaders, the Blue Book contended that stations should observe certain broad guidelines to ensure that their programming met public service obligations. The guidelines suggested that stations avoid excessive advertising and devote time to sustaining programs, local live programs, and discussion of public issues. The FCC, in turn, should examine a station's past record at license renewal time to see how well the station had met these guidelines.

The Blue Book's suggestions represented a departure from previous commission policy. Station license renewals had been passed routinely as long as all technical requirements were met. Now the FCC proposed to look at past programming. Also, while the FCC and the Federal Radio Commission had removed the charlatans—the Brinkleys, the Bakers, and all the rest—from the airwaves, this was the commission's first general criticism of "mainstream" broadcasters.

The NAB launched an attack, attempting to discredit the Blue Book. According to the NAB, any commission decision based on programming would violate the First Amendment to the U.S. Constitution and the prohibition against FCC censorship in the Communications Act. The trade press joined the battle on the side of the NAB. Invective targeted the commissioners and the FCC consultants and staff members who had prepared the book. They were likened to Communists and Fascists. Members of Congress joined the criticism. Interestingly, amidst all the *ad hominem* attacks, no one argued about the *content* of the Blue Book.

The FCC, surprised and uneasy over the reaction to its publication, did not follow its own new standards. By the end of 1946, it was clear that the Blue Book was to be an unused document. Although never officially repudiated, neither was it enforced. The FCC did, however, adopt some Blue Book recommendations, such as using license renewal

Figure 3.15 Specialization: The Negro Radio Station. WWRL, New York, was one of the first radio stations to program exclusively for a black audience. Here, Alma John is shown with her guest, Mease Booker, "Miss Golden Girl." Alma John's show "Homemakers' Club," first went on the air in October of 1952 and was broadcast from 9:00 to 9:30 A.M. daily. (*Source:* Schomburg Center for Research in Black Culture; courtesy, The New York Public Library.)

fications, and so on) and off-air (in other media).

About this time, a form of popular music arose that became known as rock 'n' roll (Figure 3.16). Top-40 radio was the perfect setting for this music. As the 1950s ground on, city after city fell under the spell of raucous, razzle-dazzle, rocking top-40 stations, and their near-fanatic youth audiences pushed them to the top of the ratings in nearly every market.

Naturally, there were imitators. Larger cities acquired two, three, and even four top-40 stations. After some stations failed, radio managers realized that the lesson of top-40 success was not top 40 itself, but specialization. In the 1960s and 1970s, radio formats diversified—country music, beautiful music, rock music, all-talk, all-news, ethnic.

While this programming change occurred, another took place in sales and advertising. Stations encouraged local retail outlets to use radio, and income from local advertising sales climbed.

Figure 3.16 Alan Freed. In the early 1950s, he moved from a Cleveland radio station to New York and became one of the most popular and important disc jockeys in the new top-40 radio format. Supposedly, he coined the name "rock 'n' roll." His confession of involvement in payola before a congressional investigating committee effectively ended his career. (Photograph courtesy of CBS. Used by permission.)

3.2.2 Networks

Network radio's adjustment to the age of television was more difficult than that of local stations. At first the radio networks tried to economize and compete with television for the mass audience. They dropped their ban on recordings and even ran a few disc jockey shows. They added telephone quiz shows, offering money and prizes to those who could answer questions posed by long-distance telephone. Audiences continued to dwindle. In the 1950s, network radio programs of long standing went off the air and were not replaced.

The importance and vitality of radio shifted from networks to stations. Network affiliation was a hindrance. If radio networks were to stay in business, they would have to adjust to the needs of the stations.

One such need was network programming designed for the change in radio listening habits. Pretelevision radio had forced the public to develop a plan-ahead, time-block audience pattern. But that pattern had shifted almost entirely to the visual medium. Now, people did not plan ahead to listen to radio; they listened when they had time and usually while doing other things. NBC responded with *Monitor*. Launched in 1955 under NBC's innovative president Pat Weaver, *Monitor* represented an attempt to adjust network programming to the tune-in/tune-out listening patterns. *Monitor* ran on weekends, for 40 hours (later 25), covering many areas of interest with short capsules of information. ABC and CBS began their own versions. NBC tried a weekday version of *Monitor*.

Mutual Broadcasting System (MBS) and ABC reduced network service to capsule news and features, usually on the hour and the half hour, giving the rest of the hour to affiliates. First NBC, then CBS adopted this pattern for weekday programming.

3.2.3 Scandals

These transitional years were unsettling. In addition to the coming of television and the proliferation of stations, the radio trade suffered from several other serious problems. Among these were McCarthyism, planted news, and payola.

3.2.3.1 McCarthyism McCarthyism transcended the field of broadcasting, pervading all aspects of American life. The late Joseph McCarthy, then junior senator from Wisconsin, did not invent the mass paranoia that bears his name. He did profit by it, building a career on finding and purging from the U.S. government people he accused of being or having been Communists.

McCarthy's tactics, fed by a growing public fear of atomic attack and internal subversion by Communists, created an aura of universal suspicion and accusation. People and ideas were labeled "Communist" just because they were different. An accusation of being a Communist or a Communist sympathizer—whether true or not—was cause enough for the accused to be summarily fired. The careers of many innocent people were ruined.

McCarthy was a master at using news media to publicize his activities and thus to build his power base among the people. Few opposed McCarthy, because he had the perfect defense—he would simply brand the opposition "un-American," synonymous in those days with "Communist" or "traitor."

One of McCarthyism's more virulent forms was **blacklisting.** It worked like this: Self-appointed protectors of the public weal, who professed concern that Communist agents were gaining control of the nation's communications channels, would supposedly investigate the background of creative personnel in stage, screen, and broadcasting. The blacklisters circulated names of performers, writers, directors, and others alleged to be Communists or Communist sympathizers to producers, sponsors, and studio heads. Blacklisted individuals lost their jobs and could not get new ones, often without knowing why; few employers would admit to being influenced by the blacklisters. The accused were presumed guilty based on allegations alone. Some never got entertainment work again. Some went through humiliating blacklister-specified rituals of "clearing," usually by publicly admitting that they had been Communists (whether or not they actually had been) and vowing to take a militant anti-Communst attitude from then on. Some committed suicide.

Leading blacklisters in broadcasting included three ex-FBI agents, who published *Counterattack: The Newsletter of Facts on Communism* and *Red Channels: The Report of Communist Influence in Radio and Television,* and **Aware, Inc.,** publisher of periodical bulletins listing supposed Communists. The blacklists were by no means nonprofit activities. Vincent Hartnett, who formed Aware in 1953, checked names for a fee on request by sponsors and producers. He also prescribed means by which blacklisted individuals could "clear" themselves—again for a fee. He was backed by Laurence Johnson, owner of a supermarket chain in Syracuse, New York. If broadcast programs persisted in using persons blacklisted by Aware, Johnson pressured the sponsors with tacit threats to prevent his customers from buying the advertised products. Agencies, networks, sponsors, stations—all ran scared, bowing to the whims of Aware because of the possibility of economic recrimination by Johnson.

John Henry Faulk, a radio personality for WCBS, New York, opposed the influence of Aware in the New York chapter of the American Federation of Television and Radio Artists, the performers' union. In 1956, Faulk helped draft a non-Communist, anti-Aware slate of candidates for election to office in the union. He was one of the candidates. Aware blacklisted Faulk. His radio program lost its sponsors, and Faulk brought suit against Hartnett and Johnson for libel. WCBS fired Faulk, saying his ratings were poor. Faulk hired Louis Nizer, a famous trial lawyer. In June 1962, Faulk's libel case went to trial. The jury found Hartnett and Johnson guilty of libel and awarded Faulk more damages than he had asked—an unprecedented $3.5 million (subsequently scaled down to $550,000 by an appellate court).

Faulk's victory signaled the end of blacklisting in broadcasting but opened no door for the victor. In 1974, a Dallas radio station broke the blacklisters' curse and hired Faulk to host a telephone call-in show. This was his first regular job in broadcasting in almost 18 years.

3.2.3.2 News Planting This involved the **Mutual Broadcasting System being paid to run favorable news items on a foreign country.** In January 1959, MBS President Alexander Guterma made an agreement with representatives of Rafael Trujillo, Dominican Republic dictator, to broadcast a monthly quota of news and commentary concerning the Dominican Republic. None of the material was to be negative. In exchange for this publicity disguised as news, MBC received $750,000. The next month, Guterma became involved in legal and business problems. The Dominican Republic sued to get its money, and the agreement came to light.

3.2.3.3 Payola In 1959, the story came out that record companies had paid disc jockeys under-the-table to promote records. The theory was that a top disc jockey on a big market top-40 station could play and push a record enough to make it become popular. Dubbed *payola*, this practice constituted advertising for which the station received no revenue; even worse, it deceived the public because it was not labeled as advertising. Some of the nation's best-known DJs were caught in this scandal (see Figure 3.16). Congress amended the Communications Act in 1959 to prohibit payola. Despite efforts by both government and broadcasters to curb the practice, however, payola recurred sporadically during the ensuing years.

3.3 FM RADIO

During the 1960s, frequency modulation (FM) radio, previously repressed and ignored, began to move and shake the trade. FM hastened the trend toward specialization and helped sharpen competition for audiences among radio stations. Now we catch up on the story of FM.

FM is almost as old as radio itself; the first patent was issued in 1902. FM broadcasting did not become practical, however, until the work of **Edwin H. Armstrong** during the period 1928–1934. RCA opposed advancement of FM on the grounds that it might detract from the development of television, in which the electronics giant had a vested interest (Section 2.2). Undaunted, Armstrong promoted FM. He showed that FM had inherent advantages over AM—higher-fidelity reproduction, freer from static, and not so subject to fading and interference from other stations. By March 1940, 22 experimental FM stations were on the air. The FCC authorized commercial FM operation, establishing 42–50 MHz as the FM band. During World War II, the FCC stopped granting applications for new FM stations.

In 1945, the FCC moved the FM band to 88–106 MHz.* With this decision, the commission rendered obsolete all transmitters at the existing 46 FM stations and all 400,000 FM receivers owned by the public.

*The frequencies 106–108 MHz, originally reserved for facsimile, were later used for FM broadcasting.

RCA's opposition, the wartime freeze, and now a major frequency shift—this should have killed any chance for development that the new aural medium had. In the long run, however, the 1945 frequency shift turned out to be a good move; it lessened the chance of FM suffering from interference, and it increased the number of FM channels from 40 to 100. In addition, the commission reaffirmed the principle of reserving channels for education. In setting up the 1940 FM band, the FCC had set aside five channels for noncommercial educational use. In the 1945 move, the commission reserved the first 20 of the new band's 100 channels for noncommercial educational stations.

FM radio was being touted as the coming medium, perhaps even replacing AM radio. In spite of the 1945 frequency shift, just three years later the FCC had authorized over 1000 new FM stations (Figure 3.17). But FM's time had not yet come. Audiences did not find FM attractive. The receivers were expensive and did not sound much better than AM receivers. In many cases, FM programming was exactly the same as AM; AM-FM licensees would duplicate AM programming on the FM station. Audiences were content with AM radio and fascinated with a new broadcast medium, television. Advertisers put their money in AM and TV. Almost without exception, FM stations lost money. From 1949 through 1952, over 350 FM station owners voluntarily returned licenses to the FCC.

In the 1950s, a small coterie of "hi-fi" enthusiasts discovered the technical delights of FM. They also enjoyed the classical music that some independently programmed FM stations featured. Then stereophonic reproduction hit the consumer market. In 1961, the FCC authorized FM stations to **broadcast stereophonically.**

In 1963, the commission adopted the **FM nonduplication rule.** This rule required licensees of AM-FM combinations in all but

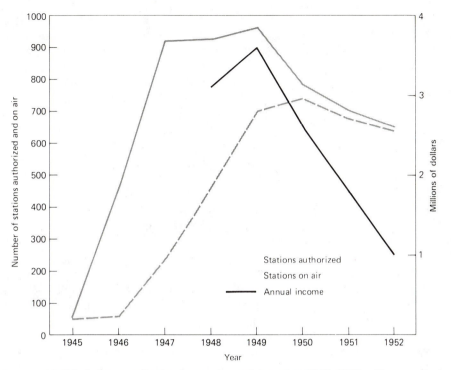

Stations authorized

Stations on air

——— Annual income

Figure 3.17 FM stations authorized, on air, and income: 1945–1952. (*Source:* Federal Communications Commission.)

the smallest cities to program the FM stations separately from AM most of the time. Such stations had to look for formats—preferably formats that did not duplicate those already in the market and that would show off FM's technical advantages. Many went to "beautiful music." Others went in an entirely different direction.

Rock music had begun to evolve and divide into increasingly esoteric forms. Large-market FM stations specialized and appealed to the audiences generated by those forms. Many new recordings were longer than normal and relied on electronic gimmickry that AM could not reproduce adequately. These were a "natural" for FM radio.

At the same time, rock fans discovered stereophonic reproduction. They formed a mass market for stereo discs, tapes, turntables, tape decks, amplifiers, speakers, and, of course, FM tuners. They put stereo in their cars. The stereo explosion boosted FM radio, and FM boosted stereo.

FM stations also competed in formatting. Programmers discovered that contemporary popular music could thrive in quieter, less frenetic surroundings than the top-40 format of the period. They found that audiences appreciated long, uninterrupted stretches of similar music. They instructed announcers to stop screaming, to play two or more selections at a time, even to track albums (play them in their entirety without interruption).

These strategies succeeded. By 1970, FM stations successfully competed for shares with AM stations in some large markets. FM programmers continued to refine techniques. More listeners discovered the superior technical quality of FM. Stereo receivers dropped in price. In 1979, FM passed AM in overall market shares, and in succeeding years FM increased its lead. FM, once the unwanted, ill-treated sibling of AM, had become the desired, admired medium.

3.4 COMPETITION

From 1950 to 1980, the number of stations increased markedly, about 276 percent. During the 1970s, the FCC made proposals that would have further increased the number of stations. One proposal involved reducing the area in which dominant stations on AM clear channels were protected from interference; the commission put this into effect and created room for some 125 new AM stations.

Another proposal would have reduced AM channel width from 10 to 9 kHz. Such a move required cooperation from neighboring countries, and the commission proposed the reduction at the international level. Most U.S. licensees, however, did not want the expense of changing frequencies, feared technical problems, and did not look forward to the hundreds of new competitors the 9-kHz spacing would create. They fought the move, and in 1981 the commission recommended that the United States stay with 10-kHz spacing.

Two years later, the commission paved the way for hundreds of new FM stations. In 1980, the FCC had proposed changes in FM; the proposal became known by its FCC file number, "docket 80-90." In 1983, the commission approved most docket 80-90 changes; modification of station and channel classifications made room for up to 1000 new stations. In 1989, the FCC authorized a new class of FM station, C3, a move that would allow yet another 200 new stations to sign on.

Even before docket 80-90, there were a lot of radio stations. By 1990, nearly 12,000 radio stations were on the air, 90 percent of them commercial. During the period 1950–1980, radio advertising sales increased tenfold, from $321 million to $3.4 billion. Despite increases in station numbers and expenses, there was money to be made, especially in medium and large markets. Competition increased.

3.4.1 Stations

The increase in competition and the success of FM led to three basic changes. First, the **programmer grew in importance.** The successful programmer used statistically based **quantitative research.** Research helped to define the station's target audience, to tailor content to capture that audience, and to spot trends in audience tastes and habits. Research helped make stations in competitive markets **highly formatted.** Research helped select records to play, news to report, jingles to insert, things to say, commercials to run, and times to do all these things—even the talent to do them.

The second change involved **decreasing reliance on local programming resources.** Successful radio programmers sometimes syndicated their services. A station could hire such a programmer to come into the market, study the competitive situation, and make programming recommendations. Or the station could automate and subscribe to a programmer's service—large reels of tape that contained all music and announcements. In the late 1970s, some syndicators went to satellite distribution for the programming.

The third change involved overall programming trends in AM and FM. **FM stations tended to program formats that featured music,** any kind of music in which reproduction of sound was important to the listener—rock, beautiful, country, jazz, classical, ethnic. **AM stations tended to program formats in which the range of**

frequencies reproduced was not as important—talk, news, nostalgia and oldies music (which featured many pre-stereo recordings), and country.

3.4.2 Technology and Regulatory Policy

By the 1980s, the tables had turned; FM was the dominant aural medium, and AM was struggling. The FCC had helped in FM's long uphill battle; now it would do the same for AM. Under one suggestion, an AM broadcaster would be allowed to use several transmitters in different locations, synchronized to increase the station's coverage.

AM licensees looked toward **AM stereo** as a means to compete. The FCC authorized AM stereo in 1982 but did not designate a specific AM stereo system. Broadcasters could use any of several competing systems; "marketplace forces" would determine which would become the trade standard. In 1989, the FCC adopted rules to curtail interference in the AM band in the hope of encouraging the manufacture of better sounding receivers.

Daytime broadcasters looked toward 24-hour operation and the possibilty of owning an FM station. The restriction to daylight-only transmission (Section 3.2) put AM daytimers at a competitive disadvantage to almost *all* other stations. The FCC began proceedings that would permit most daytimers to operate at night with reduced power. The commission also decided that a daytime broadcaster who applied for a docket 80-90 FM channel (Section 3.4) would have a slight advantage (a "preference") over other applications for the same channel.

Some AM broadcasters competed beyond the limits of their broadcast programming. They **contracted with local cable companies to provide programming**—channels for the cable audio service and even video programming such as local newscasts. Others explored new revenue-producing uses of their carriers (Section 11.5.3).

Technological advances, however, also strengthened FM's claim to superior sound reproduction. Equipment manufacturers included **digital** (Section 11.3.2.3) circuitry in the various devices and "black boxes" used by radio stations to process their signal. This allowed the audio signal to travel within the station—from source to transmitter—without picking up the distortion and extraneous signals normally acquired from even the finest nondigital equipment. Some radio networks digitally encoded their signals for satellite distribution; these signals arrived at the station as clear as they left the network. Record companies used digital technology for cleaner, purer recordings. FM stations rushed to incorporate **compact discs** (Section 5.10) into their programming. All of these things helped FM to do even better what it already excelled at—produce a superior signal.

3.4.3 Networks

The heightened competition in programming showed up at the network level as well. ABC started a trend toward **format-specific networks.** In 1968, four separately programmed ABC networks were offered—Contemporary, Entertainment, FM, and Information. Each offered brief newscasts; each was tailored to a different type of station format. None of the ABC networks dominated a station's weekend as did *Monitor*. ABC eventually increased its network services to six.

MBS followed ABC's lead four years later, adding a network for black stations and another for Spanish-language stations. MBS dropped the Mutual Spanish Network after seven months but continued the Mutual

Black Network (MBN) until 1979, when MBS sold its interest to Sheridan Broadcasting Corporation. MBN was then renamed Sheridan Broadcasting Network.

Mutual itself had passed through the hands of a number of owners. In 1978, the Amway Corporation, door-to-door marketer of home and personal products, bought the network. While under Amway, Mutual purchased two radio stations, the first Mutual had ever owned. These were later sold.

In 1973 a new organization, the National Black Network (NBN), signed on, originating hourly five-minute newscasts aimed at black stations across the country. NBN soon added sports and features.

NBC changed *Monitor* and finally dropped it in 1975. NBC retained what had become conventional network service—brief newscasts and features. In mid-1975, NBC added the News and Information Service (NIS), a program service separate from the NBC Radio Network. Designed for stations with all-news formats, NIS fed news, reports, and features throughout the hour, giving affiliates the opportunity to insert local news and advertising. Stations paid a monthly subscription to use NIS. NBC could not attract enough subscribing stations to make it pay and took NIS off the air in 1977.

National Public Radio was formed in 1970 to serve noncommercial educational radio stations. Numerous commercial state networks signed on to feed state, farm, and other special-interest news and features to affiliated stations. In the 1980s, American Public Radio formed to supplement NPR.

The late 1970s and early 1980s marked a renaissance in national networking. Most activity involved format-specific programming, a trend accelerated by increased numbers of stations and the development of domestic satellite distribution. Two ABC networks were added—Direction and Rock. CBS launched RadioRadio; NBC, The Source.

Mutual used multiple satellite audio channels to deliver various types of programming to affiliates. Sheridan and NBN expanded program offerings. AP and UPI had both operated news program services for a number of years; now AP cooperated in a country-music radio programming service and UPI started a Spanish-language news service.

A number of new networks started during this late 1970s–early 1980s period; some failed. The successes included American Public Radio, Turner Broadcasting System's (TBS) CNN Radio, RKO Radio Networks, Satellite Music Network, Transtar Radio Networks, and United Stations. The failures were Enterprise Radio and Christian Broadcasting Network's (CBN) Continental Radio. The former concentrated on sports, the latter on adult contemporary and upbeat religious music. CBN attempted radio networking again in 1987 with CBN Radio.

In the mid-1980s, electronic media businesses began a series of major corporate and financial transactions that would last for several years (Section 4.5.3). Radio networks were affected. In 1985, Capital Cities Communications, Inc., bought ABC; United Stations bought RKO Radio Networks; and General Electric bought RCA, parent company of NBC. In 1986, Transtar took over distribution and marketing of CNN Radio; TBS would continue to produce the programming. In 1987, however, Ted Turner was forced to relinquish some control over the company that bore his name (Section 5.2.5).

The two most historically notable radio network purchases were made in the mid-1980s. In both cases, the buyer was Westwood One, Inc., a producer and distributor of sponsored radio programs. In 1985 Westwood One acquired the Mutual Broadcasting System from Amway; two years later, it bought the NBC Radio Network. GE had decided that the nation's senior network—the business that had started NBC—was expendable. NBC sold all its radio stations in 1988.

All told, radio networking seemed to be on the rise, and even some state and regional networks announced plans for satellite distribution. Most of these newer networks paid no compensation, operating instead on some form of barter basis.

Radio had begun its change because of television. The arrival of television forced radio to adjust and adapt. In the meantime, even newer technologies had forced changes on television, and that is the subject of the next chapter.

NOTES

1. *Witmark* v. *Bamberger*, 291 F.776 (1923).
2. In the Matter of Mayflower Broadcasting Corporation and the Yankee Network, Inc. (WAAB), 8 F.C.C. 333 (1941).
3. In the Matter of Editorialization by Broadcast Licensees, 13 F.C.C. 1246 (1949).
4. 319 U.S. 190 (1943).

FURTHER READING

Bannerman, R. LeRoy. *Norman Corwin and Radio: The Golden Years.* University: U of Alabama P, 1986. Contributions of one of radio's most creative dramatic writers.

Barnouw, Erik. *The Golden Web.* New York: Oxford UP, 1968.

———. *The Image Empire.* New York: Oxford UP, 1970.

Broadcasting Magazine. *The First Fifty Years of Broadcasting: The Running Story of the Fifth Estate.* Washington: Broadcasting, 1982. Based on the magazine's reports.

Brown, James A. "Selling Airtime for Controversy: NAB Self-Regulation and Father Coughlin." *Journal of Broadcasting* 24 (1980): 199–224. NAB deals with the priest.

Faulk, John Henry. *Fear On Trial.* Rev. ed. New York: Grosset, 1983. Blacklisting and libel suit against Aware.

Glick, Edwin L. "The Life and Death of the Liberty Broadcasting System." *Journal of Broadcasting* 23 (1979): 117–135. McLendon's "re-creations" of sports events.

———. "WBAP/WFAA—570/820: Til Money Did Them Part." *Journal of Broadcasting* 24 (1977): 473–486. One of the last share-time operations involved two frequencies.

Harmon, Jim. *The Great Radio Comedians.* Garden City: Doubleday, 1970.

———. *The Great Radio Heroes.* Garden City: Doubleday, 1967.

Koch, Howard. *The Panic Broadcast.* New York: Avon, 1971. On the *War of the Worlds* broadcast, for which Koch wrote the script.

Lessing, Lawrence. *Man of High Fidelity: Edwin Howard Armstrong.* New York: Lippincott, 1956.

Paper, Lewis J. *Empire: William S. Paley and the Making of CBS News.* New York: St. Martin's, 1987.

Sperber, Ann M. *Murrow: His Life and Times.* New York: Freundlich, 1986.

Vane, John Mac. *On the Air in World War II.* New York: Morrow, 1979.

CHAPTER 4

Television: From 1941

In this chapter, we look at the development of broadcast television. We see how trade politics and economics helped to shape technical standards. We see how programming evolved. We see how commercial networks rose to dominate television, just as they had radio. We see how television was affected by scandal and corruption. We see how regulatory and citizen groups worked to reform the trade. We see how commercial broadcasting began to get what it had wanted for years—less regulation. We see how less regulation also had a few surprises for commercial broadcasting—more competition and structural and financial changes in the trade itself.

4.1 GROWING PAINS

Chapter 2 brought us to the point at which television was technically ready for widespread public use (Box 4.1). There would be a delay. But broadcast television would grow and evolve into the dominant form of mass communication. It would suffer growing pains ethically and even technically, but rarely economically.

4.1.1 Freeze

The Federal Communications Commission (FCC) adopted technical standards in 1941, and commercial television operation began in July of that year. A wartime stoppage on station and receiving set construction was imposed in 1942. Of the ten pioneer television stations, only six continued through the war. They broadcast four hours per week to the 7000 or so sets in existence. Even after the stoppage was lifted in 1945, shortages of materials continued. Station and set construction did not resume for almost two years.

In 1947, television began to grow at a phenomenal rate (Figure 4.1). Sales of receivers soared. Television station license applications flooded the FCC. It soon became evident that there would be many more applications than channels. In 1948, the commission ordered a **freeze** (halt) on processing station applications to allow time to work something out. The freeze was supposed to last 6 to 9 months. However, the issues involved were so complex that the freeze lasted 42 months. After a series of hearings,

Box 4.1 Forty Years of RCA Camera Tubes

From left to right, these tubes are as follows: Iconoscope (1935)—first broadcast camera tube. Orthicon (1939)—used during World War II. Image orthicon (1954)—high resolution tube, first to allow light levels low enough that performers were not nearly parboiled by the heat from studio lighting (for black-and-white TV; when used in multiples of three in the first color cameras, the lighting levels had to go back up again). Vidicon (1950)—first practical industrial camera tube, forerunner of the modern lead oxide tube. Image orthicon—improved production model. Vidicon (1954)—improved, long-lived, inexpensive production model. Vidicon (1955)—this half-inch vidicon, for years the smallest camera tube built, was used in TIROS, the nation's first weather satellite. Lead oxide vidicon (1967)—used in modern color cameras. Silicon diode array vidicon (1969)—first commercial use of the solid-state array for TV pickup. Silicon intensifier target (SIT, 1971)—highly sensitive and widely employed for day and night production; it was used on the Lunar Rover to broadcast color TV from the moon's surface on several Apollo missions. Silicon imaging device (SID, 1974)—not really a tube at all, this charge-coupled device (CCD) was the first all-solid-state TV pickup device capable of generating fully standard TV pictures, and in 1984 RCA began marketing portable electronic color TV cameras that utilized highly developed CCD descendants of the SID instead of tubes. (Photograph courtesy of RCA Corp. Used by permission of General Electric Co.)

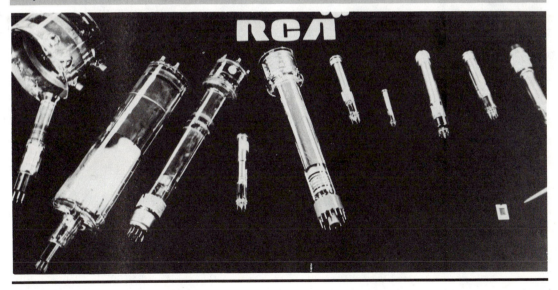

conferences, and negotiations, the FCC issued the *Sixth Report and Order*[1] on April 14, 1952, and in July it resumed processing applications for new stations. The freeze was over.

4.1.2 Sixth Report and Order

The *Sixth Report and Order* was a new plan for U.S. television. Under the order, existing VHF channels 2–13 were to remain. Seventy

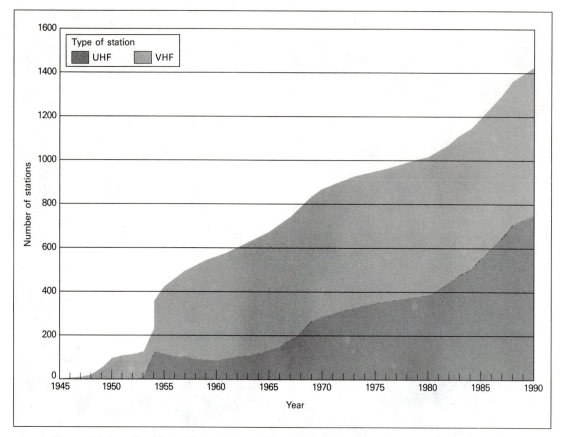

Figure 4.1 Growth of television stations.   The distance from the top curve to the baseline indicates the total number of television stations; that from the top curve to the second curve, the number of VHF stations; and that from the second curve to the baseline, the number of UHF stations. *(Source: Television and Cable Factbook.)*

additional channels numbered 14–83 were opened in the ultrahigh frequency (UHF) band. The table of assignments was revised to provide for 2053 stations in 1291 communities; 242 of these assignments were reserved for noncommercial educational use. Standards were established to reduce interference among stations—maximum power outputs were specified, and minimum distances were set to separate stations operating on the same or adjacent channels. This was the plan under which the television broadcast service continued to operate.

4.1.3 Growth

The freeze had limited the number of television stations to the 108 authorized prior to the halt on construction. During the 30 months following the end of the freeze, 308 television stations signed on the air. There were two good reasons for the rush to obtain television licenses—audiences and money. In 1948, there were 190,000 television sets in use in the United States. In 1955, the number was 32,500,000; in just seven years, 65 percent of all homes had acquired at least one television receiver. In 1948, total television station revenue was $6.2 million; in 1955, station revenue had multiplied over 6000 percent to $372.2 million.

The networks also grew rapidly. The American Broadcasting Company (ABC), the Columbia Broadcasting System (CBS), and the National Broadcasting Company (NBC) bought television stations and signed up affiliates. DuMont also formed a television network and looked for affiliates.

Network distribution required the broadband capacity of coaxial cable. One television channel was nearly six times wider than the entire AM broadcast band, much too wide for the limited capacity of normal telephone wire. Therefore, the networks expanded their reach as the telephone company extended its coaxial cable—from New York to Washington, D.C., in 1946, to Boston in 1947, to the Midwest in early 1949, and to the West Coast on September 10, 1951. Affiliated television stations that were not yet on the cable received network programming in the form of kinescope film, a pre-videotape recording medium that involved making a filmed recording from a television screen as a program was telecast.

By 1955, CBS and NBC had developed strong, nationwide lineups of affiliates in major markets. ABC had many fewer affiliates. Over three times as many stations carried the DuMont network as carried ABC. But DuMont had trouble getting affiliates in large cities, the network lost money, and there was no DuMont radio network to offset TV losses. The year 1955 was DuMont's last as a network.

As the networks expanded, so did their advertising billings (Figure 4.2). In 1948, total network billings were $2.5 million; in 1955, they were $308.9 million, up 12,300 percent. Gradually, the growth slowed. It did not stop, and overall television billings increased every year except during the early

1970s, when a legal ban on broadcast cigarette advertising went into effect.

4.1.4 UHF Television

Many would-be broadcasters applied for the new UHF channels. But the cards were stacked against them. First, all other things being equal, **UHF signals do not travel as far** as VHF signals. The FCC, in an effort to compensate, purposely allowed an *in*equality. Transmitter power affects coverage area, so the commission allowed UHF stations to operate with 5 million watts, 16 times the maximum for any VHF station. However, no UHF transmitters were available to operate with such high power.

Second, **few receivers could pick up UHF channels.** The 108 stations that were on the air during the freeze were all VHF stations. During the $3\frac{1}{2}$ years of the freeze, the number of homes with television sets had gone from 1.6 million in 1949 to 17.3 million in 1952. Naturally, the television sets were equipped to pick up VHF television stations only. When UHF stations went on the air, no one owned UHF-capable sets, so no one was able to watch the new stations. Advertising income, therefore, was difficult to obtain.

Third, **many of the UHF stations were independents,** not affiliated with a network. The major networks had grabbed most of the big-city VHF television stations as affiliates. The public, primarily interested in receiving network fare, did not buy converters to adapt existing television sets to pick up both VHF and UHF stations. Manufacturers continued to build VHF-only television sets. They offered UHF capability as an extra-cost option on some models; few buyers of new sets were interested.

UHF licensees found it nearly impossible to compete with VHF stations and lost money. Many let their stations go dark and

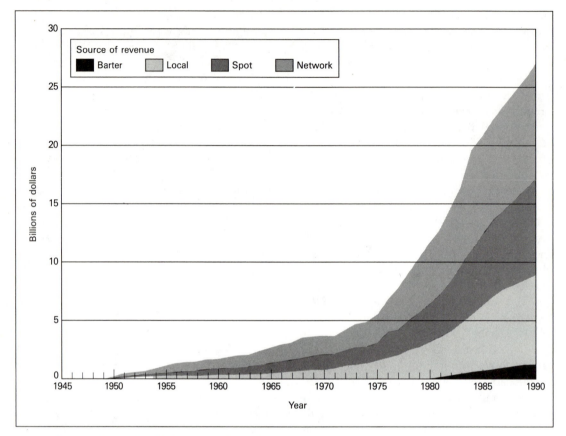

Figure 4.2 Growth of television advertising revenue. The distance from the top curve to the baseline indicates the total amount of money spent on TV broadcast advertising; distances within each horizontal segment indicate the amount spent in each of the four categories. (*Sources:* McCann Erickson and Television Bureau of Advertising.)

turned licenses back to the FCC. By 1956, the pattern of UHF television station failure was clear, and the FCC became concerned.

First, the commission tackled the transmitter problem. Transmission tests were conducted in 1961 and 1962. The FCC found that high-power transmission was feasible and did extend a UHF signal to a distance comparable to that of VHF.

The commission could not force networks to affiliate with UHF stations. But it could do something about the lack of UHF-capable receivers. At the FCC's request, Congress adopted a law that empowered the commis-

sion to require all-channel tuning. Starting on April 30, 1964, every new TV set sold in the United States had to be able to receive all VHF and UHF channels. Six years later, the commission adopted rules to make UHF tuning comparable to that of VHF; receiver design now had to be such that UHF channels were as easy and convenient to select as VHF.

The FCC took other steps, dealing with both transmitter and receiver, to make the quality of the UHF signal comparable to that of VHF. The cable must-carry rule (Section 4.5.2.1) helped, too; a cable system's channel lineup usually placed VHF and UHF stations next to each other on the dial. Eventually, FCC efforts to make commercial UHF television viable paid off. During the 1970s, UHF television stations as a group lost less money each year until 1975, when they finally showed a profit (Figure 4.3).

4.1.5 Color Television

Color television experimentation began as early as the late 1920s. Subsequently, various companies worked on and promoted different systems of color television, but the main rivalry was between **RCA's dot sequential system** and **CBS's field sequential system.**

In 1949, as a result of a petition by CBS to the FCC, the major television interests dem-

onstrated their color television systems. CBS's system was *mechanical*. Largely the work of Dr. Peter Goldmark (Figure 4.4), the CBS field sequential system used three filters—red, blue, and green. The filters rotated past the camera pickup tube in rapid succession. When the filters were synchronized with similar filters on the receiver picture tube, the viewer's eye would see the full range of natural colors. Originally, the field sequential system needed an 18-MHz channel, but CBS refined it to operate in the 6-MHz width of existing channels. The field sequential system, despite its excellent color reproduction, was *incompatible*; monochrome (black-and-white) receivers got a distorted picture when tuned to a field sequential color transmission. However, existing monochrome television sets could be adapted to receive black-and-white versions

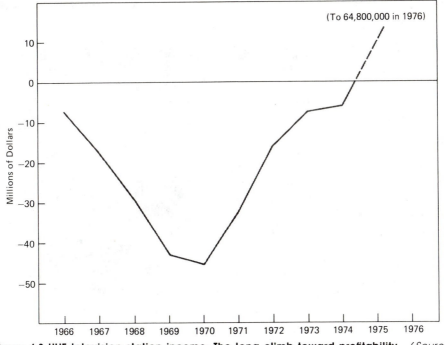

Figure 4.3 UHF television station income: The long climb toward profitability. (*Source:* Federal Communications Commission.)

Figure 4.4 The CBS field sequential color television system. Dr. Peter Goldmark with the first CBS color pickup equipment. (*Source:* William C. Eddy, *Television: The Eyes of Tomorrow.* New York: Prentice, 1945. Used by permission.)

of color transmissions for about $10 and *to receive color pictures for about $45!* Further, CBS contended that the system could eventually be refined to be completely electronic, eliminating the mechanical color disc.

The FCC adopted the CBS color system, effective November 20, 1950. The television trade was unhappy because the system was mechanical and incompatible. Before the FCC order could go into effect, RCA filed suit against its adoption. A number of manufacturers and service companies did the same. The suit delayed implementation of the order for six months while the case worked its way up the federal court system. In May 1951, the Supreme Court unheld the FCC.[2]

In October, color receiver production was halted because of the Korean War. CBS had broadcast the first network color program with the new system in June and continued technical development. Congress questioned the delay in introduction of color television, and in March 1953 the war ban was lifted.

Meanwhile, RCA and its allies had been busy. Another all-industry National Television System Committee (NTSC) of engineers was formed to study and recommend standards for an electronic, compatible color television system. By mid-1953, NTSC had completed its work, and RCA petitioned the FCC to adopt NTSC standards (Sections 12.2 and 12.3). In December, the FCC approved the electronic system.

The first RCA color sets were expensive (Figure 4.5). RCA's basic color television receiver with 15-inch screen retailed for $1000 in 1954, and no $45 conversion kits were made available. In addition, very few stations were equipped for color telecasting. The public did not rush out to trade in old monochrome receivers for new color sets. In 1955, there were only 5000 color sets in use in the entire United States (Figure 4.6). Even ten years later, less than 5 percent of all television homes were equipped for color. In 1953, CBS and NBC each carried over 22 hours of color programming weekly. Both

Figure 4.5 1954 RCA color receiver. (Photograph courtesy of RCA Corp. Used by permission of General Electric Co.)

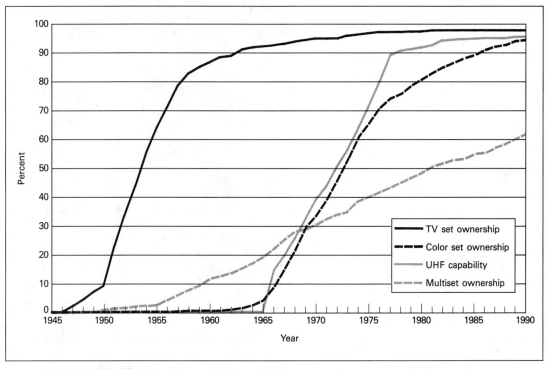

Figure 4.6 Growth of American homes with television. The top curve indicates the percentage of all U.S. households equipped with at least one working television receiver; the other curves show the households that can receive UHF stations, that have at least one color receiver, and that have two or more working receivers. (*Sources:* Arbitron Ratings Co., NBC, and Nielsen Media Research.)

cut back, and by 1958 only NBC still broadcast a regular schedule of color programs.

In the mid-1960s, prices of color receivers dropped somewhat, and sales picked up. Sales of color sets for the first nine months of 1965 doubled those of the same period in 1964. The lead oxide vidicon camera tube was introduced, resulting in better color cameras. Networks increased color telecasting and, in September 1966, began full-color programming in prime time. Stations installed color equipment; national advertisers demanded it. By 1967, it was clear that color television was an unstoppable trend. By 1969, one-third of all television homes in the United States were equipped for color. Twenty years later, color set penetration exceeded 95 percent.

4.2 TELEVISION PROGRAMMING EVOLVES

4.2.1 Station Programming

In the earliest days of television, there was no large backlog of syndicated programs to fill a station's schedule. For much local programming, stations used old feature films. These were the only films Hollywood had made available to its young rival medium, so television acquired an **old-movies** reputation. Some stations even ran silent films, adding narration and sound tracks. Some stations used **short musical films**—well-known bands, vocalists, and singing groups—and put them together in the form of a visual disc jockey show, anticipating a

Figure 4.7 Local Production. Television station WCPO, Cincinnati, did its *Al's Corner Drugstore* the same way most stations did local programming in 1950—live, on the air. This program, on which MC Al Lewis played a soda-jerk character, soon evolved into the *Uncle Al Show*. On the *Uncle Al Show*, the host's standard uniform included straw hat, colorful jacket, bow tie, and accordian. Uncle Al entertained and taught his pre-school audience using his own talent in music and art and the fantasy available from television's special effects. As the program matured, the cast increased, adding life-sized characters, puppets, and Wanda (Mrs. Al) Lewis. By 1952, Uncle Al was one of television's most-watched performers, appearing on three programs (three hours) daily, five days a week. The ABC television network carried Al and Wanda's Saturday show coast to coast for a year in 1957. In 1985, after 35 years and 14,000 episodes, the series went off the air, making the *Uncle Al Show,* according to WCPO, the country's longest running television program with the same host. During all but the last of those years, the program aired live with a studio audience of 30 or more youngsters. (*Source:* WCPO. Used by permission.)

video format that Music Television (MTV) would reinvent 30 years later. Most stations ran lots of film **travelogues.**

But when the network was not feeding programs and all the old movies and travelogues had been aired, a station had little choice other than to devise and air its own programs. There was no videotape, so they were all **live.** The stations tried **local production** (Figure 4.7) of all types of shows— soap operas; cooking programs; interview shows; the man/woman who played the piano/organ/both and sang/recited poetry; local talent shows; and children's programs, hosted by Captain/Uncle Somebody-or-other, featuring old black-and-white movie cartoons of Farmer Alfalfa or Felix the Cat.

4.2.2 Network Entertainment Programming

At the network level (Figure 4.8) there was much experimentation, attempts to find programming suitable for the visual medium. These efforts, however, had to await the spread of AT&T's coaxial cable. In June 1946, the Joe Louis–Billy Conn fight for the heavyweight boxing championship was broadcast on an ad hoc network to four East Coast cities. Sponsored by the Gillette Safety Razor Company, the broadcast reached an estimated 100,000 viewers and was reported to have convinced skeptics that television was here to stay.

Bristol-Myers became the first advertiser

Figure 4.8 CBS 1940s television studio.   Technicians felt that early TV cameras needed an even wash of bright light to make good pictures. Incandescent lights would make a studio unbearably hot, so some pioneer television production facilities were equipped with banks of fluorescent lights, as was this CBS studio. After the wash was established, spotlights beamed in additional light to give the effect of highlighting. (*Source:* William C. Eddy, *Television: The Eyes of Tomorrow*. New York: Prentice, 1945. Used by permission.)

to sponsor a network television series. It was called *Geographically Speaking* and started in October 1946 on NBC. At that time, NBC was a two-station network.

In the early days a network sometimes took a radio series and made an **adaptation** of it for television. Some series were **simulcast,** that is, aired concurrently on both radio and television. Soon, the first prime-time hit programs emerged. In 1948, the *Texaco Star Theater*, a comedy-variety show, went on the air, launching the television career of Milton Berle (Figure 4.9a). "Uncle Miltie" was so popular that he became known as "Mr. Television." That same year, *Toast of the Town* began, produced and hosted by Ed Sullivan (Figure 4.9b). This variety program was almost straight vaudeville. Later renamed the *Ed Sullivan Show*, it ran for 22 years; for 10 of those years, it was one of the 20 most popular programs. Sid Caesar and Imogene Coca (Figure 4.9c) first teamed up in 1949 on the

Admiral Broadway Revue, carried by the combined NBC and DuMont networks. They moved to NBC's new *Your Show of Shows* in 1950, and people deserted restaurants, theaters, and parties on Saturday nights to watch their comedy.

There was some reliance on film programming, but much network television was **live and produced in New York.** As today, most early dramatic programs were episodic series—a complete story each week, evolving out of the same situation, with the same main characters.

4.2.2.1 Live Anthology Drama   During the early 1950s, another type of dramatic program developed, the **anthology series.** Here, the program title remained the same, but each program featured a completely different play—different characters, different actors, different stories, different situations. The programs included *Philco Playhouse* (which

(a)

(b)

(c)

Figure 4.9 The first network superstars. (a) Milton Berle. (b) Ed Sullivan. (c) Sid Caesar and Imogene Coca. (Photographs a and c courtesy of the National Broadcasting Company, Inc. Photograph b courtesy of CBS. Used by permission.)

later alternated with *Goodyear Playhouse*), *Kraft Television Theater*, *Playhouse 90*, and *Studio One*. The plays they produced catapulted their young authors into prominence—Paddy Chayefsky, Rod Serling, Reginald Rose, Tad Mosel, Horton Foote, and others. Some of the plays were subsequently made into fine motion pictures—*Requiem for a Heavyweight, Marty, Dino, Twelve Angry Men*, and *Patterns*.

The anthology series reached their peak in 1953. By 1956, they were all but gone, victims of changing audience taste, sponsor script interference, and the economics of syndication. This brief period of live, anthology series drama is often referred to as the

golden age of television drama. This may overstate the case; much—perhaps most—of the writing was mundane. But the plays were live, they were theater, they were peculiarly television. And when they were good, they had a quality that transcended their time, that is still evident today.

4.2.2.2 Trends and Synthesis

Trends in network programming emerged in the early and mid-1950s. CBS had benefited in radio from Bill Paley's 1948 talent raid (Section 3.1.3). When the time came to beef up its prime-time schedule, CBS stuck with success. Its television forms and formats were those of radio—**fully sponsored, regularly scheduled programs.** Its programming nucleus was its stable of big-name comedians. CBS's strategy worked, and by 1953 it had captured the lead in prime-time network ratings. CBS held that lead year after year, almost continually.

NBC's programming reflected the thinking of **Sylvester L. "Pat" Weaver** (Figure 4.10). Weaver, a former advertising executive, joined NBC in 1949 as vice-president in charge of television. In December 1953, he became president of NBC. Control of network programs by sponsors and their advertising agencies, a practice that developed in radio (Section 3.1.4.1), had transferred to television; Weaver now worked to shift control to the network. He pushed for a new programming form, the **magazine concept.** The network would produce and control the program and sell time within it to advertisers for commercial messages. Each program would have a number of different advertisers. Using this concept, NBC started the *Today* and *Tonight* shows, which are both still in existence.

Another Weaver idea was the **spectacular.** Spectaculars were one-time programs made with extra care and money. Preceded by a larger-than-normal publicity campaign, they were designed to stand out from the usual programming, to create talk and excitement.

ABC, weakest of the three major radio networks, began video operations in 1948 as an even weaker television network. In 1951, ABC entered into negotiations for a merger with United Paramount Theaters, former exhibition arm of Paramount Pictures. The merger was completed in 1953, bringing Paramount's working capital and former Paramount executive **Leonard Goldenson** (Figure 4.11) to ABC. Goldenson used his Hollywood contacts to get the major studios interested in program production.

Using the themes and formulas popular with movie audiences—cowboys, cops and robbers, detective stories—ABC played a catch-up game. Its first big successes were *Cheyenne*, produced by Warner Brothers, and *Disneyland*, produced by the Walt Disney organization. ABC-TV based its programming strategies on action-adventure dramatic series—*The Untouchables, 77 Sunset Strip, The Rebel, The Rifleman, Hawaiian Eye.* All were produced on film; none was live. All were violent, but all attracted audiences.

ABC made a major commitment to sports coverage. Starting in 1959, the network acquired television rights to numerous sporting events. It also acquired Sports Programs, Inc., a production company. One of the company's young producers was **Roone Arledge** (Figure 4.12) Originally hired to produce football telecasts, Arledge brought flair and imagination to all types of sports coverage; under his leadership ABC Sports helped push the network closer to its competitive goals.

Despite having weaker affiliates in large markets and fewer affiliates overall, ABC-TV managed to close the ratings gap between itself and the other networks. In the 1975–1976 season, ABC-TV took the lead in overall prime-time ratings and did not lose it until

(a)

(b)

(c)

(d)

Figure 4.10 Pat Weaver and his programming innovations. (a) Pat Weaver while at NBC. (b) Dave Garroway, first host of *Today,* and J. Fred Muggs celebrate the program's fifth birthday. (c) The first *Tonight* cast included Gene Rayburn, Steve Allen (host), Eydie Gorme, and Steve Lawrence (at piano). (d) Betty Hutton starred in *Satins and Spurs,* the first NBC "spectacular." (Photographs courtesy of the National Broadcasting System, Inc. Used by permission.)

the early 1980s. However, by this time, ABC had picked up stronger affiliates, and its days of running fourth in a three-network race seemed to be over.

Each of these trends influenced the overall shape of network programming. Regularly scheduled programs formed the basis of the prime-time schedule. Over the years, all three networks have telecast **specials** (the successor term to *spectacular*) and *Today/Tonight*-style programs. Film production displaced live production of prime-time pro-

Figure 4.11 Leonard Goldenson. The man who headed ABC for 22 years—from its 1953 merger with United Paramount Theaters to its 1985 purchase by Capital Cities Communications. (*Source:* AP/Wide World.)

Figure 4.12 Roone Arledge. After building ABC's reputation in sports, he was put in charge of the network's news operations. (*Source:* ABC Visual Communication.)

grams (although rising production costs forced emphasis on videotape production). The television production center shifted from New York to Hollywood, and the action-adventure series became a staple of network prime-time programming.

Finally, few programs were completely sponsored. The networks had moved purposefully to take control of programming, as urged by Pat Weaver (and spurred at least in part by the quiz-show scandals; Section 4.3.3). At the same time, the cost of program production—already many times that of radio—had risen so much that most advertisers could not afford to pay for an entire program. In addition, Procter and Gamble, television's largest advertiser, adopted a policy of spreading commercials throughout a number of programs. The result was participation sponsorship—the network controlled the programs, and advertisers bought commercial positions within them.

4.2.2.3 Compared to Radio Most of radio's major program types proved successful in television. Some that were long-running features on network radio, however, were not regularly scheduled on television and appeared only sporadically as specials after the 1950s—for example, experimental drama, fine-arts programs, and programming for minority interests such as the old NBC radio program for farmers, *National Farm and Home Hour.*

Prime-time television series proved to be, on the average, much shorter lived than radio series. A television series was a veteran if it survived 5 years, but many prime-time radio series ran 10 or 15 years or even longer (Figure 4.13). Because its program turnover was higher, television was more cyclic than radio. A theatrical film or a new program type became popular, and it spawned a host of imitators. For example, in the early 1970s, the popular, so-called "social consciousness" situation comedies multiplied by means of

(a)

(b)

(c)

(d)

Figure 4.13 Long-running TV programs.   (a) Star of *The Red Skelton Show,* on the air from 1951 through 1971. (b) Vivian Vance, William Frawley, Desi Arnaz, and Lucille Ball—cast of *I Love Lucy,* which first ran on the network from 1951 through 1971 and then ran in syndication for years and years. (c) *The Jackie Gleason Show* started in 1952 and ran for 18 years. (d) Dan Blocker, Lorne Greene, Pernell Roberts, and Michael Landon, stars of *Bonanza,* 1959–1973. Thanks to syndication—long-time domestic and wide-range foreign—this program is perhaps the most popular western series in the world. (Photographs a, b, and c courtesy of CBS. Photograph d courtesy of the National Broadcasting Company, Inc. Used by permission.)

the spin-off—secondary characters from one series would become the basis on which new series were built. *All in the Family* spawned *Maude* and *The Jeffersons; Maude* spun off *Good Times,* and so on. The box office success of the 1981 theatrical film *Raiders of the Lost*

Ark inspired at least two prime-time 1982 series, *Bring 'Em Back Alive* and *Tales of the Gold Monkey.*

Television, on the other hand, popularized program forms that did not exist on radio, such as children's animated cartoons and feature films. First introduced on network prime-time television in 1961, feature films proved to be extremely popular. They also had the advantage of capturing and holding audiences for long periods of time. This inspired the networks to lengthen other prime-time programming to 1 hour, 90 minutes, and even up to 4 hours on special occasions. Sports events proved much more popular on television than on radio, from the early *Friday Night Boxing* and wrestling programs to sophisticated coverage of football, baseball, golf, tennis, Olympic Games, and other sports.

4.2.3 Network Informational Programming

Forerunners of today's early-evening network news programs began in the late 1940s (Figure 4.14). CBS's *Douglas Edwards with the News* went on first in 1948. NBC's *Camel News Caravan* with John Cameron Swayze

began the next year, and ABC and DuMont soon followed with their own newscasts. These newscasts were 15 minutes long, and the networks contracted with newsreel and other film organizations for news film.

The networks strengthened their news operations during the 1950s (Figure 4.15), adding resources, personnel, and newscasts at other times during the broadcast day. In 1963, CBS and NBC increased the length of their evening newscasts to 30 minutes; ABC followed four years later. Polls revealed that the public saw television as the most relied-on news medium as early as 1959 and as the most believable news medium by 1961 (see Figures 8.1 and 8.2).

In 1976, all three commercial television networks prepared to lengthen evening newscasts to one hour. Affiliates protested, saying expanded newscasts would take away 30 minutes of valuable, salable local time. Four years later, the networks again announced plans to expand their evening newscasts; again the affiliates protested. Net-

(a)

(b)

Figure 4.14 Early network news programs. (a) *Douglas Edwards with the News.* (b) John Cameron Swayze on *Camel News Caravan.* (Photograph a courtesy of CBS. Photograph b courtesy of the National Broadcasting Company, Inc. Used by permission.)

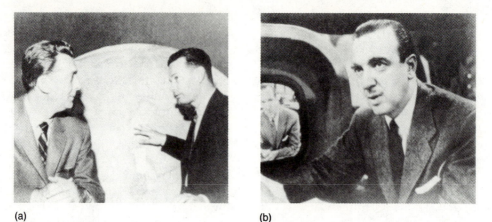

(a)   (b)

Figure 4.15 Network news stars. (a) After doing well during the political conventions in 1956, Chet Huntley and David Brinkley took over the evening news spot from John Cameron Swayze. This combination proved highly popular with viewers. NBC's showcase news program ran for 14 years as *The Huntley-Brinkley Report.* (b) In 1962, Walter Cronkite replaced Douglas Edwards as the CBS evening newscaster. Cronkite would remain in that job for two decades, helping to move CBS past NBC in the news ratings. (Photograph a courtesy of the National Broadcasting Company, Inc. Photograph b courtesy of CBS. Used by permission.)

work news did expand in other ways. Short summary newscasts—no longer than 60 seconds—were added during prime time, as well as long-form news programs during other dayparts. These were all in addition to other regular programming such as *Today, 60 Minutes,* and *Good Morning America.*

Broadcast news also expanded in two other areas—the documentary and on-the-spot coverage (Box 4.2). Edward R. Murrow, along with Fred Friendly, began network television's first news documentary series, *See It Now,* in 1951, and established standards by which television documentaries are still measured. NBC broadcast its *Victory at Sea* series in 1952, recounting U.S. naval operations in World War II. ABC's documentary efforts began in the late 1950s. By 1961, all three networks produced stimulating, vital news documentaries. Many local stations produced documentaries, too.

Some of television's finest work was live coverage of various events—national political conventions; elections; presidential inaugurations; the Kefauver Crime Committee

hearings in 1951; the Army-McCarthy hearings in 1954; the debates between presidential candidates in 1960 (the so-called great debates) and then, starting in 1976, every four years; the deaths and funerals of President John F. Kennedy (Figure 4.16), Senator Robert Kennedy, and Reverend Martin Luther King, Jr.; coverage of U.S. space efforts; and the Watergate and Iran-Contra hearings.

During the 1970s and 1980s, the networks lost impetus in documentary production and live coverage. First, they cut back on the frequency and impact of full-length documentaries. Later, they gave up extended, live coverage almost completely, allowing Cable News Network and C-SPAN (Section 8.3.2) to fill the void.

4.3 PROBLEMS AND SCANDALS

Television, like radio, suffered its share of problems. Many involved questionable ethics and occurred during the 1950s—so many that the 1950s may have been the most

Box 4.2 Documentary and Live Coverage Impact: Senator Joseph McCarthy

Even in television's earliest days, documentaries and live coverage had the power to enhance the public weal, to help citizens keep a check on their government and uncover rogues and wrongdoing, hype and hypocrisy. Such was the case with Senator Joseph McCarthy.

In 1953–1954, Ed Murrow and Fred Friendly did what others in television news could not or would not do. They focused the journalistic eye of several *See It Now* programs on McCarthy-inspired accusations of guilt by association. As discussed in Section 3.2.3.1, McCarthyism was founded on a fear of Communist subversion that had grown, cancer-like, into a national paranoia. Its basic structure was (1) a presumption (2) of guilt (3) by association; its mechanism, simple—you were guilty if accused. It had a built-in defense; those who opposed the methods of Senator McCarthy and his allies were themselves branded "un-American" or worse. The accused lost their jobs and could not find work. They included people in radio and television, as well as other areas of entertainment.

On March 9, 1954, Murrow and Friendly did a program on McCarthy himself, juxtaposing excerpts of various speeches the senator had made to show the inconsistencies and illogic of McCarthy's rhetoric. Messages flooded into CBS, overwhelmingly favorable toward the program. Senator McCarthy's rebuttal, a personal attack on Murrow, was broadcast by CBS on April 6. However, McCarthy's reply was such that it inadvertently proved Murrow's points, and the mail ran two-to-one in favor of Murrow.

Two weeks later, ABC and DuMont televised hearings before the Senate Permanent Subcommittee on Investigations over a dispute between McCarthy and the U.S. Army. The hearings ran 36 days, exposing the real, live McCarthy to many for the first time. On the thirtieth day, McCarthy launched a vicious, unprovoked, and irrelevant attack on a junior member of the Boston law firm of Joseph N. Welch, the Army's lawyer. The hastening of McCarthy's fall seemed to date from that point. The Senate voted to censure him later that year. In May 1957, he died. (Photo Source: AP/Wide World)

Figure 4.16 Live news coverage. A nation wept with this bereaved widow as she and her two children waited to be driven to the Capitol, where her late husband lay in state. Television helped stunned citizens work through their grief after the assassination of President John F. Kennedy. (Photograph courtesy of CBS. Used by permission.)

shameful, scandal-ridden ten years in the short history of radio and television. Television's share included plugola, FCC corruption, and the quiz show scandals.

4.3.1 Plugola

Plugola was discovered a few years before radio's payola revelations (Section 3.2.3.3). If a certain product was used on camera in a television program, the publicity agent for the product would pay the program's writers and directors. This constituted, in effect, advertising, but the audience did not realize it was advertising, nor was it so informed, a violation of federal law.

4.3.2 Government Corruption

In 1957, the Committee on Interstate and Foreign Commerce of the U.S. House of Representatives decided to look into the perfor-

mance of various regulatory agencies. Dr. Bernard Schwartz, a professor from New York University, was hired as chief counsel. When Schwartz produced embarrassing findings, Commerce Committee members tried to impede his investigation and finally fired him in 1958. Schwartz released his findings to the press.

Schwartz found that FCC commissioners were reimbursed for the same trip by both government and broadcasters and received from broadcasters gifts of television sets and vacation trips. He found that one commissioner, Richard A. Mack, had sold his FCC vote to an applicant for a contested Miami television channel. He discovered that Representative Oren Harris, who chaired the House Commerce Committee, had paid a cash total of $500 for one-quarter interest in an Arkansas television station, after which the station reapplied to the FCC for an increase in power—which had been refused once before—and got it. Dr. Schwartz's revelations led to the resignation of FCC Chairman John C. Doerfer and Commissioner

Mack. Harris, however, went on to a federal judgeship.

4.3.3 Quiz Show Scandals

Then there was the **quiz show scandals.** *The $64,000 Question* (Figure 4.17), first of the big-money quiz shows, started on CBS-TV in 1955. The amount of prize money, the diffi-cult questions, the suspense of the game it-self, and the gimmicky setting—all helped make *The $64,000 Question* popular. Natu-rally, it spawned imitators. By July 1955, three of the top ten programs in audience rat-ings were big-money quiz shows.

Four years and several government inves-tigations later, the truth came out. The shows had been rigged—contestants given answers in advance—on a regular basis to enhance, said the producers, their "entertainment value." Ten persons pleaded guilty to per-

Figure 4.17 The $64,000 Question. Host Hal March and a guest. (Photograph courtesy of CBS. Used by permission.)

jury for lying during the investigations, and the careers of a dozen or so other persons were ruined. The networks canceled the shows and tightened program control.

4.4 REFORM AND ACTIVISM

After the problems and scandals of the 1950s, a reaction set in. The reaction was characterized by activism—activism on the part of the regulators to see that broadcasters served the public interest, activism on the part of educators and others to provide an al-ternative television service, activism on the part of citizen groups to ensure that stations responded to the needs and interests of the communities to which they were licensed.

4.4.1 Regulation

The FCC started it. Beginning in 1960, there was to be a **new approach to regulation;** the public interest would come before the broad-casters' private interest. No more back scratching between the regulators and the regulated. The FCC issued the *1960 Program-ming Policy Statement*[3] defining what was needed in programming to meet the public interest. Licensees were to "ascertain" (find out with certainty), and then program to meet, the needs of the communities they served. An FCC Complaints and Compliance Division was created to receive and investi-gate complaints from the public. The com-mission developed a license application form that required detailed information on public interest programming. Congress amended the Communications Act to make payola and plugola illegal and to prohibit rigged quiz shows.

In early 1961, Newton N. Minow (Figure 4.18) was appointed to chair the FCC. He told broadcasters their programming was "a

Figure 4.18 Newton N. Minow, III. Appointed by President John F. Kennedy, Minow chaired the Federal Communications Commission from March 1961 to June 1963. (*Source:* Bettman.)

vast wasteland" and warned that they would have to live up to their promises regarding programming on license renewal applications. The FCC subsequently stepped up disciplinary actions against erring broadcast stations.

4.4.2 Noncommercial Broadcasting Evolves

Noncommercial broadcasting began to develop into a **viable alternative to commercial broadcasting.** Congress passed the Educational Television Facilities Act in 1962 to build and improve stations. The Carnegie Commission on Educational Television, a blue-ribbon citizen panel, issued an influential report on funding and improvement of programming in February 1967. In the same year Congress, acting on recommendations of the Carnegie Commission, passed the Public Broadcasting Act, which created the Corporation for Public Broadcasting (CPB). CPB was to serve as the funding agency for programming. Two years later, the Public

Broadcasting Service was formed to distribute television programming. In 1970, National Public Radio was set up to produce and distribute radio programming.

As a result of these changes, noncommercial broadcasting improved and increased facilities and programming, attracted audiences, and even began to influence the programming of commercial broadcasters. In the process, the generic term changed from "educational broadcasting" to "public broadcasting."

4.4.3 Citizen Groups

Citizen groups established means to force broadcast licensees to deal with them directly. In the 1966 and 1969 **WLBT cases,**[4] a federal court of appeals ruled that the FCC had to allow representatives of the public to participate in license renewal proceedings and had to give weight to their testimony in arriving at decisions. The court's ruling in the WLBT cases touched off a rash of citizen group challenges to station license renewals. Stations entered into negotiations with the groups, discussing policies, soliciting suggestions, and making agreements; in this way, the public could directly influence programming. In the 1970s, the FCC adopted rules whose net effect was to encourage the public to take a more active interest in license renewal proceedings.

4.4.3.1 Use of the Fairness Doctrine Citizen groups filed fairness doctrine complaints about commercials and other aspects of broadcast programming. According to a 1949 FCC statement,[5] a broadcast licensee whose station aired one side of a controversial public issue had to ensure that the other side was presented too. Now citizen groups attempted to use this requirement in a variety of situations and, thus, expand the types of issues to which the fairness doctrine applied.

4.4.3.2 Programming Pressures Some groups functioned on the national level. They took note of research that showed increasing evidence of links between exposure to televised violence and aggressive behavior in the viewer. Worried about the impact of such programming, they worked to curb the sex-and-violence trend. They used publicity, complaints to the FCC, and meetings with network officials. The groups themselves were varied, ranging from the American Medical Association to the PTA and Action for Children's Television.

4.4.3.3 Television Evangelism Activism came to broadcasting in a quite different form, also. During the 1970s, Christian evangelists turned to television to reach audiences. They packaged video ministries in slick, often star-studded productions and paid stations to carry them. Their audiences were small but intensely loyal. Audience contributions financed not only the programs but also ancillary organizations such as colleges, broadcast stations, and theme parks. Most television evangelists professed fundamentalist theology and conservative social values. Some took advantage of the political conservatism and "born-again" faith that swept the country to increase their influence. They played active roles in politics. They also joined an increasing number of voices that called for the television networks to eliminate gratuitous depictions of sex from programming.

4.5 THE WINDS OF CHANGE

Despite all this "reaction," television prospered. Costs, particularly programming costs, climbed alarmingly. But so did audience levels and advertising billings. Advertising rates went up every year, and advertisers had little choice but to pay the increases. After all, television pulled in the people.

There was no lack of advertisers; networks came close to selling out their entire inventories of prime-time availabilities, and stations adopted rate cards that encouraged advertisers to bid against each other for time. If you wanted video advertising, broadcast television—primarily *network* broadcast television—was the only game in town.

But the winds of change had already begun to blow. By 1990, it was apparent that these winds had caused at least two radical alterations in the structure of commercial television broadcasting. First, new competitive elements had begun to whittle away network dominance of audiences and advertising dollars. Second, Wall Street had discovered broadcasting. That, too, affected the networks.

A major factor that cleared the windbreaks and so made possible these alterations was a series of FCC actions. For years the broadcast trade had continually and repeatedly requested these same actions—the lifting of government regulation.

4.5.1 Deregulation

As the years passed, the Federal Communications Commission had made more regulations. The regulated media complained of hours and money spent on FCC requirements—checking equipment, filling in forms, completing reports, establishing and updating files. Relief started in the 1970s. President Jimmy Carter announced plans to lift regulation on transportation industries—trucking, railroads, and airlines. The FCC, in turn, started proceedings to do the same for communications media. The first major achievement of FCC deregulation came in 1981, when the commission deleted certain requirements of commercial radio broadcasters; three years later, similar requirements were lifted from commercial TV. Further deregulation was planned.

Deregulation signaled the end of reform in the FCC at least for a time. The commission even eliminated some of its 1960s cleanup provisions. For example, the FCC did away with formal ascertainment procedures. In a general reorganization, the commission replaced the Complaints and Compliance Division with a lower-level complaints branch. The FCC adopted a "postcard-size" license renewal form and, in the process, eliminated the requirement that licensees provide information about the public-interest aspects of their programming.

Among the commission's many deregulatory actions, the most conspicuous had to be its elimination of the fairness doctrine. Mark Fowler, appointed by President Ronald Reagan to chair the commission in 1981, made no secret of his dislike for the doctrine. Fowler acted as ramrod and head cheerleader to accelerate the process of deregulation, and the deletion of fairness was one of his primary goals. Fairness remained intact (if somewhat unused) during his tenure, but the commission did lay some groundwork for its deletion. In August 1987, three months after Dennis Patrick had succeeded Fowler to the chair, the commission voted to cease enforcing the 46-year-old doctrine. Several citizen groups filed court appeals, and powerful congressional leaders vowed to turn fairness into law.

For years, broadcasters had argued for less regulation. They based their arguments on First Amendment grounds and asked for the same freedom from regulation that newspapers enjoyed. They said that competition—the marketplace—should determine programming, not some Washington bureaucrat's idea of "the public interest."

In theory, deregulation seemed to be the answer to their prayers, but broadcasters found that in practice it went further than they wished. The commission agreed with the marketplace concept and applied it across the board. After all, if broadcasters were to be free to compete in the marketplace, there had to be a marketplace in which they could compete. And if there was to be a marketplace, the commission had to lift regulatory barriers to make entry easier and more available, to allow more people a chance to compete. So the FCC used the marketplace concept as a rationale for reducing regulation, adding more stations, and creating new electronic media.

4.5.2 Competitive Elements

Broadcasters now faced less regulation but more competition. Three elements in this competition directly impacted the development of traditional broadcasting: cable television, independent programming, and home video.

4.5.2.1 Competition from Cable Television Cable systems first developed during the 1948–1952 freeze on new television construction. They brought television broadcast signals to communities where stations could not be picked up directly off the air.

At first, television licensees thought cable was a good idea. They were glad to see their signals extended to new audiences and improved in areas with poor reception. As cable evolved, however, it added services and moved into towns that already had television stations. At that point, cable introduced competition to broadcast television and, according to broadcasters, not very fair competition at that.

Broadcasters complained of **signal importation** from distant stations. Local stations found themselves competing for local audiences with stations miles away. Even worse was **leapfrogging,** when a cable system carried the signal of a distant station *instead* of a local station.

But worst of all, **cable television was founded on the signals of television sta-**

tions. The product that comprised the very heart of a cable system's service was the group of broadcast signals it carried. The entities that created these signals, the television stations, had to *pay* for the programming they broadcast. Yet, the cable system got this programming *at no charge* and then *sold* it to subscribers. In effect, television licensees were actually financing and creating the vital component of the competition's product—for which the competition received payment.

Broadcasters were at least partially mollified when a number of **legal requirements were imposed on cable systems.** The FCC adopted cable programming rules in 1966 and 1972. Some rules were subsequently repealed. The survivors included **must-carry** and **network nonduplication** rules. The former required cable systems to carry the signals of local television stations; the latter required them to blank out imported broadcast network programming when it duplicated that of local affiliates.

Broadcasters complained loudly in 1980 when the FCC dropped two of the protectionist cable rules. One had banned cable systems from importing signals of distant broadcast stations. The other had protected stations' rights to exclusive use of syndicated programming in their markets. Eight years later, however, the FCC reconsidered and adopted a new **syndicated exclusivity** (syndex) rule. Under the syndex rule, a station could force local cable systems to delete programming which duplicated that of the station.

Broadcasters feared the worst when a 1985 court decision invalidated the must-carry rules (Section 14.1.1.9). They breathed somewhat easier when the FCC issued new rules in 1987, but their relief was short lived. That December, these rules, too, were struck down by a court decision. Nine months later, the FCC released results of a survey of TV stations and cable systems concerning the effects since the 1985 decision. Some systems

had indeed dropped, denied carriage of, or repositioned from one cable channel to another the signals of TV stations. Of the 912 responding stations, about one-third reported one or more such actions by cable systems.[6]

In 1976 legislation, Congress made cable systems **liable for copyrighted material on broadcast signals** they carried. But the new law granted a compulsory license to carry the material, in return for which cable systems paid a set percentage of subscriber revenues (Section 15.2.3.2). Many broadcasters argued for additional programming protection and for cable to have full copyright liability; that is, a cable system would have to arrange and pay for permission to carry each piece of copyrighted material on every broadcast signal it carried.

Most anticable rhetoric centered on the system operator's role as **carrier and gatekeeper of broadcast signals**—the ability to allow and deny access to the local audience. Implicit in these arguments was the realization that **cable subscribers constituted a large percentage of the total television audience.** For the most part, however, such rhetoric ignored the two factors with the greatest ultimate potential to impact broadcast television: cable television, both systems and networks, (1) offered a large number of **competing programming services** and (2) **competed with broadcasters for advertising.**

Historically, the three TV broadcast networks together had a 90 percent share of the television audience. Programming competition, however, started to affect viewing patterns as early as the late 1970s. By the end of the 1988–1989 season, three-network prime-time audience shares had dropped below 70. CBS predicted the drop would go as low as the 60 range by 1995. Cable caused at least part of this **share erosion** by offering expanded choices for viewers.

Competition also affected program content. For example, the networks decreased their use of theatrical films (those originally shown in theaters). Once a staple of prime-time network programming, theatricals increasingly reached audiences through other media. In fact, home video and pay cable got them *before* the networks. In response, the networks scheduled more made-for-TV films.

The networks also loosened standards to compete with the so-called adult programming that cable offered. During the first month of the 1988–1989 TV season, for example, the networks' tabloidlike offerings included an NBC special on Satan-worship; an NBC miniseries that featured bondage, masturbation, and a bisexual *ménage*; an ABC movie in which a father burned his sleeping son; and a CBS series that contained racially motivated inflammatory language and violence.[7] The producers of Fox's highest-rated entertainment show took pride in what they admitted were tasteless themes and content in their Sunday-evening prime-time situation comedy.[8] (This loosening also allowed the networks to cut standards department personnel [Section 16.2.2], part of a general downsizing of staff [Sections 4.5.3.4 and 4.5.3.5].)

Cable did *not* pose the same immediate threat in advertising, however. During the 1980s, cable systems depended on subscriber fees for 95 percent of their revenues; cable's total advertising revenue was less than 4 percent of that of broadcast television. Still, cable entities sold advertising at both system and network levels, and their advertising income increased every year. Cable continued to expand its share of the advertising dollar at the expense of broadcasting.

In addition to complaining, broadcasters reacted to cable by competing and joining. Responding to the 24-hour cable news channels (Section 8.3.2), all three networks added additional news programming. By 1990, nearly one-third of all cable systems had ownership ties with broadcast-related facilities; some of the biggest station group owners were also some of the largest cable operators. Broadcasters, including the networks, invested in cable programming ventures. Licensees of a few independent television stations profited from cable directly, becoming nationally distributed "superstations" (Section 7.4.2.2).

Many commercial broadcasters, however, felt threatened. In 1989, for example, they launched a campaign to enlist public support for their very survival. The campaign aimed to alert the populace that "free TV" was being threatened by cable. They contended that cable was draining off programming, that cable threatened to divide the nation's television service into one system for the "haves" and another for the "have-nots." "Free TV" was, of course, advertising-supported broadcast television which, at least by implication, was being threatened with extinction by the "not-free" variety, cable television.

4.5.2.2 Competition from Independent Programming

At least part of the network share erosion resulted from competing broadcast television programming. Sources included independent stations and independent programmers.

The Federal Communications Commission put the **Prime-Time Access Rule** (PTAR) into effect in 1971. The commission believed that the three commercial television networks controlled the entertainment programming market and designed the rule to encourage competition. One main provision of the rule forbade network-affiliated television stations in the 50 largest markets from broadcasting more than three hours of entertainment programming during the four hours of prime time. This prohibition included not only new but also off-net material—syndicated programming that *had* run on the network.

At first, most affiliates affected by PTAR programmed this newly vacated slot poorly. They aired the relatively few first-run (not previously on the networks) programs available—game shows, cheap action-adventure series, and other equally unappealing programs whose main virtue was low cost. However, PTAR did not apply to independent television stations.

The independents competed by programming this time slot with popular syndicated off-net series. This tactic paid off. The independents' ratings improved, not only during this particular time period but also overall, as audiences discovered they offered good, entertaining alternatives to current network fare. Meanwhile, the networks themselves, through continuous competitive schedule-shuffling, kept audiences confused—canceling new programs before they had time to gather audiences, moving older programs around the schedule, constantly substituting specials for regular programming.

4.5.2.3 More Stations: UHF and Low-Power Television

PTAR helped independent television stations to experience growing financial success. The message seemed to be that a television station had the potential to make money in almost any market. Would-be broadcasters applied for the remaining vacant channels in large and medium markets. Most VHF assignments were already in use, so unused UHF channels became attractive to prospective licensees. As the remaining channels were snapped up, applicants competed for vacant UHF assignments even in smaller markets. By the 1980s, it became rather common to read that three, four, or more parties had applied for channels and locations that no one would have wanted a few years before.

In 1980, the FCC proposed adding as many as 4000 new stations through the creation of a completely new class of broadcast service, low-power television (LPTV). LPTV stations would be awarded on a demand basis similar to AM radio stations. This meant they could be put anywhere as long as they did not interfere with existing stations. Since they would operate with low power, their signals would not reach nearly as far as those of full-power stations. On the other hand, LPTVs would operate with few of the programming restrictions and requirements that applied to full-power stations. The FCC adopted rules for the new service in 1982.

The number of applications for LPTV stations quickly reached 8000. The commission announced that it would accept no more new applications until it could deal with the backlog. Licenses were awarded by computerized lottery.

After revising its application procedures, the FCC ended the freeze in 1987. By 1990, over 630 LPTV stations were on the air, and the FCC was authorizing as many as 15 new stations each month.

4.5.2.4 Higher Off-Net Prices; More First-Run Programming

The number of television stations increased, and so did the competition to get good programming. Syndicators were able to demand and get outrageously high off-net prices for series that had proved popular on the networks. Some independents bought more than they could afford.

PTAR and the increased number of stations also encouraged production and syndication of new programming directly for stations. Once the market opened, producers turned out creative first-run syndicated programming. Advertisers and advertising agencies got back into the programming business through barter syndication (Section 7.3.2.1). The stations themselves created programming and syndicated their better efforts. Groups of stations cooperated to produce programming (Section 7.3.2.1), some of which was designed to compete directly with prime-time network offerings.

4.5.2.5 Short-Term Competition: Subscription Television

During the late 1970s and early 1980s, traditional television had competition from yet another source—subscription television (STV). Similar to a pay cable channel such as Home Box Office (HBO), an STV station offered commercial-free programming in scrambled form. Subscribers paid monthly to use a decoder that unscrambled the signal. The difference lay in the transmission medium—the STV station *broadcast* the signal, rather than sending it by cable.

Subscription broadcast systems had been tested as early as 1950. The first full-scale public tryout was launched in 1962 at WHCT, channel 18, Hartford, Connecticut. The **Hartford STV experiment** lasted seven years. In 1968, despite bitter opposition from commercial television interests (Figure 4.19) and motion picture theater owners, the FCC authorized regular STV service. The response was not exactly overwhelming. Even seven years after the Hartford experiment, no station offered subscription programming.

Cable television actually gave STV its big boost. In 1975, HBO began satellite distribution, becoming the first nationally distributed pay cable (premium) channel. It was a success. Cable customers signed up in droves to pay a monthly fee for (primarily) uncut movies. Most big cities did *not* have cable, but TV stations could provide similar service by STV.

The STV boom started in 1977. Wometco Enterprises, owner of movie theaters and previously one of STV's major opponents, bought a New Jersey UHF station and began subscription programming. Wometco's move seemed to signal the beginning. Five years later, some 30 stations offered STV programming, and subscription broadcasters formed their own trade group.

As STV grew, so did its problems. Few operations were profitable. A whole underground industry developed around signal piracy; nonsubscribers bought illegal decoders and viewed without paying. Several group broadcasters who owned STV stations ceased subscription programming, citing lack of subscribers. In some markets, two or more stations started STV service and competed with each other for subscribers.

Ultimately, however, it was cable television—the medium that had inspired the boom—that killed off subscription television. An STV station transmitted only one channel; cable, many—for about the same price. STV subscribership dropped as pay cable penetration increased. By the end of the 1980s, most stations had converted to advertising-supported, unscrambled programming.

4.5.2.6 Competition from Home Video

Although it posed negligible competition for the television broadcast advertising dollar, home video threatened to become even more formidable than cable as a competitor for audiences. The real worry for broadcasters and advertisers was the ability of the videocassette recorder (VCR) to *rearrange programming* and *eliminate commercials!* Using a VCR, a viewer could **time shift**—capture otherwise ephemeral television programming broadcast at odd hours, even when asleep or not at home, and view the programming at a convenient time; **double view**—watch programming on one channel while recording that on another; **zip** commercials—fast-forward past them during playback; and **view prerecorded cassettes**—watch material that had never been broadcast.

4.5.3 Structural and Financial Changes

4.5.3.1 Evolution

Evolutionary changes continued in television broadcasting. At the most visible level, the networks made key

Figure 4.19 Broadcasters fight pay television. This advertisement ran in the Washington, D.C., *Post* on November 29, 1973. (Used by permission of National Association of Broadcasters.)

personnel changes. Fred Silverman signed on as president of NBC in 1978. Earlier, as CBS's youngest programming vice-president, Silverman had helped keep that network firmly in first place in the ratings. Next, as ABC's head of programming, he had taken that network from third place to first. His assignment at NBC was to repeat for that network the miracle he had worked at ABC. NBC, however, stayed in third place. In 1981 Silverman resigned, and Grant Tinker, founder of the highly successful production firm MTM Enterprises, was named chairman of NBC. Slowly, the programming fortunes of NBC improved. NBC won the prime-time ratings battle for the first time in the 1985–1986 season.

Early in 1983, Frederick S. Pierce was made president of ABC, confirming his role as heir apparent to ABC chairman Leonard Goldenson. Roone Arledge, who had taken ABC to prominence in sports, was given added duties as head of news. At CBS, William Paley went through several candidates to take over as network head. In 1980, CBS brought in Thomas H. Wyman as president. Three years later, Wyman succeeded Paley as chairman.

4.5.3.2 Revolution These evolutionary changes, however, pale beside the revolution that was brewing. It started about 1983. Before it was over, two of the major broadcast networks would be under new ownership, the third drastically reorganized to win an almost Pyrrhic victory in a hostile takeover battle. And these were only the most obvious of the many changes it caused in the television trade. It was *television's financial revolution,* and—bromidic though the term may be—it was indeed a true revolution.

The initial trigger was probably the gradual **recovery of the national economy** and a **decline in interest rates.** The cost of borrowing money had dropped from record highs to a level within the reach of most people in business. This included broadcasters.

The was the year, too, in which media analysts and bankers realized that broadcasting would survive, despite cable television. Predictions that cable would decimate broadcast television's audience had not come true. And the prediction seemed to become more unlikely all the time.

Regional banks took an interest in underwriting the purchase of broadcast stations. For years, they had preferred to lend money to businesses with fixed hard assets—inventory, machines, and real estate they could sell to recover their investment if the venture went belly-up. Broadcasting had few such assets, and banks were reluctant to lend large sums for station purchases. Now, with economic recovery loosening the money available to lenders, banks looked at broadcast stations in terms of the amount of money they made—specifically, the amount available to pay off long-term debt. The banks set up communications departments and solicited business from prospective buyers of broadcast properties.

Station purchasers discovered "creative financing." Various financial devices were used to raise money to supplement that available from banks and other traditional sources. Two popular devices—the limited partnership and the leveraged buyout—were basically means of using other people's money to buy control of a business.

Deregulation also helped spur the financial revolution. The FCC had **repealed the antitrafficking rule** (Section 19.1.5) in 1982; a licensee no longer had to own a station at least three years before selling it. Two years later, the commission **raised the number of stations a licensee could control.** The limit went from seven in each service (AM, FM, TV) to twelve (Section 19.1.2.2). Station group owners at or near the previous seven-station limit now looked for additional stations to acquire.

Group owners were not the only companies to acquire stations. Management teams put together financing packages and bought out the stations and station groups for which they had worked. Individuals and companies who had no experience in the trade saw financial opportunities in broadcasting and looked for properties to buy. This rash of acquisitions drove up stations' prices drastically.

The sale of television station KTLA illustrates. In 1982, Kohlberg, Kravis, Roberts & Co. (KKR), a private investment banking firm, put together a complicated leveraged buyout to purchase KTLA, a Los Angeles independent station on Channel 5. This was KKR's first station. The deal included investments from two limited partnerships, participation by members of the KTLA management team, and a loan underwritten by a group of banks. The purchase price was $245 million. Just two years later, KKR sold the station to Tribune Broadcasting Company for $510 million, twice the original purchase price. KKR, however, had continued to put together station deals and, by the end of 1985, was one of the top ten TV group owners in terms of percentage of population covered by its station's signals.

When a company found a likely target for acquisition, it could try a number of tactics. It could buy the target company outright. It could merge with the company. It could attempt a takeover. Here, the target company was usually publicly traded (that is, owned by stockholders). In this tactic, the company attempting the takeover would try to buy up enough stock to get control of the target company. If the target was willing, the takeover was said to be "friendly"; if unwilling, "hostile."

4.5.3.3 Hostile Takeover Attempt: CBS

The most prominent acquisition activities were those involving the television networks. CBS was first to make news. In early 1985, Fairness in Media (FIM), a group associated with U.S. Senator Jesse Helms, urged political conservatives to buy stock in and assert control of CBS. They wanted to "do something" about what they perceived as a "liberal bias" in CBS news. The FIM effort failed, but the attempt demonstrated that CBS was vulnerable to takeover. In April, Ted Turner, owner of superstation WTBS and Cable News Network, announced an offer to buy the shares of CBS stockholders. In exchange, he offered no cash, only paper—a package of common stock and high-yield, high-risk debt securities in the new company (CBS would be merged with Turner Broadcasting System) that he would control. Securities analysts dubbed the debt paper "junk."

CBS fought Turner's takeover attempt and, in July, offered to buy back 21 percent of its outstanding stock at $150 a share—$40 in cash and $110 in interest-paying notes. This would cost the network $1 billion. Turner challenged the CBS move in court and at the FCC, but by August, both had ruled against him. Turner's hostile takeover had failed.

In October, CBS management announced that it had found a "guardian angel" to help fend off future takeover attempts. Loews Corporation, a New York-based conglomerate, had acquired 11.7 percent interest in CBS, and Loews' chairman and chief executive officer, Laurence A. Tisch (Figure 4.20b), had been asked to join the network's board of directors. Loews subsequently increased its CBS holdings to just under 25 percent, becoming the network's largest stockholder. In September 1986, CBS chairman Thomas Wyman was forced out, as were other top executives. Tisch was named chief executive officer, and William Paley came back to the network as chairman. The FCC later ruled that this was *not* a change of control. Nonetheless, the fact remains that CBS management had fought and won a costly battle

(a)

(b)

(c)

Figure 4.20 The next generation. Between March 1985 and September 1986, ownership of all three major broadcast television networks changed. The change brought these newcomers to the helms of their respective organizations: (a) Thomas S. Murphy, chairman of the board and chief executive officer, Capital Cities/ABC, Inc.; (b) Lawrence A. Tisch, president and chief executive officer, CBS, Inc.; (c) Robert Wright, president and chief executive officer, National Broadcasting Company. (*Source:* Photographs a and b, AP/Wide World; photograph c © 1989, courtesy of the National Broadcasting Company, Inc.)

with Turner, only to be ousted and replaced by a third party.

CBS also had a $1 billion debt to pay off, the result of its stock buy-back. The network peddled subsidiaries and laid off employees. CBS even sold the division that had given the company its original name (Sections 2.1.6.3 and 3.1.3)—CBS Records (formerly Columbia Records) was purchased by Sony Corporation in 1987. By 1988, CBS had a cash *surplus* of some $3.4 *billion.* By this time, however, hundreds of CBS employees had been released and numerous activities had been closed down. Almost all departments lost personnel, several hundred from the CBS News Division alone.

4.5.3.4 Ownership Changes: ABC, NBC, and Others   Even in a period characterized by financial and structural change, one year stands out: 1985. *Broadcasting* magazine called 1985 a "30 billion-plus year . . . a record 12 months of mergers, sales and acquisitions." It counted 108 deals that involved $10 million or more, seven worth over $1 billion each.[9] Some of these deals constituted historical changes of ownership.

In March, while CBS was still fighting FIM, American Broadcasting Companies, Inc., was acquired by Capital Cities Communications, Inc., for $3.5 billion. Capital Cities was a group station owner that also had publishing and cable properties. This was the first acquisition of a television network since ABC had merged with Paramount Theaters 32 years previously. Leonard Goldenson retired; Thomas S. Murphy (Figure 4.20a), Capital's chairman and chief executive officer, took on those same roles in the new company, Capital Cities Communications/ABC, Inc. After a reorganization, Frederick Pierce resigned. Roone Arledge was made president of ABC News and Sports, retaining direct supervision of news activities but giving up that of sports.

In December, even the ABC acquisition was dwarfed. A $6.3 billion deal was struck, and history came full circle; RCA was acquired by General Electric, the company largely responsible for its creation 66 years before. GE, a co-owner of NBC in the network's earliest days (Section 2.1.2.2), had sold off its own station group several years before. Now, with one deal, GE was back in both the network and the station-group business. Both ABC and NBC subsequently laid off employees; the latter sold its radio stations and networks (Section 3.4.3).

In 1986, Robert Wright (Figure 4.20c), a GE executive, was named president of NBC. Wright had years of experience at GE, off and on. During one of the off periods he had

served a three-year stint as president of Cox Cable. Two years after Wright took over at NBC, the network moved decisively into cable. The network first announced that it would launch Consumer News and Business Channel (CNBC), an advertising-supported cable network. Just before the end of 1988, NBC agreed to purchase a half interest in Cablevision Systems' Rainbow Program Enterprises. Rainbow, in turn, was to take a 50 percent share in CNBC. NBC already had an interest in Arts & Entertainment (A&E). The Rainbow deal, then, meant that the broadcaster would now have ownership stakes in A&E and CNBC, as well as Rainbow's programming ventures—some half-dozen SportsChannel networks, Bravo, American Movie Classics, and Long Island News 12, an elaborate local origination programmer serving cable systems and subscribers northeast of New York City.

Despite new ownership, the big three continued to suffer share erosion. This limited their ability to increase advertising rates. Yet the cost of programming and other costs rose steadily. Network executives sought ways to cut expenses and tap alternative income sources.

Rupert Murdoch (Figure 4.21a), Australian media tycoon, purchased 20th Century Fox Film Corporation and Metromedia's six independent television stations for a total of $2.5 billion. He put long-time U.S. television executive Barry Diller (Figure 4.21b) in charge. Murdoch, who became an American citizen so that the FCC would approve transfer of the licenses to his company, formed a "fourth" television network, the Fox Broadcasting Company (FBC). FBC recruited a lineup of independent stations as affiliates and launched its prime-time programs in 1987.

Home Shopping Network, Inc. (HSN) had developed a 24-hour, satellite-delivered cable program service based entirely on di-

(a)   (b)

Figure 4.21 Fox Broadcasting Company. (a) Rupert Murdoch, chief executive officer, News Corporation, Ltd., put together the new network and assigned responsibility for it to (b) Barry Diller, chairman and chief executive officer, Fox, Inc. (*Source:* Photograph a AP/ Wide World; photograph b Broadcast Magazine.)

rect marketing (Section 7.4.2.3). So successful was HSN that it formed a broadcast network and bought 12 television stations.

4.5.3.5 The Down Side

The buy-sell syndrome continued into 1987, driven at least in part by tax law changes that took effect that year. But the bloom had started to rub off the boom.

Licensees of independent television stations seemed to be having financial problems. Many found themselves beset with burdensome financing as a result of limited partnerships and crippling payments for extensive programming purchases. According to one estimate, some 24 independents filed for bankruptcy between June 1986 and January 1988.[10]

Even religious broadcasters had problems. CBN Continental Broadcasting Network, Inc., sold stations, laid off workers, and canceled programming. In 1987, a sexual scandal broke concerning Rev. James O. Bakker, president of the PTL Television Network. An investigation of the PTL ministry revealed severe mismanagement, including huge back payments due to cable and broadcast affili-

ates for carrying the programming. Some affiliates canceled PTL programming. The next year, yet another sexual scandal broke, this time involving a second TV preacher, Rev. Jimmy Swaggart.

Critics expressed concern at the changes in the trade. How could someone who planned to buy a television station, they asked, possibly have in mind to serve the public interest (as required by law) when

1. the purchase would be highly leveraged, putting a drain on resources (for example, firing personnel, lowering programming and advertising standards in order to save money) to meet the debt payments;

2. the new owner would demand that the station show an immediate increase in profits (resulting probably from reductions in expenses—which, again, meant cuts in personnel and quality— rather than from long-range planning and investment to increase revenue) so that it would look good to a subsequent buyer; and

3. the station would be sold again as quickly as possible, the whole idea of

the initial purchase being to realize a fast profit?

These types of problems were not unique to broadcasting. The fast-megabuck artists bought and sold businesses to profit from the transaction, to raise price without actually adding value, in other trades. And it had hurt these other businesses, too. But broadcasting was different. The law required the FCC to determine that the *public* interest would be served before allowing transfer of license to a new owner.

Demands came from all directions—public interest groups, the U.S. Congress, even a few broadcasters—to stop what was seen as the damage done by deregulation, to reinstitute some sort of antitrafficking rule. Such a rule was, of course, highly possible—even if the FCC chose not to impose one, Congress could still write it into law. That would certainly go a long way toward stopping profit-driven station trading.

But the changes, the fundamental changes in the broadcast trade, that we have called a revolution—these were accomplished, and they could not be undone. "The die," as Caesar said when he crossed the Rubicon, "is cast."

NOTES

1. 41 F.C.C. 148.
2. *RCA* v. *U.S.*, 341 U.S. 412.
3. Report and Statement of Policy re: Commission en banc Programming Inquiry, 25 Fed. Reg. 7291, 29 July 1960.
4. *Office of Communication of the United Church of Christ* v. *Federal Communications Commission,* 359 F.2d 994 (1966); and 425 F.2d 543 (1969).
5. In the Matter of Editorializing by Broadcast Licensees, 13 F.C.C. 1246 (1949).
6. "Real-world data on a post-must-carry world," *Broadcasting* 5 Sep. 1988: 30.
7. "Tabloid TV: 'Now You See It on the Air,'" *USA Today* 2 Nov. 1988: 1A.

8. "'Raunch' on a roll," *Broadcasting* 21 Nov. 1988: 27.
9. "Fifth Estate's $30 billion-plus year," *Broadcasting* 30 Dec. 1985: 35.
10. "Independents looking back to 1987," *Broadcasting* 4 Jan. 1988: 66.

FURTHER READING

Anderson, Kent. *Television Fraud: The History and Implications of the Quiz Show Scandals.* Westport: Greenwood, 1978. The battle for ratings leads to fraud.

Barnouw, Erik. *The Image Empire.* New York: Oxford UP, 1970.

———. *Tube of Plenty: The Evolution of American Television.* Rev. ed. New York: Oxford UP, 1982.

Bergreen, Laurence. *Look Now, Pay Later: The Role of Network Broadcasting.* Garden City: Doubleday, 1980. Details the 50-year rise of network broadcasting.

Boyer, Peter J. *Who Killed CBS News: The Undoing of America's Number One News Network.* New York: Random: 1988. Includes the effect of the Turner/FIM takeover attempt.

Brooks, Tim, and Earle Marsh. *The Complete Directory of Prime Time Network TV Shows, 1946–Present.* 3d ed. New York: Ballantine, 1985. Encyclopedic listing.

Fore, William F. *Television and Religion: The Shaping of Faith, Values and Culture.* Minneapolis: Augsburg, 1987. Critical examination of the electronic church.

Frankl, Razelle. *Televangelism: The Marketing of Popular Religion.* Carbondale: Southern Illinois UP, 1987.

Hoover, Stewart M. *Mass Media Religion: The Social Forces of the Electronic Church.* Newburyport: Sage, 1988.

Horsfield, Peter G. *Religious Television, The American Experience.* White Plains: Longman, 1984.

Powers, Ron. *Supertube: The Rise of Television Sports.* New York: Coward, 1984.

Sterling, Christoher H. *Electronic Media: A Guide to Trends in Broadcasting and Newer Technologies, 1920–1982.* New York: Praeger, 1984.

CHAPTER 5

Cable and Other Nonbroadcast Technologies: From 1950

But more happened, much more. The history of radio and television did not end with broadcast television. Electronic technology—that field of endeavor opened by Lee De Forest's 1906 invention of the Audion—continued to evolve. This evolution led to (1) additional electronic media that competed with broadcasting for advertising and audience and (2) devices and concepts that affected or became part of radio and television.

We begin with developments in electronics, the "enabling" technology for the media subsequently discussed. Then we examine six delivery systems—cable television, satellite master antenna television, wireless cable (multichannel TV), satellite distribution and relay, direct broadcast satellite, and electronic text. We follow with home devices—personal computers, video games, videocassette recorders, videodisc players, and advances in receiver technology. We look at changes in broadcast television reproduc-

tion—high-definition television and multichannel television sound. And we look at changes in the tools of the trade and the uses of those tools—miniaturization of production equipment and growth of small-format production. We end with common-carrier developments.

5.1 SOLID-STATE AND DIGITAL ELECTRONICS

Solid-state and digital electronics were much more than a simple dislacement of tubes and wires. They were revolutionary developments, such a departure from their predecessors that they gave rise to Promethean advances in the ability to manipulate and process electronic information. All phases were affected—production, distribution, transmission, and reception. Pretransistor media such as broadcasting and cable were changed and improved. Newer media, including many discussed in this chapter, were created.

5.1.1 Transistors

The vacuum tube had limitations. It cost a lot to make; many of the glass bulbs had to be hand blown. It was fragile and bulky, consumed a great deal of power, and generated heat. It changed the temperature and thus the operating parameters of the equipment of which it was part. It burned out. Despite these problems, the vacuum tube represented the state of the art in electronics for 40 years.

Then came 1948, the dawn of solid-state electronics. That year, three scientists at Bell Laboratories developed a simple, solid device that performed the same chores as the vacuum tube, except better. The scientists were John Bardeen, Walter H. Brattain, and William Shockley. Their device consisted of a sandwich of semiconducting materials, primarily germanium crystals, later silicon. A weak current entered the sandwich and, because of the arrangement of the crystals, con-

trolled a stronger current—just as in a vacuum tube. However, the device was smaller and worked faster than a vacuum tube, failed infrequently, gave off little heat, and was cheap to make. It was called the transistor.

5.1.2 The Chip

The next step was to manufacture electronic circuits with all components included in one device and in one process. Two engineers working independently, Jack Kilby and Robert Noyce, developed variations of this idea in 1959. As finally developed, the construction process produced a silicon bead or *chip* that had been treated in several stages to create an **integrated circuit**—a tiny printed circuit that incorporated transistors, diodes, resistors, capacitors, and connections. A chip could be programmed to do more than one task—play a video game, run a chronograph watch, guide a space vehicle, operate a video effects unit. The chip made possible the personal computer and other digital electronic devices. Further advances in solid-state technology allowed use of increasing numbers of components on a single chip (Figure 5.1).

Figure 5.1 Evolution of solid-state electronics. Computer chip from the late 1980s. This tiny device contains the equivalent of thousands of transistors and their associated circuits. (*Source:* AP/Wide World.)

Solid-state technology changed the concept of electronic equipment manufacture and repair. No longer was there "a circuit." TV cameras, switchers, amplifiers, receivers, satellite transponders, uplinks, downlinks—all consisted primarily of **circuit boards,** filled at first with transistors and other electronic components and later with chips. If a piece of equipment malfunctioned, technicians did not look for and replace the specific resistor or condenser at fault; they tested and replaced entire circuit boards.

5.1.3 Digital Technology

The chip was a *digital* electronic circuit. It did not measure the *size* of an electronic signal; it simply looked for the *presence or absence* of a signal—that is, on or off. The chip utilized various combinations of on (or 1) and off (or 0) to represent and manipulate any number. This was digital calculation, using the **binary** system of numbers (based on 2), the type of processing done by most modern computers.

Alec Reeves, an English scientist, demonstrated that digital techniques could be applied to information other than pure mathematics. In 1938, Reeves patented **pulse code modulation,** conversion of a telephone signal into varying combinations of 1 and 0. Years later, solid-state technology paved the way to the application of this principle to radio and television. An audio or video signal that had been digitized (converted into binary code) could be processed, altered, transmitted, or copied multiple times and then reconverted into audio or video—*with no loss of fidelity.* (With nondigital technology, each such action would almost always degrade an electronic signal.) Digital equipment could even create signals. Such capabilities led to advances in audio and video effects, in networking, in video graphics and animation, in production and postproduction, and in consumer electronic products.

5.2 CABLE TELEVISION

The first major video medium to emerge and compete with broadcasting was cable television. Originally called community antenna television (CATV), the preferred term later changed to cable television, often shortened to "cable." The solid-state revolution did not generate cable television, but it did improve the technology, eventually giving cable the ability to offer more channels and more services than had been possible with tube-based equipment.

5.2.1 Origins of Cable Television

Cable television originated to serve communities where television signals could not be received (Section 10.2.4). One early system began in 1949 in Astoria, Oregon. Other pioneer systems started in 1950 in Lansford, Mahoney City, and Pottsville, all in the mountains of Pennsylvania.[1]

An entrepreneur would erect a tower atop a tall building or mountain. Antennas on the tower picked up signals from the nearest television stations. The signals were amplified and sent by coaxial cable to TV sets of residents who paid for the service. This remained the basis of cable television—to provide **subscribers** (cable customers) with higher-quality, and usually more, television station signals than they could otherwise receive on their TV sets.

5.2.2 Cable Television Evolves—I

As cable television grew (Figure 5.2), investors and system operators looked toward larger cities. Large populations would lead to more subscribers and higher revenues. Most city dwellers, however, already received multiple TV broadcast signals. How could

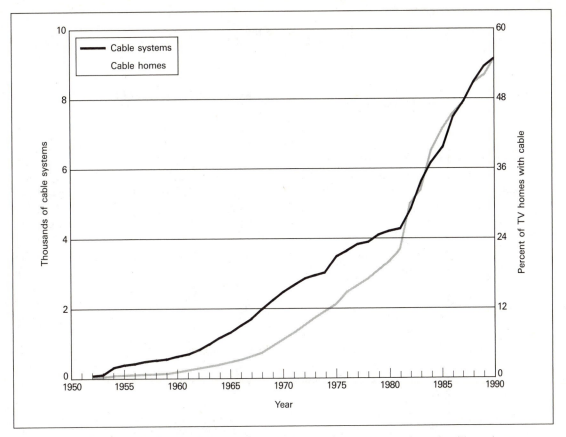

Figure 5.2 Growth of cable television.   Note that growth in the number of cable systems is shown in thousands of cable systems, while growth in cable subscribers is shown as the percentage of television homes with cable. (*Sources:* Nielsen Media Research; *Television and Cable Factbook.*)

they be sold on cable? Cable operators came up with four answers.

1. **Signal improvement.** The many electrical devices in a city could cause interference; the tall buildings could create shadow areas and ghosting (Section 10.2.4). A cable system could provide consistently strong, interference-free signals.
2. **Additional broadcast signals.** An operator could **import** signals from distant stations, giving subscribers a wider range of broadcast viewing alternatives.
3. **Cable-only basic programming.** An

operator could offer programming available only on cable. Some might be produced by the system itself. Some might come from other sources. Most would be supported by advertising. The operator could bundle this programming with the system's broadcast signals and market it as **basic service,** which provided for the system's lowest monthly rate.
4. **Pay cable.** An operator could charge extra for some cable-only programming. This programming would have to be special or exclusive—recent feature films, uncut and without commercial interruption; sports events not cov-

ered by broadcast entities; specially commissioned series and specials; stage performances and nightclub acts. The channels carrying such programming would be electronically scrambled; subscribers would pay extra to receive the signals unscrambled.

The trade was leaving the mom-and-pop stage. As cable entered larger markets, its potential to generate revenue attracted moneyed corporate interests. These companies won new franchises in a number of cities. They also bought out small entrepreneurs who had started existing systems. A firm that operated cable systems in more than one city was known as a **multiple system operator** (MSO).

5.2.2.1 The "Wired Nation"

One coaxial cable could carry huge amounts of information, 40 or more television channels. With proper equipment, signals could move not only *downstream* (to subscribers) but *upstream* (from subscribers) as well. Cable signals could also be sent to a specified destination. Such capabilities gave rise to conjecture about a "wired nation" based on a **broadband communications network.**

The wired-nation concept got its big boost in the late 1960s. The broadband communications network would consist of a grid of coaxial cables covering the entire country. We would hook into the network through an interactive home communications terminal. We could send and receive information as audio, television, cathode ray tube (CRT) display, and facsimile—to work, play, communicate, exchange written documents, file and retrieve information, do business and make financial transactions, make reservations, study, shop, visit with friends, hold group conferences, have utility meters read, and have police and fire departments monitor our homes while we were away. This would reduce traffic congestion, pollution, and the drain on diminishing supplies of fossil fuels.

5.2.2.2 Slump

Cable television ran into serious problems in the early 1970s. Many centered around Teleprompter Corporation, the nation's largest MSO. In 1971, Teleprompter and its chairman, Irving B. Kahn, were convicted of bribing city officials to keep the cable franchise in Johnstown, Pennsylvania. Several years later, Teleprompter got into financial trouble. In 1970, it had won a franchise for New York's borough of Manhattan; but the company found the city difficult to wire, encountering problems that ranged from high installation costs and low sign-up rates to vandalism and **piracy** (hooking up without subscribing). By the end of 1973, Teleprompter had invested $30 million in the franchise without showing a profit. The company undertook a major cost-cutting program, and officials announced that Teleprompter might have to write off $62 million in 22 uncompleted cable systems. The Securities and Exchange Commission investigated.

Shock waves spread through the cable trade. The financial community viewed cable as **capital-intensive,** needing a lot of money to start and a long time to pay off. Cable operators found money harder to get to build new systems. The U.S. economy lurched into recession. Profits were up. But stock prices were down, investment money scarce, and interest rates high. Several proposed mergers by large MSOs were called off because of adverse market conditions. Dreams of the wired nation, now referred to as "blue sky talk," disappeared as financial realities set in. The **National Cable Television Association** (NCTA), a trade group for cable operators, asked the Federal Communications Commission (FCC) to ease regulatory controls, which would reduce the equipment investment needed to meet technical requirements.

5.2.3 Cable Television Evolves—II

To a large extent, cable-only programming brought cable out of its slump. Previous cable-only programming had been primarily locally produced or distributed by tape. By contrast, the programming that helped revive the trade was (1) nationally distributed (2) by satellite relay. Its success generated a new subset of the trade; "cable" would mean not only "operators" but also "programmers."

5.2.3.1 Pay Cable Pay cable already existed. It had not been a big business, in simultaneously delivered network form, or offered by many cable systems. But now, pay cable grew in importance to the cable trade.

Home Box Office, Inc. (HBO) (Figure 5.3) helped launch the pay cable boom in 1975 when it announced plans for a satellite-interconnected national pay cable network. The cable trade reacted with enthusiasm. Within days, large MSOs began to sign up for the new service and acquire receive-only satellite dishes to receive HBO's signal. Cable stocks climbed, and the trade began to crawl out of its slump.

To operators, pay cable represented a source of revenue without the high investment required to expand a system's physical plant—in other words, low investment and fast return. To subscribers, pay cable represented a chance to see programming without the annoyance of commercial interruption.

HBO's success inspired others. The key seemed to be satellite distribution, a relatively low-cost means to network on a national basis. Throughout the 1970s and 1980s, myriad companies tried to emulate HBO or become "the CBS of cable" with satellite-delivered programming.

5.2.3.2 Nonpay Services National satellite-delivered nonpay services developed and proliferated. The majority sold advertising time and were called **advertiser-supported** services. Cable operators usually offered nonpay networks as part of basic service. Some of the more attractive networks might be scrambled and bundled as a separate **tier** of service. Subscribers paid extra for this tier.

Most cable networks programmed more like radio stations than like broadcast television networks; they specialized. They had much smaller audiences than ABC, CBS, or

(a)

(b)

Figure 5.3 Operations center for Home Box Office, Inc. Located at Hauppauge, New York, on Long Island, the James R. Shepley HBO Communications Center handles origination and transmission of HBO's program services. (a) Four 11-meter earth stations access HBO's satellite transponders. (b) In the master control room, technicians monitor all programming feeds and route them to the appropriate satellite transponder. (Photographs courtesy of Home Box Office, Inc. Used by permission.)

NBC; this factor prevented the cable networks from competing for national advertising on the basis of numbers. So they attempted to make their medium an efficient tool for marketing. They looked for an audience "niche," then programmed to that niche, targeting, for example, people who spoke Spanish as a first language, or black Americans, or people interested in fitness and health.

Cable programmers were willing to experiment, to attempt new programming forms. Two such attempts were the music video and home shopping formats. MTV, launched in 1981, targeted its rock music at people in their teens and twenties, an age group highly susceptible to the blandishments of advertising. Four years later, Home Shopping Network (HSN) combined continuous advertising with direct marketing to become both programmer and retailer. These format innovations led to financial success, were copied by other cable programmers, and spread to broadcast television.

Some cable networks did program to a broad, general audience. Two of these, USA Network and Turner Broadcasting System's (TBS) Superstation WTBS, were particularly successful in attracting cable affiliates.

5.2.3.3 Ancillary Services

Some "blue sky" actually came to pass. In 1977 Warner Cable began testing Qube (Figure 5.4), an interactive service, in its Columbus, Ohio, cable system. Using special home terminals, Qube subscribers participated in cable programming—playing interactive games, testing knowledge, and registering opinions. In 1981 Warner-Amex (American Express had gone into partnership with Warner the year before) started building Qube in other systems. There were even plans to interconnect local Qube systems into an interactive national network. Qube failed to pay for itself, however, and the company terminated production and distribution of interactive programming in 1984.

Other companies offered cable-based home security systems; subscribers could get police and fire surveillance of their homes while they were away. In a few systems, subscribers could make some transactions from their homes (shopping, banking, bill paying, and the like) and utilize information and scheduling services (such as news, stock prices, and airline schedules).

5.2.3.4 Shakeout

National cable programmers faced an uphill climb toward profitability. The ad-supported services did not reach large numbers of people—at least relative to broadcast television networks. Advertisers and agencies included them in media buys only reluctantly or experimentally. Most pay services also ran in the red. Several cable network ventures delayed signing on or even went out of business. For example, CBS Cable, ambitious and critically acclaimed, folded in 1982 after losing an estimated $30 million in that year alone. The Entertainment Channel, a pay service, closed in 1983 after operating less than a year. Satellite News Channel, having failed to overtake rival TBS's Cable News Network, was sold to the competition and closed in 1983 after 16 months of operation. The next year, TBS shut down Cable Music Channel after just 36 days.

During the mid-1980s, the older, larger cable networks began to turn the corner toward profitability. Cable penetration was approaching 50 percent. In cable homes, cable-only programming captured increasing audience shares at the expense of broadcast network affiliates. MSOs concluded that continued growth lay in original programming. They underwrote programming development by purchasing equity in (and thus providing funds for) various satellite cable

Figure 5.4 Interactive television: The late Qube.   A Qube subscriber used a home terminal connected to the television receiver to participate in interactive programming. (Photograph courtesy of Warner Communications, Inc. Used by permission.)

networks, including Turner Broadcasting (Section 5.2.5).

The shakeout continued, however. Few of the many Home Shopping Network clones survived. NBC considered establishing a cable news service but decided against it. In the wake of the PTL scandal (Section 4.5.3.5), many cable operators stopped car-rying that network. Pay cable subscriptions declined as home video penetration and videocassette rentals increased. Cable operators responded with **pay-per-view** (PPV) services in which the audience paid by the program; some of those PPV ventures failed. In mid-1987, *Broadcasting*[2] listed 50 nonpay services, 8 pay-cable services, and 2 pay-per-view services. There were actually more, and more signed on subsequently. Not all could succeed.

5.2.4 Cable Regulation

The mid-1980s were also years when cable operators realized a major goal in their efforts to stabilize the trade. Congress wrote cable into law.

The Communications Act of 1934 had said nothing about cable. A cable system needed no federal license; a local governmental authority—typically, a city council—granted a **cable franchise** to operate a system in a community. The FCC was at first hesitant to regulate. So it backed into cable.

The commission began to apply carriage (must-carry) and nonduplication rules (Section 4.5.2.1) to some cable systems in 1962. In 1966, the FCC asserted full jurisdiction over the medium and adopted comprehensive cable TV rules. These rules, however, caused administrative problems for the commission. After further study, revised rules were adopted in 1972. In retrospect, these 1972 rules were restrictive of cable's growth and protective of existing broadcast television stations, and in ensuing years the FCC eliminated most of them. Nonetheless, cable operators felt they could live with the rules and broadcasters were at least partially satisfied, so these 1972 rules represented a landmark for the cable trade.

The nature of franchising, however, had created friction between cable system operators and the cities. Cities awarded franchises on a competitive basis and, according to cable operators, made exorbitant demands for facilities and payments. To win big-city franchises, would-be operators felt forced to promise fantastic systems. Their investment was long range at best. Capital outlay was so large that profit depended on subscribers opting for extra-charge tiers, multiple pay

channels, and expensive ancillary services. In addition, cable systems in cities had problems with high rates of subscriber turnover (churn) and theft of service (piracy), both of which lowered earnings. Further, contended the cable operators, the cities used their rate-regulation power primarily to *refuse* cable system requests for needed increases in subscriber rates.

The cities, on the other hand, looked on operators as opportunists. Here were a bunch of outsiders (with maybe a few local people included to make it look good) requesting permission to use city easements and rights-of-way (the basis of a franchise) to lay cable. They would have a monopoly to *sell* TV signals—something citizens really did not need and could already get for free. With demands for municipal services outstripping city resources, cable operators should be happy to provide some of those services and pay a franchise fee in exchange for an *exclusive* franchise.

The FCC had little authority to deal with franchising. Congress would have to address this problem directly.

After several years of attempts, the National Cable Television Association, the National League of Cities, and the U.S. Conference of Mayors agreed on legislation. Congress enacted this legislation as the **Cable Communications Policy Act of 1984,** its first comprehensive cable law.

The Cable Act ended piecemeal local regulation of cable. It spelled out obligations of the cable operator to the franchising authority, and it limited demands the authority could make on the operator. Among the more welcome provisions for cable were those that allowed an operator to raise subscriber rates for basic service (without first getting permission), made denial of franchise renewal more difficult, and limited the franchise fee. In effect, the Cable Act ensured a profitable and predictable rate of return and, thus, made cable more attractive to investors.

The new law permitted unlimited basic-rate increases beginning in 1987. The first increases ranged from 5 to 20 percent. Many operators, in efforts to lessen subscriber shock, reduced other prices and increased services—eliminated extra-charge tiers of ad-supported networks, did away with charges for hookup of additional receivers, and decreased the price for premium channels. (As a result of the latter price drop, pay-cable networks actually gained subscribers!)

5.2.5 Structural and Financial Changes

Some of the buy-sell fever of the mid-1980s (Section 4.5.3) spread to cable. Among other large-scale transactions were those involving Group W, Storer, Turner Broadcasting System (TBS), Viacom, the USA Network, Cable Value Network, Tele-Communications, Inc., and Time Warner, Inc.

Westinghouse Corp. (Group W), one of the largest MSOs, sold most of its systems in 1986. This sale was at that time the largest in the history of cable. Group W had gone into big-time cable operation with its 1981 purchase of Teleprompter. Five years later, Group W sold out to a group of large MSOs for some $2.1 billion. Included were approximately 135 cable systems with 2.1 million basic subscribers. Even this purchase was eclipsed in 1988 when Storer Communications was sold for $2.8 billion.

Ted Turner (Box 5.1), after failing to take over CBS (Section 4.5.3.3), turned his attention elsewhere. In 1985, he made a deal to buy MGM/United Artists Entertainment Co. for $1.5 billion. United Artists was spun off as a separate company, and he later sold the MGM production and distribution businesses. He bought the company primarily for MGM's huge library of films, television series, and cartoons. The next year, he lost money on coverage of the Goodwill Games, an expensive cooperative effort with the So-viet Union. This loss presented a problem; if he could not make payments on his MGM debt, he would gradually lose control of TBS. In 1987, a group of MSOs agreed to pump $575 million into TBS in exchange for a 35 percent share of the company and 7 of the 15 seats on the TBS board. This diluted Turner's control over the company that bore his name. Nonetheless, the board approved the 1988 launch of a new, "events-oriented" cable network, Turner Network Television.

Several other cable programmers experienced ownership changes in 1987. Viacom International, part owner of Lifetime and owner of Showtime and The Movie Channel, was acquired by film theater operator National Amusements. Time Inc., sold its share of the USA Network to the other two owners, Gulf + Western and MCA. Close-Out Merchandise Buyers (C.O.M.B.), discount merchandisers and part owner of Cable Value Network (CVN), merged with CVN.

Tele-Communications, Inc. (TCI), the nation's largest MSO, pursued an aggressive program of investment and acquisition during the mid-1980s. Included among the many deals in which TCI was involved were the Westinghouse, TBS, CVN-C.O.M.B., and Storer transactions. TCI acquired stakes in several other cable programmers. In one transaction, TCI acquired Tempo Enterprises and leased the programming arm to NBC (Section 4.5.3.4).

In 1989, Time, Incorporated, and Warner Communications merged. This merger united the second and sixth largest MSOs. It brought together the largest pay cable programmer (Time's HBO and Cinemax) and one of the leading producers of motion pictures and TV programming. And it created Time Warner, Incorporated, the world's largest media and entertainment company (Section 20.3.3.1).

By 1990, the number of cable systems exceeded 8000; the percentage of subscribing

Box 5.1 Ted Turner: Atlanta's Communications Gadfly

Robert E. Turner took a shaky family outdoor advertising business and parlayed it into a communications empire. In 1970, Turner bought WTCG, a money-losing UHF television station in Atlanta, programmed it with sports and movies, and made it available by satellite to cable systems all over the country. He bought the Atlanta professional baseball and basketball teams to guarantee access to sports programming and formed Southern Satellite Systems to guarantee nationwide distribution for his station. Turner thus converted his UHF television investment from a 98-pound weakling into superstation WTBS. He used WTBS as the cornerstone for Turner Broadcasting System, the Cable News Network, Headline News, Turner Network Television, and various other broadcast and cable enterprises. His competitive tactics and his critical comments on broadcast networks made trade press headlines and upset the broadcasting establishment. (Photograph courtesy of Turner Broadcasting System, Inc. Used by permission.)

television homes, 55 percent; and the percentage of homes with pay cable, 30 percent. Cable had hit the big time. With success, however, came problems. In 1988, complaints arose that the cable trade was anti-competitive. Cable was accused of wielding undue market power, of raising rates indiscriminately, of merging into powerful ownership monopolies, and of preventing programmers from dealing with independent packagers for delivery to owners of home dishes (Section 5.6.3). There were suggestions that cable's alleged abuses should be corrected through amendments to the Cable Act and the Copyright Act (which granted cable systems a "compulsory license" to carry local television stations; Section 15.2.3.2). The National League of Cities and the U.S. Conference of Mayors both adopted resolutions urging that telephone companies be allowed to operate cable systems. Legislation was introduced, and in 1989, Congress held hearings on proposals to re-regulate cable.

5.3 SATELLITE MASTER ANTENNA TELEVISION

Satellite master antenna television (SMATV) systems began to proliferate in late 1979. That year, the FCC ended the requirement that TV receive-only (TVRO) satellite ground stations be licensed. In addition, with advances in technology the price of TVRO ground stations had dropped.

SMATV systems resembled cable systems in physical structure and operation. Unlike cable systems, however, SMATV systems were installed on private property and did not utilize public rights-of-way. An SMATV operator would contract with the owner of a multiunit dwelling or private housing development to provide cable-type service. The operator would put up a TVRO dish to receive national programming. In most cases, the building's existing master antenna system was used to distribute the signals to individual living units. In other cases, the operator had to upgrade, expand, or even build a distribution system.

Since SMATV operated on private property, it was free from regulation—it did not need a franchise, did not have the local regulations that usually accompanied a franchise, and did not have to pay a franchise fee. Further, most SMATVs did not meet the FCC's definition of a cable system, so they were exempt from federal regulation too.

5.4 WIRELESS CABLE

Wireless cable, also called **multichannel television,** emerged in 1983. It consisted of channels from the **instructional television fixed service** (ITFS), the **operational fixed service** (OFS), and the **multipoint distribution service** (MDS). All transmitted omnidirectionally (360 degrees) in the microwave frequencies (Section 12.7). Special antennas picked up the signals (Figure 5.5).

Figure 5.5 MDS/ITFS receiving antenna. This antenna features low wind resistance and is partially parabolic in shape. The square box behind it is the down-converter; it converts the signal from microwaves to frequencies that can be utilized by the television receiver. From the down-converter, the signal goes to a controller box that sits atop the receiver. The controller allows the consumer to select among broadcast and MDS/ITFS signals. (Photograph courtesy of Texscan Corporation. Used by permission.)

The FCC established the ITFS in 1963. Originally ITFS had 31 channels; 3 were later reallocated to OFS. Only educational institutions could get ITFS licenses; the channels were to be used to distribute instructional programming.

The three OFS channels were used mainly by cities and oil companies. In 1981, the commission amended its rules to allow OFS licensees to supply pay television programming to apartments, hotels, and other multiunit dwellings.

The MDS began in the early 1970s. A common carrier service, MDS consisted of two channels. Licensees leased channel time to users, who provided material to be transmitted to specific points.

MDS proved ideal for distributing pay programming (usually movies) to multiunit dwellings. At first, receiving antennas cost too much for home use. But prices dropped over the years, and as early as 1978, entrepreneurs offered MDS service to homes. By March 1980, the FCC had authorized 131 MDS systems; two years later the number of systems was over 350. As a home subscription-programming service, however, MDS was handicapped by its limited number of channels. Cable television, with its multiple basic and pay services, could offer a greater variety of channels for the money. Whenever cable penetrated a market, the MDS subscriber count dropped.

In 1983, the FCC reallocated eight channels from ITFS to MDS, thereby creating two new four-channel services (thus, **multichannel MDS,** MMDS). The FCC also permitted ITFS licensees to lease "excess" capacity (time when ITFS channels carried no instructional programming) to others. Theoretically, programmers in a given market might now be able to lease as many as 15 channels full time (2 MDS, 3 OFS, and 8 MMDS) plus as many as 20 part time (ITFS channels)—a total of 33 channels! *That* could surely compete with cable.

Some 16,000 applications for MMDS channels flooded the FCC. The commission decided to select applicants by lot. Nearly two years passed before the lottery awarded the first licenses. In the meantime, investor interest had flagged. Would-be multichannel programmers had difficulty finding start-up money and getting distribution rights to popular cable services, such as HBO and Showtime. Nonetheless, by 1990, wireless cable had appeared in a number of large markets.

5.5 SATELLITE RELAY AND DISTRIBUTION

The United States launched its first active **communications satellite** in late 1958. The satellite, in orbit above the earth, picked up signals beamed from a ground transmitting station and retransmitted them for reception by ground receiver stations. As early as 1962, AT&T launched a satellite that relayed television programming between Europe and the United States. In the same year, Congress passed the **Communications Satellite Act.** This act created the **Communications Satellite Corporation** (Comsat), a private corporation that launched Early Bird, the first commercial communications satellite, in 1965. Early Bird and its successors provided international long-distance commercial communication by use of space satellites for all types of electromagnetic communication, including radio and television programming. As time passed, satellite communications proved superior to most other forms of relay—more reliable, less distortion and noise, less expensive.

In 1972, the FCC revised its rules to encourage **domsat** service, satellite relay for domestic use. Various companies launched satellites and offered service. Cable and noncommercial broadcast networks were first in the radio-TV trade to distribute programming to affiliates by satellite relay (Figure 5.6). Eventually, nearly every major cable and broadcast network converted from land lines to satellite.

In 1984, Hubbard Broadcasting opened the door to **satellite news gathering** (SNG). Hubbard organized Conus, a satellite-based news distribution service. Stations picked up video by satellite from truck-mounted uplink dishes at remote locations. Conus coordinated the stations' satellite use. Subsequently, other organizations followed Hubbard's lead, including the commercial broadcast networks and CNN.

5.6 DIRECT BROADCAST SATELLITE

The first TVRO equipment had been expensive—$75,000 and more. But prices dropped, the necessary dish size decreased, and reception technology improved. With mass production, surely ground stations would be

Figure 5.6 Domestic satellite. Satcom III-R became one of the main satellite relay vehicles for cable and broadcast programmers. (Courtesy of RCA Corp. Used by permission of General Electric Co.)

possible for every home. Then a national programmer could transmit directly to home ground stations through a direct broadcast satellite (DBS).

5.6.1 High- and Medium-Power DBS

Comsat proposed the DBS idea in August 1979. The following June, Comsat set up Satellite Television Corporation (STC) as its DBS subsidiary. In December 1980, STC filed application with the FCC to construct a pay-supported DBS system for the United States. The system would utilize new high-power satellites whose signals could be received with roof-mounted dish antennas $1\frac{1}{2}$ to 2 feet in diameter. The DBS satellites would operate in the Ku frequency band rather than the lower C band of most existing satellites.

The FCC accepted STC's application and invited others. Broadcasters fought the idea of DBS. After all, if a programmer could transmit directly to the public, what would happen to the local station? Nonetheless, the commission authorized a number of applicants to construct direct broadcast satellites, the first of which would be in orbit no earlier than 1986. A trade group, the Direct Broadcasting Satellite Association (DBSA), was formed.

Several companies decided to get a jump on the competition. They secured FCC permission to use existing medium-power Ku-band satellites. This would require a slightly larger dish but would allow DBS service to begin immediately. United Satellite Communications, Inc. (USCI), was first, commencing its multichannel DBS pay service in the fall of 1983. USCI opened marketing efforts in Indianapolis and then rolled out the service eastward. The venture proved the technology would work and eventually signed up some 10,000 subscribers. But it did not generate enough subscribers and revenues to cover its high overhead and could not attract investors to underwrite continued operation. USCI, the only operating DBS venture, went under in 1985. Most other companies, including Comsat, abandoned their DBS projects.

By the end of the decade, Europe had launched its first direct broadcast satellites, with as many as five services projected by the early 1990s. NHK, Japan's national network, also had a high-power system operating. In the United States, only two of the original eight applicants still had active plans to go into high-power DBS. Other firms, however, had taken note of foreign DBS efforts and the growth of backyard TVRO (below). Talk of U.S. DBS heated up again.

5.6.2 Home TVRO Develops

Even when earth stations were still expensive, a few individuals—mainly the very wealthy and those who lived in remote areas beyond the reach of cable and broadcast signals—invested in dishes and picked signals off satellites for their private enjoyment. This started the **television receive-only** (TVRO) or **home satellite dish** (HSD) trade.

Retail businesses specialized in sales of "backyard earth stations" (Figure 5.7). Retailers and manufacturers formed a trade association, the Society for Private and Commercial Earth Stations (SPACE). Home dish prices dropped, eventually below $2000. As prices fell, more people bought. The Cable Communications Policy Act of 1984 sanctioned home reception of unscrambled signals; none was scrambled at the time. The number of home dishes rose from 4000 in 1980 to 1.3 million in late 1985. Sales hit 45,000 per month.

And this is where the cable operators stepped in. According to one estimate, one-third of all new home dishes went into cable franchise areas; people bought dishes and viewed *all* satellite networks *free*, rather than *pay* the local cable company to view *only* those carried by the system. Early in 1985, cable operators demanded that satellite networks scramble programming (the Cable Act provided stiff penalties for unauthorized reception of scrambled signals).

TVRO interests objected and vowed to fight any move toward scrambling. Manufacturers and dealers objected because they saw their businesses going down the drain. Home dish owners objected because they could no longer receive free programming. There was a certain irony in such objections, since satellite programming had not been intended for direct reception in the first place. The cable networks used satellites to relay programming to cable systems and had not given permission for direct reception. In effect, the home dish owners had been pirating the signals, at least until passage of the Cable Communications Policy Act.

5.6.3 TVRO Legitimized

Satellite programmers needed access to cable's large subscriber base. They acceded to the operators' demand to scramble. HBO was first. It began full-time scrambling with the Videocipher II (VC-II) system in January 1986. VC-II consisted of scramblers for programmers, block descramblers for cable systems, and addressable descramblers for home dishes.

The 1984 Cable Act had also provided for the marketing of satellite cable programming for private viewing. VC-II technology provided the means for that marketing. Signals could be transmitted to turn individual home descramblers on and off, allowing sale of satellite programming on a subscription basis. For example, home dish owners paid $12.95 a month for HBO or Cinemax, $19.95 for both. Other programmers followed HBO's lead, and VC-II became the de facto scrambling standard.

The transition to scrambling was not easy. Among many problems were the following:

> At first, no one was able to put together a comprehensive package of signals to sell to home dish owners. This was just as well, because there was a shortage of descramblers.

Figure 5.7 TVRO. The backyard satellite dish.

Home dish sales dropped precipitously; manufacturers and retailers went out of business. Shortly after midnight on April 27, 1986, an HBO movie was interrupted for about four minutes by a printed message: "Goodevening [*sic*] HBO from Captain Midnight. $12.95? No way! (Showtime/The Movie Channel Beware!)" The FCC traced the message to an Ocala, Florida, home dish retailer whose business had been crippled by scrambling; he was a part-time employee at a satellite uplink facility, from which he had transmitted the message.

By 1986, technically adept spoilers had developed illegal descrambler modifications to decode without payment.

When program packages were finally put together, TVRO interests objected that most were controlled by the cable trade, either programmers or cable operators (who promised discounted packages of programming to dish owners in their franchise areas). Noncable firms that tried to put together a package faced refusals and high prices from the cable networks.

To TVRO interests, theirs was a business on the verge of collapse, and they sought help from Congress; to the cable trade, TVRO was thriving and needed no governmental interference.

Congress passed the **Electronic Communications Privacy Act** in 1987. This law safeguarded private satellite feeds from unauthorized interception and interference. It protected broadcast television "backhauls"—relays of raw programming to network headquarters for insertion of commercials and other material before distribution to affiliated stations. Some motels and bars had used dishes to provide patrons with commercial-free sports backhauls.

Despite all the problems, TVRO seemed to be evolving into a full-time business. In 1986, SPACE merged with DBSA to form Satellite Broadcasting and Communication Association of America. By 1990, over 2.5 million homes had dishes, and about 25,000 more were sold each month. Estimates were that as many as 20 million homes would never receive cable service; these would be prime targets for home dishes.

Meanwhile, the illegal box business flourished. General Instruments (GI), VC-II's manufacturer, launched an aggressive eradication program. With government aid, they tracked down and prosecuted fabricators and sellers and then started on consumers. Electronic countermeasures shut down many illegal boxes. Congress stiffened the penalties for piracy and directed the FCC to consider encryption standards (Section 15.2.3.3). Several estimates, however, put the proportion of pirate boxes as high as half the total number of decoders. After just 18 months, some trade leaders pronounced VC-II dead as an effective scrambling standard. GI introduced a new, more secure system in 1989, the Videocipher II-Plus. The II-Plus required special security modules. Dealers could not sell these modules; consumers had to order them directly from distributors.

5.7 ELECTRONIC TEXT

Electronic text appeared at about the time cable systems entered larger markets. It consisted of printing and sometimes illustrations supplied apart from or in addition to normal video programming. Four primary forms developed: rotatext, closed captioning, teletext, and videotex.

5.7.1 Rotatext

Many people first noticed electronic text as rotatext (Figure 5.8). "Pages" (screensful) of news, weather, sports, announcements, and

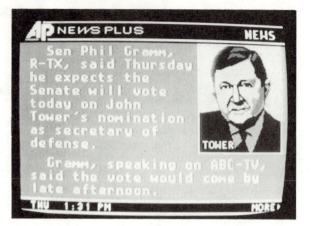

Figure 5.8 Rotatext. AP News Plus service for cable systems. (Used by permission of AP/TMS Information Services.)

advertisements were created and stored electronically. These screens were then televised in a repeating cycle on one or more **automated channels.**

5.7.2 Closed Captioning

In the early 1960s, British broadcasters developed closed captioning to serve hearing-impaired viewers. Viewers with special decoders saw printing superimposed over the regular picture; other viewers saw only the regular picture. PBS and ABC worked on a U.S. version in the early 1970s, and the FCC approved regular transmission of closed captioning in 1976. The National Captioning Institute (NCI) was established and, in 1980, began captioning selected network programming (Figure 5.9).

5.7.3 Teletext

Like rotatext, teletext presented electronic pages. Like closed captioning, teletext required a decoder and could be transmitted by TV stations along with normal programming. Unlike rotatext, teletext viewers could select specific pages. Unlike closed caption-

ing, teletext content was unrelated to and completely displaced program video.

In 1975, British broadcasters transmitted teletext on an experimental basis. Soon after, the British Broadcasting Corporation and Independent Television used teletext to offer newspapers of the air—CEEFAX and ORACLE, respectively.

U.S. interests began to experiment with teletext in 1978. They tended to follow the British pattern and use teletext to offer information—news, sports, and weather. Two incompatible systems developed—World System Teletext (WST) and the North American Broadcast Teletext Specification (NABTS). Of the two, NABTS produced better graphics but required a more complex decoder. In 1983, the FCC said that broadcasters could transmit teletext using any standard as long as it did not interfere with their broadcast signal.

In 1981, Field Enterprises, Inc., launched **Keyfax** teletext service on WFLD-TV, Chicago, using British technology. Keyfax went national in 1982 with satellite distribution on Superstation WTBS, but ceased in 1984.

CBS's **Extravision** and **NBC Teletext** started in 1983. Both used NABTS. A few affiliates promoted the service and inserted local material. But NABTS decoders were scarce and expensive (models under $300 did not reach the market until 1986). In late 1984, NBC discontinued its service; 15 months later, CBS drastically reduced its Extravision staff.

Taft Broadcasting Company launched **Electra,** a WST service, over its WKRC-TV, Cincinnati, in 1983. Taft's partner in the venture, Zenith Radio Corporation, manufactured set-top WST decoders and television receivers with built-in decoding circuitry. Satellite distribution made Electra available nationally for transmission by other television stations.

Teletext had the potential to generate additional revenues for a station. Should many persons buy and use decoders, advertisers would pay to place messages on the information pages, as with print media. On the other hand, teletext also had the potential to turn a station into its own competitor. After all, television viewers would most likely check the teletext service during the most important (to the station) part of the program schedule—the commercials!

Cable systems could also offer teletext service. A cable system could dedicate an *entire* channel—no programming, only teletext—which allowed it to carry thousands of pages (broadcast teletext was limited to about 200 pages) and a wide variety of information. What would full-channel teletext do to broadcast teletext? For that matter, what would it do to newspapers?

Cable teletext, however, was no more successful than broadcast teletext. Time Inc., after testing a 5000-page service for about a year, shut it down with the explanation that teletext was not yet economically viable as a business. Westinghouse Corp. launched Request Teletext, a 1500-page system, at its Buena Park, California, cable system in 1984. In 1985, having decided to sell its cable systems, Westinghouse phased out Request.

5.7.4 Videotex

Like rotatext and teletext, videotex provided information with electronic pages or frames. And—again, like rotatext and teletext—videotex frames could be displayed on the

(a)

(b)

Figure 5.9 Closed captioning. (a) Operator prepares captions at the National Captioning Institute (NCI). (b) In 1989, NCI captioned the first daytime serial, ABC's *Loving*, with funding from the U.S. Department of Education. (Photograph a courtesy of the National Captioning Institute. Photograph b used by permission of Capital Cities/ABC, Inc.)

screen of a TV receiver. But unlike rotatext and teletext, videotex was **interactive;** a user operated a home terminal to transmit inquiries, requests, and directions and to receive responses. And unlike rotatext and teletext, videotex could offer encyclopedic information resources.

Videotex, too, originated in England. Developed in the late 1960s to eliminate the need for live computer operators to take postal orders and train reservations, the British post office named the service Prestel. In the 1980s, France provided telephone subscribers with free terminals and electronic directory service to replace printed telephone books.

One of the biggest U.S. videotex ventures was **Viewtron** (Figure 5.10), launched in 1983. This South Florida system was operated by Viewdata Corporation of America (VCA), an arm of Knight-Ridder, Inc., newspaper and broadcasting group owner. Viewtron featured color graphics and services such as shopping, banking, news, reference, education, stock quotations, and personal message exchange (electronic mail). Telephone lines connected home terminals to the central computer. A subscriber paid initial and monthly fees, plus $600 for an AT&T Sceptre terminal. VCA found that its service did not attract users and usage enough to provide adequate revenue. Viewtron was gradually restructured. Terminal costs were included in monthly fees. A text-only version was created that allowed personal computers to substitute for the terminal. The monthly fee was dropped, and subscribers paid primarily for the time when they actually used the service. The subscriber base began to build, but VCA closed the operation in 1986.

Gateway videotex opened in 1984. This Orange County, California, service was cre-

Figure 5.10 Viewtron. The Knight-Ridder service offered many services, including electronic mail, latest news, home banking, stock market, ticket reservations, travel and vacation planning, and home shopping and ordering. Here, a family checks Little League scores. (Photographs courtesy of Viewdata Corporation of America. Used by permission.)

ated by the Times Mirror Company, owner of newspapers, magazines, broadcast stations, and cable systems. Gateway, too, was based on telephone lines and the Sceptre, but the monthly fee included use of a terminal. In 1986, with some 3000 subscribers and after 15 months of operation, Times Mirror shut down its videotex service.

In 1984, the **Keyfax** name was revived and offered as a videotex service in Chicago by Keycom Electronic Publishing. Keycom, in turn, was owned by Centel, the telephone company, in partnership with Honeywell. Keyfax lasted until mid-1985, about six months. It had attracted 800 subscribers.

Failure of systems in three large markets raised questions. Was there really a demand for consumer videotex service? If so, was this demand being met elsewhere? When these systems created text-only versions for use with personal computers (PC), they resembled existing national **information retrieval services**—CompuServe, The Source, and Dow Jones News Retrieval. Such services all served PC owners, all used telephone lines, all offered news, all featured little or no graphics—just like PC versions of videotex service. Further, financial institutions introduced competing services in 1983—for example, "HomeBanking" from California's Bank of America and "Pronto" from New York's Chemical Bank. For $8 to $12 a month, subscribers used PCs to transfer funds, get current balances, review or cancel transactions, send messages by electronic mail, and pay bills.

By the late 1980s, the success or failure of videotex seemed linked at least in part to its ability to create color graphics. One form of graphics-capable consumer videotex was already in continuous use for specialized services such as kiosk systems in shopping malls, hotel lobbies, and airports. Color graphics were also used in various professional-based videotex services, developed for such fields as engineering and agriculture.

But graphics-capable terminals were specialized, costly, and time-consuming to use. And there was some doubt as to whether consumer demand for color graphics in the *home* would grow strong enough in the near future to overcome the drawbacks.

Despite the failures and competition, companies continued to explore the possibilities of consumer videotex. In 1985, Time, Inc., AT&T, Bank of America, and Chemical Bank formed Covideo, a PC-accessible national system that would build on the banks' existing services. In 1986, Citicorp (banking), NYNEX (telephone), and RCA created CNR Partners to investigate opportunities in interactive electronic services. In 1988, Prodigy Services, a joint venture of IBM and Sears, Roebuck & Co., launched an interactive service for owners of personal computers. Several Bell operating companies had plans to offer videotex gateway services (Section 5.15).

5.8 COMPUTERS

The concept of a device to perform calculations dates back at least 2500 years to the development of the abacus in China. As early as the 1930s, computers used the binary system of numbers, now standard in digital computers. The first electronic computers used relays—electromechanical on-off switches that physically clack-clack-clacked open and shut to respresent combinations of 1 and 0.

Vacuum tubes, however, eventually replaced relays and greatly speeded calculations. Tubes were the heart of the first electronic digital computer, the ABC (Atanasoff-Berry Computer), developed during 1938–1941 at Iowa State University by Dr. John V. Atanasoff in collaboration with Clifford Berry. Five years later, a large-scale electronic computer was put into productive use at the University of Pennsylvania. This was

Box 5.2 ENIAC

ENIAC (an acronym for Electronic Numerical Integrator and Calculator) was one of the first fully electronic digital computers built in the United States. Constructed at the University of Pennsylvania to calculate artillery firing tables, ENIAC was made public in 1946. It cost $487,000, weighed 30 tons, took about the space of a two-car garage, had to be manually rewired every time a new operation was required, and contained 70,000 resistors, 10,000 capacitors, 6,000 switches, and 18,000 vacuum tubes. It worked only in short bursts; the vacuum tubes failed at an average of one every seven minutes. Nonetheless, it beat working out those artillery trajectories by hand because it could perform 5,000 additions or subtractions a second—about the same as almost any of today's home computers in the $700–$900 price range! (Photograph courtesy of the University of Pennsylvania.)

Sperry Univac's ENIAC (Electronic Numerical Integrator and Calculator) (Box 5.2).

The development of the chip resulted in a major breakthrough in computer construction. Using these miniaturized integrated circuits, designers could make computers more powerful (that is, do more in a shorter time), smaller, and more reliable. As chips improved, so did the capabilities of computers.

5.8.1 Personal Computers

The first **microcomputers** (personal computers) appeared about 1975. Many owners used television receiver screens for computer display. Most purchased "peripherals," devices that connected to, and operated in conjunction with, the computer. Entrepreneurs wrote and marketed application programs or **software.** Software allowed consumers and businesses to use computers without having to write programs.

In 1980, two dozen computer firms sold just under 750,000 units for $1.8 billion. The next year, 20 more companies sold personal computers, and consumers spent almost $3 billion for 1.4 million units. The rush was on.

Young people adapted quickly to the personal computer. They had made the **arcade video game** popular. They had brought Atari and Intellivision **video game units** into the home. Now they could use personal computers to play games, to make up their own games, to learn in school, and to explore the creative possibilities offered by the microprocessor.

5.8.2 Broadcasting and the Computer

The computer entered the broadcast station fairly early, except for the newsroom. In the 1970s, more and more stations turned to computer control of billing and accounting, payroll, proof-of-performance affidavits, and traffic (Figure 5.11). Radio stations, particularly FM, automated on-air programming. Technology existed to do the same for TV, including automation of camera shots and movement. By 1988, NBC had taken the first steps toward computerization of the entire production process (Section 6.2.1.2).

Television newsrooms seemed an obvious place for computer assistance. During the 1970s, newspapers had automated and installed computer-driven word processing systems. But TV news people circulated horror stories—one involving a station's computer that irrevocably locked up a complete

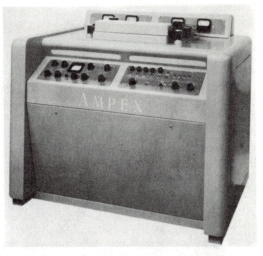

Figure 5.12 Ampex VR 1000. Ampex introduced this machine, the first commercially available videotape recorder, in 1956. Its 2-inch-wide tape was the standard for broadcast stations for years. (Photograph courtesy of Ampex Corporation. Used by permission.)

newscast script just before air time—and were reluctant to automate. Eventually, news automation systems developed that featured foolproof, user-friendly control. In the early 1980s, a few pioneer stations successfully automated newsrooms, and others followed. At last, electronic news did what newspapers had done ten years before—went electronic.

5.9 VIDEOCASSETTE RECORDERS

Ampex introduced the first commercially available **videotape recorder** (VTR) in 1956 (Figure 5.12). It used 2-inch-wide tape and four video recording heads. Later, **helical-scan** VTRs were developed using 1-inch tape, fewer heads, and a different principle for recording. Cassette versions of these machines reached the marketplace by the early 1970s.

Sony Corporation first marketed its Betamax videocassette recorder (VCR) in 1975, thereby launching the VCR or **home video** revolution (Figure 5.13). Two VCR formats,

Figure 5.11 Computerized station traffic system. An operator enters program and commercial information into the computer. The computer, in turn, generates the station's daily program log (being typed on the printer in the background).

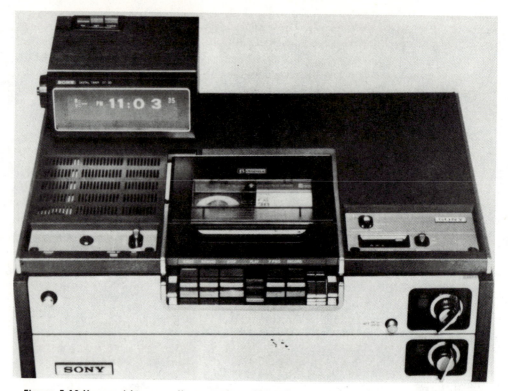

Figure 5.13 Home videocassette recorder. The VCR was first produced in 1975 by Sony. Competition forced prices to drop. Buyers used the VCR to play recorded tapes, to time shift broadcasts, and to make home movies. The VCR also gave rise to a "pirate" industry. (Photograph courtesy of Sony Corporation of America. "Sony" is a registered trademark of the Sony Corporation.)

Beta and **VHS,** evolved. Eventually, VHS began to overtake Beta in the consumer market. Competition dropped prices. Sales climbed steadily until 1979, when they soared; home VCR ownership went from less than 500,000 in 1979 to over 2 million in 1981. Six years later, Arbitron and Nielsen reported that VCR penetration of U.S. homes had surpassed that of cable television.[3] By 1990, VCR penetration had passed 66 percent.

Viewers used VCRs for time shifting, double viewing, and zipping (Section 4.5.2.6). They also used VCRs for programming other than cable and broadcast. They could rent or purchase cassettes. Their favorites were feature films, but they also viewed tapes made especially for the home market, such as how-to, self-improvement, physical fitness, and music "videos." They used portable VCRs with cameras to make "home movies."

5.10 VIDEODISCS, LASER DISCS, CDs, AND DATs

About the time Betamax hit the market, Philips Company developed the videodisc system. The videodisc player (Figure 5.14) converted information from a digital "record" into video and stereophonic audio for playback on a TV receiver.

MCA-Universal teamed up with Philips to market DiscoVision in the United States. Philips launched sales of the players through its Magnavox subsidiary during the 1978 Christmas season; MCA sold movies on

Figure 5.14 Magnavox videodisc player. Discs are seen to the right of and below the player. (Photograph courtesy of Philips Consumer Electronics Company. Used by permission.)

discs. In 1981, RCA introduced its Selecta-Vision videodisc system, and Japan's Matsushita Company (Panasonic) announced that it would market yet a third system. CBS, IBM, and GE formed partnerships with the various videodisc pioneers to get in on the action. Sales of players, however, fell far short of projections, and by 1983 most videodisc plants and operations had closed down. Pioneer Electronics continued to market players in the United States and even sold discs.

Consumers rejected videodiscs for at least two reasons. First, owners of videodisc players complained that too few interesting discs were available. Second, the videodisc was playback-only technology; it could not record. On both counts, the videodisc suffered in comparison with the VCR.

The videodisc had advantages, however, for business and education (Section 22.10). By 1987, there were indications that marketplace success of the compact disc (below) might revive the consumer videodisc, now dubbed the **laser disc.** Films looked and sounded better on laser disc than on even the best videocassettes. Consumers found laser disc players easier to use than VCRs, and newer models—*combi machines*—played both CDs and laser discs. Record companies

planned a *CDV single*—a disc containing a five-minute music video and twenty minutes of audio.

Digital technology also improved consumer audio. In 1983, the Sony Corporation launched the **compact disc** (CD), on which the very recording itself was digitally encoded. CDs were capable of clean, distortion-free reproduction of sound, loud or soft, at almost any audible frequency.

While the recording industry adapted to the CD quickly, it was less enthusiastic about another audio development, the **digital audio tape** (DAT) recorder. The Recording Industry Association of American (RIAA) threatened lawsuits to block Japanese and European companies from retailing DATs in the United States. RIAA said that the digital recorders, with their ability to make perfect copies of a CD, represented a threat to copyrights of recoding artists. In 1989, however, the two sides agreed on a compromise that would allow the sale of DATs. Under the compromise, manufactures could sell DAT recorders in the United States so long as those recorders had a built-in "serial copy management system." Using a DAT recorder that includes the sysem, a comsumer can make one digital copy from a CD machine but cannot then make a copy of that copy. The consumer can make two digital copies of audio recorded from an analog source (one copy and then one copy of that copy). The system consists of a digital subcode that signals the DAT machine when an attempt to record a second-generation tape is made and blocks the recording. The subcode is not audible when the tape is played back.

5.11 ADVANCES IN RECEIVERS

During the 1970s, manufacturers improved television receivers, particularly in color reproduction, pushbutton tuning, and remote tuning. These improvements benefited UHF stations, making them easier to tune and enhancing their reception. They also led to **flip-**

ping (tuning from channel to channel), **grazing** (constant sampling of separate program choices), and **zapping** (electronically tuning away from commercials). In the 1980s, manufacturers used digital technology on expensive models to add multiple-image screens (to view two or more programs at once [Figure 5.15]), on-screen time readouts, zoom capability (to allow the viewer to enlarge a portion of the picture), voice-actuated controls, built-in telephone answering devices, and improved sound.

Multichannel television sound (MTS) sets were equipped to receive stereophonic and second-audio-program channel (for example, foreign language) television sound transmissions. **Cable-ready** sets, capable of receiving 100 or more cable channels, connected directly to the cable system drop line (Section 12.9.3), *eliminating* the need for a converter to pick up basic cable service. The **cable television receiver** had only two channels (3 and 4) and *required* a converter to pick up all channels on the cable system.

In the **component television system,** consumers were to buy video components—video monitor, stereo amplifier and speakers, and source selector (which fed the system

Figure 5.15 Digital technology in the home receiver. This TV set can display two channels at the same time. (Photograph courtesy of RCA/Thomson Consumer Electronics, Indianapolis.)

from various sources, such as a personal computer, a broadcast TV tuner, a videotex decoder, and a VCR). Most **large-screen receivers** utilized projection on a reflective screen; since they simply blew up what was already there, imperfections and all, the picture often looked blurry.

Tiny **microminiature receivers** used electronic chips and the **liquid-crystal display** (LCD). LCD technology, often utilized for pocket calculator readouts and digital watch faces, was adapted for high-resolution video applications such as screens for lap-top computers and pocket television sets; Seiko even marketed a "wristwatch" TV receiver. The same technology also seemed to hold the key for development of the flat, hang-it-on-the-wall color television screen.

5.12 PICTURE AND SOUND IMPROVEMENTS

Various groups worked to better the video signal delivered to the viewer. Proposals ranged from improving the existing NTSC system to creating a new wide-picture, high-resolution system (Section 12.5). Most would require new television receivers especially designed to pick up the improved signals. An industrywide committee was formed in 1983 to study the various proposals and subsequently generated several recommendations for new standards.

Traditionally, television sound had received secondary consideration at best. The few telecasts that featured two-channel sound required viewers to tune in a cooperating FM station for the full stereophonic effect. Japan's NHK network launched regular multichannel television sound (MTS; Section 12.3.3) service in 1978, and U.S. manufacturers started considering standards in 1979. In 1984, the FCC established an MTS system developed by Zenith and by dbx [*sic*], Inc. as the industry standard for stereophonic and second-audio-program television sound transmissions.

5.13 PRODUCTION EQUIPMENT

Video production equipment increased in sophistication. **Digital technology** made possible advances in special video effects, audio and video editing, and video graphics and animation. **Miniaturization,** a result of solid-state electronics, led to greater flexibility in nonstudio production—smaller, more rugged video equipment, including the self-contained camera/recorder. Several firms introduced cameras that used the **charge-coupled device** (CCD)—in effect, a tubeless pickup tube.

5.14 SMALL-FORMAT VIDEO

In 1968, Sony introduced a low-cost, portable video camera in the United States. That camera, combined with helical-scan videotape recorders, made possible small-format video—use of compact equipment for nonbroadcast production.

5.14.1 Underground Television

Sony's camera attracted the attention of young people interested in nonbroadcast video. Their efforts to free video from establishment concepts led to what they called underground television. They used small-format equipment for fun, social comment, analysis, archival purposes, documentaries and documenting, and a dozen or more other purposes. They showed their efforts privately, in public storefront showings, through videotape exchanges, on college campuses, and on cable public access channels (Section 7.4.1.2).

5.14.2 Education, Business, and Industry

Small-format video also attracted notice in education, business, and industry. During the 1950s and 1960s, school systems purchased video gear for closed-circuit use.

Many schools successfully used television receivers in the classroom for instructional programs transmitted by the local educational station or by the ITFS (Section 5.4) facility.

At first, the business world utilized television primarily to scan manufacturing production lines, entryways, and security areas. As nonbroadcast video gear improved, businesses and industries of all kinds discovered that television could serve other purposes. They hired video specialists and equipped small studios. They took advantage of the small, less expensive, more rugged video equipment to create in-house production facilities for training, sales, information, and myriad other intracompany uses.

5.15 COMMON-CARRIER DEVELOPMENTS

From the earliest days of electromagnetic communication, technical innovation had come from ongoing research by common carriers—firms such as telephone and telegraph companies that hired out facilities and channels to others. During the 1970s and 1980s, common-carrier research yielded a number of devices and concepts that utilized or had the potential to affect radio and television.

A flexible strand of glass about the size of a human hair, an **optical fiber** (Figure 5.16), could carry dozens of TV signals. Charles Kao and George Hockham of ITT undertook the first industrial research in 1966. Corning Glass marketed optical fibers as early as 1970. Experimental communications links were set up in 1976. During the 1980s, optical fiber supplanted some telephone lines, replaced coaxial cable supertrunks in a few cable systems, and connected New York and Washington on an experimental basis for ABC. Common carriers began to build the first links for a national grid of optical fibers, a fiber-optic network.

Teleconferencing developed as an alternative to some business travel during the 1970s and early 1980s. A teleconference allowed groups of people to confer without

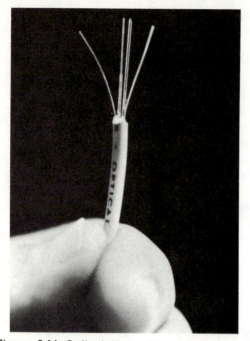

Figure 5.16 Optical fiber. Storer Communications has been a pioneer in the use of optical fiber in cable television. (Photograph courtesy of Storer Communications, Inc. Used by permission.)

leaving their home cities. These electronic meetings were primarily person-to-person (through audio or video) but could also be conducted by computer. For interconnection, they utilized telephone company channels, cable, satellite relay, or some combination of these.

Teleconferences were set up and marketed by common carriers, some cable companies and television stations, and specialized consultants. The telephone company offered elaborate and expensive facilities for interactive (two-way) video/audio teleconferences among certain cities. On the other hand, technology was such that most teleconferences featured one-way video and were interactive only for audio.

The FCC paved the way for **cellular radio** in 1982. Cellular radio used multiple transmitter/receiver units to increase the number of automobile telephones that could operate in an area. Many radio news departments installed cellular radio telephones in station automobiles to enhance spot news coverage activities.

Perhaps the biggest common-carrier development was the **breakup of AT&T.** In 1984, under federal court supervision, the giant firm divested its seven regional Bell operating companies (RBOCs). Each former Bell System telephone company now competed with the other six and with AT&T. As a result, all were allowed to enter new businesses—computer manufacturing, cellular telephony, joint ventures with foreign companies, and various innovative services—and to pursue aggressive marketing and product development strategies.

Four years later, the court gave the RBOCs permission to establish **videotex gateways.** These telephone-computer systems would provide links between information service providers (ISP) and users. ISPs could include companies ranging from newspapers to legal research firms to travel bureaus. Users would include anyone—individuals, businesses, institutions. In connection with these gateways, the RBOCs could also offer certain electronic services—voice messages, mail, and "white pages" directories. Within six months after receiving court permission, the telephone companies had gateway services up and running on a test-market basis.

The telephone companies wished to expand into video delivery, too. To a large extent, legal restrictions prevented such expansion (Section 19.5.1). Nonetheless, RBOCs invested in cable systems outside their telephone areas and lobbied for unrestricted ownership.

The RBOCs could *carry* information, but they could *not provide* it. Neither could AT&T. The 1982 court judgment that led to the breakup of the giant telephone company prohibited the eight resulting firms from entering the field of electronic publishing for at least seven years. The RBOCs requested that their ban be lifted. The court refused, and the regional companies appealed the decision. In 1989, AT&T asked that its ban be allowed to expire on schedule and not be renewed.

Marketplace regulation advocates (Section 4.5.1) within the federal government urged further freedom for RBOCs. They argued that the telephone companies could provide "universal information service" for consumers, an optical-fiber delivery system that would handle telephone service, data transport, videotex, and cable television programming. But the telephone companies earned huge revenues, many times larger than those of even the largest mass media empires. Publishers, cable operators, and many broadcasters feared that the RBOCs would use their overwhelming financial resources to crush or control existing newspaper and television media. The first two groups fought telephone company entry into their areas of endeavor. Television broadcasters also worried that they would have to pay for telephone company carriage of station signals.

NOTES

1. E. Stratford Smith, "The Emergence of CATV: A Look at the Evolution of a Revolution," *Proceedings of the IEEE* 58 (1970): 967–82.
2. "Cable programing [sic] status report," 18 May 1987: 41.
3. "VCR penetration eclipses cable," *Broadcasting* 27 July 1987: 96.

FURTHER READING

Aumente, Jerome. *New Electronic Pathways: Videotex, Teletext, and Online Databases.* Newbury Park: Sage, 1987.

Compaine, Benjamin M., ed. *Understanding New Media: Trends and Issues in Electronic Distribution of Information.* Cambridge: Ballinger, 1984. Direction and consequence.

Dizard, Wilson P., Jr. *The Coming Information Age: An Overview of Technology, Economics, and Politics.* 2d ed. New York: Longman, 1985. Impact of changes.

Ganley, Gladys D., and Oswald H. Ganley. *Global Political Fallout: The First Decade of the VCR, 1976–1985.* Norwood: Ablex, 1987.

Garay, Ronald. *Cable Television: A Reference Guide to Information.* Westport: Greenwood, 1988. Organizes, classifies, and provides access to cable literature.

Graham, Margaret B. W. *RCA and the Videodisc Player: The Business of Research.* New York: Cambridge UP, 1987.

Lardner, James. *Fast Forward: Hollywood, the Japanese, and the VCR Wars.* New York: Norton, 1987. History.

McCavitt, Willaim E. *Television Technology: Alternative Communication Systems.* Lanham: UP of America, 1983.

National Association of Broadcasters. *Tomorrow's TVs: A Review of New TV Set Technology, Related Video Equipment and Potential Market Impacts, 1987–1995.* Washington: NAB, 1987. Changes in receivers.

Ostroff, David H. "A History of STV, Inc. and the 1964 California Vote Against Pay Television." *Journal of Broadcasting* 27 (1983): 371. Early try with pay cable.

Rogers, Everett M. *Communication Technology: The New Media in Society.* New York: Columbia UP, 1986.

Schramm, Wilbur, *The Story of Human Communication: Cave Painting to Microchip.* New York: Harper, 1988.

Singleton, Loy A. *Telecommunication in the Information Age: A Nontechnical Primer on the New Technologies.* 2d ed. Cambridge: Ballinger, 1986. Nontechnical descriptions.

Weinstein, Stephen B. *Getting the Picture: A Guide to CATV and the New Electronic Media.* New York: IEEE, 1986.

Williams, Frederick. *Technology and Communication Behavior.* Belmont: Wadsworth, 1987. Impact on human behavior.

TWO

CREATIVE/INFORMATIONAL PERSPECTIVE

Chances are good that you will feel this section is the real meat of this book.

And you may be right.

The glamour and excitement of radio and television definitely grow out of programming and program creation. There is a feeling of creativity and accomplishment and vitality in programming that stretches from the disc jockey shift at the local cable radio station to the highest-paid directing positions for network television.

It's fun. It's hard. It's long hours, crises, and heartbreaks. You have to *want* to do it—more than pay, pride, or privacy. And if you don't, you had better choose something easier for your life's work, such as brain surgery or corporate accounting.

End of sermon.

At any rate, this is the section in which you find out how it all works—how programs are put together, Chapter 6; how programmers operate, Chapter 7; how news works, Chapter 8; and how commercials are created, Chapter 9. But watch out! It's addictive.

CHAPTER 6

Production, Programs, and Performance

A program is like a many-faceted jewel that can be examined from many different angles. At this point, we are interested in its structure, the program as a creative endeavor. Thus we focus on five of the facets: audio and video production, types of programs, procedures for getting programs on the air, talent, and critical review.

6.1 AUDIO PRODUCTION PROCESS

The production process in almost any medium can be divided into three phases. **Preproduction** includes activities necessary to prepare for broadcast or recording; **production,** actual broadcast or recording; and **postproduction,** creative treatment after production to put the production into final form for the audience. We shall look at the production process for audio—radio and other aural-only media—in these terms.

6.1.1 Audio Preproduction

The exact procedures covered by the term preproduction vary with the medium and the intended finished product. In a radio station, preparation for broadcast includes a variety of activities, from choosing the overall programming specialization and devising the format to selecting recordings for air play and preparing newscasts. Preproduction for a radio program or a commercial often involves preparation of a script or rundown sheet, selection of talent, and acquisition of special music and other creative components. In the recording industry, preproduction may cover selection of artists, music, backup musicians, and the recording facilities themselves.

6.1.2 Audio Production

In most cases, audio production centers on the **mixing** process. Audio from several sources is fed to a central point for selection, control, and amplification, then sent on to broadcast or recording. Audio sources may include microphones and playback devices, such as tape machines, turntables, and compact disc players. Mixing takes place at an audio control board (Section 11.3.2.1).

Titles and duties of audio production personnel vary—in radio broadcasting, they even vary from one station to the next. In a fairly common arrangement, one person makes on-the-spot creative decisions and supervises (but does not actually manipulate) control board operation. Board operators are usually given the title **audio technician** (or audio engineer). In the recording industry, the supervisor is a **producer.** In radio, the supervisor is a **director;** however, more times than not, the same person is both technician and director and is called the **producer.** On most local disc jockey programs the technician works alone, combining two jobs—talent and audio technician. This is called **combo** (combination) operation (Figure 6.1).

Radio stations that broadcast live telephone call-in programs use a special production technique, **audio delay,** to retain control over content. (The term "delay" is also used to refer to an audio technique, the effect of which sounds similar to echo or reverberation.) A delay device picks up the audio signal coming from the audio console and holds it up a specific number of seconds. If someone utters an objectionable remark during a program, the station has those several seconds in which to react and cut the remark before it actually goes over the air.

The recording industry strives for absolute control of audio quality (Figure 6.2). When a studio makes a record of a musical group, it sets up a **separate microphone** for every section, often every performer. In popular music the studio may even **record each component separately.** The band may record one day, the special rhythm section the next, the background voices on the third day, and the soloist on the fourth. The result is a **multitrack recording;** each signal records on a separate track or channel (horizontal section) on the

Figure 6.1 Radio combo operation.   In front of the operator is the audio console. Meters at the top of the console indicate relative loudness of the audio signal. The microphone, over the console, is on an adjustable boom. Note the stack of audiotape cartridges (lower left) and the line of cartridge playback units (below the console); this station "carts" (transfers to audiotape cartridges) all records, and the operator plays the cartridges instead of records over the air.

Figure 6.2 Recording session. The recording engineer and the producer work at the audio console. The recording artist sings and plays into the microphone in the studio next door. (*Source*: Wolinsky, Stock, Boston)

same special wide audiotape. (So it is entirely possible that the musicians on your favorite pop music record have never even met each other!) Production houses sometimes use the same technique for radio commercials, sound tracks for television commercials, and some radio programs.

6.1.3 Audio Postproduction

For ongoing radio station programming, any postproduction processing is normally passive. A station may put electronic devices in the line that **process** the audio signal before transmission. The usual aim of such processing is to make the average audio level louder so that radio receivers will pick up and reproduce the transmitted signal "loud and clear." Some devices, however, add effects such as echo.

Radio programs and commercials produced on audiotape often require postproduction **editing.** The producer or director (or an editor under supervision) edits the tape. The editing process involves cutting out, adding, or rearranging segments of the taped material or splicing together two or more tapes. Typical motivations for editing include time (to lengthen or shorten) and continuity (to append, delete, or restructure material).

In preparing a popular music recording for final release, the studio plays back the completed multitrack tape while adding **effects** to the various channels, making some louder than originally recorded, some softer, some in echo, and sundry other electronic gimmicks. After such effects have been added, the multichannel recording is **rerecorded** down to two channels. Again, production houses may do the same for commercials and other elaborate audio projects.

6.2 TELEVISION PRODUCTION

An entertainment television program begins as someone's idea. The idea, typed in a brief descriptive form called the **presentation,** is submitted to a production company. If the company likes the submission, it buys the idea from the **creator,** sometimes outright, sometimes on a royalty or percentage basis. Often the creator is hired as **story consultant** or **script consultant.**

Most production companies do not accept unsolicited program ideas from an individual. Instead, a recognized **agent** deals with the company on behalf of the individual. The agent is extremely important in television production; a larger agency may, on its own, put together a program idea and pitch it to a production house or network as a package deal—concept, writer, director, stars, all under contract to the agency, of course.

The production company may decide to aim the program idea at the syndication market. In that case, a pitch is made to local outlets and, often, to advertisers. If the pitch draws enough commitments to pay for the program, the company puts it into production.

The company pitches an idea for a network program to network executives. The network may commission (contract for) an elaboration of the idea, ranging from a **treatment** (simple outline or descripton of a sample show) to a **pilot.** A full pilot is a sample program, often in the form of a made-for-television movie, and is generally produced only for proposed prime-time broadcast television network shows. The network may then commit to a limited number of episodes, in which case the program goes into production.

By the time it hits the production stage, the original program concept has gone through many changes at the hands of agents, production company executives, network people, and so on. Sometimes the fin-ished product resembles the creator's first idea only in the most general manner. The script, for example, will be changed continuously, even during production.

The **producer** is in overall charge of the program. The producer first shepherds the program through preproduction—has the script written, cost estimates and budgets made, personnel hired, sets built, and so on. Then the producer oversees production as the **director** chooses various camera shots to translate the written script into visual images. Generally, these shots include the following: close-up shots showing the head and shoulders of performers; medium shots showing the upper part of performers; long shots showing all or most of the performers and a large part of the background; reaction shots showing performers seeming to watch or listen to someone or something else; and cutaway shots of objects showing, for example, the close-up of the murder weapon or the glass with the lipstick on it.

Finally, the producer supervises postproduction, in which the visual images are turned into a finished program. Sometimes writers or directors, to retain creative control of their material, take on the role of producer. They are called **hyphenates** because of the hyphens in their job titles—for example, producer-writer.

We can divide television production techniques into two overall classifications. In electronic production, the resulting medium—the output of the production process that carries the picture information—is video, an electronic signal. Video may be transmittted immediately or stored on videotape. In film production, the output is exposed and developed motion picture film.

6.2.1 Electronic Production Techniques

The following paragraphs describe electronic production. Four electronic production techniques have evolved—multicamera, automated multicamera, multivideotape, and single-camera—as well as the stop-and-go method, which is sometimes used in corporate video settings.

6.2.1.1 Multicamera

As the name implies, multicamera production involves two or more cameras. During production, every camera produces a picture different from that of every other camera, and all cameras produce pictures at the same time. Only one picture, however, is used—broadcast or recorded—although that one may be a combination of several that are available. Multicamera production involves a series of on-the-spot, as-it-happens answers to the question, "What *one best* picture should be the ultimate video product of this production *right now*." Multicamera production is traditionally used in many studio and location productions—for example, news programs, sports remotes, and comedy/variety shows.

For a dramatic program, the **director** *blocks* (plans) all performer and camera movement in advance. Television studio time is expensive, so the director rehearses performers elsewhere, perhaps in an empty rehearsal hall. By the time they move into the studio, sets have been erected, dressed (props put in place), and lighted. Only then are cameras and performers rehearsed together.

When the program is finally telecast or taped, the director usually works in the control room. There, the director has two principal tasks, selection and instruction.

Selection involves the decisions discussed above, the ongoing choices of video for inclusion in the production from among the varied sources available, such as studio and remote cameras, videotape playback, and character generators. The control room (Figure 6.3) contains video monitors (television screens), each showing the output from one video source. The director observes these monitors and "calls the shots," that is, instructs which picture or combination of pictures is to be selected. A **technical director** (TD), also in the control room, operates the mixing controls and other devices to carry out the director's commands.

The instruction task consists of issuing directions to production crew members. Most crew members are usually located outside and away from the control room, so the director communicates through two-way headsets. Each studio and remote camera has an **operator,** and the director tells the operator what camera shot to get. Similarly, the director gives other instructions to the production assistants and technicians who make up the rest of the crew. Thus, the director **simultaneously directs** (tells the camera operators what shots to get) **and edits** (tells the technical director which shots and what order of shots to use.

Television **audio** uses basically the same equipment and follows the same principles as audio-only production. Unlike audio-only production, however, the performer in television is often in motion. Therefore, TV sound pickup (the capture of sound by microphone) requires some specially adapted equipment and techniques.

The postproduction phase includes videotape editing (Box 6.1). The amount of editing varies with the program. For example, many local public affairs programs use **live-type videotaping.** Here the videotape recorder (VTR) begins recording, and the program is done as though it were being televised live. The tape is later broadcast with little or no editing. At the other extreme is a program produced in segments and assembled later, almost like editing a film (Section 6.2.2.5). Somewhere in between is the videotaped situation comedy. Typically, the program is recorded several times all the way through; then separate scenes or shots are recorded again as needed. The best of each recording is edited together to make one complete program.

(a)

(b)

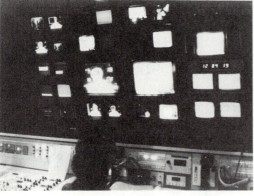

(c)

(d)

Figure 6.3 Production control room.   (a) The technical director (TD; left) and the director for the noon news at WESH-TV sit at the video mixing console and face a bank of monitors. (b) Looking over the shoulder of the director (right) to see the TD and the controls he operates. The box to the left of the video mixing console (partially obscured by the TD's head) contains controls for videotape machines that are located in another room. (c) The director's view of the video monitors. (d) At Channel 2's Orlando studio, the audio control operator sits behind and slightly above the TD in the production control room.

6.2.1.2 Automated Multicamera

A variation of the multicamera technique eliminates production crew members, particularly camera operators, through automation. This works best in one-set studio situations with little or no movement by on-air talent—primarily in newscasts. A **remote-control** device allows one person to manipulate all cameras. Levers, switches, and pushbuttons on a central panel activate servomotors that pivot the camera and move its zoom lens. Most remote-control systems allow advance programming of all camera movements.

In 1988, NBC News introduced **robotics** to production; it put into use a remote-controlled camera (Figure 6.4) that could pivot, zoom, and *move around the studio floor*. The network also planned to replace technicians who play back videotapes and video graphics with robotics technology and then tie all robotically operated devices into a computer. At that point, one individual could produce a newscast from the computer keyboard.

6.2.1.3 Multivideotape

Multivideotape production also employs two or more cam-

Figure 6.4 NBC's remote-controlled camera. (Photo © 1989, Courtesy of the National Broadcasting Company, Inc.)

eras. In this technique, however, all pictures are used—that is, recorded for postproduction editing. Each of a number (say, four) of electronic cameras feeds a separate VTR. All operate simultaneously. The result is four complete videotapes of the same scene, each from a different angle or shot. On-line switching is completely eliminated, and the director works in the studio with the performers. After production, an editor selects various shots and angles from the four videotapes and edits them together into the finished production. Thus all editing is done in the post-production phase, in motion picture style.

6.2.1.4 Single-Camera/Electronic Field Production A single-camera production employs one camera, usually a high-quality minicamera, which feeds a VTR. Through stop-and-go taping, the camera records every scene and sequence in the script, one shot at a time. The various shots may even be taped out of sequence, just as in film production (Section 6.2.2.3). However, when well done and skillfully edited, the shots go together to form a unified whole that looks as slick as the best standard multicamera production. The single-camera technique works well in situations where the program creator wants hands-on control of production or must work with less than a full production crew.

When used out of the studio, the single-camera technique is called *electronic field production* (EFP) (Figure 6.5). It is particularly well suited for production of commercials and documentaries, and independent video documentary makers and corporate television producers often use it. Some broadcast and cable program producers have experimented with single-camera production and predicted that it would become the norm, particularly in high-definition television (Section 12.5.3).

6.2.1.5 Corporate Video Corporate video refers to in-house use of small-format video by a business, governmental, or educational organization. Therefore, it is not so much a separate production technique as it is a *purpose* for *use* of production techniques.

In some corporate settings, however, a special technique has developed. Often, the organization does not staff its "media department" on a grand scale. So the corporate television producer may not only produce

Figure 6.5 Electronic field production. EFP crew sets up in a county courtroom. The director checks out the videotape recorder (right background). Channel 2 used the single-camera technique to produce this series on the criminal justice system for use by Orange County middle schools.

the production but also direct, make do with a skeleton crew, and—even with multiple cameras—use the **stop-and-go** production technique mentioned above. For example, suppose the director (the corporate television producer acting as director) has three cameras and only one other person to help. The director could switch and run audio, and the helper could run the cameras and give cues. But at some point, the director will need two cameras moved at once, and there just are not enough people to do it. In such a situa-

Box 6.1 The Videotape Editing Process

Typical equipment in a videotape editing suite (a) includes two editing recorders (lower left; operator's left hand is on bottom recorder), three video monitors (on desk—two 19-inch and one 5-inch); editing controller (on desk, under operator's right hand), special effects generator (to right of operator—control board on top, electronics below), and a printer (above small monitor). Minimum equipment for videotape editing consists of two VTRs (b). One plays back and the other records program material in the order in which it is to appear in the final edited version. This recording becomes the edited tape. More sophisticated editing can be done by adding a control console (c). The tape editor operates the console to command electronically the two recorders when and where to cue up, play back, and record. The most elaborate consoles (d) allow insertion of special effects such as fades, dissolves, mattes, and keys. (Photograph courtesy of JVC PROFESSIONAL PRODUCTS CO. Used by permission.)

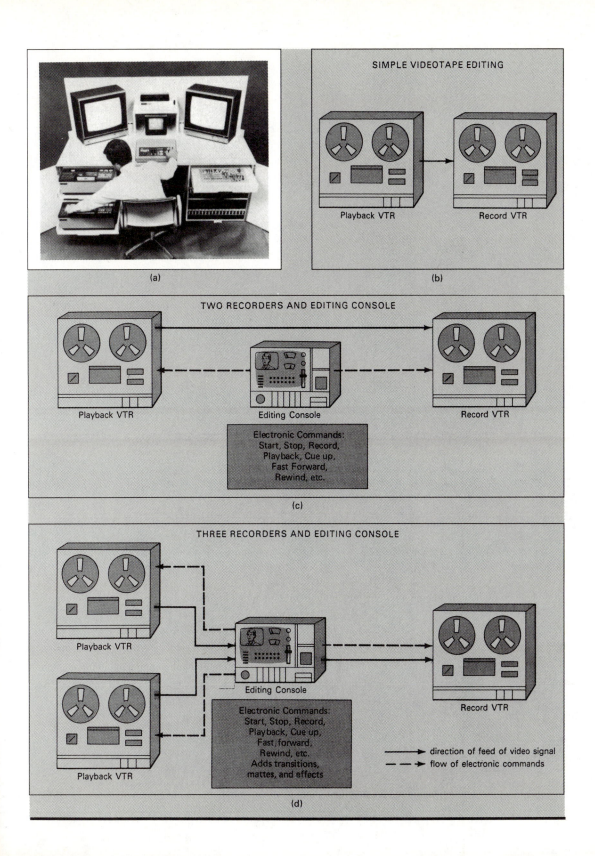

(a)

SIMPLE VIDEOTAPE EDITING

Playback VTR

Record VTR

(b)

TWO RECORDERS AND EDITING CONSOLE

Playback VTR

Editing Console

Record VTR

Electronic Commands:
Start, Stop, Record,
Playback, Cue up,
Fast Forward,
Rewind, etc.

(c)

THREE RECORDERS AND EDITING CONSOLE

Playback VTR

Editing Console

Record VTR

Playback VTR

Electronic Commands:
Start, Stop, Record,
Playback, Cue up,
Fast forward,
Rewind, etc.
Adds transitions,
mattes, and effects

→ direction of feed of video signal

- - → flow of electronic commands

(d)

tion the director would set up all cameras on their shots, turn on the VTR, tape as much as possible, stop the VTR, reset the cameras for the next group of shots, and tape some more, until the entire production is on tape and ready for editing.

6.2.2 Film Production

Much television program material is produced on film. After discussing multicamera and kinescope, this section focuses on the feature film technique, film animation, and film postproduction.

6.2.2.1 Multicamera Film Production Some half-hour situation comedies use electronic-style production technqiues with film cameras. The program is often performed on a stage before an audience. A number of film cameras are placed so as to film the production simultaneously from different angles.

The result is a number of film copies (prints) of the program.

6.2.2.2 Kinescope Recording Though not currently used in cable or broadcasting, another method of film production uses electronic cameras and a switcher. The picture is fed to a **kinescope,** a high-intensity television picture tube. A film camera is aimed at the tube and films the picture. This prevideotape method of recording television is called *kinescope recording.*

6.2.2.3 Feature Film Production Most film television dramas and many commercials (Figure 6.6) are produced using feature film production techniques (Figure 6.7). One camera is used. Each time the camera moves, it is a new **setup,** and often the lights and microphones must be reset as well. A setup takes anywhere from a few minutes to most of a day, according to its complexity.

Scenes are filmed **out of sequence;** that is,

Figure 6.6 Location film production.   (Photograph courtesy of Victor Duncan, Inc. Used by permission.)

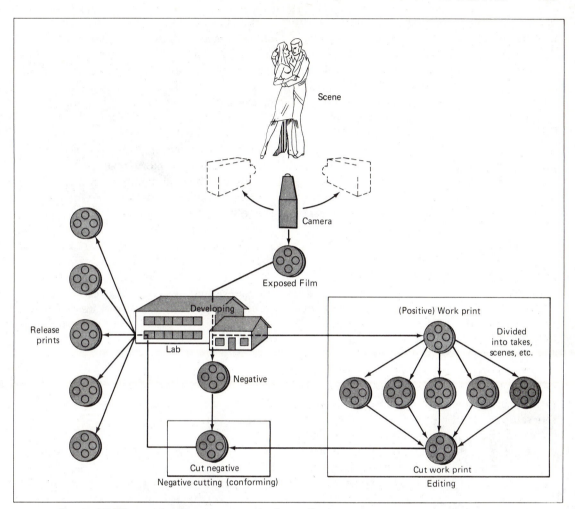

Figure 6.7 Film production process. Audio, opticals, and many other steps have been omitted for the sake of clarity.

they are not filmed in the order in which they appear on the program. In the finished program, a particular section might open on a close-up of a performer speaking the first line, cut to a reaction shot of another performer as the original performer speaks the second line, and then cut to a long shot as the third line is spoken. In filming, however, the entire section was first filmed in one or a series of long shots. These **master shots** correspond to the scenes as written in the script.

Then the director filmed supplementary scenes—first, medium shots; then, close-up shots; and finally, reaction shots and cut-away shots. By the time the director has filmed the section from all angles and views, much more film has been shot than will be used. On the average, 10 feet of film are shot for every one used in the program.

To confuse matters further, the sections of the program are also filmed out of sequence. The script may call for the first section to take place in an office, the second in a house, the third in the office again, the fourth in a bar, the fifth in the house, the sixth in the office, and the seventh back in the bar. But in filming the program, the first, third, and sixth sections will be filmed one after the other in the office set; the second and fifth, in the house set; and the fourth and seventh, in the bar set. This filming method saves time and money by reducing major camera movements from one set to another, thus cutting fees for sound stage rental and location (at someone's actual office, house, and bar) usage.

Dialogue is recorded at the same time as the picture, but separately. While the camera records the picture, sound is recorded on audiotape.

The **director** supervises the entire production, directs performers in rehearsal and during filming, and decides how to film each scene and section. The **director of photography** is in charge of the camera crew, advises the director on how to use the camera in filming a scene, and designs and directs the setup of lighting. The film production crew consists of specialists, and there are individuals or teams that handle properties, sets, lighting, heavy equipment, sound, clerical functions, logistics, and transportation.

6.2.2.4 Film Animation   Film animation begins with a series of drawings, and each second of screen time may require at least 24 separate drawings. The total number of drawings required for even a short animated section can be in the tens of thousands. These drawings are then photographed using special cameras that film one frame at a time, stopping after each frame to allow the drawing to be changed.

Highly articulated, lifelike film animation, such as that used in the Walt Disney classics, is very expensive compared with live-action filming. Computer animation, on the other hand, allows the artist to draw the basic shapes once and then animate them electronically. This saves a great deal of time and, thus, money. Despite the high initial costs for equipment, television makes increasing use of computer animation.

6.2.2.5 Film Postproduction   Each day, exposed film is delivered to the processing laboratory. The laboratory processes the film overnight. The next day the film is viewed as **dailies** or **rushes** to determine whether any scenes need to be refilmed.

The film next goes to the **editor.** The editor chooses scenes, sets them in the order that will best tell the story, and edits the dialogue to match the picture. Other sound is added—sound effects, music, voice-over narration (if used). Finally, picture and sound are put together on one film, the completed program.

6.2.3 Electronic Production *Versus* Film Production

We have described two different types of television production. In traditional electronic production the program is largely produced in sequence and in real time. There may be some postproduction editing, but for the most part the shots have gone together in the proper, finished order at the time of production. In film production, on the other hand, the program is produced out of sequence and is edited after production. The director films; then the editor assembles.

There is a difference, too, in quality of picture. As viewed on home receivers by audience members, electronic cameras give brighter, sharper pictures, more intense colors, better color reproduction, and greater feeling of simultaneity—of watching a performance as it happens. Film programs seem less alive than electronic productions (and remember, we mean here only quality of picture, not program content) chiefly because of their intermedium nature.

Intermedium nature simply means that a program is produced on film and played back on television. Film stores information by photochemical means; television transmits information using electrons. Each medium has its own limitations on amount and types of information it can reproduce. The combination of these two sets of limitations makes for a picture that is not as crisp as a direct, electronic picture. Videotape, on the other hand, is actually part of the electronic production medium. Videotape avoids loss of crispness because it stores signals from electronic cameras, reproducing them with nearly total fidelity on demand. In fact, unless the viewer is so informed, it is impossible to tell whether a production is live or on videotape.

Film production, however, is still the method that allows greatest flexibility in production—scheduling performers, crews, and sets—and moving from location to location. Hollywood, California, is the home of most major production companies, and film is the medium with which they are most experienced. And though videotape production is slightly less costly, the initial investment for equipment is much higher than for film production.

A sort of trichotomy has evolved based on live, videotape, and film production characteristics. Programs in which the element of time is important—to get it on the air as soon as possible—are produced live using electronic techniques. These include news, sports play-by-play, on-the-spot coverage, local church services, and, occasionally, informational and public affairs.

However, most television programs are produced on either videotape or film. Both allow some degree of flexibility in production

scheduling and postproduction editing. Perhaps more important from an economic standpoint, both allow the program to be syndicated.

Videotape is used for programs in which the illusion of aliveness and simultaneity is thought to be important. These include soap operas, a number of network prime-time situation comedies, almost all of the Public Broadcasting Service's dramatic programs, talk shows, children's programs, game shows, commercial network music and variety programs, some syndicated religious programs, and various pay television specials such as plays and nightclub acts. Videotape is also used for most instructional television programs, for the time and money saved over comparable film production.

Film production is used for programs where production flexibility is important, while time and apparent simultaneity are not. These include most regularly scheduled commercial network dramatic programs, some situation comedies, and made-for-television movies. Film is the oldest and the traditional medium for animation as well; thus children's cartoon programs are on film. Most film sizes are also compatible all over the world, an advantage in international production and syndication.

6.2.4 Electronic Production *and* Film Production

On the other hand, in production the boundaries among various media have become blurred. Film uses production techniques once associated only with video, and vice versa. For examples, look at earlier paragraphs in this chapter—multicamera film, multi-VTR video, single-camera video, stop-and-go production, computer animation. The first four mix film and video production techniques. The last marries video and computer technology to produce moving drawings, an effect developed in, and for years possible only in, film. Yet even theatrical film production now uses computer animation.

Also, film crews routinely use video equipment. They strap a video camera onto the film camera. The video camera feeds a VTR. When they film a scene, they switch on both the film camera and the VTR. Immediately afterward, they play back the tape and determine whether the shot was good—without having to wait for the next day's rushes. In postproduction the tape becomes a video work print, and the editor uses a video editing console to assemble a tape version of the completed production. Finally, the editor physically cuts and splices the film to match the tape. This saves time and work.

High-definition television (HDTV; Section 12.5.3) opens even more possibilities. HDTV differs from conventional television in at least one respect and perhaps two—resolution and aspect ratio. Resolution refers to the amount of picture elements or information in the frame, and HDTV features such high resolution that it can be projected onto a motion picture screen and look as sharp as film. Aspect ratio refers to the height of the picture as compared to its width. Some HDTV proposals would widen the television screen so that its shape more closely matches that of the motion picture screen. Thus, a director could make a movie using HDTV video cameras and record it on videotape. The completed movie would then go to the theaters in two ways. For smaller theaters, the studio would transfer the tape to film to be shown by the traditional method, on a film projector. For larger theaters, the studios would play the taped "movie" and relay it by satellite to the theaters. The theaters would feed the satellite signal directly to large video projectors to show the movie on their screens.

6.3 RADIO PROGRAMS

Most radio stations emphasize *programming* as a whole (Section 7.2.1), not individual programs. Radio audiences tend to listen to rock radio stations, not rock radio programs; to country music stations, not country music programs; to jazz stations, not jazz programs. However, many stations air individual programs, and even an ongoing programming format is a program. Therefore we examine types, scripting, and syndication of radio programs.

Live programming at most radio stations consists of the disc jockey, the telephone call-in, or the news format. Except for some commercial copy (script) that must be read live, the disc jockey and call-in formats do not use a script in the formal sense of the term. Even a public affairs program often takes the form of extemporaneous discussion, with the moderator's list of questions being the only written script. News programs, sports programs, and weather reports are fully scripted, and sports play-by-play broadcasts uses partial scripts. For the most part, scripted network- and station-produced programs are commentary, editorials, documentaries, and (rarely) dramas and comedy.

A great variety of scripted, recorded radio programs is available from **syndication sources.** The term syndication implies production, sale, and distribution of programs designed primarily for the station to attract and interest an audience. There are firms that produce such programs, and the programs themselves range from one minute to several hours in length and from commentaries and features to drama and musical anthologies. Syndicated music services offer automated stations literally weeks of music programming. Some syndicated material is offered to stations on a **barter** basis—the station pays little or no money, and the programming contains positions into which the station may insert commercials, but it also contains commercial messages (which the station must carry) that the syndicator has sold.

Programs are available that promote the opinion or stand of the producing organizations. These organizations include churches and church-related groups, various levels and branches of government, educational institutions, political organizations, industry and trade groups, labor unions, and other special-interest groups. Sometimes stations are asked to air these programs free; at other times they are paid rate card prices (the amount charged to advertisers) to run them.

6.4 TELEVISION PROGRAMS

Television programming consists of individual programs. Some cable programmers, independent television stations, and low-power television outlets have adopted ongoing programming formats, most of which are based on comtemporary music. But, for the most part, television schedules comprise discrete units of entertainment and information. In this section, television programs are divided into eight broad categories—entertainment, information, sports, advertising, special audience, cultural, educational, religious, and miscellaneous.

6.4.1 Entertainment

The first concern of any TV programmer is entertainment. To a certain extent, this holds true even for television news (Section 8.1.5). Most TV programming consists of *pure entertainment*—it has no other purpose but to hold our attention so as to bring us pleasure (and, of course, to expose us to the advertising messages it contains). Nearly every broadcast and cable network and outlet telecasts the various entertainment program

types; these may be categorized as drama, comedy, music, variety, talk, game, and reality.

6.4.1.1 Drama The weekly **dramatic series** is a continually popular program type, especially in prime time. A program in a dramatic series is generally one hour. Each program in the series features a complete and different play. The same performers play the same main characters every week; only supporting characters change.

The **daily serial,** also called **soap opera** (Figure 6.8) or simply "soap," runs 30, 60, or 90 minutes per daily episode. Usually, several main plots unfold at once in a soap. Dramatic pacing is slow, and plot and characters carry over from one program to the next. Soaps generally air during the day; however, themes and characters in some popular prime-time network weekly series bear a strong resemblance to those in the daytime soaps and are even called **prime-time soaps.**

The **miniseries** (Figure 6.9) combines elements of both the dramatic series and the soap. The miniseries is finite; it runs for a specific number of episodes and then ends. Individual episodes have continuing characters, and each program is a complete story. But the series also tells an overall story—for example, a family evolving with the times or an individual going through a particularly critical phase of life. There may be a trace of the soap's cliff-hanging element in the miniseries; an individual episode, while complete in itself, may close with a tacit question concerning the fate of a major character or endeavor.

As is the case with a number of other programming innovations adopted by commercial broadcasting, the first successful miniseries appeared on public broadcasting. This was *The Forsyte Saga,* a British Broadcasting Corporation production aired by the Public Broadcasting Service in 1969. By the late

Figure 6.8 Soap opera. ABC's *General Hospital* is one of daytime television's most popular network programs. (Photograph © 1989, Capital Cities, ABC, Inc.)

1980s, the most popular miniseries was still ABC-TV's *Roots*, broadcast over eight days in 1977.*

The **docudrama** recreates an actual incident, situation, or individual, usually in the form of a made-for-television film. The docudrama is scripted to highlight the dramatic elements, uses professional actors, and is produced as an entertainment program.

Rarely, a broadcast network telecasts a theatrical production. Plays and revues are

*The single program that had the largest audience was CBS-TV's 1983 "Goodbye, Farewell and Amen," the 2½-hour final episode of the long-running comedy series *M*A*S*H;* CBS estimated that over 125 million people watched some part of that program. The highest-rated program was a January 1953 episode of *I Love Lucy,* in which the female lead gave birth to a son (Lucille Ball, the actress, was pregnant in real life); that show averaged a 71.8 rating and a 92 share, but the total number of television homes in the country was only 21.2 million at that time.

seen slightly more often on some cable networks.

6.4.1.2 Comedy Comedy programs may feature a funny person, the humor that derives from putting certain types of people in certain types of situations (the situation comedy [Box 6.2]), or a string of seemingly unrelated funny lines and situations.

6.4.1.3 Music and Variety In pure form, **musical programs** would feature only music, and **variety programs** would feature various changing acts and performers. Early in television's history, there were such pure forms; later, however, music and variety were usually combined. For example, an individual gained fame as a singer of popular music and, as a result, hosted a network musical variety series; on the program the star introduced performing guests and acted in comedy skits, as well as singing in musical numbers. By 1990, musical variety TV shows were mostly a thing of the past. However, comedy programs sometimes still contain music and variety; *Saturday Night Live* is an example. Even some dramatic programs may include musical numbers.

Two musical program forms really qualify more as television disc jockey shows. One, the dance program, dates from the 1950s. A host introduces each recording, and the video accompanying the music shows the dancing of a studio full of audience participants. The other program form is the music-

video show, a product of the 1980s. Inspired by the success of Music Television (MTV), a national cable program service, this program features "videos"—videotapes of visual interpretations of popular music—often introduced by a "video jockey." Cable programmers and TV stations put such programs in their schedules; a few devoted their entire program day to music videos, becoming, in effect, television radio stations.

6.4.1.4 Talk The basic talk show format features a moderator who converses with one or more guests. Talk shows may have elements of comedy, music, and variety as well. In another variation, the moderator

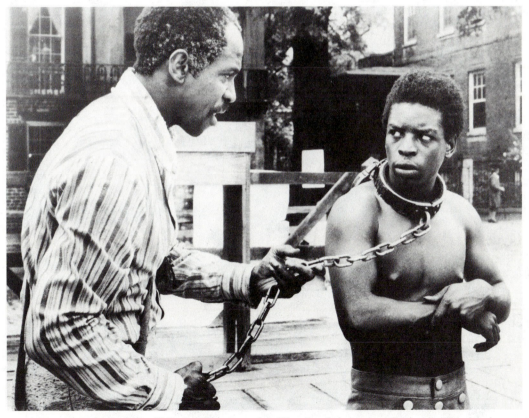

Figure 6.9 Miniseries. ABC aired the record-setting *Roots*, based on the best-selling book by Alex Haley, in 1977. (*Source:* AP/Wide World.)

Box 6.2 Cosby: The Sitcom Phenomenon

A hit from the outset, *The Cosby Show* founded an unbeatable Thursday night comedy lineup for NBC during the middle and late 1980s and helped push the network into its first-ever prime-time-season ratings victory. *Cosby* set records in syndication, too; Viacom, distributor for the off-net *Cosby* episodes, used an ''auction'' format to demand and receive the highest prices ever paid for a syndicated series. Trade press reports had WWOR-TV, New York, paying slightly more than $40 million for the initial cycle of *Cosby* episodes; KCOP-TV, Los Angeles, paid close to $40 million. This first cycle was said to have generated a total of $600 million to $650 million in revenue. Most came from fees paid by the station. Not only the most expensive, *Cosby* was also the first off-net strip to be sold on a cash-plus-barter (Section 7.3.2.1) basis. More than $100 million of its total revenue was generated by the one minute of barter time in each episode. Here, Theo (played by Malcolm–Jamal Warner, right) has brought his friend Denny (Tory Winbush, center) to seek advice from Cliff (Bill Cosby) in the episode titled ''What He Did For Love.'' (Photograph © 1989, courtesy of the National Broadcasting Company, Inc.)

Figure 6.10 Confrontational talk.   Television newspeople often described these and other "reality" programs as "cheap," "sensationalist," and "exploitative." Along with *The Morton Downey Jr. Show,* one of the most condemned (and one of the most popular with viewers!) was *Geraldo!* A melee during a November, 1988, taping of the latter program resulted in the host suffering a broken nose—which, in turn, was milked for its publicity value. (*Source:* AP/Wide World.)

also calls for studio audience participation. In the advice show variation, an "expert" responds to questions from the audience; during the 1980s one of the most popular and, at the same time, titillating such shows featured Dr. Ruth Westheimer answering queries concerning sexual conduct.

By the end of the 1980s, personality-based, audience participation talk shows had emerged as one of the staples of "reality" programming (Section 6.4.1.6). Among the best-known such programs were *Donahue, The Oprah Winfrey Show, Geraldo!* (Figure 6.10), and *The Morton Downey Jr. Show.* The latter two, particularly, gained notoriety for their confrontational nature. *Downey,* however, suffered loss of audience and advertisers, and its syndicator took it out of distribution in 1989.

6.4.1.5 Game   Game shows use a host or hostess who sets up the game situation or asks the questions and one or more contestants who try to win the game and collect a prize. This theme seems to have endless variations, and television broadcast schedules nearly always include game shows. During the late 1980s, one company, King World, distributed the three most popular syndicated shows (Figure 6.11)—*Wheel of Fortune* and *Jeopardy!*, both game shows, ranked one and two, while *Oprah Winfrey,* a talk show, came in third.

6.4.1.6 Reality   In the early 1980s, programming interests in the trade began to use the term *reality programming* to cover a number of different types of programs. By the latter part of the decade, a two-part distinction had

(a)

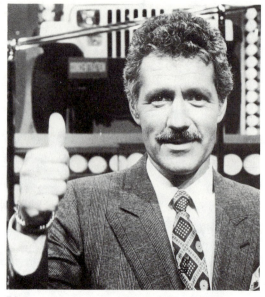

(b)

(c)

Figure 6.11 King World's winners. During the late 1980's, one company, King World, distributed the three most popular syndicated shows. (a) *Wheel of Fortune* and (b) *Jeopardy!*, both game shows, ranked first and second, while (c) *Oprah Winfrey*, a talk show, came in third. (*Source:* AP/Wide World)

emerged. "Reality programming" featured nonactors dealing with issues of personal concern. It included shows such as *The People's Court, Group One Medical, On Trial,* and *America on Trial*. In "reality-*based* programming" paid talent dealt with nonfictional material. Examples included Fox's *The Reporters, A Current Affair,* and *America's Most Wanted*; NBC's *Unsolved Mysteries*; and al-

most any Geraldo Rivera special (such as the syndicated *Mystery of Al Capone's Vaults* and NBC's *Devil Worship: Exposing Satan's Underground*).

These programs resembled both fiction and news or public affairs but were neither. Most were strictly entertainment fluff yet left the viewer with the impression of "having learned something." Some TV news personnel condemned them as **trash TV** and worried that they blurred the line between journalism and entertainment for TV audiences.

6.4.1.7 Miscellaneous Into this subcategory go the entertainment programs that do not easily fit into the other slots. For example, various exercise and aerobics shows might conceivably be construed as educational, since they supposedly aim at how-to and self-help needs. On the other hand, most such programs feature well-developed, attractive people clad in skintight clothing who bounce around energetically to popular music—more than a little entertainment even for the most unathletic voyeur. Similarly, *Entertainment Tonight* and its clones are not readily categorized, nor are the several movie-review programs.

6.4.2 Information

Information programs include news, discussion, documentaries, on-the-spot coverage, and commentary and editorials. Section 8.4 deals with these at some length. Cable networks have greatly expanded the availability of information programming. On the other hand, there are cable networks and television stations that broadcast little or no informational programming.

6.4.3 Sports

Sports programs fall into two categories— sports reports and play-by-play. A **sports report** is structured much like a newscast. An anchor reporter reads sports news—who won, who got hired, what stadium is nearing completion. Sometimes the sports report includes an interview with a prominent sports figure. In broadcast television, local stations do most of the regularly scheduled sports reports. In cable television, however, several national networks telecast daily sports reports.

Play-by-play is a remote telecast of an entire sports event—a football game, a horse race, a golf tournament. Several sports announcers offer commentary, statistics, explanations, and interviews during the event.

In addition to reports and play-by-play, there are **documentaries** on sports personalities or events, program **series** devoted to a single sport (such as fishing or hunting), and **sports magazine** programs (spot coverage of various events on one show, sometimes live, sometimes recorded and edited for time).

The major broadcast networks and some independent stations carry sports programming. In cable, at least one national network (ESPN) and several regional networks specialize in sports and telecast extensive play-by-play programming. Superstations and some other cable networks carry sports programming. Various pay television outlets occasionally offer full play-by-play coverage of individual sporting events on a pay-per-view basis.

6.4.4 Advertising

This category comprises programs designed solely to sell things (Section 9.1.2.1). An advertising program may contain elements of entertainment, information, or instruction, but these are incidental to the advertising message.

6.4.5 Special Audience

Special-audience programs are designed to appeal to a particular segment of the public (Figure 6.12). Common special audience programs include those for women, children, farmers, and specific ethnic groups. This program category overlaps others somewhat;

(a)

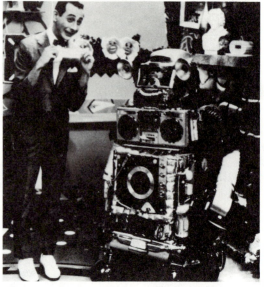

(b)

Figure 6.12 Special-audience programming. Examples of programs for (a) women, Lifetime's *Attitudes;* (b) children, *Peewee's Playhouse;* and (c) racial minorities, Univision's *Portada* (Cover Story). (*Source:* a courtesy, Gene Nichols & Associates, b AP/Wide World, c Univision)

(c)

many of these programs could also be classified as entertainment or information.

In recent years, stations have done less and less locally produced programming for women and children and have relied more and more on network and syndication sources. Cable systems, however, have begun to provide **women's programs.**

The Public Broadcasting Service runs some of the finest **children's programming** in existence. Cable networks also offer good children's programming; Nickelodeon, in fact, aims its entire program schedule at children. By contrast, CBS systematically squeezed out its fine, long-running daily *Captain Kangaroo* and reduced it to a weekend slot in the Saturday morning children's programming ghetto. On the other hand, critics have noted improvement in both intellectual and entertainment levels of Saturday morning broadcast network programming.

Stations and cable systems produce programs for **farmers.** Such programs occur particularly in agricultural areas, usually in the early morning.

Programs for **special ethnic groups** originate from local stations, cable systems, cable networks, and PBS. Racial and ethnic minorities are targeted by some cable networks, for example, Black Entertainment Television and Univision (Spanish language). The combination of cable television and the low-power television service (Section 4.5.2.3) offers possibilities for even more programming for ethnic groups, as well as for other groups such as women, farmers, and country music fans.

6.4.6 Cultural

Cultural programs focus on arts, letters, and scholarly pursuits. This is perhaps the broadest of all program categories, the one that offers the most diversity. While most programs must focus on the "now," the current, and the popular or are otherwise limited as to content, cultural programs select subjects from the whole range of human achievement and study, from the past as well as the present. They range from films to plays to symphony concerts to dramatizations of lives and literature to documentaries of wild life and archaeological explorations. Public television broadcasts much cultural programming. At least three cable channels—Arts & Entertainment, Discovery, and Bravo—focus

all or most of their programming on cultural subjects. Advertising-supported broadcast stations rarely carry cultural programs.

6.4.7 Educational

Educational programs are designed to teach or to supplement the teaching process. Many focus on conventional educational goals, particularly those related to schools and the teaching of children. They may take the form of for-credit lessons for classroom or home use. They may supplement or offer assistance in formal school instruction; these programs range from PBS shows that have been integrated into school curricula to local "homework hot line" programs. They may offer informal, less traditional instruction that aims, nonetheless, at teaching some of the concepts taught in a classroom, as does the perennial *Sesame Street*. They may teach more abstract concepts, such as the self-esteem and positive social values offered by another perennial, *Mister Rogers' Neighborhood*.

The educational category also includes programs that focus on self-improvement, health, and how-to instruction, subjects that often have little to do with schools or children. Subjects range from beauty and makeup hints to home repair, from fitness and health to landscape painting and cooking.

Most educational broadcast programs are telecast by public television sources. The Learning Channel, a national cable network, specializes in educational programming, and some cable systems carry instructional programming originated by local school systems. Self-improvement/how-to programs, once the nearly exclusive domain of public television, grew in popularity during the 1980s, appearing on local commercial stations, on cable networks, and in home video stores.

6.4.8 Religious

Religious programs are telecast chiefly on commercial and religious broadcast stations and religious networks. They originate locally, from networks, or from religious syndication sources, such as a denominational radio-television-film agency or an evangelistic association. The programs themselves range from local worship services to slick, star-studded productions of major evangelists, from children's programs that teach moral lessons to intellectually stimulating, professionally produced dramatic presentations.

6.5 ON THE AIR

Somehow, the programs must be transmitted. They must be strung together into some sort of whole and then embedded into the proper channel and dispersed to the intended audience. The *decisions* that go into that "stringing together" are called *programming*, the subject of the next chapter. In this section, we are concerned with the *procedures* by which those decisions are translated into the stuff you hear and see on your receiver, how it gets on the air (or the cable or whatever).

6.5.1 Program Log

In the United States, radio and television programs begin and end at exactly the time they are supposed to, and every second during the programming day is accounted for. Most broadcast stations (and many other media outlets) achieve this precision with the program log (Box 6.3). The log lists in chronological order information such as the following: each program and announcement, its length, when it begins and ends, the type of program material (such as news, religion,

---

Box 6.3 Deciphering the Program Log

The program log provided is used to control and keep track of programming content. Many stations use a computerized system to schedule programming elements and to generate the log. The page pictured here is the 11 to noon segment of a computer-generated log for a radio station. Abbreviations are defined across the top. The Sponsor-Program-Title-Product column lists programming elements that will run during the hour. Entries under Scheduled Time indicate when each element is to be aired; those under Length specify how long each lasts in hours, minutes, and seconds (HMS); and those under Source and Type show the origin and classification of the element, respectively. The remainder of the columns apply to commercials. The numbers under INST (instructions) indicate audiotape cartridges that contain the recorded commercials; Reference No. entries refer to the client contract and the affidavit (the certification that the commercials have run); Ordered Time shows the daypart during which the commercial is to run. An entry under Make Good for Date would indicate a commercial scheduled for previous broadcast that had not run correctly or had not run at all. This station originates its own AOR format (Quality Rock n' Roll), so the first entry is marked LIV (live) under Source. The *Psychedelic Psnack* entries list WWO as the source, indicating that they come from Westwood One. (Log courtesy of WRUF-FM. Used by permission.)

TIME	SOURCE/NETWORK	PROGRAM TYPE		TYPE	
@ EXACT (ALL OTHERS APPROXI-MATE) A – AM P – PM N – NOON M – MIDNIGHT	CBS NBC ABC MUT – MUTUAL NET – OTHER NETWORK REC – RECORDED LOC – LOCAL	A – AGRICULTURE E – ENTERTAINMENT I – INSTRUCTIONAL N – NEWS O – OTHER P – PUBLIC AFFAIRS	R – RELIGIOUS S – SPORTS ED – EDUCATIONAL ET – EDITORIAL PL – POLITICAL ID – STATION • – IDENTIFICATION	COMMERCIAL MATER OR ANNOUNCEMENT TYPE CM – COMMERCIAL MATTER MRA – MECHANICAL REPRODUCTION ANNOUNCEMENT PRO – PROMOTIONAL ANNOUNCEMENT PSA – PUBLIC SERVICE ANNOUNCEMENT (✓) – ANNOUNCED AS SPONSORED	FCC – LOCAL NOTICE ANNCT. OSC – GENERAL SYSTEMS CUE NCA – NON COMMERCIAL ANNCT.

PROGRAM LOG   WRUF 103.7 FM

EST 33   WRUF–FM   GAINESVILLE, FL   TUESDAY   02-28   PAGE 13

SCHEDULED TIME	SPONSOR-PROGRAM-TITLE-PRODUCT	LENGTH HMS	SOURCE	TYPE	INST	REFERENCE NO.		MAKE GOOD FOR DATE	ORDERED TIME
						CONTRACT LINE NUMBER	SPOT NUMBER		
1100.00A	QUALITY ROCK N' ROLL	1 00 00	LIV	E					
1120.00A	PIZZA HUT/SPRING BRK	60		CM	146	2128 02	158		10-3P
1121.00A	ALLSTATE INSURANCE/INS	30		CM	079	2158 01	138		6A-7P
1121.30A	FLA LOTTERY/JACKPOT	30		CM	031	2080 04	129		6A-7P
1122.00A	ABC ROCK NEWS	1 30	ABC	N					
1123.30A	WEATHER	15	LIV	N					
1137.00A	GODFATHER'S PIZZA	30		CM	114	2229 01	214		10-1230P
1137.30A	ORKIN/EXTERMINATOR	60		CM	061	2205 02	178		10-3P
1145.00A	RECORD ABC NEWS @45								
1150.00A	DELTA COMAIR/COMAIR	60		CM	086	2179 02	151		10-3P
1151.00A	CHESNUTS/OFFICE SUP	30		CM	081	2213 01	185		6A-12M
1151.30A	GATOR SUBARU/AUTOS	30		CM	098	2177 01	197		10-3P
1153.00A	PSNACK NETWORK SPOT	60	WWO	CM					
1154.00A	PSYCHEDELIC PSNACK	5 50	WWO						

or entertainment), whether it is recorded, the source of the audio and (in television) the video, and sponsor and advertiser information.

In a broadcast station the **traffic department** publishes the log. The staff maintains and constantly updates records concerning the program elements that are to go on the air. Program elements are all individually scheduled items, such as programs, commercials, and public service announcements; relevant information includes when and how these items will run and for how many days, weeks, or months they will run. Each day, the traffic department uses its records to compile information about the next day's programming and to generate the log, ready for the sign-on crew the next morning.

6.5.2 Program Sources

To understand how the log is translated into ongoing programming, you must know about the physical places from which the programs originate. We shall call these places of origin *sources,* although it must be understood that this is a special use of the term. Sources of programs here mean where the programs come from when they are actually transmitted, not who produced or distributed them. The term *program* is also used here in a special sense to refer to anything listed on the program log and thus includes commercials, station identifications, and other such elements, as well as the productions we normally think of as programs. With that understanding, programs originate from four main sources—studio, network, remote, and recordings.

6.5.2.1 Live from the Studio Most programs that originate in the studio also have input from other sources. For example, a disc jockey radio program includes disc recordings and audiotape commercials and jingles. A tele ision news program includes film and tape reports and commercials.

6.5.2.2 Network Sources In this category, we include interconnected program services as we!l as networks. For example, a radio station may subscribe to a satellite-delivered music program service and, at the same time, be affiliated with a national radio network, a network to broadcast major league baseball games, a network to broadcast the state university's football games, and a farm news network. Even an independent television station (a station not affiliated with one of the three major commercial networks) may occasionally carry programs from a network of one kind or another.

6.5.2.3 Remote In a remote, the program is relayed live to the studio from a distant location. The transmission of a local high school basketball game, the weekly service at a local house of worship, and the annual Thanksgiving Day parade are examples of remotes.

6.5.2.4 Recordings These may be syndicated programs or locally produced programs. Most syndicated radio material arrives at stations on tape or disc; the stations, in turn, usually "cart" (transfer to tape cartridges) for easy handling and instantaneous cuing those programs not already in cartridge form. Recorded television programs are on film or videotape. Short program material is often transferred to videotape cartridges for ease of handling. Television audio and video can originate from separate sources; a news story, for example, might consist of a silent film narrated live by the newscaster.

6.5.3 Gatekeepers: People and Machines

The **operator** at a radio station (usually the announcer or disc jockey on duty) sits at the audio console and feeds the programs to the transmitter as prescribed by the log—originating some live, throwing the switch to bring in the remote, loading and playing back taped programs, opening the microphone in the booth for the newscaster, bringing in the network on time.

The person in charge of getting television programs on the air on time and in correct order is the **duty director** (Figure 6.13) or **residue director.** The duty director starts and stops film projectors and videotape play-

Figure 6.13 Duty director.   At Orlando's Channel 2, the duty director's station is a centrally located, glass-enclosed booth. A computer feeds an electronic version of the program log to a video monitor (lower left). The switching equipment (lower center, in front of the duty director) handles video and audio simultaneously, so one person operates both. In the background—actually on the other side of the booth's glass wall—video monitors show the various program sources available.

back units, joins the network, cues the booth announcer, signals directors of live studio and remote programs when to begin, and goes into and out of various program sources.

Sometimes no person actually throws switches or pushes buttons. Instead, technicians program sophisticated automation devices to choose sources and get programs on. These devices can operate at varying levels of automation. For example, all television switching functions can be funneled to a limited number of simple control devices; an operator watches clock and log to punch the button at the correct time, and the automation system programs that one button to punch up a VTR playback, punch out of the VTR playback, join the network, cut away from the network, punch up an identification frame, cut away from the frame, and so forth.

Or, the system can handle the whole routine, with no human intervention. In this case, the logging information can go directly into the system, without first having to be printed out. Listen to a good automated radio station (the good ones do not sound automated!), or watch certain pay cable services. They are smooth, they never make mistakes, they do exactly what they are told, and they work literally for pennies.

6.6 TALENT: CREATORS AND PERFORMERS

The two major production centers for nationally distributed television programs are **New York** and **Hollywood**. People who wish to write, direct, and perform in "the big time" congregate around these two cities. While the pay is high and the life seems glamorous, the work is hard and long, and job security is low. To put together an hour-long television film show every week is all-involving and demanding, requiring early morning to late evening production schedules and, for the director, producer, and other key creative personnel, seven-day work weeks for most of the year. Programs using electronic production techniques take just as much time; taped half-hour situation comedies are usually produced on a seven-day-per-week schedule.

Perhaps the hardest grind of all is the daily soap. Writers must prepare five scripts a week in advance. The directors must work out camera and actor blocking on five programs per week. Actors must memorize lines from five scripts a week.

The term *the big time* does not necessarily equate with *stardom* or *fame*. In the talent realm, it can mean simply *getting steady work*. The foregoing discussion of hard work applies only to the few—the *very* few—who stay employed. Bit parts, small supporting roles, commercial work—such jobs are not glamorous, do not qualify you as one of "the beautiful people," and do not grant you automatic entry into the current fad night spot. But they do bring in paychecks, and that equates with *success*. Even at this level, getting to "the big time" as talent in television usually involves "paying your dues." Chaper 21 discuss the concept of dues paying at some length.

6.7 CRITICISM

A play in the theater runs for a number of performances. A motion picture plays for days or even weeks at theaters around the country. A book remains on sale in bookstores over a period of time. A painting or sculpture exists for the ages. Critics of theater, motion pictures, literature, and other fine arts report on what they see as good,

bad, or indifferent and can influence future attendance and sales. A television critic cannot do this. A television program is here and gone in an instant, to be repeated rarely and at widely spaced, unannounced intervals as reruns or in syndication, making it difficult for the TV critic to influence future attendance.

What is **criticism**? You have probably heard some people say they never watch television because it is so bad, so violent, so immoral, or so commercial. That is criticism, but it is not the type we mean here. Usually, the I-never-watch-TV criticism implies (1) use of critical standards from other media such as literature or painting to judge television and (2) judgment of the medium as a whole, rather than its individual parts. After all, few people have stopped reading books because there is so much "trash" in the bookstores; why then should television be judged by such an inclusive standard? To condemn television out of hand is to condemn the consistently high standards of network news organizations; the occasional presentation of outstanding drama, music, dance, and film; and the entire schedules of PBS and the arts cable services, much of which qualifies as fine art by any standards.

Aside from television's presentation of journalism and fine art, one should be able to distinguish between good and bad television, even among the more popular entertainment programs. This is the job of professional critics, people who review programs and other aspects of television, particularly broadcast television, in newspaper and syndicated columns. These critics look at a television program and, recognizing the **limitations of the medium**—it has to draw a large audience, has to fit within a time slot, has to be sponsorable, and all the rest of the "has-tos"—judge the worth of the program. They look at its overall premise or theme or idea, the writing, the directing, the acting, the opening and closing titles and credits, the music, the setting. They judge these elements on originality, cleverness or quality, depth, and taste. And based on prior experience and their individual, absolute standards, they make distinctions between good and bad situation comedies, game shows, comedy-variety shows, action-adventure dramas, soap operas, sports play-by-play, talk shows, children's programs, political convention coverage, documentaries, and so on.

Critics pay particular attention to the new broadcast network programs each September and January. The repetitive nature of television series allows a critic to look at the first one or two programs and to make fairly accurate judgments about the entire series. If the initial judgment is wrong, the critic can reexamine and rereview the series later in the season.

Unlike their colleagues in art, music, drama, and literature, television critics are expected to comment on nonprogram aspects of their medium. So you read in their columns information and observations on business developments, laws and regulation, station and network personnel changes, and advertising practices.

FURTHER READING

Blum, Richard. *Television Writing*. Rev. ed. Stoneham: Focal, 1984. From proposal to marketing the script.

————. *Working Actors: The Craft of Television, Film and Stage Performance*. Stoneham: Focal, 1989.

Breyer, Richard, and Peter Moller. *Making Television Programs: A Professional Approach*. White Plains: Longman, 1984. Production—the trade and the mechanics.

Burrows, Thomas D., and Donald N. Wood. *Television Production Disciplines and Techniques*. 3d ed. Dubuque: Brown, 1986. Equipment functions and crew positions.

Compesi, Ronald J., and Ronald E. Sherriffs. *Small Format Television*. Boston: Allyn, 1985. Light, portable gear.

Dudek, Lee J. *Professional Broadcast Announcing*. Boston: Allyn, 1982.

Gayeski, Diane M. *Corporate and Instructional Video: Design and Production*. Englewood Cliffs: Prentice, 1983.

Hindman, James, Larry Kirkman, and Elizabeth Monk. *TV Acting: A Manual for Camera Performance*. New York: Hastings, 1979. Guide to TV acting.

Hyde, Stuart W. *Television and Radio Announcing*. 5th ed. Boston: Houghton, 1987. Standard text.

Keith, Michael. *Broadcast Voice Performance*. Stoneham: Focal, 1988.

————. *Production in Format Radio Handbook*. Lanham: UP of America, 1984. Producing commercials that match station format.

Kindem, Gorham. *The Moving Image: Production Principles and Practices*. Glenville: Scott, 1987.

Levinson, Richard, and William Link. *Off Camera: Conversations with the Makers of Prime-Time Television*. New York: NAL, 1986. How programs are created and made.

Medoff, Norman J., and Tom Tanquary. *Portable Video: ENG and EFP*. White Plains: Knowledge, 1986.

Meeske, Milan D., and R. C. Norris. *Copywriting for the Electronic Media: A Practical Guide*. Belmont: Wadsworth, 1987. How to write for cable and broadcast.

Millerson, Gerald. *The Technique of Television Production*. 11th ed. Stoneham: Focal, 1985. Why and how.

————. *Video Production Handbook*. Stoneham: Focal, 1987. Low-cost video.

Newcomb, Horace, ed. *Television: The Critical View*. 4th ed. New York: Oxford UP, 1987. Analyses.

O'Donnell, Lewis B., et al. *Announcing: Broadcast Communicating Today*. Belmont: Wadsworth, 1987.

————. *Modern Radio Production*. Belmont: Wadsworth, 1985.

Oringel, Robert S. *Audio Control Handbook: For Radio and Television Broadcasting*. 6th ed. Stoneham: Focal, 1989. Guide to audio production equipment.

————. *Television Operations Handbook*. Stoneham: Focal, 1984. Guide to television production equipment.

Pekurny, Robert. "The Production Process and Environment of NBC's 'Saturday Night Live,'" *Journal of Broadcasting* 24 (1980): 91.

Perlmutter, Martin. *Producing Interactive Television.* White Plains: Knowledge, 1986. Analysis of interactive video's special timing and capability requirements.

Rose, Brian, ed. *TV Genres: A Handbook and Reference Guide.* Westport: Greenwood, 1985. Critical, historical survey.

Shaefer, William Drew, and Richard Wheelwright, eds. *Creating Original Programming for Cable TV.* White Plains: Knowledge, 1983. Basic how-to manual.

Slide, Anthony, ed. *Selected Radio and Television Criticism.* Metuchen: Scarecrow, 1987. 1920s–1950s.

Verna, Tony, and William Bode. *Live TV: An Inside Look at Directing and Producing.* Stoneham: Focal, 1986. Professionals tell their experiences, techniques, and philosophies.

Wurtzel, Alan, and Stephen Acker. *Television Production.* 3d ed. New York: McGraw, 1983. How-to textbook. Senior author is an ABC executive.

Zettl, Herbert. *Television Production Handbook.* 4th ed. White Plains: Knowledge, 1984. Long-time standard text.

CHAPTER 7

Programming

The "product" of commercial radio and television is time—time *you* spend listening and viewing. You donate such time to stations, cable channels, and networks; they, in turn, sell it to advertisers to air commercial messages. In exchange, you receive elements of entertainment and information put together in a particular way. This is *programming*. Attractive programming convinces you to donate time to a particular radio or TV outlet. Poor programming results in few listeners and viewers, low prices for commercial messages, few advertisers, and low profit. Ultimately then, success in commercial programming is measured in terms of profit, and successful programming is vital to a commercial radio or television operation.

To a large extent, pay programming is driven by the same motivations. The audience pays for programming directly; in theory, at least, this could bring in enough money to allow the programmer to appeal to narrow, minority tastes. By and large, however, through the 1980s, most pay programmers still selected materials and arranged schedules to attract mass audiences.

In this chapter we start with the daypart concept and radio programming. Then we look at television programming—local and network, broadcast and nonbroadcast. Fi-

nally, we examine audience promotion and its role in programming.

7.1 AUDIENCES AND DAYPARTS

The trade divides the programming day into standard time periods—dayparts (Box 7.1). Much planning and evaluation in radio and television revolve around the concept of the daypart. Programmers, sales personnel, advertisers, audience research firms—all deal in dayparts.

For the most part, audience levels and patterns define dayparts. For example, during television's daytime daypart (morning until about 4:30 p.m.), homemakers, preschool children, and, later, school-age children do most television viewing. During early fringe, audience composition and size change as wage earners return home. Radio's audience patterns differ from those of television, so it also has different dayparts.

7.2 RADIO PROGRAMMING

Physically, broadcast radio is portable, more so than any other medium. People turn on the radio primarily when doing something

Box 7.1 Dayparts

TELEVISION*

Early morning	6–9 a.m.
Daytime**	9 a.m.–4 p.m.
Morning	9 a.m.–12 Noon
Afternoon	12 Noon–4 p.m.
Early fringe	4–6 p.m.
Early evening	6–7 p.m.
Access hour	7–8 p.m.
Prime time	8–11 p.m.
Late fringe	11–11:30 p.m.
Late night	11:30 p.m.–2 a.m.
Overnight	2–6 a.m.

*Times given for Eastern time zone. Daypart groupings differ slightly depending on time zone. Saturdays and Sundays are divided into fewer and different dayparts.
**Defined and used primarily by networks.

RADIO*

Morning drive	6–10 a.m.
Mid-day	10 a.m.–3 p.m.
Afternoon drive	3–7 p.m.
Evening	7 p.m.–12 Midnight
Overnight	12 Midnight–6 a.m.

*Times given for Eastern time zone.

else. The radio audience is the commuter driving to work, the homemaker cleaning and cooking, the student doing homework, the counter people scooping ice cream at Baskin-Robbins. The radio audience tunes in and tunes out; it does not listen for extended lengths of time. Yet, radio reaches over 95 percent of all persons 12 years and older every week.

Radio draws its largest audience 7:00–9:00 a.m. Figure 7.1. Audience levels decline gradually until early afternoon, then build to a secondary peak 5:00–6:00 p.m. Radio audiences abate as television sets light up.

The implication for the programmer is clear. Program elements must be arranged so that audience members may tune in and tune out and not feel they have missed anything. This usually means that program elements will be short—music, $2\frac{1}{2}$ to 3 minutes; news, 1 to 4 minutes; commercial messages, no longer than 60 seconds. It also means there will be repetition; if you do not hear the news or your favorite record while getting dressed in the morning, listen as you drive to work, and you will probably hear both. Stations and networks design most radio programming around these concepts.

7.2.1 Radio Stations

Most radio stations specialize. Rather than attempting to program for the general public, a radio station chooses a target audience, then devises a programming format to reach that audience. The format is often built around music that appeals to the target audience, and a disc jockey/host alternates among records, commercials, and self-contained information capsules.

Essential to format programming is *consistency*—insurance that the listener can hear the expected programming at any time. Most programmers use some variation of a **clock** chart (Figure 7.2) to control for consistency. The clock specifies which program elements are to be aired at what time during each hour. A news station's *news wheel* indicates when to run the various types of hard news (local, state, national, international), sports, weather, business news, headlines, traffic reports, time checks, features, station identifications (ID), and commercials. A music station's *hot clock* or *music wheel* stipulates types of music, when and for how long the disc jockey is to speak, when to air commercials, when to give time checks, when to play

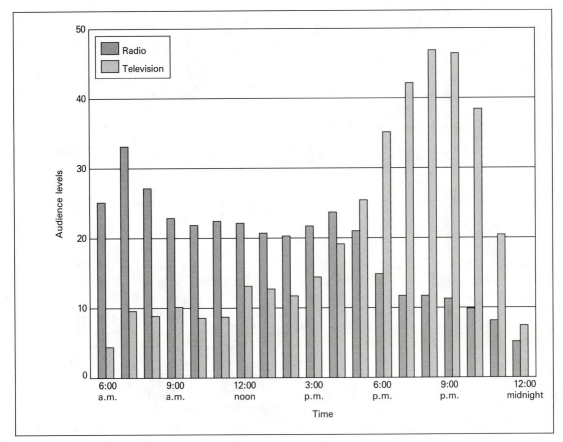

Figure 7.1 Radio and television audience levels. Radio's audience patterns are almost exactly opposite those of television. (*Source:* Radio Advertising Bureau. Used by permission.)

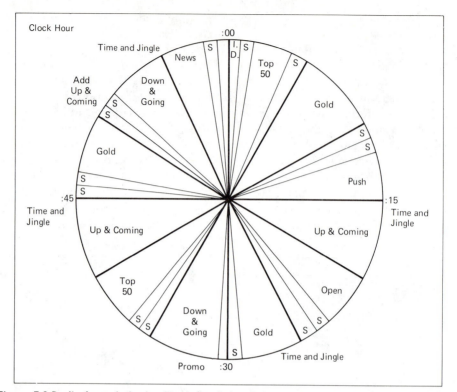

Figure 7.2 Radio format clock. The large S stands for "spot," indicating a commercial or a public service announcement. (*Source:* KNTU(FM).)

a musical station ID jingle, and so on. Stations may have different clocks for different dayparts. The news station might increase traffic and weather reports during drive time; the music station might vary the music according to time of day and types of people in the audience.

7.2.1.1 Formats The term *format* in this context refers to the type of content a radio station uses to attract listeners. Formats, especially music formats, vary with time and changes in taste. No firm definitions exist for most formats. One station calls its music mix adult contemporary; another using the same mix calls it soft rock. During the late 1980s, country and adult contemporary were, by far, radio's most widely programmed formats. The others followed in the order listed below.

Country attracted a broad audience. It attracted listeners aged 25 to 64, in all parts of the country, from urban as well as rural areas. Despite its universality, country competed more successfully in markets below the 25 largest. Country's variations extended from a traditional, down-home style featuring older songs to a smooth, big-city mode with a wide-ranging play list (often called "modern country").

Adult contemporary (AC), comprised a number of variations, each aiming at a segment of the aging post–World War II "baby boom" generation. In one form, AC aired current hits mixed with popular music from the preceding few years and attracted a young, nonteen audience (ages 18–34). A second form featured personalities and news during drive times, played music that included AC standards (artists such as Neil Diamond and Barbra Streisand), and focused on the 25–54 age group. A third form, "soft rock" or "soft adult contemporary," programmed in a less-talk-more-music setting and went after an older (35–54) audience. AC was particularly successful in large markets.

Contemporary hit radio (CHR) used a *tight* (relatively few records on it) play list of the week's most popular recordings. It appealed to a young (12–24) audience. Essentially a 1980s revival of the pioneer top-40 format, CHR was consistently one of the most popular in large markets.

Religious radio stations increased in number dramatically during the 1970s and 1980s. Fundamentalist Christian groups operated most. They programmed religious music, talk, advice, preaching, and worship services. Music ranged from traditional hymns to gospel to so-called "Jesus rock" to beautiful-music-style songs of worship. A few stations, licensed to mainstream religious groups, aired less didactic programming.

Middle-of-the-road (MOR) featured pop and jazz standards from the big-band era mixed with compatible music from recent years. One of the oldest formats, MOR originally played what was then mainstream pop, avoiding minority-taste music such as rock and country. Over the years, popular music tastes changed, and the audience for standards aged. By the 1980s, MOR itself had become a minority format, targeting an audience aged 45 and older. Still, MOR (also called "nostalgia" or "big band") was one of the four most widely programmed formats.

Easy listening, also called **beautiful music,** comprised melodic recordings, often lush orchestral arrangements, in a less-talk-more-music setting. It drew an affluent, well-educated 35–64 audience. As the general population matured and new generations moved into this age range, easy listening expanded from an instrumentals-only play list, adding compatible vocals and even popular recordings from past years. In most large markets, the top ten stations usually included at least one that programmed easy listening.

Album-oriented rock (AOR) featured album cuts and, often, whole albums (Figure 7.3). Originally, AOR had targeted males, 18–34. In the 1980s, AOR stations went after aging baby boomers by playing more album selections from the late 1960s and early 1970s. In fact, one growing AOR variant was *classic rock*, which focused on such older albums.

Oldies formats usually feature 1950s and 1960s hits on AM and 1960s and 1970s hits on FM. Oldies stations encountered increasing competition in the 1980s as AC and AOR "aged" their demographics by including older recordings. The oldies format is also called *golden oldies.*

Talk and **news/talk** were more expensive than most music formats and therefore usually limited to medium and large markets. The basis for talk radio programming was the telephone call-in show. Most talk stations also made a hefty commitment to news. News/talk stations programmed news full time during drive times then talk, interspersed with frequent news and information, during other dayparts. Audiences for these formats often included a high percentage of older people. Much of the audience actually *listened to* these formats (unusual for modern radio) instead of using them for background.

Black and **urban contemporary** (UC) featured records, news, features, and comment aimed at the black community. The music of black radio encompassed a range from gospel to rhythm 'n' blues to jazz. UC, primarily

```
**********************************
*            WRUF-F              *
*  1 AM  Wednesday  03-01-89     *
**********************************
          ARTIST              TITLE              C    SOURCE    TIME
=================================================================================

---------------------------------------------------------------------------------
          QUALITY ROCK AND ROLL                                           :05
---------------------------------------------------------------------------------
HEART                   THESE DREAMS           F    CD H-6     4:12
          HEART


---------------------------------------------------------------------------------
     4:17      WRUF-FM LEGAL ID CART                                       :05
---------------------------------------------------------------------------------
QUEEN                   BOHEMIAN RHAPSODY      J    CD Q-99    5:55
          A NIGHT AT THE OPERA

GUNS AND ROSES      KNOCKING ON HEAVENS DOOR D  CD G-60    4:40
          GUNS AND ROSES LIVE    UNRELEASED LIVE IMPORT TRACK

ZOMBIES                 TIME OF THE SEASON     G    CD Z-15    3:30
          ODYSSEY AND ORACLE

FABULOUS THUNDERBIRDTUFF ENUFF                 L    CD F-26    3:21
          TUFF ENUFF


---------------------------------------------------------------------------------
     21:48 LINER/ABC NEWS/SHORT WEATHER                                  2:00
---------------------------------------------------------------------------------
U2                      GOD PART II            A    CD U-6     3:15
          RATTLE AND HUM

TRAFFIC             LOW SPARK OF HIGH HEELED   J    CD T-35   12:01
          LOW SPARK OF THE HIG

TOMMY CONWELL           I'M NOT YOUR MAN       E    CD C-75    4:15
          RUMBLE


---------------------------------------------------------------------------------
     43:19     SPEED BREAK - PRE-SELL "C" RECORD                          :05
---------------------------------------------------------------------------------
FIXX                    DRIVEN OUT             D    CD F-9     4:00
          CALM ANIMALS

SUPERTRAMP              GIVE A LITTLE BIT      I    CD S-29    4:07
          EVEN IN THE QUIETEST

BULLET BOYS         FOR THE LOVE OF MONEY      C    CD B-61    3:44
          BULLET BOYS


---------------------------------------------------------------------------------
     55:15     OPTION RECORD (PLAY ONLY IF NEEDED)                        :05
---------------------------------------------------------------------------------
GUESS WHO          NO SUGAR TONITE/NEW MTHR    K    CD G-9     4:52
          AMERICAN WOMAN


---------------------------------------------------------------------------------
     60:12     LINER/COMMERCIAL BREAK                                    1:00
---------------------------------------------------------------------------------
```

Figure 7.3 AOR play list. In the WRUF-FM control room, air personnel use printed play lists instead of a music wheel. The programming department issues the lists, which specify the selections to play and the order in which they are to be played. WRUF-FM features an AOR format, employs Jeff Pollack as consultant, and consistently places first in ratings in the Gainesville market. (*Source:* WRUF-FM. Used by permission.)

a large-market format, tended to feature melodic recordings with a prominent beat—music that could be hummed and danced—but the precise mix varied from market to market. UC audiences consisted of a plurality of blacks, with large percentages of whites and Hispanics.

Spanish radio stations targeted Hispanics. During the 1980s, American citizens or residents of Spanish descent were the fastest-growing segment of the U.S. population.

Block programming was done primarily in small, one-station markets. Block or *diversified* programming offered something for everyone, changing format every two or three hours according to who was in the audience—for example, farmers in early morning, homemakers during the day, teens at night.

Classical/fine arts, ethnic, all-news, and **jazz** were primarily large-market formats. Commercial classical/fine arts audience members were few, were well educated, had high incomes, were fiercely loyal, and used the format for foreground listening. Ethnic stations broadcast to minority or nationality groups, often in their own languages. All-news stations programmed in repetitive cycles, focused on state and local stories, and required a large, expensive staff. Some commercial jazz stations did very well, although they frequently competed for audiences with noncommercial and new-age stations.

Commercial programmers experimented continually, especially in large markets. They changed existing formats and created new ones, striving to define and reach audiences efficiently. In the late 1980s, for example, a *new-age* format developed to target upscale baby boomers with light instrumental jazz/fusion music ("yuppie jazz") in a relaxed setting. New age, in turn, generated *new adult contemporary*, a light jazz–soft rock format.

AM programmers spearheaded the search for new formats. Hoping to regain lost listeners (Section 3.3), AM stations tried highly targeted formats—all-weather, all-comedy, all-business. One station even focused on traffic reports.

Educational radio is used here as a generic term to mean *no advertising*. The largest number of educational stations was in the reserved part of the FM band, but some were AM stations or on commercial FM channels. Frequently, programmed formats included fine arts/classical, jazz, AOR, black, and CHR. Many programmed electrically, combining a variety of programming types in one format. Most were operated for genuine educational purposes, but dozens were licensed to sectarian organizations that programmed a "religious" format promoting their particular brand of orthodoxy.

The forgoing does not cover all formats. With over 10,000 radio stations, one short listing could hardly be inclusive. Even among the categories we have discussed, permutations are legion. The larger, more diverse the community, the more format variations are broadcast. Categorization is confused, too, by **crossover records.** For example, the popularity of a recording made by a country music performer may spread beyond country music fans and show up on other types of stations.

7.2.1.2 Competition   Various elements can be manipulated in the competition for audience. A station will improve methods to determine locally popular records. It will adjust play lists and clock hours, seeking just the right mix of current top-10 hits, golden oldies, and hit-bound records. It will change on-air personnel—shift them to different time periods, hire new ones, remove those who have lost rating points. The station will alter, juggle, add, or delete various nonmusic elements—news, sports, features. It will upgrade weather and traffic reports with new equipment, personnel, and services. It will change production gimmicks, air personalities' deliveries, musical station identifications.

Some stations hire **programming consultants.** The consultant studies the market, listens to the client station and the competition, lays out a competitive strategy, then alters the format of the client station. The consultant is often highly successful, pushing a station low in the ratings to first, second, or third in its market.

Some radio programming firms offer **syndicated music services.** Used mainly in automated or semiautomated programming situations, they give even a small-market station a big-market sound. Some syndicators function much like a consultant; they customize their services for each situation and can help a station's ratings. Most syndicators send the music on big reels of tape; some have gone to satellite transmission and deliver a "live" service, much like a full-time music network.

7.2.1.3 Cable Audio Services

Many cable systems offer audio services. Cable audio services frequenty take three forms—cable radio stations, audio basic services, and audio premium services. Outfit a studio for radio production, feed the output to a cable system, and you have a **cable radio station** (Figure 7.4). Station operation may take three forms—local origination (the system does the programming; Section 7.4.1.1), access (programming comes from the public or public institutions; Section 7.4.1.2), and leased–channel (programming comes from a third-party operator who pays the system; Section 7.4.1.3). Access operation often parallels that of a college's student station; the others, a commercial station.

Cable subscribers receive audio services by attaching the drop line (cable lead-in) to an FM receiver. **Audio basic service** often

Figure 7.4 Cable radio station. A cable radio station needs no license from the FCC and is not subject to broadcast regulation, not even call-letter requirements. Many cable stations, however, adopt and use call letters for promotional reasons—for example, "KRNB: Kable Rhythm 'N' Blues." Further, the actual operation of a successful commercial cable radio station often parallels that of a successful commercial broadcast radio station—right down to control room checks by the general manager to ensure that commercials for a new advertiser are aired properly.

comes as part of the basic fee for cable service. Typically, the service includes signals from cable stations, local radio broadcast stations, and radio superstations (Section 7.2.2). Subscribers pay an extra fee for **audio premium service.** Premium service frequently consists of commercial-free national services (Section 7.2.2) and special audio channels, such as stereophonic sound for the MTV cable network.

7.2.2 National Networks and Program Services

By the late 1980s, any listing of major national radio programmers would include at least the following (Figure 7.5). Still predominant were the "traditional" networks, those that programmed news, features, and enter-

ABC Contemporary

ABC FM

ABC Information

ABC Rock

ABC Entertainment

ABC TalkRadio

ABC Direction

Radio's business solution.

CABALLERO SPANISH RADIO

TRANSTAR

CBS RADIO NETWORK

CBS RADIORADIO

CNN RADIO

TNNR

Satellite Music Network

UNITED STATIONS RADIO NETWORKS

WESTWOOD ONE RADIO NETWORKS
MUTUAL BROADCASTING SYSTEM

THE SOURCE
A Division of Westwood One, Inc.

THE WALL STREET JOURNAL RADIO NETWORK

NBC RADIO NETWORK
A Division of Westwood One, Inc.

TalkneT
A Division of Westwood One, Inc.

Figure 7.5 National radio networks.

tainment scattered throughout the hour aimed at a general or "adult" audience— CBS Radio Network, NBC Radio Network, Mutual Broadcasting System (the latter two owned by Westwood One), United Stations Radio Network Two, and three ABC networks, Information, Entertainment, and Direction. NBC, Mutual, and ABC also offered talk program services.

A number of programmers packaged news and information for specific segments of the national audience. Young adults were targeted by CBS's RadioRadio, NBC's The Source, United Stations Radio Network One, and three ABC networks, Rock Radio, Contemporary, and FM; blacks, by Sheridan Broadcasting Network and National Black Network; Hispanics, by Cadena Radio Centro, Spanish Information Service, and UPI Spanish Radio Network.

AP Radio Network, UPI Audio, and CNN Radio all programmed news; Reuters fed a financial news service. Opryland USA, Inc., and Group W Satellite Communications operated The Nashville Network Radio. Satellite Music Network and Transfer both fed a number of music program services.

National firms also distributed cable system services. Several offered multiple channels, each carrying a different format. Some offered specialized programming—reading service for the sight-impaired, background for text channels (Section 7.4.5), religious. Some offered radio superstations such as WFMT, Chicago (fine arts, music), and KKGO, Los Angeles (jazz).

7.3 BROADCAST TELEVISION PROGRAMMING

Unlike radio, television typically demands blocks of time and full attention from its audience. Despite miniaturization, television is not a mobile medium. We sit down to watch at home, and we usually watch in blocks of half or whole hours. Such blocks are available to most of us in the evening, after dinner. Audience levels (Figure 7.6) build rather gradually until 7:00 p.m. eastern time, when they shoot up, far out of proportion to previous levels. The levels stay up until bedtime, and after 11:00 p.m. they drop dramatically. This 7:00–11:00 p.m. period is **prime time** for getting large audiences.

7.3.1 Broadcast Networks

Broadcast television programming aims to attract and hold large, general audiences. Therefore, the dominant programming in television, in terms of audience drawing power, is that produced by and for the broadcast networks. The networks, through their affiliated stations, draw huge, nationwide audiences for which they charge advertisers the sums necessary to finance programming. An affiliate benefits from its network's audience-pulling power; network programming draws high audience levels, which allow the station to charge more for its own advertising. Whereas in radio the emphasis in programming rests with stations, in television it rests with networks.

7.3.1.1 Costs and Control   Prime-time program production is expensive. And it gets more expensive every year. By 1990, one episode of a half-hour situation comedy could cost anywhere from $325,000 to $500,000. Hour-long action shows started at $750,000. Networks do not pay the full cost; nonetheless they encouraged videotape production as a way to save money. They changed the system of pilot programs for prospective series. They used more extended treatments (Section 6.2) and scripts and fewer pilots to make decisions on proposed series. In some cases they ordered partial pilots—two or three scenes—rather than a finished program. Even when a project reached the full-

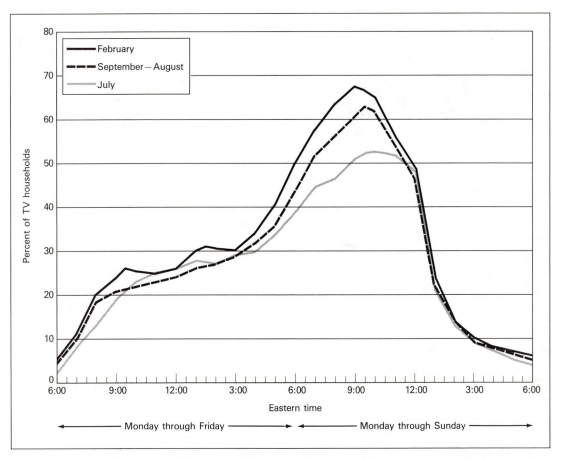

Figure 7.6 Average daily home television viewing. Television viewing levels increase gradually through the day. They climb sharply from about 5:00 p.m. as people arrive home from work, peak between 8:00 and 10:00 p.m., and drop rapidly at bedtime. During the winter, when many people stay indoors a good part of the time, viewing levels are high. In summer, more people go out and viewing levels are lower, particularly in late afternoon and early evening. (*Source:* Nielsen Media Research. Used by permission.)

pilot stage, the network might order it as a television movie; if rejected as a series, the pilot could still run as a movie.

Early on, the high per-episode cost of prime-time series programming led to two developments—**repeats** of an episode and increasing importance of syndication. In most cases, advertising revenue from one broadcast does not cover the cost. A repeat, however, generates enough additional revenue to yield a profit. Over the years, the networks ordered fewer new episodes for each

series. By 1979, the norm was 22 or less a year; most were repeated. A decade later, however, competing media had lured away so much prime-time audience (Section 4.5.2) that the networks increased new-episode orders to 25 or 26 for most series, 28 to 30 for prime-time soap operas (Figure 7.7).

The majority of network entertainment programming comes from independent producers. The networks purchase exclusive rights—to air the program first and to air it a designated number of times—that last a

Figure 7.7 Brandon Tartikoff and the 52-week season. Brandon Tartikoff, NBC's chief programmer, has advocated a 52-week season—*all* prime-time episodes new, none repeated. He would use this all-new-programming scheduling as one means to stem the drain of TV audiences to other media. (Photograph © 1988, courtesy of the National Broadcasting Company, Inc.)

specified period of time. Network payment often covers only about two-thirds of the huge production costs cited above. In other words, the producers may take a loss in making prime-time network programs. This is **deficit production.** When series episodes have completed their run on the network, they are put into **syndication** (made available at a price for use by local stations, cable programmers, or other media). This is where the producers hope to recoup their investment and make a profit.

7.3.1.2 Competitive Tactics So far, this discussion of programming has applied primarily to ABC, CBS, and NBC. However, many of the concepts presented in the paragraphs that follow pertain to other networks and to individual stations as well. Fox Broad-

casting Company, for example, programs directly against "the big three" in selected dayparts. Specialized networks such as Univision (Spanish language) use these scheduling practices and, insofar as they vie for a targeted segment of the general audience, may even counterprogram the big three. (*Highly* specialized programmers such as MTV do not schedule in quite the same way; they counterprogram with *format*, their entire programming concept, instead of individual programs.)

The networks **strip program** (Figure 7.8) during every weekday daypart except prime time. This means that they schedule series programming Monday through Friday, the same series at the same time each day. Traditionally, ABC, CBS, and NBC have scheduled informational "magazines" to start the day, game shows and dramatic serials in daytime to capture homemakers, and major newscasts in early evening. They program weekends and prime time individually. Children's shows air Saturday morning. Saturday and Sunday afternoon sports lineups target adult males. In other words, they schedule programs that appeal to the group most prevalent in the audience during any given daypart. This is **dayparting** (Section 7.1).

Within each daypart, the commercial television networks compete for audiences. But network competition for audiences is greatest during prime time, and we shall use this 8:00–11:00 p.m. period to illustrate broadcast network program competition at its sharpest.

The aim of a network is to capture a large share of audience and to keep it throughout the evening. This is **audience flow.** One way to achieve audience flow is to schedule **long-form** programming. All other things being equal, an hour program gives a viewer only half the opportunity to switch networks as do two half-hour programs. Over the years, networks have lengthened many program

	Station A (ABC affiliate)	Station B (PBS affiliate)	Station C (Independent)	USA	CBN
			Monday through Friday		
10:00 A.M.	Family Feud (Game)	Electric Company (Children)	Big Valley (Western)	Alive and Well (cont.) (Health)	700 Club (Religious talk)
10:30	Leave It To Beaver (Situation comedy)	3-2-1 Contact (Children)	↓	↓	
11:00	Benson (Situation comedy)	Mister Rogers (Children)	Jim Bakker (Religion)	Designs for Living	↓
11:30	Loving (Serial)	Wild, Wild World of Animals (Nature)	↓	The Great American Homemaker	Another Life (Serial)
12:00 Noon	(Local interview)	In-School Programming	I Love Lucy (Situation comedy)	Movie	Movie
12:30 P.M.	Ryan's Hope (Serial)		Movie		
1:00	All My Children (Serial)				
1:30	↓				
2:00	One Life to Live (Serial)		↓	Sonya (Talk)	Sewing, cooking and other homemaker programs
2:30	↓		Woody Woodpecker (Children)	↓	I Married Joan (Situation comedy)
3:00	General Hospital (Serial)		Inspector Gadget (Children)	Alive and Well (Health)	700 Club (Religious talk)
3:30	↓	Electric Company (Children)	He Man and the Monsters (Children)		↓
4:00	Edge of Night (Serial)	Sesame Street (Children)	Tom and Jerry (Children)	↓	Another Life (Serial)

Figure 7.8 Strip programming.   During weekdays, stations and networks generally program the same shows at the same time, Monday through Friday.

slots from the traditional 30 minutes to 60 and even 90 minutes, with regularly scheduled slots for movies of two hours and more.

More vital than length, however, is the strength of individual programs. If one program has high ratings, the following program has a built-in advantage because it "inherits" the **lead-in** (high audience level). If the following program is strong, it will maintain or improve the rating; if weak, it will "waste" the lead-in by losing audience and may even reduce audience levels for a stronger third program. A network attempts to capture and keep its audience (positive audience flow) on any given night through **block programming.** It schedules—one after another—either similar programs (for example, all comedy and musical variety) or different types of programs that have proved individually strong. If block programming is successful, the network could win the ratings race for the entire evening.

ABC also came up with the idea of the **seamless night.** In 1989, the network proposed to schedule prime–time advertising so that it would not interrupt the flow of an evening's series. Commercials would air in clusters, with fewer breaks throughout the evening. This practice would start probably with one night a week and no earlier than 1990.

At any given time, total prime-time audience levels for ABC, CBS, and NBC are fairly constant, and one gains audience at the expense of the other two. In planning its schedule, a network will try to **counterprogram,** to figure what types of shows (say, comedy and musical variety) the competition will put in a certain time slot, then program a completely different type (say, crime drama or reality) in that slot. The hope is that the other networks will fragment the audience, leaving the greatest share to the counterprogrammer.

Another counterprogramming tactic involves length of program, as when one network starts an hour-long program 30 min-

utes before a competitor's popular half-hour situation comedy; this is **bridging.** A network may counterprogram by ratings, as CBS did in January 1975 when it replaced *Paul Sand's Friends and Lovers*, a show relatively weak in ratings, with *The Jeffersons*, which turned out to be one of the most popular shows of the season. With this change, CBS also improved the ratings of the program that followed in its Saturday night comedy block; this is an example of lead-in placement. Other tactics that attempt to use programs with high ratings to build audience for weaker shows include the **tent-pole**—putting a strong program between two weak ones—and the **hammock**—putting a weak or new show between two strong ones.

In January or February, network executives begin to plan schedules for the following fall. They use a *scheduling board*, a graphic display of days and time slots. Programs that rival networks are expected to offer are placed in their proper slots, each rival represented by a different color. The executives then enter programs of their own network, yet another color, in an attempt to program competitively. They must determine which programs to keep and which to drop, what the other networks will do at each time slot, what programs are needed to maintain successful audience flow and to counterprogram on evenings that are not so successful, and what is available as new programming.

In most cases, the factor that determines whether a series is continued is its **share**—the percentage of all homes using TV that tune to the series (Section 18.2.4.2). When ABC, CBS, and NBC attracted 90 percent of all viewing, a program was a hit with a 30 share—about one-third of the audience. With the drop in network viewing (Section 4.5.2.1), the share needed to qualify a hit dropped also. By 1990, the figure was in the low to middle 20s. Nonetheless, network competition for ratings is still keen—so keen that a network will often cancel a new series with a low share, even before the end of the season. The practice of canceling some series and adding others at midseason began in the late 1960s. ABC gave these January changes the name *second season.* By the end of the 1970s, the second season had evolved into one with nearly continuous programming changes.

7.3.2 Stations

Network affiliates receive highly promoted, big-audience programming for relatively little effort. As a result, in most markets network affiliates usually draw the highest overall ratings and earn the greatest revenues. Rarely can an independent station become first overall in market ratings. But it can win in certain dayparts and among certain segments of the audience. However, when the network is *dark* (not feeding programming), the affiliate and the independent compete head to head.

7.3.2.1 Competitive Programming Elements A key element in competitive programming is syndicated material. **Syndicated programming** includes that which ran previously on networks **(off-net)** and original material prepared especially for syndication **(first-run).** A station looks for programming that will be popular in its market, then buys the rights to that programming. Typically, these rights allow the station sole use of the programming in the market for a stated period—say two years—during which time the station may broadcast it a specified number of times, frequently two or three.

There is no set or "catalog" price for a syndicated program. The price varies with factors such as success of the program (on the network or in other markets), size of the market in which it will be run, and the number of stations in the market that want it.

Buying and selling television programming resembles the proverbial Persian marketplace—the price paid represents a compromise between all the syndicator can get and as little as the station can pay.

As the number of stations increases, competition for successful programming grows more keen. A station may buy and **shelve** (not use) a series; this keeps the series off the market and out of the competition's schedule until the buyer is ready to use it. Stations sometimes buy **futures** on hit network series (pay for first off-net rights in its market), an investment of which they may not be able to take advantage for years. Syndicators even have stations **bid** on futures, one market at a time, for an especially desirable off-net series. This can drive prices very high.

In the past, syndicators avoided topical programming. It went out of date quickly—even while being shipped!—and could not be stored and used again. However, the development of satellite communication offered distribution that was instantaneous and relatively inexpensive. In the 1980s, syndicators successfully offered topical programming via satellite (Figure 7.9).

Some syndicated programming is offered on a **barter** basis. A barter program is offered to a station free, but it contains some commercials (for which the syndicator has been paid) that must be run. The station may sell the remaining availabilities (slots for commercials). In the **time banking** variation, the program contains *no* commercials; the station may sell every availability locally. Availabilities are, however, "banked" by the syndicator, often an advertising agency or independent media-buying firm (Section 17.2.1). This means the station "owes" the syndicator a specified number of commercials, which the syndicator will use at a later time.

Yet another wrinkle in the distribution of syndicated programming is **cash-plus-barter.** Here, the program contains some com-

Figure 7.9 Syndication and the satellite.   With satellite relay offering the possibility of instantaneous delivery, syndicators could offer programming that contained dated material, such as the daily *Entertainment Tonight*. (*Source:* Exley, © 1988, Paramount Pictures Corp.)

mercials that the station must air (plus availabilities that it can sell), and the station must pay a fee. Syndicators contend that such an arrangement helps pay for better production and allows higher-quality shows without raising the price to the station. In the past, most programming distributed on a barter or cash-plus-barter basis has been first-run.

Another source of programming is the **stations themselves.** In the Operation Prime Time (OPT) venture, for example, cooperating stations provided financing for production of their own miniseries. Large-market stations occasionally put their production efforts into syndication. Group-owned stations sometimes cooperate to produce programming for use among themselves; if successful, this programming may be syndicated to other stations. For example, Group W's KPIX, San Francisco, created *Evening*, a program that focused on the town's people, places, and things. *Evening*, aired in KPIX's access time, drew impressive audiences and

good reviews. The other Group W stations produced their own versions of *Evening*. They agreed to exchange *Evening* portions and features among themselves. The exchange succeeded, and Group W decided to syndicate the formula and certain key segments. The result went into general syndication in 1978 as *P.M. Magazine.*

A second key element in successful competitive programming is **feature films.** Films need not be new to attract large audiences. For example, local-station showings of the film *Casablanca* have often given network fare heavy competition for ratings. Widespread conversion of black-and-white films to color began in 1986 when Turner Broadcasting *colorized* a number of old MGM movies. Film buffs decried the practice. But—in a generation raised on color television—many who would tune away from the original monochrome version might watch these colorized movies.

A third element—perhaps first in importance for affiliates—is **local news programming.** A strong news department takes time, money, and effort. But local news, well done, draws high audience levels, good advertising rates, and enough revenue to pay for itself and turn a profit.

Local productions can be assets or liabilities in overall programming strategy. Well-planned and slickly produced local programs—discussion programs, cooking shows, children's programs, community magazines—can augment local news efforts in building a positive public image and high circulation for the station. Poorly done programs drive audiences away and give the station a bad name.

Stations use many of the programming tactics discussed in Section 7.3.1.2. Dayparting, audience flow, counterprogramming, lead-in programs, block programming—all are concerns of the station programmer. In 1986 and 1987, a few stations revived a tactic from earlier days. They used **checkerboard programming** (Figure 7.10)—a different series (same type and length) each weekday at the same time. Most tried five half-hour first-run situation comedies in access time.

7.3.2.2 The Network-Affiliated Station

ABC, CBS, and NBC supply nearly two-thirds of a station's program schedule. Affiliation thus significantly reduces the station's programming burden. On the other hand, network affiliation can cause problems with **positioning**—making the station stand out in the minds of the audience. As you have probably noticed, the big three TV networks program very much alike. Differences exist in program titles and specific performers, but basically all run the same type of programming. That means the affiliates, too, look very much alike. An affiliate often puts great effort into overcoming this sameness, into convincing viewers that it really does differ from the other two affiliates. Such effort focuses on promotion (Section 7.6) and local programming, primarily news. A station advertises its helicopters, or its satellite news capability, or its pretty, chatty anchor reporters, or whatever to convince the public that it is unique.

With local news programming filling part of the schedule, an ABC/CBS/NBC-type affiliate has relatively few hours to fill with syndicated programming. Often, too, affili-

	Source	Time	Program Type	Programs				
				Monday	Tuesday	Wednesday	Thursday	Friday
A	NBC owned and operated stations (Fall 1987 to Fall 1988)	7:30 P.M. (Eastern)	Situation Comedies*	Marblehead Manor	She's the Sheriff	You Can't Take It with You	Out of This World	We've Got It Made
B	A Public Broadcasting Station	12 Noon	Cooking	Frugal Gourmet	You Can Cook	New Southern Cooking	Madeleine Cooks	International Cooking School
C	Discovery Cable Network	1:00 P.M.	Nature	Cranes - Cold Water Survival	Living Isles	New Explorers	New Animal World	Roaming Wild and Free

*Some series switched broadcast days before NBC O&O's dropped this checkerboard.

Figure 7.10 Checkerboarding.

ated stations are financially the strongest in the market. In other words, a network affiliate usually has more money and fewer slots to spend it on than an independent station. So the affiliate, when playing the game of programming, should hold the winning hand at every deal. Independent station programmers, however, take the opposite view: affiliates are *most vulnerable* during those few key times (below) when they use syndicated entertainment to compete directly with independents.

The FCC actually created one of these direct-competition times. The commission's prime-time access rule (PTAR; Section 14.1.3) had the effect of prohibiting network programming during the period 7:00–8:00 p.m. eastern and Pacific time, 6:00–7:00 p.m. central and mountain time. Even before PTAR, the three networks had not programmed the first half-hour of prime time, so they actually gave up only 30 minutes. Further, the top-50 markets contain such a large percentage of the total television audience that the networks did not find it economically feasible to program entertainment during that period for affiliated stations below the top-50 markets. So this first hour of prime time became **access time,** a programming arena that pits affiliates against independents in a battle of syndicated entertainment.

7.3.2.3 The Independent Station
An independent station builds its schedule from scratch and can usually position itself more easily. It might, for example, program and promote itself as "the more movies station." Some independents target particular audiences with specialized programming. Most, however, compete for a general audience; they counterprogram the local affiliates and, therefore, the networks. In this respect, the chief programmer plays a more crucial role at an independent than at an affiliate, literally matching wits against "the best program-

ming minds in New York." A programmer who can utilize research, gauge audience taste, purchase series rights on favorable terms, and effectively package and promote programming is a living profit center.

In pursuing these goals, independent stations have perfected the art of counterprogramming. When networks schedule game shows in the morning, independents may counter with movies or situation comedies. Later, when networks run soap operas, independents air situation comedies, musical variety programs, children's shows, and feature films. During early fringe time, affiliates aim for adults with syndicated courtroom, game, and talk shows and off-net action-adventure; independents target children. In early evening, independents do particularly well, capturing a large number (often a plurality) of people who would rather watch situation comedies or *Star Trek* reruns than news. Competition is more difficult against network prime-time programming; however, an independent may get enough tune-in/tune-out audience to raise its average ratings to respectable levels. At 10:00 p.m. eastern time (ET), independents begin to recapture audiences and often put their major news efforts at this time. Then, while network affiliates run news at 11:00 p.m., independents are back to entertainment programming.

Independents achieve success through creative packaging and marketing of feature films and off-net series. They group old and familiar films into thematic packages—for example, "The Films of Bogart," "The Charlie Chan Series"—and draw respectable ratings. They count on the fact that most people in the TV audience did not see series episodes when they aired on the network.

Some independents have gone heavily into local production. They produce talk shows, interview programs, children's shows, and community magazines. Some broadcast play-by-play of local sports events.

Independents occasionally carry programming from one of the networks. If an affiliate decides not to run a particular network program, the network will offer it to another station in the market, often an independent. Independents may also broadcast programs from special networks, such as the ad hoc chain Mobil put together in early 1983 to broadcast *The Life and Adventures of Nicholas Nickleby*. Some specialty networks even offer programming primarily for independent stations; Independent Network News, for example, provides the daily *USA Tonight* news program. Fox Broadcasting commenced programming in 1986 and drew its affiliates entirely from the ranks of independents.

7.3.2.4 The Narrowcast Station
As mentioned above, some television stations narrowcast—they target particular segments of the general audience with special programming. Examples include religion, ethnic, music-video, direct marketing, and information. By 1990, most ethnic stations programmed for the burgeoning Hispanic population; most religious stations, primarily for conservative Christians.

Narrowcast station programmers often took advantage of existing networks. For example, a number of the Spanish-language broadcasters were actually Univision affiliates. The religious stations frequently aired programs from the cable religious networks. The information-based stations took feeds from Cable News Network, The Weather Channel, and Financial News Network.

Many narrowcast programmers actually broadcast a variety of program types; Hispanic stations, for example, may schedule Spanish-language programming that includes everything from comedy to news to sports play-by-play. Others operate much more like radio stations, programming a continuous schedule of rock videos, or news and information, or direct marketing. Most of the narrowcast stations are licensed to big cities. Full-service (that is, *not* low-power) narrow-

cast stations tend to be in the UHF band; many narrowcast stations, however, are low-power.

7.3.2.5 The LPTV Station
The Community Broadcasters Association (CBA), trade group for low-power television (LPTV) stations, held its first convention in November 1988. By that time, 427 LPTV stations had signed on the air. One CBA official estimated[1] that about 150 produced local news, sports, and public affairs programs and sold local advertising. Another 60 stations were affiliated with educational institutions or PBS, 15 aired subscription programming, 75 were "satellators" (transmitting programming received from a satellite), and the remainder were translators, automated repeaters of other TV stations. Most locally programmed LPTVs also aired syndicated material and programs from national networks (Section 20.3.7). Most were also narrowcasters. The range of LPTV ethnic programming, for example, included Hispanic, black, Indian, Hunan, and Korean. The one major key to success was cable carriage. In some cases, LPTV licensees aired programs that promoted their local cable system in exchange for being carried on the system.

7.4 NONBROADCAST TELEVISION PROGRAMMING

In this section we focus on a number of alternatives to the programming of full-service, advertising-supported broadcast stations. Sources of these alternatives include *local production, satellite-delivered basic services, satellite-delivered pay services, TVRO packagers*, and what we shall call *unconventional services*.

Locally produced programming is created in the area served by, and often using the facilities of, the local outlet. Our "unconventional" category embraces several disparate programming options. They may be locally originated or national.

Satellite-delivered services ordinarily program for national audiences. Local outlets receive them by satellite and put them on local channels for relay to homes in the community. Most originated to serve cable systems and are called *national cable programmers, satellite networks,* or *cable networks.* Other media, however, also distribute them. Hotel/motel, wireless cable (multichannel TV), and satellite master antenna television (SMATV) systems carry them. LPTV stations may carry them, particularly in areas without cable. Some services allow TVRO packagers to retail their signals to home dish owners.

7.4.1 Locally Produced Programming

Cable system practices have evolved three types of locally produced programming. *Local origination* is programming produced by the cable system's staff; *access programming,* that produced by others for which the cable system neither pays nor receives direct payment; *leased-channel content,* that produced by others and which the cable system is paid to carry.

LPTV stations that have production capability may also originate programming. Other video distribution systems rarely have the capability or desire.

7.4.1.1 Local Origination Programming
Local origination efforts by cable systems (Figure 7.11) range from automated camerascan of temperature, news, and advertising cards to feature films, high school and college sports, and live telecasts of city council meetings. Some systems and LPTV stations operate their own studios and produce a daily schedule of newscasts, discussions, children's shows, educational materials, commercials, and other programming.

7.4.1.2 Access Programming
Access programming is cable program material provided by groups or individual members of the community. If your community's cable system has an access channel, you can probably use it to cablecast your own TV program. The choice of subject and presentation is yours. You can do a round-table discussion on macramé, play-by-play coverage of a chess game, your own dramatic efforts, political commentary, whatever you want.

Access channels have other uses. They may carry meetings of governmental bodies—city commission, zoning and planning council, school board. They may run material for the school system or community college—enrichment, courses, announcements. For this reason, access channels are often called **PEG** (public, educational, government) **channels.**

7.4.1.3 Leased-Channel Content
A cable system may lease channels to others on a full-time or part-time basis. Possible uses for these **leased-access channels** vary. Some lessees might offer regular programming—advertising-supported or pay. Others might use leased channels to provide home security service (Section 5.2.3.3). Still others might use them for exchange of computer data among several locations; access to such content would, of course, be restricted.

7.4.2 Satellite-Delivered Basic Service Programming

Any description of cable networks (Figure 7.12) risks being dated as soon as it is published. However, by 1990 some patterns had emerged. Satellite-delivered basic services, for example, divided into *advertiser supported, superstations, direct-response marketing,* and *noncommercial.* They were *basic* services because most were designed to run on a cable system's basic tier (Section 5.2.2).

(a)

(b)

(c)

(d)

Figure 7.11 Local cable origination. (a) This cable crew videotapes an interview with a member of the U.S. House of Representatives for later playback on a local origination channel. (b) An announcer adds commentary to a cablecast of a Little League game. (c) For more elaborate out-of-studio cablecasts, the cable company uses a remote unit—a control room that travels in a van—the interior of which is seen here. (Photographs courtesy of National Cable Television Association. Used by permission.)

Figure 7.12 National cable networks.

7.4.2.1 Programming by Advertiser-Supported Services

In some ways, advertiser-supported satellite services resemble broadcast networks. They program nationally and depend on advertising revenues. They have also started to go after original programming.

In other ways, ad-supported services resemble modern radio and magazines. Most focus on content. Their programming divides into seven broad categories. One group includes cable services that program *horizontally*. Like the broadcast networks, they aim for a general audience. The other groups make up the majority of ad-supported services, those that program *vertically*. Like radio stations and magazines, these networks aim for specificity.

General and consumer. USA Network and the CBN Family Channel both offer a mix of programs for all types of people. USA focuses on entertainment. CBN takes a family entertainment approach and also carries religious programming (below). The Nashville Network features country programming—music, comedies, game and variety shows, and sports. Turner Network Television (TNT; Section 5.2.5) focuses on major programming events (specials), plus a regular schedule with increasing amounts of original (made-for-TNT) programming. In 1989, both HBO and MTV networks announced plans for all-comedy basic networks—The Comedy Channel and the "HA" Comedy Network, respectively.

Information. Cable News Network (CNN), Galavision's ECO, and CNN's Headline News present general news. CNN programs frequent news updates and a variety of informational features and material. ECO does somewhat the same in Spanish. CNN often provides continuous live coverage of breaking news events. Headline News uses a tightly formatted half-hour news cycle. Financial News Network (FNN) reports on finance, business, and the economy during the business day. Consumer News and Business Channel (CNBC; Section 4.5.3.4) programs market reports, business and news updates, and consumer pieces in an hourly format during weekdays and talk and other business–consumer programming evenings and weekends. The Weather Channel originates weather information, forecasts, and features.

Sports. Entertainment and Sports Programming Network (ESPN) has grown into one of the most successful networks with its schedule of professional, amateur, and collegiate sports events. ESPN experienced significant audience increases in 1987 when it first carried National Football League games. SCORE, a sports news service, shares distribution channels with FNN. In 1989, FNN increased its evening and weekend financial programming, reducing SCORE to a part-time weekend schedule and eliminating a companion overnight shopping channel, Telshop.

Regional sports networks. Typically based on a large market, a regional sports network features play-by-play of professional and college teams identified with the market. It feeds programming by satellite to cable systems in the market and the surrounding area. These networks carry advertising, and most cable systems put them on the basic tier. Some systems put them in a pay tier at the center of the market and on basic in the outer areas. Some of the sports networks include Home Sports Entertainment (Texas), Home Team Sports (Washington/Baltimore), Madison Square Garden Network (New York), New England Sports Network, Pirates on Cable (Pittsburgh), Prime Ticket (Los Angeles), Prism (Philadelphia), Pro-Am Sport Systems (Detroit), SportsChannel America (a national service that provides programming for co-owned and affiliated regional services); SportsChannel Florida, SportsChannel Los Angeles, SportsChannel New England, SportsChannel New York, SportsVision Chicago, and Sunshine Network (Florida).

Music. MTV pioneered music-video programming and enjoyed great success. It inspired others to try the format. MTV includes some series programming but focuses on the latest rock-music recordings. The co-owned VH-1 uses a more inclusive popular-music play list. Country Music Network plays the music indicated by its name.

Special-interest. Arts & Entertainment (A&E) targets people who enjoy drama and fine arts. A&E almost qualifies as a general network. Its programs, many British in origin, include dramatic, adventure, and comedy series; family classics; plays; documentaries; variety specials; movies; music; opera; and dance. The Discovery Channel (TDC) appeals to the intellectually curious. TDC's programs feature science, nature, history, technology, adventure, and world exploration. The Learning Channel offers adult education courses, business and career development, hobby, how-to, and personal improvement and enrichment. Lifetime programs for women, including medical and health information. Movietime appeals to film fans with previews of movies, celebrity interviews, profiles, and local movie listings. Nickelodeon, a children's service, broadens its appeal to family/nostalgia entertainment in the evening as Nick at Nite. Nostalgia Channel aims for an older audience. The Silent Network serves deaf and hearing-impaired audiences with information and entertainment in sign language, open captions, and sound.

Racial and ethnic. These services schedule a variety of programming and, in that respect, resemble general and consumer networks (above). The difference, of course, is that these networks target major subgroups in the U.S. population. Black Entertainment Television (BET), for example, provides black family programming around the clock. Univision (Section 20.3.2.1) and Telemundo (Section 20.3.2.4) both present a full schedule of Spanish-language family programming to cable systems as well as to their affiliated stations. Galavision also programs in Spanish, both its ECO news service and its entertainment programming.

Religion. The CBN Family Channel, which schedules family fare during most of the day (above), programs religion evenings and weekends. Evangelist and CBN founder M. G. "Pat" Robertson hosts the network's best-known program, *The 700 Club.* Vision Interfaith Satellite Network reflects the ecumenical nature of its support with both religious and value-oriented programming. In 1988, Rev. Jerry Falwell's (Section 7.6.2) Liberty Broadcasting Network cable service transformed into FamilyNet, production arm of the for-profit Family Television Network. FamilyNet planned to acquire family-oriented programming that would capture ratings and advertisers. That same year, the Southern Baptist Radio and Television Commission sold its ACTS Satellite Network to Friends of ACTS, a for-profit corporation.

7.4.2.2 Superstation Programming A superstation is a television broadcast station whose signal is distributed by satellite to many cable systems. A firm picks up the station's programming and utilizes satellite relay for national distribution. A cable operator that takes the station's programming off the satellite and puts it on a system must pay the firm.

The most popular superstations are independents. Like the majority of full-service independents, the superstation programs to a general audience. Beyond this, however, its "superstation" appeal—the reason the station attracts audiences across the country—is usually its heavy schedule of professional sports and movies.

As a broadcast station, the superstation must serve the market to which it is licensed. If the station does not actively promote its "super" status, that may be as far as it goes—it's a good independent that serves its market, and its national audience can take it or leave it. On the other hand, Atlanta's WTBS actively seeks such status and programs with its national audience in mind. It counterprograms the broadcast networks around the clock but, because of time zone differences, not specific stations in specific markets. Instead, WTBS schedules to provide alternative program choices throughout the broadcast day.

During the 1980s, three firms turned six independent TV stations into superstations. Eastern Microwave distributed WWOR, Secaucus, New Jersey (New York City). Tempo Enterprises carried Atlanta's WTBS. United Video distributed KTLA, Los Angeles; KTVT, Fort Worth; WGN-TV, Chicago; and WPIX, New York.

Some firms distributed the signals of other stations, mostly network affiliates. They marketed these to small cable systems that did not carry a full complement of broadcast TV signals and to the television receive-only (backyard) dish market (Section 7.4.4).

7.4.2.3 Programming by Direct-Response Marketing Services

Direct-response marketing services retail goods to their audiences. Programming consists of pitches for the various items. Viewers are encouraged to call toll-free telephone order lines and make credit card purchases. Since these services generate revenue directly from viewers, they normally do not need to sell advertising time to others or pay heed to ratings.

Direct marketing developed as full-time cable programming during the 1980s, thanks largely to the success of Home Shopping Network (HSN; Section 20.3.2.3) (Figure 7.13). The idea of these services *seemed* great—the ultimate merger of show business and marketing. Skip the programming costs; let's get down to business and *sell* full time. Low investment; high return. Many tried it. Many went under. They could not get cable systems to carry them. Even large-capacity systems resisted carrying more than one or two specimens of such a specialized service.

Figure 7.13 Home Shopping Network. Others tried to cash in on HSN's initial success. (*Source*: Home Shopping Network)

In researching this chapter, one count showed ten national services. These included two HSN channels plus America's Shopping Channel, Cable Value Network, Fashion Channel, QVC Network, Shop TV, Telshop, Travel Channel, and Video Mall Network. Not all will survive, not even until this book reaches print. Some local and regional services have also developed. In 1988, GTE began testing Main Street, a two-way interactive home shopping service.

7.4.2.4 Programming by Noncommercial Services Noncommercial services carry no paid advertising. The best known is *C-SPAN*, an acronym for Cable Satellite Public Affairs Network. C-SPAN consists of two channels. They normally carry coverage of the U.S. House and Senate. When Congress is not in session, they carry other public affairs programming. C-SPAN is financially supported by cable system operators.

This noncommercial category includes some religious services. Although their programming may include appeals for donations, they do not run commercials as such. Eternal Word Television Network, a Roman Catholic service, originates a limited schedule from Birmingham and features spiritual-growth programming. PTL provides multidenominational religious programming. Fighting for survival in the wake of scandal (Section 4.5.3.5), PTL changed its name to the Inspirational Network in 1987 and considered advertising support. The Trinity Broadcasting Network offers Christian religious programming all day long.

Two services program to the Jewish community. The Jewish Television Network (JTN) schedules material in the areas of news, arts, Israel, religion, and features. In 1988 JTN considered accepting advertising. The National Jewish Television Network offers a Sunday afternoon program of informational, cultural, and religious material.

7.4.3 Satellite-Delivered Pay Service Programming

Satellite-delivered pay services may be categorized as *pay cable* and *pay-per-view*. Cable subscribers who opt for such channels are normally charged fees over and above the cost for basic service (Section 5.2.2); thus, they are *pay* services.

7.4.3.1 Programming by Pay Cable Services Pay cable services are also called *premium* or *subscription* services. Most offer three inducements to potential subscribers. First, they offer material that is **uncut.** A pay cable service generally does not cut programming to eliminate objectionable content or to squeeze it into a time slot. Second, they offer **uninterrupted** material. A pay cable service may declare a recess in the middle of a long presentation to give viewers a break, but it does not insert commercials or promotional announcements (promos).

Third, they offer **unique** material. The pay cable services acquire some original material. You see it first (or only) on pay cable. They also acquire much material that is not original—movies, for example, that have shown in theaters. But they acquire it on an exclusive basis. Networks and stations may not program such material while a pay cable service has it.

Pay cable services look at cumulative ratings for the month, rather than per-program or daypart ratings. They try to run a variety of material so that, over a month's time, they appeal to both sexes and diverse ages. Viewers usually turn to most pay-service channels to watch a particular offering, rather than for continuous viewing. Nonetheless, pay cable services do make some attempt to counterprogram the broadcast networks and establish audience flow.

In the development of pay cable services, **movies** played a key role. They figured large in the initial success of the services. Since the services made money directly from viewers, they could pay premium prices for first TV rights, rights that allowed them to show recent films long before their release to broadcasting.

By the mid-1980s, however, so many consumers owned videocassette recorders that the home video trade could outbid pay cable services. Films were released on videocassette before they went to cable. The novelty of premium movie channels wore off. Subscribers complained of repetition (not enough good new films) and duplication (the various services all showed the same films).

The services responded in several ways. First, they produced more original programming. Second, they signed contracts with film studios to get exclusive rights for movies during the cable *window* (the time during which they can be shown on cable); this strategy involved primarily archrivals Home Box Office and Showtime/The Movie Channel. Coincidentally, cable systems dropped subscriber rates for premium channels, a result of deregulation under the Cable Communications Policy Act (Section 5.2.4). By the end of the 1980s, subscriber defections had slowed. Still, predictions were made that the future of pay cable was pay-per-view.

Pay cable networks attempt to position themselves through programming and promotion. Home Box Office and Showtime compete head to head. Each promotes the variety on its programming schedule—movies, specials, documentaries, sports, comedy series, music, and original programs. Cinemax, HBO's companion service, aims at a young adult audience with select and broad-appeal films and with original music and comedy programming. Bravo focuses on feature films and the performing arts. Playboy At Night (formerly the Playboy Channel) and the Disney Channel program polar-opposite material. Playboy At Night, which op-

erates in the evening and overnight, uses mature-audience feature films and made-for-Playboy original programming. Disney uses family entertainment from its own studios and other sources. (In 1988, Festival, created by HBO as another family-oriented service, closed after operating one year.) The Movie Channel (TMC) and American Movie Classics (AMC) promote their film content. TMC's schedule includes recent films and aims at young adults. AMC emphasizes older movies that have been critically acclaimed or otherwise made their mark. During the late 1980s, AMC was considering conversion to a basic service.

7.4.3.2 Pay-Per-View Programming Movies, sports events (often, championship boxing matches and wrestling matches), rock concerts, hit plays and revues—these are the types of material that pay-per-view (PPV) services program. By 1990, several satellite-delivered services provided PPV programming for cable systems and other pay outlets. Technical systems had improved, including true *impulse technology* (permitting the viewer to watch simply by pressing a button). Still, relatively few cable systems had the necessary equipment, so overall PPV audiences figures were low compared with those for pay cable. Pioneer PPV services include Viewer's Choice (merged with competitor Home Premiere Television in 1988) and Request TV. In 1989, the Playboy Channel converted to Playboy At Night, available on either a per–night or a monthly basis.

The NBC-Cablevision Systems deal (Section 4.5.3.4) included PPV plans. Under that agreement, NBC's broadcast coverage of the 1992 summer Olympic Games in Barcelona, Spain, was to be complemented by PPV coverage. Some predicted that carriage of such popular and prestigious programming would constitute a landmark in the development of PPV.

7.4.4 TVRO Programming Packages

TVRO packagers retail groups of programming services to backyard dish owners. Most satellite programming services scramble their signals to prevent unauthorized reception. Packagers provide the TVRO audience with legal means to pick up and descramble the services.

The packager must get permission from and make arrangements with the individual program services. To subscribe, a dish owner buys a descrambler and then contacts a packager. Once the packager has signed up the dish owner, the descrambler is activated *for the services in the package.* The dish owner can pick up satellite signals other than those of the services in the package, but they remain scrambled. The dish owner pays a monthly fee for the package.

The packages consist primarily of basic and pay cable services, such as those described in the preceding sections. C-band satellites carry most of these services, and the majority of the TVRO audience can pick up only C-band transmissions. Packagers often sell pay cable channels separately from their groups of services. National Rural Telecommunications Cooperative (NRTC), one of the largest packagers, retails through its local co-ops. Other packagers retail through local cable systems or directly to the customer. These include Netlink, Tempo Development, and Showtime/The Movie Channel. A few programmers do not scramble so that TVRO dishes can pick them up; one of these is the Public Broadcasting Service. Some individual services have begun specifically to serve the TVRO market.

7.4.5 Programming in Unconventional Services

Most of us think of television programming in terms of "shows"—formal, fixed presentations by people for a relatively large audience that normally cannot affect the nature of the presentations. This has been the convention in TV since its beginnings. By extension, content that does *not* fit this mold is *unconventional,* and that is the subject of this section.

We discussed **electronic text** at some length in Section 5.7. Cable systems commonly use rotatext (Section 5.7.1) to program a channel with news, weather, announcements, advertising, even cable channel program listings. Several firms provide satellite-delivered text services of various types—news, sports, and financial information; customized (to the local system) electronic program logs; and even specialized services a cable system could feed to its subscribers' personal computers.

By contrast, none of the 1980s attempts at teletext (Section 5.7.3) and videotex (Section 5.7.4) service succeeded. Still, both seemed to have the potential for success, given the right combination of equipment, cost, and, most important, content.

Videotex, of course, is an **interactive** medium. There are others. Warner-Amex, for example, operated Qube for seven years before shutting it down in 1984 (Section 5.2.3.3). Other cable systems have experimented with or operated other types of interactive services, particularly those involving PPV programming and direct marketing. Additional interactive video services include information retrieval, home banking, and kiosks, all discussed in Section 5.7.4.

Some cable systems and program services offer a form of interactive programming involving the telephone. Viewers watch programming on a cable channel and interact by using the telephone. According to the specific program, they can ask for more information or order advertised merchandise, call in opinions for polls, and participate in talk and game shows. Direct-response marketing cable services (Section 7.4.2.3) consist of such telephone-interactive programming.

7.5 CABLE SYSTEM PROGRAMMING

Most cable systems offer four distinct types of services—the signals of local broadcast television stations, local productions, satellite-delivered basic networks, and satellite-delivered pay services. Many also program rotatext channels; a few offer home security and other unconventional services. These can add up to a lot of channels. For example, a market may have seven or more full-service broadcast television signals, and the cable system carries them. Big cable systems—may carry a large number of local origination and access channels. And, according to when and how you count, there are 55 to 65 nationally distributed basic and pay services.

Certain requirements and restrictions apply to cable system programming. The franchise agreement, for example, may call for access programming and put curbs on obscenity. Federal regulation includes the network nonduplication rule, the syndicated exclusivity rule (Section 4.5.2.1), and the political-candidate equal-opportunities requirement (Section 14.1.1.4).

Some cable systems have marketed their service using a scheme called **tiering.** Typically, the basic tier consists of all local broadcast signals, all local origination and access channels, and a number of national basic services. Subscribers pay a certain monthly sum for this first tier of service. The second tier may consist of additional national basic services. Subscribers pay an additional fee to get the second tier. The third tier may consist of one or more pay channels in various combinations and at various prices.

For years, cable systems sold additional services only in combination with basic service. In 1988, the first operator broke that marketing custom. Cablevision Systems offered residents in its New York franchise pay-cable-only service.

One of cable's major selling points is the variety of programming it offers. Nonetheless, a 1982 study sponsored by NCTA, the cable trade association, showed that most viewers would be happy with just five non-broadcast channels in addition to local broadcast television signals. This could be achieved any number of ways by rival media without the high capital outlay needed to install cable. For example, wireless cable (multichannel television; Section 5.4) could grow into a real threat. Direct-broadcast satellites (DBS; Section 5.6) could also provide multichannel service. Cable systems, however, could offer to carry (and share the proceeds from) both wireless cable and DBS signals as additional tiers. Also, each person's combination of five favorite channels could be different. Two years later, another NCTA study reported that consumers overwhelmingly favored cable over wireless cable or DBS; further, lower installation charges and greater channel capacity would allow cable to continue its dominance in the multichannel marketplace.

7.6 CONSTRAINTS ON PROGRAMMING

Certain limitations affect programming. Some are set by law or federal regulation. These limitations are discussed in Sections 14.1.1 and 15.3. Various government bodies and elements of the court system restrict coverage of their activities (Section 15.2.4). For years, the Radio Code and the Television Code of the National Association of Broadcasters (NAB) influenced radio programming. However, the NAB eliminated its code operations in 1983 (Section 16.2.1). Each operator of a radio/TV outlet has a set of personal values that affect programming (Section 16.1).

Factors outside law, regulation, and ethics also affect programming. Two of these include the fact of advertising support and the activities of some pressure groups.

7.6.1 Advertising Pressures

Advertisers today rarely attempt to dictate policy to programmers. Occasionally, an advertiser will attempt to influence programming or news coverage, threatening to withdraw advertising unless the programmer takes some specific action. But, for the most part, the decline of single-sponsor programs caused a parallel decline of direct *advertiser control* of content.

On the other hand, **advertising support**—the fact that advertising revenue pays for programming—affects content directly. Consider the three major TV broadcast networks, for example. The larger the audience, the more money ABC, CBS, and NBC can charge for advertising time. Therefore, they attempt to maximize audiences by programming material that **appeals to the broadest spectrum of the public** and that **avoids themes and depictions that might alienate** major segments of the audience. Such programming ordinarily precludes that which challenges or might offend prevailing established political beliefs, economic systems, social norms, standards, or customs.

Critics contend that the practice of maximizing audience limits not only the range and treatment of subjects within programs but also the amount of certain types of programs. Programming that draws relatively low audiences—usually "serious" drama and music, documentaries, public affairs, and discussion programs—is scheduled rarely or at odd hours and, when programming changes are made, is first to be cut.

Defenders say that networks give the audience what it wants, that the consistently high ratings for entertainment programming prove it. The question then arises: How does the audience know it does not want more serious programming if it rarely has access to it? Still, ratings are relatively low for even the finest public television programs and for serious artistic and public interest programs* from the commercial networks. Yes, the networks lost audience in the 1980s, but most was lost to entertainment—on independent stations, cable, and home video—not culture and public affairs.

7.6.2 Pressure Groups

Occasionally, outside groups attempt to influence programming. One example is the blacklist of the 1950s, discussed in Section 3.2.3.1. Another is the continuing efforts of Action for Children's Television to improve programming for youngsters (Section 4.4.3.2). Still another is the fight against excessive or gratuitous depictions of violence and sexual activities. As mentioned in Section 4.4.3.2, several organizations have opposed overuse of sex and violence on television programming. None was as large or had as much potential clout as the **Moral Majority,** with its estimated 21 million sympathizers (which meant that it was actually a *minority*). When Moral Majority entered the debate, it focused on sex more than violence. Many critics felt the issues had taken a frightening turn.

Moral Majority was led by Rev. Jerry Falwell, a television preacher. An evangelical Christian conservative movement, the group took an active role in the 1980 election of Ronald Reagan to the presidency. Later, Falwell focused efforts of the Moral Majority on television programming. The networks had discovered sex in 1977 and started the T 'n' A[†] programming fad with series such as

---

*The exception was CBS's *60 Minutes.* In 1976, *60 Minutes* began to earn ratings in the top ten programs. By the 1980s, it often placed first. By any measure, *60 Minutes* was the most popular public affairs series in television's history.

[†]Approximate translation: "bosoms and buttocks"; characterized by camera shots of women's bottoms and what the trade called "jiggle"—bouncing female breasts. Themes and dialogue were often suffused with sexism, leering innuendo, and suggestive language, usually unrealistic and unmotivated.

Charlie's Angels and *Three's Company.* Falwell organized opposition and threatened consumer boycotts of products advertised on programs that featured gratuitous sex.

Detractors said that Moral Majority's very name epitomized its tactics, the implication being that those who did not agree with its stand were not moral and, by extension, not Christian. Thus many who might also have objected to the T 'n' A fad did not join Falwell's campaign. A rival group organized to counter the Moral Majority's stand on television programming. This group, People for the American Way, included a number of mainstream religious leaders and was organized by Norman Lear, producer of television series including *All in the Family.* They used TV spots and other publicity vehicles to fight the Moral Majority philosophy.

7.7 ROLE OF AUDIENCE PROMOTION

Effective as a programming strategy may be, it will not do any good unless the potential audience knows about it. Networks and stations cannot rely on audience dial switching and schedule listings in newspapers to inform the public of new programs and time changes in old ones. The role of **audience promotion** is to *draw* an audience. It is, of course, up to the programming to *keep* the audience. No amount of clever promotion can hold an audience for poor programming.

For a broadcast medium, one effective promotion tool is its own airwaves. On-air promotion includes contests, promos for upcoming programs, mentions on programs of other programs, call letters ("KBIV—Best in Viewing"), thematic graphic designs (to create an easily recognized symbol or **logo** of the station) worked into local production, clever station identification devices (special musical signature or animation), and even public service ("The KBIV Action Line Ombudsman").

Figure 7.14 Promotional materials. WOGX-TV, an independent television station, uses outdoor advertising along a busy street to promote itself as "The Great Entertainer." Signs in other parts of the WOGX coverage area promote individual programs on its schedule. Outdoor advertising is just one part of the station's extensive promotional activities. (Used by permission of WOGX-TV.)

Off-air promotion may include advertisements in other media (newspapers, magazines, billboards, [Figure 7.14], even other stations); stunts and personal appearances by station personalities; display of the logo on station vehicles, equipment, and jackets; and giveaways, such as bumper stickers and program guides. In many promotional activites, the station seeks additional publicity through a printed **release** of information about the station, its personnel, and its programs to newspapers and trade publications to be run as news stories.

Good programming and good promotion are year-round requirements. During ratings surveys, however, stations want to maximize audiences, so promotion efforts intensify. Some even run promotional contests. Contests violate the spirit of Arbitron and Nielsen guidelines and, when staged during a survey period, are noted in the resulting rating report. Broadcasters refer to such practices as **hypoing** the ratings and, over the years, have come to tolerate it as part of the promotion game. (Ratings *distortion*, however, is another matter; see Section 18.2.11.3.)

The promotion function has grown in importance for broadcasters. Television stations, for example, faced increasing competition during the 1970s on at least four fronts. First, affiliates' local news efforts developed into fierce rivalries. Second, independent stations made audience gains in all dayparts. Third, many more television stations signed on. Fourth, rival video media developed. Stations responded by increasing promotional activities. They started promotion departments or expanded existing ones, budgeted additional money for promotion, and, in general, changed promotion from a sideline to a major activity.

Cable and other media use some of the same promotional activities as broadcasting—promos, catchy logos, musical and animated identifications, advertising, and program guides. They use others that are quite different. Cable systems, for example, use door-to-door and telephone sales to sell services. They may offer special limited-run "packages" as inducements (for example, no installation fee for new subscribers, or three pay services for the price of one for one month). At the national level, a pay network may offer a free week of programming. It will urge affiliated cable systems to run the network's programming unscrambled on a vacant channel in the basic service so that every subscriber can see it; then it will schedule "commercials" that urge subscribers to sign up for the service.

By 1990, both broadcast and cable television networks had tried promotional tie-ins with national retailers and marketers. For example, certain Sears 1989 customer mailings included a contest designed to familiarize viewers with new NBC shows for the up-

coming prime-time season. CBS had a similar tie-in with K mart. ABC planned to give away a million promotional video cassettes through the Pizza Hut chain. Showtime Networks, Inc. worked out a promotional tie-in with Beatrice Hunt Wesson, marketer of Orville Redenbacher Gourmet Popping Corn; Home Shopping Network, with Maxwell House Coffee.

NOTE

1. "Low-power riding high," *Broadcasting* 14 Nov. 1988: 79.

FURTHER READING

Allen, Robert C. *Speaking of Soap Operas.* Chapel Hill: U of North Carolina P, 1985. Content and appeal.

Barwise, Patrick, and Andrew Ehrenberg. *Television and Its Audience.* Newbury Park: Sage, 1988. How and why we watch.

Bergendorff, Fred L., et al. *Broadcast Advertising and Promotion: A Handbook for Students and Professionals.* New York: Hastings, 1983. Written with participation of the Broadcast Promotion Association.

Blum, Richard A., and Richard D. Lindheim. *Primetime: Network Television Programming.* Stoneham: Focal, 1987. Creation, development, marketing, decision making.

Cantor, Muriel G. *The Hollywood Producer: His Work and His Audience.* New Brunswick: Transaction, 1987. How and why of series selection.

Eastman, Susan Tyler, and Robert Klein, eds. *Strategies for Broadcast and Cable Promotion.* 2d ed. Belmont: Wadsworth, 1985. Standard text in the field.

Eastman, Susan Tyler, Sidney W. Head, and Lewis Klein, eds. *Broadcast/Cable Programming: Strategies and Practices.* 3d ed. Belmont: Wadsworth, 1989. Includes public broadcasting.

Gitlin, Todd. *Inside Prime Time.* New York: Pantheon, 1987. How American broadcast TV networks create programs.

Howard, Herbert H., and Michael S. Kievman.

Radio and TV Programming. Ames: Iowa State UP, 1983. Textbook.

Kaminsky, Stuart M., and Jeffery H. Mahan. *American Television Genres.* Chicago: Nelson, 1985. Program types.

Keith, Michael C. *Radio Programming: Consultancy and Formatics.* Stoneham: Focal, 1987. All aspects.

Matelski, Marilyn J. *Broadcast Programming and Promotions Worktext.* Stoneham: Focal, 1989.

Newcomb, Horace, and Robert S. Alley. *The Producer's Medium: Conversations with Creators of American TV.* New York: Oxford UP, 1983. Views, relations with networks.

Oringel, Robert S., and Sue Miller Burke. *The Access Manager's Handbook: A Guide for Managing Community Television.* Stoneham: Focal, 1987. Programming, outreach.

Rose, Brian, ed. *TV Genres: A Handbook and Reference Guide.* Westport: Greenwood, 1985. Critical, historical survey.

Schneider, Cy. *Children's Television: The Art, the Business, and How It Works.* Lincolnwood: National, 1987. Views of producers on content, advertising, impact.

Shanks, Bob. *The Primal Screen: How to Write, Sell, and Produce Movies for Television.* New York: Fawcett, 1988. Author is well-known program producer.

Smith, V. Jackson. *Programming for Radio and Television.* Rev. ed. Lanham: UP of America, 1983.

CHAPTER 8

News

"Did you see the news last night?" someone asks. You assume the question refers to a *television* news *program* or *service*, and you are probably right. The wording of the question and your assumption illustrate a fact of life—most of us rely on television news reporting so much that we think of it as *the news*. Dating from 1963, biennial national polls show that people mention television more than any other medium as one of their main sources of news (Figure 8.1). Dating from 1961, the same polls show people choosing television as the most believable news medium (Figure 8.2).

Radio is also an important source of news for many people, although it does not dominate the news field as does television. Large numbers of individuals listen to radio news as they get ready for work in the morning, travel in automobiles, and work in their homes or businesses. In a 1982 nationwide survey, respondents specified local, national, and world news, along with traffic and weather reports, as the most important elements of their radio listening.[1]

In this chapter, our subject is radio and television news. We first explore the meaning of "news." Next, we inspect radio newscasts, television newscasts, and television news services. Finally, we look at other forms of news programming—documentaries, on-the-spot coverage, interviews.

8.1 NATURE OF NEWS

As a broad definition, we can say that news is the **reporting of recent happenings.** But more specifically, we are interested primarily in **processed** news—news that has been **gathered to a central point, put into a form suitable for public distribution and presentation, and disseminated to a mass audience.**

8.1.1 What Are the Origins of News?

Technology has played a crucial role in the history of news processing. The very origins of mass news—and, in fact, all mass communication—derive from a technological development: reusable metal type combined with ink, paper, and a compress; in other words, the **printing press.**

8.1.1.1 The Newspaper Evolves According to tradition, Johannes Gutenberg of Mainz, Germany, introduced movable metal type in

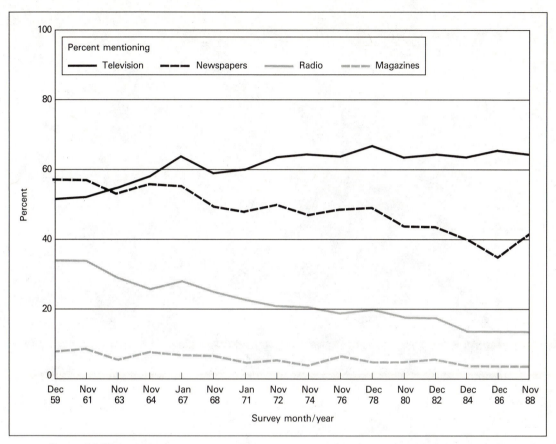

Figure 8.1 Where people get most news. About every two years, from 1959 through 1988, the Roper Organization conducted nationwide surveys of people 18 and older for the now defunct Television Information Office. Television has led all other media as a source of most news since 1963. In the 1988 survey, out of the sample of 2000 people, 65 percent mentioned television as a source of most news—a full 30 percentage points higher than the next most frequently mentioned source, newspapers. (Survey respondents could name more than one medium.) (*Source:* Television Information Office.)

Europe about 1450. Just over 50 years later, newspapers appeared in Germany and Holland aimed at merchants and other persons in business. These first primitive newspapers contained mainly news of shipping and commerce. England's first regularly published newspaper began in 1621; its first daily newspaper, in 1702.

Juan Pablos brought printing to the New World in 1539 when he set up a press in Mexico City. Stephan Day came to Massachusetts Bay in 1638 and helped to start a printing establishment. In 1690, Benjamin Harris published *Publick Occurrences*, a news sheet. Authorities closed it down after one issue.

The *Boston News-Letter*, America's first continuously published newspaper, began in 1704, and by 1715 it had some 300 subscribers. The *News-Letter* contained local financial news and foreign political news. It copied the latter from English newspapers. By 1750, the American colonies had 12 newspapers; 25 years later the number had multiplied fourfold. All were weeklies; America did not get its first daily until 1783.

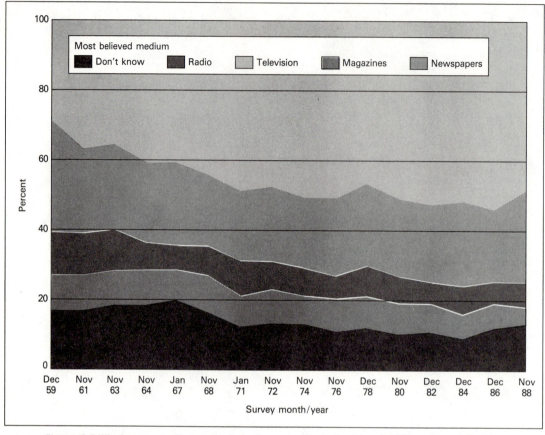

Figure 8.2 What news medium people believe most. In the biennial TIO surveys, television has led as the most believable mass medium since 1961. In the 1988 survey, however, television lost ground, while newspapers gained. (The distance from the bottom of the chart to the top represents all responses; distances within each horizontal segment indicate the percentage of survey respondents who gave each reply.) (*Source:* Television Information Office.)

In 1765, England imposed on the colonies the Stamp Act, a heavy tax on paper. Most colonial newspapers united to oppose the Stamp Act. The act was repealed in 1766, but a majority of the colonial press continued to be active in the cause of rebellion and revolution.

After the American Revolution, newspapers retained partisanship but lost unity, splitting over politics. Some newspapers supported the Federalist party, made up of large landowners, merchants, manufacturers, and bankers. Others backed the Republican party, made up of salaried workers and farmers. There was little attempt at objectivity. Newspapers freely mixed news and opinion in the same report.

The first newspapers had published mainly news sent to their offices by interested parties or copied from other newspapers. Early in the nineteenth century, newspapers made an important change in news gathering practices; they started hiring reporters to go out and gather news.

8.1.1.2 Metamorphosis to Mass Communication
Before the 1830s, newspapers had been written primarily for the privileged

classes. Prices were high, circulations low. However, a new class—wage earners—moved to the cities, received the right to vote, and learned to read in free, tax-supported schools. Publishers saw opportunities for large-circulation newspapers. Power had been added to the printing press in 1811, and by 1833 the steam press produced thousands of copies per hour. Publishers altered content to attract these newly enfranchised readers, filling papers with material the urban masses found interesting and easy to read. Circulations grew so large that publishers could sell space in their newspapers for commercial messages aimed at the public, and the revenue from this advertising financed the publication. Newspapers were almost given away at one cent (later two) per copy, earning them the name **penny press.** The first penny newspaper, the New York *Sun,* started in 1833 and, by 1836, had a circulation of over 30,000. The press was on its way to becoming a mass medium, **dependent on large circulations and large advertising revenues.**

8.1.1.3 The News Wire Services

In 1848, the first news agency wire service was organized. Six New York newspapers agreed to share the costs of telegraphing national news from Washington, D.C., and foreign news from Boston through formation of the **Associated Press** (AP) of New York. Other newspapers asked to join. Newspapers still slanted reports to match party, cause, or editorial policy. The papers AP served had a variety of editorial policies. So AP decided to adopt *no slant*—to report only facts. Each AP newspaper would be free to rewrite the wire service stories to fit its editorial slant. Some did. Many more did not, printing stories as they came over the wire. Eventually, this became the practice at most newspapers. Thus, necessity gave birth to **objective reporting,** fathered by the telegraph, a technical development.

A competing wire service, the United Press, was organized in 1882 but went bankrupt in 1897. In 1907, E. W. Scripps founded the United Press Association (UP), and in 1909, William Randolph Hearst formed the International News Service (INS). In 1958, UP and INS merged into **United Press International** (UPI).

8.1.1.4 Metamorphosis to Big Business

A bitter rivalry led to the age of **yellow journalism.** Joseph Pulitzer's *New York World* and Hearst's *New York Morning Journal* (and imitators across the nation) emphasized sensationalism in efforts to appeal to working-class audiences and to build huge circulations. Yellow journalism peaked in the 1890s; both the *World* and the *Morning Journal* circulated to some 700,000 readers each. As they grew, however, newspapers also became big business. Publishers identified with working-class readers less and less and with business interests more and more. By 1910, the age of yellow journalism had ended. It left its mark on the shape and form of the daily press—comics, editorial crusades against crime and corruption, and investigative reporting.

Sensational journalism reappeared in the 1920s. During this era of **jazz journalism,** the tabloid newspaper appeared. New York provided three leading examples, the *Daily News,* the *Daily Graphic,* and the *Daily Mirror.* All played up sexual and sensational aspects of news, featured lots of photographs, and were printed on smaller paper sheets than other newspapers, which made them easy to read on crowded subways and buses.

Despite the excesses of jazz journalism, newspapers overall had become distinctly middle class in outlook. This complemented another trend that began when Scripps put together the first chain of commonly owned newspapers. Hearst and others followed, buying newspapers in different cities and managing them from one central office. Gradually, chain and absentee ownership became the norm, and interests of owners shifted away from editorial influence to profits.

8.1.2 What Are News Outlets Like?

As we have seen, the pattern for mainstream, public news media was set early in the twentieth century. These media evolved into what LeRoy and Sterling[2] have called **mass news**—distributed by organized, large, imposing systems; attended by huge audiences; relied on by the public for reports of recent happenings.

8.1.2.1 Ownership and Motivation The main news outlets—organizations that package and present news to the public—are generally big business, large, bureaucratic. Typically, they are **owned by publicly held corporations.** The corporate-owned news outlet is an investment and may be one of many commonly owned businesses. Corporate officers answer to stockholders and are **interested chiefly in profits,** not editorial policies. The manager of a particular news outlet is usually free to adopt any editorial stance, as long as the outlet earns a profit. With this freedom, editorial policies vary among commonly owned outlets, from conservative to liberal. Even liberal outlets, however, identify primarily with a middle-class, within-the-system approach to political and social issues.

8.1.2.2 Content Although editorial policies vary, most news outlets report most news as objectively as they know how. (More subtle aspects of news reports, such as story placement, phrasing, and emphasis may contribute to the public's perception of bias.) Some observers attribute objective reporting to a feeling of responsibility on the part of news outlet managers. Historically, **objectivity** also springs from at least two other sources—**reliance on wire services** and **need for large circulation.**

News outlets are linked together by the two dominant domestic wire services, AP and UPI, and to a lesser degree by a number of specialized, limited, and foreign-based services. AP and UPI provide the bulk of national and international news for many different news outlets, a situation which—as pointed out in the preceding section—requires the services to be objective. Because of the wire services, this news **tends to be identical,** often verbatim, from outlet to outlet, city to city.

As to circulation, news outlets are supported primarily by advertising revenues. To keep advertising rates up, outlets need the largest possible circulation or audience, including people who disagree with editorial policies. Therefore mainstream news outlets—and here we do not mean *National Enquirer*-type publications—**report the news straight and objectively and reserve opinion for clearly labeled editorials.**

As part of the effort to increase and hold circulation and audience, news outlets produce **much that is not, strictly speaking, news.** Look carefully at your daily newspaper; most of its space is devoted to advertising, syndicated features and columns, sports, family, and other specialized information. The national cable news services allot a great deal of time to commercials, sports, weather, features, and other nonnews content. Broadcast stations and networks, of course, are primarily entertainment/advertising media. Yet even on newscasts, much of the already limited time goes to material other than hard news.

8.1.3 What Is News?

Which brings us to the problem of defining news. What exactly is this thing we have been calling "news"? Earlier we said that news is the reporting of recent happenings that have been gathered and prepared for dissemination to an audience. We have added to that definition by describing the development and present structure of news outlets and their motivations for turning out the type of product they do.

8.1.3.1 News Value News is further defined by the way in which news outlet managers decide on a news story's news value—its **ability to attract a large audience.** A major factor in determining news value is whether a story is hard or soft. **Hard news** is the reporting of current events that are of interest because of their timeliness and general importance or their violence (crimes and accidents). Hard news declines rapidly in news value with passage of time. **Soft news,** on the other hand, consists of features and news of current events that lose news value relatively slowly. Although there are exceptions, sports and other specialized news are usually of secondary importance to hard news.

8.1.3.2 Controls over News There are other characteristics of news, characteristics that serve as means of control over, and thus limitations on, content. One classification system lists seven types of control[3]—**monopoly, source, government, internal, advertiser, self,** and **public.** The giant ownership monopolies that control news media tend to reduce the diversity of, and impose sameness on, content. Soruces—people and institutions, private and government—control news about themselves through secrecy, news management, and manipulation and shaping of news before it reaches the media. Government influences news media through the court system, agencies, and policies. Internal control is exercised by media personnel. Publishers, managers, editors, producers, reporters, camera crews—all act as informational **gatekeepers,** allowing some news to flow through media pipelines (to mix metaphors!) to the audience, stopping other news. Advertisers exercise control sometimes directly but usually indirectly through media acceptance of establishment viewpoints and conceptions of reality. Self-control through professional codes and standards of good practice and public control have relatively little effect (although some citizen groups succeeded in affecting broadcasting during the 1970s [Section 4.4.3]).

8.1.4 What Is Radio and Television News?

So far we have discussed news in general terms. Now we examine radio and television news specifically. Broadcast stations transmit news, for the most part, at regularly scheduled times. A station occasionally interrupts other programming (but never commercials) to present a news **bulletin,** a news report so important that it cannot wait for the regular news broadcast. News radio stations and the cable news services use news as their primary programming content; they run news and news-related material throughout the day. Electronic text services can also offer news full time.

8.1.4.1 Characteristics As yet, no medium matches radio for its ability to do on-the-spot reporting. A radio reporter needs little equipment and can telephone a report from the scene of a news event, even getting it on the air live. A television reporter is also mobile, but camera operation usually requires at least one other person at the scene, plus some coordination and frequently on-line or postproduction editing at the studio. Cable news services have been notably successful in overcoming these problems and presenting extended, live on-the-spot coverage of protracted news events.

Cable news services and radio stations have the ability to report immediately. Electronic text services can update news continuously. Broadcast television, on the other hand, programs on a relatively rigid schedule that inhibits extending newscasts or breaking into other programs with bulletins. Nevertheless, broadcast television will have a report on a late-breaking news item—often with tape—long before the newspaper is published. But the newspaper account often includes detail and background information for which broadcast and cable have no time and electronic text has no space. The newspaper also contains a good many stories that the other media did not even report.

8.1.4.2 Local News Outlets   Radio stations that carry news (other than those with all-news formats) typically schedule it once an hour, at the same time each hour. (This pattern can vary by daypart; music stations, for example, may carry newscasts during morning and afternoon drive times, but not during midday and at night.) For the most part, major news items are rewritten and repeated on each newscast, with perhaps a few changes in details. The five-minute newscast, once standard, is now the exception and has been all but replaced by the $3\frac{1}{2}$-minute newscast (which, after commercials, may contain just over two minutes of actual news). One-minute newscasts are not uncommon, and many stations broadcast no news at all.

To be fair, some radio stations present additional news each hour, perhaps a network newscast for national and international news and a local follow-up for area and state news. They may also carry extended or more frequent newscasts during morning and afternoon drive times.

All-news radio stations broadcast continuous news interspersed with features and commercials. News is repeated in cycles, 20 minutes or longer in length, so that a listener may tune in at any time and hear the full complement of news stories within a short period.

Television stations broadcast news less frequently but for longer periods than most radio stations. As a rule, network affiliates carry more news than independents. There is usually an early morning newscast that may range from a 15-minute summary off the wire to an elaborate, hour-long, locally produced *Today*-type magazine-format program. A second newscast, 5 to 30 minutes in length, airs around noon. The station broadcasts its **showcase** news program—longest, most elaborate, with the greatest number of recent or updated stories and videotape—in the early evening. This lasts 30 minutes or longer. Affiliates broadcast this program either before or after, or before *and* after, the network news. A final newscast airs at 10:00 or 11:00 p.m. and is 15 to 30 minutes in length. Some television stations also present short news summaries at sign-off and sign-on and one-minute news capsules between prime-time programs.

8.1.4.3 Network News   There are many radio networks (Sections 20.3.8 and 20.4–20.6), and most provide a news service. Radio networks usually schedule news at least once an hour, increasing news feeds during morning and afternoon drive times. Larger radio networks may feed newscasts two or more times an hour along with features, commentary, and sports. National Public Radio's *Morning Edition* and *All Things Considered* air during morning and evening drive times, respectively.

The three commercial broadcast television networks feed extended presentations in the early morning, the oldest being NBC's long-running *Today*. The television networks all air weekday showcase newscasts in the early evening (Figure 8.3). They have shorter feeds at other times, do one-minute news summaries during prime time, and provide individual reports that affiliated stations can record and use on their own newscasts.

The year 1982 seemed to constitute a peak in the development of network news programming. That year, in response to the rise

(a)

(b)

(c)

(d)

Figure 8.3 Broadcast television network anchor reporters. During the late 1980s, these reporters anchored the network early evening news programs: (a) Peter Jennings, ABC; (b) Dan Rather, CBS; (c) Tom Brokaw, NBC; and (d) Robert MacNeil and Jim Lehrer, PBS. (Photograph a courtesy of Capital Cities/ABC, Inc., b of CBS, Inc., c of the National Broadcasting Company, Inc., and d of WNET and WETA. Used by permission.)

of the cable news services, all three networks converted their news divisions into 24-hour operations and added a variety of late night and early morning newscasts. Just three years later, they weakened their reporting ability. During the period 1985–1987, the networks went on a staff-cutting binge; among those eliminated were hundreds of news employees, including respected and well-known veterans.

The programming of the cable news services varies. Cable News Network (CNN), for example, carries a number of extended newscasts interspersed with other informational programs. When important news breaks, CNN does not hesitate to suspend regular programming and provide extended coverage. C-SPAN (Section 7.4.2.4) supplements congressional cablecasts with unique, in-depth reporting on politics and public affairs. Informational programmers such as Financial News Network (FNN) and CNN's Headline News schedule repeating cycles, similar to those of news radio stations. ECO programs news and information in Spanish.

Public Broadcasting Service feeds its affiliates the *MacNeil/Lehrer News Hour* a little later than the commercial networks' early evening newscasts. This PBS news program differs from those of the commercial broadcast networks in that it has a full hour. The *News Hour* covers major news in summary fashion and also selects a few stories for treatment in depth. Weekend news schedules are different for all four television networks.

8.1.4.4 Other Radio-TV News Sources

During the 1980s, satellite relay capability spawned additional sources of television news. The birth of satellite news gathering (SNG; Section 5.5) (Figure 8.4), for example, gave rise to **SNG cooperatives.** A co-op consists of SNG-equipped television stations and a coordinating unit. The coordinator surveys the co-op's stations daily to assess what they will cover, identifies stories of general interest, and puts them on the satellite for other cooperating stations to use. It also helps arrange individual news exchanges—a co-op station in one city covers a story that is relayed to the requesting co-op station in another city. Co-ops formed at national, regional, and state levels. Organizers included

(a)

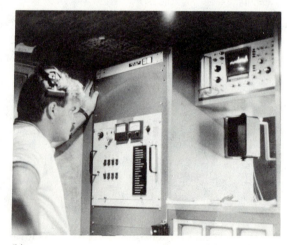

(b)

Figure 8.4 Satellite news gathering. (a) WESH-TV's SNG vehicle being readied to transmit a story through Conus. (b) Inside the truck, the Channel 2 technician establishes contact with the Conus coordination center by satellite relay.

Conus Communications (Section 5.5), Group W's Newsfeed, the three major broadcast networks, and the stations themselves.

The communications satellite spurred growth of firms that **syndicate video news, provide custom video coverage services,** and **create video public relations releases.** The news syndicators put together news and information packages, which they distribute to stations and other clients. Their product ranges from soft news to hard, from individual stories to complete programs. A custom-service firm provides news coverage support in its market for out-of-town news outlets. A Jacksonville TV station, for example, wants to do a story in Washington, D.C., and contracts for support with a Washington firm. Support varies with the client's need and may consist of a production crew, editing facilities, raw footage (unedited video), or even a complete news package (a finished story). Some companies offer the same support for public relations purposes. Businesses and special-interest groups contract with these firms to create and disseminate video news releases and other promotional material to television news outlets and other destinations. By 1990, among companies that provided one or more of these services were AP Express, Broadcast News Service, Financial News Network, Independent News Network, Los Angeles News Service, Medialink, Mobile Video Services, Newslink, Potomac Communications, Professional Video Services, Sun World Satellite, Turner Broadcasting, TV Direct, Visnews, and Washington Independent News.

8.1.5 Limitations and Problems of Radio-Television News

Time is a major factor. How many stories can be reported in a two-minute "news summary"? How many details can be given for each story? In both cases, not many. Formal newscasts are longer, but the problem is still the same. The script of an evening 30-minute network newscast actually accounts for only 22 to 23 minutes; commercials, credits, and a station break take up the rest of the time. A "half-hour" network news script, if set in type, would not even fill the front page of the *New York Times.*

News radio stations and cable news services operate continuously and would seem to have all the time they need. On occasion, they do operate that way, particularly C-SPAN and CNN. But most of the time, most all-news programmers package news in short, repeating cycles. Thus television news, news radio, and cable news service editors must be extremely selective in the detail they include in each story.

Television's **visual** element presents a whole set of problems. First, what gets videotape and SNG coverage? Those **events that are predictable,** where the assignment editor can schedule the equipment and personnel and the crews can set up in advance. This means heavy visual coverage of public figures arriving and departing; of meetings; of ribbon cuttings, grand openings, and the like; of speeches; and of press conferences.

Second, what gets on the air? Those **stories that have visual coverage**—videotape and SNG. Coverage of the opening of a new building, with tape of the mayor cutting the ribbon, may get as much newscast time as the less visual but more important story of the city auditor's report of a missing $3.5 million dollars in city revenues, or the story of a violent school bus accident that happened too late for camera crews to get to the scene. Of course, people turn to television news to *see* things, and if the station does not use a lot of pictures—regardless of content—the audience tunes to a station that does. Thus we see the trivial given as much or more coverage than the important.

Third, there are those who **manipulate news coverage**—demonstrators who await the arrival of television cameras before beginning action; political thugs who plant bombs, hijack airplanes, take over embassies, and kidnap people in such a manner as to make the 6:00 p.m. newscasts in the United States; major political parties that orchestrate national conventions to take advantage of television coverage; public figures who plan announcements and news conferences for major visual impact.

A fourth problem stems from subtle pressures on news crews to **emphasize certain aspects** in covering stories—action, blood, simplification, and, above all, conflict. These are visual news values that get audiences. Unfortunately, real life is rarely so clear-cut that it can be accurately depicted as a battle of two sides, us versus them, good versus bad, black versus white. Camera crews feel they must *force* their coverage into these terms, and the result gives a distorted picture. For example, during the war in Southeast Asia, network news film from Vietnam emphasized conflict and blood because reporters knew that was what the New York offices wanted. Supposedly, the sight of wounded and dead American military personnel brought war home to the public as never before, helping turn public opinion against the war. Yet subtle and equally important issues of the war were undercovered or unreported, simply because they did not lend themselves to visual presentation.

Questions of ethics confront television reporters and technicians. Certainly, faking a scene and coaching responses from subjects for the camera is unethical, and most television news organizations have established policies to prevent faking. But some situations are not easy to define as ethical or unethical. Suppose you were covering a demonstration protesting atomic weapons, taping a group of people praying in unison. You could hear the prayer clearly, but your microphone could not pick it up. What would you do? Ask the group to pray louder?

Would that be ethical? Further, the very introduction of a television camera into a situation changes the nature of that situation. People behave differently from the way they would if the camera were not there. How would you correct for that? Would you tape them (in spite of their changed behavior) and use the tape anyway? Would that be ethical? Would you hide the camera? That, of course, would be clearly unethical—in most situations. But what would you do?

Some problems with camera coverage derive from the conception held by news personnel of **how it should be shot.** Warren Breed[4] once noted that novice newspaper reporters adopt news practices not from perceptions of audience needs but from what older newsroom hands do and say. It was the same in television news, including production of spot news reports and documentaries. News film and documentary producers put together products that *looked* good. In the process, they used production and editing techniques that did not necessarily depict exactly the way the event had happened. They did this not to distort or alter reality but because that was the way they had learned to produce news film and documentaries. The results often came as a shock to those who had been filmed. The film would appear on television, and subjects would see themselves seeming to say or emphasize things they had not intended, commenting on things they had never seen, arguing with people they had never met.

Television's **ability to alter reality** was noted as early as 1952.[5] However, it was not until 1967 that this ability assumed the proportions of a public issue. During the 1960s, American news media reported on the civil rights movement, riots, assassinations, and the war in Vietnam. Angered and frustrated by such reports, certain politicians and segments of the public began to look askance at the media carrying these reports, particularly television. In 1968, television provided pictorial coverage of demonstrations and events surrounding the Democratic National Convention in Chicago. Charges were leveled that coverage was biased and unfair, that news reports had been staged and distorted through editing. Subsequently, similar charges were made against a number of television documentary projects (Section 8.4). As a result, most television news and documentary personnel have become sensitized to production techniques that they had previously taken for granted; the networks and many stations have instituted policies to eliminate deceptive use of production techniques.

A final problem involves the charge that television news is **more show business than news.** In the past, critics made the case that television management, striving for high news ratings, has emphasized entertainment values at least as much as news values in news operations. Television personnel even refer to newscasts as news "shows." Television trade and news leaders have responded that theirs is a legitimate journalistic endeavor, albeit limited in comprehensiveness and depth compared with, say, a large city daily newspaper. Then along came the **news consultants,** and the trade blew its whole argument as licensees and managers stumbled over each other in efforts to turn their newscasts into the prettiest, warmest, fuzziest, most likable (and, therefore, most highly rated) news "show" in town.

In the early 1970s, competition for local-news audiences became so keen that some stations hired news consultants to boost ratings. Many in TV news felt the consultants' suggestions emphasized cosmetic changes— use of youthful and attractive anchor reporters with little or no actual reporting experience; light and humorous banter ("happy talk") among anchor personnel; emphasis on stories with pictorial coverage, even when content might be inconsequential; inclusion in the newscast of more human interest (soft news) stories; weather reporters with a shtick as well as a forecast. Often, experienced station news personnel resented the consultants, saying their changes degraded journalistic integrity of news.

8.2 RADIO NEWS

Radio station news efforts vary greatly from station to station. At one extreme is the profitable service-oriented station with five or more full-time news and public affairs staffers. At the other extreme is the station that runs no news at all, in the belief that radio deregulation (Section 8.4) lifted the "burden" and "intrusiveness" of even a minimal news operation. Just above this is the station whose sole news effort is its rock network's one-minute "newscast" each hour. Or the **rip 'n' read** operation, where the disc jockey on duty runs to the wire service machine, rips off the latest five-minute news summary, runs back to the control room before the record ends, and then—without even looking over the copy first—opens the microphone and reads the latest news "from the news room of KXZX" or wherever.

Many stations fall somewhere in between. Let's look at a hypothetical small-market station with a full-time news staff of two. Although we call these staffers *reporters*, each actually fills additional roles as producer, editor, writer, and newscaster. A typical day might start at 5:00 a.m. The early-shift reporter arrives at the station before sign-on to prepare for a group of extended newscasts— 10 to 15 minutes each—starting at 6:30 and scheduled several times through wake-up and morning drive time. There may even be a **news block** of 30 to 60 minutes starting at 7.

First, the reporter **clears the wire.** The reporter examines the copy that the AP or UPI wire machine has printed and *pulls* (separates for immediate use) the most recent hard news. Other material—sports, features, stock reports, commodity prices—is filed for later use. If the station is not a network affiliate, the reporter prepares local, state, national, and international news; if it is an affiliate of a network with full-service news, the network covers national and international news, and the reporter concentrates on state and local.

A station may have more than one wire service and network. For example, in addition to AP or UPI and a national network, some stations subscribe to a financial news wire and affiliate with a state news network. Also, AP and UPI produce extensive audio services that carry both regularly scheduled newscasts and feeds of **actualities** (voices of people involved in a news event) for use in locally originated newscasts.

The reporter **checks other news sources.** There may be audiotape cartridges made the evening before that could be used on the morning newscast—local reports telephoned to the station, local news makers' statements or comments, special network **news feeds** (reports by network personnel sent as individual news stories to stations for use in locally originated newscasts).

The morning newspaper is checked. If it contains late-breaking local news on which the station has no information, the reporter *may*—although the practice is ethically and legally questionable—rewrite the story in broadcast news style directly from the newspaper and use it on the air.

Then the reporter makes telephone calls (Figure 8.5)—to the police station, sheriff's office, hospital, U.S. Weather Service, highway patrol, and any other institutions that might have had overnight activity that is newsworthy—the university, the U.S. Coast Guard, the army base, and so forth. During the telephone calls, the reporter sometimes records (with permission) the voice of the respondent for playback on the air; other times the information is simply jotted down.

After gathering all available, pertinent news material, the reporter **assembles the**

Figure 8.5 Radio newsroom. Inside reporters use telephones to track down stories and record sound bites. These are two of the work stations in the newsroom of WRUF and WRUF-FM, Gainesville.

newscast. Some items are standard features every morning and are automatically included—the commodity report, the farm report, the extended weather report. In hard news, however, decisions must be made as to which stories will be included and how much time to devote to each one. The newscast format allows a preset amount of time, and the reporter must select and prepare news, based on news value judgments, to fit within that time.

News material must be **processed** for use. Processing varies from **editing** (adding or subtracting a word here and there, deleting a sentence or two) a wire service story to writing a local story from scratch and preparing a tape actuality for playback as part of the story.

After the stories have been processed and the newscast is assembled, the reporter **confers with the audio technician** or disc jockey on duty. Both reporter and technician have **format sheets** that indicate when and how long each part of the newscast is to be— the weather, the local news, the commercials, and so on. Both have done this together many times, every weekday morning. Hence, the conference is less a matter of how to do the newscast than of what is unusual or different from the norm today. If the technician handles technical duties during the newscast, the reporter hands over tapes for playback on cue. A well-equipped station, however, will have a small studio set aside just for news, complete with audio control board and tape playback, and the reporter can engineer the newscast.

At the scheduled time, the reporter **goes on the air.** Although they are in separate rooms, technician and reporter can see each other through a window of soundproof glass. They exchange hand signals to communicate information such as when to start news tapes and when commercials are almost over.

Between newscasts, the reporter **updates** (rewrites to include new information) some stories, deletes some, adds others. After the heavy early-morning schedule of newscasts, the reporter has only two-minute hourly news summaries to prepare until the next extended newscast at noon.

After a well-deserved cup of coffee, the reporter begins **gathering local news.** A number of **sources and tools** are available. The handiest is the telephone, and the reporter makes liberal use of it, calling news makers for comments (to be recorded and aired), calling for background information, confirming news tips and leads. The reporter may call and record on-the-spot reports by colleagues at stations in other cities, when big state or regional stories break in those cities.

The newsroom may contain radio receivers that monitor police, fire, and other emergency frequency bands so the reporter will know when and where something happens as soon as it happens. Stories may be telephoned in by **stringers,** people—often residents of outlying communities or regions— whom the station pays on a per-story basis to be part-time reporters. Listeners may call in tips on news stories.

The publicity and public information offices of various institutions mail, bring, or call in material they hope the station will use. Some is legitimate news; some, puff pieces or self-serving propaganda. Individuals and organizations send or call in notices of meetings, elections, actions, stands taken, and press conferences.

Sometimes groups of commonly owned stations share exclusive news stories and coverage among themselves; a large station group may even maintain its own news bureaus in key cities. Finally, the station monitors the competition, checking other radio stations, television news, and newspapers for leads on major local stories.

Notice of a coming event is filed in a **future folder.** There are 31 such folders, numbered consecutively for days of the month. Each day's folder is examined to see what news conferences, meetings, and special events are scheduled. This is where a second reporter comes in handy. Usually, a radio reporter uses the telephone to cover most **beats** (places where news often originates, which are checked on a frequent, periodic basis, for example, city hall and the police station). Nonetheless, someone has to attend, physically, the school board meeting, the mayor's press conference, and the senator's address at the Rotary Club. With a second reporter going on duty at midmorning to cover outside events, the first reporter can stay at the station, run the newsroom, prepare newscasts, and receive and record telephone reports from the second reporter for use on the air.

When the first reporter goes off duty, the operation reverts to semi-rip 'n' read. The announcer reads wire-service copy until the second reporter returns to the station to prepare the afternoon drive-time newscast. If there is no second reporter, afternoon and evening newscasts are network-only or rip 'n' read. Night events, if covered, require overtime or juggling of schedules.

8.3 TELEVISION NEWS

Addition of the visual element makes television news much more complex than radio news. Whereas in radio news one or two people may do everything, television news usually requires more people and more specialization.

8.3.1 Local Television News

We shall look at the news operation of a hypothetical typical television station in a market of, say, 150,000 to 300,000 homes. News operations for larger and smaller stations and for cable system news departments constitute variations—elaborations and truncations—on this theme.

The head of the department is the **news director,** usually a television news specialist by training and experience. The news director sets policy for and acts as overall supervisor for news activities and personnel. The **producer** is in charge of a news program and decides what news stories go on, how long they are, and in what order they are presented.

The **assignment editor** designates personnel to cover specific stories. **Reporters** are the station's on-the-spot observers and explainers. They cover stories, interview people, write reports, supervise camera crews, and appear in taped spot coverage. A **camera crew** usually consists of a reporter, a camera operator, and sometimes an audio technician. **Videotape editors** help prepare, trim, and arrange visual reports for the newscast.

Writers (Figure 8.6) take material from various news sources and type them into script form, to assigned length, and in the writing style preferred by the station. They write the script to include instructions on how and when live location shots, videotape, electronic still frames, slides, and other pictorial materials are to be used.

Newscasters or **anchor reporters** narrate the newscast on the air, reading the script and tying together the various visual and aural elements of the program. Separate staffs prepare sports and weather news, often with a graduate meteorologist in charge of the latter. There may be additional news employees—clerical and research personnel, drivers, SNG operators, and even pilots of helicopters and light planes.

News sources are basically the same as those for radio. Tips and leads come from the public and competitive media. Stories and visuals (stills, tape, satellite feeds) come from the station's own news staff, special network feeds, news syndication services, stations in other towns, stringers, public relations offices of private and public institutions, and station group news bureaus. In addition to

Figure 8.6 Television station newsroom. Midmorning in the WJXT newsroom, and writers work at their CRTs preparing stories for the upcoming newscast. Looks are deceptive— television newsrooms usually appear chaotic, but they produce smooth, polished newscasts. Television newsrooms are mechanisms that require frequent lubrication with copious supplies of coffee and soft drinks, as is evident from the many cups in this picture, from the foreground all the way to the back wall. (Photograph courtesy of WJXT.)

the broadcast news wire machines of both AP and UPI, the station may have the AP and UPI newspaper wires, special sports wires, a financial wire, photo transmission wires, weather wires, and city news service wires.

The time actually available for news in a newscast is absolute; it cannot be stretched or compressed. The producer, therefore, prepares a news **lineup** (Figure 8.7). All news material available or due is reviewed. Each item is judged by standard news values, whether there are pictures to go with it, and how it would fit in the program for maximum appeal. Then specific items are chosen for inclusion on the newscast. They are put into a certain order and assigned running times. This is the news lineup.

Using the news lineup, writers put to-

gether the stories. They type scripts into the computer, work with reporters and tape editors, and select other visual materials from slides and electronic still frames. As stories are completed, the producer calls them up on a monitor screen and adds them to the master script being assembled in the computer. The producer adds instructions on each page, where appropriate, indicating such directions and procedures as which newscaster is to read the story and when to lead into or out of a commercial. Meanwhile, the videotape editor is preparing all tape stories so they can be called up on the newscast in sequential order. Slides and other visual elements are stacked in order. During this time, the newscasters have been reading over and rehearsing the script (Box 8.1).

Finally, the deadline arrives. Copies of the

NewsCenter 2

DATE _____ TIME __12P__ PRODUCER _____

CAMERA	PAGE	TALENT	VISUAL	SLUG		VIDEO	AUDIO	TIME
	1	AC		HEADS: MTA, COOKING		EJ'S	VOT	:15
	2			BREAK AND OPEN		ACR	ACR	1:40
	3	AC	IRIS:MTA	MTA RADIO DEBATE	11PM	EJ	VO/SOT	1:30
	4	AC		HIGH SPEED RAIL	AP	NC	NC	:25
	5	AC		HIGH SCHOOL REZONING	11PM	EJ	VOT	:30
	6	AC	IRIS:DEATH PENALTY	DEATH PENEALTY VOTE	AP	NC	NC	:30
	7	AC		MACHINE GUN SALES	NET	EJ	SOT	1:30
	8	AC		SOVIET SPACE WALK	NET	EJ	VOT	:30
	9	AC		SOVIET-AID		NC	NC	:15
	10	AC		TX WX/FADE		NC	NC	:05
	11			BREAK #1		ACR	ACR	1:40
	12	AC/DS	MONITOR	WEATHER		WP/DB	LIVE	2:00
	13	DS/AC	MONITOR	TAG/TX SPORTS		NC	NC	:10
	14			BUMP SPORTS		ACR	SOT	:10
	15			BREAK #2		ACR	ACR	2:00
				MORE ⟶				

Figure 8.7 News lineup. Each element of the news program is assigned a sequential number; that is the figure in the "page" column. The "talent" column contains the initials of the individual(s) in the studio who will introduce or report news items. "Visual" lists accompanying pictorial matter. The "slug" is the "title" at the top of the script page that describes the news item's content (Figure 8.10). The "video" and "audio" columns identify sources for sound and picture. "Time" gives the length of each element. The program director uses the leftmost column to plan and mark assignment of studio cameras to the various elements of the program.

Box 8.1 The Noon News at Channel 2

These are the activities at WESH-TV, the NBC affiliate for Orlando–Daytona Beach, just moments before the 12 o'clock newscast. (a) The producer (back to camera) finishes last-minute details. The program's director (right) marks her copy of the script. The glass wall in front of the video monitors (right background) shows a reflecton of other parts of the newsroom. (b) Just moments before the program begins, Andrea Coudriet, anchor reporter, studies and marks her script. In the background, the floor manager walks by toward her crew position. (c) Cue her! The floor manager receives the command from the director through the intercommunication headset she wears and signals Andrea to begin. (The lens of the camera that made this photograph was adjusted to the relative darkness *behind the cameras* so that details of the cameras and crew would be visible; that is why the background appears overlighted or washed out.)

(a)

(b)

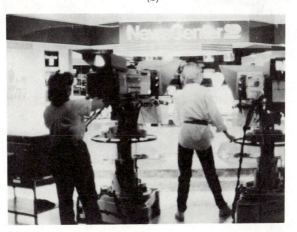

(c)

script are printed and distributed to the producer, the newscasters (Box 8.2), the director of the newscast program, and key members of the production crew. Tapes go to the videotape operator, still pictures are loaded in the frame store (Section 12.2.7), and captions are created on the character generator.

The director marks the script with standard directing cues (Box 8.3) and checks to ensure that all elements are in place and ready to go. At the instant the newscast is to begin, master control gives the go-ahead, and the director starts the program. As with the radio newscast, the television news team and the production crew have used the same format for so long that actual production (Box 8.4) is second nature, a matter of plugging each day's script into the routine.

8.3.2 Network Television News

Broadcast network television news programs are put together much like those at local stations. Their emphasis, of course, is on national and international news. The networks' news operations include bureaus at key cities across the nation and around the world. Pictorial coverage from these bureaus is transmitted by satellite to the New York studios. Evening showcase network news programs do not include sports and weather news on a regular basis.

Cable news services rely heavily on up-to-the-minute news and video, with live video feeds whenever possible. They operate continuously, 24 hours per day. Much like the broadcast networks, CNN operates an extensive system of domestic and foreign bureaus. CNN also picks up international material from video news services and stringers and domestic material from television stations with which it has reciprocity agreements.

As mentioned earlier, the two C-SPAN channels operate differently. First, they are noncommercial. Second, their coverage of Congress (Section 7.4.2.4) exemplifies their significant departure from the very concept of television news; whenever possible, C-SPAN covers an event in its entirety, from beginning to end, with no interruptions or cutaways.

Headline News (Figure 8.8) focuses primarily on hard news in capsule form, using as much video as possible. During any particular half-hour, the anchor reporter may appear on camera as little as two minutes. Informational programmers such as Financial News Network and the Weather Channel concentrate on a particular type of news.

8.4 OTHER FORMS OF NEWS PROGRAMMING

Full-service news departments often produce not only newscasts but also other types of programs. These may include interviews, news panel programs, remote (on-the-spot) coverage, news specials, editorials and commentary, and documentaries.

Interviews are programs in which a news maker or knowledgeable person is questioned at length. If two or more people ask questions or answer them, the format is a **panel program.** NBC's long-running *Meet the Press* is an example of the former; PBS's *Wall Street Week,* the latter. A panel program may also feature a group of people discussing a subject among themselves, often with a moderator. PBS's *Washington Week in Review* is an example.

Remote coverage is live transmission from the scene of a news event. On-the-spot reporting of the national political conventions; the Watergate hearings of 1973; the space shots of the late 1960s; the space shuttle landings of the 1980s; the funerals of John Kennedy, Robert Kennedy, and Martin Luther King, Jr.; the presidential debates of 1976 and succeeding campaigns—all are examples of remote news coverage.

Box 8.2 Why They Don't Often Look at the Script

They use prompters in front of the camera lenses. A prompter is a closed-circuit television system that feeds an image of a large-print version of the script to small video monitors, one of which is attached to each of the television cameras. A one-way reflecting glass mounted in front of the camera lens reflects the images from the monitor like a mirror. The image is not visible from the lens side of the glass, so the camera shoots through it as if it were not there. But a newscaster looking at the camera sees the image of the script. The script "scrolls" upward on the monitor as the newscaster reads, its speed controlled by the operator. This device allows the newscaster to read and deliver the news by looking directly (and sincerely) at the camera during the newscast, glancing down at the desk copy of the script only occasionally and for effect. (a) The operator (left) gets ready to put the script on the lighted horizontal stage (left center). Just above the stage are two lamps. Just to the right and above the lamps, a small, vertically mounted TV camera points down toward the light stage. At right, the bottom video monitor will show the script, allowing the operator to see what the newscaster sees and control the speed of the scrolling script. The top monitor will show the program video. Through the window (center) is a view of the news studio. (b) Close-up view of the stage (lower left) with a script on it, the words of which can be seen in the monitor on the right. Above the stage are the lamps. Look carefully for the camera's fixed-focus lens between the lamps, about one-quarter down from the top of the picture. (c) The newscaster (left) can look straight at the camera to read the script. The floor director stands between cameras so the newscaster can see cues without looking off-camera.

(a)

(b)

(c)

Box 8.3 TV News Script: Deciphering the Director's Copy

Each news story is typed on a different page. The writer, Vihlen, has slugged the story at upper left, indicating that it deals with the mayor and has videotape (V-T) as part of the story. The writer has also indicated that during the opening of the story, the newscaster should be seen in front of a picture of the city hall. The newscast producer has noted that the story contains 13 lines (not counting the single-word lines) which, at a reading speed of 2 seconds per line, add up to 26 seconds. The videotape lasts 31 seconds for a total of 57 seconds on the story. The big ''3'' in the upper left means that the story will be the third one reported on the newscast. Newscaster Ball will read the story, and (as noted at the bottom), Wekerle will read the next story. The director has marked the script, too. The story will open on camera 3 with camera 6 (in a film chain) on the city hall slide matted in behind. Videotape rolls on the term ''four-year,'' and the director dissolves to videotape on the word ''finances.'' During the tape, the director readies camera 2 with a close-up of Ball and, at the end of the tape, dissolves to 2. As Ball wraps up the story, the director readies camera 4 with a shot of Wekerle, who will read the next story and, on Ball's last word, takes (cuts to) camera 4.

Box 8.4. Those Weather Graphics Are Really *Not* on That Back Wall

The weather reporter appears on-screen in front of a huge map on the wall, periodically turns to and looks at the map, and points out things we should notice about the weather patterns. That map is replaced by other huge graphics—another map, satellite pictures of the continental cloud cover, a summary of the five-day weather forecast—and the reporter looks at and works with each of them in turn. How do they change those graphics so fast? Actually, that wall behind the weather reporter is blank. The graphics are electronically generated stills, prepared in advance, stored in a frame store (Section 12.2.7), then called up by the director according to cues in the script. The director uses an electronic effect called a *matte* to superimpose the camera image of the reporter over the electronic graphic. While appearing to look at the back wall, the reporter is actually viewing an off-camera video monitor showing the composite picture, the reporter-over graphic. By watching that monitor, the reporter can tell where to stand so as not to block vital information from the audience's view and where to point. The director switches background graphics instantaneously simply by calling the next still from the frame store.

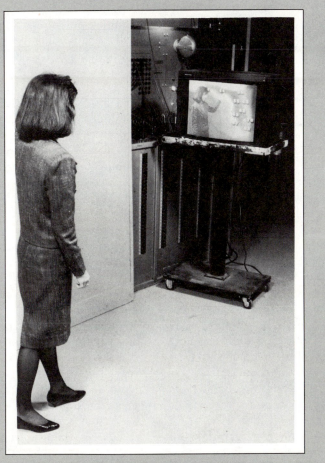

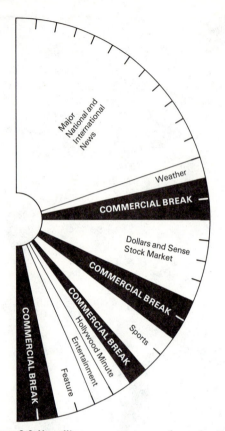

Figure 8.8 Headline news program format. This Turner Broadcast news service operates on a 30-minute cycle. Each half-hour contains four segments.

News specials are coverage or programs that deviate from the regular schedule. As such, they may include interviews, panel programs, remotes, election returns, and wrap-ups or summaries of important stories, as well as a group of correspondents evaluating and discussing a news event.

Commentary and **editorial** are expressions of opinion. The word "editorial" carries the connotation of taking a for or against position, of being more hard-hitting than commentary. Networks and cable news services label most expression of opinion as commentary. Some local news operations air true editorials, usually on local issues and delivered by the news director or the general manager. Most do not editorialize; they either just do not care or they fear that editorials could alienate advertisers and the community. Many broadcasters said they did not editorialize because of fairness doctrine implications (Section 15.3.4.1).

A **documentary** shows or analyzes an issue—for example, a news event or a social conditon—in nonfictional but dramatic form. Documentaries are primarily television programming. However, a few radio stations occasionally put together and air a news documentary. Broadcast networks and stations both air television documentaries. They range in length from minidocumentaries of 5 to 10 minutes to (rarely) two or more hours; most single "stand-alone" documentaries are 30 to 60 minutes long. Subject and approach vary.

Television minidocumentaries often run daily as a regular feature in a station's early evening newscast. Each may deal with a separate subject, or one subject may be serialized over several evenings. Each *60 Minutes*- and *20/20*-type program consists of several minidocumentaries. Some cable news service reports are actually minidocumentaries.

Television documentaries have generated public controversy and criticism. In the late 1960s, when politicians and others attacked general news practices (Section 8.1.5), television documentaries also came under fire. Congress investigated a number of network documentaries for bias and deception in production. Following that, the private sector took over. Gun clubs, food trade associations, a psychiatric professional association, and others attacked various documentaries during the 1970s. Accuracy In Media (AIM), a Washington-based organization, sprang up and devoted full time to searching for biased reporting on the networks, as well as in major East Coast newspapers and magazines.

Various tactics were used against documentaries—pressure on advertisers, publicity, civil suits for libel and trespass, complaints of fairness doctrine violation to the Federal Communications Commision (FCC). Normally, the FCC acts in such matters only if it has extrinsic (i.e., outside the documentary itself) evidence of deliberate distortion or staging involving a licensee or station management. However, in 1973, the FCC agreed with an AIM complaint that NBC's *Pensions: The Broken Promise* violated the fairness doctrine because it described only the negative side of private industrial pension programs. The commission told NBC to explain how it would rectify the situation. An appeals court, however, reversed the FCC's decision, saying opposing viewpoints do not have to be presented on the same program.[6]

Over the years, CBS faced a number of legal problems stemming from documentary efforts. Two involved former military officers and the Vietnam War. In 1969–1970, Anthony Herbert, a lieutenant colonel, received widespread media attention when he accused his superiors of atrocities and other war crimes. In early 1973, *60 Minutes* did a report on the matter. Herbert, now retired, sued, saying the report portrayed him as a liar. Herbert sought a court order to force the producer, Barry Lando, to submit to questioning. The questions would inquire into Lando's state of mind, his thoughts and reasoning as he had edited the program. In 1979, the U.S. Supreme Court ruled in favor of Herbert.[7] CBS won the *overall* libel case on appeal in 1986; the 1979 state-of-mind decision, however, remained as precedent.

In early 1982, CBS News broadcast *The Uncounted Enemy: A Vietnam Deception.* As a result, General William Westmoreland, former U.S. commander in Vietnam, sued CBS for $120 million, charging that the 90-minute documentary falsely implicated him in an alleged conspiracy to misrepresent enemy troop strength. The general dropped his suit in 1986.

Some entertainment programs masquerade as news documentaries or remote coverage of news events. They take the form and tone of news yet focus on subjects such as Al Capone's bank vault, the opening of an Egyptian tomb, or interviews with convicted murderers. This type of coverage is more accurately classified as *reality programming* (Section 6.4.1.6) than as news.

NOTES

1. R. H. Bruskin Associates, New Brunswick, NJ, completed the survey of 1012 adults (18 and older) in August 1982. CBS Radio had commissioned the study. Reported in "AM and FM listeners have a lot in common," *Broadcasting* 27 Sep. 1982: 81.
2. David J. LeRoy and Christopher H. Sterling, *Mass News: Practices, Controversies, Alternatives* (Englewood Cliffs: Prentice, 1972).
3. Peter M. Sandman, David M. Rubin, and David Sachsman, *Media: An Introductory Analysis of American Mass Communication* (Englewood Cliffs: Prentice, 1972).
4. "Social Control in the News Room? A Functional Analysis," *Social Forces* 33 (1955): 326–335.
5. Kurt Lang and Gladys Engel Lang, "The Unique Perspective of Television and Its Effect: A Pilot Study," reprinted in *The Process and Effects of Mass Communication*, ed. Wilbur Schramm and Donald F. Roberts (Urbana: U of Illinois P, 1971).
6. *NBC* v. *FCC*, 516 F.2d 1101 (1974 and 1975). The U.S. Supreme Court refused to review the decision (424 U.S. 910, 1976).
7. *Herbert* v. *Lando*, 441 U.S. 153 (1979).

FURTHER READING

Barnouw, Erik. *Documentary: A History of Non-Fiction Film.* Rev. ed. New York: Oxford UP, 1983.
Bennett, W. Lance. *News, the Politics of Illusion.* 2d ed. New York: Longman, 1988. Flaws; reality shaping.
Emery, Edwin, and Michael Emery. *The Press and America: An Interpretative History of the Mass*

Media. 5th ed. Englewood Cliffs: Prentice, 1984. History of U.S. news

Fang, Irving E. *Television News, Radio News.* 4th ed. St. Paul: Rada, 1985. How to do it, and what is needed.

Garrison, Bruce, and Mark Sabljak. *Sports Reporting.* Ames: Iowa State UP, 1985. How to do it.

Goldstein, Tom. *The News at Any Cost: How Journalists Compromise Their Ethics to Shape the News.* New York: Simon, 1985.

Hesse, Jurgen. *The Radio Documentary Handbook: Producing and Selling for Broadcast.* Vancouver: International, 1987. A how-to book.

Lewis, Carolyn D. *Reporting for Television.* Irvington: Columbia UP, 1984. Concentrates on local reporting.

MacDonald, R. H. *A Broadcast News Manual of Style.* White Plains: Longman, 1987. Formats, wire copy, usage, etc.

Madsen, Axel. *60 Minutes: The Power and the Politics of America's Most Popular TV News Show.* New York: Dodd, 1984. History of the program.

McCabe, Peter. *Bad News at Black Rock: The Sell-Out of CBS News.* New York: Arbor, 1987. *CBS Morning News* troubles.

Medoff, Norman J., and Tom Tanquary. *Portable Video: ENG and EFP.* White Plains: Knowledge, 1986.

Nimmo, Dan, and James E. Combs. *Nightly Horrors: Crisis Coverage in Television Network News.* Knoxville: U of Tennessee P, 1985. Case studies.

Shook, Frederick, and Dan Lattimore. *The Broadcast News Process.* 3d ed. Englewood: Morton, 1987. Text.

Stephens, Mitchell. *Broadcast News.* 2d ed. New York: Holt, 1986.

———. *A History of News: From the Drum to the Satellite.* New York: Viking, 1989.

Turow, Joseph. *Media Industries: The Production of News and Entertainment.* White Plains: Longman, 1984.

Weaver, J. Clark. *Broadcast Newswriting as Process.* White Plains: Longman, 1984. By noted late educator.

White, Ted, et al. *Broadcast News Writing, Reporting, and Production.* New York: Macmillan, 1984.

Wulfemeyer, K. Tim. *Beginning Broadcast Newswriting: A Self-Instructional Learning Experience.* 2d ed. Ames: Iowa State UP, 1984. Programmed workbook.

Yoakam, Richard D., and Charles F. Cremer. *ENG: Television News and the New Technology.* New York: Random, 1985.

CHAPTER 9

Commercials and Other Persuasive Announcements

Commercials. Everybody has something to say about them, mostly bad. But they work. And for those who pay for the sponsored programming which you listen to and view, that is good. It is almost impossible to show direct cause-effect relationships—that one buys a product *because* of a commercial. Still, the fact remains that increased sales follow effective radio and television advertising.

"Commercial" is short for *commercial announcement*, and we sometimes forget there are other kinds of announcements. In this chapter, we use *announcement* to include any (usually relatively) short unit of programming created to attract your attention in order to persuade you. We deal with the following aspects of announcements: types, creation (pitches, approaches, and production), criticism, praise.

9.1 TYPES

Announcements may be classified in several ways. Some of the more common classifications include the following: distribution medium, placement, length, purpose, marketing interest of advertisers, basis of payment, production medium, and method of production.

9.1.1 Distribution Medium

Commercial broadcast stations and **basic cable services** carry advertising.* Can we say that other forms of radio and television do *not*? For example, what about **noncommercial educational broadcast stations?** By legal definition, those stations may not run advertising. But, as discussed in Section 22.5, they do carry persuasive announcements, many of which bear a strong resemblance to commercials. In fact, there have been proposals to allow public stations to run commercials.

Generally, pay services do not run advertising. After all, that is one of the major reasons why we pay for such services—for uncut, advertising-free programming. But is

*Proposals for some direct-broadcast satellite (DBS) and wireless cable (multichannel TV; Section 5.4) systems have also included advertising support.

211

it really advertising-free? Look at pay service programming *between* movies and features. It consists of promotional announcements, advertising for upcoming programming and the service itself. True, it is self-advertising and runs between (rather than interrupting) program material. Nonetheless, it is advertising. Also, some sports-oriented pay services and pay-per-view sports telecasts *do* carry regular commercials.

9.1.2 Placement

When classified by placement, announcements may be divided into five types as follows: as programming, within sponsored programs, within participation programs, within barter syndication programs, and at major programming breaks.

9.1.2.1 Advertising Programs and Formats
In some cases, the advertising *is* the programming. An advertising program may sell one product or many different products. It may, for example, take the form of a half-hour program that extols the virtues of a home exercise machine. It could show up as a five-minute "infomercial" on nutrition or cooking "brought to you by" a manufacturer of food products. On the other hand, the direct-marketing program format (Section 7.4.2.3) and cable advertising channels both feature a variety of brands or advertisers. For many years, radio and television did not run long-form advertising (Section 9.1.3.3) except for political and campaign messages.

9.1.2.2 Sponsored Programs
Most other programs, by contrast, clearly separate advertising from program content into *availabilities* (places for announcements). In the sponsored program, all advertising pertains to a single sponsoring entity (two, if the program is cosponsored). A sporting goods store may sponsor a five-minute radio sports report on weekday evenings. An automobile company may sponsor a network television special to introduce its new models.

9.1.2.3 Participating Advertising
In participating advertising, each availability may contain an announcement for a different advertiser. Advertisers usually prefer to spread announcements over a number of different days and dayparts during the week, so participating advertising is the dominant form of radio and television advertising.

The form of advertising time buying varies with the medium. An advertiser who buys 100 availabilities on television or on network radio usually contracts for 100 **specific dates and times.** An advertiser who purchases 100 availabilities on a radio station usually buys **time periods;** the station decides exact times. For example, the radio advertising contract may specify that the purchased availabilities will all occur within two weeks and during a particular daypart (say, morning drive time) or scattered throughout the day—**ROS** (run of schedule), **BTA** (best times available), or **TAP** (also called *maximum impact*—a certain number to run in each of a number of different time periods).

Although not the norm, an advertiser can buy specific positions on a radio station (for an additional charge), buy ROS on a radio network, or sponsor a program on a radio station or network. The advertiser can also buy **rotations** on a television station. In rotations, an advertiser's commercial runs either at different positions in the same program every day (horizontal rotation) or in different programs during the same time period every day (vertical rotation).

At the local level, advertisers may "participate" on both syndicated and network programs. Programming from radio networks and advertising-supported national cable services contains **local windows** (availabilities) that affiliates may sell. Broadcast television network programs contain local availabilities, too, in some dayparts. One exception is prime time; here, the affiliate has little to sell except at programming breaks (Section 9.1.2.5).

Advertiser-supported basic cable networks sell time in much the same way as broadcast TV networks. Cable systems, however, sell time in terms and for rates similar to those of local radio.

9.1.2.4 Barter Syndication
Advertisers may place announcements on a barter or cash-plus-barter program in two ways. As explained in Section 7.3.2.1, such programs contain some advertising sold by the syndicator and some availabilities that the local programmer may sell. Therefore, an advertiser may deal with the syndicator or with the local programmer. The form is usually participating advertising.

9.1.2.5 Programming Breaks
Programming breaks consist of formal interruptions for local advertising during network television programming. They include **station breaks** and **middle break positions.** Station breaks are the announcement positions between programs; middle breaks are those within the temporary cut back to affiliates every 30 minutes during programs of one hour or longer. Advertisers pay hefty prices for program-break availabilities during prime time; viewing levels are high, and affiliates charge dearly. An advertising-supported national cable service normally does not draw nearly as large an audience as a broadcast network. Nonetheless, some cable systems charge higher prices for programming-break availabilities during prime time on the more popular services.

9.1.3 Length

When classified by length, announcements may be divided into three categories. These consist of 60 seconds and less, longer, and program length.

9.1.3.1 Sixty Seconds and Less
At one time, the normal length for radio and television announcements was **60 seconds.** Radio's standard length is still the 60, although more and more advertisers buy **30s.** Also available in radio are **20s** and **10s.**

The cost of television advertising, however, rose to expensive levels, and research seemed to show 30-second commercials to be about as effective as 60s. A shift to the shorter length started during the late 1960s, and television adopted the 30 as standard. You still see a few 60s, particularly on cable services and late at night on television stations. These are often direct-response marketing spots run as PIs (Section 9.1.6.5) or as a standing order for unsold availabilities, bought at the lowest possible rate (Section 17.3.6).

Television stations also offer a *limited* number of 10-second availabilities. Some are called **IDs** because they constitute the "extra" ten seconds immediately before the station identification during a station break or middle break. Normally, 10s cost about 50 percent of the price of a 30.

By 1990, however, another "standard" length emerged—the **15.** The cost of television advertising had continued to rise unabated. Some advertisers sought to save money by **piggybacking**; they would attempt to buy one availability and put in it short commercials for two different products. For example, if a 30 cost $100, the advertiser could run two 15-second commercials in a **split 30** for $100—the same price as two IDs. The Television Code of the National Association of Broadcasters (Section 16.2.1) prohibited piggybacking availabilities of less than 60 seconds, unless the pitches for the two products were integrated and appeared to be a single commercial. However, in 1984, with the Code barely one year in its grave, the unintegrated split 30 became a fact of life. Alberto-Culver, marketer of personal grooming products, had used various means (including an antitrust suit) to persuade the networks and several large-market station group owners to drop bans on the split 30. By 1987, all three networks sold **stand-alone 15**s (individual availabilities); by 1988, 15s accounted for one-third of all network commercials. The 15 was not yet *the* standard, but advertisers regarded it as an attractive alternative to the 30.

9.1.3.2 Longer Announcements Some announcements run longer than one minute. Some single-sponsor television specials, particularly certain fine-arts presentations, are of such a nature that the sponsor forgoes the usual number of interruptions, opting instead to let commercial announcements run at natural breaks in content—between acts, or at the end of a long piece of music. In these cases, the sponsor uses specially prepared commercials of 90 seconds or longer.

During election years, candidates for office sometimes use longer announcements. In presidential races, networks edit down scheduled programs (generally in prime time) to make time available for five-minute political announcements.

9.1.3.3 Program-Length Announcements Until the 1980s, responsible broadcasters did not air advertising programs for products and services. Some advertisers attempted to disguise their extended pitches as programs. These "program-length commercials" would interweave "program content so closely with the commercial message that the entire program must be considered a commercial."[1] For example, a group of garden supply dealers sponsor a program on home garden care, a program liberally sprinkled with mentions of the dealers' products. The Federal Communications Commission (FCC) banned such commercials, and the NAB Code said they were "not acceptable."

These length restrictions, however, applied to *broadcast* television. Cable had none. The cable trade touted its freedom to develop long-form commercials, to mix program and commercial content, as an advantage over broadcast television. Cable television, therefore, provided advertisers with the opportunity to develop and refine the program-length commercial or advertising program. "Infomercials," half-hour commercials, advertising channels, the home shopping format—all were nurtured on cable.

Prohibition against program-length broadcast commercials disappeared in the 1980s. The FCC, as part of an ongoing program of "deregulation" (Section 4.5.1), lifted its ban in 1984. The Television Code had died the year before. As a result, some television stations air programs; some, advertising formats.

9.1.4 Purpose

The purposes of announcements can be divided into four broad categories. These categories are straight advertising, institutional advertising, issue advertising, and corrective advertising.

9.1.4.1 Straight Advertising A straight advertising announcement is one whose ultimate aim is to have you do something that will supposedly benefit someone—you, someone else, or both. Many persuasive advertising announcements contain a direct call for action. These include commercials that try to get you to purchase some product or service, political advertising that urges you to vote a particular way, public service announcements (PSAs) that ask you to donate time or money, and promotional announcements (promos) that urge you to tune to the advertised programs.

Some announcements do not contain a direct call for action but instead attempt to create awareness, promote understanding, shape attitudes, or enhance recall. However, the ultimate aim of many such announcements is still to get you to do something, and thus they may be included in our definition. For example, during the 1970s, the Advertising Council (Section 9.4) developed television PSAs that showed an American Indian shedding a tear over litter and pollution. Their immediate purpose was to create awareness that we each play a role in the quality of the environment with the slogan, "People start pollution. People can stop it." Ultimately, of course, this PSA asked us to put trash in receptacles, commute by car pool or public transportation, and take other actions to reduce environmental abuses.

9.1.4.2 Institutional Advertising The aim of institutional advertising is to enhance a company's image, that is, the general public's concept of the company. In other words, institutional advertising attempts to make you feel a certain way toward the advertiser. As an example, in the wake of the 1973–1974 fuel shortage, prices for gasoline and other petroleum products rose. At the same time, major oil companies ran television commercials, not to sell gasoline, but to show what they were doing to alleviate the shortage—offshore drilling, construction of the Alaska pipeline, and research into alternative forms of fuel. Several years later, American Telephone and Telegraph (AT&T) tried to dispel its image of a faceless, corporate bureaucracy. AT&T's "Hello America" television commercials depicted the company as a group of smiling employees whose only concern was to make America's telephone system the best in the world. More recently, Dow Chemical commercials have encouraged young people to "do great things."

9.1.4.3 Issue Advertising In issue advertising, the advertiser pays for broadcast time to expound one side of an issue. In the past, issue advertising sometimes resulted in fairness doctrine (Section 15.3.4.3) problems. For example, Esso (which later changed its name to Exxon) paid for and NBC ran the commercials on the Alaska pipeline mentioned above (Figure 9.1). Environmental groups filed a fairness doctrine complaint

1. GRANDFATHER: So what are you doing at Dow these days, Peggy?

2. GRANDDAUGHTER: Well, right now, I'm working in agricultural research, Grandpa.

3. We're trying to help farmers find new ways to make every dollar work harder.

Figure 9.1 Institutional advertising. Frames from the "Farm" commercial of the series "Dow lets you do great things." (Courtesy of the Dow Chemical Company)

about the Esso spots. NBC maintained the commercials were institutional advertising, but the FCC ruled that they presented one side of the controversial issue of the pipeline's ecological impact in Alaska and thus were subject to fairness doctrine obligations.[2]

9.1.4.4 Corrective Advertising The goal of corrective advertising is to set the record straight concerning previous advertising. Corrective advertising is a regulatory device used by the Federal Trade Commission (FTC). If the FTC finds certain advertising to be false or misleading, it may seek a consent order by which the advertiser promises to devote a certain percentage of its advertising expenditures for a certain period of time to corrective advertising.

The first such advertisers were ITT Continental Baking Company in 1971 and Ocean Spray Cranberries, Inc., in 1972. Both ran television commercials as part of their corrective advertising. ITT Continental had allegedly touted its Profile bread as a dietary product and so agreed to advertise that Profile had about the same number of calories per ounce as other breads. Ocean Spray had said that its cranberry juice cocktail had more "food energy" than orange juice or tomato juice; its corrective advertising made clear that food energy was not protein and vitamins but calories.

The FTC won judicial sanction for corrective advertising in 1978. Three years earlier the commission had ordered Warner-Lambert Co. to state in future advertising that its Listerine mouth wash would not help prevent colds or sore throats as previously advertised. Warner-Lambert appealed. In 1978, a federal appeals court ruled in favor of the FTC and thereby upheld the commission's authority to order corrective advertising.[3] Listerine advertising, including broadcast commercials, had to contain the message, "Listerine will not help prevent colds or sore throats or lessen their severity" until the

company had spent $10 million in advertising.

At one time, the FTC attempted to create yet another announcement category—the **countercommercial.** The FTC proposed *counteradvertising* to the FCC as an extension of the fairness doctrine; consumer groups would have the right of access to radio and television to present negative aspects of advertising claims. In 1974, the FCC rejected the idea of countercommercials, and therefore they have never been run as such on television and radio.

9.1.5 Advertiser

Announcements may be classified by marketing interest or scope of advertiser. These classifications include local, network, barter, spot, and cooperative advertising.

9.1.5.1 Local Advertising Local advertising aims at people living in the advertiser's community. The owner of a hardware store, a hairdresser, or a restaurant advertises on local broadcast and cable channels to reach local consumers.

9.1.5.2 Network Advertising An organization that has some product or service used by all types of people and distributed nationwide would probably wish to place advertising on one or more of the national networks—broadcast and cable. Almost everyone brushes teeth, drinks beverages, and uses soap, so manufacturers of such products buy advertising on networks to reach large, nationwide audiences.

9.1.5.3 Barter Advertising In barter advertising, a company pays to have its commercial announcements run on a barter or a cash-plus-barter program (Section 7.3.2.1). The syndicator tries to place the program in every market, so barter advertising appeals to firms that offer widely used, nationally marketed goods and services.

9.1.5.4 Spot Advertising

The same types of firms that use network and barter advertising may also use spot advertising. In national spot, the advertiser "spots" commercials around the country by choosing specific media outlets, programs, and time periods that deliver the desired audience. A household detergent manufacturer may, in addition to network advertising, use national spot to get commercials on radio stations, television programs, and cable channels whose audiences have high percentages of women.

National firms with specialized products and regional advertisers also use spot. A tractor manufacturer, for example, places advertising in markets where it reaches many farmers. A brewery whose beer is available only in a three-state area advertises only within that area. In both cases, network advertising would be inefficient, reaching too many people, and local advertising would reach too few.

Vertically programmed cable services (Section 7.4.2.1) could pose a threat to national spot business. Consider, for example, a cable network that specializes in health programming, aiming at people concerned with health and fitness across the country. A marketer of vitamins would pay less money and encounter less paperwork if it advertised on such a network rather than using national spot. (Choice of advertising media, however, involves additional factors; the advertiser still might have to use national spot.)

9.1.5.5 Cooperative Advertising

Cooperative (co-op) advertising combines spot and local advertising. In co-op, the local dealer buys advertising. The ad features the product of a national firm and ties it to the local dealer; for example, "Gant shirts are available at Silverman's, downtown." The manufacturer then shares the cost of the advertising time with the retailer.

9.1.6 Payment

Announcements are classified by payment to the medium. Categories include rate card, cut rate, sustaining, make-good, per inquiry, barter, plugola, promotional announcements, and payola.

9.1.6.1 Rate Card

A rate card is a published list of a medium's charges for advertising time (Section 18.1), including discounts and other price differentials. In most cases an advertiser pays rate card prices for a commercial.

9.1.6.2 Cut Rate

Some media sell **off the card**—that is, below their published rates—an ethically questionable practice (Section 18.1.3). In such cases, the advertiser is said to pay a "cut rate."

9.1.6.3 Sustaining

The medium receives no payment for running a sustaining announcement. This category includes, for example, most PSAs.

9.1.6.4 Make-Good

A medium will reschedule a paid announcement that does not run correctly—that runs, for example, distorted, at the wrong time, not at all, or with some element missing. The medium does this to "make good" the problem; the advertiser does not pay for the rescheduling.

9.1.6.5 Per Inquiry

In per inquiry (PI) (Figure 9.2), the advertiser pays the medium based on the number of responses to the PI announcement. PIs include, for example, most of those 60-second commercials that give a toll-free number on which to order knives, pots, food steamers, or three-record

Figure 9.2 Per inquiry. The how-to-order frame. (Used by permission.)

albums of the greatest hits in gospel or country or oldies rock. Each medium has a different telephone number and receives payment according to the number of viewers who order on its number.

9.1.6.6 Barter In barter, the advertiser pays the medium in some form other than money. As a category, barter encompasses several forms of exchange. In one, the payment consists of goods or services. A cable system, for example, runs commercials for an office supply firm in exchange for new furniture; a television station runs commercials for a radio station in exchange for radio advertising. At the local level, this is **tradeout;** at the national level, **barter.** In **time banking,** a national barter firm offers a radio or TV outlet the opportunity to obtain goods-and-services payment *before* running any advertising; the outlet then *owes* the firm availabilities.

In another variation, the payment consists of programming. This includes **barter syn-**

dication and **time banking syndication** (Section 7.3.2.1).

9.1.6.7 Plugola In plugola, a program includes a *plug*—a free boost or advertisement for a product or service. The "advertiser" pays the *individual* who slipped in the plug, a performer, writer, director, or someone else affiliated with the program's creation. Neither audience nor medium is aware of the payment. Plugola is illegal.

9.1.6.8 Promotional Announcement A thin line divides a promotional announcement from plugola. With a promotional announcement, however, the *medium* receives payment and *is* aware of the announcement. Television game shows contain examples. Appearance and description of the prizes are plugs. Donation of prizes (and sometimes even additional compensation to the programmer for using them!) is payment. Phrases such as "Prizes, courtesy of . . ." and

"Promotional fees paid by . . ." identify the donors. Promotional announcements are often *not* based on rate card prices.

9.1.6.9 Payola Payola is payment by a record company to a disc jockey for playing the company's records. Again, neither audience nor station is aware of the payment. Plugola and payola are both illegal and unethical (Sections 3.2.3.3 and 4.3.1), but evidence of both surfaces from time to time.

9.1.7 Production Medium

Radio announcements may be **live,** on **tape,** or (rarely any more) on **record.** Sometimes an announcement will **combine** elements— for example, a co-op commercial produced on tape by the national manufacturer's advertising agency followed by a live *tag* giving the local dealer's name.

Television announcements may be (in descending frequency of use) on **videotape,** on **film,** on **slides, live,** or some combination. For example, a television co-op commercial might consist of a sound film featuring the manufacturer's product, followed by a slide displaying local dealer information with a booth announcer reading additional copy.

9.1.8 Production Mode

In radio, a **straight announcement** features an announcer reading copy, with no production frills. A **production announcement** mixes in effects, music, and multiple voices. On a **musical announcement** or jingle, one or more persons sing the advertising message. Many radio announcements combine elements of two or more production techniques.

In the television **on-camera talent** technique, the performer speaks and is in view; in the **voice-over,** the speaker does not appear on screen. Either technique may be used with realistic or nonrealistic action. **Realistic action** features real people. Nonrealistic action often takes the form of some kind of animation. **Animation** includes drawn cartoon characters, charts, and two-dimensional models with moving parts. It includes "real" but normally inanimate objects given life by **stop-motion** techniques—Pillsbury's Poppin' Fresh doughboy and various raisins, stomachs, and other commercial anthropomorphisms. Another production technique is to use a series of **still pictures.** And, of course, one commercial may combine several production techniques.

9.2 CREATIVITY IN ANNOUNCEMENTS

While marketing may claim to be a science, much of advertising is still art. The effectiveness of an announcement depends in large part on the creative elements that make it up—format, appeals, approach, production skill.

9.2.1 Formats

The format of an announcement is the way the message is presented. Formats include description, demonstration, problem, dramatic, spokesperson, testimonial, interview, suggestion, symbolic, and abstract.

9.2.1.1 Description In the description format the announcement simply *describes* the product. The description is phrased in terms, for example, of what the product can do for you, why your help is needed, what the product's properties are, or how it works.

9.2.1.2 Demonstration The demonstration format *shows* what the product is or does. The commercial shows, for example, how the product removes spots from clothing, how it coats the stomach, or what a one-dollar donation will do.

9.2.1.3 Problem The problem announcement poses a problem, preferably one with which the audience can identify, and shows how the product solves that problem. You must, for example, shop for a specific item; the solution: use the Yellow Pages, and let your fingers do the walking.

9.2.1.4 Dramatic The dramatic (also called *slice-of-life*) format is often based on a problem situation, too. But it sets up the problem within a miniature dramatic plot. Over the years, for example, we have watched dramatic commercials in which Mrs. Olson recommended Folger's coffee, Mr. Goodwin told youngsters to use Crest, and Mr. Whipple tried to prevent the squeezing of Charmin (Figure 9.3). In the late 1980s, we saw youngsters with personal problems and heard "Grandpa" Jimmy Stewart's voice offering Campbell's soup as a solution.

9.2.1.5 Spokesperson Some announcements take the form of a recognized spokesperson extolling a product's virtues. Ed Reimers, Ed McMahon, and Arthur Godfrey were for years associated with Allstate Insurance, Budweiser, and Lipton Tea, respectively. More recently, Bill Cosby has appeared on commercials for Jello; Telly Savalas, for Players Club; and John Houseman for Smith Barney (Figure 9.4).

9.2.1.6 Testimonial The testimonial format is autobiographical, allowing individuals to describe personal experiences with the product. The testimony may be given by a famous person, by experts, or by unknown citizens—or a combination, such as the "nurse and mother" who touts Pampers.

9.2.1.7 Interview The interview format features one person asking questions and another responding. Campbell Soup used a variation during the late 1970s on radio com-

(a)

Because Folger's has that "just right"...mmm,

(b)

Your teeth need extra protection, too. (SFX)

(c)

WHIPPLE: Ladies, please don't squeeze the Charmin.

Figure 9.3 Dramatic format. (a) Mrs. Olson recommends Folger's coffee. (b) Mr. Goodwin advises the use of Crest. (c) Mr. Whipple asks that Charmin not be squeezed. (Photographs courtesy of The Procter & Gamble Company.)

Figure 9.4 Spokesperson commercial format. The late John Houseman telling us "Smith Barney makes money the old fashioned way; they *earn* it." (Photograph courtesy of Smith Barney Harris Upham & Co., Inc. Used by permission.)

mercials that were recordings of an announcer telephoning homemakers and getting them to sing the Campbell theme song.

9.2.1.8 Suggestion   The suggestion format takes an oblique approach. Instead of emphasizing the product's merits, the commercial shows it being used in happy or desirable settings or otherwise associates it with a particular way of life. Before they were legislated off the air (Sections 15.3.1, 15.3.4.3), tobacco companies often advertised cigarettes this way. The Marlboro man and Salem's cool glades and icy springs sold many more packs than would any straightforward description of the benefits that derive from drawing smoke from a burning weed into the lungs. Coca-Cola has used this format cleverly and successfully (from "I'd like to teach the world to sing . . ." [Figure 9.5] to the Florida A&M University Marching Band) to sell its caramel-colored carbonated beverage.

Figure 9.5 Suggestion format.   Still photo from one of Coca Cola's original "I'd Like to Teach the World to Sing" commercials. (Courtesy of the Coca Cola Company.)

9.2.1.9 Symbolic The symbolic format uses analogy, representing traits of the product by featuring completely different objects. Animals have been particularly popular. In the 1960s, television commercials for the Dreyfus Fund showed a lion strolling through New York's financial district, finally jumping onto and becoming part of the company's logo, to represent the strength and solidity of that mutual fund. During the 1980s, cattle grew in popularity; for example, bulls appeared in commercials for Schlitz malt liquor and for Merrill Lynch (Figure 9.6).

9.2.1.10 Abstract A final production format could best be described as abstract. Unconventional editing, the synthesizer, digital effects, computer animation—all are utilized to produce acoustically or graphically offbeat announcements. Advertisers often employ the abstract format to appeal to younger audiences, to represent the product as innovative, to represent concepts and forces in abstract symbols. Exciting at first, use of this production style in countless music videos eventually made it almost a cliché.

9.2.2 Appeals

Appeals are implicit or explicit arguments used to get the attention of the audience. Most of us share certain psychological needs and wants, and an announcement plays on these. An insurance company's television commercial shows a family breadwinner ill or incapacitated and poses the question, "How well would your family be provided for if you were not able to work?" The commercial then urges that you be sure of such provision by taking out a policy with the company. The commercial targets your desire for security.

There are many ways to categorize the various motivational needs and urges to which broadcast commercials appeal. One

At Merrill Lynch, we know that size and strength can be very valuable...

(a)

ALL SING: No one does it like the Bull!

Figure 9.6 Symbolic format. (a) Merrill Lynch uses a bull in its "A Breed Apart" campaign, as typified here in the "China Shop" commercial. (b) Schlitz Malt Liquor also uses a bull, as shown here in its "Bachelor Party" commercial. (Photograph a courtesy of Merrill Lynch Co. Photograph b courtesy of The Stroh Brewery Company. Both used by permission.)

set of appeals is that listed by Heighton and Cunningham (see bibliography), which includes the following: **security, threat, sex, love and sentimental, humorous, convenience, curiosity, ego, hero worship, and sensory.** Usually, an emotional appeal by itself is an inadequate persuasive device; facts and arguments must be presented to support and augment the appeal.

9.2.3 Approaches

The approach is the way the appeal and its supporting data are presented. Approaches include straightforward, hard sell, direct humor, self-ridicule or understatement, direct comparison, and suggestion.

9.2.3.1 Straightforward
The most effective approach is often the simplest—straightforward. The straightforward approach features no yelling, no humor, no direct comparison, just persuasive arguments and data.

9.2.3.2 Hard Sell
A second approach—and one its adherents contend is particularly effective for brand name recall—is the hard sell. The hard sell is a high-pressure, unrelenting pounding at the audience with persuasive data and repetition. In hard-sell announcements the audio often sounds loud—even louder than most commercials—and there is a lot of copy read by the announcer. Television hard-sell announcements often flash key words and phrases on the screen as the announcer says them and pound home the sales point with simplistic diagrams and demonstrations.

9.2.3.3 Direct Humor
Another approach is to use direct humor. Over the years, Alka Seltzer has been particularly successful in using direct humor in television commercials. Alka Seltzer's "Stomachs," "Meatball Commercial" ("Mama mia, that's a spicy meatball!"), "I can't believe I ate that whole thing," "Try it; you'll like it"—all became classics of commercial humor. Humorous television commercials for Wendy's Old-Fashioned Hamburgers generated what developed into a national catch phrase—"Where's the beef?" (Figure 9.7). And Michael J. Fox in a reprise of the silent movies made getting a Pepsi almost as funny as a Charlie Chaplin short.

CUST. #3: Where's the beef?

Figure 9.7 Direct humor approach. This performance by the late actress Clara Peller recycled the phrase, "Where's the beef?" (*Source:* The Wendy National Advertising Program.)

9.2.3.4 Self-ridicule or Understatement
Closely related to direct humor is self-ridicule or understatement. Benson and Hedges ran a whole series of television commercials illustrating the disadvantages of smoking their long cigarettes—they bent or burned a hole when the smoker got too close to some object. This campaign continued in print long after cigarette advertising left the air in 1972.

9.2.3.5 Direct Comparison
Until the late 1960s, commercials for a product never mentioned the name of a rival product. Advertisers equated stimulus (brand name) with response (purchase). They assumed that if the audience saw or heard a competitor's name, that was free advertising for the competition. Comparisons were made between the advertiser's product and Brand X or "the other two leading manufacturers" or "greasy kid stuff." Most advertisers have abandoned this simplistic view of consumer psychology, and commercials do occasionally compare a product to its rival by name. Two of the best-known comparative-commercial series were those by Schick for its Flexomatic electric shaver, challenged by competitors before an advertising industry self-regulatory group

Figure 9.8 Direct comparison approach.   Pepsi won in this one. (Copyright PepsiCo, Inc., 1981. Reproduced with permission.)

(Section 16.2.2) in 1973, and those by Coca-Cola and Pepsi Cola (Figure 9.8), comparing the two rival beverages by taste test, which led to a comparative advertising battle in a number of markets in 1976.

9.2.3.6 Suggestion   A final approach is part and parcel of the suggestion format (Section 9.2.1.8). Here, the announcement features something intangible, often not an intrinsic part of the product. It suggests—without actually saying—that use of the product leads to the good life, or sexual attractiveness, or power and domination over others.

9.3 CREATION AND PRODUCTION

The history of an announcement begins with the origin of the advertising campaign of which the announcement is part. To illustrate, we posit a national advertising campaign, a fairly complex situation compared with, say, the corner hardware store advertising a special on the local radio station. The advertiser has secured the services of an advertising agency (Section 17.2.1) and established a budget for the campaign.

The agency first analyzes the product that is to be advertised. The analysis is a process of asking and answering questions about the product—for example, What is it? What does it do? What is better about it than its competitors? At the same time, the agency makes a similar analysis of the product's buyers—Who are they? What is their life-style? When do they buy? Where? This study is called **marketing research** and is carried on before, during, and after an advertising campaign.

After analysis of product and buyers, **advertising objectives** are formulated. Contrary to what we might think, advertising objectives do not aim toward goals such as increasing sales by 15 percent or share of the market by 5 percent. These are marketing goals. Advertising is certainly one means of working toward a marketing goal, but advertising objectives are stated in specific terms and reach toward communication goals, such as introducing a new product, suggesting new uses for an old product, or publicizing a new feature for an existing product.

After objectives are defined, **strategies** are planned to meet those objectives. Campaign strategies include at least the following: devising content and form of messages, choosing the target audience at which to aim the messages, and selecting media to deliver messages to the audience.

As a result of the first strategy, a **copy policy** (or **copy platform** or **campaign platform**) is developed. Copy policy guides the creation of advertising in all media; it states the theme or idea of the campaign, consumer appeals, and significant product characteristics.

The second strategy results in a **consumer profile.** This is a detailed analysis of the target audience by age, sex, life-style, buying habits, education, and other factors.

The third strategy, the **media strategy,** builds a **media profile** to match the consumer profile. The media profile is the selection of vehicles that will best deliver the message to the target audience—*this* kind of mailing list for direct mail; *that* type of magazine; newspapers and spot television in *these* areas; spot radio on *this* type of station in *those* markets; participating advertising during *that* time of day on network television or cable; sponsorship of *this* special on network, cable, or barter syndication.

The agency prepares the **campaign plan** for presentation to the advertiser client. The plan includes general advertising strategy and concepts as well as creative, media, and marketing recommendations. Storyboards, commercials, layouts, and copy are presented.

If the campaign is approved (usually with client-suggested changes), the **media-buying** phase begins. After careful study, the agency recommends specific media; in radio and television, this means particular stations, cable systems, broadcast networks, national cable services, times, and programs. Upon client approval, the agency prepares a final schedule and cost estimate. When the client signs the schedule, the agency negotiates contracts for purchase of advertising time.

Agency writers develop commercials. They work from the copy platform, the advertising objectives, the campaign role assigned to electronic media, and the product, its buyers, and other market data.

Storyboards and sometimes even *precommercials* are prepared for television commercials. *Fact sheets* may be prepared for certain radio stations. A **storyboard** is a depiction of what the finished commercial will look like. Similar to a comic strip in appearance, it represents each scene of the planned commercial with a small sketch, below which is typed dialogue, sound, and description of action.

A **precommercial** is an actual production of the commercial. However, it is done by the agency on its own videotape equipment and is not broadcast quality. The precommercial serves the same purpose as the storyboard—to help the client visualize what the commercial will look like—and is not used on the air.

A **fact sheet** is not a complete script but contains only key facts on the product or service. Fact sheets are supplied to radio personalities who are especially effective at ad-libbing commercials.

9.3.1 Radio Commercials

The entity that produces a radio commercial varies with the situation. In the local advertising of small markets and small retailers, the **radio station** often produces the commercial at no charge above that for broadcast time. For example, the owner of the corner hardware store might deal directly with station sales personnel; no agency is involved. The station staff writes and records the commercial, then plays it back as scheduled for broadcast; occasionally, the announcer on duty will read a commercial live each time.

Most large advertisers have commercials professionally produced on tape and sent to stations for use. In this case, the advertising agency either puts the job out for bids to production houses or handles the production itself.

A **production house** does all creative work. Often, this even includes the script, based of course on the copy platform and subject to agency and advertiser approval.

If done in-house, the script is written at the agency. A staff **producer/director** handles talent and creative arrangement—auditioning and hiring talent, contracting for original music, securing musicians and a music director. Completed, taped, client-approved commercials are duplicated, and copies are sent to radio stations.

9.3.2 Television Commercials

Before a commercial commences production, the client (the advertiser) must approve the storyboard. The advertising agency production supervisor then writes a **spec** (specification) **sheet** describing the commercial and its production requirements and puts the project out for bids to selected **production houses.** The production houses submit **bids,** statements of how much money they would need to produce the commercial. Usually, the agency accepts the low bid, subject to negotiation over certain cost factors.

Once the client has accepted the agency's bid recommendation, representatives from agency and production house meet to iron out preproduction details—set design, location, crew, talent, director. An agency representative is designated producer. Agency producer and contract director work closely

during the production phase. The commercial is completed during postproduction, the finished commercial is duplicated, and copies are sent to the networks, stations, cable systems, and other media selected for distribution.

At the local level, production may be handled by the **media outlet**—TV station, cable system, or whatever. Local outlets are usually eager to rent facilities at bargain prices (relative to the cost of large-market production houses). With local production, a commercial rarely has the same high quality and slickness as one produced by a large production house. However, for local advertising the savings may more than make up for the lack of slickness.

9.4 ADVERTISING COUNCIL

Established as the War Advertising Council in 1942, the Advertising Council reorganized under its present name after World War II. Its constituent and sponsoring organizations include major advertising and media trade groups. The Ad Council selects noncommercial organizations as clients, for which advertising campaigns are prepared as a public service. Advertising agencies volunteer their services to the Ad Council, and each volunteer agency is assigned a client for which to plan and execute a campaign. The client pays only for materials—art, engraving, printing, paper, tape, slides. The various media carry the campaign free. Materials may cost up to several hundred thousand dollars annually, but this out-of-pocket expenditure by a client yields millions of dollars worth of advertising and publicity. Ad Council campaigns have created memorable symbols and slogans (Figure 9.9)—Smokey Bear; Iron Eyes Cody, the Indian whose eyes brimmed with a single tear; A Mind Is a Terrible Thing to Waste. Some of radio and television's finest minutes have been Ad Council-produced PSAs.

(a)

(b)

(c)

Figure 9.9 Memorable symbols from the Ad Council. (a) For years, Smokey Bear reminded us that only we could prevent forest fires. (b) The Indian with a tear was part of an eloquent and poignant visual appeal to stop pollution. (c) ''He could be delivering crates instead of babies. A mind is a terrible thing to waste. Give to the United Negro College Fund.'' (Photographs courtesy of The Advertising Council, Inc. Used by permission.)

Stations and cable systems also produce PSAs. They run these for local charities and other good works.

9.5 CRITICISM

Commercials are the announcements most often criticized. This is understandable. In American radio and television, commercial announcements are ubiquitous, frequent, interruptive, repetitive, intense, unavoidable, packed with highly persuasive elements, and often the product of (what many see as) large, profit-at-any-cost businesses.

In print, the **audience** controls the situation. You choose whether, how much of, and when to read a newspaper or magazine ad-

vertisement. In radio and television, the *medium* controls the situation. Without a remote control or a VCR, you must endure *all* advertising on the channel you view. If you switch to another channel to avoid commercials, you find more commercials. If you turn off the set or leave the room, you miss the program.

Any feature that conspicuous and unavoidable on media as popular as radio and television is bound to come in for at least some criticism. A great deal of criticism is leveled at television commercials particularly, since television is the more popular and attention-getting medium.

Critics fault commercials for **lying,** for making claims for products and services that are not true. The commercial might, for example, misrepresent some features of the product or service. It might falsely describe the advertiser's financial situation or ability to do business. It might feature bait-and-switch advertising; the bait (often a bargain price advertised for a particular product) lures you into a store, whose personnel pull the switch (attempt to sell you a higher-priced model once you are there). Local and federal authorities, better business bureaus, and others bear down hard on false advertising, and there is relatively little outright lying on commercials.

Puffery, however, is another matter. Puffery denotes use of superlatives and general terms, such as "new," "improved," "better," "best." It is the half-lie, telling only the good points about a product or service, making good points even better, not mentioning negative aspects. Puffery traditionally formed the basis of most advertising. But in 1971, the Federal Trade Commission adopted a requirement that advertisers be able to substantiate claims about performance, quality, effectiveness, safety, or comparative price. No longer could the advertiser tout a product as "number one in performance" or "more effective than the three leading competitors" without defining terms and proving claims.

Somewhere between lying and puffery goes the **false demonstration.** Here, the commercial shows that a product has certain qualities, but special techniques are used during production to display these qualities. In other words, the product is not like or will not do exactly what the commercial purports to show. Two notorious false demonstrations took place on television commercials for Rapid Shave and Libbey-Owens-Ford auto-glass (Section 14.2.2).

Critics complain that commercials assume and aim at insultingly **low intellectual levels.** Wording, repetition, arguments, format—every element seems to patronize listener and viewer.

Many people object to the **salience** of commercials, their unavoidable conspicuous-

ness. At least three elements contribute to salience—number of interruptions per program, clutter, and loudness.

As for the **number** of commercials, there actually is a high ratio of commercial minutes to program time. The NAB Television Code allowed stations to program over 25 percent of every hour during most of the day in commercials, promos, and other nonprogram content. The Radio Code allowed advertising to constitute 30 percent of every hour, with provision for even more in special circumstances. The FCC adopted restrictions on commercial time that paralleled those of the NAB Codes. However, the Codes are gone and the commission repealed its restrictions, so the broadcast trade no longer has even these liberal guidelines to restrict total commercial time. Stations may now cram in as many minutes of commercials as they feel the audience will tolerate; some do (Sections 9.1.2.1 and 9.1.3.3). The cable trade, of course, never even had a code that restricted commercial minutes.

As for complaints about the **number of interruptions** per program, again there would seem to be justification. The Television Code placed liberal restrictions on the number of interruptions and the number of commercials per interruption. Even then, advertisers and audience complained of **clutter,** too many different announcements during each program interruption. Advertisers said that clutter caused their messages to be lost and forgotten in the sea of other commercials at each break. The audience just felt there were too many. The Radio Code placed no restrictions on interruptions; neither does the cable trade.

Women's and minority groups have complained that commercials **reinforce negative stereotypes.** For years, women were depicted as dependent on men, concerned primarily with children and household, unable to cope with financial or mechanical complexities, valued primarily as ornaments or sex objects, and, when seen in occupations other than homemaker, employed as secretaries and teachers. Commercials rarely included racial and ethnic minorities except in highly stereotyped roles—servants, cooks, and peons who were lazy, shuffling, inscrutable, or sombrero'd.

Since the early 1970s, many advertisers have attempted to eliminate from their commercials objectionable role depictions. They contend, however, that they have to use some stereotypes to set up and resolve a situation within a commercial's 15 or 30 seconds. As a result, we still see an unreal TV commercial world, in which middle-class families buy hamburgers, fried chicken, and new automobiles and women worry about clean clothes and shiny floors and succumb to men wearing after-shave lotions.

Consumer groups say that commercials attempt to sell products to the wrong people or to sell the **wrong products** to all people. Over the years, commercials have been criticized for selling toys, vitamins (which can be fatal if swallowed in large doses), and junk food to children; for selling quack medicines, nostrums, money-hungry religious charlatans, useless gadgets to those least able to afford them—the old, the poor; and for selling large cars and leaded gasoline (which contribute to atmospheric pollution), cigarettes (Section 15.3.4.3), and over-the-counter drugs to everybody.

Critics question the **value** that commercials promulgate. Commercials teach. And, goes the argument, they teach more than advertising slogans. They teach the values, philosophies, and behaviors they depict, values that may be dysfunctional (i.e., working toward undesirable goals) for both the individual and society. Commercials teach that it is good to be acquisitive, highly competitive, and conscious of status. They teach narcissism and that physical beauty is an end in itself. They teach us to take a pill when we feel bad, to see issues—no matter how complex—in black-and-white terms, to think in slogans, to look no farther than the surface,

to aim for a Ken-and-Barbie doll existence of eternal, middle-class, plastic-wrapped youth.

Many people criticize the **way in which commercials appeal to certain human motivations.** In the 1973 *CBS Reports: You and the Commercial*, Dr. Eric Fromm, the late renowned psychoanalyst, noted that commercials often use as motivation the fear of not being loved—attributable to body odor or split ends or baggy panty hose—which some product promises to alleviate. A second and related theme is the miracle; use this soap or that cooking oil and a miracle will happen. Commercials imply that love depends on a gadget. Use the advertised gadget, and attain the good life. Commercials promise the fountain of youth, that the product will turn us into beautiful young people who never change. Fromm also said advertising molds us, makes us greedy, makes us *want* more and more instead of trying to *be* more and more.

Commercials do not convince, Fromm said; they suggest. Convincing attempts to persuade through rational argument. Suggesting breaks down rationality and powers of criticism to get audiences to believe the promises of commercials. Therefore, concluded Fromm, people *know* on a rational basis that claims for the products are nonsense, but at the same time, they would like to hope there might be something to the claims. The result is a mixture of reality and fantasy that operates on the subconscious level.

While most criticism is directed at commercial announcements, **PSAs** have also come under fire. In 1976, public service groups and sympathizers in Congress petitioned the FCC to require that broadcasters air PSAs from a wider variety of sources. Over 70 disparate parties called for new rules, including Action for Children's Television, Sierra Club, National Gay Task Force, Public Media Center, and the United Church of Christ (UCC). The UCC commented that licensees had abdicated responsibility for

Box 9.1 ". . . Such a Big Production"

Stan Freberg produced this one-minute extravaganza for Great American Soup. Asked by her husband what was for dinner, Ann Miller replied by chucking her apron and tap dancing out of the kitchen and into a fantasy world of a chorus line, a huge soup can that rose out of the floor, and sundry visual effects—all while she belted out a song about "Great American Soup," accompanied by a brassy, fully orchestrated musical arrangement. She finally danced back into the kitchen and into her apron. The commercial ended with her husband asking why she had to "make such a big production out of everything." (Photograph courtesy Heinz U.S.A. Used by permission.)

PSAs to outside agencies, such as the Ad Council, which provide broadcasters with slick, noncontroversial PSAs. (See Section 22.5 for complaints about public broadcasting announcements.)

9.6 PRAISE

Not all words spoken about commercials are critical. For example, there is no doubt that, well done, broadcast advertising is effective.

Merchants and manufacturers who use radio and television successfully are among the first to praise broadcast commercials.

Certainly, too, the skill and imagination that go into making a commercial must be admired. Commercials are among the most carefully, painstakingly crafted productions in radio and television. Their original use of locations, props, actors, animals, and other elements to translate the fantasies of a copywriter into 30 seconds of sales pitch is legend (Box 9.1). The Clio, cousin to Oscar and Emmy, is awarded to the winning commercial in each of several categories based on cleverness and artistry.

The skilled personnel and persuasive techniques honed on advertising are used to create messages designed to improve the common good. The success of Ad Council campaigns is due almost entirely to the selling skills of its agencies.

Let us not forget, too, that advertising pays for programming on commercial broadcast stations and cable channels. The music, the stars, the news operations—all are financed by advertising dollars. Even some programming on public broadcasting is funded by advertising or restricted forms of advertising (Section 22.5).

Finally, commercials, as integral parts of advertising, serve as key forces in the American economy. Our economy is based in large part on mass production, mass distribution, and mass consumption. Commercials and the rest of advertising are vital to the maintenance of such an economic system.

NOTES

1. FCC, Program Length Commercials, 26 R.R.2d 1023 (1973).
2. In re Wilderness Society and Friends of the Earth, 30 F.C.C.2d 643 (1971).
3. *Warner-Lambert* v. *FTC*, 562 F2d 749, *certiorari* denied, 435 U.S. 950 (1978).

FURTHER READING

Arlen, Michael. *Thirty Seconds.* New York: Farrar, 1980. Creation of a television commercial.

Baldwin, Huntley. *Creating Effective TV Commercials.* Chicago: Crain, 1982.

Book, Albert C., Norman D. Cary, and Stanley I. Tannenbaum. *The Radio and Television Commercial.* 2d ed. Chicago: Crain, 1984. Copywriting workbook.

Geis, Michael L. *The Language of Television Advertising.* New York: Academic, 1982. Use of words to deceive.

Gradus, Ben. *Directing: The TV Commercial.* Stoneham: Focal, 1985. Step-by-step process in making a spot.

Hall, Jim. *Mighty Minutes: An Illustrated History of Television's Best Commercials.* New York: Harmony, 1984.

Heighton, Elizabeth J., and Don R. Cunningham. *Advertising in the Broadcast and Cable Media.* 2d ed. Belmont: Wadsworth, 1984. All aspects of commercials.

Orlik, Peter. *Broadcast Copywriting.* 3d ed. Boston: Allyn, 1986. How to write—including commercial copy.

Schudson, Michael. *Advertising, The Uneasy Persuasion: Its Dubious Impact on American Society.* New York: Basic, 1985. Role in developing a nation "born to shop."

White, Hooper. *How to Product Effective TV Commercials.* 2d ed. Lincolnwood: National, 1986. TV production process.

Witek, John. *Response Television: Combat Advertising of the 1980's.* Lincolnwood: National, 1981.

THREE

PHYSICAL PERSPECTIVE

Broadcasting was the first nonmechanical mass medium. Printing, recording, and cinema each originated from different technological devices. All, however, were mechanical contrivances.

Broadcasting's bases—electronics and electromagnetic radiation—were radically different from those of older media, so different that they even involved a different branch of physics. These physical bases have, in turn, affected all other aspects of broadcasting, from audience size to station licensing. The fact that broadcasting travels by electromagnetic energy, energy that has certain properties, has profoundly affected the history, regulation, and economics of radio and television, including nonbroadcast forms of radio and television. If you are going to understand radio and television, you must understand those physical properties.

We begin this section with a review of radio energy in Chapter 10. We look at its nature and some of its propagation characteristics. In Chapter 11, we survey the physical aspects of aural media—the sound and audio, AM and FM, and other radio services. We conclude the section by examining the workings of television and other electronic visual media, from light and the human eye, through video and various video services.

CHAPTER 10

Radio Energy

Programs from broadcast stations, wireless cable (multichannel TV; Section 5.4), and direct-broadcast satellites (DBS) are radiated from a transmitting antenna and sent to your receiver via radio energy. You cannot smell, feel, or see it, yet radio energy is the basis on which the entire structure of broadcasting, wireless cable, and DBS are built. To a large extent, the peculiar characteristics of radio energy determine how these media are organized—the frequencies assigned to transmitters, the power they may use, their physical location, their very licensed status. In this chapter, we examine the concept of radio energy waves and then the various characteristics of waves in different frequency bands. The term *radio* is used here in the generic sense to include television, microwave, and other such transmissions.

10.1 WAVES

Imagine that you hold one end of a long rope. Shake the rope rapidly up and down. Your arm's oscillation sets up a wave motion that travels the length of the rope. Hit a water glass with a spoon, and the glass vibrates, creating waves of sound that you can hear.

Radio waves, too, result from **oscillation.** Unlike the rope waves and the sound waves, however, radio waves require no material medium (such as a rope or molecules of air) for transmission. They can travel not only in the earth's atmosphere but also in the near vacuum of space.

A radio transmitter produces radio waves by feeding an oscillating form of electric current into a transmitting antenna. The current alternates direction of flow, first in one direction, then the other. Each change of direction is a half-cycle. Two successive half-cycles, one in each direction, make one complete oscillation or **cycle** (Figure 10.1). Called *alternating current* (AC), this form of electricity includes normal household current, which flows at a rate of 60 cycles per second. The rate for radio transmission is much higher, usually above 400,000 cycles per second.

In the transmitting antenna, the electric current creates coexistent **electrical** and **magnetic fields of force** around the antenna (Figure 10.2). The direction in which the current flows determines the direction toward which these fields' lines of force point, that is, their *polarity*. When the alternating current in the antenna reverses direction, it creates new electrical and magnetic fields

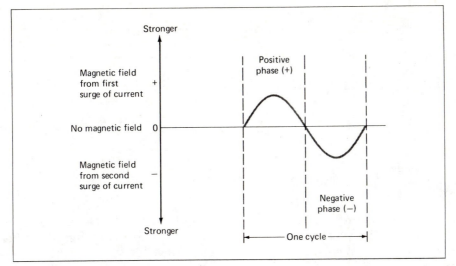

Figure 10.1 Sine wave as radio wave. The sine wave is a graphic representation of a radio wave. (To further confuse things, the sine wave is also used to represent the radio-frequency current that generates the radio waves, the audio that modulates the radio frequency, the sound waves that cause audio, and the vibration of the sound source from which the sound waves originate!)

around the antenna. These new fields, opposite in polarity, push the old fields away from the antenna (Figure 10.2). The alternating current again reverses direction, and the whole process starts over again.

Since newly created fields push previous fields away from the antenna, they continu-

ally radiate outward. Two successive sets of electrical and magnetic fields of force—the **positive phase** and the **negative phase,** according to their respective polarity—constitute one radio wave.

The strength or **amplitude** (Figure 10.3) of the alternating current in the transmitting

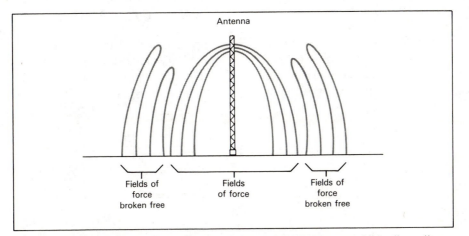

Figure 10.2 Lines of force radiating from antenna. If the frequency of the alternating current is high enough, the fields of force break free and continue to travel as electromagnetic waves.

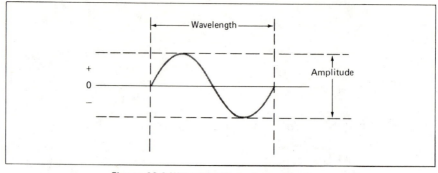

Figure 10.3 Wavelength and amplitude.

antenna determines the strength of the radiated waves. The amplitude of the waves, in turn, determines the strength of the signal you get on your receiver.

At the receiving end, radio waves are "picked up" with yet another antenna. They **induce** (cause) in the receiving antenna a pattern of alternating current exactly like the oscillations in the transmitting antenna, although of much lower amplitude.

10.1.1 Attenuation

As they travel, radio waves **attenuate** (lose strength) for a number of reasons. This is illustrated in Figure 10.4. A radio wave radiates outward from a transmitting antenna. As the wave travels, the circle becomes larger and the wave spreads itself ever more thinly, diminishing in amplitude as it covers a greater area. Eventually, the point is

reached at which the amplitude is so low that, for purposes of reception, there is no more wave. This is when the signal fades on your radio or television receiver.

Certain structures and electrical interference (particularly in cities) and terrain obstacles may create **dead spots** within a station's coverage area; that is, places where you should be able to receive the station but cannot. **Overlapping signals** or **interference** occurs when the radio waves from one station collide with and distort or weaken those from another.

Absorption involves expenditure of energy by a wave as it travels. When radio waves travel through a vacuum, there is little absorption. But in anything denser, such as the earth's atmosphere, radio waves lose energy. The denser the medium, the more absorption occurs. In AM radio, for example, the earth conducts (allows to travel) the ground wave (Section 10.2.2.1), but it also

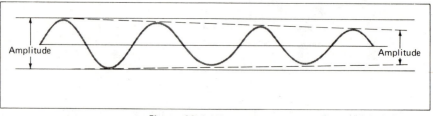

Figure 10.4 Attenuation.

absorbs much of the wave's energy. The ground waves of even the most powerful U.S. AM radio stations, operating with 50,000 watts of power and no interference, lose most of their punch after about 100 miles of travel. Sky waves, on the other hand, do not undergo much absorption. If the transmission is powerful and meets with minimal interference, its sky waves may bounce from the ionosphere to earth and back again to deliver powerful, clear signals thousands of miles away.

10.1.2 Velocity

Radio energy has a **velocity** of (travels at) 300 million meters per second in a vacuum (it travels somewhat slower in the atmosphere). That figure should sound familiar to you because it is the speed of light. All electromagnetic energy (which includes radio waves and visible light) travels at that speed.

10.1.3 Frequency

Transmitters emit radio waves at a rate of thousands and millions per second, the exact rate varying according to service (AM or FM radio, TV broadcast, MDS, and so forth). The number of waves a transmitter emits per second is, of course, determined by the number of cycles per second of alternating electrical current energy flowing to the transmitting antenna. The term **hertz** has been adopted as a name for cycles per second, honoring Heinrich Hertz, the scientist who first demonstrated the exitence of radio waves. The number of hertz a station generates is its **frequency.** Since such large numbers are involved, prefixes are used as shortcuts; **kilo-** means times 1000, and **mega-** means times 1,000,000. Thus 850 kilohertz (kHz) would be 850,000 cycles per second, and 98.3 megahertz (MHz) would be 98,300,000 cycles per second.

10.1.4 Wavelength

Since radio energy's velocity is constant, the only way to increase frequency (number of cycles/waves per second) is to shorten **wavelength** (Figure 10.5). This is easy to illustrate. Draw a horizontal line 3 inches long. Now use it as the middle line, and draw on it three sine waves (backward Ss, lying on their sides; see Figure 10.5) representing three radio waves, each of equal length, so that they take up the whole space. How long will each sine wave have to be? Obviously, 1 inch. Now draw another line 3 inches long, and put four sine waves on it. This time each will have to be $\frac{3}{4}$ inch long. You have to shorten wavelength to get more waves in the same 3-inch space.

Now, reread the previous sentence, substituting "time" for "3-inch space," and the same principle applies—**speed being constant at all frequencies and wavelengths, you have to shorten the wavelength to get more waves** (that is, to increase frequency) **in the same time period.** If you are confused at this point, just remember "longer and lower"—the longer the wave, the lower the frequency. And the converse holds, too—the shorter the wave, the higher the frequency.

With radio energy velocity constant at about the speed of light, we should be able to figure frequency if given wavelength and wavelength if given frequency. The formula is **frequency equals velocity divided by wavelength** or **wavelength equals velocity divided by frequency.** For example, an AM broadcast station operating at 1500 kHz is using a wavelength of 200 meters (300,000,000 ÷ 1,500,000 = 200); that is, the length of each wave the station transmits is 200 meters long.

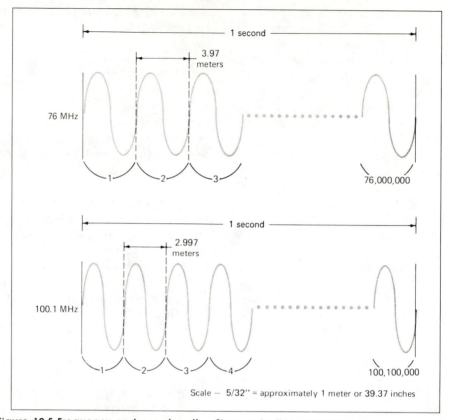

Figure 10.5 Frequency and wavelength. Since velocity is constant, the only way to increase frequency (say, from 7.6 MHz to 100.1 MHz) is to decrease wavelength (here, from 3.97 meters to 2.997 meters).

10.1.5 Review

Before going on, let us review. Alternating electrical current sets up thousands or millions of oscillations in the transmitting antenna. These oscillations produce radio waves, each with a positive phase and a negative phase, which travel outward from the tower at close to the speed of light. When the waves contact a receiving antenna, they set up similar oscillations, which the receiver amplifies and uses as the signal. The strength of a radio wave is directly related to its amplitude. The wave attenuates (and the amplitude decreases) as the wave travels. Speed is constant, so frequency and wavelength are inversely related.

10.2 FREQUENCY-RELATED CHARACTERISTICS

Since radio waves consist of electrical and magnetic fields, radio energy is a form of **electromagnetic energy,** as are infrared rays, visible light, ultraviolet light, and other types of radiation. All radiate from a source and travel in waves at the speed of light. As mentioned in Section 10.1, electromagnetic energy needs no conduction medium; in fact, it travels most efficiently through a vacuum.

10.2.1 Electromagnetic Spectrum

If you were to arrange all forms of electromagnetic energy in order of frequency, from lowest to highest, you would have what is called the **electromagnetic spectrum** (Figure 10.6). At the highest frequencies (and shortest wavelengths) are cosmic rays. Below that, in descending order of frequency, come gamma rays, X-rays, ultraviolet rays, visible light, infrared rays, and, near the bottom, radio waves.

As shown in Figure 10.6, the **radio portion** of the electromagnetic spectrum has been further divided. AM radio is in the medium frequency (MF) band; television channels 2–13 and FM radio are in the very high frequency (VHF) band; TV channels 14–70, the instructional television fixed service (ITFS), the multipoint distribution service (MDS), and the multichannel multipoint distribution service (MMDS) are in the ultrahigh frequency (UHF) band; and direct-broadcast satellites (DBS) are in the superhigh frequency (SHF) band. Wavelengths in the ITFS, MDS, MMDS, and DBS services are so short they are called **microwaves.**

10.2.2 Propagation

The manner in which radio waves travel—the paths they take—is called **propagation.** Propagation varies greatly with frequency.

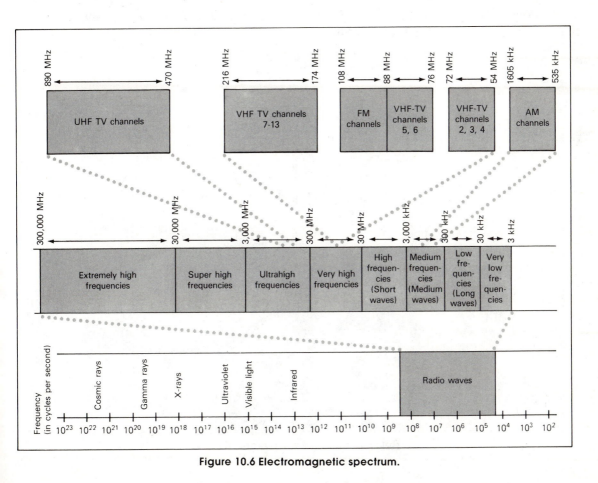

Figure 10.6 Electromagnetic spectrum.

10.2.2.1 Ground Waves and Sky Waves In the MF band, ground waves and sky waves determine propagation. Ground waves follow the curvature of the earth (Figure 10.7). Ground waves are relatively constant; at a given distance from the transmitter, they usually provide the same quality of reception most of the time.

Sky waves radiate away from the earth (Figure 10.8). During the day, they travel unimpeded into space and serve no use to terrestrial propagation. At night, however, changes in the ionosphere, 30 to 200 miles above the earth's surface, cause many sky waves to bend and to land back on the ground hundreds of miles from the transmitter.

During nighttime, then, sky waves expand a transmitter's reception area beyond that provided by ground waves. But the quality of the signal in this expanded area varies more

than in the ground-wave coverage area. As the ionosphere changes, the strength of the sky waves changes, and listeners hear the signal "fade" in and out on their radio receivers. At times, freak ionosphere conditions make possible clear sky-wave reception at distances of half a continent or more from the transmitter. Such reception is usually subject to severe fading.

10.2.2.2 Direct Waves Higher radio frequencies are closer to visible light in the electromagnetic spectrum and behave more like visible light rays. In VHF, UHF, and SHF, propagation is primarily by direct waves. Like light, direct waves travel in straight lines, may be blocked by physical objects, and may be reflected. This is illustrated in Box 10.1.

Like light, direct waves are also subject to

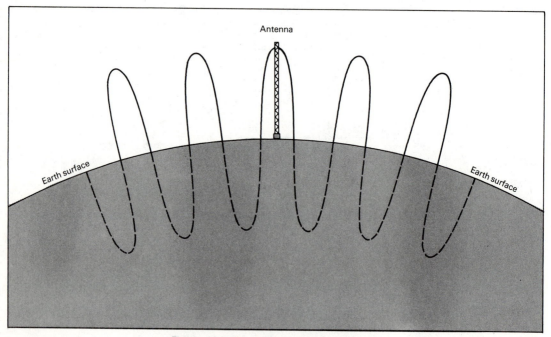

Figure 10.7 Ground wave propagation.

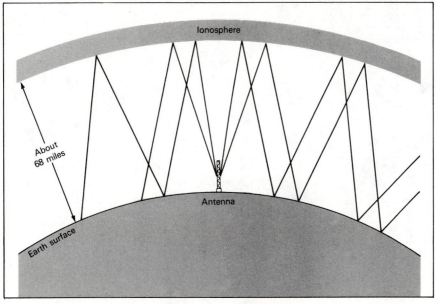

Figure 10.8 Sky wave propagation.

refraction or bending. Perhaps you have had the experience of putting a straight pole into clear water and seeing the pole appear to bend. The pole seems to enter the water at one angle, then bend at the surface to another angle. The pole has not really bent, of course, but the light rays have. The light rays reflected from the submerged part of the pole travel through a relatively dense medium, water, then enter a less dense medium, air, and in the process they bend. This is called **refraction,** and it is why the straight pole looks bent. Similarly, VHF, UHF, and SHF waves can be bent as they pass through varying temperatures and weather conditions that affect density.

Attenuation, absorption, interference, reflection, refraction—all affect propagation at all frequencies to a certain extent. Some of them affect some frequencies more than others. Climate and weather play a large role in propagation. The next time a cold front, a warm front, a high-pressure area, or a low-

pressure area is scheduled to move into your vicinity, note the changes in broadcast reception before, during, and after.

10.2.3 MF Coverage

Coverage refers to the physical area within which a radio wave may be received. Medium-frequency coverage is affected by three factors—ground, frequency, and power.

10.2.3.1 Ground The term *ground* refers to electrical grounding. In MF transmission, part of the antenna is buried beneath the ground, and the whole antenna structure, ground and all, transmits. The object is to make maximum use of the ground waves, which requires a good electrical ground connection. Wet soil gives a better electrical ground than does dry, so that in medium-

Box 10.1 Direct Wave Propagation

Television and FM radio propagation have been described as *line-of-sight,* and to a large extent that is true. If you were to climb to the top of a television transmitter tower, for example, you could (on a clear day) literally see most of the station's primary coverage area—the area reached by its actual off-the-air, not delivered-by-cable signal. You see to the horizon but no farther; for all practical purposes, that is how far the television signal reaches. A series of hills looms up close on one side of you, blocking your view; they block the television signal, too, and people living on the other side of the hills cannot receive the station directly. Some neighborhoods are partially obscured from your view by tall buildings or other large structures; the people living in these areas pick up the television station with difficulty or not at all. Some tall buildings seem especially bright, reflecting quite a bit of light; they also reflect television signals. Residents living near these buildings receive one television signal directly from the station's transmitting antenna and another from the bounce off the reflective buildings. The result is ghosting (double image) on the screen.

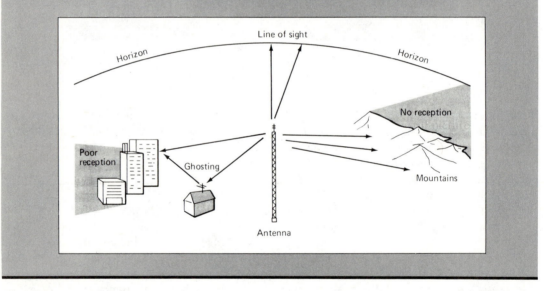

frequency transmission, the transmitting antenna is better off in a low swamp than on top of a dry, well-drained hill (Figure 10.9).

10.2.3.2 Frequency Frequency affects coverage just the opposite of what you may think. In MF transmission, as in all transmission, the *lower* the frequency, the better the coverage (Figure 10.10). This is because lower frequencies result from longer waves, and the longer the wave, the greater the distance one wavelength covers. For example, a station transmitting at 1600 kHz generates a wavelength of 187.5 meters, while a station at 540 kHz generates a wavelength of 555.6 meters. For every one wavelength the waves at 540 kHz travel, the waves at 1600 kHz must travel nearly three wavelengths, ex-

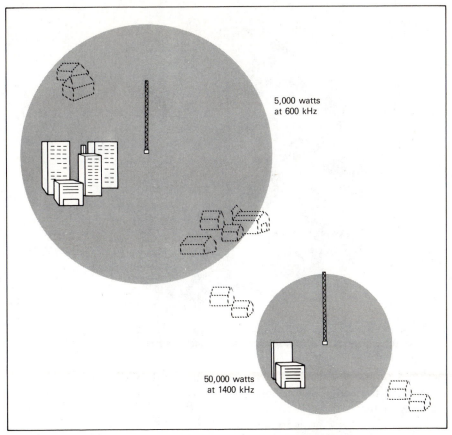

5,000 watts
at 600 kHz

50,000 watts
at 1400 kHz

Figure 10.9 Relative broadcast coverage.

10.2.3.3 Power Power works just the way that seems most logical—the higher the power the transmitter pumps into the antenna, the farther the wave will travel and the better the coverage. Because of ground wave propagation, radio transmission in the MF range is not so affected by hills and line-of-sight considerations as VHF and UHF transmission. Given enough power, ground waves surmount hills and range beyond the horizon.

10.2.4 VHF, UHF, and SHF Coverage

Coverage in the VHF, UHF, and SHF frequencies is affected by **antenna height, frequency,** and **power.** VHF and UHF propagation is by direct waves and is line-of-sight (although, in reality, FM and TV station signals do spread beyond line-of-sight). Just as the higher you fly in an airplane, the more area of ground you can see, so, too, the higher the antenna, the greater the coverage. Line-of-sight also means natural terrain features and human-constructed obstacles can block coverage, yielding dead spots and poor reception areas. ITFS and MMDS operate so high in the frequency bands that their coverage is literally line-of-sight; the transmitting antenna must be *seen* from the receiving antenna, and even leaves and foliage can block reception. Also, in DBS, the receiving dish must have a clear "shot" at the satellite.

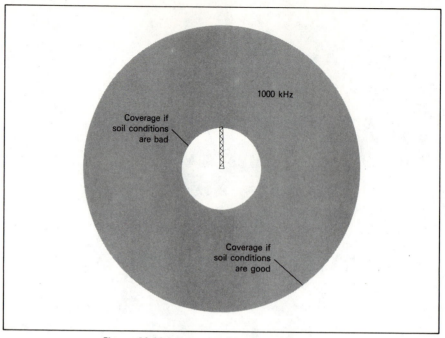

Figure 10.10 Influence of Soil Condition.

Frequency and power affect VHF, UHF, and SHF coverage as they do in all frequency ranges—lower frequencies and higher power yield greater coverage. Wavelengths in these frequency bands are so much shorter than in the MF band that TV and FM broadcast stations operate with higher average power than AM stations. DBS satellites, however, can operate at much lower power because the waves they transmit travel most of their journey through near-vacuum and low-density atmosphere.

FURTHER READING

Carr, Joseph L. *The TAB Handbook of Radio Communications.* Blue Ridge Summit: TAB, 1984.

Miller, Gary M. *Modern Electronic Communication.* 2d ed. Englewood Cliffs: Prentice, 1983. Chapter 11 deals with electromagnetic waves and wave propagation.

CHAPTER 11

Radio Channels

How can more than 12,000 radio broadcasting stations in the United States fit into just over 200 channels? How does sound become radio and vice versa? What is the difference between AM and FM?

These are some of the questions we shall answer in this chapter. In addition to the AM and FM bands, we shall look at other radio broadcasting channels, the international service, and various forms of wired radio.

11.1 AM BROADCAST SERVICE

According to the FCC, an AM broadcast staion is one **licensed for transmission of radiotelephone** (voice, music, and the like) **emissions** (radio waves) **primarily intended for reception by the general public and operated on a channel in the band** [that begins with] **535 kHz** (535,000 Hz).[1] This places AM radio in the medium frequency (MF) band.

For years, the AM broadcast band had ended at 1605 kHz (1,605,000 Hz). In 1979, action by an international conference added another 100 kHz, which would expand the band to 1705 kHz (1,705,000 Hz). Technical details were to be worked out at the regional

level. The ten added channels would open for use by new stations in mid-1990.

In the broadcast services, a place for a station is a **channel.** An AM channel consists of its carrier frequency plus the upper and lower sidebands of the AM broadcast signal. (You will learn more about these terms in Section 11.3.3.1. For now, the *carrier* is the frequency at the center of the channel; *sidebands* are groups of frequencies generated by the process of broadcasting and are located directly above and below the carrier.) Each channel is **identified by its carrier frequency.** The carriers are **spaced at 10-kHz intervals,** with the first at 540 kHz. This works out to **107 channels** with the AM band at 535–1605 kHz, **117 channels** at 535–1705 kHz. Most channels are used by more than one station, although a (relatively) small number of channels contain a large percentage of all stations.

11.1.1 Interference and Coverage

Interference—the mutual action of two sets of radio waves affecting each other—takes the form of **static** and **station interference** (Figure 11.1). Static is electrical discharges

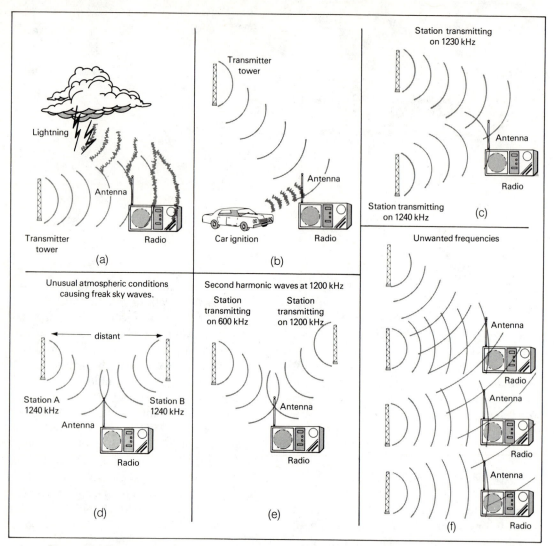

Figure 11.1 Types of interference in AM radio.   (a) Static—natural (lightning in this example). Radio simultaneously receives station signal and static. (b) Static—human-created. Radio simultaneously receives signal and static. (c) Station interference—adjacent channel. Radio tuned to 1230 simultaneously receives station transmitting on 1230 kHz and station transmitting on 1240 kHz. (d) Station interference—co-channel. Radio tuned to 1240 to receive station A simultaneously receives signals from both stations A and B. (e) Station interference—second harmonic. Radio tuned to distant station transmitting on 1200 kHz simultaneously receives nearby station transmitting on 600 kHz through its second harmonic frequency (1200 kHz). (f) Station interference—splatter. Station transmitting on one frequency overmodulates, and radios tuned to stations on other frequencies receive audio from the overmodulating station.

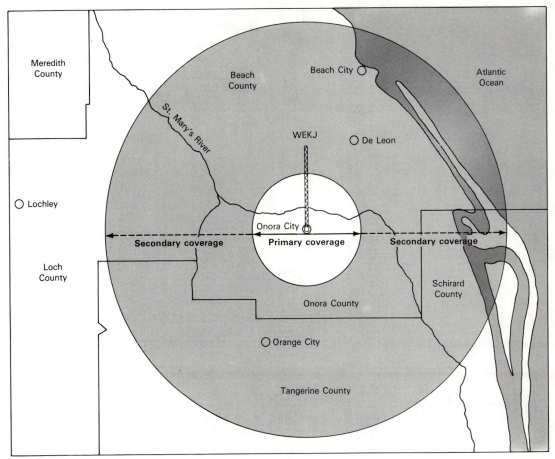

Figure 11.2 Primary and secondary coverage areas.

and can be either **natural** or **induced.** Natural static results from atmospheric disturbances such as lightning. Induced static originates from electrical machines and devices—the faulty ignition system of an automobile, a vacuum cleaner or mixer running in another room, a noisy starter in a fluorescent light fixture. These sources generate electromagnetic waves that mix and are received with incoming radio waves.

Station interference involves signals of two or more radio stations. You tune to one station but receive others on the same setting at the same time.

Coverage is the area within which a station's signal can be received. Since AM operates in the MF band, a radio station's coverage is dependent on **ground, power,** and **frequency** (Section 10.2.3). All other things being equal, wetter soil, higher power, or lower frequency results in greater coverage. The FCC has defined two types of coverage areas—**primary** and **secondary** (Figure 11.2).[2] Generally, a station's primary service area is that served by its ground wave; its secondary service area is that within which its sky wave is received with some degree of strength and consistency.

11.1.2 Channel and Station Classification

Early in the history of broadcasting, it became apparent that a system was needed to prevent massive interference among AM radio stations. Sky waves, particularly, caused problems; they were unpredictable and could skip long distances. The system that finally evolved included two related classifications—(1) **AM frequencies are classified as clear, regional, or local channels**, (2) **stations, as I, II, III, or IV.** As you read the remaining paragraphs in this section, refer to Figure 11.3, which shows channel classification and its relationship to station classification.

11.1.2.1 Clear Channels Clear channels are used by dominant stations and secondary

Channel classification				Frequencies (kHz)	Station classification	
Clear (60)	A (25)			640, 650, 660, 670, 700, 720, 750, 760, 770, 780, 820, 830, 840, 870, 880, 890, 1020, 1030, 1040, 1100, 1120, 1160, 1180, 1200, 1210	Dominant I-A	Secondary II
	B (19)	U.S. Clears (11)		680, 710, 810, 850, 1080, 1110, 1170, 1500, 1510, 1520, 1530	I-B	II
		Clears shared by U.S. and foreign countries (8)	with Canada (2)	1070, 1130		
			with Mexico (5)	1000, 1060, 1090, 1140, 1190		
			with Cuba (1)	1560		
	Foreign clears (16) (No U.S. dominant stations)	Canada		540, 690, 740, 860, 990, 1010, 1580	None	II
		Mexico (6)		730, 800, 900, 1050, 1220, 1570		
		Canada & Mexico (2)		940, 1550		
		Bahamas		1540		
Regional (41)				550, 560, 570, 580, 590, 600, 610, 620, 630, 790, 910, 920, 930, 950, 960, 970, 980, 1150, 1250, 1260, 1270, 1280, 1290, 1300, 1310, 1320, 1330, 1350, 1360, 1370, 1380, 1390, 1410, 1420, 1430, 1440, 1460, 1470, 1480, 1590, 1600	III	
Local (6)				1230, 1240, 1340, 1400, 1450, 1490 (These frequencies are classified as regional for Alaska, Hawaii, Puerto Rico and the Virgin Islands.)	IV	

Figure 11.3 AM channel and station classification.

stations. Of the 107 AM channels, 60 are designated clear channels.

Dominant stations provide primary and secondary service over an extended area and at relatively long distances. They may operate with no less than 10 kilowatts (kW; 1 kW = 1000 watts) nor more than 50 kilowatts of power. On 25 of the 60 "clears," the FCC limits the number of dominant stations to one per channel, and it requires that one station to operate at 50 kW, the maximum allowed in the United States.

Of another 22 clears, the commission allows multiple dominant stations. These stations must operate so as to minimize co-channel interference. During the day, for example, two dominant stations on the same clear channel might use nondirectional transmitting antennas (to radiate their ground waves equally in all directions) and then at night switch to directional antenna arrays (to direct their sky wave transmissions away from each other).

Some of the latter 22 clear channels are shared; both the United States and another North American country operate dominant stations on them. The remainder of the 60 clears are foreign; the United States may operate no dominant station on any of these channels without prior agreement from the other country.

In addition to dominant stations, one or more **secondary stations** may transmit on a clear channel. Secondary stations are licensed so as to **protect** the signal of the dominant stations, that is, not interfere with their primary service areas and much of their secondary service areas. They must use restrictive operational modes—transmit with relatively low power, or reduce power at night, or operate only in the daytime, or use a directional antenna array, or employ some combination of these measures.

11.1.2.2 Regional Channels Forty-one frequencies are regional channels. A regional channel is one on which a number of stations may operate, each serving a population center and adjacent rural areas. None dominates; each station operates in order to avoid interference with all others on the same channel, and some must use restrictive operational modes. The most powerful use 5000 watts.

11.1.2.3 Local Channels The remaining six frequencies are local channels. A local channel is one on which many stations, 150 or more, may operate. These stations serve one city or town and the adjacent suburban and rural areas. Most operate with 1000 watts day and night.

11.1.2.4 Station Classification The dominant stations on a clear channel are class I stations. The secondary stations that operate on a clear channel are class II stations.* Stations assigned to regional channels are class III stations. And stations on local channels are class IV stations.

11.1.2.5 New Stations Should you wish to construct a new AM radio station, you will find slim pickings. All class I stations were taken years ago. If you want a clear-channel dominant station, you will have to buy it.

In putting on a new AM station, the frequency you use determines the type of station you build. Therefore you must first find a frequency. You hire a consulting engineer, who makes a **frequency search,** that is, studies existing AM radio assignments and measures the strength of their signals in the area where you wish to build. Again, pickings are slim. Most of the better frequencies have already been taken. In your application to the FCC, you must show that your proposed station would not interfere with existing stations.

---

*The FCC makes further breakdowns of class I and class II stations.

11.1.2.6 Spectrum Management Most of the 5200 AM radio stations operate on regional and local channels. These 47 channels—44 percent of the total—account for about 70 percent of the stations. Of the 60 clear channels, 14 have five or fewer stations operating on them.

Despite the apparent crowding of the AM dial, ways do exist at the policy-making level to add new stations. In the 1980s, for example, the FCC reduced the area in which the signals of class I stations were protected. This made room for additional stations of other classes. Treaties between the United States and other North American countries would permit construction of new stations. And, of course, the 1979 expansion of the AM band (Section 11.1) seemed to hold out the promise of spectrum space for hundreds of additional stations. On the other hand, given AM's diminishing audience shares, the *need* for so many new stations might legitimately be questioned.*

Also during the 1980s, the FCC attempted to improve the lot of the 2400 "daytimers." As explained earlier, a number of class II and class III stations have had to operate in the daytime only. This dawn-to-dusk operation can be extremely limiting. The winter sun rises late and sets early in the colder latitudes of the United States. During certain months, a station that must restrict its programming to a sunrise-to-sunset schedule misses one or both of the two drive times, the most listened-to and potentially lucrative parts of the radio broadcast day.

The daytimers requested help, and the commission responded along several fronts. Post-sunset operations were authorized for some daytimers operating on domestic clear channels. The FCC worked with the U.S. State Department to negotiate agreements with Canada and Mexico that would allow many daytimers on foreign clears to extend their broadcast day (including some that would be allowed 24-hour operation). The commission promised daytimer licensees preferential treatment when they applied for new FM stations. Rule changes in 1987 permitted most daytimers operating on clear and regional channels to operate at night. Finally, in order to ensure that the "daytimer problem" did not get worse instead of better, the FCC stopped accepting applications for new AM daytimers.

11.2 FM BROADCAST SERVICE

The FM radio broadcasting band is 88 to 108 MHz, in the VHF portion of the radio frequencies, located just above television Channel 6. There are 100 channels in the FM band, each 200 kHz wide (108 MHz − 88 MHz = 20 MHz ÷ 0.2 [which is 200 kHz] = 100). For convenience, the FCC customarily refers to FM channels by **channel number,** as in television. The first FM channel is 201; the last, 300. Stations identify themselves to the public by **frequency,** similar to AM radio. The first FM channel frequency is 88.1 MHz (the center of a band of frequencies, 88–88.2 MHz), and the last is 107.9 MHz (107.8–108 MHz).

11.2.1 Interference and Coverage

Interference is rarely the problem in FM radio that it is in AM. As discussed in Section 10.2.2.2, propagation is primarily by direct waves and, therefore, is fairly predictable. Ground waves and sky waves do not figure into FM coverage. Additionally, the VHF band contains less static and other noise than the lower frequencies. Frequency, power,

---

*FM radio, already the dominant aural medium by 1979 (Section 3.3), increased its audience share at the expense of AM throughout the 1980s. Consequently, the value of AM radio stations, relative to FM stations, dropped. AM licensees who wished to sell their stations often had difficulty finding buyers.

tower height, and terrain and human-constructed obstacles all affect coverage.

FM receiver design also contributes to reduction of station interference and static. In co-channel and adjacent-channel interference situations, an FM receiver has a much greater ability to suppress the weaker signal than does an AM receiver. Static signals attach themselves to positive and negative peaks of a radio wave, and FM receivers eliminate static by **clipping** (removing) these peaks.

11.2.2 Station Classification

The FCC has adopted rules to provide for the orderly growth of the FM radio service, while minimizing possibilities for interference. The commission has divided the country into three zones, designated **I, I-A,** and **II.** Stations have been classified as **A, B1, B, C1, C2, C3,** or **C** according to power and antenna height. Figure 11.4 shows the zones and the classification system.

11.2.2.1 Commercial FM Commercial FM stations operate on the **80 channels** (221–300) in the nonreserved (that is, commercial) portion of the FM band. In 1963, the FCC adopted a table assigning nonreserved channels to specific communities. Should you wish to build a new commercial FM station, you go to the FM **table of assignments,** look up your city, choose an unused channel assigned to that city, and apply for it. If there are no vacant channels, you either find a city that does have vacant FM channels or petition the FCC to amend the table of assignments to add a channel to your city.

In 1983, the FCC opened the FM band to additional stations. It adopted a new station classification system (the present one) and changed the required minimum distances between stations on the same and adjacent channels. The commission estimated that

this action would allow room for up to 2000 new FM stations.

11.2.2.2 Noncommercial Educational FM FM **channels 201–220 are reserved for noncommercial educational stations.** These 20 channels are not included in the FCC's table of assignments (except as noted below). Noncommercial FM stations are assigned on an individual application-demand basis, much like AM. Noncommercial FM stations are classified A, B, C, and D. Stations classes A, B, and C parallel those in the commercial band. A station that operates with a transmitter power output of no more than 10 watts is a class D station. In 1978, the FCC adopted rules designed to free channels for full-service (classes A, B, and C) noncommercial stations and to encourage existing class D stations to upgrade facilities to full service. Under these rules, the FCC stopped accepting applications for new class D stations. Existing class D stations were informed that they had four choices if they wished to continue to operate:—(1) increase power to at least 100 watts; (2) move to an unused commercial channel; (3) move to a newly created FM channel 200 (87.9 MHz); or (4) operate as a secondary station on a commercial or noncommercial channel.

The commission also proposed adopting a table of assignments for educational FM. In the meantime, a table of assignments already existed for various communities in Arizona, California, New Mexico, and Texas. These assignments lay within 199 miles of the border between the United States and Mexico and were the result of agreements between the two countries.

11.3 SOUND AND AUDIO

We use the term **audio frequency** (AF, or simply "audio") to refer to a certain type of electronic signal. Audio is, in most cases, an

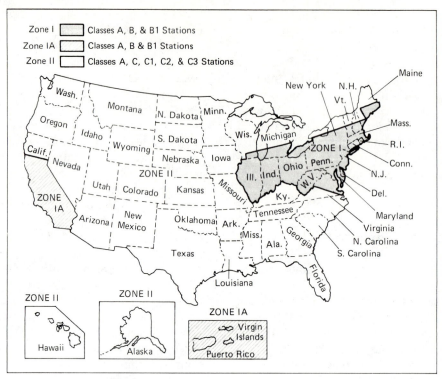

(a)

Station Class	Effective Radiated Power (ERP in kilowatts—kW)		Maximum Antenna Height Above Average Terrain [HAAT in meters (and feet)]	Zones to which allocated
	Minimum	Maximum		
A*	.1 (100 watts)	3/6	100 (328)	I, I-A, II
B1	over 3	25	100 (328)	I, I-A
B	over 25	50	150 (492)	I, I-A
C3	over 3	25	100 (328)	II
C2	over 3	50	150 (492)	II
C1	over 50	100	299 (981)	II
C	100		600 (1968)	II

*Selected Class A FM stations may operate with 6 kw.

(b)

Figure 11.4 FCC's FM zones and station classification. (a) Geographic boundaries of zones. (b) Station classification and assignment to zones.

analog of (that is, resembles or is comparable to in certain respects) sound. In other words, audio is an **electric current that carries the pattern of sound in a form suitable for electronic manipulation.** Manipulation includes transmission. So we need to find out how sound originates and how it is converted to audio.

11.3.1 Sound

Sound originates with the **vibrating body** of a **sound source**—the human vocal folds in the larynx, the strings of a harp, the reed of a clarinet. A plucked harp string, for example, vibrates rapidly back and forth, compressing and rarefying adjacent air molecules. As the string moves in one direction, it pushes together molecules in front while creating a partial vacuum and rarefying (making less dense) the molecules behind. After it reaches the outermost point of movement in one direction, the string begins to swing back the other way, and the condensation-rarefaction process reverses sides.

11.3.1.1 Sound Waves

As the string displaces the nearest air molecules, these molecules hit the next molecules, which then hit the next molecules, and so forth. This chain reaction creates repeating patterns of alternating condensation and rarefaction radiating outward from the vibrating body. If these patterns reach your ear, they set up vibrations in your eardrum similar to those of the harp string. The vibrating eardrum activates tiny mechanisms in your middle ear that transmit sensations to your auditory nerve, which, in turn, sends the information to your brain. Your brain interprets the result as sound. Figure 11.5 illustrates this process.

Each condensation-rarefaction combination is one wave. Each set of back-and-forth movements of the vibrating body is one cycle.

11.3.1.2 Frequency, Wavelength, Amplitude, and Pitch

The number of cycles per second—the frequency—determines the length of the sound waves. (We first used these terms in Sections 10.1.3 and 10.1.4 when discussing radio waves. But keep in mind that this is sound energy, not electromagnetic energy.) Amplitude determines loudness. As the body vibrates harder, amplitude increases and the sound grows louder. Frequency determines pitch. If the body vibrates at a frequency of 440 Hz, your brain hears the musical pitch A, sixth tone in the scale of C major. A frequency of 258 Hz is middle C; twice that number is C above middle C; and so on. Figure 11.6 shows the relationships among frequency, wavelength, and amplitude.

11.3.1.3 Fundamentals and Overtones

Any given sound usually contains many different pitches. For example, let us say that you pluck the A string of a harp. You hear the note A above middle C, the fundamental tone, the one to which the string is tuned. But at the same time that the whole string moves back and forth at a rate of 440 Hz, segments of the string also move back and forth independently and at faster rates. These vibrating segments also produce pitches called overtones. The shorter the segment, the faster it vibrates, and the higher the pitch it produces. The drawing in Figure 11.7 illustrates overtone production.

Overtones vary according to the type of vibrating body. When overtones are *consonant*, you perceive the sound as pleasing, even musical; when *dissonant*, as upsetting or jarring or as noise.

Although overtone frequencies go much higher, most of us cannot hear above 15,000–17,000 Hz. As we grow older, or if we damage our hearing, the upper limit drops. But most fundamentals are below 5000 Hz, and most speech sounds go no higher than 3000 Hz.

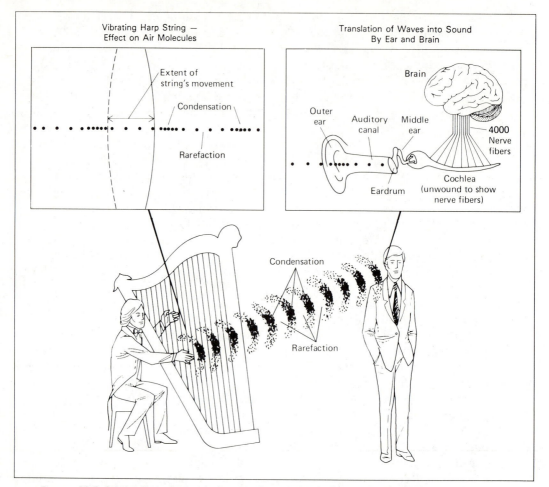

Figure 11.5 Origination, transmission, and reception of sound. The condensation-rarefaction patterns (in the air molecules) radiate outward in all directions from the sound source. For clarity, the illustration shows the waves going only to the listener's ears, and the inserts show only one line of air molecules.

Structure and enclosure of the sound source also play a major role in what you hear. The vibrating body and its sound waves cause other parts of the source to vibrate and amplify the sound. This is called *resonance*, and the nature of resonance varies from sound source to sound source.

Vibrating body, overtones, and resonance are the factors that allow you to tell one sound source from another—a human voice from a harp from a trumpet from a clarinet—

even though each produces the same fundamental tone. These factors also help you to tell one voice from another.

Most sound waves are highly complex. Overtones and resonance both complicate sound wave structure, as do factors such as two or more sound sources used in combination (orchestra, singing group, even one instrument on which two or more notes may be sounded simultaneously) and acoustical properties (the qualities that determine how

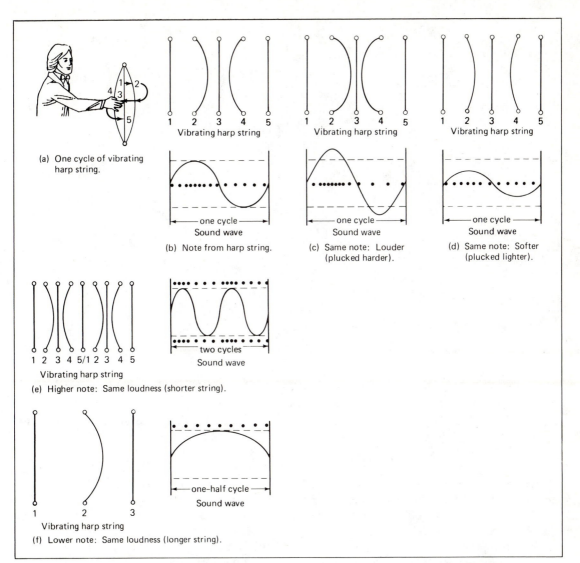

(a) One cycle of vibrating harp string.

(b) Note from harp string.

(c) Same note: Louder (plucked harder).

(d) Same note: Softer (plucked lighter).

(e) Higher note: Same loudness (shorter string).

(f) Lower note: Same loudness (longer string).

Figure 11.6 Sound waves: frequency and amplitude.   In drawings (b) through (f), the numbered lines show what movements the harp string makes within a given time period (the same for each drawing, (b) through (f)), while the sine wave forms show what the resulting sound waves are like. Variations in the degree of string displacement ((c) and (d)) result in variations in amplitude. Variations in the number of cycles of string movement ((e) and (f)) result in variations in frequency and pitch.

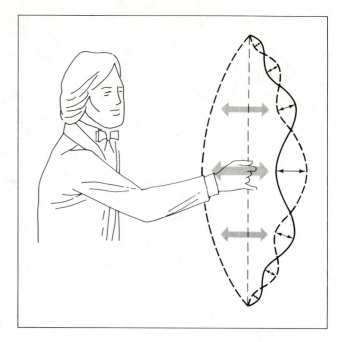

Figure 11.7 Creation of overtones.

clearly sound can be heard) of the room in which sound is produced.

11.3.2 Audio

When sound energy is translated directly into electrical energy, the result is audio. To illustrate, let us use a 1000-Hz tone, a pitch nearly two Cs above middle C. We shall make this a pure tone, that is, a tone with no overtones, resonance, echoes, or what-have-you, such as might be produced by an electronic tone generator.

11.3.2.1 Audio Sources A microphone converts this sound into electrical energy. The sound waves cause a diaphragm in the microphone to vibrate, and its vibrations cause current to flow, the amount of current varying with the amount of sound pressure on the diaphragm. The result is a weak electrical current of 1000 Hz (which is the same as 1

kHz). This electrical current is the audio, also called the *audio signal* and the *audio frequency* (AF). Figure 11.8 shows a microphone converting sound to audio.

The microphone is an audio source; that is, it originates an audio signal. Other sources include playback units for recordings and electronic tone generators. A recording is simply a stored version of sound. An audio source—a compact disc player's optical sensor, a phonograph turntable stylus, a tape machine's playback head, a film projector's photocell—translates the recording into audio. Typically, the heart of a tone generator is an oscillator. This oscillator produces an electrical signal that, when fed to a speaker, produces a tone. In other words, an electronic tone generator, such as a synthesizer, creates audio first and then converts it to sound.

The signal from one or more sources is fed to an **audio control board.** One major purpose of the board is to allow the audio tech-

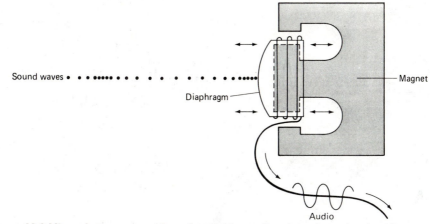

Sound waves

Diaphragm

Magnet

Audio

Figure 11.8 Microphone: conversion of sound to audio. In a dynamic microphone, a diaphragm and a voice coil are connected; when the diaphragm moves, the coil also moves. The voice coil is positioned between the poles of a magnet. Sound waves cause the diaphragm to move back and forth. Movement of the voice coil within the magnetic field sets up a weak current in the coil. Each back-and-forth movement results in one cycle of current. Sound waves cause the movement so that the current is an electrical reproduction of the sound waves. A wire connected to the voice coil carries off the current as audio.

nician to select the signal or combination of signals to be put **on the line,** that is, to be amplified and sent to the next point on the way to broadcast or cablecast (Figures 11.9 and 11.10). From the audio board, the signal may be routed to either of two destinations. First, the signal may go live, that is, directly to the transmission point for immediate modulation and distribution to the public. At a radio broadcast station, that point is the transmitter; at a cable radio station, the cable system's headend (Section 12.9.1); at a network, the network operations center.

11.3.2.2 Audiotape The second possible destination of the audio signal is a machine that records it. In most cases, the recording medium is audiotape, usually thin plastic coated with magnetic oxide. In recording, the **audiotape machine** moves the tape past an electromagnetic record head; the record head impresses the audio on the tape in the form of magnetic patterns (Box 11.1). To re-create the audio signal, the machine moves the recorded tape past a playback head, also elec-

tromagnetic; the playback head detects the patterns on the tape and translates them into electrical impulses. A recorded tape may be played back immediately, replayed repeatedly, edited, *sweetened* (have special effects added), duplicated (called a **dub**), erased, or used again for another recording.

Some audiotape machines are record-only units; some, playback-only; many do both. Two popular formats in professional audio are reel-to-reel and cartridge. The former is used primarily for recording and editing, particularly in critical situations (such as making master recordings for records and long-form radio programs); the latter, for recording and playback in broadcast and cable outlets.

11.3.2.3 Analog Versus Digital (To understand the terms analog and digital, refer to Figure 11.11 as you read this section.) In Section 11.3 we noted that audio usually takes the form of an analog of the sound it represents. As such, the audio signal is normally complex, just as complex as the sound that

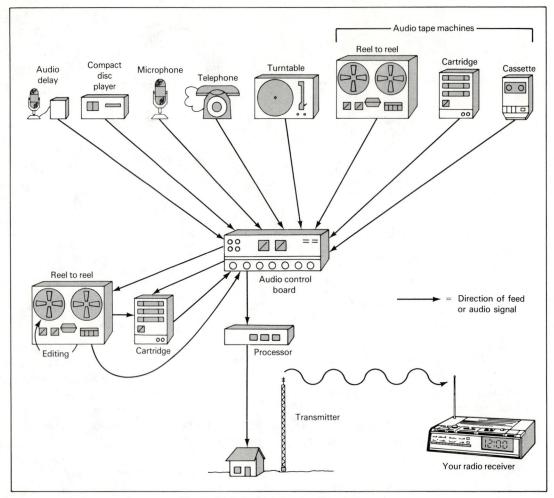

Figure 11.9 Combining audio sources.

created it (and most sounds are *very* complex). In analog form, however, audio is subject to problems. Every time an analog audio signal passes through an electronic processing device—amplifier, equalizer, compressor—the device itself introduces **noise** (unwanted sounds). Additionally, some signal information is lost. The more devices, the more noise and loss.

The process of recording, for example, both introduces noise and artificially limits the range from softest to loudest sounds **(dy-**

namic range). The noise problem becomes particularly bad when recordings are made of recordings; the more "generations" (that is, removed from the original recording), the more noise.

Digital technology can eliminate such problems. In the process of digitization, the audio signal is sampled periodically, and these samples are encoded into off-on pulses. The pulses do *not* resemble (are not analogs of) the wave form of the audio.

The signal is sampled many times per sec-

Figure 11.10 Radio automation.   An automation unit combines computer and mechanical technologies. Radio automation entails setting up a machine to carry out standard technical procedures and to play back recorded programming elements in such way as to simulate the "live" production process. On this unit, the control panel for the programmer is the device that juts out about midway down the right rack. The three large wheels in the middle rack hold tape cartridges of commercials and will select, load, and play back the proper cartridge as programmed. (Photograph courtesy of Sono-Mag Corporation.)

Box 11.1 Audio Tape Recorders

Photo (a) shows a reel-to-reel machine; photo (b) a cartridge (cart) machine. Both have their advantages—the reel-to-reel machine generally produces better quality recordings and playbacks and allows easy access to the tape for editing; the cart machine is quick to use and load and allows for automatic stop and re-cue of tape. Both use $\frac{1}{4}$-inch tape (which, in the cart, is in the form of a continuous loop enclosed in a flat plastic box) and, for broadcast work, usually operate $7\frac{1}{2}$ inches per second (i.e., $7\frac{1}{2}$ inches of tape pass the heads each second). (c) To record audio, the tape—which is oxide-coated—moves past the heads at constant speed. The heads are actually small electromagnets. The magnetic properties of the record head vary with the audio signal fed into it and thus induce varying patterns on the oxide as the tape moves past. By putting these patterns on the tape, the tape machine has encoded the audio into a form that may be stored then retrieved many times. When the tape is played back, the playback head "reads" these patterns and converts them back into audio. During recording, the erase head clears off all previous signals from the tape so that the record head encounters a "clean" (unrecorded) tape. (Photograph (b) courtesy of Harris Corp. Used by permission.)

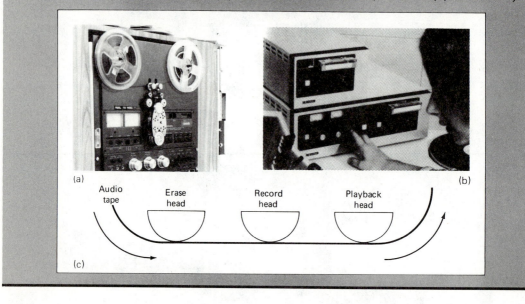

(a)   (b)

Audio tape   Erase head   Record head   Playback head

(c)

ond. This sampling rate lies far beyond the range of human perception to recognize discrete entities, so you never sense "something missing" when the digital signal is reconverted into analog audio and into sound. Yet because the basic code is simply off and on, unwanted signals may be deleted and lost information may be restored. Audio engineers use the term *transparent* to describe digital processing. Digital recordings, for example, contain almost no spurious or system-induced noise, allow an expanded dynamic range, and reproduce faithfully even after many generations of dubs.

Digital technology has proved particularly useful for postproduction processing (Section

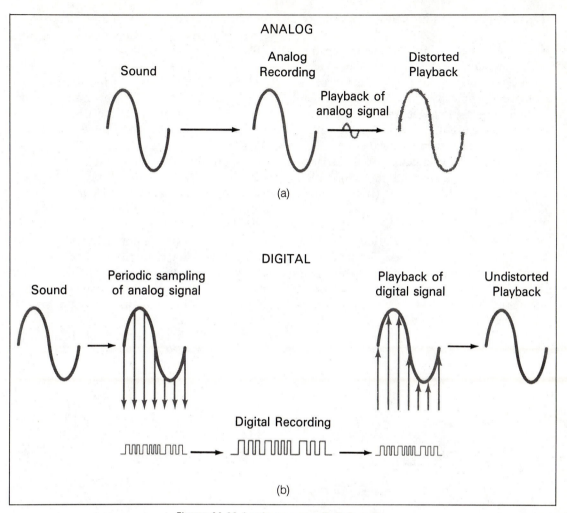

Figure 11.11 Analog versus digital audio.

6.1.3). For years, the only way to edit was to cut and splice the tape physically, and many radio stations still use this method. However, electronic digital (Section 5.1.3) devices now allow an editor to delete, add, and rearrange without cutting, even to preview material with *proposed* edits—listen to what it will sound like with the edits in place—*before* the edit decisions are made final. Other digital devices stretch or compress recorded material without altering pitch, that is, speed it up or slow it down without making it sound like animated mice or sounds from beyond the grave. They can also change pitch without changing speed, add echo and delay, and otherwise alter or distort the quality of the material. Such gimmicks are used extensively in popular music recording and in creation of radio and television commercials (Section 6.1.3).

As yet, the complete digital system is not possible. A production facility may create and process a digital audio production. But that digitized signal must be converted to analog form for modulation and transmission to the public.

11.3.3 Modulation Process

Modulation occurs in telecommunication when one electrical signal causes another to change. The first signal usually consists of information—typically, audio or video. The second signal is a carrier frequency, product of a carrier current, a high-frequency alternating electrical current. Thus (before we get lost in detailed explanations) the carrier is changed so that it contains the information of the audio or video signal. That, basically, is modulation.

11.3.3.1 Amplitude Modulation

To illustrate how modulation works, let us look at amplitude modulation. For our example, we shall use a carrier frequency of 1000 kHz and the audio signal of 1 kHz (1000 Hz) that we originated in Section 11.3.2.

In the AM radio transmitter, three main operations occur. The first two happen simultaneously—the oscillator generates the 1000-kHz carrier frequency, and the incoming audio-frequency signal is boosted and fed into the modulator. In the third operation, these two frequencies meet in the power amplifier, interact, and generate new frequencies. This is illustrated in Figure 11.12.

Two of these new frequencies are particularly significant—the **upper side frequency** and the **lower side frequency.** As a result of these new side frequencies, the amplitude or strength of the carrier is no longer constant. The carrier's amplitude now varies, rising and falling periodically. The rise-and-fall variation of the carrier amplitude forms a pattern matching that of the audio signal. We have placed information about the sound wave on the carrier wave.

We now have a carrier of 1000 kHz,

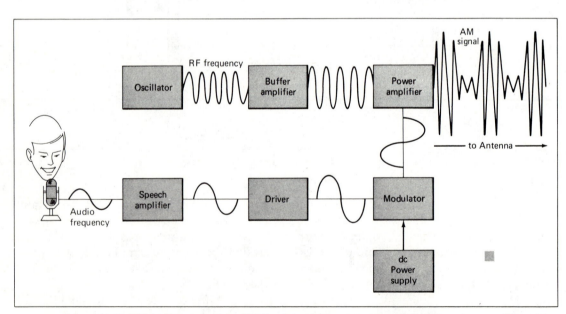

Figure 11.12 Block diagram of an AM broadcast transmission. This diagram includes a few elements not mentioned in the narrative. The speech amplifier boosts the weak audio-frequency (AF) signal to feed the driver. The driver converts the AF signal into a large voltage and enough current to drive the modulator. The buffer amplifier boosts the radio frequency and prevents the modulated signal from reflecting back from the power amplifier. The DC power supply provides power to both the modulator and the power amplifier.

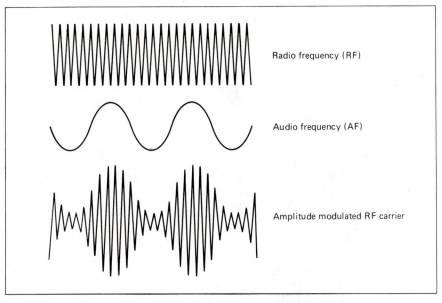

Figure 11.13 Amplitude modulation.

whose amplitude is modulated or varied so that it reproduces the pattern of the 1-kHz audio frequency. Thus the term *amplitude modulation.* Because there are both upper and lower frequencies, the pattern is repeated so that the negative phase of the carrier now bears a mirror image of the pattern carried by the positive phase. This is illustrated in Figure 11.13.

Side frequencies are generated on a sum-and-difference basis. The upper side frequency is equal to the sum of the carrier frequency plus the audio frequency. In our example, this sum would be 1001 kHz (1000 kHz [carrier frequency] + 1 kHz = 1001 kHz). The lower side frequency is equal to the difference between the two frequencies, 999 kHz in our example (1000 kHz − 1 kHz = 999 kHz).

So far we have dealt with a single audio frequency, one representing a pure tone. As mentioned in Section 11.3.1.3, however, most sounds are complex. They result in a complex audio signal, containing a number of different frequencies—a **band** of frequencies, as shown in Figure 11.14. When this complex audio signal modulates the carrier, it creates bands of side frequencies—an **upper sideband** and an identical **lower sideband.**

11.3.3.2 Frequency Modulation In frequency modulation, amplitude remains constant, while frequency varies. Figure 11.15 shows this process. During the positive phase of one cycle of an audio signal, the modulated carrier increases frequency; during the negative phase, the modulated carrier decreases frequency. Audio *frequency* is reflected in the number of *times* the modulated carrier increases and decreases frequency each second. Audio *amplitude* is reflected in the number of *carrier frequencies* in *each increase and decrease.* For example, an audio signal of 440 Hz shows up in the modulated carrier as 440 increases and decreases of frequency per second. Low audio amplitude (say, a whisper) may increase and decrease

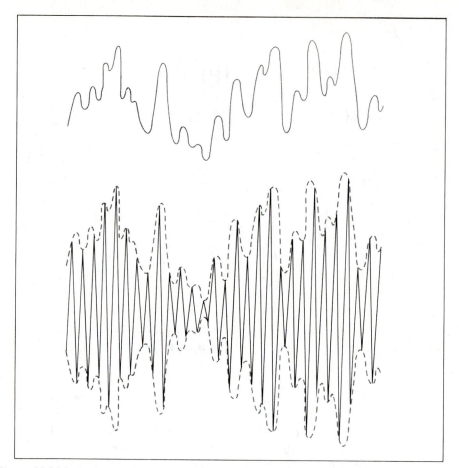

Figure 11.14 Complexity of signals. Most sounds are complex and produce audio signals similar to the top drawing, above. Should this signal modulate a carrier in an AM transmitter, the result would be similar to the bottom drawing. Note the mirror image at top and bottom; these are the sidebands. On the drawing of the modulated carrier, the pattern of the audio signal is drawn in dashed lines to point out that the carrier's amplitude now reproduces the pattern. Technically, the audio signal itself is not part of the carrier; that is, the carrier does not carry the audio signal, only the pattern of that signal.

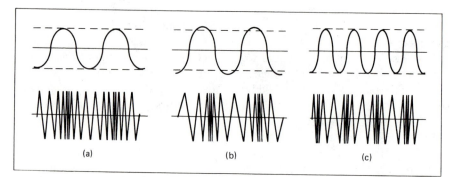

Figure 11.15 Frequency modulation of frequency and amplitude. (a) Initial signal. (b) Increased amplitude. (c) Increased frequency.

frequency only 2 kHz; high audio amplitude (a shout) may increase and decrease carrier frequency by as much as 75 kHz.

11.4 RADIO TRANSMISSION AND RECEPTION

After the carrier is modulated, it is fed to the transmitting antenna. The presence of the modulated carrier in the antenna results in radiation of electromagnetic waves, as described in Section 10.1. The electronic pattern or structure of these waves corresponds to that of the modulated carrier, and thus the waves carry the encoded information.

When these waves reach a receiver, they must go through several processes so that you can hear the audio information as sound (Figure 11.16). First, the waves come into contact with a receiving antenna. They induce a small electrical signal, a weak reproduction of the modulated carrier frequency. The signal moves into your receiver to the tuner. The tuner blocks all other frequencies except those of the frequency or channel to which you have tuned. The signal is then fed into an RF (radio frequency) amplifier that boosts the signal. The amplified signal next goes into a detector. Detection is the reverse process of modulation and recovers audio from the carrier.

In monaural radio, the recovered audio signal is fed to an AF (audio frequency) amplifier for boosting, then to a speaker. In a stereophonic receiver, a stereo signal is split into component right and left channels, each of which is separately amplified and sent to separate speakers; a monaural signal simply goes to both amplifiers unchanged, exactly the same in each.

A speaker consists of a voice coil, a paper or fiber cone, and a magnet. The voice coil consists of a number of turns of wire wound around a lightweight form that is, in turn, attached to the cone. Voice coil and cone can move back and forth. The voice coil is mounted between the poles of the magnet. The audio signal (which, remember, is a varying electrical current) is fed into the voice coil, which acts as an electromagnet. The varying magnetic field created by the voice coil interacts with the stationary field of the magnet on either side, causing the voice coil to move back and forth at the audio-frequency rate. The cone, attached to

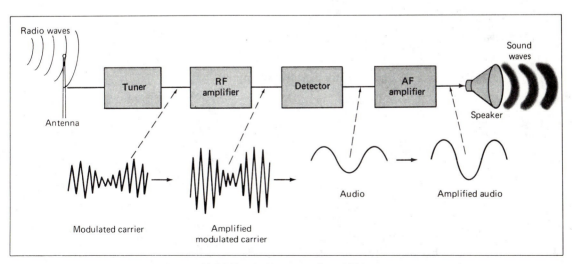

Figure 11.16 Block diagram of an AM receiver.

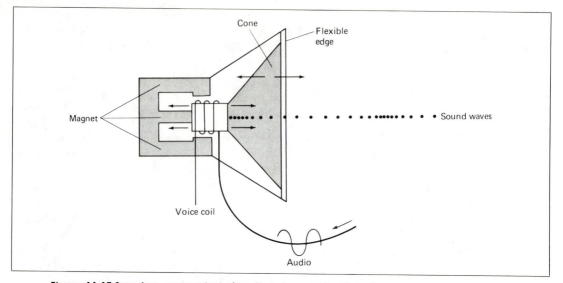

Figure 11.17 Speaker: conversion of audio into sound. Note the similarity in construction and operation to the dynamic microphone (Figure 11.8).

the voice coil, also moves back and forth, alternately compressing and rarefying adjacent air molecules. If you are near the receiver when this happens, you identify the result as sound. Figure 11.17 illustrates the speaker process.

Headsets (once called "earphones") are essentially miniature speakers. Basically, they work on the same principle as speakers.

11.5 THE AM CHANNEL

For years, FCC regulations allowed each AM radio station to occupy a 30-kHz bandwidth. Since the 30 kHz had to contain identical upper and lower sidebands (Section 11.3.3.1), this meant an AM station could transmit a 15-kHz audio response bandwidth.

11.5.1 Frequency Response

In theory, 15 kHz was enough audio bandwidth to qualify as "high fidelity." In practice, however, AM was a low-fidelity me-

dium for a number of reasons. First, technical limitations in AM systems prevented transmission of the full 15 kHz.

Second, many radios were cheaply made. They had the simplest of circuits and tiny speakers. As a result, they reproduced a narrow audio-frequency bandwidth. On such receivers, the sound of both AM and FM stations was little better than that of a telephone.

Third, AM was trapped in a cycle of degenerating fidelity for many years. Despite the 30-kHz occupied bandwidth (which equaled 15 kHz of audio bandwidth) allowed by the FCC, transmission of more than 20 kHz (10 kHz of audio) increased chances for interference from second adjacent channels. To mitigate interference, AM receiver manufacturers made sets that picked up less than the full 30 kHz. With reduced bandwidth capability, the receivers were not as liable to pick up interfering stations on second adjacent channels. But they would also not pick up the stations' high audio frequencies! As a result, the stations did not sound as good. To compensate, AM broadcasters used preemphasis; that is, they boosted the high frequencies of their audio signal. This caused even more interference, so the receiver manufacturers made AM radios that picked up an even narrower bandwidth. As a result of this cycle, the typical AM radio set reproduced an audio bandwidth of no more than 4 kHz, compared with the 15-kHz response of FM.

Trade groups for broadcasters and receiver manufacturers formed a National Radio Systems Committee (NRSC) to study and make recommendations concerning this third problem. In 1987, the NRSC voted approval of new standards, and two years later, the FCC adopted them as requirements. These standards limit the bandwidth of audio a station can transmit to 10 kHz rather than the 15 kHz allowed by previous FCC rules. The standards call for a specific preemphasis curve—how much boosting of high frequencies the stations can do. While AM stations appeared to give up 5 kHz of audio bandwidth under these standards, they would actually more than double their frequency response to a true 10 kHz, generally considered the low end of high fidelity. This would work, however, only *if* manufacturers produced AM receivers that would reproduce a full 10-kHz audio bandwidth.

11.5.2 Stereophonic AM

When the FCC voted to allow AM stereophonic broadcasting in 1982, proponents of four different systems pushed aggressively for marketplace acceptance by receiver manufacturers and AM licensees. The four were those of Harris Corporation, Kahn Communications, Magnavox (North American Philips), and Motorola.*

Each system was compatible with mon-

*Belar Electronics had proposed a fifth system but dropped out of the running early on.

aural AM, but none was compatible with the other stereo systems. A broadcaster who invested money to install one system was gambling. If that system became the standard—that is, if the majority of licensees and receiver manufacturers adopted it—then the broadcaster would be well positioned to take advantage of trends in audience listening to AM stereo. If another system became the standard, the broadcaster would be in the unenviable position of having expended a considerable amount to transmit a stereo signal that few could receive. The audience would be able to pick up the station's nonstandard signal, but in monaural only for most. Several Japanese electronics manufacturers sought to finesse the compatibility issue and developed multisystem receivers, AM radios that would pick up and reproduce in stereo the signals from all four systems.

Delco Electronics Division of General Motors (GM) tested two of the systems (the other two companies refused to participate). After completion of the tests, Delco endorsed the C-Quam system proposed by Motorola. This endorsement represented a major victory for Motorola, since Delco was the largest domestic manufacturer of radio receivers and the supplier of sets to GM's five auto divisions.

Both Magnavox and Harris eventually dropped out of the race. Kahn continued to promote his single-sideband system and the idea of multisystem receivers.

In 1987, the U.S. Commerce Department's National Telecommunications and Information Administration (NTIA) announced the results of a five-month study of AM stereo's progress. The NTIA said that stereo was vital to the future of AM broadcasting but concluded that the AM stereo marketplace had "stagnated." The only way to get it moving again was to produce multisystem radios—receivers capable of reproducing the stereophonic signals produced by both the Motorola system and the Kahn system.

Motorola, by contrast, believed that the marketplace was active and heading directly toward C-Quam. Five times as many stations broadcast with C-Quam as with the single-sideband system. A number of automobile receiver manufacturers had followed Delco's lead and were manufacturing C-Quam-only sets. And several other countries had adopted C-Quam as their national standard for AM stereophonic broadcasting.

Many AM broadcasters looked to receiver improvements and AM stereo as means to stop the flow of music listeners to FM. And, indeed, the various proposals did sound promising. None would eliminate static and station interference. But AM did have one major advantage—the ability to cover large areas, thanks to sky wave propagation.

11.5.3 Other Uses of Carriers

In 1982, the FCC adopted a rule that allows AM licensees to use their carrier frequencies for utility load management. Under this rule, a utility company may lease the carrier of an AM station to transmit a subaudible (beneath the level of human hearing) signal. A utility company usually offers special rates to its customers who participate in this load management service. The utility installs a special receiver in the participating customer's home, business, or factory. During periods of peak load (that is, whenever the most electricity or whatever is being used in the utility's service area), the utility transmits the subaudible tone via the AM station's signal. The special receivers pick up the signal and turn off the customers' appliances. When the peak load subsides, the utility transmits another subaudible tone that signals the receivers to turn the appliances back on.

In 1984, the FCC broadened its ruling. Under this action, AM stations may devote their carrier signals to any broadcast or non-broadcast use that does not interfere with their main broadcast channel programming or the signals of other stations. This expanded ruling allows AM licensees to offer many of the same subsidiary services as FM (Section 11.6.2).

11.6 THE FM CHANNEL

FM is said to be a **high-fidelity medium** because it is capable of reproducing most of the pitches that most of us can hear, from a low of 50 Hz to a high of 15,000 Hz. That wide range takes 15 kHz of each FM channel; sideband duplication accounts for another 15 kHz; and 25 kHz guard bands (frequencies not used for transmission) at either extreme of the channel use an additional 50 kHz. That leaves 120 kHz unused out of the 200-kHz FM channel. The FCC has authorized FM stations to use these frequencies to broadcast **stereophonically** and to transmit nonbroadcast channels in the **Subsidiary Communications Service.** Box 11.2 represents the upper sideband of an FM channel and shows some of these additional signals.

11.6.1 FM Multiplex

In developing a system of stereophonic broadcasting, there were three major requirements. First, one broadcast channel had to accommodate two audio channels. Second, some method had to be provided so that both stereophonic channels could be transmitted independently without interfering with each other (that is, without causing crosstalk). Third, stereophonic broadcasts had to be compatible with existing receivers.

The **FM multiplex system** met all requirements. The word "multiplex" refers to the sending of two or more signals simultaneously over the same channel. FM stereophony uses *frequency multiplex;* that is, in addition to the main carrier frequency of a

Box 11.2 The FM Channel

We are looking at the upper sideband (100 kHz) of an FM channel. The channel's center frequency is at extreme left, where the solid horizontal line begins. The lower sideband (the other 100 kHz of the channel) lies unpictured to the immediate left of the "Audio L + R" block. Numbers indicate the number of frequencies in (kHz) above the center frequency. The station using this channel broadcasts stereophonically and transmits one SCS. A monaural receiver utilizes only the "Audio L + R" signal and reproduces a monaural signal. A stereophonic receiver utilizes the subcarrier at 19 kHz above the center frequency to recover the "L − R" signal. The stereo receiver combines the L + R and L − R signals to produce separate left and right channels. Since this station transmits in stereo, the subcarrier for its SCS (and for any other SCSs it may wish to add) must operate between 53 and 99 kHz. This station's SCS subcarrier operates at 67 kHz and generates sidebands 7.5 kHz to either side (59.5–74.5 kHz). Only receivers equipped to utilize the SCS subcarrier can pick up the SCS signal. The guard band consists of frequencies left unused so as to avoid adjacent channel interference.

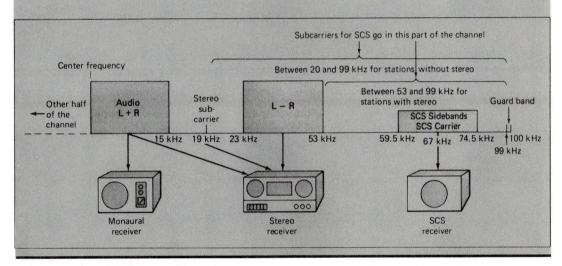

channel, subcarriers are generated and modulated to carry additional information. The right and left stereophonic channels are combined and transmitted on the main carrier, and certain accessory signals are transmitted on a subcarrier (Box 11.3). A stereophonic receiver has special circuitry that picks up the subcarrier and uses the accessory signals to separate the right and left stereophonic channels and to feed them to individual speakers. A monaural receiver can pick up the transmission but does not have the circuitry to utilize the subcarrier signals. A listener hears a monaural broadcast, the combined right and left stereophonic channels.

11.6.2 SCS

Even with a stereophonic signal, there is still enough room left in an FM channel for still more subcarriers to transmit additional information. Some FM stations avail themselves

Box 11.3 Monaural and Stereophonic Sound Systems

In monaural broadcasts (a), all sound sources are funneled down to one channel (here represented by one microphone picking up sound sources A, B, C, and D. When more than one microphone is used, audio signals from all microphones are simply blended together.) The listener hears the sound as a blend (A + B + C + D) and perceives the source of the sound to be the speaker. In stereophonic broadcasts (b), all sound sources are funneled down to two channels—"right" and "left" (here represented by two microphones picking up A, B, C, and D. Other microphones may be used, but their signals are blended into one of the two channels). The two signals are kept separate until transmission, at which time they are multiplexed together. A stereophonic receiver re-separates the right and left audio signals and feeds them to separate right and left speakers. The listener hears the sound binaurally, as though in the studio with the sound sources. When properly positioned, the listener perceives the sources of sound not to be the two speakers, but to be at various locations around the listening room, the same relative (to the microphones) locations of the sound sources in the studio.

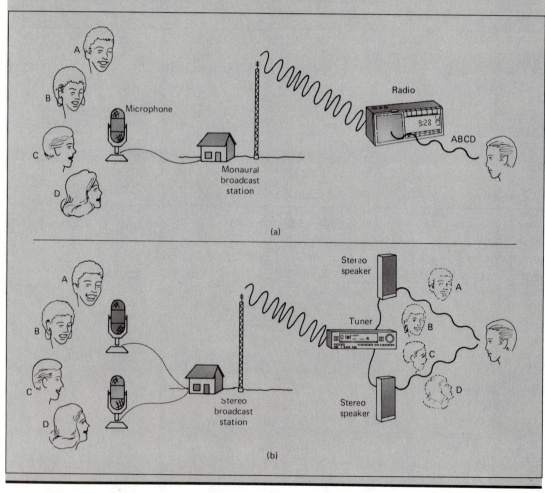

(a)

(b)

of the FCC's liberal Subsidiary Communication Service (SCS)* rules and transmit non-broadcast material. Users (the "audience") are equipped with special receivers tuned to the station's frequency. The receivers, in turn, have circuitry that allows them to pick up the SCS subcarrier. Home sets receive the station's normal broadcast programming, but most cannot receive the simultaneous SCS signal.

FM stations may use SCSs for any purpose, including point-to-point communication and common carrier-like services, and may offer multiple SCS subcarriers in a single FM channel. In most cases, SCS provides a background music service. Some stations, however, provide specialized informational material for physicians, lawyers, or stockbrokers. Others offer radio paging (beeper) services, data transmission, and dispatch services. An SCS subcarrier can even transmit slow-scan video. Many noncommercial stations have used their SCSs to provide reading services for the blind, but they may also use them to earn a profit (as long as the reading service remains on a nonprofit basis).

11.7 INTERNATIONAL BROADCAST SERVICE

By international agreement, certain groups of frequencies in the 6–25 MHz (high frequency or **shortwave**) bands are allocated for broadcast between nations. Propagation characteristics change with the seasons, and a station usually wishes to broadcast programs simultaneously to different parts of the world, so that each international broadcasting station uses a number of different frequencies and multiple transmitters.

The FCC licenses nongovernmental international broadcasting stations in the United

*Called Subsidiary Communication Authorization (SCA) until 1983, when the commission liberalized the rules and changed the name.

States. Minimum power is 50 kW. Both private and governmental international broadcast stations are discussed in Chapter 23.

11.8 WIRED RADIO

So far, we have discussed broadcast radio, that which goes "over the air" to reach your receiver. However, there are also radio services that use wire and other conductors for distribution.

You could draw parallels between the wired systems and **cable audio services.** Many cable television systems charge a low extra fee to hook your FM receiver to the cable. You, then, use the FM tuner to select among the various services carried on the system.

A number of colleges have **carrier current** stations. These feed a very low-power AM signal to the dormitory water pipes or power lines, which, in turn, act as an antenna system. Radio receivers within the building are close enough to receive the station, but the signal does not carry beyond the walls. For this reason, such stations are also called "campus-limited" and "wired wireless." With their transmissions limited to prevent interference, the FCC does not require them to be licensed.

Finally, the FCC licenses stations in the **Travelers Information Service** (TIS). A TIS station uses a low-power roadside radio transmitter to feed conductors that parallel the highway. The conductors act as an antenna, and the transmission can be picked up on automobile radios in the immediate vicinity. A TIS station transmits information concerning hazards; directions to parking lots, food, and lodging; and other such information. TIS stations operate at the extreme ends of the AM band, near or at busy air, train, and bus terminals, public parks, historical sites, interstate highway exchanges, bridges, and tunnels.

NOTES

1. 47 CFR §73.1.
2. 47 CFR §73.11.

FURTHER READING

Alten, Stanley R. *Audio in Media.* 2d ed. Belmont: Wadsworth, 1986. Radio, TV, film, sound recording.

Ballou, Glen, ed. *Handbook for Sound Engineers: The New Audio Cyclopedia.* Indianapolis: Sams, 1987. Latest ideas, innovations, discoveries in audio technology.

Carr, Joseph L. *The TAB Handbook of Radio Communications.* Blue Ridge Summit: TAB, 1984.

Crutchfield, E. B., ed. *NAB Engineering Handbook.* 7th ed. Washington: NAB, 1985. Broadcast engineer's "bible."

Eargle, John. *Handbook of Recording Engineering.* 3d ed. New York: Van Nostrand, 1986. Sound, stereophony, microphones.

Miller, Gary M. *Modern Electronic Communication.* 2d ed. Englewood Cliffs: Prentice, 1983. Chapters 2–6 deal with AM and FM radio.

Olson, Harry F. *Music, Physics, and Engineering.* 2d ed. New York: Dover, 1967. Physics of sound.

Oringel, Robert S. *Audio Control Handbook: For Radio and Television Broadcasting.* 6th ed. Stoneham: Focal, 1989. Guide to audio production equipment and operation.

Prentiss, Stan. *AM Stereo and TV Stereo: New Sound Dimensions.* Blue Ridge Summit: TAB, 1985.

Woram, John M. *The Recording Studio.* Plainview: Sagamore, 1976.

CHAPTER 12

Television Channels

The basic process of television transmission is the same as that of radio. The major difference, of course, is that television involves visual (picture) information. The visual signal is complex and requires wide bands of frequencies.

In this chapter, we start with visual perception—how our eyes and brains make use of light. Then we discuss the video signal—the conversion of light into an electronic analog. Next, we look at the television channel—the band of frequencies that carries the video signal and its various accessories. After that, we see how the television receiver makes use of that channel. Finally, we discuss the various modes of transmitting and receiving the television channel—wireless and wired distribution—and the mechanics of some alternative video services.

12.1 VISUAL PERCEPTION

Television requires a lot of complex and expensive equipment. But the most complex part of the whole system is the device on which television depends for its very existence—your eyes. Television takes advantage of certain characteristics of the eye. If we

want to know how television works, we must start with these characteristics.

12.1.1 Light

We see because our eyes are sensitive to light, electromagnetic radiation in the frequency range 3.85×10^{14} to 7.90×10^{14} Hz.* All that we "see" is simply light—some direct, most reflected. For example, you can see this page that you are now reading because light falls on the page, and the page reflects some of the light. Your eyes receive the light reflected from the page and, together with your brain, translate the particular pattern of light into a particular pattern of visual images. Your brain interprets this pattern as a page in a book.

Light is part of the electromagnetic spectrum (Section 10.2.1). Light—like radio—

*To read figures expressed in *exponential* notation, start with the whole number (the one before the decimal point) of the *mantissa* (the first number), followed by enough digits to equal the *exponent* (the little number above and to the right of the 10). For these digits, start with the numbers after the decimal point in the mantissa, then add zeros to fill. Thus, 3.85×10^{14} would be 3 plus 14 more digits—85 plus 12 zeros—or 385,000,000,000,000 (385 trillion).

travels in waves and is measured by frequency and wavelength. Light, however, is far up the electromagnetic spectrum, and whereas radio waves are measured in meters, light waves are measured in millimicrons (mμ), each of which is one thousandth of a millionth of a meter.

12.1.2 Color

Our eyes are sensitive to light in different ways at different frequencies, and the different sensations that light produces are called colors. For example, we may perceive light in the range 400–490 mμ as blue, 500–560 mμ as green, and so on.

The sensation we call color may be described by three distinct psychological aspects—**hue,** the color itself (red, blue, green, yellow, etc.); **saturation** (also called *chroma*), the purity or strength of a color as pale, rich, washed out, and so on; and **brightness** (also *luminance* or *value*), whether the color is dark or light. These aspects are psychological because they are subjective, and each affects our perception of the others; if one changes, we see the result as a different color.

Keep in mind that we are discussing light, not pigment such as paint or crayons. Also remember that we are dealing with **physiological** color, not physical color. A physical color is pure, monochromatic, unmixed with other colors and can be precisely described in terms of frequencies and wavelengths.

However, most light that reaches our eyes is not monochromatic, but a mixture of frequencies. White light, such as ordinary daylight (or the light reflected from this page), is a mixture; the various frequencies have, in a sense, canceled out each other so that we see no color. When one frequency in the mixture is stronger than the others (highest intensity), we see color. If the highest intensity occurs in the yellow frequency region, we see yellow.

In some cases there is more than one strong frequency in the mixture. There could be, for example, one strong frequency in the red region and another in the green. We would interpret the light hitting our eyes not as separate red and green but (given the proper frequencies) as yellow. This is an example of physiological color and is apparently determined by the ratios of light picked up by the red-, blue-, and green-sensitive cones (color receptors) in our eyes. Given proper mixtures, we would see no difference between the pure, monochromatic yellow and the physiological yellow created from red and green.

These physiological colors are possible because of the **trichromatic nature of vision;** that is, over a wide range of brightness levels, our eyes can match almost any color by specific combinations of two other colors. Color television takes advantage of this to work its chromatic illusion. The camera breaks down light reflected from a televised scene into three colors—red, blue, and green (at wavelengths of 610, 472, and 534 mμ, respectively)—called **primary colors.** When your home receiver screen reproduces the three colors in the same proportions, your eyes see all the various and assorted colors present in the original scene.

12.1.3 Persistence of Vision

We watch an exciting automobile chase scene unfold on our television screens. But the movement that we think we see is an illusion.

This illusion was first used for mass audiences in another medium, motion pictures. A movie camera actually photographs a scene as a series of still pictures (frames) taken one after another, 24 per second. The exposed film must be chemically processed (developed) to bring out the photographs and make them permanent. The film is semitransparent so that light beamed through it projects an enlargement of the pictures.

When used in a movie projector, these separate still pictures are shown in such a way as to create the illusion of motion. The projector places one frame in front of a light source, the light projects the picture twice very briefly, and the projector moves the first frame out and the next one in. This action is repeated 24 times per second.

The TV screen, similar to the movie projector, is capable only of reproducing a series of electronic still pictures or frames. In the case of our chase scene (or any apparent movement), each still picture is slightly different from the others.

At this point, we still have a series of still pictures, but a trick of the eye called *persistence of vision* translates the still pictures into motion. When you look at an object then glance away, the retina of your eye retains the image of the object for the briefest of instants; this is persistence of vision. As you watch a motion picture or a television program, your eye retains the image of each frame long enough so that by the time the next picture appears, your brain has connected the two, and you see an illusion of motion instead of a series of still pictures.

12.2 VIDEO SIGNAL

We are now ready to investigate the mechanics of video, to find out how light, the primary colors, and persistence of vision make pictures. We begin with the key device, the color camera, origin of the video (picture) signal.

12.2.1 The Color Camera

Three main parts of the color television camera help create the video signal—the **lens,** the **internal optical system,** and the **video pickup.** The lens is external to the camera but attached to it. The lens gathers light reflected from the scene to be televised and focuses it onto the internal optical system inside the camera. The internal optical system consists of various combinations of prisms, mirrors, and color filters, the purpose of which is to break up the light from the scene into its red, blue, and green components. Each of these three components is focused onto a separate video pickup or *imager.*

12.2.2 The Video Pickup

Most video cameras use one of two overall types of pickup. One is the **camera tube;** the other, the **charge–coupled device** (CCD).

Modern "tube-type" cameras (Figure 12.1) actually consist of solid-state circuitry. Their only remnant of electronic vacuum-tube technology (aside from the viewfinder screen) is the video pickup itself, the cylindrically shaped camera tube (Figure 12.2). At one end of the tube is the **target** (Figure 12.3). The target consists of a transparent electrode covered with many thousands of tiny photosensitive segments that form the picture elements or **pixels.** When light hits one of these segments, the segment reacts in a way that alters certain of its electrical properties or characteristics, the degree of alteration varying directly with the intensity of the light falling on the segment. Therefore when the image (incident light reflected from the scene being televised) is focused on the target, the pattern of light in the image creates a pattern of reaction on the target.

The **electron gun** in the other end of the tube fires a hair-thin stream of electrons at the target. This electron beam systematically travels over each part of the target (and thus the pattern on it) guided by electromagnets (coils) that surround the camera tube. This is called **scanning.** As the electrons hit each part of the target, the result is an electrical

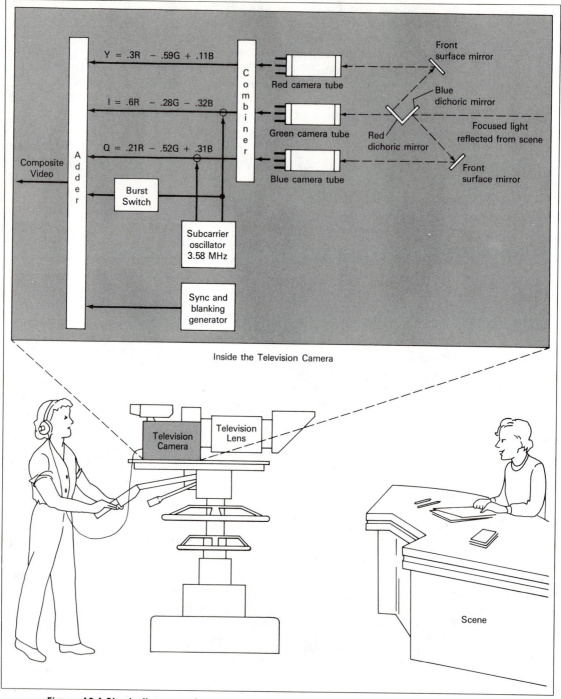

Figure 12.1 Block diagram of a color television camera. The Y signal represents brightness; and I and Q signals, orange-cyan colors and green-purple colors, respectively.

scale integrated circuit measures about $1\frac{1}{2}$ inches long by 1 inch wide by $\frac{1}{16}$ inch thick. The scene being televised is focused on the CCD's imaging surface or optic. The imaging surface consists of some 200,000 "photosite" capacitors—the pixels—arranged in columns and rows on an area with a 3×4 aspect ratio. Similar to a camera tube, the reception of light energy by a photo site liberates electrons proportionate to the intensity of light at that location. A potential well holds the light-generated charge. The charge then transfers, first to a vertical (digital) store (Section 12.2.7) register, and then to horizontal (analog) storage, a shift register from which it is clocked out as a continuous video signal. This transfer process passes the charge pattern from one capacitor to the next.

12.2.3 Scanning Pattern

When the electron beam scans the target of a camera tube, it follows a pattern somewhat like that of your eyes as they read this book. The beam starts at the top of the target, scans left to right, drops down, scans left to right, drops down, and so on. On each line, the beam scans roughly 425 pixels. Once the beam scans the entire target, the camera tube

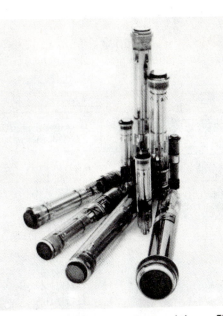

Figure 12.2 Plumbicon camera tubes. They come in various sizes and styles for various cameras and applications. (Photograph courtesy of Amperex Electronic Company. Used by permission. Plumbicon is a registered trademark of Philips.)

current that varies according to the part of the pattern being scanned. This current leaves the tube and is used as the video signal.

The charge–coupled device (CCD; Figure 12.4), a solid-state imager, makes possible the tubeless television camera. This large-

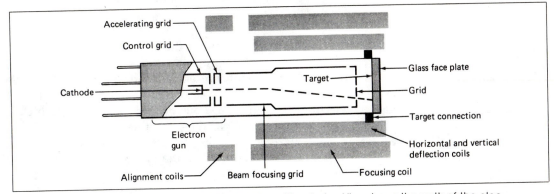

Figure 12.3 Structure of the lead oxide tube. The dashed line shows the path of the electron beam. The video signal is conducted from the tube via the target connection, a metal ring that circles the tube.

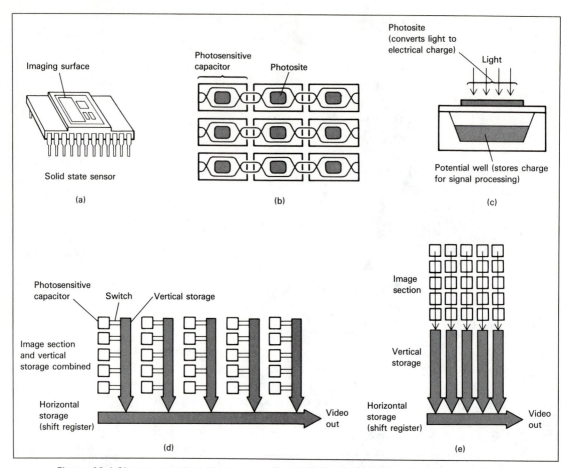

Figure 12.4 Charge-coupled device. (a) The CCD itself. (b) Detail of a section of the imaging surface. (c) Side cutaway view of one photo site capacitor. The configuration of the vertical storage area defines two basic CCD technologies—(d) an *interline transfer* CCD integrates the storage area with the optic; (e) a *frame transfer* CCD uses a separate storage area.

has created the electronic equivalent of one still picture, then has converted it into a video signal, emitting each electronic element of the picture, one by one, in a specific, sequential order. One complete electronic still picture is called a **frame.** The electron beam scans **525 lines per frame** and **30 frames per second** (fps).

Thirty per second would *seem* to be enough to make us see an illusion of smooth motion, especially considering that silent

film achieves the illusion at 16 fps. However, a film projector shows each frame twice, so silent film actually utilizes *32 frame projections* per second. Also, as screen brightness increases, our eyes are not as easily tricked into blending together a sequence of pictures. The television screen is so much brighter than the motion picture screen that even at 30 fps we would still see **flicker**—a constant, regular variation in the overall brightness of the television screen. Therefore, to eliminate flicker, American television actually shows **60 half-pictures per second.** The electron beam scans **every other line** until it reaches the bottom of the target; then it jumps back to the top and starts over, scanning the lines it skipped the first time. This is called **interlace scanning** (Figure 12.5). The beam scans $262\frac{1}{2}$ lines on each pass, called a **field,** so there are **two fields per frame** and **60 fields per second.**

Signal readout from a CCD follows this same pattern. Each photo-site capacitor includes a switch. All switches open in alternating rows, and the accumulated charges transfer to the first (vertical) frame store. Next, they transfer to the second (horizontal) frame store, from which they emerge to become the video signal. (Additionally, some CCD cameras include a mechanical shutter that completely shuts out light during transfers.)

12.2.4 Signal Processing

Video signals from the camera tubes combine in various ratios to form three intermediate signals—one for brightness, two for colors. These are added to produce the **composite video signal,** which consists of **luminance** and **chrominance** components.

12.2.5 Camera Configurations

A **camera control unit** (CCU) provides power and drive pulses (to direct the scanning pattern) for the camera; the CCU is usually located apart from the camera, and one technician operates several CCUs at once. A **camera cable** connects camera and CCU, delivering drive pulses to, and composite video from, the camera. Camera, cable, and CCU are known collectively as a **camera chain.**

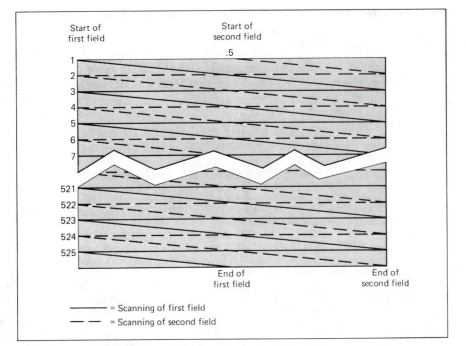

Figure 12.5 Interlaced scanning pattern.

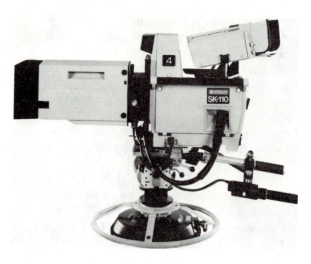

Figure 12.6 Electronic studio camera. Hitachi SK-110 camera. (Photograph courtesy of Hitachi Denshi America, Ltd. Used by permission.)

The cameras discussed above (Figure 12.6) are the type used for studio productions and for scheduled remotes (broadcasts of planned events that take place outside the studio). Two other types of camera are the film chain and the minicamera. The **film chain** is basically a camera that has been mounted permanently in a stationary position. Adjacent film and slide projectors focus their beams into the lens of the camera. The whole works—camera, projectors, and associated control equipment—is the **telecine unit** (Figure 12.7) and is a means to integrate slides and films into a television program. The **minicamera** (Figure 12.8) often uses no cable; its video can be recorded or relayed short distances via radio waves.

12.2.6 Videotape Recorder

Not all video signals originate from a camera. For example, a videotape recorder (VTR) (Box 12.1 and Figure 12.9) may serve as a video source. Like an audiotape recorder, a VTR records the electronic signal in the form

Figure 12.7 Telecine unit. The telecine operator loads a motion picture projector. Special tape and a film splicer (right foreground) serve for emergency film repairs. In the lower left foreground, 35-mm photo slides sit in a box before being loaded into the round drum (behind them) of a slide projector. The slide drum partially obscures another motion picture projector (at left). The dark gray box at right holds the film-chain camera. The box suspended from the ceiling is a video monitor; we are seeing the back of it.

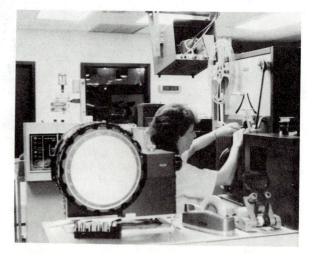

Figure 12.8 Tubeless electronic minicamera. An operator can hoist a self-contained minicamera to shoulder and take it places not easily accessible to larger studio cameras. This particular minicamera, RCA's CCD-1, made use of a technological revolution, the charge-coupled device (CCD). The small gadget being held above the camera is one of three CCD chips used instead of camera tubes in this RCA camera. (Photograph courtesy of RCA Corp. Used by permission of General Electric Co.)

(a)

Figure 12.9 Open-reel and cartridge videotape recorders. Broadcast stations often play back (a) programs on open-reel (reel-to-reel) VTRs and (b) short segments (such as commercials and news stories) on cartridge machines. This video cartridge machine uses two stacks for loading the cartridges (you see one of them at left, partially obscured by the operator) and can be programmed in advance (keyboard and screen at right) for near-instant random access. In (a) the reels can be seen through the front glass of the VTRs' cases. In (b), a cartridge sits on the counter between the operator and the keyboard.

(b)

Box 12.1 Two Types of Videotape Recorders

The quadraplex recorder (a) is so-called because it utilizes four tiny recording heads for the video signal. They are mounted on a small wheel that spins at 14,400 revolutions per minute as the two-inch-wide tape moves past at $7\frac{1}{2}$ or 15 inches per second. These heads thus put the video signal on the tape at right angles to the long axis of the tape while several fixed recording heads put on the audio, cue, and control tracks. The recording heads on a helical-scan or slant-track recorder (b) are mounted on a short, wide cylinder. The tape is threaded so that it winds around the cylinder on a slant. As the tape moves, the cylinder turns, and the video heads put a slanted track on it. Fixed heads add audio, cue, and control tracks. When first introduced, helical-scan recorders were unstable and produced inferior pictures. Over the years, however, continuing research and development improved slant-track technology, and helical recorders using 1-inch tape became the standard for television broadcast station use. Open-reel (reel-to-reel) tape threading was phased out. Newer recorders pulled the tape from a cassette—a container that held both feed and take-up reels—and automatically threaded the tape around the drum. The U-matic (c) was developed in 1969 and hit the market in 1971. Betamax (d) was introduced in 1976 followed in 1977 by video home system (VHS). More recent configurations for digital VCRs include the Ampex D-2 (f). Manufacturers also pushed the technology toward narrower tape—$\frac{1}{2}$-inch, $\frac{1}{4}$-inch, even $\frac{1}{8}$-inch.

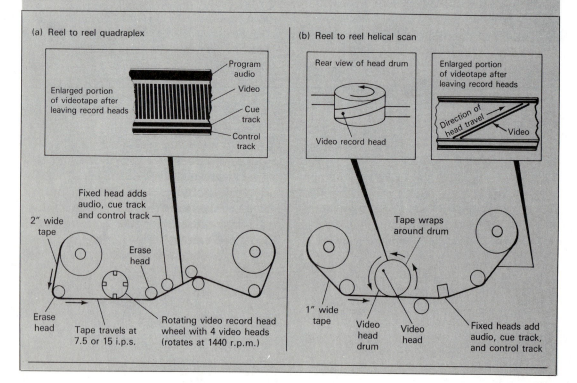

(a) Reel to reel quadraplex

Enlarged portion of videotape after leaving record heads

Program audio
Video
Cue track
Control track

Fixed head adds audio, cue track and control track

2" wide tape

Erase head

Erase head

Tape travels at 7.5 or 15 i.p.s.

Rotating video record head wheel with 4 video heads (rotates at 1440 r.p.m.)

(b) Reel to reel helical scan

Rear view of head drum

Video record head

Enlarged portion of videotape after leaving record heads

Direction of head travel

Video

Tape wraps around drum

1" wide tape

Video head drum

Video head

Fixed heads add audio, cue track, and control track

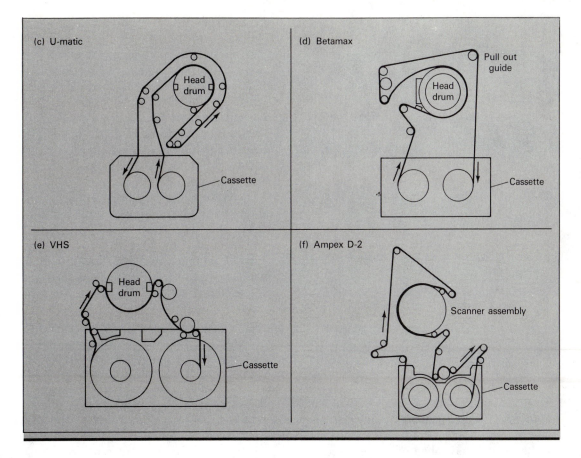

of magnetic patterns on tape. Like an audiotape recorder, the VTR can play back a recording immediately; no further processing or developing is necessary. Unlike an audiotape recorder, however, a VTR records the complex video signal as well as the comparatively simple audio signal.

12.2.7 Other Video Sources

Several devices utilize computer technology to produce "pure" (not originated by a camera) video signals. These include the frame store, character generator, paint system, and 3D graphics and animation system.

The **frame store** (electronic still store) performs somewhat the same task as the slide projectors in the telecine unit. An electronic camera scans a live scene or artwork, and the resulting electronic image (the frame) is stored in digital form in a memory unit along with dozens of other frames. Any of these frames may be recalled instantaneously for broadcast, production, or alteration. Frame storage is electronic, uses few moving parts, and so avoids many of the problems that plague slide projection—hung-up changers, burned-out lamps, and dirty, scratched, broken, backward, or upside-down slides.

A **character generator** (Figure 12.10) contains a repertoire of shapes that can be placed on the screen. Its circuitry creates letters and numerals in several different fonts,

Figure 12.10 Character generator. The operator uses the keyboard to select shapes and typefaces and to adjust size and position on screen. The resulting title shows up on the rightmost small preview monitor just above the keyboard. The operator saves the titles on an 8-inch data disk (inserted in the slot just above the preview monitor). During broadcast, the titles are called up from the disc and matted into the regular video picture; the audience sees (for example) an individual speaking to the camera with the individual's name printed in the bottom one-third of the picture. This operator sees this composite picture in the large monitor at center.

styles, and sizes. It may also have the ability to produce a limited number of other figures. Material produced by a character generator can be stored then called up when needed. Most often, such material takes the form either of captions and identifying titles placed on another picture or of full frame messages (as, for example, the screen that tells you how to use your bank card and the 800 telephone number to order at the end of a per-inquiry or direct-marketing TV commercial).

A **paint system** consists of computer and software, electronic stylus, digitizing tablet, and color video monitor. It may also include a character generator and a frame store. When the system is being used to create video graphics, the video signal is held in a buffer for a modification and display. The artist watches the monitor while using the stylus to draw on the flat graphics tablet. The stylus, simply a pencil-shaped solid rod, puts no mark on the tablet. Instead, each

movement of the stylus shows as a corresponding mark on the monitor screen. The artist may create a completely new image "from scratch" or may alter an existing video image—perhaps to change an advertiser's logo slightly or to add art to a frame from a videotape shot on location. The more elaborate systems provide so many control functions that the artist creating video graphics actually has greater flexibility than one who uses traditional paints and brushes.

The video graphics artist can create the illusions of three dimensions (3D) and animation with a **3D animation system.** With this system, an object may be drawn in one position and then rotated to show it in other positions. The system has built-in logic circuits and large-scale frame storage that assist in creating the many individual "slightly different" frames needed for animation. Once an initial drawing is completed, the human input required to animate it is minimal—especially when compared with old-fashioned film animation that required hand-drawn cels for each frame (Section 6.2.2.4). Once created, an animated sequence is stored for recall and use in production.

The broadcast and cable networks use computer art and animation extensively, especially for logos, promos, and program graphics for news and sports. The equipment to create such graphics costs a great deal, and local stations and cable systems usually must think long and hard before making the investment.

12.2.8 Combining Video Signals

Most television programs use video signals from a number of sources. Any source or combination of sources may be **put on the line,** that is, selected to send the video on to the next point in the production process (Figure 12.11). The selection of the video signal

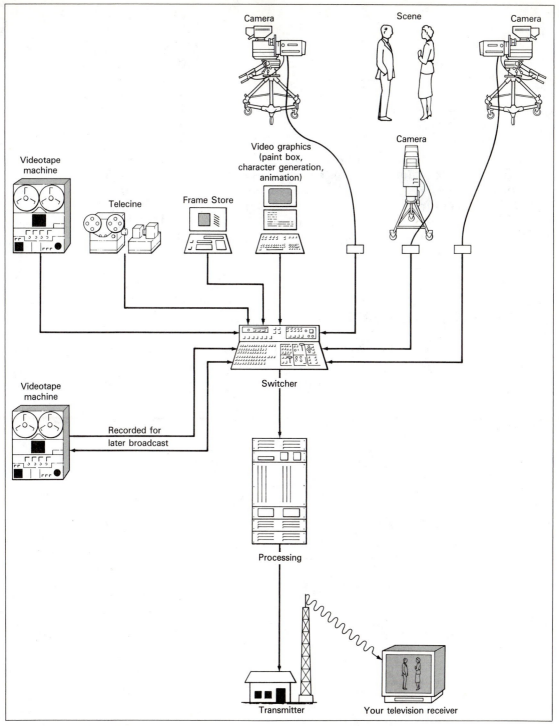

Figure 12.11 Combining video sources. Video sources include the playback head of a videotape machine, the pickup tube of the film chain in the telecine unit (for slides and film), frame (still) store, video graphics generator, and live studio and remote cameras. These feed to the switcher for mixing and special effects. From there, a number of things may happen to the video signal—it may be recorded for later broadcast; it may be sent to the transmitter for immediate transmission; or it may be both recorded and transmitted at the same time.

or combination of video signals to go on the line is **mixing,** also called **switching.**

The mixing controls are known collectively as the **switcher.** In addition, there is usually an **effects generator** associated with the switcher, and between the two devices various visual effects may be achieved, ranging from a simple **cut** (instantaneous replacement of one picture by another) to exotic **mattes** and **keys** (part of one picture is inserted into another). Newer effects generators utilize digital technology and offer almost unlimited manipulation of the picture and its component parts.

12.3 THE TELEVISION CHANNEL

The 6-MHz-wide television channel accommodates two carrier frequencies. The first is at 1.25 MHz (from the channel's lowest frequency) and is modulated by the composite video signal; the second, at 5.75 MHz, is modulated by the audio signal.

12.3.1 Modulation

As you can see in Figure 12.12, the upper and lower sidebands of the video signal are *not* mirror images of each other. The former extends 4.5 MHz above the carrier; the latter, only 1.25 MHz below, a result of **vestigial sideband** modulation. This is normal amplitude modulation with one of the sidebands partially suppressed. The color component is in the sidebands of the **color subcarrier.**

Figure 12.13 shows that the luminance and chrominance sidebands overlap. The technique by which these two different signals share the same frequency space is called **frequency interlace** or **interleaving**—placing the clusters of color energy between the clusters of video energy.

As mentioned at the beginning of this section, the luminance signal modulates the amplitude of the video carrier. The saturation part of the chrominance signal modulates the amplitude of the color subcarrier. And the hue part of the chrominance signal modu-

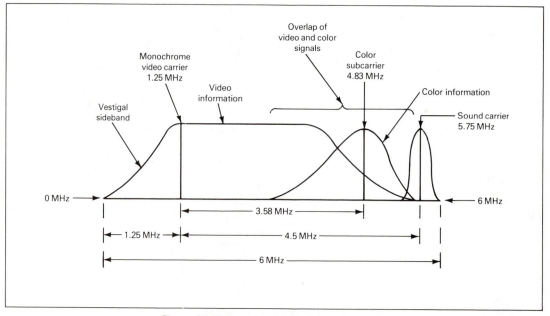

Figure 12.12 Broadcast television channel.

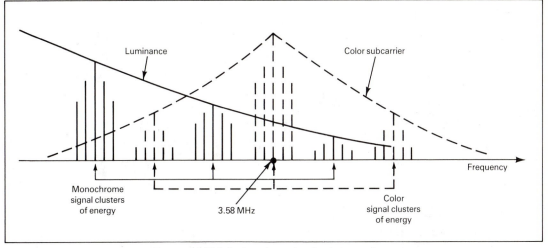

Figure 12.13 Interleaving of color information.

lates the phase of the color subcarrier, varying the angle of the wave slightly for each hue. Thus the **video signal is amplitude modulated** (AM), while the **color signal is both AM and phase modulated.**

12.3.2 Accessory Signals

In order for the home color receiver to recover the phase-modulated hue information, a special signal is sent as part of the composite video signal. This is the **color burst** (Figure 12.14), and its purpose is to ensure that the electronic circuits in your home color receiver are exactly in phase with the original subcarrier frequency. The color burst is an accessory signal—a nonpicture signal sent as part of the video signal—that accompanies color transmissions.

Two other accessory signals are part of all television transmissions, both color and monochrome. These are **sync pulses** and **blanking pulses.** Sync pulses keep your receiver's scanning beam synchronized with the camera's scanning beam. Blanking pulses cut off the electron beam when it moves from the end of one line or field to the beginning

of the next. This between-lines movement is called **retrace,** and the blanking pulse prevents retrace lines from showing on the screen.

The video signal is **negatively modulated.** This means that as darker areas of the scene are scanned, the video signal increases in amplitude. The amplitude of the signal can be boosted to a point beyond the darkest shade a television set can reproduce. Sync, blanking, and color burst pulses are transmitted between each line of scansion, all at this **blacker than black level** of amplitude (Figure 12.15). The same technique is used to send signals for closed captioning and teletext (Sections 5.7.2 and 5.7.3) in the vertical blanking interval, that is, during the period when the scanning beam returns from the end of one field back up to the top of the frame to begin scanning another field.

12.3.3 Audio

While the video signal is amplitude modulated, the **audio signal is frequency modulated** (FM). The audio signal sidebands extend 25 kHz to either side of its carrier.

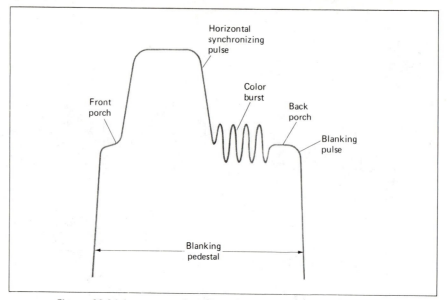

Figure 12.14 Accessory signals: color burst, sync, blanking.

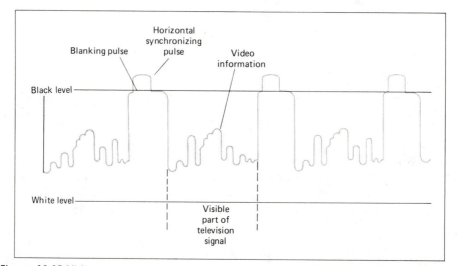

Figure 12.15 Video and accessory signals. This diagram shows three horizontal lines of video signal with accessory signals.

FCC rules allow broadcasters to use any system for **multichannel television sound** (MTS). However, on recommendation of an industrywide Broadcast Television System Committee (BTSC), the FCC specified that all systems had to "protect" (not interfere with) the workings of an MTS system developed by Zenith and dbx [*sic*], Inc. The FCC thus set a standard but at the same time encouraged marketplace advances in technology.

BTSC MTS allows both stereophonic and second-audio-program (SAP) transmission. The TV stereo sound system is similar to that of FM radio in that it consists of a main channel (which combines both left and right channels) and a stereo subcarrier. The SAP is transmitted by means of yet another subcarrier. An example of use of the SAP might be a television station whose service area includes a large number of Hispanics and transmits a Spanish translation of program audio on the second channel.

12.4 THE TELEVISION RECEIVER

The existing color television system is **compatible**—you may watch the same color telecast on either a color receiver or a monochrome receiver (in black and white, of course). Compatibility is possible because both the color receiver and the monochrome receiver utilize the video signal ("the picture" without color). Color receivers have special circuitry that detects and makes use of the color signal (which colors the picture), so when you watch a color telecast on a color receiver, you see color pictures. A monochrome receiver lacks this circuitry, but since it receives the video signal, you see color telecasts in black and white.

Your television receiver must reconstruct the various picture components from the composite signal. Using the color burst and the chrominance component, it retrieves the green, red, and blue signals. Other circuits detect and make use of sync and blanking pulses.

The **color picture tube** (Figure 12.16) is the device that creates the picture. The three separate color signals feed into the base of the picture tube, where there is an **electron gun** assembly. The inside of the face of the tube—that is, the other side of the glass screen that you watch—is coated with many thousands of tiny separate **color phosphors**—red, blue, and green. Just in back of the phosphor screen is a **mask**.

The gun assembly fires at the screen three separate electron beams, the intensity of each controlled by its respective red, blue, or green signal voltage. (Remember, electrons themselves have no color; they only carry information about color.) The beams scan the

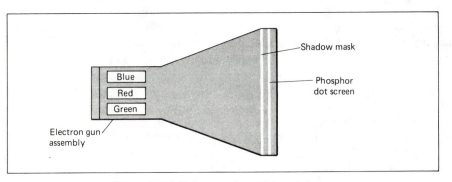

Figure 12.16 Color receiver picture tube.

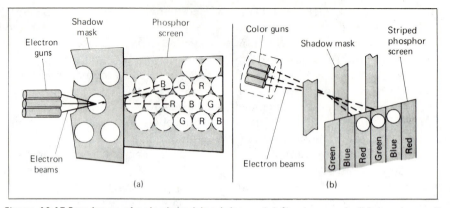

Figure 12.17 Two types of color television tubes. (a) Shadow mask. (b) Aperture grill.

screen, and their scanning matches that of the camera tube—30 frames (60 interlaced fields) per second. The mask helps to direct and sharpen the three electron beams so that they hit the proper color phosphors. The beams strike the phosphors, making them glow briefly at intensities that vary with those of the beams (Figure 12.17). However, the beams scan so quickly that we cannot see those brief instances when phosphors are not glowing.

This means that the only colors actually on the screen are red, blue, and green (in varying proportions, of course). At normal viewing distances, characteristics of our eyes are such that we do not see the individual phosphors. As discussed in Section 12.1.2, we blend together these three physical primary colors so that we see a full range of physiological colors.

Sound reproduction is less complicated. After being split from the video signal, the audio signal goes through its own circuitry. The process is similar to that for radio (Section 11.4). The end result is that sound is reproduced by the television speaker.

Monochrome receivers pick up only the luminance signal from a color telecast. The single video signal feeds into the base of the

monochrome picture tube. The gun assembly fires a single beam at the rear surface of the screen. Since there is only one beam, there is no mask. The phosphors all glow white.

12.5 ADVANCED TELEVISION SYSTEMS

The television system just described gave many years of service, since proposed by National Television System Committees in 1941 and 1953 (Sections 2.2 and 4.1.5). But as time passed and technology progressed, complaints developed. Critics compared NTSC picture quality unfavorably to the newer, higher-resolution systems found in some foreign countries. Engineers pointed out the difficulty of achieving color consistency when switching from one video source to another—even from one camera to another in the same studio!—and suggested that NTSC stood for "Not Twice the Same Color."

One major source of NTSC color problems was the composite nature of the signal, the fact that the luminance and chrominance components were frequency multiplexed (Section 12.3.1). The overlap of their sidebands resulted in what was termed *cross-color and cross-luminance effects* that degraded the picture. Further, the very process of production and distribution made the problem worse. At every point between camera pickup and home screen where something had to be done to video, the NTSC signal had to be first taken apart (decoded) and then reassembled (encoded). Each manipulation further degraded the signal.

By the 1980s, three overall approaches to improve U.S. video picture quality had emerged. These included improved NTSC, enhanced NTSC, and high-definition television.

12.5.1 Improved NTSC

The improved-NTSC approach retained all 1941 and 1953 standards but utilized advanced technological developments to upgrade the quality of the picture before transmission and after reception. Production and postproduction devices would utilize component analog video and digital technologies (Section 5.1.3) to reduce signal degradation. "Smart receivers" would contain a silicon chip capable of storing an entire television field. Such receivers digitally process the NTSC signal to eliminate video noise and cross-color. The digital-frame-store chips also allow smart receivers to scan sequentially—that is, to interpolate an additional 262.5 lines for each field and thus scan a complete 525-line picture in one pass every $\frac{1}{60}$ of a second (60 frames per second, as opposed to 60 interlaced fields per second). Sequential scanning eliminates additional picture defects. Finally, receivers equipped with digital field stores have some of the same capabilities as special-effects generators (Section 12.2.8)—for example, freeze frame and picture within another picture.

12.5.2 Enhanced NTSC

The enhanced-NTSC approach retained the 1941 NTSC standards of 525 scanning lines and a 3-to-4 aspect ratio.* But they did away with frequency multiplexing of the video signal components. Instead they *time-multiplexed* luminance and chrominance. This means they allocated specific time intervals in lines or frames for each component, compressed the components to fit into the intervals, and thus transmitted them sequentially. Called **multiplexed analog component** (MAC), this sytem did away with the need to interleave sidebands and the resulting interference. The receiver, in turn, was required to decompress the components and put them back into their proper position. The enhanced signal could be displayed on an NTSC video monitor. It could also be "down-converted" with some loss of picture quality to an NTSC signal for modulation and display on a regular television set. MAC would also time-multiplex the audio signal; a whole family of MAC systems developed, all differing mainly in how they handled the digital sound. The MAC signal required slightly more bandwidth than a regular NTSC signal, so would probably be utilized in direct-broadcast satellite, cable, or special-channel terrestrial transmission.

12.5.3 High-Definition Television

The third approach would, in effect, abandon the NTSC standard and start from scratch. This high-definition televison

---

*This refers to the height-to-width radio of the television screen—three units high by four units wide. Screen measurements usually refer to the diagonal dimensions. The height is 60 percent of the diagonal; the width, 80 percent. So for a 21-inch screen (diagonal measurement), the height/width dimensions are (0.6 × 21 inches =) 12.6 inches by (0.8 × 21 inches =) 16.8 inches.

Figure 12.18 NTSC versus HDTV. Side-by-side comparison: NTSC picture on the left and the NHK HDTV system on the right. (*Source:* AP/Wide World.)

(HDTV) approach would increase the number of scanning lines, thereby increasing resolution. The resulting picture would be sharper, clearer, and show more detail than an NTSC signal (see Figure 12.18).

A number of different HDTV systems were developed. One that received a great deal of attention and support in the United States was that developed by Japan's NHK television network. The NHK HDTV system featured 1125 scanning lines, 60 fields per second, interlace scanning, and a wide-screen 3-to-5.33 aspect ratio. You could not, of course, receive telecasts using this system on your present television receiver. Other HDTV systems, however, did promise varying degrees of compatibility with existing NTSC receivers. Most required more than 6 MHz for the full HDTV effect and so were aimed at DBS, cable, or special-channel terrestrial transmission.

12.5.4 Commission, Committees, and Centers

The HDTV problem was to set a standard— one single system that everyone could agree on, use, and market. The standard-setting problem actually encompassed two issues. One involved a search for a **production standard**—a system for *making* HDTV images. The other had to do with a **transmission standard**—a system for *broadcasting* HDTV images. In practice, the two could be considered separately; any HDTV transmission standard could broadcast images made with any HDTV production standard. The idea, however, was to have just one of each.

In 1988, the Federal Communications Commission made a tentative decision concerning U.S. HDTV transmission standards. HDTV broadcasts would have to be compatible with existing NTSC receivers in the same way NTSC color broadcasts were compatible with monochrome receivers (Section 12.4). Further, no additional spectrum space would be provided for HDTV outside the existing VHF and UHF bands. The commission said there was enough space within the broadcasting bands to accommodate HDTV.

The FCC had plenty of help in its continuing inquiry into HDTV standards. An Advanced Television Systems Committee (ATSC) had been formed in 1983. ATSC consisted of representatives from the various trades and companies that would be affected by changes in consumer television technology. The commission itself had formed an Advanced Television Services (ATS) advisory committee. The networks and the major broadcast trade associations sponsored an Advanced Television Test Center (ATTC). ATTC would provide facilities for ATSC and ATS to test the various advanced systems. Major cable operators formed Cable Television Laboratories, Inc., which would also test proposed new systems.

12.6 TELEVISION BROADCAST SERVICE

The television broadcast service operates on **68 channels** spread across two different frequency bands. Television channels are identified by numbers, 2 through 69. Each channel is **6 MHz wide,** so wide that all 100 FM radio channels could fit in the space of $3\frac{1}{2}$ television channels, while the entire AM radio band could be repeated nearly six times within the space of one television channel.

12.6.1 Transmission Band and Allocations

Television channels 2 through 13 lie in the very high frequency (VHF) band. Channels 2, 3, and 4 encompass the frequencies 54 to 72 MHz; 5 and 6, 76 to 88 MHz; and 7 through 13, 174 to 216 MHz. The FM radio band lies just above channel 6 (which is why you can often pick up television channel 6 sound on the lower end of your FM radio dial), while frequencies between channels 4 and 5 and between the FM band and channel 7 are used for other purposes.

Channels 14 through 69 are in the **ultra-high frequency** (UHF) band, encompassing a continuous band of frequencies from 470 to 806 MHz. Thus there is a big gap of 254 MHz (used for other purposes) between channels 13 and 14.

When the FCC first opened UHF for television broadcasting in 1952 (Section 4.1.2), it created 70 new channels—the UHF television band extended all the way up to 890 MHz, and the highest channel number was 83. However, in 1970, the FCC reallocated channels 70 through 83 in the UHF broadcast band to the land-mobile radio services.* Next, the commission reallocated certain unused UHF assignments involving channels 14–20 in the 25 largest markets to the land-mobile services. Channel 37 was reallocated to radio astronomy use. During the 1980s, the FCC considered additional proposals from land-mobile users to reallocate and to share UHF broadcast channels.

Like FM radio, television signal propagation is primarily by direct waves. Coverage is determined largely by antenna height, frequency, power, and terrain. With careful planning, co-channel and adjacent-channel interference are rarely problems.

Also as in FM radio, the FCC table of assignments allocates specific television channels to specific communities. But unlike FM, the television table assigns educational noncommercial channels to specific communities; the TV table reserves about 20 percent of the specific allocations for noncommercial use.

12.6.2 New Stations

Should you wish to build a new full-service television station, you must do one of three things. First, you look for a vacant channel allocated to the community in which you want to build the station. If there is such a channel, you apply for it. But you will probably find all local channels taken.

Second, you look for a vacant channel assigned to a nearby smaller market. Using that channel, perhaps you can locate the sta-

*Two-way radio for public safety.

tion so that it puts a signal over the desired community; there is a limited amount of freedom in locating a station. Again, most of those channels have been taken.

Third, you petition the FCC to amend the table of allocations, probably to have a vacant channel moved from another location to the desired community. The petition would have to demonstrate that the move would meet all relevant mileage separation requirements as spelled out in the FCC rules to prevent interference. Then, if the FCC were to grant the petition, you could apply for permission to build a television station. But the channel is open for other applicants, too; convincing the FCC to amend the TV table of allocations does not mean that you automatically get the channel. So at least a half-dozen other parties would probably also apply.

Theoretically, you would have a much easier time applying for a low-power television (LPTV) station. LPTVs are not included in the table of allocations. Instead, you apply for an LPTV on a demand basis, somewhat similar to the situation in AM radio. When the FCC opened the LPTV service in 1982, however, thousands applied to construct stations. For each of the choicest channels and locations, there were usually a number of different applications. So even LPTV might be out as an option.

12.6.3 TV Transmission and Reception

A televison broadcast transmitter actually consists of two transmitters—one each for the video and audio signals (Figure 12.19). The output of both the video transmitter and the audio transmitter are combined, and the combined signals power the antenna to generate transmission waves.

Just as in radio, the transmitted waves induce a weak electrical signal in the television receiving antenna. This signal feeds to a tuner, which blocks all frequencies except those for the channel to which you are

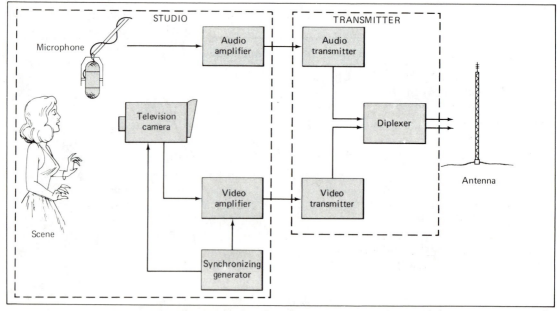

Figure 12.19 Block diagram of television station and transmitter.

tuned. The signal is boosted, and video, audio, and accessory signals are recovered from the carrier and used as described earlier.

12.7 ITFS, MDS, AND OFS

The **instructional television fixed service** (ITFS), the **multipoint distribution service** (MDS), and the **operational fixed service** (OFS) consist of 20, 10, and 3 channels, respectively, in the 2-GHz (2000–3000 MHz) band. The waves at these frequencies are so short they are called **microwaves.** When radiated omnidirectionally at 100 watts of power, as in ITFS, MDS, and OFS, these waves have a range of 30 miles. Any obstruction in the path between transmitting and receiving antennas will block the signal. This includes foliage, as well as more solid objects. ITFS, MDS, and OFS are separate services, but in 1983 the FCC adopted rules that allowed programmers to mix channels from the three services and offer the subscription service that became known as "wireless cable" (multichannel TV; Section 5.4).

In an ITFS or MDS system, the video and audio signals originate just as they do in broadcast or cable television. Then they are combined and used to modulate the carrier frequency for transmission. The ITFS or MDS transmitting antenna radiates the signal. Receiving antennas, built especially to pick up these high frequencies, capture the signal. A converter demodulates the video and audio signals down, then feeds them to a descrambler (when necessary) and on to an unused channel on your television set.

12.8 DBS

The FCC authorized high-power **direct-broadcast satellite** (DBS) service in 1982. Direct-broadcast satellites were to transmit with 200 watts of power and utilize directive transmitting antennas. The receiving antenna on the ground would need no more than a 30-inch reflector (dish) within the relatively narrow "footprint" (reception area) of a direct-broadcast satellite. The frequencies 12.2 to 12.7 GHz in the K_u band (the middle of the SHF band) were allocated for satellite-to-ground transmission (downlinks), 17.3 to 17.8 GHz for uplinks. The 500 MHz band was broken down into 32 channels.

By 1990, no U.S. direct-broadcast satellites had been launched. Meanwhile, an ad hoc **C-band direct** service had developed. When the cable networks scrambled their satellite feeds (Section 5.6.3), television receive-only (backyard) dish owners had to purchase descramblers and pay subscription fees to view a "clear" signal. C-band satellites transmit to broad areas using only 5 to 15 watts of power. This requires a dish of 3 to 5 meters at the receiving antenna.

In a satellite system, the combined video and audio signals go to the transmission point called the **ground station.** There they modulate the carrier, which, in turn, feeds a transmitting **dish,** a special antenna that focuses the signal into a beam. A receiving antenna on the satellite picks up the signal and feeds it to a **transponder.** The transponder amplifies the signal, modulates it to the proper frequency for retransmission, and sends it to the transmitting antenna. The satellite transmitting antenna radiates the signal so that it can be picked up over a wide area—for example, major parts of the country. A home receiving dish picks up the signal and feeds it to a low-noise amplifier* and a down-converter. The down-converter demodulates the signal from its satellite channel and feeds it to a descrambler (if necessary) and several additional devices to

---

*The term "low noise" means that the device itself does not add much spurious information ("noise") to the incoming signal.

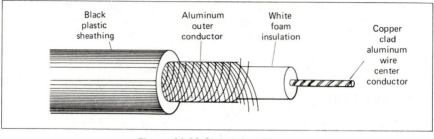

Figure 12.20 Coaxial cable.

amplify the signal and get it ready for display on an NTSC receiver.

12.9 CABLE TELEVISION

Coaxial cable is a **broadband** medium; that is, it conducts a wide range of frequencies. A coaxial cable (Figure 12.20) acts as a "pipe," down which an electromagnetic wave may be propagated. The wave resembles those transmitted by broadcast stations. It suffers and causes little external (to the cable) interference and, through modulation (Box 12.2), can carry as many as 80 or 90 6-MHz television signals, depending on the quality of the cable and the amplifiers used in the system.

12.9.1 Headend and Signal Origins

Cable television system signals are sent from the headend to subscribers' receivers. A tall tower (Figure 12.21) usually sits close to the building housing the headend. This tower contains the various types of antennas needed to pick up nearby television stations, any local radio stations the system carries, and microwave signals that relay in the signals of distant television stations. Nearby will be at least one large satellite receiving dish to bring in cable networks. Additional signals may be fed to the headend from studios, videotape machines, telecine units, and

other video production sources; from rotatext, teletext, and other electronic text sources; and from videotex, home security services, and other two-way and ancillary sources.

The headend (Figure 12.22) contains distribution amplifiers, interference filters, multiplex equipment, switching gear, and other devices that process incoming signals. Therefore, all signals—direct off-the-air, microwave-relay, satellite, local origination—go to the headend for processing.

Figure 12.21 Cable system tower and receiving antennas. (Photograph courtesy of National Cable Television Association. Used by permission.)

have installed the necessary equipment to offer two-way service.

12.9.3 Signal Distribution

A cable system that serves a large area or population will establish a number of distribution hubs (Figure 12.23). A **hub** serves a smaller area and 10,000 to 15,000 subscribers and may contain a headend. Processed signals from the headend proceed to the hubs by way of a coaxial **supertrunk, microwave,** or **optical fiber.** Three or four **trunk lines** branch from each hub. A **tap** on the feeder carries signals into homes via **drop lines.** In-line amplifiers keep the signals boosted throughout the length of the system.

12.9.4 Subscriber Hookups

If the cable system offers 12 or fewer channels of service, it puts all signals on the 12 VHF channels on the cable. In this case (and if the system offers no pay channel), the drop line can be attached directly to the receiver's antenna terminal. For example, suppose your cable system carried over-the-air channels 4, 8, 17, 24, and 39 plus a superstation, three satellite-distributed advertiser-supported services, and a community access channel. The cable system would probably set up its service so that you, as a cable subscriber, would receive broadcast channels 4 and 8 on (cable) channels 4 and 8.* But you would pick up broadcast channels 17, 24, and 39 on, say, (cable) channels 2, 3, and 7 and the supersta-

Figure 12.22 Cable system headend. A technician adjusts a control at Cox Cable-University City's headend. At left is the front of one rack of equipment; at right, the back of another—two of many that fill the small cement-block building. All signals feed to the box at top, the first amplifier in the system. From the other side of the amplifier emerges the trunk line, which carries programming throughout the franchise area.

12.9.2 Cable Channels

Cable systems carry a television signal with the same AM format as used in broadcast television. A cable system need only "translate" an incoming signal onto the frequency of the proper cable channel. Cable channels 2–13 operate with the same carrier frequencies as broadcast channels 2–13. A set of midband channels fills most of the gap between channels 6 and 7, and superband and hyperband appear above channel 13. The 5–30-MHz bandwidth is dedicated to upstream (return) transmission, although few systems

---

*A cable system may place a VHF broadcast signal on a different cable channel in order to avoid "ghosting." When a cable system carries a nearby VHF television station's signal "on-channel" (broadcast channel 4 on cable channel 4), the station's signal may be so strong that it gets onto the cable wiring (and into your receiver) directly. In such a case, you would see a double image on channel 4—the stronger one by way of the headend, the weaker from the direct pickup.

Box 12.2 Modulation and "Stacking" of Communications

A relatively simple example will help explain how modulation lets us use a single communications channel to carry multiple messages simultaneously. Imagine that you run a telephone company that serves two neighboring towns. Each town has one telephone, and the telephone subscriber in one town calls the telephone subscriber in the other town quite often. All of a sudden, business in both towns booms, and another person in each town applies for telephone service. You know that there will be times when both telephones will be in use in both towns, interurban acquaintances using their telephones to talk to each other. Your long-distance telephone channel capacity between cities will have to increase 100 percent. You find that construction of another line between towns would be prohibitively expensive.

You decide to use *modulation*. How does it work? What happens when two conversations travel over the same line? Why don't they interfere with each other? The frequency response range of a telephone is roughly 400–2,800 Hz. One conversation can go over the long-distance line at this "voice frequencies" range, just as it used to. The second conversation goes from the subscriber's phone in one city to a modulator in that same city. Your modulator uses a carrier frequency of 6,000 Hz. Through the voice frequencies interacting with the carrier frequency on a sum-and-difference basis, the frequency range for the second call is 3,200–6,280 Hz. Notice that this frequency band is so high that even the lowest frequencies are higher than the highest frequencies of the first conversation. The second conversation can now be sent over the same long-distance line simultaneously with the first conversation. At the other end of the line, a demodulator recovers the voice frequencies (gets them back down to the range of 400–2,800 Hz) of the second conversation and sends them on (and here you *do* need a second line) to the subscriber. Obviously, you need a modulator and a demodulator in both towns. But you get the idea. This form of modulation, carrier current telephony, allows a single conducting medium to carry as many as 1,860 messages simultaneously. Use of coaxial cable increases this tremendously; optical fiber, even more.

Pulse code modulation (PCM) also allows multiple simultaneous telephone conversations. This is the way it works. Samples are taken of the amplitude of the waves made by the voices. When sampled often—thousands of times per second—enough information is obtained to make a listener hear what sounds like the full conversation. Since only samples are taken, there can be spaces between the samples of one conversation into which samples from other conversations can be inserted. So long as the timing is correct for insertion and recovery, one line can carry several dozen conversations at the same time. The samples of conversations are encoded and transmitted digitally, and many foresee this **digital compression** as a way to squeeze broad-band communications (such as television channels) into narrow-band channels (such as normal telephone lines).

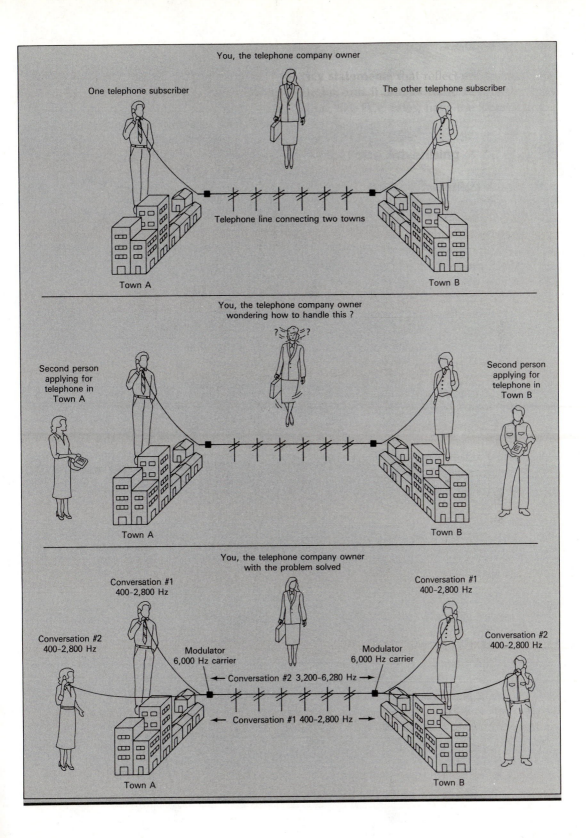

You, the telephone company owner

One telephone subscriber

The other telephone subscriber

Telephone line connecting two towns

Town A

Town B

You, the telephone company owner
wondering how to handle this ?

Second person
applying for
telephone in
Town A

Second person
applying for
telephone in
Town B

Town A

Town B

You, the telephone company owner
with the problem solved

Conversation #1
400–2,800 Hz

Conversation #1
400–2,800 Hz

Conversation #2
400–2,800 Hz

Conversation #2
400–2,800 Hz

Modulator
6,000 Hz carrier

Modulator
6,000 Hz carrier

← Conversation #2 3,200–6,280 Hz →

← Conversation #1 400–2,800 Hz →

Town A

Town B

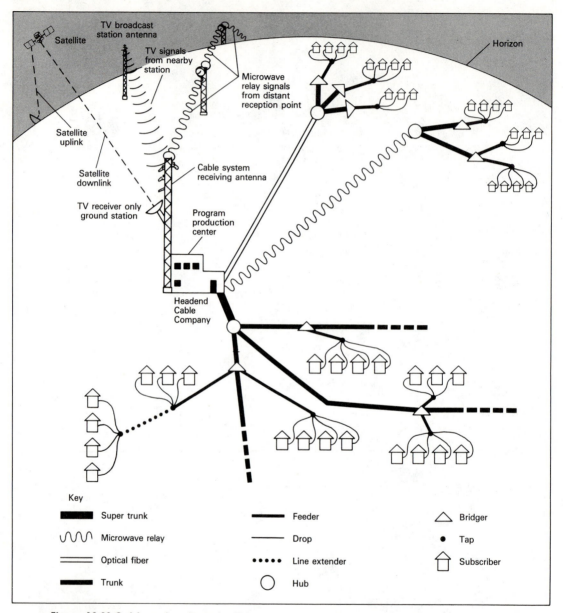

Figure 12.23 Cable system layout.   This system uses a combination of direct off-air reception, microwave relay (to bring in signals of stations too distant for direct off-air reception), and satellite reception.

Figure 12.24 Cable adapter box. The subscriber end of the Jerrold IMPULSE 7000 system by General Instrument consists of this sophisticated, feature-packed addressable converter. The subscriber may operate the converter using either the control buttons on top of the box or the remote control. Among the many features of the IMPULSE 7000: channel selection; volume control; mute button; favorite-channel programming; last-channel recall; parental-control channel lock-out; time-controlled programming (for unattended VCR recording); response capability for video opinion polling; and both planned and impulse pay-per-view event buying. (Converter courtesy of Cox Cable-University City.)

tion and nonbroadcast services on cable channels 9, 10, 11, 12, and 13.

If the cable system offers more than 12 channels, additional channels are used—midband, superband, hyperband, according to the capacity of the system. If you, the subscriber, have a **cable-ready receiver,** you will probably be able to pick up most or all of these additional channels by selecting channels numbered above 13. If your receiver is not cable-ready, you will have to use a **converter** (Figure 12.24). The drop line connects to the converter, which sits on or near your receiver, and a short cable connects the converter to the receiver. A *block converter* moves all cable channels to either the VHF band or the UHF band; you use your receiver's channel selector. A *general converter* feeds all signals into one channel (say, channel 3) on your receiver, so you leave the receiver set on that channel; you use a channel selector on the converter to change channels.

A cable system utilizes converters for pay channels, even when total service is 12 channels or less. In this case, the converter unscrambles the pay signal.

A satellite master antenna television (SMATV) system operates much like a cable system. However, it distributes only to the multiple-unit dwelling with which it has a contract. And the array of programming signal inputs may not be as extensive.

12.9.5 Addressability and PPV

Many cable systems have installed technology that permits **signal addressability.** This refers to the capability to send over the system a signal that applies only to one specific point and to nowhere else. In **one-way addressability,** the cable operator's computer sends a signal directly to cable system equipment located in or near a subscriber's home. This equipment could be an electronic "gate" at the tap, or it could be a converter on top of the subscriber's television receiver. The signal directs the equipment to turn on or off basic cable service, premium channels, or other services, according to what the customer has ordered. In **two-way addressability,** the subscriber can send a signal directly to the cable operator's computer.

Most cable pay-per-view systems (Box 12.3) make use of addressability. In a system that has one-way addressability, the subscriber must request unscrambling (and willingness to pay for) a PPV offering through other technology, usually the telephone. The request is programmed into the computer. The computer, then, generates and transmits through the cable the code that turns on the converter's unscrambling electronics. A two-way addressable system would permit the subscriber to send the request simply by pressing a button on the PPV converter.

12.10 ELECTRONIC TEXT AND VBI SERVICES

Electronic text services consist of informational frames created by a character generator and stored electronically. These pages are then recalled and distributed on broadcast

---

Box 12.3 Pay-per-View Technology

PPV requires direct two-way information flow. The PPV transmission facility must not only get programming *to* the customer, it must also get viewing information *from* the customer for billing purposes. Five types of PPV technology predominated in the cable trade by 1990. A cable system might use any one of the following: (1) Customer service representative (CSR): A customer service representative at the cable system answers a viewing-request call from a PPV subscriber. The CSR programs the computer that sends the unscramble code to the addressable decoder box in the requesting subscriber's home. The code tells the box to unscramble the incoming PPV signal so the requesting subscriber can see the programming. (2) Automatic response unit (ARU): A subscriber uses a touch-tone telephone to access the system's computer directly. The subscriber makes a PPV viewing request by pushing the correct telephone buttons when cued by a recorded message. The computer then automatically sends out the unscramble code. (3) Automatic number identification (ANI): Usually, a cable system contracts with the telephone company for ANI service. The telephone company allocates a block of telephone numbers for PPV use. Each number corresponds to a different PPV event. To order a PPV event, the subscriber dials the number assigned to that event, then waits for an electronic beep tone to confirm that the order has been placed. Again, the computer automatically sends out the unscramble code. (4) Store-and-forward impulse pay-per-view (IPPV): The subscriber can activate the decoder at any time; no telephone call is needed. The subscriber uses the decoder's remote control to give the unscramble command. The decoder unscrambles the PPV programming and stores the command. A telephone line connects to the decoder, and, periodically, the cable system's computer dials up the decoder to collect the stored information. (5) Two-way RF IPPV: (Cable systems must have the capability for two-way addressability to use this method.) Again the subscriber punches a button on a remote control to request unscrambling. The decoder picks up the order from the remote control. The cable system's computer picks up the order through the coaxial cable and sends out the unscramble code.

With every system, the customer receives a bill for PPV viewing through the mail. Other media could and do use all of these systems, except two-way RF IPPV. Wireless cable and TVRO PPV, for example, can use CSR, ARU, and ANI by sending the unscramble code "over the air."

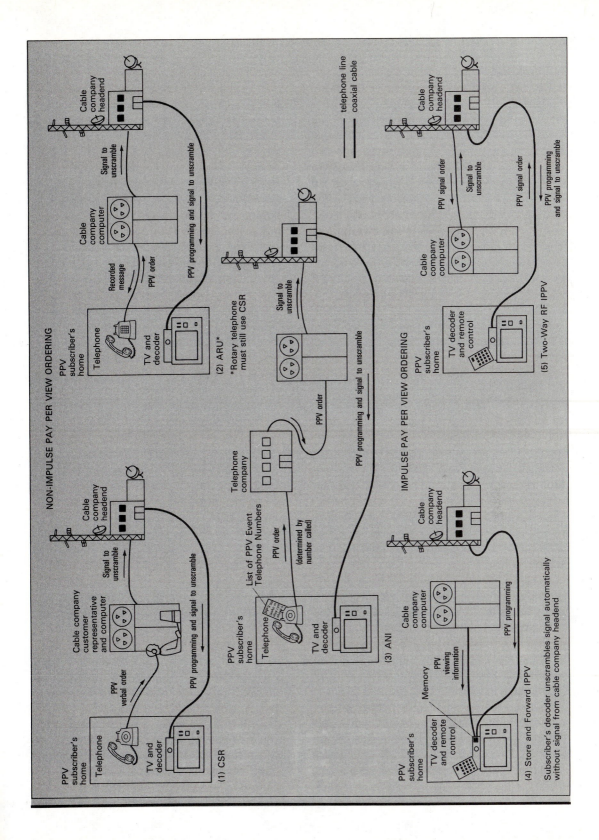

NON-IMPULSE PAY PER VIEW ORDERING

PPV subscriber's home

Telephone

TV and decoder

Cable company headend

Signal to unscramble

PPV programming and signal to unscramble

Cable company customer representative and computer

PPV verbal order

(1) CSR

Cable company headend

Signal to unscramble

PPV programming and signal to unscramble

Cable company computer

Recorded message

PPV order

Telephone

PPV subscriber's home

TV and decoder

(2) ARU*

*Rotary telephone must still use CSR

telephone line

coaxial cable

PPV subscriber's home

Telephone

List of PPV Event Telephone Numbers

(determined by number called)

PPV order

Telephone company

PPV order

PPV programming and signal to unscramble

Signal to unscramble

Cable company computer

TV and decoder

(3) ANI

IMPULSE PAY PER VIEW ORDERING

PPV subscriber's home

TV decoder and remote control

Memory

PPV viewing information

Cable company computer

PPV programming

Cable company headend

(4) Store and Forward IPPV

PPV subscriber's home

TV decoder and remote control

PPV signal order

PPV signal order

Signal to unscramble

PPV programming and signal to unscramble

Cable company computer

Cable company headend

(5) Two-Way RF IPPV

Subscriber's decoder unscrambles signal automatically without signal from cable company headend channels, cable, or telephone lines, according to the specific type of service. They include closed captioning, rotatext, teletext, and videotex. The latter three are usually information services, but each uses a different technology.

Closed captioning is designed to serve hearing-impaired viewers. The dialogue of a television program is typed into short strips or "captions"; these captions are then placed on the screen at appropriate times in appropriate positions to show what each person said and encoded onto line 21 of the vertical blanking interval (VBI) between transmissions of television picture fields. Special decoders detect and recover the information from the VBI and insert the captions on the screen. Viewers without decoders see no captions.

Rotatext is technologically rather simple. A cable system televises "pages" (full screens) of information—news, weather, sports, announcements, advertisements—in a continuously repeating cycle on one or more nonbroadcast channels. No special rotatext decoder is needed to receive the service. The viewer has no control over the order or the timing of the screen display. A viewer who turns to a rotatext channel to check the weather forecast just *after* the weather screen has been televised may have a long wait; for example, if the rotatext service contains 45 screens and each is displayed 20 seconds, the weather screen will take 15 minutes to cycle through again. Most cable systems put such channels on their basic tier, making them available to all subscribers.

Teletext gives the viewer more control and usually carries a greater number of pages than rotatext. The pages are encoded onto a television channel and transmitted in a repeating cycle, one after the other, with no pause. To see a specific page, the viewer punches the page number into a special decoder attached to the television receiver.

When that page comes up in the transmission cycle, the decoder "grabs" and uses a frame store to display it on the receiver screen. That page remains on screen until the viewer punches another order into the decoder.

Even with this page selection capability, teletext is *not* a true interactive medium. The system consists of a number of continuously transmitted screens, a one-way flow of information from source to user. It does not provide for the user to send information back to the source.

Broadcast teletext uses technology similar to that of closed captioning; a television station loads the pages onto several lines in the VBI. As mentioned in Section 5.7.3, two rival and incompatible broadcast teletext systems developed during the 1980s. These were the World System Teletext (WST; based on British standards) and the North American Broadcast Teletext Specification (NABTS; based on French and Canadian technologies). The WST decoder was relatively inexpensive. But the system was *alpha-mosaic*; text and graphics were limited to a fixed set of letters and shapes in fixed-sized character spaces. Illustrations often looked as though they had been created on a typewriter. NABTS was *geometric*; each pixel (the individual picture element on the screen) could be controlled. NABTS could generate illustrations with much greater resolution and subtlety than WST (whose character space was 6 pixels by 10 pixels), but it also required a much more expensive decoder.

Theoretically, a broadcast teletext system could carry any number of pages. Practically, it is restricted by the viewer's "wait." Since teletext transmits a continuing cycle of pages, each additional page lengthens the cycle. With only a limited number of lines in the VBI available for transmission, even a few pages could extend the cycle by seconds. Also, the teletext transmission cycle is *not* continuous, since it is "interrupted" by the transmission of the 490 lines of picture information every $\frac{1}{30}$ of a second. In a 200-page cycle, for example, a viewer who selects page 37 just as page 38 is received (so that pages 38–200 and 1–36 have to cycle through) has to wait 10–12 seconds before page 37 appears on the screen. Most viewers would find even that short wait unacceptable.

With **full-frame teletext,** 30 times as much data can be sent each second. The text-loading techniques are the same as for broadcast teletext. But instead of only the VBI, the entire video channel is utilized for full-frame teletext; there is no picture transmission. For that reason, full-frame teletext is also known as *cable teletext*, cable generally being the only medium able to dedicate an entire video channel to textual information.

Of all these systems **videotex** provides by far the greatest degree of user control. Videotex is a two-way interactive video system that can offer schedule and transactional services, as well as literally encyclopedic information resources. The user controls a home terminal to access directly large-capacity data banks in a central computer. From here, *gateways* provide entry to computers of service providers, such as banks, travel agencies, and catalog order merchants. The user may view information and response frames on the screen of a television receiver or some similar video display.

Since information must flow two ways, broadcast channels may not carry videotex service. Most cable systems cannot carry it, either. While coaxial cable does have the potential for two-way information flow, the typical cable television system does not have the sophisticated switching equipment needed to provide the on-call point-to-point communication channels needed by videotex. The telephone system does have this capability, and most attempts at videotex service have been based on telephone lines. A telephone line, unfortunately, does not have the broadband information-carrying capacity of coaxial cable. Consequently, a frame that consists of large quantities of information takes a long time to complete on a telephone line-based videotex system; an elaborate graphics frame, for example, requires nearly 10 seconds, even longer if the frame includes a photograph. A hybrid system might utilize the best of both media. Telephone lines could carry user requests, and the broadband capability of a switched cable system could rapidly download information, supplying most screens in a fraction of a second.

The FCC allows television stations to utilize lines 10–14 of the vertical blanking interval for data transmission services in addition to teletext. This allows television broadcasters to offer **VBI services** similar to the SCS services of radio broadcasters (Section 11.6.2). Like the SCS services, they may take almost any form and may be operated private carrier-like (operated for selected customers or purposes) or common carrier-like (available for all for many purposes).

FURTHER READING

Benson, K. Blair, ed. *Television Engineering Handbook*. New York: McGraw, 1986. Technical but complete explanation, from light and vision to electronic editing.

Miller, Gary M. *Modern Electronic Communication*. 2d ed. Englewood Cliffs: Prentice, 1983. Chapter 7 deals with television.

Oringel, Robert. *Television Operations Handbook*. Stoneham: Focal, 1984. How to operate production equipment.

Rszeszewski, Ted, ed. *Color Television*. New York: IEEE, 1983. Technical articles on all aspects.

———. *Television Technology*. New York: IEEE, 1985. Includes articles on new developments.

Weinstein, Stephen B. *Getting the Picture: A Guide to CATV and the New Electronic Media*. New York: IEEE, 1986. Also explains the TV signal, STV, MDS, SMATV, DBS, VCRs, the telephone network, videotex, and teletext.

FOUR

LEGAL/ETHICAL PERSPECTIVE

Each of us has a stake in this next section. Most regulation aims at ensuring that mass-media operation (1) does not harm individuals—in some cases, that it actually furthers the common good—and (2) at the same time allows the operator to profit. Theoretically, then, as citizens and consumers we play at least some role in the regulation of radio and television. Also theoretically, the more effectively the media voluntarily operate with our good in mind, the less the government needs to regulate.

We divide our investigation of regulation into four chapters. In Chapter 13, we focus on the Communications Act of 1934 and its various amendments; Chapter 14, governmental regulation; Chapter 15, First Amendment issues; and Chapter 16, media ethics.

Like the business to which they apply, law and regulation of radio and television constantly change. New issues arise. Old ones evolve. Arguments, court cases, hearings, and investigations continually explore and define the uses of electronic mass communication.

CHAPTER 13

Communications Law

The basic law of radio and television is the **Communications Act of 1934.** This law provides for use of the radio frequencies. It also singles out broadcasting as being a use of the frequencies that is special and different from all others. It provides for both the existence of broadcast stations and their regulation. In this chapter, we first trace the origins and authority for government regulation and then survey the overall nature and status of broadcasting under the 1934 law. Next we review results of growing dissatisfaction with the Communications Act. Finally, we look at some of the amendments that Congress has made to the law since 1934, including the Cable Communications Policy Act of 1984.

First, we need to sort out use of the term "section." Up to now, when the narrative in this book has contained an unusual or specialized concept, we have referred you to the place in the book where that concept is discussed with a note such as "(Section 27.3.2)." In this chapter and the next two, we deal with the legal aspects of radio and television. Most laws and regulations consist of numbered sections, and in explaining their

workings we must refer to them as, for example, "Section 315." To forestall confusion, *for Chapters 13, 14, and 15 only,* we shall refer to numbered sections in *Perspectives on Radio and Television* with the initials PRT—for example, "(PRT 26.3.2)."

13.1 ORIGINS AND AUTHORITY

Article I, Section 8, of the Constitution of the United States contains the *commerce clause,* giving Congress **power to regulate interstate commerce.** Early on, the U.S. Supreme Court ruled that Congress's power extends to all kinds of commercial dealings involving more than one state and to the formulation of rules to regulate those dealings.[1] Later, the Court ruled that the term "commerce" includes interstate electrical communication.[2] Still later, the Court held that all radio communication is, by nature, interstate.[3] These decisions established the right of Congress to regulate broadcasting (and other uses of the radio frequencies), and a 1968 Supreme

Court decision affirmed federal regulation of cable television.[4]

Congress wrote the basic law of radio, but it also created an independent agency and delegated to it authority to make specific rules and regulations. A federal court ruled in 1929 that Congress had the power to establish such an agency.[5] Five years later Congress passed the Communications Act,[6] which created the present agency, the Federal Communications Commission. Although amended continuously, over a half-century later this 1934 act continues to serve as the law under which civilian electronic media are regulated. Congress, of course, still has ultimate control over these media and monitors the functioning and adequacy of the Communications Act, including FCC regulation, through the commerce committees of its two houses.

13.2 THE LAW OF RADIO AND TELEVISION

The Communications Act of 1934 deals with more than broadcasting. Its purposes include "regulating interstate and foreign commerce in communication by wire and radio so as to make available, so far as possible, to all people of the United States a rapid, efficient, nation-wide, world-wide wire and radio communication service with adequate facilities at reasonable charges, . . . [aiding] the national defense, . . . [and] promoting safety of life and property through the use of wire and radio communication. . . ."[7] The act applies "to all interstate and foreign communication by wire or radio and all interstate and foreign transmission of energy by radio which originates and/or is received within the United States, and to all persons engaged within the United States in such communications or such transmission of energy by radio and to the licensing and regulating of all radio stations. . . ."[8]

13.2.1 Structure of the Communications Act

The Government Printing Office publishes federal laws in the **United States Code (U.S.C.)**. **Title 47** of U.S.C. contains the Communications Act of 1934 as amended. The act itself consists of major divisions called *titles*. Within each title are numbered paragraphs called *sections*.

Title I defines the purposes of the act and specifies terms, organization, duties, and general powers of the Federal Communications Commission. Title II covers communications common carriers (PRT 13.3).

Title III deals with radio and is divided into four parts. While Parts II and III apply to uses of radio on ships and boats, Parts I and IV apply directly to our area of concern—(I) radio licensing and regulation in general (including sections that deal specifically with broadcasting), and (IV) special provisions pertaining to noncommercial educational broadcasting.

Title IV spells out procedural and administrative provisions. Title V prescribes penalties and forfeitures for violators of law or FCC regulation.

The Communications Act originally had six titles. However, in 1984, Congress passed the Cable Communications Policy Act. The act put cable legislation into Title VI and moved the former content of Title VI into a newly created Title VII. As a result, Title VI now deals with cable communication, and Title VII deals with unauthorized reception of communication and the president's war emergency powers.

13.2.2 Characteristics of the Communications Act

From our perspective of interest in radio and television, three apsects of the act stand out—its **comprehensiveness,** its **flexibility,** and its **establishment of the FCC.** Profiting from the lesson of the Radio Act of 1912 (PRT 2.1.7), Congress wrote the Radio Act of 1927 to be comprehensive enough to cover all types of radio communication—maritime, broadcasting, amateur, common carrier. Seven years later Congress wrote most of the provisions of the 1927 law into the Communications Act. This means that principles first written into law in 1927 continue to cover interstate communications. Their comprehensiveness is such that they provide for regulation of technology and developments that were brand new, still in the laboratory, or not yet even dreamed of in 1927—for example, microwave relay, television, FM radio, uses of subcarriers, ultrahigh frequencies, direct-broadcast satellites, and teletext.

Congress wrote the Communications Act to be flexible. The law set forth basic principles and created the FCC to carry out the intent of those principles. It established a general legal framework and provided the FCC with **discretionary powers** to make specific rules and regulations concerning licensing and operational requirements. Within this legal framework, the FCC has power to set up criteria for licensing, to grant or refuse licenses, to attach conditions to licenses, to revoke licenses, to specify how and where stations are to operate, and to change regulations to keep up with changing conditions and technology.[9] Further, FCC rules and regulations have the force of law, yet the Communications Act provided for their challenge in the federal courts,[10] adding yet another dimension to the concept of flexibility.

Finally, the Communications Act established the Federal Communications Commission. The commission carries out the specific functions prescribed by the act, makes rules and regulations, checks to see that they are being followed,[11] and takes corrective or punitive action where they are not.[12] In other words, the FCC regulates.

13.3 STATUS OF BROADCASTING UNDER LAW

In writing the Communications Act, Congress defined the legal status of broadcasting, that is, set forth its legal characteristics—what it is, what rights are assigned to it, how it is to be treated. Under this law, broadcasting is (1) a unique form of electrical communication, unlike any other; (2) a function of the private sector, not of the government; and a form of expression (3) that is distributed via radio frequencies, a scarce natural resource in the public domain (4) to which the government may limit access, and (5) that has limited protection under the First Amendment. Let us examine each of these characteristics.

13.3.1 Unique Form of Electrical Communication

First, the Communications Act of 1934 recognized broadcasting as a unique form of radio communication. Section 153(b) defines *radio communication* as any transmission by radio of intelligence. Section 153(o) then defines *broadcasting* as **radio communication intended for reception by the general public,** clearly distinguishing broadcasting from other forms of radio communication. The act contains a number of sections that apply to radio communication in general, but it also contains provisions that apply only to broadcasting. Section 315, for example, deals with use of broadcast stations by political candidates (PRT 14.1.1.4).

Note that the law's definition of broadcasting emphasizes reception. Such emphasis distinguishes broadcasting from common carriers. Section 303(b) defines a common carrier as radio or interstate wire communication facilities for hire, a definition that emphasizes the sender of the message. Telephone and telegraph are both examples of common carriers. Common carriers render essential services, and Congress wrote Title II of the act to ensure reliability and continuity of these services.

How does this make a common carrier different from a broadcast licensee? The following comparison illustrates the difference. A common carrier is *closely regulated, even to the rates it may charge and the services it may provide.* For example, you have only one telephone company in your town, and it provides service for local calls and for access to long-distance communications. The FCC regulates the companies that provide the network of *interstate* long-distance telephone communications to which your phone company is attached. And the state public utilities commission usually regulates your local telephone company and *intrastate* long-distance communications.

A broadcast licensee, on the other hand, *competes and has the freedom to determine charges and services.* True, a broadcast station must be licensed and is subject to some regulation. But the licensee is basically an entrepreneur in competition with other broadcast licensees and may charge whatever rates and (to a large extent) may provide whatever services the market will bear.

Note, also, that the law's definition of broadcasting does not limit it to the traditional services, AM and FM radio and TV channels 2–69. Thus, law and regulation of broadcasting can be applied to any other wireless medium the FCC may authorize, as long as it is intended for reception by the general public.

13.3.2 Function of the Private Sector

Second, the Communications Act affirms that private entities—people or corporations—may use the radio frequencies.[13] By the time Congress passed the Radio Act of 1927, the pattern for broadcasting in the United States was set. Radio broadcasting had developed primarily as a function of private enterprise and had evolved into an advertising medium operated to earn a profit. Congress accepted the status quo. Contrary to the arrangement in many other countries—in which broadcasting was some combination of monopoly, noncommercial, and government-operated or -chartered—the U.S. Congress wrote in private operation as one of the basic assumptions of its first comprehensive radio law. The FCC has since reserved channels for noncommercial FM and television stations. And Congress has also set up and funded the national and noncommercial Corporation for Public Broadcasting. But by and large, the broadcasting system in the United States is still privately operated and commercial.

13.3.3 Distributed Through Radio Frequencies

On the other hand, the government retains ultimate control of the radio frequencies and requires all broadcast licensees to meet certain responsibilities and operate within certain limitations. Congress wrote this into the law because broadcasting is a form of expression distributed through use of a scarce natural resource in the public domain. The natural resource is the electromagnetic spectrum, and it is scarce because a finite number of stations can operate in any given geographic area (PRT 11.1.1). The FCC may allow individuals to use the frequencies for limited periods of time,[14] but only after ensuring that those individuals will use the frequencies to serve the public interest, convenience, and necessity.[15] Furthermore, the FCC must see that everyone receives radio services.[16]

A parallel could be drawn between a broadcast licensee and a concessionaire—restaurant, inn, gasoline station—in a national park. Both operate in the public domain, and both are in business to earn a profit, but the government allows them to operate only insofar as they serve and help make the natural resource more useful to the public.

13.3.4 Government May Limit Access

The fourth legal characteristic of broadcasting is a logical extension of the previous two—the government may restrict access to the radio frequencies. Section 301 of the Communications Act **restricts use** of the radio frequencies **to those so licensed.** But licenses are not granted automatically on application. Not everyone who wants full-time use of a channel in the broadcast frequencies can have it. This means the FCC must choose who does and who does not get a license. Sections 308(b), 310, and 313 suggest basic **criteria that an applicant must meet** to be eligible for a license. The FCC has adopted additional criteria (PRT 19.1.2.1).

Even if the applicant meets all criteria and the FCC grants a license, Sections 304 and 309(h) (1) make clear that the licensee **does not own the frequencies.** Further, the licensee must operate the station within all applicable conditions, rules, and regulations or, as prescribed in Sections 307(d) and 312(a), **lose the license.**

13.3.5 Limited First Amendment Protection

Finally, the Communications Act applies the constitutional guarantee of free speech to broadcasting. Section 326 states that the FCC does not have the power of censorship and may make no regulation or set any condition that would interfere with the right of free speech by means of radio. The fact is, however, that broadcast licensees do not have the same degree of First Amendment protection enjoyed by publishers of print media. Certain types of broadcast content may be restricted or required when it would be in the public interest to do so[17] or when it would enhance the public's First Amendment right to *hear* all points of view.[18] Licensing, legal requirements, FCC standards on programming—none of these applies to print.

In Chapter 15 we discuss in detail the complicated relationships involved in broadcasting and the First Amendment. For now, let it suffice to say that the broadcast licensee does have protection of freedom of speech under the First Amendment; however, that protection is circumscribed by requirements to operate in the public interest—the result of utilizing a scarce natural resource in the public domain—and thus is less than that enjoyed by a publisher.

13.4 DISSATISFACTION

The Communications Act is flexible, and it has served well over the years. Congress has amended the act almost continuously, but most amendments have supplemented the basic thrust of the act; change was evolutionary. However, beginning in the 1970s and continuing into the 1980s, demands mounted for radical change or replacement of the Communications Act.

13.4.1 Congressional Rewrite Attempts

U.S. Representative Lionel Van Deerlin (Figure 13.1) of California kicked off the revision attempts in 1976. He announced plans for a "basement to attic" revision of the Communications Act. Van Deerlin, who chaired the communications subcommittee of the House

Figure 13.1 Lionel Van Deerlin. He attempted a complete overhaul of the Communications Act with wholesale deregulation of the broadcasting trade. In 1979, one attempt behind him, Representative Van Deerlin stood in his Washington office with an old radio and announced his determination to try again. "Cancel the wake," he said. "Stay tuned." (*Source:* AP/Wide World.)

Commerce Committee, felt existing law was dated and inadequate for regulating contemporary electronic communications.

By the end of 1981, a number of bills had been introduced to change the Communications Act. No consensus formed around any of them, so none made the transition to law. One problem had to do with the number of issues and interests involved—*all* interstate wire and wireless communication. A bill that made common carriers happy, for example, made cable operators unhappy. A bill that made cable operators happy made broadcasters unhappy. Another problem stemmed from interest groups who perceived change as a threat. Van Deerlin, for example, proposed to levy fees on users of the spectrum; this drew opposition from broadcasters and other types of licensees. His revision would also have eliminated many requirements and restrictions on broadcasters and deleted the concept of "the public interest"; this drew opposition from citizen and public interest groups.

13.4.2 Marketplace Regulation

Mark Fowler (Figure 13.2) assumed the chair of the FCC (PRT 4.5.1) and continued the push for revision. Fowler echoed President

Reagan's commitment to eliminate what the administration saw as the unnecessary regulation of business. Fowler translated this commitment to mean that program regulation was no longer needed for the electronic

Figure 13.2 Mark Fowler. While chairing the FCC, Fowler took every opportunity to advance "the marketplace philosophy" of regulation for electronic media. (*Source:* Bettmann.)

media. He labeled the commission itself a "New Deal dinosaur." He referred to the concept of scarcity,* on which much FCC program regulations was based, as an "assumption" and said that it was no longer valid. He offered as evidence the large number of broadcast stations and, beyond that, the expanding number of channels available from other technologies, especially cable. He urged that broadcasters and other programmers be allowed to program with few or no FCC requirements or restrictions. He believed that "the marketplace" would regulate programming adequately; audiences would tune to those channels, broadcast or otherwise, that best catered to the public's wants and needs.

In 1981, the FCC sent Congress legislative proposals that reflected Fowler's philosophy. Under one proposal, Congress was to redefine the general purposes of the Communications Act. The redefinition was to state that marketplace forces would normally be favored over regulation. These marketplace forces would determine how and what telecommunications services would be made available to the public. Further, the FCC was to step in and regulate only when necessary for the protection of the public and the efficient functioning of the marketplace.

In 1982, Fowler and others suggested that broadcasters be granted property rights to the frequencies they used. In effect, they called for elimination of a basic assumption underlying the Communications Act—the public nature of the radio frequencies. Under their proposal, the frequencies would no longer be in the public domain. The broadcasters would own them. They could buy,

sell, and program their frequencies for whatever the market would bear without having to get FCC permission and without having to make any promises or commitments concerning programming.

Critics scoffed at the marketplace argument. They labeled it sophomoric, the result of muddled thinking. Some, however, took it seriously, not all of whom were knee-jerk reactionaries. Congress, for the most part, did not heed Fowler's calls for change. (Section 15.3.4.7 discusses the commission's relationship with Congress during the post-Fowler years.)

13.5 AMENDMENTS

As previously mentioned, Congress has amended Title 47 of the United States Code rather frequently. Some of the more important amendments included all-channel television receiver legislation passed in 1962 (PRT 4.1.4), the Communications Satellite Act of 1962 (PRT 5.5), the Educational Television (ETV) Facilities Act of 1962 (PRT 22.1.2), and the Public Broadcasting Act of 1967 (PRT 22.1.3).

In 1973, Congress amended Title 47 to deal with television coverage of professional sports. Prior to 1973, professional football teams routinely blocked local television coverage of home games even when they were broadcast in other parts of the country. In response to complaints, Congress amended the Communications Act to bar such professional sports "blackouts" if all tickets were sold 72 hours before game time. The statute expired in 1975. An attempt at a permanent law failed in 1976, but the National Football League promised to follow the expired sports blackout rule.

Congress approved a number of amendments during the 1980s. Some, perhaps reflecting the mood for revision mentioned

---

* The scarcity factor derives from physical limitations on the number of stations that can operate in an area (PRT 11.1.1 and 13.3.3). Program regulation was rationalized as follows: since not everyone can broadcast, those who do must be regulated so that they use their stations for the benefit of all.

above, changed basic aspects of the Communications Act.

The 1981 amendments contained the most changes. They lengthened the license term for broadcast stations from three years to five for television and seven for radio. They cleared the way for public broadcasting to run commercials on an experimental basis. They allowed the FCC to use a lottery in choosing broadcast licensees. Previously, when two or more parties applied for the same facility, the commission held hearings and, based on a complicated formula involving (among other things) programming promises and type of ownership, selected a licensee. Now they could ignore most such factors and use some variation of "odd man out" to make the choice.

The 1981 amendments also changed the nature of the commission. Previously, the FCC had been a permanent agency. Now it was put on a short-term basis; Congress had to reauthorize it every two years, otherwise it would cease to exist. The next year, Congress reduced the size of the commission itself. In 1982, Congress decreed that the FCC—comprising seven commissioners since 1934—would become a five-member commission in mid-1983. The 1982 amendments also revised the previous year's lottery-licensing legislation (the FCC had not been able to make it work as originally written) and allowed the commission to license noncitizens as operators for the first time.

13.6 CABLE COMMUNICATIONS POLICY ACT OF 1984

Congress enacted an extensive communications amendment in 1984. This was the Cable Communications Policy Act. For the first time, the FCC and the courts could deal with cable under direct law, rather than by attempting to infer from legislation intended for broadcasting and other forms of interstate communication.

The Cable Act sets forth its purposes as follows:[19]

1. To establish
   a. A national policy concerning cable communications,
   b. Guidelines for federal, state, and local regulation of cable systems,
   c. Franchise procedures and standards, and
   d. An orderly process for franchise renewal;
2. To encourage cable systems to
   a. Grow and develop,
   b. Respond to the needs and interests of their local communities, and
   c. Provide the widest diversity of information and services to the public;
3. To protect cable operators against unfair denials of renewal;
4. To promote competition in cable communications; and
5. To minimize "unnecessary regulation that would impose an undue economic burden on cable systems."

The act defines cable as one-way video programming and other services. It includes pay-per-view programming and one-way transmission of video games and electronic text. It does not include two-way communications services.[20] It affects cable system franchising (PRT 19.5.2.2 and 19.5.2.6), operation (PRT 15.2.3.2, 15.3.6, and 19.5.2.4), and regulation (PRT 14.1.1.8 and 19.5.2.5).

Just as there was dissatisfaction with the overall Communications Act, so was there also dissatisfaction with the Cable Act. As cable operators increased subscriber fees during the latter half of the 1980s, the cities regretted the regulatory power they had given up (PRT 5.2.4). They lobbied Congress. They joined broadcasters in demanding the re-regulation of the cable trade (PRT 5.2.5). In 1989, Congress held hearings on bills that would do the following: restore the cities' authority to regulate subscriber rates; force vertically integrated cable companies to make their programming available to competing technologies (such as wireless cable) on "fair terms"; and ban cable systems from serving more than 25 percent of subscribers across the nation.

NOTES

1. *Gibbon v. Ogden,* 9 Wheat 1 (1824).
2. *Pensacola Telegraph Co. v. Western Union Telegraph Co.,* 96 U.S. 1 (1878).
3. *Federal Radio Commission v. Nelson Brothers Bond & Mortgage Co.,* 53 Sup. Ct. 627, 633–634 (1933).
4. *United States v. Southwestern Cable Co.,* 392 U.S. 157 (1968).
5. *General Electric Co. v. Federal Radio Commission,* 31 F.2nd 630.
6. 48 Stat. 1064, 19 June 1934.
7. 47 U.S.C. §151.
8. 47 U.S.C. §152.
9. 47 U.S.C. §§154(i), 303, 307, 309.
10. 47 U.S.C. §402.
11. 47 U.S.C. §§303(n), 403.
12. 47 U.S.C. §§307(d), 312, 501–503.
13. 47 U.S.C. §307(a).
14. 47 U.S.C. §301.
15. 47 U.S.C. §§307(a), 307(d), 309(a), 311(b), 303(f).
16. 47 U.S.C. §§ 151, 307(b).
17. *National Broadcasting Co. v. United States,* 319 U.S. 190, 227 (1943).
18. *Red Lion Broadcasting Co. v. Federal Communications Commission,* 395 U.S. 367, 390 (1969).
19. Paraphrased and quoted from Communications Act, Section 601 (47 U.S.C. §521).
20. Communications Act, Section 602 (47 U.S.C. §522).

FURTHER READING

Bensman, Marvin R. *Broadcast Regulation: Selected Cases and Decision.* 2d ed. Lanham: UP of America, 1985.

Holt, Darrel. "The Origin of 'Public Interest' in Broadcasting." *Educational Broadcasting Review* 1 (1967): 15.

Kahn, Frank J., ed. *Documents of American Broadcasting.* 4th ed. Englewood Cliffs: Prentice 1984. Includes many of the important legal instruments in the development of regulation.

National Association of Broadcasters. *Legal Guide to Broadcast Law and Regulation.* Washington: NAB, 1988.

Whitley, Jack W., and Gregg P. Skall. *The Broadcaster's Survival Guide: A Handbook of FCC Rules and Regulations for Radio and TV Stations.* New York: Scripps, 1988.

CHAPTER 14

Regulation

Regulation means **control or direction by government agency according to rule, principle, or law.** Primary responsibility for regulation of radio and television belongs to the Federal Communications Commission. However, since commercial radio and television are advertising media, they are also subject to regulation by the Federal Trade Commission. Each of the three major branches of the federal government influences regulation. Even state and local governments can affect radio and television, especially cable television.

14.1 FEDERAL COMMUNICATIONS COMMISSION

The Federal Communications Commission (FCC) (Figure 14.1) consists of **five commissioners** who set policy and a **federal agency** that carries it out. The president of the United States appoints the commissioners with the advice and consent of the Senate. Commissioners must be citizens and have no financial interest in any industry the commission regulates. No more than three may belong to the same political party. Each commissioner chooses a small personal staff, which can include various combinations of

secretaries, lawyers, engineers, and economists.

The terms of the commissioners are five years. Terms are fixed; for example, if one individual leaves the commission three years into a term, the replacement is appointed for the remaining two years. When the term expires, the two-year commissioner may then be reappointed to a full five-year term.

The president designates one of the five commissioners to **chair** the commission. This individual presides at meetings of the commissioners, serves as chief executive, and represents the commission before Congress and other agencies and groups. The commission conducts its business in meetings and must meet at least once each month at its Washington, D.C., headquarters.

The agency consists of **four bureaus** and a number of **staff offices.** Each bureau has responsibility for one of the main areas of FCC concern—**mass media** (which deals with broadcasting and cable), **private radio** (point-to-point communications, such as amateur and citizens band), **common carrier** (interstate telephone and telegraph), and **field operations.** The field operations bureau oversees district FCC offices, whose personnel carry out various duties, including monitoring, investigation, technical inspection,

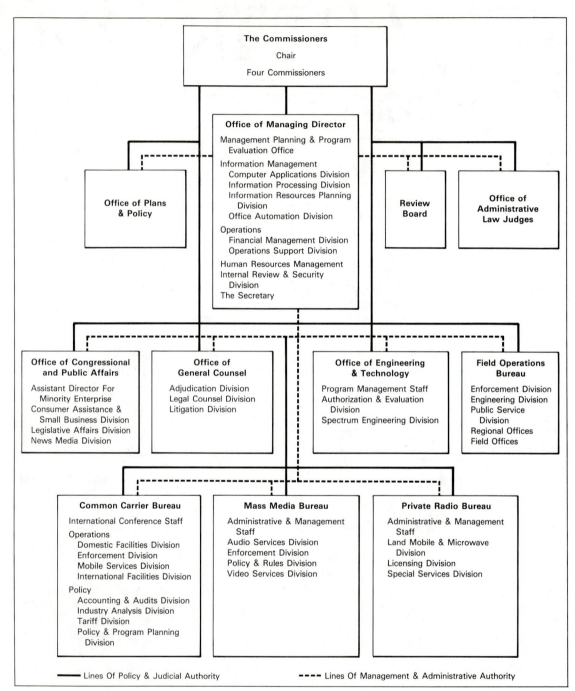

Figure 14.1 FCC organization.

and examining applicants for operator licenses.

The FCC has **executive, legislative,** and **judicial** functions. It performs the duties specified in the Communications Act, it makes rules and regulations, and it holds hearings, weighs evidence, and renders decisions on certain matters.

The commission has **delegated authority** to the bureaus to act on most routine business. For example, the Mass Media Bureau takes final action on most broadcast station license and renewal applications. However, all rule formulations, all license revocations, all major policy decisions, and many decisions on actions appealed from lower levels of the agency are made directly by the five commissioners.

14.1.1 Statutory Requirements and Regulatory Implementation

The Communications Act says what to do, and FCC rules say how to do it. The how is often much longer than the what. A single phrase—one or two lines in the Communications Act—is often supplemented by pages of specifics in FCC rules. In addition to the Communications Act, other laws affect broadcasting as well, such as the U.S. Criminal Code, the Federal Trade Commission Act, the Copyright Act, the Civil Rights Act, and the National Labor Relations Act.

14.1.1.1 General Powers Section 303 of the Communications Act spells out the general powers of the FCC. Several of these powers center on traffic duties, that is, ensuring that stations operate in such manner that they do not interfere with each other. This section also gives the FCC power to license operators, to inspect stations, to regulate network-affiliated stations, to require that stations keep certain records and paint and illuminate transmission towers, to assign and require

stations to use call letters, and to require that new television receivers be equipped to pick up all channels (PRT 4.1.4).

Two important provisions in Section 303 direct the commission to study new uses and otherwise encourage more effective use of the radio frequencies in the public interest, and to make rules and regulations necessary to carry out the intent of both domestic laws and all international agreements to which the United States is a party. These international agreements deal with traffic problems—who uses what frequencies—and are made at both regional (neighboring countries) and worldwide levels. The world organization is the International Telecommunications Union (ITU; PRT 23.4.1).

One ITU responsibility is to assign first letters for call letters in each country. ITU assigned to the United States the letters K, N, W, and part of the A's. The FCC, in turn, has assigned to stations call letters beginning with W east of the Mississippi River and K west of the Mississippi. Some pioneer broadcast stations, however, received call letters before the government set up the present rules. WBAP, for example, is in Fort Worth, while KDKA is in Pittsburgh.

14.1.1.2 Licensing Sections 307–311 and 319 give the FCC **discretionary power to license and to set up criteria** for licensing. No station may operate without a license, and thus licensing is one of the FCC's most important powers. FCC rules specify when and which licenses come up for renewal. All radio stations in a state come due on the first day of a particular month every seven years; television stations, every five years. The licensing process for broadcast stations is discussed in PRT 19.1.3.

14.1.1.3 Sponsorship Identification Section 317 requires identification of sponsors and advertisers. If any program or program element is paid for or furnished by parties other than the station licensee, the station must make an announcement to that effect and identify the sponsor or donor. This requirement pertains even if the station is non-commercial. It also applies to a cable system's local origination programming (PRT 7.4.1.1). With respect to commercials, mention of the advertiser's trade name or product meets the requirement. While Section 317 applies to the licensee or cable operator, Section 508 prohibits plugola and payola (PRT 9.1.6.7 and 9.1.6.9) by applying the sponsorship identification requirement to employees, program production and creative personnel, and program distributors.

The sponsorship identification requirement does provide for exceptions. It excludes material furnished to the station free or at a nominal charge with no reciprocal obligation on the station's part. In other words, the exception applies when the material comes "with no strings attached." For example, many radio stations normally get records free from distributors. The distributors hope the stations will play them over the air and thus stimulate retail sales of the records. However, the stations may use the records or not, as they prefer, so the commission requires no sponsorship identification announcement when they are broadcast.

The FCC may also waive the requirement, which it has done for certain types of "want ad" (listener swap shop) programs and for films produced originally for theatrical release. Many films contain plugs that are not disclosed as such; without the waiver they would have to be substantially altered for television use.

14.1.1.4 Political Programming Section 315 contains the **equal opportunities** requirement. If a licensee allows a candidate for public office to use a broadcast station, the licensee must then allow all other candidates for that office the chance to use the station for the same length of time and for the same cost. You may hear this called the "equal time" requirement. Section 315, however, requires "equal opportunities," not equal time. The station does *not* have to *give* an impecunious candidate matching time to reply to an opponent who *bought* time.

Section 315 **excludes certain types of news and public affairs programs** from the requirement. It also specifies that a station **may not censor** broadcasts by political candidates. It stipulates that a station may charge candidates no more than its **lowest unit rate** during a period of 60 days prior to a general election, 45 days prior to a primary. The quantity discounts and other rate advantages the station gives its most favored advertiser must also be given to a political candidate, no matter how little time the candidate buys. This rule applies only to spots of the same class or type. A station does not, for example, have to sell a candidate prime-time spots at overnight prices, nor must it figure in barter and per-inquiry spots when calculating the lowest unit rate. Section 312(a) (7) contains the **candidate-access requirement;** a station must make available (by gift or by sale) reasonable amounts of time to candidates for federal elective office.

The **Zapple doctrine** applies a "quasi-equal opportunities" rule to supporters of and persons who represent a candidate. When a licensee allows such persons to use a station's facilities during an election campaign to urge their candidate's election, to discuss campaign issues, or to criticize an opponent, the licensee must afford "comparable time" to supporters of other candidates for the same office.[1] (Zapple actually derives from the fairness doctrine, discussed in PRT 15.3.4.)

These political-programming requirements apply to operator-produced locally originated cable programming as well as to broadcast licensees. During the 1980s, several suggestions and attempts were made to delete or ease the equal opportunities requirement for both broadcasting and cable.

14.1.1.5 Editorializing by Noncommercial Licensees

The Public Broadcasting Act of 1967 (PRT 22.1.3) added Section 399 to the Communications Act. Section 399 prohibited noncommercial stations from editorializing. Congress subsequently changed the wording to prohibit editorializing only by public stations that received funds from the tax-supported Corporation for Public Broadcasting. Nonetheless, in 1984, the U.S. Supreme Court ruled that Section 399 was too broadly written and, therefore, unconstitutional.[2]

14.1.1.6 Equitable Distribution

Section 307(b) provides for the "fair, efficient, and equitable distribution of radio service to each" state and community. This *seems* to say that all cities and states should have the same number of stations. But there are far fewer broadcasters who want to serve the beautiful, relatively unpopulated reaches of Wyoming than who wish to serve the wall-to-wall people (and potentially far greater return on investment) of Los Angeles.

The FCC has made some effort to see that all persons benefit from local broadcast service. For example, the commission constructed the table of assignments in both television (PRT 12.6.1) and FM (PRT 11.2.2.1) in an attempt to serve the intent of 307(b). In dealing with competing applications (PRT 19.1.4), the FCC gives a slight advantage (a "preference") to applicants who propose to serve a community with few or no local stations. Docket 80-90 FM channels (PRT 3.4) went primarily to communities that lacked full-time radio stations. In 1983, on the other hand, the commission eliminated policies designed to ensure that a station serves its community of license rather than nearby large markets.[3]

14.1.1.7 Other Requirements

Section 325 prohibits willful transmission of false distress signals and requires a station planning to rebroadcast the signal of another station to get permission first from that other station. Section 326 **forbids censorship** by the FCC.

For years, the final word on broadcast of lottery information was Section 1304 of the Criminal Code. That statute placed a flat ban on the broadcast of lotteries or information about lotteries. During the 1970s, Congress passed a measure that allowed stations to broadcast information about official state lotteries in states that had them.[4] In 1988, Congress loosened the prohibition further to **permit announcements promoting all *legal* lotteries.**[5]

Section 1464 of the Criminal Code **prohibits transmission of obscene, indecent, or profane language** (PRT 15.2.1 and 15.3.5). Section 1343 of the Criminal Code **prohibits fraud** by wire, radio, or television. Sections 312 and 503 of the Communications Act authorize the commission to use license revocation or forfeiture against those who violate any of these three sections of the Criminal Code.

FCC rules require stations to establish a continuing program to afford equal employment opportunities to all persons (PRT 19.1.7). The commission has enacted rules to implement the National Environmental Policy Act. These rules are designed to minimize negative impact on the environment by construction of communications facilities.

Similar restrictions and requirements apply to cable. Local origination programming is subject to lottery and obscenity restrictions, and cable systems must establish equal opportunity employment programs. The **Emergency Broadcast System** (EBS), however, is based entirely on broadcast stations. The FCC has established rules for operation of EBS. EBS is designed to deliver emergency information quickly to the public. In the event of war or other large-scale disasters, EBS may be activated at the local, state, or national level.

14.1.1.8 Additional Cable Requirements

Sections 611 and 612 deal with cable access channels. Section 611 permits the franchising authority to require that the cable system provide for channel capacity for public, educational, and governmental (PEG; PRT 7.4.1.2) use. Section 612 requires that some channels be designated for "commercial" (lease-out) use on systems of 36 or more channels. On systems with 36 to 54 and 55 to 100 channels, the operator must so designate 10 and 15 percent, respectively, of its channels not required to carry local stations; systems with 100 or more channels must designate 15 percent of all channels. Persons not connected with the cable operator may use these channels on a leased-access basis (PRT 7.4.1.3). The operator sets the rates for use. The operator may not censor access programming on either PEG or leased channels. On the other hand, the operator may run other types of programming on these channels when they are not needed for access use. Furthermore, Section 638 relieves the cable operator of criminal and civil liability for access programming.

Section 613 permits the government—a state or a franchising authority—to own a cable system. The government-owner must set up an entity separate from the franchising authority to carry out the actual operation of the cable system. The government may, however, directly control programming on the system's educational and government access channels.

14.1.1.9 Must-Carry, Syndex, and Network Nonduplication

Three FCC cable rules that have had as their purpose the protection of broadcast stations are the must-carry, syndicated exclusivity, and network nonduplication rules (PRT 4.5.2.1). While the first two had an off-and-on existence, some form of

the latter was on the books continually since the 1960s.

Must-carry required a cable system to carry the signals of local television stations. Excluded were the signals of LPTV stations and broadcast teletext. Court decisions invalidated different versions in 1985[6] and 1987.[7] The latter decision, however, left in place A/B switch requirements from the second set of must-carry rules.[8] A/B switches would allow a cable subscriber to change the input of a home television receiver. The subscriber could use the device to switch easily between the cable system feed and over-the-air reception. Cable operators were to provide these switches and training in their use to subscribers.

Under syndicated exclusivity (syndex), a TV station could force local cable systems to delete syndicated programming which duplicated that of the station. Network nonduplication required a cable system to blank out imported broadcast network programming when it duplicated that of local affiliates. The FCC eliminated the syndex rule in 1980. Eight years later, it adopted new syndex rules and expanded the network exclusivity rules.

In programming, exclusivity is the right to be the only outlet in a market to show a syndicated program. The resurrected syndex rule permits a station to enforce its exclusivity against local cable systems that carry distant stations (those whose signals are imported from other markets) which show the same program. A syndicator may also enforce exclusivity for a program in all markets for the first year after that program is first sold to a TV station. A station may negotiate for national exclusivity; thus, a superstation can try for national rights to a syndicated program and be the only station to show it. Syndex excludes cable systems with less than 1000 subscribers.

The old network nonduplication rule covered only simultaneously aired duplicative network programming. The revision allows an affiliate to demand protection against all duplicative network programming, even when it airs at another time.

14.1.1.10 Rule-Making Procedure

As mentioned in PRT 14.1.1.1, the Communications Act authorizes the FCC to make "rules and regulations."[9] The process begins with a suggestion to make, amend, or delete a rule. The suggestion can come from almost any source—in or out of the commission, in or out of the government. All suggestions go to the appropriate FCC bureau or office for evaluation. A suggestion that survives staff screening goes to the full commission.

In some cases, the proposal involves only editorial changes to an existing rule. Here, the commission may issue a Report and Order adopting the change with no further action necessary. Some rule proposals take the form of a formal petition. If the FCC does not belive such a proposal has value, it issues a Memorandum Opinion and Order (MO&O) that denies the petition.

The process grows more complicated when the FCC likes a proposal that calls for substantive change. Here, the commission issues a **Notice of Proposed Rule Making** (NPRM), a **Notice of Inquiry** (NOI), or a combination of the two. The NPRM calls for comment on a specific proposal to change the rules. The NOI asks for information or suggestions on a certain topic. When the commission issues an NOI, it must eventually follow up with either an NPRM that proposes a specific rule or an MO&O that concludes the inquiry.

Interested parties or any member of the public can file comments. Later, they can also file responses to the comments. Occasionally, the commission may decide to hold oral arguments or hearings on the matter. Hearings or not, after everyone has had a chance to comment and the record is closed, the FCC considers all comments and either changes the proposal, adopts it in its original form, or decides not to adopt it. The commission then issues a **Report and Order** announcing its action.

A rule goes into effect 30 days after it is published in the *Federal Register*. During that time, any interested party may file a petition for reconsideration. Failing that, the rule may be challenged in court. If no one successfully challenges it, the rule stands as an enforceable FCC regulation until the commission changes or repeals it or Congress overrides it with new legislation.

The FCC may also utilize a less formal **policy-making** procedure. The commission examines a particular area of concern, reviews previous decisions in the area, and establishes guidelines or expectations. The Government Printing Office publishes regulations, including policy formulations, from all agencies in the *Code of Federal Regulations.*

14.1.1.11 Hearings and Appeals

The Communications Act requires that the FCC hold hearings on certain matters. The purpose is to ensure that all parties involved **have a chance to make their views known** so that the FCC may take them into account in reaching a final decision. Hearings are required in the following situations: when the commission decides to deny the grant of an application for a new license or for renewal, modification, or transfer of an existing license (Section 309[e]); when a licensee whose station frequency, power, times of operation, or other operation mode the commission proposes to change so requests (Sections 303[f] and 316); when the FCC wishes to revoke a license or construction permit or to issue a cease and desist order (Section 312[c]); when a second party files a petition to deny an application for license (*if* the FCC finds the petition raises valid points [Section 309(d)]); when two or more parties apply for the same frequency (PRT 19.1.4); and when an operator whose license has been suspended so requests (Section 303[m][2]).

An **administrative law judge** (ALJ) presides over most hearings. ALJs are commission employees. They have authority to administer oaths, examine witnesses, rule on admission of evidence, and issue decisions. An ALJ must render an impartial and independent opinion.

After conclusion of the hearing, the ALJ issues an **initial decision.** Unless reviewed, the initial decision eventually becomes final and effective. **Review** may result from appeal by one of the parties involved or by direction of the commission. Most initial decisions go to the **Review Board,** a permanent body composed of senior commission employees. The board issues a final decision, which, in turn, is subject to review by the commissioners meeting and acting together as the **full commission.** Some initial decisions, however, go directly to the five commissioners.

Section 405 of the Communications Act allows persons who are "aggrieved or whose interests are adversely affected" by a commission decision to **petition for rehearing.** Many decisions, however, are appealed directly to the federal courts. The case then becomes [*aggrieved party*] v. *FCC.* In its decision, a federal **appeals court** either **affirms** or **reverses** the commission's decision. If the latter, it **remands** the case to the FCC, sending the case back for the commission to carry out the judgment of the court. The party that loses the case may petition the **U.S. Supreme Court** to review the decision of the appeals court. If the aggrieved party petitions, the case remains [*aggrieved party*] v. *FCC*; if the FCC appeals, it becomes *FCC* v. [*aggrieved party*]. The Supreme Court may or may not grant *certiorari*—in effect, decide to review the decision—depending on the principles involved. If the Supreme Court denies *certiorari*, the decision of the lower court stands.

14.1.1.12 Enforcement The Communications Act gives the FCC six ways to deal with a broadcast licensee that violates the act, FCC rules, or terms of the license. Sections 401, 501, and 502 authorize the commission to call on any U.S. district attorney to **prosecute violators in court.** Section 503(b) allows the commission to levy a **forfeiture,** a fine of up to $2000 for each day the violation occurs, $20,000 maximum. Section 312(b) authorizes the FCC to issue a **cease and desist order.**

Section 307(d) allows the FCC to grant **short-term renewals,** that is, to renew a broadcast license for a period of less than five (for TV stations) or seven (for radio stations) years. The commission uses the short-term renewal when it wishes to review a station's performance sooner than the normal five- or seven-year interval.

Section 307(d) also gives the commission the option to **deny renewal,** and Section 312(a) allows it to **revoke** the license, to take it away before renewal time. Denial of renewal and revocation of license are both serious sanctions—the trade refers to them as "the death penalty" for a station—and the FCC rarely uses them. Nor does the commission often use court prosecution or cease and desist orders, since other sanctions are easier to apply.

In addition to the sanctions granted by the Communications Act, the commission uses three other methods of enforcement. In one, the FCC simply writes a **letter** to the licensee. The letter describes the matter under question and asks, in effect, "What about this? Please explain," or "What do you plan to do about this?" Some call this the **"raised eyebrow"** technique. A second method involves a **consent order.** Here, the alleged violator signs an agreement to comply with specified laws, rules, or policies. This does not, however, constitute admission to the alleged violations. In a third method, the FCC grants a **conditional renewal** of a license. The commission may condition renewal of a license on specific licensee behavior—for example, fulfilling promises to serve the community of license better, or improving hiring practices to bring in more women and minority staff members.

The FCC does not license cable systems, so it cannot use license-affecting enforcement methods on an erring cable operator. But it can use any of the others.

14.1.2 The Public Interest

The Communications Act gives the commission very little specific control over programming. Yet it directs the commission to grant licenses and renewals only if the **public interest, convenience, and necessity** will be served thereby. Over the years, the commission has taken the position that one primary means by which a station serves the public interest is its programming; therefore, of necessity, the FCC has to examine broadcast programming. The federal courts have consistently supported this view (PRT 15.3.3.1). Congress has not seen fit to amend the Communications Act to preclude FCC programming regulation and, in committee hearings, has even scolded the commission for not paying enough attention to programming.

In the past, the FCC has trod a thin line between censorship and program regulation. The commission would not tell a station that it could or could not air a particular *program*. But it did hold that the station had a responsibility to provide *programming* that **met the varied needs of its home community** and adopted policy statements, rules, and procedures to ensure that the station met that responsibility. The *station* decided how it would meet the needs of the community. The *station* designed its own programming. Then, when the station's license came up for renewal, the *FCC* had the authority and duty to review *overall* programming, to compare the station's *performance* during the preceding license period to *promises* it made on the last renewal application, and to determine whether it had operated *in the public interest.*

This routine, while nice in theory, rarely worked in practice. The commission granted most license renewals if the applications were filled out properly. Normally, the commission questioned a station's renewal only if there were problems with its application form or if the station's file contained serious and frequent complaints from the public. So, in fact, very little was lost in 1981 when the FCC adopted a postcard-size renewal form that required no information on programming and dropped formal ascertainment requirements (PRT 15.3.3.5) for commercial radio and television.

Nonetheless, there are still mechanisms for ensuring that a station serves the public interest. Every three months, each station must put in its public file (PRT 15.3.3.6) a list of its programs that dealt with community issues during the preceding three months. And citizens can make their views known to the station and, if necessary, to the commission. Serious and frequent complaints may lead the commission to order a hearing; quite often, one of the questions the hearing seeks to answer concerns whether renewal of the station's license would serve the public interest.

The anti-"public interest" rhetoric of the 1980s (PRT 13.4) left its mark in at least one respect. Congress did not use the words "public interest" even once in the Cable Communications Policy Act of 1984. Instead, the act contains phrases such as "responsive to the needs and interests of the local community," "meet[s] the standards established by this title,"[10] and "complied with the material terms of the franchise and with applicable law."[11]

14.1.3 Network Regulation

The Communications Act **does not require that networks be licensed.** However, the FCC does license network-owned stations, and Section 303(i) gives the commission authority to make special regulations for network-affiliated stations. When the FCC adopted its **Chain Broadcasting Regulations** in 1941 (PRT 3.1.5.4), the rules applied through affiliated stations. Most began "No license shall be granted to a . . . broadcast station . . ." and then went on to spell out what the FCC prohibited.

The Chain Broadcasting Regulations were designed to end network control of affiliated stations, to shift control from the networks back to those who were legally responsible for the stations, the licensees. They did their job. But over the years, conditions changed and eliminated the need for several of the regulations. In 1977, the FCC repealed most Chain Broadcasting Regulations as they applied to radio, retaining as a formal rule only that **prohibiting territorial exclusivity** (so that when an affiliate rejected a network program, the network could offer it to another station in the market). At the same time, the commission redefined the concept of a network to include news-agency audio services, such as those of Associated Press and United Press International.

All network regulations were retained for television. Four additional rules applied only to television networks. One said that a network **may not act as national sales representative for nonnetwork time on affiliated stations** (except for those it owns). The **network syndication rule** prohibited a network from syndicating programming in the United States. The **network financial interest rule** prohibited a network from owning in whole or in part any of its programs that it did not produce itself. And the **prime-time access rule** (PTAR) prohibited network affiliates in the 50 largest markets (in effect, all markets) from airing over three hours of network programming (including off-net programming) during the four hours of prime time. In adopting the network syndication and financial interest rules, the FCC broke precedent and applied the rules directly to the networks—"No television network shall. . . ."

Over the years, PTAR changed in detail, but the principles remain intact. The ban includes both current network and off-net programming (PRT 4.5.2.2). It created the access hour (PRT 7.3.2.2). The FCC did specify certain exemptions, so the networks can schedule (and large-market affiliates can air) certain children's, documentary, and public affairs programs (except on Saturdays), along with certain news, political, and sports programming in the access slot. *Affiliates in markets below the top 50* and *all independent stations* can program off-network (and "on-network" were it available) programming in the access hour. So can affiliates of a new network whose prime-time programming totals less than 15 hours a week.

In 1978, the FCC hired a special staff to inquire into network practices. Two years later, the network study staff issued its findings, one of which was that the network syndication and prime-time access rules had failed. Heartened by this, the networks lobbied the commission. In 1982, the FCC proposed repeal of the "finsyn" rules as trade press headline writers dubbed them. In 1981, Chronicle Broadcasting Company had petitioned the FCC to change PTAR so that top-50 affiliates could broadcast off-net programming during the access hour. The commission dismissed Chronicle's petition, saying it might take up the entire prime-time access rule when it examined the network inquiry staff's recommendations.

But the rules had not failed. They had generated competition and diversity in the programming marketplace (PRT 4.5.2.4). Original programming developed for the syndication market that might never have seen the light of day without the network syndication and financial interest rules and PTAR—programming for access (such as *Entertainment Tonight*) and for other dayparts (such as *The Oprah Winfrey Show*).

PTAR also yielded unexpected benefits. First, it strengthened independent stations. Through competitive programming, the independents significantly improved their ratings (PRT 4.5.2.2). Second, affiliates made money. Their access programming typically generated lower ratings than network programming would have. Still, the affiliates made much more from their own time sales for the access slot than they would have received in compensation if the networks had programmed the slot. As a result, affiliates were reluctant to support network efforts to have the FCC drop the financial interest and syndication rules and, in fact, did so only after the networks backed off their drive to repeal PTAR.

In 1983, the FCC reached what was termed a "tentative" decision to repeal the financial interest and network syndication rules. Meanwhile, the program producers and independent TV stations had lobbied hard and effectively. In 1984, under pressure from the president and Congress, the FCC postponed its plans to repeal the rules. In 1989, however, the commission eliminated its rule limiting the length of network-station affiliation agreements to no more than two years. The FCC also proposed to delete its rule prohibiting a TV network from acting as its affiliates' rep (above).

14.1.4 Advertising and Commercial Limitations

During the 1980s, the FCC eliminated most of its restrictions on advertising. These included regulations or policies on commercial minutes per hour (PRT 15.3.3.7); program-length commercials (PRT 9.1.3.3); false, misleading, or deceptive advertising;[12] alcohol advertising;[13] and advertising aimed at children.

14.1.5 Children's Programming and Advertising

Over the years, individuals and citizen groups have asserted that children have special requirements as a radio-TV audience. Children need protection, for example, from accidentally tuning in certain types of sexually oriented material. The FCC responded by channeling such programming to late night (PRT 15.3.5).

In the area of children's programming, however, the commission has a spotty record. In 1970, Action for Children's Television (ACT), a citizen group, petitioned the FCC to require that TV licensees carry worthwhile children's programming. Four years later, the commission issued a policy statement.[14] It asked licensees to increase the amount of such programming, air more of it on weekdays, and broadcast educational and informational programming aimed at specific age levels. Their efforts would be reviewed at license renewal time.

Things went downhill from there for children's programming advocates. The FCC revisited the issue in 1979, found little improvement, and asked for comment on several rule-making options.[15] These ranged from setting children's programming quotas to rescinding the 1974 policy statement. In 1984, the commission—well into its deregulatory phase (PRT 4.5.1)—chose the latter.[16] The amount and variety of children's programming, said the FCC, were substantial and diverse; mandated quotas were not needed. At license renewal time, a station would have to show that programming needs of children in its community had been met. But in making that showing, the station could count programming by other media in the market, such as cable and public television.

The commission's record in the area of advertising is equally spotty. The 1974 policy statement had placed limitations on advertising during children's programming. It called for a clear separation between programming and advertising, prohibited program hosts or characters from selling products, and limited ad time to 9½ minutes an hour on weekends, 12 minutes on weekdays. In 1986, the FCC said that those 1974 limitations had been eliminated as part of the general deregulation of television two years previously.

Other commercialization issues came up, and the commission refused to deal with them. In 1983, ACT and the National Association for Better Broadcasting (NABB) complained to the FCC that children's programs based on toys (Figure 14.2) violated a com-mission policy against program-length commercials (PRT 9.1.3.3). In another action, ACT asserted that toy companies' offers to share profits with stations airing their shows might lead to program choices based on profit rather than the public interest. The FCC rejected both complaints[17] in 1985.

Then, along came interactive children's shows. Several companies announced plans for this product tie-in scheme. The programs would transmit inaudible signals causing specially designed toys to react. ACT filed a petition asking that the FCC declare the toys against the public interest.

Efforts of children's programming advocates began to pay off in 1987. ACT had appealed the FCC's 1984 decision to abolish its 1974 children's commercial guidelines, and the court remanded the case, saying that the FCC had presented inadequate justification for eliminating those limitations.[18] NABB had appealed the FCC's program-length-com-

Figure 14.2 Toys as televison.   G.I. Joe dolls, shown here, are popular toys for young boys. There is also an animated television program featuring G.I. Joe as a character. (*Source:* Courtesy, Hasbro.)

mercial decision, and the court overruled that commission action.[19] In response, the FCC opened a rule-making procedure, requesting comments on commercial guidelines for children's shows, the nature of commercial matter, and interactive toys.[20]

ACT and others had also lobbied Congress for legislation on children's programming and advertising. In 1988, both houses passed a bill requiring TV stations to provide programming that would serve the special needs of children. It would also have limited advertising in children's programming. President Reagan vetoed the measure, but a similar bill was introduced and shepherded through Congress soon after George Bush suceeded Reagan to the presidency.

14.1.6 Regulatory Weaknesses

We have described what should be an ideal mechanism for regulation. Feed in a problem—an erring licensee, competing applications, need for corrective action or new policy; spin it through regulatory and decision-making machinery, powered by the desire to ensure service in the public interest; and out should come the perfect solution— the sanction, the choice of best applicant, the proper action or cure-all policy. But, unfortunately, it does not work that way. Anyone who has ever dealt with government agencies knows that even the best are not too efficient and are prone to make mistakes. Historically, the FCC has not been one of the best; some critics have even said it was one of the worst. Critics generally list the following as the FCC's major weaknesses over the years.

14.1.6.1 Politically Motivated Appointments to the Commission Commissioners often have not been of the quality needed to guide the civilian communications policy of the United States. Individuals have been ap-

pointed to the commission, not because of their ability to regulate in the public interest, but as political favors and, during the 1980s, to mold the commission to conform to an ideological bent.

14.1.6.2 Decisions Made Without Citizen Involvement For years, the commission did not encourage citizen participation in licensing matters, rule-making procedures, and hearings. During the 1970s, the FCC reversed that policy and attempted to encourage such public participation.

14.1.6.3 Decisions Made Under Pressure from Trade Lobbyists The commission, bombarded by myriad trade lobbying efforts, loses sight of the public interest. Commissioners find it hard *not* to adopt the view of the regulated companies—that is, let the trade run itself, but regulate all competitors to the hilt. Broadcasters, cable system operators, and their lobbyists and lawyers are in constant touch with the commissioners. They are always ready to provide information, help, and advice. They are the milieu within which the commissioners work. Theirs is the veiwpoint most often heard. Some commissioners even go to work for regulated industries after leaving the commission. In 1987, for example, Mark S. Fowler left the commission chair and joined a law firm where, among other things, he planned to represent communications clients before government agencies.

Commissioners who have bucked the trend and tried to force the issue of public interest from the *public's* point of view have been branded as mavericks and troublemakers. They have been vilified and harassed by broadcasters and the trade press. These commissioners were not playing the game according to the rules of the trade.

14.1.6.4 Decisions Made with Inadequate or Biased Information The agency is a bureaucracy. It consists of a massive hierarchy of chiefs and a staff of entrenched civil servants, many of whom are more interested in keeping pensions intact than in problem solving, innovation, and clearing up backlogs. The commissioners must deal with matters and base decisions on information these middle-level staff personnel put before them. These staffers often choose matters for FCC consideration based not so much on what will serve the public as on what will serve their own private interest. In addition, as communications become even more technically complex, commissioners have difficulty educating themselves adequately to make competent technical judgments.

14.1.6.5 Unreasonable Delays in Resolving Matters
Efficiency has been strangled in red tape. Huge backlogs of work have built up, causing unreasonable delays. The commission has taken months, often many years, to resolve individual matters.

14.1.6.6 Inability to Plan
The commission has seemed incapable of devising procedures, of adopting innovative solutions, to deal with chronic regulatory weaknesses. In the 1970s and 1980s, two individuals worked to institute long-range planning and reduce delays and achieved some measure of success. Richard E. Wiley, who chaired the commission in the mid-1970s, cut backlogs and brought efficiency to FCC decision making. Commissioner Fowler appointed to the chair in 1981, introduced the concept of management by objectives to all levels of the commission and reorganized the agency.

14.1.6.7 Decisions Made Without Consideration of Precedent
In reaching a decision on a matter, commissioners have often ignored past FCC decisions. As a result, decisions have been inconsistent; that is, the commission has applied different principles in different ways in similar cases.

14.1.6.8 Sanctions Not Used; Policies Not Followed
The commission has not followed its own guidelines or used the sanctions available to it. As a result, licenses were renewed routinely, irrespective of how well the stations met the public interest standard. Rarely were licenses revoked, even for the most serious violations of law and regulation, and license transfers were granted that concentrated station control into fewer and larger corporate structures and created more and more absentee owners (see PRT 19.1.2.2).

14.2 FEDERAL TRADE COMMISSION

Like the FCC, the Federal Trade Commission (FTC) is an independent federal regulatory agency created by Congress under its constitutional power to regulate interstate commerce. Congress passed the **Federal Trade Commission Act** in 1914,[21] establishing the FTC and prohibiting "unfair methods of competition." Twenty-four years later, Congress amended the act by passing the Wheeler-Lea Act.[22] The Wheeler-Lea Act prohibits "unfair and deceptive acts or practices in commerce" and thus allows the FTC to protect the consumer from deceptive advertising.

The FTC exercises primary jurisdiction over maters involving unfair or deceptive broadcast advertising. The trade commission is also concerned with deception and misuse in audience rating surveys.

14.2.1 Organization and Operation

The FTC's structure resembles that of the FCC. Both have five commissioners, working bureaus, field offices, and ALJs.

A complaint of deceptive advertising may arise from the FTC's own monitoring activities, from a trade competitor, from other federal agencies (such as the FCC), from the Better Business Bureau, or from the public. If the FTC finds the complaint valid, it may attempt to secure a **stipulation agreement,** an informal agreement to discontinue the practice under question. For more serious cases, the commission may seek a **consent order,** legally binding on the advertiser but with no admission of guilt. Failing that, the matter goes to an ALJ for **hearing.** If evidence sustains the complaint, the ALJ (or the FTC on appeal or review) issues an order requiring the respondent to **cease and desist** the deceptive advertising.

The **federal courts** figure in FTC operation in three ways. First, cease and desist orders may be **appealed.** Second, the government may **sue violators** of cease and desist orders. Third, in some cases, the FTC may seek a court **injunction** to halt advertising even before a hearing. The injunction remains in effect until final FTC or court disposition of the case. Violators of a cease and desist order or of the FTC act are subject to **fines** and **imprisonment.** The FTC also uses **publicity** for enforcement, publicizing complaints and cease and desist orders.

In 1971, the FTC introduced another regulatory option—**corrective advertising.** The Profile Bread, Ocean Spray, and Listerine television commercials discussed in PRT 9.1.4.4 are examples of corrective advertising. Also in 1971, the FTC began its **advertising substantiation program.** The trade commission selects certain advertisers and asks them to prove advertising claims they make for their products. Responses are made public.

The FTC also plays a positive role in prevention of deceptive practices. It will respond to advertiser inquiries with informal **staff opinion letters.** It also responds with more formal **advisory opinions,** which go on the public record. It publishes **industry guides** that give its opinion on how certain products should be marketed. It issues **pol-**icy statements** that reflect enforcement attitude. And it adopts **trade regulation rules** that, like FCC rules, have the force of law.

14.2.2 False Advertising

Section 15 of the Wheeler-Lea Act defines a "false advertisement" as one that is "misleading" in a material respect. **Misleading** refers not only to what an advertisement says but also to what it does not say. In other words, the FTC looks for both **direct falsehoods** and **failure to reveal material facts**—for example, facts concerning consequences from use of a product, or facts concerning a product's value in treating illness or pain.

Three of the most famous cases of deceptive broadcast advertising are the **sandpaper case,** the **Libby-Owens-Ford** (L-O-F) **glass case,** and the **Geritol case.** In the fall of 1959, three new commercials began running on television to advertise Rapid Shave. They purported to demonstrate how the aerosol shaving cream was "super-moisturized" to shave "a beard as tough as sandpaper." As part of the demonstration, Rapid Shave was spread on sandpaper, and a razor shaved a swatch clean of grit. What the commercials did *not* say was that the "sandpaper" was really a piece of Plexiglas covered with sand. The FTC found that to actually shave off the grit, sandpaper had to soak in the lather for about 80 minutes. The FTC issued a cease and desist order. The U.S. Supreme Court upheld the decision, ruling that undisclosed use of Plexiglas constituted a "material deceptive practice."[23]

In the L-O-F glass case, a television commercial invited the audience to compare views through the glass of two different automobiles. One showed distortion in ordinary auto glass; the other represented the minimum distortion in L-O-F safety glass. What the audience was not told was that scenes purported to be camera shots through L-O-F safety glass were actually filmed through an open window! The FTC issued a cease and desist order, which a federal court upheld.[24]

J. B. Williams Company advertised its patent medicine, Geritol, heavily on television. The commercials touted the product as a remedy for tiredness, loss of strength, nervousness, or irritability due to iron deficiency anemia. The Geritol advertising failed to explain that among people who suffered from those particular symptoms, only a relative few actually had iron deficiency anemia, and therefore Geritol would not help most such persons. The FTC issued a cease and desist order in 1964. It also required Williams to make an **affirmative disclosure** in its advertising that a great majority of persons who experience such symptoms do so *not* because of vitamin or iron deficiency.[25]

14.2.3 Regulatory Problems

Four basic structural problems of the FTC include lack of prior restraint, extended case lengths, lack of penalty provisions, and inadequate budget and personnel. A fifth stems from the trade commission's vulnerability to pressure.

14.2.3.1 Lack of Power of Prior Restraint The trade commission does not have the power to censor advertising materials. We do not mean to imply that it should have this power; such would be inimical to the First Amendment of the U.S. Constitution and would smack of totalitarianism. Yet the fact remains that an individual can perpetrate false and misleading advertising until the FTC acts. Meanwhile, the false advertiser has bilked many customers.

14.2.3.2 Extended Length of Cases Even after the FTC has stepped in, years may pass before a case is settled, years in which the advertiser may continue to use the techniques under question. In the Geritol case, for example, the trade commission began its investigation in 1959. Fourteen years of appeals, complaints, and suits passed before a federal court imposed a fine of $812,000 on J. B. Williams and its advertising agency. During that time, some $60 million had been spent on television advertising for Geritol, generating sales in 1971 alone of an estimated $90 million, which accounted for 90 percent of the tonic market.[26]

14.2.3.3 Lack of Penalty Provisions That $812,000 probably sounds like a great deal of money to most of us—but it is little more than a minor business expense to a company that generates $90 million in one year. Even here, the monetary fine is unusual. The court imposed the fine not because of Williams's deceptive advertising but because the company had violated the FTC order for affirmative disclosure. In most cases, the only "penalty" imposed is an order to stop the deceptive practice. No provision requires the advertiser to pay for what has already been done. And the constructive semipenalty of corrective advertising can easily be rendered innocuous; a clever advertising copywriter can devise wording to follow and neutralize—or even turn into a selling point—the FTC-required corrective statement.

14.2.3.4 Inadequate Budget and Personnel With its budget and minuscule staff, the FTC is a David in a nation of Goliaths. FTC personnel number less than 1000. Its fiscal year 1987 budget was just over $66 million. But in calendar year 1987, *every one* of the top 25 broadcast network advertisers spent more than that in network TV advertising alone, while total U.S. advertising expenditures in 1987 were over $104 billion.

14.2.3.5 Vulnerability to Criticism, Congressional Whim, and Ideological Ap-

pointments Radical changes in the commission's operation have been caused by the complaints of two groups—consumer advocates and the advertising community (advertisers, agencies, and media). Consumer advocates say that the commission is not active enough; the advertising community, that it is too active. The FTC, like the FCC, is a creature of Congress. And Congress may whipsaw, chastise, and mold the trade commission to fit the desires of the group with the most influence at the particular time. Also as with the FCC (PRT 14.1.6.1), the president may attempt to mold the trade commission to an ideological bent, sometimes to the detriment of the agency's effectiveness in regulating advertising.

For example, during the 1960s, consumer groups and Congress complained that the FTC was not doing its job. As a result, the FTC reorganized and took on a more consumer-oriented, activist bent. As late as 1977, a House committee report implied that the trade commission should do even more about advertising abuses.

The commission started to deal with *unfair* advertising in the mid-1970s. In 1975, President Gerald Ford signed into law a bill that gave the agency authority to issue broad trade regulation rules to prohibit unfair or deceptive practices.[27] The FTC then proposed rules that would prohibit certain advertising practices as unfair. The business and advertising communities contended that *unfair* was too vague a term and opposed these rules.

In 1978, the FTC responded to petitions from two public interest groups and started procedures to adopt a rule to ban certain types of television advertising to young children. The commission reasoned that any advertising aimed at children who were too young to understand the intent of commercials was unfair and, therefore, deceptive. The proposal would have banned all commercials directed to preschool children. It would have prohibited commercials for foods with high sugar content aimed at children under 12. And it would have required advertisers who ran commercials for products such as presweetened cereals to air other TV spots that would promote nutritional and health information.

The FTC would hold a series of hearings on the proposal, giving all concerned a chance to have their say. Following the hearings, the commission would consider the comments and the evidence and take action on the proposal. Certainly, this seemed to be an adequate response to previous congressional criticisms.

Advertisers, agencies, and broadcasters were outraged. The National Association of Broadcasters hosted a meeting to organize a fight against the FTC proposal. Attendees included representatives of the American Association of Advertising Agencies, the American Advertising Federation, the U.S. Chamber of Commerce, ABC, CBS, NBC, the National Association of Manufacturers, and several food trade groups—the Cereal Institute, the Nutrition Foundation, the National Soft Drink Association, the Grocery Manufacturers Association, and the Foodservice [*sic*] and Lodging Institute.

The broadcast, food, and toy trades pulled their strings in the national legislature. As early as 1978, threats emerged from Congress to cut off FTC appropriations if the commission continued its children's advertising inquiry. The threats affected two areas vital to the functioning of the commission, reauthorization and appropriations. In fact, the commission went out of business briefly twice in 1980—once because Congress had not yet reauthorized it, the second time because Congress had not granted full funding and the commission ran out of money. Agency shutdowns and restarts entail added expenses, so this congressional game playing cost the taxpayers.

Eventually, Congress approved full funding and reauthorization of the trade commission. But the reauthorization legislation[28] included a few punitive measures. It said that the children's advertising inquiry could continue, but it had to be based on false and deceptive advertising, rather than unfair advertising. The act prohibited the FTC from issuing trade regulation rules based on unfairness. And Congress gave itself veto power over any action of the FTC. A 1983 U.S. Supreme Court decision, however, nullified legislative vetoes by Congress.[29]

Meanwhile, the advertisers had been busy on other fronts. A group of advertisers tried to have Commissioner Michael Pertschuk disqualified from participating in the children's advertising inquiry. Pertschuk chaired the FTC and had pushed for the inquiry. The plaintiffs argued that comments by Pertschuk in a speech showed he had prejudged the issue and could not be impartial; therefore he should be removed from the inquiry. A federal appeals court disagreed. Pertschuk then voluntarily removed himself, saying that he did not wish to inhibit the proceedings.

Nonetheless, in 1981, the FTC suspended its investigation. An attempt to persuade the industry to adopt voluntary curbs on children's advertising had failed. After reviewing the testimony—more than 200 witnesses and over 1 million words on the record—the commission concluded that there was a problem, but they could probably do nothing about it.

Ending the inquiry, however, did not end the attempt to debilitate the FTC. During the administration of President Ronald Reagan, proposals emerged to cut and limit the trade commission's power and resources. In 1981, Reagan appointed James C. Miller to chair the FTC. Miller subscribed to the same "marketplace philosophy" (PRT 13.4.2) as other Reagan appointees—the best regulation was no regulation. Under Miller's tenure, the commission decided that deceptive advertising, by itself, did not necessarily warrant FTC concern; the advertising had to mislead a *reasonable consumer* to sustain a complaint. Miller left in 1985, but the agency continued on the course he had charted.

14.3 EXECUTIVE, LEGISLATIVE, AND JUDICIAL BRANCHES

The FCC, the FTC, and other such agencies are **independent regulatory agencies,** created to operate outside regular departments of government. However, the three regular branches also affect regulation.

14.3.1 Executive Branch

A number of departments in the executive branch deal with radio and television. Some of the more important include the Executive Office of the President, the National Telecommunications and Information Agency (NTIA), the Department of State, and the Department of Justice.

14.3.1.1 Executive Office of the President Section 706 of the Communications Act gives the president authority to assume certain powers during war and other national emergencies. Under these powers the president may regulate, operate, and even appropriate civilian stations.

Section 305 gives the president responsibility to allocate radio frequencies used by the federal government. Such allocations are coordinated through the NTIA and the Interdepartmental Radio Advisory Committee (IRAC). IRAC includes representatives of major frequency users among governmental agencies. NTIA advises, chairs, and facilitates IRAC. The FCC represents Congress and frequency users other than the federal government at IRAC meetings.

The Office of Management and Budget (OMB) coordinates agency budget requests and draws up the administration's budget for submission to Congress. It also evaluates and suggests changes in agency structure and functioning. An agency that wishes to adopt a new application or information-gathering form or change an old one must first secure OMB approval. All of these directly affect the FCC, the FTC, and other agencies involved in regulation of radio and television.

The president has at least four ways to influence ongoing civilian communication policy and regulation. First, the president can **recommend legislation.** For example, the Communications Act of 1934 resulted in large part from a recommendation by President Franklin D. Roosevelt. Second, the president can use the **appointive power.** With careful appointments, the FCC's ideology can be molded to reflect that of the president. Third, the president can use **departments and offices in the executive branch.** For example, all agencies funded by the government must submit annual budget requests to OMB. Since OMB is a unit of the Executive Office of the President, the potential exists for the president to exert economic pressure. Fourth, the president can use **informal means** such as prestige of office and speeches.

14.3.1.2 National Telecommunications and Information Agency

The NTIA is a division of the Department of Commerce. In addition to the duties mentioned above, NTIA has the responsibility to advise the secretary of commerce and the president on overall communications policies, international treaties and agreements, federal research and development activities, and spectrum management. NTIA also makes public broadcasting facilities grants. The director of the NTIA answers to an undersecretary of commerce and represents the president in FCC proceedings.

14.3.1.3 Department of State

The Department of State makes arrangements for treaties and agreements involving international communications and prepares delegations for regional and world conferences on radio (PRT 23.4). To prepare for and staff delegations for such activities, the State Department draws heavily on personnel and expertise of the FCC and, to a lesser degree, other agencies and even trade organizations involved in communications.

The FCC, the NTIA, and the State Department all have responsibilities in the area of international communications. A key person in this increasingly important area is the State Department's coordinator for international communication and information policy. As the title implies, this person attempts to coordinate the work of, and makes suggestions to, all federal agencies involved in international communications matters, including interagency task forces and committees. The coordinator has the rank of assistant secretary of state and heads the department's Bureau for International Communications and Information Policy.

14.3.1.4 Department of Justice

The FCC and the FTC may call upon the Justice Department and its federal district attorneys to prosecute enforcement and punishment proceedings in the federal courts. The Justice Department's Antitrust Division may prosecute violations of the antitrust and preservation of competition sections (313, 314) of the Communications Act. The Criminal Division prosecutes licensees who broadcast and cable operators whose locally originated programming includes illegal lottery information, fraud, obscene or indecent language, or false advertising (Sections 1304, 1342, and 1464 of the U.S. Criminal Code and 14 of the

FTC Act). The department's Solicitor General office represents the agencies in decisions that have been appealed to the federal courts.

In 1972, the U.S. Department of Justice filed antitrust suits against ABC, CBS, and NBC. The suits charged that certain network practices with regard to programming were monopolistic. In 1976, NBC settled out of court and signed an agreement with the Justice Department to reduce network interest in production of entertainment programming, as well as to ecourage production by independent companies. ABC and CBS held out until 1980 and then signed similar agreements.

14.3.2 Congress

Congress shapes regulation directly through **legislation** and indirectly through **appropriation** and the Senate's **confirmation** power over presidential appointees. Both chambers rely heavily on recommendations of the appropriate committees. Congressional **appropriations committees** hold the purse strings for the regulatory commissions and the CPB. **Special committees** may be appointed, whose activities affect radio and television and their regulation.

The House and Senate **commerce committees**—specifically, their **communications subcommittees**—review proposed and existing legislation that deals with radio and television. They investigate regulation, regulators, and regulated to determine whether additional legislation is needed.

The Senate Commerce Committee examines appointees to the FCC, the FTC, and the CPB board and recommends for or against the appointees' confirmation by the Senate. Presidential appointments may also be held up in committee. In 1988, the FCC had only three commissioners because the Senate Commerce Committee did just that.

Like the president, Congress also uses informal means to influence regulation. One such means is the **hearing.** When the FCC takes some action that congressional leaders do not like, they hold a committee hearing and demand the presence of the commission for testimony and chastisement.

Individual senators and representatives also influence regulation. If the commission makes a decision that licensees or cable system operators do not like, they complain to contacts in their state's congressional delegation. The senators and representatives, in turn, pressure the FCC.

14.3.3 Federal Courts

Violators of law or of regulatory commission rules, decisions, or orders may be tried in federal courts. The courts may issue **writs** (formal legal documents ordering or prohibiting some action), impose **fines, sentence to jail,** and even **revoke broadcast licenses.** The courts also hear and rule on appeals from commission decisions and orders. Over the years, court decisions have played a major role in shaping radio and television regulation. See, for example, accounts of the Brinkley, Shuler, and WLBT cases in PRT 15.3.3.1 and the *Red Lion* in PRT 15.3.4.2.

14.4 STATE AND LOCAL GOVERNMENTS

All broadcasting is interstate in nature and therefore subject to primary regulation by Congress and the FCC. Congress has established federal regulation over cable television, too. State and local governments, however, may also affect broadcast stations and other media. For example, several states have forbidden the advertising of alcoholic beverages; such a ban includes beer and wine commercials. Ownership of most media outlets takes the form of a corporation; each state has its own statutory requirements for **incorporation,** and a licensee or operator must meet those requirements and file for approval with the state. States and municipalities **tax** and **regulate** businesses. State legislatures have enacted laws that pertain to **noncommercial broadcasting**—to establish state agencies; to fund stations, agencies, and programming projects; or to specify procedures and operations. City **zoning and safety ordinances** affect location of studios, headends, and towers.

Cable, dependent as it is on a local franchise (PRT 19.5.2), is especially subject to city, county, and state regulation. A local governmental authority issues the franchise and adopts the ordinance that will govern cable television within its boundaries. Some states have enacted cable legislation, and a few have established cable television commissions or councils to ensure uniform franchising and regional planning.

NOTES

1. Letter to Nicholas Zapple, 23 F.C.C.2d 707 (1970); and First Report, Docket No. 19260, 36 F.C.C.2d 40 (1972).
2. *FCC* v. *League of Women Voters of California,* 468 U.S. 364.
3. Suburban Community Policy, 53 R.R.2d 681.
4. 18 U.S.C. §1307.
5. "Congress, in overtime, passes TVRO, children's ad bills," *Broadcasting* 24 Oct. 1988: 27; and "NAB approves," *Broadcasting* 14 Nov. 1988: 73.
6. *Quincy Cable TV, Inc.* v. *FCC,* 768 F.2d 1434; certiorari denied, *National Association of Broadcasters* v. *Quincy Cable TV, Inc.,* 106 S.Ct. 2889 (1986).
7. *Century Communications Corp.* v. *FCC,* 835 F.2d 292.

8. *Century Communications Corp.* v. *FCC,* 837 F.2d 517 (1988).
9. 17 U.S.C. §303(r).
10. 47 U.S.C. §521.
11. 47 U.S.C. §546(c)(1)(A).
12. Unnecessary Broadcast Regulations, 57 R.R.2d 913 (1985).
13. In the Matter of Elimination of Unnecessary Broadcast Regulation and Inquiry into Subscription Agreements Between Radio Broadcast Stations and Music Format Service Companies, 54 R.R.2d 1043, 1049 (1983).
14. Children's Television Report and Policy Statement, 50 F.C.C.2d 1; affirmed on reconsideration, 55 F.C.C.2d 691 (1975).
15. Children's Television Programming and Advertising Practices, 75 F.C.C.2d 138 (1980).
16. Children's Television Programming, 55 R.R.2d 199.
17. Action for Children's Television, 58 R.R.2d 61; and Children's Programming (Profit-Sharing Arrangements), 58 R.R.2d 90.
18. *Action for Children's Television* v. *FCC,* 821 F.2d 741 (1987).
19. *National Association for Better Broadcasting* v. *FCC,* 830 F.2d 270 (1987).
20. Revision of Programming and Commercialization Policies, Ascertainment Requirements, and Program Log Requirements for Commercial Television Station, 53 R.R.2d 365 (1987).
21. 38 Stat. 717 (1914).
22. 52 Stat. 111 (1938).
23. *FTC* v. *Colgate-Palmolive Co.,* 380 U.S. 374, 390 (1965).
24. *Libby-Owens-Ford Glass Co.* v. *FTC,* 352 F.2d (1965).
25. *J. B. Williams Co.* v. *FTC,* 381 F.2d 884 (1967).
26. Donald M. Gillmor and Jerome A. Barron, *Mass Communication Law: Cases and Comments,* 2d ed. (St. Paul: West, 1974), p. 693.
27. 88 Stat. 2183 *et seq.*
28. 95 Stat. 374 *et seq.*
29. *Immigration and Naturalization Service* v. *Chadha,* 462 U.S. 919.

FURTHER READING

Baughman, James L. *Television's Guardians: The FCC and the Politics of Programming.* Knoxville: U of Tennessee P, 1985.

Besen, Stanley M., et al. *Misregulating Television: Network Dominance and the FCC.* Chicago: U of

Chicago P, 1984. Contends network regulation does not work.

Brotman, Stuart N., ed. *The Telecommunications Deregulation Source Book.* Boston: Artech, 1987. Proderegulation.

Carter, T. Barton, Marc A. Franklin, and Jay B. Wright. *The First Amendment and the Fifth Estate: Regulation of Electronic Mass Media.* 2d ed. Mineola: Foundation, 1989. Case book with yearly supplements.

Le Duc, Don R. *Beyond Broadcasting: Patterns in Policy and Law.* White Plains: Longman, 1987. Examines regulation over time.

National Association of Broadcasters. *Legal Guide to Broadcast Law and Regulation.* Washington: NAB, 1988.

Powe, Lucas A., Jr. *American Broadcasting and the First Amendment.* Berkeley: U of California P, 1987. Argues for elimination of most regulations.

CHAPTER 15

Radio, Television, and the First Amendment

Earlier we said broadcasting enjoys limited protection under the First Amendment to the Constitution of the United States (PRT 13.3.5). In this chapter, we look at how that protection is limited and why.

15.1 ORIGINS AND PURPOSES OF THE FIRST AMENDMENT

The intellectual and philosophical climate of the seventeenth and eighteenth centuries provided ideal conditions for growth of faith in pure reason and natural rights. The individual was thought to be a rational being, one who could listen to all arguments, weigh their merits, and, through the power of reason, make an intelligent choice. Given the power to reason, continued this line of thought, the people needed no lawgiving absolute ruler; they could govern themselves. But if they were to govern themselves well, they needed **access to the greatest possible flow of information and opinion**—to an uninhibited **free marketplace of ideas.**

Earlier, John Milton had urged that authority should open up the closed philosophical arena for debate. Now, John Locke argued that each individual has a "natural right" to life, liberty, and property. Liberty included freedom to speak and to publish, rights considered indispensable to self-government.

Yet the U.S. Constitution, when it emerged from the Federal Convention in 1787, contained no declaration of natural rights. A clamor arose demading that such be added. Democratic leaders, farmers, the mercantile class—all demanded that the new national charter guarantee their hard-won rights. The result was a series of ten amendments—the famous **Bill of Rights,** the first of which states in part, "Congress shall make no law . . . abridging the freedom of speech, or of the press. . . ." The means to keep the marketplace free had been provided.

15.2 EXCEPTIONS TO FREEDOM OF PRESS

Some legal scholars have argued that rights guaranteed by the First Amendment are **absolute.** They agree with the late Supreme Court Justice Hugo Black, who said, "[The

First Amendment] says 'no law,' and that is what I believe it means."[1] The majority of courts and legislatures, however, do not share Justice Black's absolute interpretation. They recognize situations in which a medium loses First Amendment protection and may be punished for something it has published. Exceptions to an absolute freedom of speech and press include defamation law, right of privacy, material protected by copyright, court proceedings, prior restraint, lack of access, lack of reporter's privilege, and prohibitions against obscenity.

Are radio and television part of "the press" as the term is used in the First Amendment? For purposes of this section, the answer is yes. Radio and television must endure all limitations imposed on print media. These limitations apply equally to all media—broadcast and cable networks; programmers who produce and originate their own material in cable systems, the multipoint distribution service, and direct-broadcast satellite; electronic text and data base services; producers of materials for videodiscs and videocassettes; and all the rest.

15.2.1 Defamation

Defamation is **communication that harms a person's reputation.** In a defamation case, the defamed person (the **plaintiff**) brings **civil suit** against the defamer (the **defendant**) for **damages** (monetary compensation for suffering caused by the defamation) in a **court** of law. Defendants who lose defamation suits often must pay large damage awards.

Defamation consists of two categories, **libel** and **slander.** Historically, **spoken** defamation was slander; **written or printed** defamation, libel. Since libel resulted in a permanent form of defamation, it was con-

sidered more serious and brought higher damages.

A defamation by radio or television most resembles slander in form, libel in effect. For example, a defamation spoken (slander) on a popular network television program reaches tens of millions of persons (seriousness and effect of libel). In addition, most radio and television programming exists in permanent form—as a script, a recording, or both—from which defamation could be deleted before transmission. Courts tend to treat **radio and television defamation as libel.**

When defamation occurs on a broadcast station, the **licensee is liable** (legally responsible) for damages, no matter when it occurs, who said it, or who supplied it (including commercials produced by others). In the 1959 **WDAY case,**[2] the U.S. Supreme Court provided one exception. Section 315 of the Communications Act forbids a licensee to censor material aired by political candidates. Therefore if a candidate, using a station's facilities (broadcasting) under Section 315, utters a defamation, the licensee pays no damages. This immunity is called **absolute privilege.**

Congress built similar immunity into the Cable Communications Act of 1984. When a PEG or leased-access channel carries access programming (PRT 14.1.1.8), the cable operator may exercise no editorial content except to censor obscenity. Section 638, therefore, protects operators from liability for defamation in access programming.

The plea of **truth** is the oldest and was, for years, the news media's most used defense against defamation suits. If the medium can prove in court the defamation to be true, the plaintiff, in most cases, cannot recover damages. But truth is often hard to prove. In 1964, the U.S. Supreme Court expanded constitutional protection against defamation judgments. In its decision in *New York Times* v. *Sullivan,* the court wrote that fear of libel judgments might cause some who had legitimate criticisms of government conduct to keep their criticisms to themselves. This defeated the purpose of the First Amendment. Therefore **public officials** who wished to sue for defamation could not recover damages unless they could prove the defamatory statement "was made with **'actual malice'**— that is with knowledge that it was false or with reckless disregard of whether it was false or not."[3] Subsequently, the court expanded the actual malice requirement to include **public figures,** defined in its 1974 decision *Gerts* v. *Welch*.[4] Public figures comprised persons of widespread fame or notoriety and, to some extent, people who had injected themselves into the debate of a controversial public issue for the purpose of affecting the outcome.

The "actual malice" requirement gave news media added protection against libel suits. For example, even if a radio or television news operation defames a person who is a public official and the defamation is false, that official still cannot recover damages without proving (1) the news operation knew it was false or had serious doubts about it, but aired it anyway, or (2) the operation aired it without first taking normal precautions to check its validity. Both are hard to prove. Proof of actual malice requires an examination of the "state of mind" of writers and editors, and that is precisely what the U.S. Supreme Court permitted in its 1979 *Lando* v. *Herbert* decision (PRT 8.4).

Gertz v. *Welch* gave some protection to news media in suits brought by persons who qualified as neither public officials nor public figures. All persons must prove some form of fault or media error. Most states require that private persons prove negligence (often the failure to check information adequately or to use the right kind of sources) or a lack of reasonable care on the part of the media. In 1986,[5] the Supreme Court ruled that private

persons involved in matters of public concern must also prove a defamation is false to win a libel suit.

Such protections all assume *ethical and responsible news practices.* They provide effective defenses most often when the news medium has used sound journalistic techniques to determine and report the communication under question. They do not usually protect slipshod and unprofessional news gathering. Further, they do not normally protect against defamations carried in entertainment programming or advertising. Thus a radio or television outlet can still be successfully— and expensively—sued for defamation.

15.2.2 Right of Privacy

Should radio or television carry material that seriously invades the privacy of an individual, courts in most states allow that individual to recover damages. A medium invades privacy and opens itself to a civil suit if it does any of the following to or concerning someone *without permission:* releases intimate, private facts; intrudes (physically or technologically invades the privacy); creates a false public impression; appropriates for commercial purposes elements of personality or identity. This pertains to all programming, including advertising.

The potential for invasion of privacy is inherent in the very technology of cable television. After all, if a wire carries information into a home, that wire could also carry information out of the home—without the residents even being aware! Congress recognized this technological fact of life and built privacy protection for the cable subscriber into the 1984 cable act.

A cable operator may collect data used in the aggregate—so long as it does not identify individual subscribers. On the other hand, the law restricts the collection and use of information about personal viewing habits and, if those restrictions are violated, allows the subscriber to sue for invasion of privacy.

15.2.3 Copyright

As a general rule, a programmer must get permission to air material created by another person. To do otherwise is to risk suit for infringement of copyright. Copyright is the **right to control or profit from a creative work.** Copyright provisions are spelled out in Title 17 of the United States Code. Copyright covers the following works of authorship: literary; musical (including words); dramatic (including any accompanying music); pantomimes and choreographic; pictorial, graphic, and sculptural; motion pictures and other audiovisual works; and sound recordings. Literary works include books, newspapers, magazines, corporate house organs, newsletters, and annual reports. A copyright holder's exclusive rights last for the life of the work's creator plus 50 years. Exclusive rights for a company-held copyright last 100 years or 75 years from the date of publication, whichever is shorter.

Among the rights included in copyright law are those to perform or display the work publicly and to authorize someone else to perform or display it publicly. In the latter case, the copyright holder usually requires payment. This is just compensation for the effort put into creation of the work. Presentation on radio or television is a public performance. Thus when a medium leases a motion picture, program, or series, it pays for more than just the tape or film. It also pays for the right—that is, permission from the copyright holder—to air the work a number of times within a certain period of time.

Copyright law does spell out **exceptions.** For example, noncommercial broadcasters can get special breaks on certain copyrighted material in particular situations. Clearance and payment are not necessary to use U.S. government works and works in the public domain (those that have not been copyrighted or those on which the copyright has expired).

15.2.3.1 Radio-TV Music and Copyright
Most commercial radio stations depend on music for most programming. And most of the music they use is copyrighted. Two organizations represent the majority of music copyright holders in the United States, **American Society of Composers, Authors, and Publishers** (ASCAP) and **Broadcast Music, Inc.** (BMI).

An all-industry committee, representing station licensees, negotiates individually with ASCAP and BMI. They agree on an all-industry contract, one each for ASCAP and BMI. Under terms of the contract a licensee agrees to pay a certain percentage of gross revenues (minus specified deductions) to the music copyright organization, and in return the station may use any composition in the organization's catalog (list of compositions it represents). No station has to accept the all-industry contract. A licensee may wish to negotiate individually or may elect to use no copyrighted music. Most, however, accept the all-industry contract (or **blanket license,** as it is often called) for both ASCAP and BMI. Both organizations also offer a **per program license;** stations pay a percentage of advertising revenue derived from a program in return for use of ASCAP or BMI music on that program.

Those who wish access to literally all music also contract with the **Society of European Stage Authors and Composers** (SESAC). ASCAP, BMI, and SESAC distribute money collected from stations to the copyright holders.

In some situations, those who *receive* broadcast music should pay royalties. This probably does not apply to you. It does not even apply, for example, to a small restaurant or bar where the radio or TV plays for the enjoyment of a few customers without becoming a public performance. It does apply when over-the-air broadcasts are retransmitted (as over a speaker system) to a large number of people for commercial purposes. In this case, the retransmission has become a public performance for which royalties should be paid.[6]

Television stations have long been unhappy with the blanket license. Much of their programming came to them already packaged—programs from networks and syndicators and commercials from advertisers and agencies—and the content, including music, was beyond their control. They objected to paying revenue-based fees that gave them access to over four million compositions (in the BMI and ASCAP catalogs) for which they had little use. They argued for "source licensing"; the producers of syndicated programming should acquire the music performance rights when they produced the programs. Then the stations would need licenses only for music used in the relatively few programs and commercials they used themselves, perhaps even obtaining them directly from the copyright holders. However, BMI and ASCAP refused to grant such an option. The stations brought suit, contending that the blanket license constituted unreasonable restraint of trade, but lost on appeal.[7] Subsequently, several bills were introduced in Congress that would require source licensing.

15.2.3.2 Cable Television and Copyright
With respect to copyright responsibility, we can divide cable system video content into two broad categories, nonbroadcast programming and the signals of broadcast stations. Nonbroadcast programming consists of satellite-delivered services (except for superstations), PEG (PRT 7.4.1.2) and leased-channel programming (PRT 7.4.1.3), and

local origination (LO; PRT 7.4.1.1). The satellite-delivered services generally contract for nationwide performance rights, so local cable operators do not pay royalties to the copyright holder. The operator has no editorial control over access programming and so does not pay royalties for copyrighted material used therein. The operator bears full copyright responsibility for programming the system acquires itself or produces itself and puts on the system, including both standard-television LO and locally created nonstandard material such as electronic text channels.

The copyright law of 1976 grants a cable operator a **compulsory license**[8] to carry distant nonnetwork broadcast signals. This includes satellite-delivered superstations as well as any nonnetwork distant signals the system imports on its own (say, through microwave relay). Every six months the operator pays a royalty based on a percentage of subscriber revenues to the Register of Copyrights. The fee is set by a presidentially appointed **Copyright Royalty Tribunal** (CRT). The Register of Copyrights turns the funds over to the CRT, which distributes them to copyright holders.

The operator does *not* have to pay royalties to carry the signals of local stations or broadcast network programs, whether on local or distant stations. The reasoning is that they do not diminish the value of programs from either source. Local signals would be available with or without the cable system, and the networks pay royalties on the basis of reaching all markets.

15.2.3.3 TVRO and Copyright In 1988, Congress passed a bill that created a compulsory license for satellite distribution of broadcast signals to backyard satellite dish owners (television receive-only [TVRO, PRT 5.6.2]). TVRO packagers (PRT 7.4.4) such as Satellite Broadcast Networks and Netlink (PRT 20.6) that deliver station signals to rural dish owners would receive a six-year compulsory license.

The same bill attempted to deal with TVRO piracy. It established stiffer penalties for piracy of satellite signals and made the manufacture, assembly, and modification of unauthorized descramblers a felony punishable by a stiff fine and imprisonment up to five years. It required the FCC to conduct an inquiry to determine whether a universal encryption standard was needed.

15.2.3.4 Home Recording and Copyright
The development and marketing of the home videocassette recorder (VCR) opened a whole new area of problems with copyright. Film studios and television production houses did not want viewers to record movies and other programming off the air. In 1976, Universal City Studios and Walt Disney Productions brought suit against the Sony Corporation (whose Betamax started the whole VCR boom), Sony's advertising agency, some Sony dealers, and a Betamax owner for copyright violation. The case wound its way up the federal court system. Finally, in 1984, the Supreme Court ruled[9] that use of a home VCR to tape broadcast programming for later viewing ("time shifting") was exempt from copyright law. The court said that time shifting was "fair use" of copyrighted works and therefore beyond liability for copyright royalties.

A video store can buy videotapes and rent them to the public under the **first-sale doctrine.** The copyright statute does not specifically mention it, but court decisions have interpreted the act as allowing such.[10] Under this doctrine, a copyright owner who sells a copy of a copyrighted work receives a royalty from the sale but does *not* receive *further* royalties as long as the copy is rented or resold for private use. The copyright owner retains all other rights.

The first-sale doctrine does not apply to phonograph records. Congress specifically amended Section 109(b) (1) of the copyright act to exclude the rental of phonograph records without permission of the copyright holders, except by nonprofit libraries or educational institutions. The reasoning derived from presumed intent—about the only reason you would rent a record would be to copy it. (See also Section 5.10 for a discussion of the copyright worries that devolved from the digital audio tape recorder.

15.2.4 Free Press Versus Fair Trial

Two constitutional rights seem to conflict, with the result that reporting of federal and some state court proceedings is restricted. The Sixth Amendment guarantees individuals the right to a fair trial. The First Amendment guarantees freedom of speech and press, which, presumably, includes the right to report public trials. But many attorneys maintain that media coverage often destroys the rights of a defendant before the trial can even start. Media publicity, they say, prejudices people so much that it is impossible to select an impartial jury and to get a fair trial. Reporters and editors reply that media reporting is essential and that the First Amendment takes preference over the Sixth.

During the 1980s, the U.S. Supreme Court handed down rulings that emphasized the First Amendment right of the public and the press to attend judicial proceedings. In a series of four decisions,[11] the court said that a judge may close a trial only after demonstrating a compelling need to protect the rights of the defendant to a fair trial. The judge must first consider alternatives to closing the trial and must limit the closing to as short a time as necessary. Grand jury and juvenile proceedings are still ordinarily closed.

Some judges have issued **gag orders.** Here, the judge *tells* reporters what they can and cannot report and how they are to report it. Violations are prosecuted as contempt of court, which can result in fines and jail sentences.

U.S. Supreme Court decisions seem to indicate disapproval of most such prior restraints on publication. Its 1976 decision in *Nebraska Press Association* v. *Stuart*[12] strictly limited gag orders. A year later, the court affirmed its reluctance to allow prior restraints in *Oklahoma Publishing* v. *District Court.*[13] Over the next several years, the court indicated that most attempts to punish the media for violation of restraint orders after publication do not meet constitutional muster.[14] Judges have been successful, however, in restraining officers of the court and others involved in a case from talking to the press.

For years, judicial proceedings could not be covered by electronic and photographic means. This is because of two factors that kept radio, television, and photography out of courtrooms—Canon 3A(7) of the ABA's code of judicial ethics and the U.S. Supreme Court's 1965 *Estes* decision.

Canon 3A(7) had recommended that a judge prohibit microphones and cameras in a courtroom except in specified situations, none of which provided for broadcast or other public dissemination. Adopted in 1972, Canon 3A(7) superseded an even more restrictive Canon 35, which the ABA had asopted in 1937 and amended in 1952. The rationale was that the presence of photographic and electronic media distracted participants and witnesses.

In the 1965 *Estes* v. *Texas* decision[15] the Supreme Court reversed Estes's conviction because his trial had been televised. The Court said that the televising of the trial had denied Estes the constitutional right of due process. This decision reinforced the tendency of the legal profession to refuse to open trials to cameras.

A few years later, however, a few state court systems moved toward allowing cameras and microphones in the courtroom. Fol-

lowing a successful one-year experiment, Florida state courts in 1979 adopted rules that allowed nearly restriction-free courtroom coverage by radio and television. Two years later, the U.S. Supreme Court upheld Florida's rules. In *Chandler* v. *Florida,*[16] the Court said that states could develop such rules so long as they did not violate the defendant's right to a fair trial. No one had offered data that the mere presence of radio-TV coverage automatically impaired fundamental fairness. In order to make a successful Sixth Amendment appeal, the defendant would have to *demonstrate* such an impairment—that radio-TV coverage had adversely affected witnesses or jurors or the ability of the jury to decide the case fairly.

Following the *Chandler* decision, the ABA amended Canon 3A(7). The new rule still recommended the prohibition of courtroom broadcasting, reporting, and photographing. The judge, however, could allow visual and aural coverage (1) if authorized by supervising appellate courts or other authorities and (2) if consistent with fair trial rights—being unobtrusive, not distracting, and not interfering with administration of justice. Other states experimented with or permitted photographic and electronic coverage. By 1990, over 80 percent of all states allowed some form of camera coverage of courtroom proceedings.

Federal courts, however, continued to ban cameras. Most television coverage of federal court proceedings consisted of oral descriptions, sketches, and watercolors.

15.2.5 Prior Restraint

Prior restraint refers to the government preventing publication; normally, the First Amendment forbids such. In the 1931 *Near* decision,[17] Chief Justice Charles Evans Hughes said that the main purpose of the constitutional guarantee of freedom of expression is to prevent prior restraint. Chief Justice Hughes did not say that the prohibition on prior restraint is absolute. In fact, he listed specific instances in which the government could legitimately prevent publication.

Federal courts issued injunctions to prevent publication of the **Pentagon papers** for 15 days in 1971. The Pentagon papers were a massive top secret Defense Department study entitled *History of the United States Decision-Making Process on Vietnam Policy.* First, the *New York Times*, then the *Washington Post* obtained copies and began to publish articles on the study. Injunctions halted publication, and the newspapers appealed. The U.S. Supreme Court lifted the injunctions but not before it, too, had voted 5–4 to halt publication until it could hear the case and render a decision. In addition, its brief 6–3 decision seemed to allow the government to exercise prior restraint any time it could meet the "heavy burden of showing justification."[18]

15.2.6 Access and Reporter's Privilege

Two exceptions to freedom of press involve a reporter's sources of information. One has to do with access; the other with reporter's privilege.

Access here refers to **the ability to get to sources** of information. The idea of necessity of access grows from the same philosophical soil as the First Amendment. The government of the United States is based on the presumption of an informed citizenry. That being the case, news media have an obligation to enhance the media's ability to report. The government should allow reporters access to information on its own performance and operation, except where national security or public welfare would be compromised. But such is not always the case.

Denial of access takes several forms—**classification** (as "top secret," "secret," or "confidential"), supposedly to protect against unauthorized disclosure in the interests of national defense; **agency-created barriers and dodges** (also called "the runaround") to avoid releasing information; and **executive sessions** or **secret meetings** of decision-making bodies. Many states and the federal government[19] have enacted **government in the sunshine** (open meetings) and **open records laws** designed to tear down barriers to access. Such laws help, but a determined official can stll sometimes delay or even deny access.

News reporter's privilege refers to **the ability to protect a confidential source from identification** in legal and legislative proceedings. The news media contend that if a source provides information to a reporter, with the provision that the source's identity remain secret, the First Amendment protects that reporter from having to reveal the source or to yield notes, tape, film, and other unpublished information about the source. The media maintain that confidential communications between reporter and source are privileged (do not have to be revealed) in a manner somewhat similar to those between lawyer and client or priest and penitent. Besides, conclude the media, if the courts force reporters to reveal confidential sources, the sources will stop being sources. This affects the public's right to know and thus violates the First Amendment.

A number of states have adopted **shield laws** to ensure that reporters do have some form of privilege. There is no national shield law, however. And in its 1972 *Branzburg* v. *Hayes* decision,[20] the U.S. Supreme Court refused to recognize any sweeping reporter's privilege. On the other hand, a majority of the justices suggested that in all cases except grand jury proceedings, a reporter's wish to protect a confidential source must be balanced against the government's need to know; one must be weighed against the other to determine which should prevail.

Even a grand jury may not use a reporter's notes for a "fishing expedition," that is, just to see if anything turns up. Since 1972, lower courts have relied on the concurring and dissenting opinions in *Branzburg* to create a limited First Amendment privilege from testifying. Further, reporters seldom have to testify when criminal defendants or litigants in civil suits (except those to which the medium is a party) seek information. Still, reporters from both print and electronic media have spent time in jail, not because they were criminals, but because they wished to preserve the confidentiality of their sources.

Newsroom searches, however, are a different matter. Congress provided a measure of relief against newsroom searches by law enforcement authorities in 1980. In its 1978 ruling in the *Stanford Daily* case,[21] the U.S. Supreme Court had interpreted the Fourth Amendment to the Constitution to mean that police need only have a warrant to search a newsroom. Police took advantage of this ruling and made a number of such searches in 1980. Congress responded by passing the Privacy Protection Act of 1980,[22] also called the News Room Search Law. Under this act, law enforcement officials must get a subpoena before searching a newsroom in all but a few specified situations. A subpoena must specify what is sought, is generally more difficult to obtain than a warrant, and may be challenged in court. Some state legislatures have passed similar laws.

15.2.7 Obscenity

Most persons agree that obscenity does not deserve First Amendment protection. The disagreement comes in defining obscenity, that is, saying what is and what is not obscene. After all, something you consider art might be pornography to someone else, and vice versa. Over the years, legislatures and courts have attempted to define *obscene*, to draw the line between the permissible and the prohibited. Most attempts have centered on sexual matters.

The U.S. Supreme Court provided a (usually) workable definition in its 1973 **Miller** decision.[23] In the *Miller* decision, the Court ruled that material would have to meet all three of the following criteria before it could be regarded obscene: (1) the **average person, applying contemporary community standards** (local standards, not national), **finds the work, taken as a whole, appeals to prurient interest;** (2) the work **depicts or describes, in a patently offensive manner, sexual conduct specifically defined by state law;** and (3) the work **lacks serious literary, artistic, political, or scientific value.** Material that meets all three criteria is obscene and therefore, said the court, does not merit First Amendment protection.

15.3 EXCEPTIONS TO FREEDOM OF RADIO AND TELEVISION

Even with all the exceptions described above, the United States still enjoys one of the greatest latitudes for freedom of expression of any country. Radio and television, however, have an additional set of restrictions.

15.3.1 Exceptions by Law and Regulation

The **Communications Act and FCC rules** impose on broadcast licensees myriad and varied programming requirements—things they must or must not do. As examples, consider the following: Broadcast stations must operate a minimum number of hours each day;[24] certain types of recorded material must be identified as such;[25] broadcast stations must identify themselves to listeners at certain times and in a certain manner;[26] cigarette advertising is prohibited on radio and television.[27] Additional requirements are discussed below and in PRT 14.1.1–14.1.5.

15.3.2 Section 315 and Candidate Debates

One of the most important programming requirements—a major fact of regulatory life for broadcasting and cable—is **Section 315** of the Communications Act. Congress wrote the equal opportunities provision (PRT 14.1.1.4) into Section 315 to ensure that broadcasters treat all candidates for the same political office equally. The legislators reasoned that the public interest and the free marketplace of ideas are better served when the audience can hear all candidates equally, rather than only those favored by the licensee. However, some broadcast licensees say they find the mechanisms of Section 315 so intricate and so burdensome that they avoid the whole thing by allowing no candidates to use station facilities.* In these cases the provision literally defeats its own purpose; it silences the very political debate the Congress intended to promote.

For years, the broadcast networks ran no election-time programming featuring candidates for president and vice president. Network officials said they wanted to produce programs on the Democratic and Republican candidates, but under Section 315 they would also have to provide equal opportunity for a score of minor party candidates. And, they argued, most of the electorate is interested only in major party candidates.

In 1960, Congress suspended the equal opportunity requirement on an experimental basis. Special legislation applied the suspension to the presidential and vice-presidential

---

* Except as required under Section 312(a)(7) (PRT 14.1.1.4).

races only and for that election only.[28] The networks jointly arranged and broadcast on radio and television four one-hour question-and-answer sessions featuring Senator John F. Kennedy, the Democratic candidate, and Vice President Richard M. Nixon, the Republican candidate. Kennedy, relatively unknown before these so-called **Great Debates** (Figure 15.1), went on to win the election by a slim margin. Sixteen years passed before the broadcast of another presidential debate.

The FCC made possible candidate debates on a continuing basis with its 1975 adoption of the **Aspen rule.**[29] Under this rule, candidate news conferences and debates both qualified as "on-the-spot coverage of a bona fide news event" and, as provided in Section 315(a) (4), were exempt from equal opportunities requirements. The only qualification was that the debate had to be under control of someone other than broadcasters or candidates.

Third-party organizations organized debates among candidates at all political levels across the country. The League of Women Voters was particularly active, organizing and sponsoring debates in the 1976 and succeeding presidential elections. The commission subsequently eliminated the third-party requirement. The spot-news exemption was extended in 1983 to permit coverage of debates arranged by broadcasters[30] and in 1987 to permit coverage of debates arranged by political candidates themselves.[31]

15.3.3 FCC Concern with Programming

As discussed in PRT 14.1.2, the FCC has examined programming as one means to determine whether the public interest would be served by granting or renewing a broadcast license. Broadcasters have objected that FCC review of programming violates both the First Amendment and Section 326 of the

Figure 15.1 The Great Debates, 1960.   (Used by permission of CBS.)

Communications Act (which forbids FCC censorship). Yet, the courts have consistently upheld the FCC.

15.3.3.1 Judicial Affirmation   The first ruling came in the 1931 **Brinkley case,** *KFKB* v. *FRC*.[32] The Federal Radio Commission (FRC), forerunner of the FCC, had denied John Brinkley's application for renewal of KFKB's license based on his use of the station to peddle patent medicines. Brinkley appealed on the grounds that the commission's actions amounted to censorship. The Court of Appeals affirmed the denial. In its decision, the court equated "censorship" with "prior scrutiny," ruling that FRC review of **past conduct** to determine whether a license renewal would serve the public interest does not constitute censorship.

The next ruling came in the 1932 **Shuler case,** *Trinity* v. *FRC*.[33] The FRC had denied Reverend Bob Shuler's application for renewal of KGEF's license because of his alleged use of the station for defamatory and otherwise objectionable utterances. Shuler

appealed on both First and Fifth Amendment grounds. The court ruled that the FRC had not denied Shuler's freedom of speech (Shuler could continue to say whatever he wished; he just could not do so on the radio any more). Rather, the commission had applied legitimate regulatory power. As to the Fifth Amendment appeal, the court ruled that since KGEF's frequency was not Shuler's property but a grant or permit from the government, the government had the right to withdraw it without compensation. The Supreme Court refused to review,[34] which allowed the appeals court decision to stand.

15.3.3.2 FCC Statements   But what was programming in the public interest? What did it consist of? What should a station program to avoid trouble at renewal time? The commission hesitated to set forth specific programming guidelines. After all, the law forbade censorship, and guidelines smacked heavily of prior restraint. Once the Brinkleys and Shulers were cleared off the air, the FCC rarely used its program review power. The commission routinely approved renewal applications, based entirely on engineering reports, without examining past programming.

During the late 1930s and early 1940s the FCC received a number of complaints on programming. Commissioner Clifford J. Durr investigated and found widespread programming abuses. The commission decided to act. It hired Charles Siepmann, former executive with the British Broadcasting Corporation, to direct a study and suggest criteria the FCC might use to evaluate program service. The result was the 1946 **Blue Book** (PRT 3.1.5.5). The broadcasters were so successful in fighting the Blue Book that the commission never revoked or denied renewal of a license based on Blue Book criteria.

The commission did, however, adopt several Blue Book recommendations. One of these was a new renewal application form that called for information on past and proposed programming. A station was to base its report of past programming on a **composite week.** Just before renewal time, the FCC would notify the station of seven specific days—a Monday, a Tuesday, and so on—scattered over the (then) three-year license period just ending. In processing the renewal application, the commission could thus compare **performance**—as reflected by programming during the composite week—to the programming **promises** made on the previous renewal application.

In 1960, the FCC adopted a policy statement that defined what it felt was needed in programming to meet the public interest. The **1960 Programming Policy Statement** provided no pat formula. It contained two broad guidelines. First, the broadcaster should **ascertain the tastes, needs, and desires of the community** to which the station was licensed. Second, the broadcaster should **decide what specific programs and program types** would meet these needs. The policy statement named some program types that had evolved as usually necessary to meet the public interest but added that the

list was "neither all-embracing nor constant," that the commission relied primarily on the broadcaster's own judgment. A court decision in the 1962 **Suburban case**[35] affirmed the FCC's right to require ascertainment of local needs.

15.3.3.3 Public Participation in the Licensing Process

Until 1966, the broadcast audience had almost no say in the licensing process. The FCC interpreted two previous court decisions[36] to mean that only other licensees alleging economic interest or electrical interference could intervene in a station's license renewal proceedings; you, as a member of the public, could not. The **WLBT cases** changed that.

In 1964, the Office of Communications of the United Church of Christ (UCC) petitioned the FCC on behalf of black citizens of Jackson, Mississippi. UCC asked to intervene in (present evidence and arguments opposing) renewal proceedings for television station WLBT, Jackson. The church said the station practiced racial discrimination in programming. The commission contended UCC had no standing and granted WLBT a short-term renewal of one year. UCC appealed.

The appeals court reversed the commission's decision. The court ruled that the public (here represented by the UCC) **could intervene in renewal proceedings.** So the FCC held hearings and listened to UCC's testimony. It then gave the station a *full three-year license term*, saying UCC had failed to prove its case. Again, the church appealed.

This time the court ordered that the license not be renewed. It ruled that **public intervenors do not bear the burden of proof.** Rather, said the court, intervenors present evidence, and the commission must investigate, gather facts, and, if it finds cause to believe a violation has occurred, prosecute or regulate.

As a result of the WLBT cases, the public gained a mechanism to affect programming of a broadcast station, to ensure that it served the interests of the community. The fact that the public could intervene meant that many licensees not only opened their doors to citizen and audience groups but also listened and negotiated. Such negotiations were usually most effective when carried on by an organized group representing interests of a particular segment of the community, for example, blacks, Hispanics, or classical music lovers.

15.3.3.4 Entertainment Formats During the 1970s, such groups formed all over the country, encouraged not only by the WLBT cases but also by the WHDH decision (PRT 19.1.2.3). Some audience activist groups even attempted to affect entertainment programming, including radio station formats. One such attempt led to the *WEFM* case.[37] WEFM, Chicago, had programmed classical music since it signed on in 1940. WEFM's licensee, contending it lost money on the operation, contracted to sell the station to a group owner in 1972. The prospective new owner proposed to program rock music. A group of listeners formed the Citizens Committee to Save WEFM. Citizens Committee filed a petition with the FCC to deny transfer of license or, barring that, to conduct a hearing. The FCC refused, Citizens Committee appealed, and the court reversed the commission, remanding the case for hearing.

Uneasy in its court-sanctioned role as arbiter of formats, the FCC issued a policy statement on the matter in 1976.[38] In its statement, the FCC said it would no longer get involved in format disputes; selection of a format was up to the licensee, and its success or failure should be determined by the marketplace. This led to the 1981 **WNCN case**.[39] A situation developed over WNCN, New York, similar to that of WEFM. The WNCN Listeners Guild, joined by several other groups, appealed the FCC's policy statement. In its decision, the U.S. Supreme Court upheld the FCC policy of licensee discretion in entertainment formats. Subse-

quently, the commission was fairly successful in staying out of the format business, although an appeals court did rule that misrepresentation of programming intentions by a licensee warrants FCC attention.[40]

15.3.3.5 Ascertainment The requirement that a station licensee ascertain community needs, set forth in the 1960 Programming Policy Statement, grew in importance. The FCC issued guidelines that specified that a licensee had to ask members of the community what they saw as the community's needs. The licensee had to ask at two levels—leaders of significant groups in the community and a random sample of members of the general public. Each year the licensee had to place in the public file (PRT 15.3.3.6) **a list of no more than ten significant problems, needs, and interests ascertained** during the preceding 12 months, along with descriptions of typical and illustrative **programs broadcast in response** to these problems, needs, and interests.

The commission eliminated formal ascertainment requirements as part of its 1980s general deregulation.[41] These cuts did away with the prescribed formal contact with community leaders and the public. Each quarter, however, a station still had to put in its public file a list of programs that provided its most significant treatment of community issues during the preceding three-month period.[42]

15.3.3.6 1973 License Renewal Rules In 1973, the commission revised license renewal procedures in an effort to encourage dialogue between the public and the broadcast stations. The actions included adoption of an Annual Programming Report, a revised television renewal application form, and rules requiring stations to maintain a public file and to broadcast periodically certain public notices. The programming report, based on an annual composite week, called for information on news, public affairs, and other programming. The renewal form required information concerning specific programming areas, for example, public service announcements and children's programming.

The rules required the **public file** be kept at the station or other accessible place for members of the public to request and examine during regular business hours. The file was to contain (among other things) the following: copies of applications and reports the station had filed with the FCC, the station's equal opportunity model program, a copy of the FCC publication *The Public and Broadcasting—A Procedural Manual*, letters received from the public, requests for time by political candidates, documentation of ascertainment procedures, and a list of the station's programs that had addressed community needs.

The rules also required that stations broadcast **public notices** of their license renewal. They called for announcements that the public could examine a copy of the renewal application and could comment on it and the station's performance in meeting the public interest to the FCC.

15.3.3.7 Deregulation

Subsequent deregulation (PRT 4.5.1) eliminated a number of the requirements of ascertainment and of the 1973 renewal rules. At the same time, deregulation seemed to repudiate the rationale for program regulation, a rationale that had been spelled out over a period of more than 50 years by the FRC and the FCC, the federal court system, and the Congress of the United States.

Commercial radio was deregulated in 1981; commercial television and noncommercial broadcasting, in 1984.[43] In these two actions, the commission eliminated programming-related requirements in three key areas. First, the FCC discarded a set of guidelines the staff had used in processing license applications. These guidelines had, in effect, limited commercial minutes per hour and re-

quired at least some news, public affairs, and other nonentertainment local programming. Elimination of the commercial-time guidelines also lifted a prohibition against program-length commercials (PRT 9.1.3.3). Second, the commission got rid of a requirement that stations use program logs and retain and allow the public to examine them. Third, the FCC dumped formal ascertainment requirements, described above.

In 1981, the commission adopted a short-form renewal application (Figure 15.2). The short form replaced a complicated, multipage application that required detailed submissions and attachments to explain various aspects of station operation, including programming. The short form consisted of five questions (four of which were to be answered yes or no) and a statement whereby the person who signed certified that all information on the form was true. Adoption of the short form automatically eliminated any composite week reporting, programming promises for the upcoming licensing period, reports on ascertainment procedures, and information on programming areas of special concern, such as children's and public affairs. The commission also eliminated the Annual Programming Report and a requirement for broadcast of a twice-monthly announcement of licensee obligation.

The commission rationalized such actions with a "marketplace" argument. This argument asserted that electronic media outlets should survive or fail because of public preferences. If the public wanted news, public affairs, special programming for children, controls on advertising, or local programming, the public would support such things by tuning in the electronic media outlets that provided them. Those media outlets would thrive; others would either change or not do as well, perhaps even go out of business. If the public did not want these things, the media would change to reflect what they did want. Government should not mandate programming requirements or restrictions. The main point was that it would be the media and the public that would determine survival, and government should not interfere with the process.*

15.3.4 The Fairness Doctrine

Another victim of the deregulation frenzy (PRT 4.5.1) was a nearly four-decades-old public-issue programming requirement. The FCC articulated the requirement in a 1949 statement[44] that reversed the Mayflower decision (PRT 3.1.5.3) and announced that broadcast licensees could editorialize. The commission noted that in the American system of broadcasting, the right of the public to be informed took precedence over the right of a station to air the licensee's private opinion and exclude all others. That being the case, concluded the commission, (1) a licensee **must afford reasonable opportunity for discussion of contrasting points of view on a controversial issue of public importance,** and (2) a licensee has an **obilgation to provide some programming that deals with controversial public issues.** The requirement for overall balance in treating controversial issues became known as the *fairness doctrine.*

15.3.4.1 Fairness and Implementation Basically, it worked like this. If a broadcaster aired a particular view on a controversial issue of public importance, that broadcaster had the duty to afford *reasonable* (not necessarily equal) opportunity for presentation of contrasting views at some time (not necessarily on the same program) in the station's broadcast schedule. The mechanics of achieving a balanced presentation—for ex-

ample, types of programs, when and how long they run—were up to the licensee. When the FCC received complaints concerning a station's treatment of a particular issue, the commission considered the station's program service as a whole, not specific programs, to determine if the balance had been fair.

Fairness seemed to be written into law in 1959. That year, Congress amended Section 315 of the Communications Act to exclude news-type programming from the equal opportunities requirement. It also added, "Nothing in the foregoing shall be construed as relieving broadcasters . . . from the obligation imposed on them . . . to afford *reasonable opportunity for the discussion of conflicting views on issues of public importance* [emphasis added]."

A 1963 FCC decision became known as the **Cullman doctrine.**[45] Under this fairness corollary, a licensee had to ensure that opposing views were presented, irrespective of ability to pay. A station that aired sponsored programming which addressed one side of a controversial issue could not reject a reply just because it was not paid for.

In 1967, the FCC converted two aspects of fairness into formal rules—the **personal attack and political editorial** rules.[46] These rules required a station to notify and give reasonable opportunity for reply to (1) an individual who had been attacked during a broadcast discussion of controversial public issues, (2) a political candidate against whom the station had editorialized, and (3) all candidates running against a candidate who had been editorially endorsed by the station. The commission developed the **Zapple doctrine** (PRT 14.1.1.4) in 1970.

15.3.4.2 Fairness and *Red Lion* The U.S. Supreme Court upheld the constitutionality of fairness in the *Red Lion* case (Figure 15.3). In 1964, WGCB, Red Lion, Pennsylvania, aired a program in which Reverend Billy

---

* The marketplace argument also assumed that the scarcity factor was no longer valid. This aspect is discussed in PRT 13.4.2.

James Hargis reviewed *Goldwater—Extremist of the Right*, a book critical of the Republican presidential candidate, Senator Barry Goldwater. Hargis attacked the book's author, Fred J. Cook. Cook asked to reply, the station refused, so Cook complained to the FCC. Basing its decision on the fairness doctrine, the commission ordered WGCB to give Cook reply time. The station appealed on grounds that the fairness doctrine was unconstitutional. The appeals court in Washington, D.C., ruled against WGCB, and the station appealed to the Supreme Court.

Meanwhile, the FCC had adopted the personal attack and political editorial rules. The Radio-Television News Directors Association (RTNDA) challenged the rules in another court. An appeals court in Chicago declared the rules and fairness unconstitu-

tional. The FCC appealed, and the Supreme Court consolidated both cases as *Red Lion* v. *FCC*.[47]

In 1969, the Supreme Court reversed the Chicago judgment and affirmed the D.C. court. It ruled that Congress had authorized both application of the fairness doctrine and promulgation of the rules, that they enhanced rather than abridged the freedoms of speech and press protected by the First Amendment, and that they were constitutional.

15.3.4.3 Fairness and Advertising

Several groups attempted to apply the fairness doctrine to advertising. The FCC sparked these attempts with a 1967 ruling on cigarette commercials. The federal government had recently begun to assert that smoking could

Figure 15.2 FCC broadcast renewal application. (a) Although the FCC adopted a post-card-size renewal application in 1981, a 1988 revision increased the size of the form to the (b) front and (c) back of a half-sheet and expanded the number of questions from five to eight. (*Source:* FCC.)

| Federal Communications Commission
Washington, D.C. 20554 | APPLICATION FOR RENEWAL OF LICENSE FOR
COMMERCIAL AND NONCOMMERCIAL AM, FM OR TV BROADCAST STATION | Approved by OMB
3060-0110
Expires 5/31/91 |

For Commission Fee Use Only	FEE NO:	For Applicant Fee Use Only
	FEE TYPE:	Is a fee submitted with this application? ☐ Yes ☐ No
	FEE AMT:	If No, indicate reason therefor (check one box): ☐ Nonfeeable application
	ID SEQ:	Fee Exempt (See 47 C.F.R. Section 1.1112) ☐ Noncommercial educational licensee
For Commission Use Only: File No.		☐ Governmental entity

1. Name of Applicant

Mailing Address

City | State | ZIP Code

2. This application is for: ☐ AM ☐ FM ☐ TV

(a) Call Letters: | (b) Principal Community: City | State

3. Attach as Exhibit No. _____ an identification of any FM booster or TV booster station for which renewal of license is also requested.

4. Have the following reports been filed with the Commission:

(a) The Broadcast Station Annual Employment Reports (FCC Form 395-B) as required by 47 C.F.R. Section 73.3612? ☐ Yes ☐ No

If No, attach as Exhibit No. _____ an explanation.

(b) The applicant's Ownership Report (FCC Form 323 or 323-E) as required by 47 C.F.R. Section 73.3615? ☐ Yes ☐ No

If No, give the following information:
Date last ownership report was filed _____
Call letters of station for which it was filed _____

FCC 303-S
May 1988

(b)

5. Is the applicant in compliance with the provisions of Section 310 of the Communications Act of 1934, as amended, relating to interests of aliens and foreign governments? ☐ Yes ☐ No

If No, attach as Exhibit No. _____ an explanation.

6. Since the filing of the applicant's last renewal application for this station or other major application, has an adverse finding been made or final action been taken by any court or administrative body with respect to the applicant or parties to the application in a civil or criminal proceeding, brought under the provisions of any law relating to the following: any felony; broadcast related antitrust or unfair competition; criminal fraud or fraud before another governmental unit; or discrimination? ☐ Yes ☐ No

If Yes, attach as Exhibit No. _____ a full description of the persons and matters involved, including an identification of the court or administrative body and the proceeding (by dates and file numbers) and the disposition of the litigation.

7. Would a Commission grant of this application come within 47 C.F.R. Section 1.1307, such that it may have a significant environmental impact? ☐ Yes ☐ No

If Yes, attach as Exhibit No. _____ an Environmental Assessment required by 47 C.F.R. Section 1.1311.

If No, explain briefly why not.

8. Has the applicant placed in its station's public inspection file at the appropriate times the documentation required by 47 C.F.R. Sections 73.3526 or 73.3527? ☐ Yes ☐ No

If No, attach as Exhibit No. _____ a complete statement of explanation.

The APPLICANT hereby waives any claim to the use of any particular frequency or of the electromagnetic spectrum as against the regulatory power of the United States because of the previous use of the same, whether by license or otherwise, and requests an authorization in accordance with this application. (See Section 304 of the Communications Act of 1934, as amended.)
The APPLICANT acknowledges that all the statements made in this application and attached exhibits are considered material representations and that all the exhibits are a material part hereof and are incorporated herein as set out in full in the application.

CERTIFICATION: I certify that the statements in this application are true, complete, and correct to the best of my knowledge and belief, and are made in good faith.

Name	Signature
Title	Date

WILLFUL FALSE STATEMENTS MADE ON THIS FORM ARE PUNISHABLE BY FINE AND IMPRISONMENT. U.S. CODE, TITLE 18, SECTION 1001.

(c)

be a health hazard. In light of these assertions, the commission ruled that cigarette advertising involved a controversial issue of public importance to which the fairness doctrine applied. A station that broadcast cigarette commercials had to present the other side of the issue.[48]

The FCC attempted to limit its decision to cigarette advertising. Nonetheless, the commission received additional fairness challenges on other commercial advertisements, on military recruiting announcements, and on paid editorial announcements. In 1974 the FCC adopted a policy that specifically dealt with application of the fairness doctrine to advertising.[49] Fairness would apply to regular product or service advertising only when it discussed public issues in an obvious and meaningful way. A 1977 appeals court decision affirmed the commission's policy on regular advertising.[50]

15.3.4.4 Fairness and Stations   The FCC received thousands of complaints involving the fairness doctrine but found only a handful worth its attention. Only one station lost its license for violation of the fairness doctrine—**WXUR,** Media, Pennsylvania. Rever-

end Carl McIntire bought this radio station in 1965 to bring conservative, fundamentalist religion and his syndicated *Twentieth Century Reformation Hour* to the Philadelphia area. After complaints from local citizens, the FCC denied renewal in 1970, based in part on what it saw as the station's failure to comply with the fairness doctrine and the personal attack rule. McIntire appealed, and the court upheld the FCC decision.[51]

Most fairness cases involved reasonable opportunity to respond. But the fairness doctrine also held that a licensee had an obligation to provide some programming that dealt with controversial public issues (PRT 15.3.4). The commission enforced this doctrine only once, in the **WHAR case.** Radio station WHAR served Clarksburg in the West Virginia strip-mining country. In 1976 the commission, in response to a complaint, informed WHAR that it had failed to cover adequately the controversial issue of strip mining. This violated the doctrine, and the station was directed to notify the commission on how it planned to remedy its failure.[52]

15.3.4.5 Fairness and Reevaluation   During the 1980s, new appointees to the com-

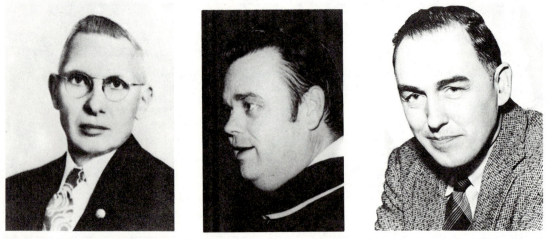

Figure 15.3 The lions of *Red Lion.* Reverend John M. Norris (*left*), president and majority stockholder of Red Lion Broadcasting Co. Reverend Billy James Hargis (*center*), host of *The Christian Crusade* radio series. Fred J. Cook (*right*), author of *Goldwater—Extremist of the Right.* (*Source: Left,* Red Lion Broadcasting Co., Inc; *center and right,* AP/Wide World.)

mission resulted in a radical change of its political tenor. Much regulation was marked for
elimination, and the fairness doctrine was
announced as a prime target (PRT 4.5.1).

In its **1985 Fairness Report,**[53] the FCC asserted that things had changed since the U.S.
Supreme Court's *Red Lion* decision. The
"broadcast marketplace" had evolved, and
"compelling documentation" showed that
fairness had a "chilling effect," that it actually caused broadcasters *not* to air controversial-issue programming. Fairness violated
the First Amendment. The courts, however,
would have to decide the question of constitutionality. The commission would give
Congress opportunity to review the fairness
doctrine before taking any action. Meanwhile, the FCC would continue to enforce
fairness because it was the law.

Congress instructed the commission to
make no changes until 1987. At that time,
the FCC was to report alternatives to enforcing and administering fairness.

Federal court decisions seemed to give indications that FCC action on fairness might
survive judicial review. In 1984, for example,
the Supreme Court indicated a willingness to
reassess the scarcity factor[54] (PRT 13.4.2 and
13.3.3), a basis for *Red Lion*. A 1986 appeals
court ruling held that 1959 amendments to
Section 315 of the Communications Act
(PRT 15.3.4.1) had *not* written the fairness
doctrine into law. Instead, according to the
court, the wording in question aimed to
make clear that the amendment did not ne-
gate fairness *as the Commission* had previously applied it.[55] A 1987 decision noted
that, in the light of the 1985 Fairness Report's findings, the FCC's failure to start procedures to eliminate or modify fairness was
subject to court review.[56]

Finally, in the 1987 **Meredith** decision,
the federal appeals court in Washington said
the FCC *had* to consider the constitutionality
of the fairness doctrine. Meredith Corporation's Syracuse TV station, WTVH, had run
advertisements that promoted construction
of a nuclear power plant. The Syracuse Peace
Council complained to the FCC. The complaint demonstrated that the plant's construction constituted a controversial issue
and that WTVH had not presented opposing
viewpoints. Meredith invoked the 1985 Fairness Report in an attempt to argue that the
doctrine was unconstitutional. The commission refused to consider the argument, found
that WTVH had violated the fairness doctrine, and ordered Meredith to air opposing
views. Meredith appealed.

The court ruled that the FCC had erred.
After all, the commission itself had concluded the fairness doctrine was unconstitutional. The decision that Meredith had violated fairness, then, was arbitrary and
capricious. The court remanded the case to
the FCC, and the FCC was to consider Meredith's constitutional arguments.

15.3.4.6 Fairness and Recantation The
commission reviewed Meredith's arguments
and reconsidered. In its 1987 **Syracuse Peace
Council**[57] decision, the FCC concluded that
the fairness doctrine contravened the First
Amendment *and its enforcement was no
longer in the public interest.** Therefore, the
Constitution barred enforcing the fairness
doctrine against WTVH.

In other words, the commission eliminated the fairness doctrine. Bolstering its
case with frequent references to the 1985
Fairness Report, the commission said, among
other things, that fairness had a "chilling effect," actually causing broadcasters *not* to air
controversial-issue programming; that it in-
hibited the expression of unorthodox opinions; and that it caused unwarranted government intrusion into program content. The
amount and type of information sources had
increased so much since 1969 and *Red Lion*
that fairness was no longer necessary. Constitutional protection should cover broad-

---

* The public interest obligation itself, however,
continued.

casting and print equally, focusing on similarities between the two media, not differences.

15.3.4.7 Fairness and Residue

The FCC's action did not include all fairness-related policies. It eliminated the basic requirements of fairness—provide opportunity for discussion of contrasting points of view on a controversial issue of public importance and provide some controversial-issue programming—and the Cullman doctrine. It left in place the personal attack and political editorial rules and the Zapple doctrine. The RTNDA and the National Association of Broadcasters asked the FCC to eliminate the personal attack and political editorial rules.

The Commission's *Syracuse Peace Council* action angered many members of Congress. Congress had directed the FCC to report alternatives before making any changes to fairness (PRT 15.3.4.5). The commission complied—technically. The FCC staff presented the report and the commission approved sending it to Congress at the same meeting—but about 30 minutes before—*Syracuse Peace Council* was adopted. Earlier in 1987, Congress had attempted to write fairness into law, but President Reagan had vetoed the bill. Now, the legislators tried again and failed again, withdrawing their attempt after threat of another presidential veto. Several powerful members of Congress vowed to enact a fairness law eventually, even if they had to wait until President Reagan left office.

Mark Fowler had actively worked to eliminate fairness for years (PRT 4.5.1). But Dennis Patrick (Figure 15.4) had succeeded Fowler to the FCC chair some three months earlier, so it was actually under Patrick's leadership that the commission took its *Syracuse Peace Council* action. Subsequently, Patrick found Congress ill-disposed to cooperate with or help the commission in any way. The Senate refused to move on nominations for two vacant commission seats,

Figure 15.4 Dennis Patrick. (*Source:* AP/Wide World.)

leaving the FCC for months with only three members. Congress also "micromanaged" the FCC, writing into law instructions on matters before the commission, matters that—at one time—would have been left to the discretion of the commissioners.*

The Syracuse Peace Council, the organization at the heart of the case, appealed the FCC's decision. The appeals court affirmed the FCC on the basis that fairness did not serve the public interest. The court did not rule on the constitutional issue.[58]

---

* In April 1989, Patrick announced his plan to step down as FCC chair. By that time his relationship with Congress had thawed somewhat. The FCC had earlier replaced AT&T's historic rate-of-return regulation with price-cap regulation and proposed to do the same for federally regulated services of local telephone companies. But before Patrick had the FCC act, he provided lawmakers with details of the price-cap proposal, listened to their concerns, and modified the proposal accordingly. As a result, Congress did not challenge this FCC action, and Patrick had mended at least some fences.

In mid-1989, President George Bush nominated Alfred C. Sikes to the FCC and designated Sikes to chair the commission. Sikes, head of the NTIA, was described as "a political moderate, . . . not ideological, [and] expected to develop closer, more cordial ties with Congress and [the other] commissioners" than either Fowler or Patrick. ("Closing in on a new FCC," *Broadcasting* 19 June 1989: 27.)

Some broadcasters, too, apparently did not necessarily feel that abolition of fairness was necessary. Westinghouse Broadcasting's KDKA actually urged that viewers write Congress to support putting fairness into law. Two powerful trade organizations—the Association of Independent Television Stations and the Television Operators Caucus (PRT 19.8.1)—both made statements favoring public interest regulation, of which fairness was a primary example.

15.3.5 Indecency

Section 1464 of the Criminal Code provides fines and prison penalties for anyone who uses "obscene, indecent, or profane language" on the radio waves. The courts have defined *obscene* (in the *Miller* case, PRT 15.2.7). They have also defined *profane*—language that invokes divine condemnation or contains blasphemous statements,[59] such as "damn you" or irreverent use of "by God" (although the FCC does not normally penalize for an occasional "damn" or "by God"). But they did not define *indecent*.

Most broadcast language that offends through sexual connotation does not meet all three *Miller* tests and thus is not legally obscene. Yet, radio and television—unlike books, magazines, and motion pictures—are directly available in the home, requiring no more audience initiative than the turn of a switch. They occupy large percentages of time for many persons. They easily reach children, as well as adults who take offense at sexually oriented material. Most years, the FCC receives more complaints about objectionable language than for any reason. Therefore, the FCC felt that the public interest required establishment of a standard for radio and television that was stricter than *Miller*. This standard defined *indecent* material, and it received judicial sanction in the WBAI case.

15.3.5.1 WBAI Case   This case began with a complaint from a man who, with his son, happened to hear Pacifica-owned WBAI-FM, New York, broadcast a cut from a record album by George Carlin, a comedian. The cut contained several common sexual and scatological slang terms. The FCC ruled the broadcast "indecent" and took the occasion to issue a declaratory ruling[60] to tell what the term meant.

The commission said indecent refers to **words that describe sexual or excretory activities and organs in a patently offensive manner.** The indecency standard did not include the dominant-appeal-to-prurient-interest criterion from *Miller*. And only if (1) a program containing indecent material was run late at night when children were least likely to be in the audience and (2) the programmer had made a solid effort to warn adults in advance that the program contained such material[61]—only then would literary, artistic, political, or scientific value redeem it (make it worthwhile). In 1978, the U.S. Supreme Court affirmed the FCC's "indecent" standard.[62]

15.3.5.2 New Enforcement Standards   The FCC dealt with succeeding cases as though the "indecent" standard referred only to the specific words at issue in the WBAI case. Further, the commission defined "late at night" as after 10 p.m. During the mid-1980s, citizen groups put pressure on the commission to do more about enforcing Section 1464 of the Criminal Code (PRT 15.3.5).

In 1987, the FCC responded by announcing[63] its intention to use the judicially sanctioned definition of *indecency* from the WBAI case. Future enforcement would extend beyond the "seven dirty words" of the WBAI case to a broader range of patently offensive programming. Further, even at 10 p.m., the audience might contain significant numbers of children. Broadcasters, therefore, should not assume that indecent programming could safely air after 10 p.m. (The indecency standard apparently did not apply to cable operators [PRT 15.3.6.1].)

The commission also took action against three radio stations about which it had received complaints. KPFK-FM, Los Angeles, had broadcast excerpts from "Jerker," a play that included explicit descriptions of homosexual fantasies. WYSP-FM, Philadelphia, had aired objectionable language in a pandering and titillating fashion during the morning drive-time shift of Howard Stern, a "raunch radio" personality. KCSB-FM, Santa Barbara, had broadcast a recording that contained explicit sexual language, "Making Bacon," by the Pork Dukes.

The commission had problems with the time element. It established a "safe harbor" from midnight to 6 a.m.,[64] during which indecent (but not obscene) programming could be aired. On appeal, a 1988 court decision[65] upheld the WYSP-FM ruling but vacated those on KPFK-FM and KCSB-FM; their programming had aired *after* the commission's *previous* safe harbor of 10 p.m. Further, the court said the FCC had not adequately justified changing the safe harbor to midnight.

Several months later, the president signed into law a measure instructing the commission to enforce the ban on indecency 24 hours a day.[66] An appeals court, however, granted a stay of the FCC's rule implementing the law until such time as the court could hear the case. The FCC then asked the court to remand the case so that the commission could open a proceeding aimed at justifying the 24-hour-a-day ban. At the same time, the FCC initiated proceedings against three more radio stations, alleging indecency on the part of "shock jocks" at KSJO, San Jose, California, WLUP, Chicago, and WFBQ, Indianapolis.[67]

Media Central's KZKC-TV, Kansas City, Missouri, had also run afoul of the new indecency enforcement. In 1987, the station aired the movie *Private Lessons* at 8 p.m. The film contained, among other sexually oriented material, scenes of a nude female attempting to seduce a young boy. The FCC levied a $2000 fine. A subsequent court decision, however, overturned in part the policy on which the commission had based the KZKC action, and the FCC rescinded the fine.[68]

15.3.6 The First Amendment and Cable Television

In passing the Cable Communications Act of 1984, Congress attempted to sort out program control of cable systems. It gave franchising authorities the power to regulate cable systems, but they did so within the parameters of federal law and FCC regulation.

The 1984 act required that most cable operators provide leased channels (PRT 14.1.1.8). The franchising authority could require public, educational, and governmental (PEG; PRT 14.1.1.8, 19.5.2.2) channels. The franchising authority could take an active hand in programming educational and governmental channels but otherwise could not control programming content. The system operator was not to censor programming on PEG or leased channels.

15.3.6.1 Obscene and Indecent Cable Programming   The cable act made cable operators and programmers fully liable for programming abuses. This included defamation, obscenity, incitement, invasion of privacy, deceptive advertising, and similar misdeeds.[69] It excluded PEG and leased-channel programming. With respect to obscene or indecent programming, a subscriber could require the operator to supply a device that shut off access to certain cable services. This would prevent accidental viewing, for example, by children.

The act allowed the operator and the franchising authority to agree that the system would not provide obscene programming, and it specified fine or imprisonment for anyone who transmitted obscenity by cable. In both cases, the statute's wording referred to content that was "obscene or otherwise unprotected by the Constitution. . . ."[70]

Apparently, however, "otherwise unprotected" content did not include "indecent" programming. The Utah legislature had attempted to define and prohibit indecent cable programming with passage of the Cable Television Programming Decency Act. This state law authorized fines for cable operators who programmed depictions or descriptions of naked human buttocks and genitals and female breasts. A 1987 U.S. Supreme Court decision[71] affirmed lower court rulings that the Utah statute violated the First Amendment.

15.3.6.2 The First Amendment and Cable Franchising   Just two years after Congress passed the cable act, court decisions seemed to question its constitutionality. They opened the franchising process to examination in the light of the First Amendment. One such proceeding reached the Supreme Court—the **Preferred case.**[72]

Preferred Communications, Inc., applied for a cable franchise in Los Angeles. The city refused the application because Preferred had not participated in an auction for the single franchise in the area. Preferred contended the refusal violated the company's First Amendment rights; the area contained sufficient space on public utility structures and public demand to support more than one cable system. The question of whether the First Amendment was a legitimate consideration in the franchise process was argued all the way to the U.S. Supreme Court. The court said that attempts to secure a cable franchise "plainly implicate First Amendment interest." On the other hand, the court refused to set a *specific* First Amendment

standard for cable and, instead, sent the case back to the trial court for more information. Subsequently cable operators used the *Preferred* decision in court attempts to challenge single-system franchises and franchise requirements.

15.3.7 The First Amendment and Other Media

Generally, newer FCC-regulated media have fewer content restrictions and requirements than broadcasting. In adopting rules for these media, the commission attempted to use the print model; they were given, as much as possible, freedom from government regulation of editorial decisions similar to that enjoyed by newspaper, magazine, and book publishers. Most of these media may not transmit obscenity, tobacco advertising, information on illegal lotteries, and similar statutorily forbidden material. On the other hand, the less they resemble broadcasting—service intended for reception by the general public—the more they tend to be free of what we shall call *broadcast-type regulation.* This includes requirements such as equal opportunities for political candidates, candidate access (PRT 14.1.1.4), and the personal attack and political editorial rules.

The LPTV service *is* broadcasting. But even LPTV stations have fewer programming rules than their full-service competitors. LPTVs do not even have minimum schedule requirements (PRT 15.3.1). Broadcast-type regulation applies on a sliding scale based on the station's ability to originate programming. For example, LPTV stations that have no local origination facilities, that simply rebroadcast full-service stations or satellite programming, have no political programming or access obligations. Neither version of the must-carry rule (PRT 14.1.1.9) included LPTV; that is, cable systems did not have to carry local LPTV stations.

Regulation of other wireless media operators varies with the type of service. If others originate programming over which the transmitting licensee exercises no editorial control, the licensee is a **common carrier** and is so regulated.

The programmer, however, whether the licensee or simply a common-carrier customer, is regulated according to the *intent* of the programming service.[73] If the programmer intends transmissions for reception by the public at large, it is **broadcasting,** and broadcast-type regulation applies.

If the programmer intends to limit access to the transmissions—as in subscription programming—the process is *not* broadcasting. Instead, it is **point-to-multipoint communication,** according to the FCC, and therefore *not* subject to broadcast-type regulation. Here, the programmer uses transmission techniques to prevent the reception of programming by nonsubscribers. The signals cannot be received without special antenna converters or decoding equipment supplied by the programmer.

Common carrier, broadcasting, and point-to-multipoint—these regulatory categories cover direct-broadcast satellite (DBS), subscription television stations (STV; PRT 4.5.2.5), and, to some extent, wireless cable (multichannel TV; PRT 5.4 and 12.7). A multichannel medium may even be regulated *by channel* according to the use of that channel. In a six-channel direct-broadcast satellite or a four-channel multipoint distribution service (MDS; PRT 5.4) facility, for example, two channels could operate (and be regulated) as broadcast services and the others as subscription services. MDS was originally strictly a common-carrier service; in 1987, however, the FCC gave MDS licensees the option to operate as *noncommon carriers,* freeing them to program their own channels.

The FCC does not apply broadcast-type regulation to subsidiary communications services (SCS; PRT 11.6.2) offered by radio stations. A radio licensee may lease out an SCS channel for programming by others but must retain control over material transmitted. A 1986 court decision ruled that the FCC may not preempt state public utilities commission regulation when regulated intrastate carrier services are offered by SCS.[74]

Broadcast teletext is not subject to broadcast-type regulation[75] with the exception of equal opportunities for political candidates.[76] The FCC applies common-carrier regulation when a station leases its vertical blanking interval for data transmission. Most attempts to provide videotex service have used telephone lines, so broadcast-type regulation did not apply. The 1984 cable act excluded satellite master antenna television (SMATV) systems from federal requirements for cable systems, and, of course, local franchise requirements do not apply to SMATVs, either.

NOTES

1. "Justice Black and First Amendment 'Absolutes': A Public Interview," *New York University Law Review* 37 (1962): 548.
2. *Farmers Educational and Cooperative Union* v. *WDAY,* 360 U.S. 525.
3. 376 U.S. 254, 279–280 (1964). Boldface added.
4. *Gertz* v. *Robert Welch, Inc.,* 418 U.S. 323 (1974).
5. *Philadelphia Newspapers* v. *Hepps,* 475 U.S. 767 (1986).
6. *Solar Music* v. *Gap Stores,* 516 F. Supp 923 (1981), affirmed 688 F.2d 84 (1981); *Broadcast Music, Inc.* v. *United States Shoe Corp.,* 678 F.2d 816 (1982).
7. *Buffalo Broadcasting Company* v. *American Society of Composers, Authors, and Publishers,* 744 F.2d 917, *certiorari* denied 469 U.S. 1211 (1985).
8. 17 U.S.C. §111.
9. *Sony Corporation of America* v. *Universal Studios,* 464 U.S. 417.
10. *United States* v. *Atherton,* 561 F.2d 747 (1977).
11. *Richmond Newspapers* v. *Virginia,* 448 U.S. 555 (1980); *Globe Newspaper Co.* v. *Superior Court,* 457 U.S. 596 (1982); *Press-Enterprise* v.

Superior Court (I), 464 U.S. 501 (1984).; and *Press-Enterprise* v. *Superior Court* (II), 478, U.S. 1 (1986).

12. 427 U.S. 539.
13. 430 U.S. 308 (1977).
14. *Landmark Communications* v. *Virginia*, 435 U.S. 829 (1978); and *Smith* v. *Daily Mail*, 443 U.S. 97 (1979).
15. 381 U.S. 532.
16. 101 S.Ct. 802 (1981).
17. *Near* v. *Minnesota*, 283 U.S. 697.
18. *New York Times* v. *U.S.* and *U.S.* v. *Washington Post*, 403 U.S. 713, 714 (1971).
19. 5 U.S.C. §522.
20. *Branzburg* v. *Hayes,* In the Matter of Paul Pappas, and *U.S.* v. *Caldwell*, 408 U.S. 665.
21. *Zurcher* v. *Stanford Daily*, 436 U.S. 547.
22. 42 U.S.C. §2000aa.
23. *Miller* v. *California*, 413 U.S. 15.
24. 47 CFR §§1740.
25. 47 CFR §73.1208.
26. 47 CFR §73.1201.
27. 15 U.S.C. §1335 (1969).
28. Public Law 86-677, 74 Stat. 554 (1960).
29. Petitions of Aspen Institute and CBS, 55 F.C.C.2d 697 (1975). A federal appeals court upheld the commission's interpretation in *Chisolm* v. *FCC* and *Democratic National Committee* v. *FCC*, 588 F.2d 349 (1976); *certiorari* denied, 429 U.S. 890 (1976).
30. Petitions for Henry Geller, 95 F.C.C.2d 1326.
31. Request for Declaratory Ruling by WCVB-TV, 63 R.R.2d 665.
32. 47 F.2d 670.
33. 62 F.2d 850.
34. 288 U.S. 599 (1933).
35. *Henry* v. *FCC*, 302 F.2d 191; *certiorari* denied, 371 U.S. 821 (1962).
36. *NBC* v. *FCC*, 132 F.2d 545 (1942), affirmed, 319 U.S. 239; and *FCC* v. *Sanders Bros.*, 309 U.S. 470 (1940).
37. *Citizens Committee to Save WEFM* v. *FCC*, 506 F.2d 246 (1974).
38. Development of Policy re: Changes in the Entertainment Formats of Broadcast Stations, 60 F.C.C.2d 858.
39. *FCC* v. *WNCN Listeners Guild*, 450 U.S. 582.
40. *Citizens for Jazz on WRVR, Inc.* v. *FCC*, 775 F.2d 392 (1985).
41. Deregulation of Radio, 84 F.C.C.2d 968 (1981); Deregulation of Commercial Television, 98 F.C.C.2d 1076 (1984).
42. Deregulation of Radio, 104 F.C.C.2d 505 (1986); Programming and Commercialization

Policies (Reconsideration), 104 F.C.C.2d 526 (1986).
43. Note 41 above.
44. In re Editorializing by Broadcast Licensees, 13 F.C.C. 1246.
45. Cullman Broadcasting Co., 40 F.C.C. 576.
46. 47 CFR §§73.123, 73.300, 73.598, 73.679.
47. 395 U.S. 367 (1969).
48. *Banzhaf* v. *FCC*, 405 F.2d 1081 (1968); *certiorari* denied, 396 U.S. 842 (1969). Congress later banned cigarette advertising completely. See note 27.
49. Handling of Public Issues Under the Fairness Doctrine and the Public Interest Standard of the Communications Act, 48 F.C.C.2d 1.
50. *National Citizens Committee for Broadcasting* v. *FCC*, 567 F.2d 1095, *certiorari* denied, 436 U.S. 926 (1978).
51. *Brandywine Main Line* v. *FCC*, 473 F.2d 16 (1972). Only one of the three judges who heard the case affirmed the denial because of the fairness issue.
52. Representative Patsy Mink, The Environmental Policy Center and O. D. Hagedorn re Radio Station, WHAR, Clarksburg, West Virginia, 59 F.C.C.2d 987.
53. General Fairness Doctrine Obligations of Broadcast Licensees, 58 R.R.2d 1137.
54. *FCC* v. *League of Women Voters of California,* 468 U.S. 364, 376 n. 11.
55. *Telecommunications Research and Action Center* v. *FCC*, 801 F.2d 501, rehearing denied, 806 F.2d 1115, *certiorari* denied, 107 S.Ct. 3197 (1987).
56. *Radio-Television News Directors Association* v. *FCC*, 809 F.2d 860.
57. 63 R.R.2d 541.
58. "Court upholds FCC's fairness repeal," *Broadcasting* 13 Feb. 1989: 28.
59. *Duncan* v. *U.S.*, 48 F.2d 128 (1931). Subsequent rulings interpreting the constitutional guarantee of freedom of religion have all but negated profanity as an offense.
60. Pacifica Foundation, 56 F.C.C.2d 94 (1975).
61. In the Matter of a "Petition for Clarification or Reconsideration" of a Citizen's Complaint against Pacifica Foundation, 59 F.C.C.2d 892 (1976).
62. *Pacifica* v. *FCC*, 438 U.S. 726 (1978).
63. New Indecency Enforcement Standards to Be Applied to All Broadcast and Amateur Radio Licensees, 62 R.R.2d 1218.
64. Infinity Broadcasting Corporation of Pennsylvania (Indecency Policy Reconsideration), 64

R.R.2d 211 (1987); and "FCC creates adult country: Midnight–6 a.m.," *Broadcasting* 30 Nov. 1987: 51.

65. *Action for Children's Television* v. *FCC*, No. 88-1064 (July 29, 1988) (1988 U.S. App. LEXIS 10094).

66. "Congress says 'safe harbor' is safe no more," *Broadcasting* 3 Oct. 1988: 28.

67. "FCC turns up the heat on indecency," *Broadcasting* 28 Aug. 1989: 27.

68. "FCC drops fine for indecency in KZKC case," *Broadcasting* 14 Aug. 1989: 59.

69. 47 U.S.C. §558.

70. 47 U.S.C. §§544 and 559.

71. *Wilkinson* v. *Jones*, 107 S.Ct. 1559.

72. *City of Los Angeles* v. *Preferred Communications*, 476 U.S. 488 (1986).

73. Subscription Video, 2 F.C.C.Rcd. 1001 (1987); affirmed, *National Association of Better Broadcasting* v. *FCC*, No. 87-1198 (1988 U.S. App. LEXIS 8331).

74. *California* v. *FCC*, 798 F.2d 1515.

75. Amendment to the Commisson's Rules to Authorize the Transmission of Teletext by TV Stations 53 R.R.2d 1309 (1983); affirmed on reconsideration, 101 F.C.C.2d 827 (1985).

76. *Telecommunications Research and Action Center* v. *FCC*, 801 F.2d 501 (1986).

FURTHER READING

Baughman, James L. *Television's Guardians: The FCC and the Politics of Programming*. Knoxville: U of Tennessee P, 1985.

Carter, T. Barton, Marc A. Franklin, and Jay B. Wright. *The First Amendment and the Fourth Estate: The Law of Mass Media*. 4th ed. Mineola: Foundation, 1988. Casebook.

Holsinger, Ralph L. *Media Law*. New York: Random, 1987.

Middleton, Kent R., and Bill F. Chamberlin. *The Law of Public Communication*. White Plains: Longman, 1988. Well-researched, readable law-of-the-press text; good section on electronic media. Annual updates.

Nelson, Harold L., Dwight L. Teeter, Jr., and Don R. Le Duc. *Law of Mass Communications: Freedom and Control of Print and Broadcast Media*. 6th ed. Westbury: Foundation, 1989.

Overbeck, Wayne, and Rick D. Pullen. *Major Principles of Media Law*. 2d ed. New York: Holt, 1985.

Parsons, Patrick. *Cable Television and the First Amendment*. Lexington: Lexington, 1987. Suggests new model for regulation.

Pember, Don R. *Mass Media Law*. 4th ed. Dubuque: Brown, 1987. Widely used text.

Zuckman, Harvey L., et al. *Mass Communication Law in a Nutshell*. 3d ed. St. Paul: West, 1988. Outline summary.

CHAPTER 16

Ethics and Self-Regulation

Radio and television are highly competitive businesses. They can also be very lucrative. Therefore why not bend the rules just a little and get the jump on the competition? Or go ahead and run that questionable advertising for an extra few hundred dollars? Some managers do. Many do not. Why not? Certainly they fear the wrath of the federal government. But there are two other factors also—factors that both deter misconduct and stimulate performance above the required legal minimum standards. These factors are ethics and self-regulation. In radio and television, *ethics* refers to a personal sense of what is right and what is wrong on the part of individuals who make major policy decisions for the operation—persons such as licensees, members of the board of directors, corporate officers, general and system managers (for convenience, we shall use the term *managers* to refer to these policy makers). *Self-regulation* is the translation of those personal ethics into systematic rules of conduct.

16.1 ETHICAL CONSIDERATIONS

Contrary to the implications of some critics, there is nothing inherently wrong about running an electronic medium to make money. Given a capitalistic economic system such as that of the United States, earning a profit is a desirable goal. However, some of the means employed to the end of making money could be considered inherently wrong, means that seem to violate certain obligations and responsibilities. We call such means unethical. Means that do meet these obligations are ethical.

What do we mean by "ethical means," "ethical practices," and "ethical operation"? The nouns in these terms are easier to define than their common adjective. For illustrative purposes, let us use the example of a broadcast licensee who runs a commercial radio or television station. *Means* are ways to earn a profit. A commercial broadcast licensee operates a station to earn a profit; therefore *operation* of the station is the licensee's means.

Practices refer to things a licensee does in operating a station. All three terms are closely related, and they apply to almost any kind of radio-TV entity—a cable system, a broadcast network, or whatever. We shall use these terms interchangeably to refer to **the things managers do in operating a radio-TV entity to earn a profit.**

As for "ethical," it would seem logical to employ our definition of "ethics"—the individual manager's personal sense of what is right and what is wrong. But **"right" and "wrong" are relative concepts.** For example, in 1973, Reverend Carl McIntire announced plans to open a pirate radio station (Figure 16.1) on board a ship just outside the U.S. territorial limit off Cape May, New Jersey. Doubtless, this was an act of pure conscience on the part of the minister; the FCC had not renewed the license of his seminary's radio stations (Section 15.3.3.4), and Reverend McIntire told reporters he was ready to risk going to jail to broadcast "the message God wants me to preach." Yet, while Reverend McIntire may have believed his plan to be the right thing to do (given the circumstances in which he found himself), it is conceivable that the federal government and the licensees with whose station signals the pirate transmitter would interfere would have viewed the pirate station as wrong. Therefore, our first definition of "ethics" is not entirely adequate for our present discussion of "ethical."

The dictionary defines "ethical" as "conforming to professional standards of conduct." There are at least two problems with this definition, First, it seems to imply existence of a *profession*. Radio-TV, however, **does not fit many of the characteristics attributed to a profession.** A profession often requires advanced academic training, as in medicine and law; radio-TV does not. A profession stresses service; we have already discovered that commercial radio-TV emphasizes profit, while service is both a function

of individual managers' decisions and mandated by legal documents, such as laws and franchises. Second, our dictionary definition does not tell us to what or whose standards to conform, beyond that of the vague and probably invalid term "professional."

16.1.1 Moral Obligations

Somehow, then, our definition of "ethical" should include the concepts of (1) effects on other persons and (2) specificity—that is, kinds of acts or things that are ethical. Perhaps we can combine these two concepts by speaking in terms of obligations, duties radio-TV managers are bound to perform as a result of moral responsibility. There would seem to be at least three sets of such obligations—those of any business; those of a medium of mass communication; and those of an entity that uses means of delivery held in trust for the common good.

16.1.1.1 Obligations of a Business There are laws to protect the individual consumer. There are laws to preserve competition and prevent restraint of trade. But over and above legal regulatory requirements, there are also moral responsibilities. Businesses are expected to produce good products and services at fair prices. They are expected to pay and deal with their employees on a fair and equitable basis. They are expected to contribute toward the betterment of the community in which they do business. They are expected to follow the Golden Rule in dealing with customers and competitors. In short, they are expected to be good neighbors, to do voluntarily more than the law requires, as good neighbors do. And, just as in any other business, managers are expected to accept this general responsibility and run a radio-TV entity so as to **produce a good product, treat employees fairly, contribute to the com-**

Figure 16.1 Reverend McIntire's pirate radio station.   "Right" versus "Wrong." (*Source:* AP/Wide World.)

munity, **be an honest competitor,** and **be a good neighbor.**

16.1.1.2 Obligations of a Medium of Mass Communication Like newspaper publishers, the managers of a radio-TV entity are subject to laws and judicial decisions involving defamation, invasion of privacy, pornographic material, and false and misleading advertising. But also like publishers, radio-TV managers operate instruments of tremen-

dous potential for contribution to the public weal. As such, publishers and managers have certain obligations to society, corollaries of the **social responsibility theory of mass communication.**

According to this theory, the press, which includes all media for reporting news, is guaranteed freedom by the Constitution and so is obliged to perform certain essential functions of mass communications in modern society. In 1948, the Commission on Freedom of the Press, a University of Chicago project funded by private enterprise and staffed by scholars, suggested five such functions. The **media should**

1. **present a truthful account of the day's news in such way as to give it meaning,**
2. **serve as a forum for the exchange of ideas,**
3. **present a representative picture of the various groups that make up society,**
4. **present and clarify the goals and values of society, and**
5. **provide full access to the day's intelligence.**

Over the years, national surveys have indicated that the public increasingly relies for its news on the broadcast media, particularly television. For this reason, it has become increasingly important for broadcast licensees to meet this second set of obligations and to carry out the five important functions the commission has outlined.

16.1.1.3 Obligations from Use of Resources Held in Trust

Unlike other businesses and media, many radio-TV outlets do not own means of distribution. Broadcast stations, wireless cable systems, direct-broadcast satellites, and other wireless media use radio frequencies, natural resources in the public domain. Cable operators use the right of way in their service areas, areas held and controlled by local governmental authorities on behalf of residents.

The Communications Act of 1934 directs that the FCC determine that the public interest would be served before the grant of any license for use of the radio frequencies. It also allows the commission to place certain requirements on licensees consistent with the public interest. The Cable Communications Policy Act of 1984 aims to ensure that cable systems are responsive to their community and provide the widest possible diversity of information sources and services to the public.[1]

These are minimum requirements. The manager has a positive obligation to regard them as such and to use the outlet to serve the good of the overall public.

Justice Byron R. White, in writing the U.S. Supreme Court's *Red Lion* decision, alluded to this obligation with respect to broadcasting. He noted that only a few persons in each community can be licensed to operate a broadcast station. However, those few who do receive licenses could be required to operate as proxies or fiduciaries. In making this point, Justice White was explaining the rationale for FCC regulation under the fairness doctrine. But the same reasoning applies to extralegal, moral obligations—**the outlet has been authorized to employ resources held in trust for the common good and should use them for the common good.**

16.1.2 Ethics of Fulfilling Requirements

The term "ethical" also seems to imply the concept of **voluntary.** No one requires managers to operate a radio-TV entity in an ethical manner; managers should do so voluntarily. The FCC has fewer than 2,000 employees to regulate all interstate common carriers and millions of radio transmitters in the various services, to say nothing of over 8,000 cable systems and 15,000 broadcasting stations in all 50 states, the District of Columbia, Guam, Puerto Rico, and the Virgin Islands. With this workload, it is impossible for the commission to check the performance of every outlet. A careful but unethical manager could bend or break a few rules, and no one would ever know.

There are also **degrees** of ethicality in meeting the regulatory minimums. Regulatory requirements can be fulfilled to the best of the manager's ability, or they can be fulfilled grudgingly, with the least amount of effort possible. Most persons would probably feel the first operation to be the more ethical of the two.

16.1.3 "Ethical" Defined

Having looked at some of the implications of the term "ethical," let us now attempt to define "ethical practices" as they apply to radio-TV. Ethical practices are **the things a manager does to operate a commercial radio-TV entity for profit in such way as to fulfill certain obligations it has as a business, as a medium of mass communication, and as an entity authorized to use resources held in trust for the common good.** The manager **operates this way voluntarily and in response to a personal sense of what should be done, of what is right and what is wrong.**

16.1.4 Ethical Managers

It is possible for a manager to be both ethical and unethical. For example, a radio station might program so as to serve well its obligation to the community, yet at the same time engage in all manner of unfair business practices. Generally, however, **a radio-TV entity is either mostly ethical or mostly unethical,** especially at the local level.

Size has little to do with ethicality. You might think that a large, successful group-owned outlet could afford to be more ethical than a mom-and-pop operation. You could also argue that the locally owned small outlet has to operate ethically since it is so close to and so dependent on its public and its advertisers. But you can find examples of both kinds of outlets that do as little as they can for as much as they can get.

An ethical manager does not have to be a hero. But it does take **compassion**—empathy and the milk of human kindness. And **strength**—when the chips, the ratings, the subscribers, the rates, and the gross are down, when the profit-and-loss statement (Section 19.2.1) is full of red ink, or when the competition is hot, it takes a strong will to resist certain unethical practices.

Specifically, what are the types of things an ethical manager might do that make the operation ethical? As we said earlier, simply doing what is required could be considered ethical. But some managers have taken a more positive approach. Some examples from small-market radio stations include the following: airing the weekly high school speech and drama class program at a time when people are listening rather than 10 a.m. Sunday morning; employing a full-time news reporter and stringers when, as the only radio station in town, a rip 'n' read operation would do; lending space or equipment to a competitor whose station has been destroyed; mounting an appeal for clothing, shelter, and food for a destitute family; scheduling a hard-hitting investigative documentary in spite of opposition from several advertisers; running an editorial favoring the side that seems best for the community in a heated local controversy; establishing paid internships to help young people get started in broadcasting; hiring and training handicapped persons; hiring and training poor youngsters from the barrios and the black ghettos.

16.1.5 Unethical Managers

Motivations for unethical conduct in radio-TV are the same as in any other field—drive for power, promotion of a cause, desire for prestige. But in most cases the immediate stimulus is much simpler—**money.** A radio-TV outlet has the potential of being a very lucrative business. When an outlet loses money, the manager often continues to operate it in the hope that it will turn the corner and begin to pay off. In the meantime, however, the outlet may sacrifice ethics to cut costs enough to stay in business.

At the other end of the spectrum is the already sucessful outlet whose management feels it must squeeze maximum profit from the business. The owner in this case is often a corporation whose owners are hundreds or thousands of stockholders. When profits, subscribers, sales, or ratings drop, so do stock prices; the stockholders suffer, and managers get fired. Thus managers run the outlet as a profit machine, reacting more to financial pressure than to their own good taste and sense of responsibility.

Some persons assert that radio-TV seems to be particularly vulnerable to the lure of money and is often unfavorably compared to the daily press. At least three factors seem to support this assertion. First, **time is limited.** If a newspaper wishes to make more money, it adds more pages and sells more advertising to fill them. A broadcast station or a cable channel, however, cannot add more time. To earn more money it must either add more commercials or attract a greater audience so that it can charge more for advertising time. A radio-TV outlet attracts greater audiences by airing more popular programs, which, because of audience tastes, means programs with little or no serious or worthwhile content.

Second, **advertising-supported radio-TV does not maintain strict separation of content and advertising considerations.** In preparing a daily newspaper, all space not taken by advertising belongs to the editor, and the editor is relatively free to select news, information, and entertainment to fill this "news hole." In radio-TV, most content is selected specifically for the purpose of attracting an audience for advertising. This content/advertising relationship is deeply rooted in the very origins of commercial broadcasting (Section 2.1.5).

Finally, the **policy makers in radio-TV come, by and large, from the areas of sales and marketing.** In newspapers, the editor makes content decisions, and editors have come up through the content ranks—copy, rewrite, and reporter. In broadcast stations, the manager makes the content decisions, and most station managers have come up through the ranks of sales. They see their medium as a sales vehicle and so do not hesitate to do whatever is necessary to make their medium attractive to prospective advertisers. In cable, the route to the policy-making level often originates in marketing; policy makers view their selection of channels as a "package" to be marketed to the maximum number of homes passed, to generate additional revenue with subscribers upgrading to ancillary services and multiple pay cable channels. With these three factors—limited time, strong content/advertising relationship, and sales/marketing orientation of managers—it would be surprising if radio-TV were not more vulnerable to the lure of the dollar than the daily press.

16.1.6 Unethical Business Practices

For our purposes, unethical practices show up in two main areas of radio-TV operation—business and programming. Unethical business practices include rate cutting, double billing, ratings distortion, clipping, and blacklisting.

In **rate cutting** or **selling off the card,** an outlet retains its existing rate card. But if sales personnel cannot sell time at rate card prices, they are allowed to make special deals with clients at lower prices. This practice can set off rate-cutting wars involving all outlets in a market, and in the end no one benefits.

Double billing is tied to cooperative advertising (Section 9.1.5.5). In double billing, the outlet issues two bills to the local advertiser. One reflects the amount the advertiser actually paid, for example, "50 one-minute spots in class AAA time @ $5.00 = $250." The other shows a higher amount, for example, "50 one-minute spots in class AAA time @ $10.00 = $500." The local advertiser sends the higher bill to the manufacturer and, according to the amount involved and the terms of the co-op deal, recovers most or all of the expenditure or even makes a little money.

Ratings distortion—a broadcast station's attempt to inflate ratings—has been condemned by the trade itself (Section 18.2.11.3). Station advertising rates are based on ratings, so the station that distorts the ratings process sets itself up to charge advertisers for audience it does not have. At the same time, it gets an unfair, unearned competitive advantage over other stations in the market.

A broadcast station that deletes network programming or superimposes local material over it is **clipping.** The affiliate usually clips off the opening or closing of a program to gain a few more seconds of local time to sell. Clipping is unethical because the station deletes material it has promised to air in its affiliation contract with the network.

Clipping may be illegal as well. If the station clips programs but certifies to the network (for affiliate compensation) that it carried the programming in full, or if the clipped material contains legally required sponsor identification, the licensee may be subject to forfeiture or other FCC sanctions.

A **blacklist** is a scheme that causes persons to be refused employment. The broadcasting blacklists of the 1950s are explained in Section 3.2.3.1. Blacklists still exist in various forms. A common one is the "you'll-never-work-again" ploy. Here, management passes the word that a former employee is alcoholic or undependable, has a drug problem, or has some other habit or characteristic that makes a person a poor job candidate. If this is untrue, the individual spreading such stories may become a defendant in a libel suit. A second common blacklist type might be called "don't hire my employees." Typically, this results when an outlet is not doing well and is operating in the red. Employees sense that the operation may cease and they would be without jobs, so they start applying at other outlets in the market. To prevent experienced personnel from leaving, management asks the other outlets not to hire them.

16.1.7 Program Practices Under Question

Unethical practices seem to show up most blatantly in the programming area of commercials. One such practice is **deception in production,** often a false demonstration. Two of the most famous false demonstration cases were the sandpaper and the Libby-Owens-Ford auto glass cases (Section 14.2.2). A second problem involves the **number of commercials** as discussed in Section 9.5.

Some radio-TV outlets accept advertising for **borderline products.** These are products that may not be exactly illegal, but an outlet exhibits questionable ethics in advertising them. Borderline products include quack medicines and nostrums; services of palm readers, fortune tellers, and faith healers; certain religious articles; shady real estate promotions; overpriced and useless gadgets; get-rich-quick schemes; automotive devices that purport to increase horsepower or allow a car to run on water.

Unethical outlets may accept **questionable advertising.** Such includes deceptive advertising (such as bait and switch) and program-length commercials (Section 9.1.3.3). The latter increased in number markedly during the 1980s.

Some unethical outlets sell time to **charlatans,** the modern-day Brinkleys, Shulers, and Bakers (Sections 2.1.7 and 15.3.3.1). The outlets inquire into the backgrounds and motives of such persons no further than the color of their money. The charlatans use the time to get money from the poor, the uneducated, the elderly, the non-English-speaking—that is, those who can least afford it. Their schemes are as varied as their methods are nefarious, ranging from religion and politics to real estate.

Closely related are **phony products** and **shady advertisers.** The commercial describes the phony product in glowing terms, says that it is not sold in stores, cautions that supplies are limited, and urges you to write or call immediately ("Operators are standing by!"). Then (1) you get the product and either (a) it does not come anywhere near the commercial's description or (b) you find the stores flooded with them at half the price two months later. Or (2) you send in money and receive nothing; subsequent inquiries are returned to you marked "Moved; left no forwarding address." In this case you have encountered a shady advertiser. Other shady advertisers include the discount merchant who uses bait-and-switch advertising, the used-car dealer who sells primarily to racial minorities and enlisted military personnel for low down payments and usurer's interest rates, and almost any business that promises much more than it can deliver without some catch. No ethical manager knowingly accepts such advertising.

So far, our discussion has centered on advertising. But unethical practices show up in other types of programming as well. For example, in Section 4.3.3 we discussed rigging of big-money quiz shows in the 1950s. The rigging supposedly enhanced "entertainment values," which, interpreted, meant "ratings." In Section 8.1.5 we discussed ethical problems in television news, most of which grew out of the drive for high ratings—emphasis on stories that feature conflict, that are particularly visual, or just are on videotape; staging and deceptive editing of news film.

There is also the question of news bias. Each of us perceives the same thing in different ways, a result of differential learning (Section 24.1). One person's objective report is another person's lie. As long as human beings report the news, there will be this kind of bias. Far different is the situation in which a manager orders news slanted, often for commercial reasons. If the nightly 30-minute local newscast features a $2\frac{1}{2}$-minute film story on the arrival of a trainload of new pickup trucks at the local Chevrolet dealer, you can bet the car dealer is or soon will be one of the outlet's big advertising clients. Such practices hardly present a truthful account of the news, serve as a forum for the exchange of ideas, or fulfill any of the other obligations of a medium of mass communication.

16.2 SELF-REGULATION

When ethics are translated into policy, the result is self-regulation. Since managers' ethics are reflected in an outlet's operation, each outlet has some sort of self-regulation. Many outlets have no formal written policies; new employees must learn policy by osmosis—posted memos, the grapevine, and the like. Some outlets have policy books that each new employee must read. These range in size from a couple of double-spaced typewritten pages to large and detailed tomes that attempt to cover every department and every eventuality.

16.2.1 NAB Codes

For years, many broadcast stations relied on the codes of the National Association of Broadcasters (NAB) as the basis for their policies, either formally, as subscribers, or informally, through the codes' general influence on the trade. The codes were the best-known products of broadcasting self-regulation.

There were two—the Radio Code and the Television Code—and they represented the collective average ethics of the subscribing stations, a set of rules that the licensees agreed should serve as minimum ethical standards. The first Radio Code was written in 1929; the first Television Code, in 1951. Both were revised many times.

A Code Authority carried on the day-to-day operations of the codes, under supervision of broadcaster committees of the NAB. Stations voluntarily subscribed to the codes. Code subscription and NAB membership were independent of each other; a licensee could have one without the other. A code-subscribing station could advertise that it was such and could display the appropriate "seal of good practice." Penalty procedures provided for the ouster of subscribing stations that violated the code.

The heart of the codes was their standards. These were divided into program standards and advertising standards. Both were a mixture of positive statements of general principles and negative statements of things that should not be done. For example, the Television Code, on the one hand, directed the licensee to "provide for reasonable experimentation to the development of programs specifically directed to the advancement of the community's culture and education." On the other hand, it warned, "The use of liquor in program content shall be de-emphasized." Elements of both program and advertising standards eventually led to the demise of the codes.

As a result of pressure from the FCC and Congress, the NAB (with the support of some network initiatives) amended the program standards of its Television Code in 1975 to include a **"family viewing" standard.** The standard was aimed at reducing sex and violence in content and said, "Entertainment programming inappropriate for viewing by a general family audience should not be broadcast during the first hour of net-

work entertainment programming in prime time and in the immediately preceding hour. . . ." Guilds representing television writers, producers, directors, and actors challenged the family viewing standard in court. In 1976, a federal judge ruled that the standard was unconstitutional. An appeals court threw out the ruling in 1979,[2] and the Supreme Court denied a petition for review in 1980, allowing the decision of the appeals court to stand. But the NAB had suspended enforcement of the program standards four years before (at the time of the first ruling).

Meanwhile, the advertising standards had come under attack. In 1979, the U.S. Department of Justice filed an antitrust suit against the NAB. The Justice Department charged that the TV Code's **limitations on advertising** restricted the amount of television advertising time available and, therefore, kept TV commercial rates artificially high. Specifically, the department objected to limitations on the following aspects of advertising: number of commercials per hour, number of commercial interruptions per program, and number of products or services advertised in a single commercial of less than 60 seconds. In 1982, an initial court ruling went against the NAB, and so the association suspended the advertising standards. After negotiations, the NAB agreed to delete the contested standards and the Justice Department dropped the suit.

At this point, the codes were empty shells. Both programming and advertising standards—the primary content of the codes—were suspended. The NAB closed down the Code Authority, released its staff, and shut its offices. Early in 1983, the NAB officially dissolved the codes.

There is more than a little irony in this episode. The government—in the form of the Justice Department—dealt a blow to the codes. Yet the case could be made that one main purpose of the codes' very existence was to appease the government. Repeatedly over the years, Congress, the FCC, or the FTC would perceive some problem with broadcasting and propose a law or rule; the NAB, in turn, would amend the codes to take care of the problem, to demonstrate that government action was not needed and that the trade could regulate itself. Indeed, according to the court decision in the family viewing standard case, the NAB adopted that standard as a result of pressure on the trade by Commissioner Richard Wiley, when he chaired the FCC. As for the advertising standards, the FCC's Blue Book (Section 3.1.5.5) had criticized stations for airing too many commercials; the NAB subsequently tightened standards. At one point, the commission had instructed its staff to question any license renewal application in which a station proposed to exceed NAB code guidelines on number of commercial minutes per hour. Here was a case in which the government actually (but unofficially) adopted code standards as its own!

The codes were by no means perfect. Critics contended they were picky and overly specific, an open invitation to work around them and to observe the letter but not the spirit of the standards. They criticized the codes for their voluntary nature, which meant that at any given time a large number of stations were nonsubscribers. They noted that the public did not know what the codes and the seals were or did; few in the audience knew or cared whether a station subscribed to the code, or even whether it had violated the code and lost the right to display the seal. They criticized the codes for being defensive and reactive and said that changes came only after the threat of government action. Within the trade, there were those who said the codes were not tough enough. There were also those who said that there should be no codes at all, that they did not do what they were supposed to do, and that true self-regulation had to occur at the level of the individual station licensee.

Defenders argued that the codes were industry standards against which all stations could be measured. If there was a movement toward growth of a professional spirit in broadcasting, it was best reflected in the codes. The codes acted as a shield against intrusion by government; according to strict libertarian interpretation of First Amendment theory, the less government interference, the better off we are. And despite their voluntary nature, the codes did have an overall effect on programming and advertising standards. For example, code bans on the advertising of whiskey and depictions of people drinking alcohol in commercials were so effective and so widely known that many believed them to be federal law or regulation (which they were not).

Immediately after dissolution of the codes, there was some indication of change. The big three broadcast TV networks announced willingness to accept piggyback commercials (Section 9.1.3.1). Several stations began to advertise hard liquor. An advertising industry study found that, in some instances, nonprogram material such as commercials, credits, and promos exceeded the networks' own standards (see below) in prime time. There was also some talk in the NAB and in Congress about reestablishing the codes.

16.2.2 Other Vehicles for Self-Regulation

For years, each of the three national commercial television networks had its own **broadcast standards department.** Staff editors would review thousands of commercials and programs annually to ensure that they met network standards. If they found problems—of taste, deception, or whatever—they suggested deletions or changes, requested substantiation, or referred to outside experts for an opinion. They could check at all stages of production, from script to release print, and request changes at any or all points along the way. Even outside organizations checked with network standards departments in advance. Advertising agencies, for example, asked for review of commercials that would run on the network, starting with storyboard or script. During the latter 1980s, however, the networks substantially reduced their standards departments. At least four factors contributed to this action: general personnel and expense trimming, lessening of regulatory pressures, the "need" to compete with less restricted programming on cable, and a marketplace-driven perception that the moral climate had changed.

The **National Advertising Review Board** (NARB) acts on complaints concerning advertising. Although NARB is concerned with national advertising in all media, a substantial number of cases have involved television commercials.

The NARB was formed in 1971 through the efforts of various trade groups in the advertising community. Representatives from advertisers, agencies, and the general public sit on the board. Complaints about a firm's advertising go to the National Advertising Division of the Council of Better Business Bureaus. If the matter is not resolved at that level, it goes before the NARB. The final decision of the NARB is sent to the advertiser and made public. If the decision goes against the firm, the firm is expected to modify or withdraw the advertising in question. Otherwise the NARB informs the appropriate government agency.

NARB is *corrective* (after the fact), as opposed to trade association codes and network standards departments, which are *preventive* (before the fact). The NARB was formed primarily to forestall government regulation as well as expensive and publicly damaging lawsuits against advertisers by the public and even by other, competing advertisers.

For 11 years, a somewhat parallel group operated for news, the **National News Council** (NNC). Its origins date from 1972, when a Twentieth Century Fund task force published a report that urged establishment of an independent and private national news council. NNC was organized and opened for business in 1973. Funds came from a variety of private, research, media, and industrial foundations. The council consisted of ten persons representing the public and eight representing the media. Complaints about accuracy and fairness of news reports went to the NNC, which transmitted to all parties and made public its actions and decisions.

The NNC was not really self-regulation, however. Like the NARB, the NNC was a corrective, nongovernmental regulatory body, set up to forestall government involvement. But unlike the NARB, the NNC was not set up by practitioners to police themselves. In fact, some news personnel tended to resent any kind of watchdog agency, contending that the agency infringed on the very First Amendment it sought to protect.

Through the years, the council experienced increasing cooperation from news media. All three TV broadcast networks cooperated, as did the wire services and many other news organizations. Nonetheless, its adversaries were powerful and influential, including (among others) the *New York Times* and the American Society of Newspaper Publishers. After fighting an uphill battle for acceptance for more than a decade, the NNC voted itself out of existence in 1984.

Some other self-regulation efforts that affect broadcasting include those of **major advertising and trade groups** and of **organizations of individuals** who work in broadcasting. For example, various trade groups in the advertising community have adopted the "Advertising Code of American Business." The Council of Better Business Bureaus has a "Fair Practice Code for Advertising and Selling." The Proprietary Association, trade organization of over-the-counter drug manufacturers, has its own code that covers advertising. Financial institutions have a code of ethics and specific guidelines for advertising. The Radio Television News Directors Association, an individual membership organization for broadcast news personnel, has a "Code of Broadcast News Ethics" that describes, in positive terms, what broadcasters should be and do. Many broadcast newspeople belong to the Society of Professional Journalists, Sigma Delta Chi; this group also has a code of ethics.

NOTES

1. Communications Act, Section 601 (47 U.S.C. §521).
2. *Writers Guild of America* v. *FCC*, 423 F.Supp. 1064.

FURTHER READING

Brogan, Patrick. *Spiked: The Short Life and Death of the National News Council.* New York: Priority, 1985. Why it failed.

Brown, James A. "Selling Airtime for Controversy: NAB Self Regulation and Father Coughlin." *Journal of Broadcasting* 24 (1980): 199.

Christians, Clifford G., Kim B. Rotzoll, and Mark Fackler. *Media Ethics: Cases and Moral Reasoning.* 2d ed. White Plains: Longman, 1987. Real-life problems involving ethical choices.

Commission on Freedom of the Press. *A Free and Responsible Press.* Chicago: University of Chicago Press, 1947. This is the report discussed in Section 16.1.1.2.

Fink, Conrad. *Media Ethics: In the Newsroom and Beyond.* Hightstown: McGraw, 1988.

Gillmor, Donald M., and Jerome A. Barron. *Mass Communication Law: Cases and Comment.* 4th ed. St. Paul: West, 1984. Case book.

Goodwin, H. Eugene. *Groping for Ethics in Journalism.* 2d ed. Ames: Iowa State UP, 1987. Questions (and ways of answering them) of persons working in the media.

Hulteng, John L. *The Messenger's Motives: Ethical Problems of the News Media.* 2d ed. Englewood Cliffs: Prentice, 1985.

Kowet, Don. *A Matter of Honor.* New York: Macmillan, 1984. Careful, critical look at CBS's treatment of General Westmoreland (Section 8.4).

Lambeth, Edmund B. *Committed Journalism: An Ethic for the Profession.* Bloomington: Indiana UP, 1986. Ethical bases of liberty and restraint in journalism.

Peterson, Theodore. "The Social Responsibility Theory of the Press." In *Four Theories of the Press.* Frederick Siebert, Theodore Peterson, and Wilbur Schramm. Urbana: University of Illinois Press, 1956. Explains the social responsibility theory.

Powell, Jon T., and Wally Gair, eds. *Public Interest and the Business of Broadcasting: The Broadcast Industry Looks at Itself.* Westport: Greenwood, 1988.

Rivers, William L., Wilbur Schramm, and Clifford G. Christians. *Responsibility in Mass Communication.* 3d. ed. New York: Harper, 1980. Obligations of a medium of mass communication.

FIVE

ECONOMIC PERSPECTIVE

The desire for profit drives the dominant form of radio and television in the United States. People invest in and operate local and national outlets to make money. So here we examine electronic mass media as businesses. Successful businesses generate enough revenue to cover expenses and to yield a profit. We divide our survey of the economics of radio and television as follows: techniques and institutions involved in the sale of time, Chapter 17; rate card structure and audience research, Chapter 18; structure and operation of local outlets, Chapter 19; and structure and operation of networks, Chapter 20.

People also invest time, experience, talent, and skill in radio-TV as employees. These individuals, too, hope to earn enough in salary and commissions to meet personal expenses as well as long-range savings goals. Many also enjoy the work, which is why they have chosen a career in radio-TV instead of brain surgery, corporate accounting, nuclear physics, or some other less demanding field. We look at careers in radio and television in Chapter 21.

CHAPTER 17

Sales and Advertising

In commercial radio and television, advertising revenues are vital. Advertising underwrites programming and supports operations. Advertising also generates profit, the whole point of running a commercial radio or television outlet. It is no coincidence that promotions to manager often go to those on the sales staff.

We begin this chapter with a discussion of advertising in general. Next we look at advertisers and advertising agencies. Then we focus on radio and television—time sales, advertising representatives, and network time sales.

17.1 ADVERTISING

The dictionary defines *advertising* as "the business of preparing and issuing public notices or announcements, usually paid for, as of things for sale, needs, etc." Most of us take advertising for granted. We encounter so much of it so often that we almost accept it as an inevitable part of the environment. But look at the nature of the basic transaction involved. It is *indirect*.

Consider, for example, radio and television advertising. A conventional advertising-supported radio or television medium uses programming to attract an audience, a process that generates considerable expense but no revenue. To earn revenue, the medium must sell time during the programming to an advertiser, who wishes to expose the medium's audience to commercial messages. After the medium airs the message, the advertiser can receive estimates of the audience for the message. The advertiser may even experience a change in sales.

The medium must *appeal* to the *audience*. That costs money for which there is no direct return. The medium must *earn revenue* from a third party, the *advertiser*. The advertiser usually has no direct measure of the message's effectiveness, no way to tell if commercial A led audience member B to purchase product C.

Two major types of commercial advertising are institutional and product. **Institutional advertising** attempts to have the public think of the advertiser in a certain positive way. **Product advertising,** a subset of *straight advertising* (Section 9.1.4.1), attempts to sell a specific commodity by creating a new market or by winning a bigger share or increasing the size of an existing market.

The advertising trade—the people who pay for and produce advertisements—consists of **advertisers, advertising agencies, sales representatives, the media,** and **specialty firms** (for example, research companies and media buying services). **Major advertising media** include newspapers, broadcast television, cable television, radio, magazines, direct mail, and outdoor (billboards and rental signs). **Minor media** include vehicles such as car cards, matchbook covers, subway posters, giveaways (pencils, pens, bumper stickers, and the like), and merchandising tie-ins (for example, shirts imprinted with a product's name, toy trucks with a real company's name on the trailer, toys and other items based on characters or incidents in movies or TV).

Advertisers, agencies, and media have formed trade organizations. Some of the important organizations include the following: American Advertising Federation, the American Association of Advertising Agencies, the Association of National Association of Broadcasters, and the National Cable Television Association.

The **American Advertising Federation** (AAF) represents all segments of the advertising industry—advertisers, media, agencies, advertising service companies, various media and advertising associations, and local advertising clubs. When a single voice must speak for advertising—to Congress, the Federal Trade Commission, or whatever—the AAF usually provides that voice.

The **Association of National Advertisers** (ANA) includes more than 300 major corporations comprising over 2000 companies that advertise products and services on a national basis. ANA provides informational, educational, and representational services for its members. It also works with other trade groups and the actors' unions to negotiate union contracts for talent in broadcast commercial production.

American Association of Advertising Agencies (AAAA), **National Association of Broadcasters,** and **National Cable Television Association** are the trade associations of advertising agencies, commercial broadcasting, and cable, respectively. In addition, **Radio Advertising Bureau** and **Television Bureau of Advertising** promote the broadcast media as advertising vehicles, while **Cabletelevision Advertising Bureau** does the same for cable.

The ANA, the AAAA, and the AAF all helped organize and support the National Advertising Review Board (Section 16.2.2). And the AAAA and the ANA founded the Advertising Research Foundation (ARF) in 1936 to encourage research in advertising. ARF has grown to include more than 300 advertiser, agency, media, research, association, academic, and international member organizations and institutions.

Advertising subsidizes (pays part of the cost of) many media outlets in the United States (Table 17.1). Advertising takes up about 60 percent of newspaper and magazine space, yet generates over 75 percent of their revenues. Advertising supports commercial broadcasting almost entirely. It contributes to the support of many national and regional program services distributed primarily by cable. Cable systems derive most revenue from subscriber fees but also sell advertising.

Some media derive almost total financial support directly from the audience. These include pay cable services (for example, premium and pay-per-view programming), records, books, and movies. Look carefully, however, and you will see that in some cases advertising has come to these media. As noted in Section 9.1.1, some pay cable programming does, indeed, carry advertising. Records, books, and movies carry advertising

Table 17.1 TOTAL U.S. ADVERTISING
EXPENDITURES (IN MILLIONS).

Newspapers		$3,788
Magazines		5,390
Business publications		2,231
Farm publications		166
Newspaper supplements		422
Outdoor		703
Television		17,210
Network	$8,814	
Spot	8,396	
Network cable TV		607
Radio		2,055
Network	609	
Spot	1,446	
Total		32,572

Table 17.1 Total U.S. advertising expenditures.
National advertisers spent over $35.5 billion in measured media in 1987. (*Measured* means that something—such as copies of magazines or viewers of programs—was counted by someone—such as an audience rating company.)
Source: Advertising Age.

in the form of promotional material for their own products. And although you pay $5 and up for a ticket, you still may have to sit through commercials in a movie theater!

17.1.1 Pros and Cons

In Section 9.5 we reviewed criticisms of radio and TV commercials. Critics also complain about advertising in general. Concerning content, they charge that advertising induces us to buy things we cannot afford and do not need, appeals primarily to emotions (rather than to intellect), is biased, makes conflicting claims about competitive products (have you ever seen a soap advertised as second best?), is repetitious, annoying, and forced on people. Some economists condemn advertising as wasteful and unnecessary, for adding to the cost of advertised products.

Social critics charge that advertising ma-

nipulates our lives, molds us, and makes us believe that consumption is a major goal of life, irrespective of social consequences. They say advertising emphasizes private and political interests at the expense of human and social interests.

Critics contend that advertising monopolizes consumer information, depriving the public of the diversity of opinion needed for informed choices. Many persons believe that advertisers, agencies, and media have no ethics; that the advertising trade uses any means, no matter how unscrupulous, and tells any story, no matter how untrue, to get us to buy products, no matter how shoddy or dangerous. Broadcast advertising, particularly television, receives special attention from critics for loudness, frequency, intrusiveness, clutter, and other complaints discussed in Section 9.5.

In reply, defenders say that advertising does not coerce. They remind that we as consumers must exercise judgment in the marketplace. They explain that advertising appeals to emotions because we are motivated largely by emotional drives, that advertising is out in the open (unlike some propaganda which is hidden), and that repetition is needed to reach those not reached previously.

Advertising, assert its defenders, really serves a desirable social purpose. Our economy is based on fast turnover of merchandise. Advertising "provides selective buying information, assures us of uniform quality, saves us time in shopping, helps to lower prices through mass production and mass selling techniques, improves our standard of living by educating us about new products, serves cultural and intellectual ends, as well as those of a purely material nature, and enables us to enjoy the mass media at small expense."[1] The advertising trade contends that all advertisers should not share the blame for the few who use poor taste and unethical practices. The trade points to rising standards and self-regulation efforts.

17.2 ADVERTISERS AND AGENCIES

We can classify advertisers into three categories based on marketing interest or scope—local, regional, and national. A **local advertiser** serves one community and aims advertising messages at the citizens of that community. For example, an automobile dealer's business comes primarily from the town in which the dealership is located; the dealer advertises in local media, to reach local people only.

A **regional advertiser** sells goods and services in more than one community, but not on a national basis. A regional brewery, for example, advertises beer only in the three states in which it is available.

A **national advertiser** distributes products nationally and advertises all over the country—for example, automobile manufacturers and nationally distributed beer. National advertisers often spend huge sums on advertising (Figure 17.1). During the late 1980s, Procter & Gamble spent so much that

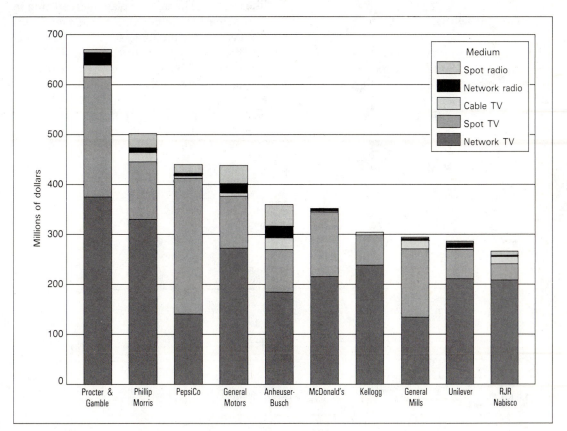

Figure 17.1 Ten largest electronic media advertisers. Huge sums, indeed. In 1988, for example, these ten companies alone spent nearly $4 billion in electronic media advertising. Their *total* advertising expenditure was even more; this figure does not reflect spending for newspapers, magazines, direct mail, and other nonelectronic advertising. (*Source: Advertising Age.*)

their yearly billings in cable and broadcast TV alone totaled well over two-thirds of a *billion* dollars.

Many advertisers, particularly local advertisers, deal directly with the media. Sometimes the medium prepares some or all advertising, as with the hardware store and the radio station in Section 9.3.1. Sometimes the local advertiser is large enough to have in-house advertising departments to plan campaigns, prepare newspaper layouts, write broadcast commercials, and buy space and time.

17.2.1 Advertising Agencies

Most large advertisers hire advertising agencies (Figure 17.2), firms that specialize in creation and placement of advertising. Actually, any size advertiser may use an agency, including our locally owned corner hardware store. Just as there are local, regional,

and national advertisers, so there are **local, regional, and national advertising agencies.**

The main products of an advertising agency are its services, evident from our look at agency operation in Section 9.3. These services include **creativity** (the ideas around which a campaign is built), **research and planning** (how best to get those ideas across in specific media), **supervision** (of production of materials and their use by media), and **media selection and buying.**

Oddly enough, most agency services come free to the client advertiser. It works like this: (1) The agency places advertising in the media for the client. (2) The client pays the agency for media space and time based on the media's full rate card (Section 18.1) prices. (3) The agency, in turn, pays the media full rate card prices minus a **15 percent commission.** If a broadcast station or cable system charges $1000, the agency collects $1000 from the advertiser and pays the

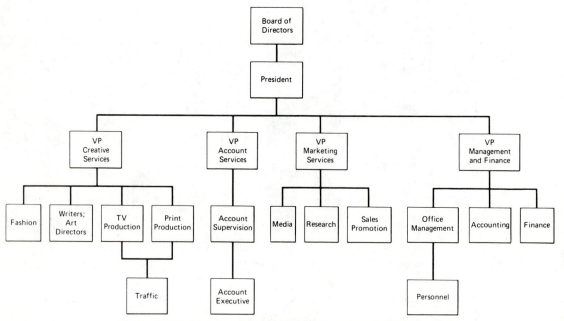

Figure 17.2 Full-service advertising agency organization chart.

medium $850. So, in effect, the media pay for these basic services.

Full-service agencies earn an average of about 75 percent of their income from media commissions. Clients pay the other 25 percent for materials and services used in preparing advertising—typography, filmed or taped commercials, printing, and subcontracted artwork and photography. Some agencies have dropped the commission system and operate entirely on a fee basis.

In addition to independent, full-service agencies, there are two other types of advertising agencies, house and boutique. When an advertiser establishes its own agency, it is called a **house agency.** The advertiser may run a house agency in an attempt to save the 15 percent commission or to get better, more efficient advertising. A **boutique agency** (or modular agency) sells each service separately. The client buys the specific service needed and usually pays on a fee basis.

Yet another specialist is the **media buying service.** Such an organization specializes in buying radio and television time, attempting to drive better bargains for its clients than agency media buyers.

17.2.2 Target Audiences

Most advertisers do not wish to reach all people. Instead, they want to reach only those who might be interested in buying their goods and services. These people are the target audience. The job of advertising research is to **identify and suggest means to reach the target audience**—describe its characteristics, specify media that will best reach it, and suggest approaches to persuade it to buy.

Crucial to identifying and reaching the target audience are the concepts of market, demographics, CPM, and efficiency. The trade uses the term **market** in two ways. First, it refers to specific cities and surrounding areas in which a product is sold. That regional brewery (Section 17.2), for example, is interested in reaching only the ten markets within the three state where its beer is sold.

Market also means prospective buyers for the product—who and where they are. This is where **demographics** come in. Demography is the statistical study of populations—how many persons there are in various age brackets, of each sex, who earn annual incomes of stated amounts, who have completed specific amounts of schooling, and so on. Analyses of population by age, sex, income, education, and other characteristics are called *demographic breakdowns* or simply *demographics*. Research can establish that a certain type of product should appeal to individuals who have certain characteristics. The advertising researcher studies the demographics of media usage to determine which media reach great numbers or high percentages of the persons to whom the product should appeal. Those are the media in which the product will be advertised most heavily.

Advertisers compare costs of media outlets by computing how much they would pay to reach 1000 persons. This is **CPM,** cost per thousand (M stands for *mille*, Latin for thousand). For example, a radio station may use a contemporary music format to gain top ratings and charge $27.50 to air a one-minute commercial. Another station may program country music and charge only $18. The country station seems less expensive. But the contemporary station reaches 5000 persons, whereas the country station reaches only 3000. The contemporary station's CPM is $5.50 ($27.50 ÷ 5 = $5.50); the country station's, $6.00 ($18 ÷ 3 = $6.00). So the contemporary station is really less expensive.

The lowest CPM is not always best, however. If a farm tractor manufacturer were to advertise on the contemporary station, the audience might contain a high percentage of persons with no interest in buying tractors.

This is **waste circulation.** On the other hand, the country station's audience might be packed with potential tractor buyers. Here, the tractor manufacturer would find the country station more efficient—less waste circulation and a lower CPM (based on target audience).

CPM is difficult to use across media, however. The "M" represents different things in different media. In radio, it usually stands for thousands of persons reached. In broadcast television, it can mean thousands of persons or households. In newspapers and magazines M denotes number of copies sold; but two or more persons often read one copy, so the M is no indication of the number exposed to an advertisement.

17.3 LOCAL TIME SALES

At the local level, the broadcast station or cable system must sell itself as an advertising medium to merchants, businesses, and advertising agencies in its community. This is the job of the sales staff.

In broadcasting, the sales staff is usually an integral part of the station. Some cable systems, however, contract with outside firms that specialize in selling local cable advertising. In the following section, the discussion focuses on "in-house" sales departments, although most of the points also apply to contract sales units.

17.3.1 Sales Staff

The **sales manager** is a key figure in radio and television. A major executive answering directly to the general manager, the sales manager supervises the local sales staff and maintains liaison with the sales representative firm (in larger operations there may be assistants for each of these functions). The sales manager may also oversee the traffic department (Section 17.3.2).

The **local sales staff** attempts to convince businesses in the community to buy advertising time. Before they buy, advertisers are **prospects;** afterwards, **clients.** Staffers usually sell **availabilities,** small segments (60 seconds or less) of time in which commercial announcements are run. Occasionally, they sell **sponsorship** of a program.

The sales job does not end when a client signs a contract. The salesperson oversees in-house handling of the client's advertising and periodically checks back with the client to improve the schedule and ensure satisfaction. This sale plus follow-through is **servicing the account,** and media outlets call their sales personnel **account executives.**

The sales manager holds a staff meeting at least once a week—often daily—to exchange ideas and monitor activities. In these meetings, the sales manager points out new prospects, listens to problems and suggests solutions, explains policy and procedures, describes the company's competitive position among media in the area, and encourages greater sales effort. The sales manager may also work with individual salespersons, even accompany them on sales calls, when more experience and ability to bargain are needed.

The sales manager is paid a salary plus a percentage of total station sales. Compensation arrangements for salespersons vary with the company; all involve a commission (percentage of individual sales)—straight commission, salary plus commission, and draw (in which the salesperson receives a regular salary but must sell a minimum dollar amount of advertising) plus commission. The sales manager assigns each salesperson a quota, the minimum revenue the salesperson has to bring in. The sales manager assigns a client list to a new salesperson, but the salesperson is expected to expand the list, adding new clients or persuading old ones to buy more advertising.

17.3.2 Tools for Selling

A good salesperson makes maximum use of available tools and resources. One tool is the **rate card,** a list of the cost to advertise in the outlet under various conditions (Section 18.1). The salesperson must know the rates backward and forward and be ready to suggest an advertising schedule that meets the client's needs and budget.

A second tool is **ratings.** The salesperson has to understand ratings thoroughly—their meaning, their limitations, their demographic breakdown. Only one outlet in town can have the largest audience. But others may have the largest audience at certain key times, or the largest number of women 18 to 34 years old, or the largest black audience, or some other salable feature. The salesperson must know this information to show the prospect how the outlet is a must-buy for reaching potential customers or a more efficient buy than competing outlets (as with the country station and the tractor manufacturer in Section 17.2.2).

Where ratings are concerned, cable system sales personnel operate at somewhat of a disadvantage. Broadcast-style rating methodologies are not always appropriate for cable (Section 18.2.10). Cable sales personnel can sometimes finesse the lack of audience data by offering prospects the chance to advertise on television at radio prices. They also emphasize the opportunity to target audiences precisely. A client's advertising circulates only to the franchise area (local broadcast advertisers may pay for waste circulation because many station signals spill over to other towns). And the client can reach customers directly by placing advertising in complementary programming contexts (a sporting goods store, for example, could buy local availabilities in Lifetime and ESPN).

A third tool is **knowledge of the outlet and the market.** The salesperson must know information such as potential audience (signal coverage or cable penetration), production capabilities, who buys what and where they shop for it, and strengths and weaknesses of rival media.

A fourth tool consists of outlet-supplied **support resources.** For example, the salesperson depends on the traffic department to schedule client advertising properly. The outlet may provide personal computers with special software—from programs that suggest advertising schedules to on-line (connected by telephone line) research services that provide custom-tailored analyses of audience life-style and purchasing patterns. Larger outlets create sales-support departments to prepare material for and help salespersons.

A fifth tool is the help of **advertising media trade organizations**—Cabletelevision Advertising Bureau, Radio Advertising Bureau, and Television Advertising Bureau. They supply member outlets with direct sales aids—sales ideas, case histories, examples of effective commercials, statistics on the dimensions of their respective media. They also conduct seminars to improve skills of members' local sales personnel. They work with major advertisers and agencies, selling them on their respective media.

17.3.3 Art of Sales

One of the most creative jobs in radio and television is sales. It is an art. True, there are sales personnel whose primary approach is to wander into a prospect's place of business and ask, "Wanna buy some time today?" These people are rarely successful. A good salesperson sells not time but (1) **radio or**

television advertising (2) on **a particular outlet.** The salesperson must match the outlet's capabilities and resources to the prospect's advertising needs, then demonstrate that match to the prospect.

17.3.3.1 An Educational Process

At the local level, the salesperson often has to start from scratch, educating the retailer on the value—perhaps even the existence!—of local radio or television advertising. If the retailer has advertised, it has probably been in the newspaper. Newspaper advertising is tangible; the retailer can admire the proofs or tear sheets and post copies all over the establishment. Radio and television advertising is ephemeral; it has nothing the retailer can hold. The salesperson must expand the retailer's view of advertising, educate the retailer away from any print-only, tangible-copy orientation.

Even the best sales job rarely persuades a prospect to increase the advertising budget to include radio or television. More often, the successful salesperson uses the educational process to convince the retailer to divert part of the advertising budget from some other medium—usually the newspaper—and put it in the station or cable system.

The educational process must often include *how* to use broadcast advertising. For example, Thursday newspapers usually contain supermarket advertising. Each ad lists dozens of items and prices. The homemaker can browse the newspaper food section to see which store has the best prices. Some supermarket managers expect radio and television advertising to do the same thing; they want direct conversion of their newspaper ads to electronic media—lists of products and prices. Consumers cannot browse commercials, and "list" commercials are largely ineffective. The salesperson has to convince the manager to use commercials to advertise a few items or some special feature—such as a special sale, the fine quality of the store's meat, or the ease and convenience of shopping at the store.

17.3.3.2 The Presentation

The salesperson's formal proposal to a prospect is the *presentation*. Considerable preparation goes into this presentation. Before beginning to assemble the presentation, the salesperson visits and gets to know the prospect. They discuss marketing and advertising aims and problems, but no attempt is made to sell time. The salesperson researches the prospect's business—notes best-selling lines and features, observes customer types, and tracks sales and advertising patterns. Using this research and the various selling tools, the salesperson puts together a package of plans and materials to show how advertising on the station or cable system would help achieve goals and reach consumers. This is the presentation.

The presentation often takes the form of a booklet. It may contain specific suggestions of how and when to advertise on the outlet, recommendations on how to tie that advertising with other advertising (even suggesting additional advertising on other radio or television outlets or in other media!), cost breakdowns, sample scripts, success stories of similar businesses that have used the outlet, and standard promotional material adapted to fit the particular prospect (for example, coverage maps and ratings data showing how the outlet reaches the prospect's customers). The salesperson talks through the booklet with the prospect. Accompanying materials may include a tape or a storyboard of a commercial done on **spec** (speculation, hoping to get the sale).

17.3.3.3 Sale and Service

Chances are, the sale will not be closed at this point. The salesperson may have to return several times, work with the retailer to revise the plan, bring the sales manager along on a call, or even bring the prospect to the studio for a tour and red-carpet treatment.

Once the contract has been signed, the salesperson must service the account (Section 17.3.1). A radio or television salesperson sells a service; clients who get that service tend to remain clients.

17.3.4 Tradeout and Barter as Sales

If based on the rate card and retail prices, tradeout and barter (Section 9.1.6.6) are perfectly ethical. Some firms specialize in barter on a national basis; they offer anything—automobiles, furniture, vacations—in return for which they put the outlet's availabilities into their time bank (Section 9.1.6.6). Too much barter and tradeout cause cash flow problems; employees and creditors prefer to receive payment in legal tender rather than movie tickets, car washes, and McDonald's coupons.

17.3.5 Impact of Barter Syndication on Sales

Barter syndicators make their money from advertising sales (Section 7.3.2.1). They *give* the programming to local outlets; sometimes they even *pay* outlets in top-10 markets to carry their programming. This makes barter programming sound like a good deal, but it does have drawbacks. It **reduces salable inventory** (total number of availabilities). That could *cost* an outlet money (Box 17.1). Also, in both barter syndication and time banking, the contract may specify that the **outlet owes the full amount of commercial time, whether or not the programming is used.** Cancellation of a barter series could result in many "free" spots.

Additionally, television station licensees and their reps (who sell spot advertising for stations; Section 17.4) have expressed concern over the **effect of barter syndication on national spot advertising revenue.** As a national advertising vehicle, barter yields basically the same result as network and national spot—national advertising runs on local stations. So when a national advertiser invests in barter, where does the money come from? Barter syndicators say that most advertising dollars they attract come from money that would otherwise have gone to the networks. Reps and some station executives contend that barter takes money away from spot advertising budgets.

17.3.6 Per Inquiry Advertising

Per inquiry (PI; Section 9.1.6.5) can be an excellent revenue producer. Some PI advertisers, for example, give a television station a standing order for all unsold inventory. The station then runs the ad for record albums or kitchenware or whatever in any availability not otherwise purchased. And the revenue earned by the station usually equals or even exceeds the comparable grid cost (Section 18.1.2) for the time.

17.3.7 Time Brokering

In time brokering, the outlet sells large blocks of time to a third party, the broker, at a discounted rate. The broker, in turn, resells segments of the time to advertisers at a higher rate and pockets the difference. The outlet then runs the advertising. The broker is usually an independent contractor, not an employee of the station. A radio time broker may even program the brokered time block. In broadcasting, however, the licensee is still responsible for everything transmitted and

Box 17.1 How an Outlet Can Lose Money with a "Free" Program

Let's say the local outlet is a VHF television station in a growing, dynamic market. The station normally sells out at close to 100 percent of inventory in most dayparts. In one of these dayparts, a syndicated half-hour series is about to end, and the station needs to find another to replace it.

The choice narrows down to two series, both about the same quality. Both have an inventory of $6\frac{1}{2}$ minutes (thirteen 30-second slots) of commercial time. One is a straight cash deal; the station would get the entire $6\frac{1}{2}$ minutes but would have to pay $2,750 per episode.

The other possibility is a barter series. The syndicator takes six 30-second slots for national advertising, leaving seven availabilities for the station. Of course the station pays no money for the program.

In this particular daypart, the station sales staff can get at least $750 per 30-second availability. So, we can figure the revenue for the cash series as follows:

$$\$750 \times 13 = \$9,750$$

But we must deduct the syndication payment:

$$\$9,750 - \$2,750 = \$7,000$$

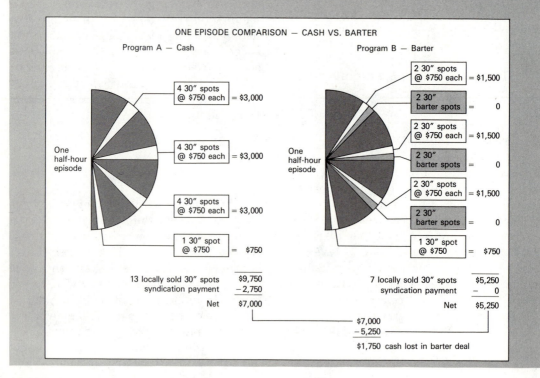

How much would the station make from the barter program? We figure the revenue as follows:

$$\$750 \times 7 = \$5,250$$

Wait a minute. The net figures are $7,000 per program from the cash series and $5,250 from the barter series? That means our "free" program would actually *cost* us *$1,750!*

The choices a program director faces are not usually so clear-cut as in this example. We have assumed that both series had about the same quality. But it is entirely possible that a certain barter program is just what the station needs to be competitive in a particular daypart; nothing as good is available from cash syndication sources. In that case, the barter program may well be worth the "extra" $1,750. We have also assumed that the station does well financially. If, however, the station were just getting started, or had cash-flow problems, or consistently had leftover inventory in the daypart in question—then the barter show might be the better choice.

so must monitor and maintain control of the programming.

17.3.8 Leased Cable Channels

A cable system operator may lease a whole channel to another party. The other party then programs the channel, sells time on it, or whatever. Some firms, for example, have leased cable channels and used them to carry exclusively, or to experiment with effectiveness of, advertising. Here, the cable system's situation resembles that of a common carrier. The system operator does not control programming so the leasing party is responsible for content.

17.4 THE REP

In spot advertising, the advertiser "spots" commercials around by choosing specific markets, media outlets, programs, and time periods that deliver the desired audience (Section 9.1.5.4). National and regional spot advertising account for more than 20 percent of all radio station revenue and more than 50 percent of all television station revenue.

This brings up the question of how a local outlet gets spot business. Ideally, the outlet would hire a person just to sell time to advertisers and agencies. That would be impossible. First, each spot advertiser would be inundated with thousands of salespersons, each working for a different outlet. Second, spot advertisers and their agencies are spread among nearly all the large cities in the country; a radio or television outlet would have to keep one full-time salesperson in New York, another in Los Angeles, a third in Chicago, and so on. This would be economically absurd for all but the largest group-owned stations and cable multiple-system operators. Instead, outlets contract with **advertising representatives—"reps"** for short.

Reps are **independent firms that attempt to persuade spot advertisers to buy time on client outlets** (Figure 17.3). Reps must be able to provide advertisers with immediate

Figure 17.3 Major broadcast rep firms.

and current information on rates and availabilities. Each rep has branch offices in various major advertising centers and represents many outlets. National reps have offices in at least three of the largest markets; regional reps, fewer. The national trade organization for broadcast reps is the **Station Representatives Association.**

Reps work on a commission basis. Reps for radio and most cable systems receive 15 percent of the advertising revenues they generate. Television station reps receive anywhere from 8 or 9 to 15 percent, the percentage decreasing as station market size increases. Some reps supply additional services to client stations, providing advice, research, and materials on everything from sales and promotion to management and programming.

The sales manager or national sales manager maintains nearly constant contact with a rep, advising on availabilities, sending copies of station promotional material, notifying of changes in rates and programming, ensuring that the rep is doing the job in representing the outlet to national and regional advertisers.

17.4.1 Trends in Station Representation

Three developments in broadcast station representation should be noted. One is the **house rep** or **self-representation,** terms used when a group licensee sets up a national sales department at the corporate level to represent stations in the group.

A second development is the **spot network,** also called the **unwired network.** A spot network is not interconnected and carries no common programming. It is a group of stations in various communities put together by a rep to make spot advertising easier for the advertiser to buy. The unwired network may consist solely of the organizing rep's client stations. A smaller rep may add nonclient stations, particularly in important markets where the rep has no clients. One primary aim of a spot network is convenience. The advertiser signs one contract and receives and pays a single bill from the rep. Some spot networks also feature flexibility; a rep may organize spot radio networks on a state-by-state basis, so a regional advertiser could reach, for example, the Kansas agriculture market. The spot network may also be a bargain; when television network and barter advertising time gets scarce and expensive, some national advertisers try to negotiate with rep firms for better prices on unwired TV networks.

The third development involves **multistation representation.** Originally, broadcast reps handled only one station in any given market to avoid representing direct competitors. During the 1970s, the number of stations per market increased dramatically. There was no commensurate increase in the number of reps; several existing rep companies restricted their client lists, merged, or went out of business. As a result, many radio stations found it difficult to get good representation. Radio reps eased the problem somewhat by representing several noncompeting (appealing to different target audiences) stations in one market. Television reps did somewhat the same. Typically, a TV rep formed two competing divisions, one that would represent network affiliates; the other, independent stations.

17.4.2 Cable Interconnects

An interconnect groups nearby cable systems as a single advertising buy for regional and national advertisers. A rep handles sales for the interconnect.

Typically, an interconnect ties together systems in contiguous or nearby urban and suburban franchise areas. A **hard interconnect** links them together by microwave network or coaxial cable. The interconnect downlinks advertiser-supported cable networks, inserts commercials in the **local windows** (availabilities within network programming for use by affiliates), and distributes them to the interconnected systems. The systems receive compensation, free network-produced programming, a division of the interconnect's profits, or some combination thereof.

A **soft interconnect** parallels an unwired network in broadcasting. There is no electrical interconnection. Instead, a rep has power to sell availabilities on the whole group of systems or any one system.

17.5 SELLING NETWORK TIME

The business of network sales is more than simply that of local outlet sales writ large—much more. A major complicating factor for networks involves their relationship with affiliated local outlets. First, networks compete with their own affiliates. Both networks and stations go after the national advertising dollar.

Second, networks *need* affiliates. A network without affiliates could reach no audience, could make no money, would be no network. This dependency functions in but one direction. A local outlet can exist—even thrive—without network affiliation. Many broadcast stations do just that. Even cable systems, given the franchise monopoly most enjoy, could probably survive without networks.

Satellite or optical fiber technology may eventually alter this relationship. Network programmers could send signals directly to individual homes (in which case they would no longer be networks!). At this writing, however, the traditional network-affiliate relationship is in place and a major background element in network sales.

17.5.1 Television Broadcast Networks

In television broadcast network time sales, stakes are high and competition is fierce. Programming, overhead, everything in television networking is expensive. Returns can more than justify the investment, so each network attempts to sell 100 percent of inventory.

Some advertisers still invest in **sponsorship** (Section 9.1.2.2), usually sponsoring specials. Most network advertising, however, is done on a **participation** basis (Section 9.1.2.3)—the network provides the programs and advertisers buy availabilities within those programs. Formal rate cards are rare. Prices are based roughly on ratings, season of the year, and time of day.

Network inventory is sold in three ways—up-front, scatter, and opportunistic. Each spring the networks announce their program schedules for the following fall. Heavy network advertisers wish to reserve the best availabilities, so their advertising agencies begin bargaining with network sales personnel right away. This is **up-front** buying. The agency buyer purchases specific commercial positions in specific weekly program series.

On conclusion of up-front buying, the rest of the network inventory goes on the **scatter** market. Here the buyer purchases any combination of availabilities. The purchase may be a continuing position in a weekly series for several months, or it may be a number of positions scattered over the entire schedule for a week or two.

As air dates draw closer, the networks drop prices of unsold positions. Agency buyers can often pick up good positions at bargain prices. This is **opportunistic** buying.

17.5.2 Radio Broadcast Networks

The purchase of radio network time is less frantic, less expensive, and more flexible than that of television. There are no "new seasons" in radio networks.

In radio, most availabilities are in news, sports, commentary, features, or, in some of the newer networks, music. The buyer can buy sponsorship or participation advertising, fixed position, or run-of-schedule. Prices vary by time of day, number of affiliates, size and type of audience, and other factors. Network radio is difficult to sell to new clients; most agency buyers prefer to invest in television broadcast networks to reach large numbers of persons and in spot radio to reach specific audiences.

17.5.3 Cable Networks

Sales on some advertising-supported cable networks are similar to those for radio networks. They target narrowly defined audiences (relative to those of the broadcast TV networks), often with cyclical or repetitive programming, such as that of Cable News Network and MTV. They schedule no weekly entertainment series and no fall "season" in which to introduce new and returning shows. There is little in the way of upfront and scatter buying of these channels.

Other cable networks, however, schedule broad-appeal programming and compete head-on with the broadcast networks for audience. These include some of cable's most successful program services, such as Superstation WTBS and USA Network. Such channels elicited a nascent "season"—bolstered by increases in original programming, audiences, and advertiser investment—which fostered time-buying patterns that increasingly paralleled those of the broadcast networks.

17.5.4 Compensation

Broadcast stations derive most revenue from sale of advertising time; when they **give up time to network programming that contains advertising,** they expect to be paid. Therefore, networks share advertising revenues with affiliated stations. The affiliates' share is *compensation.* The rate of compensation is specified in the contract (Section 20.1.2) between network and station and is usually based on some percentage of the affiliate's network hourly rate. This rate is determined by negotiation between station and network and is specified in the affiliation contract. The percentage varies by daypart (for example, 30–32 percent for the 6:00–11:00 p.m. period). The program rate varies with factors such as size of the station's mar-

ket and the affiliate's competitive position within that market. An affiliate sends monthly reports to the network listing each network program and commercial carried; the network pays the affiliate based on this report. During the late 1980s, ABC, CBS, and NBC all worked to reduce compensation payments as one means to reduce network expenses (Section 20.1.2).

Radio compensation involves much less money than television. Radio networks pay monetary compensation to large-market affiliates. In smaller markets, the **compensation may be the programming itself and local windows** (Section 17.4.2).

Most advertising-supported cable networks do not compensate the cable systems that carry them. They charge a cable operator to carry their signals, typically 10–20 cents a subscriber a month. This might seem unfair, but keep in mind the origins of cash flow. Cable systems earn most money from subscribers' fees. The operator touts to prospective subscribers the number and variety of channels on the system. Thus, advertising-supported cable networks do not *deprive* a cable operator of revenue-producing *time;* instead they **contribute to the revenue-producing *value* of the system.** In addition, the networks carry local-window availabilities that affiliates may sell to advertisers.

The pattern does vary. Some religion-oriented services come to the operator free of charge. Direct-response marketing channels come free and even pay a percentage of all sales made in the operator's franchise area. A few ad-supported networks pay their affiliates—for example, a one-time incentive stipend to a system when it first affiliates. Occasionally, a network that has increased its advertising revenues reduces affiliate rates or even pays affiliates. Networks that make affiliate payments often avoid the term "compensation," instead using "support package," "incentive," or "bonus package" and tying it to promotional and satellite reception expenses.

NOTE

1. Edwin Emery, Phillip H. Ault, and Warren K. Agee, *Introduction to Mass Comunications* (New York: Dodd 1965), 163–164.

FURTHER READING

Barr, David Samuel. *Advertising on Cable: A Practical Guide for Advertisers.* Englewood Cliffs: Prentice, 1985.

Berkman, Harold W., and Christopher Gilson. *Advertising: Concepts and Strategies.* 2d ed. New York: Random, 1987.

Berman, Ronald. *Advertising and Social Change.* Beverly Hills: Sage, 1981. Influence on society and individuals.

Bovée, Courtland L., and William F. Arens. *Contemporary Advertising.* 2d ed. Homewood: Irwin, 1986. All aspects.

Eicoff, Al. *Eicoff on Broadcast Direct Marketing.* Lincolnwood: National, 1988. Direct-response commercials.

Fox, Stephen R. *The Mirror Makers: A History of American Advertising and Its Creators.* New York: Vintage, 1987.

Heighton, Elizabeth J., and Don R. Cunningham. *Advertising in the Broadcast and Cable Media.* 2d ed. Belmont: Wadsworth, 1984. Comprehensive; uses and techniques.

Jones, Kensinger, et al. *Cable Advertising: New Ways to New Business.* Englewood Cliffs: Prentice, 1984.

Kaatz, Ronald B. *Cable Advertiser's Handbook.* 2d ed. Lincolnwood: Crain, 1985.

Schudson, Michael. *Advertising, the Uneasy Persuasion: Its Dubious Impact on American Society.* New York: Basic, 1985.

Warner, Charles. *Broadcast and Cable Selling.* Belmont: Wadsworth, 1986. Sales procedures and techniques.

White, Bart, and N. Doyle Satterthwaite. *But First These Messages . . . The Selling of Broadcast Advertising.* Boston: Allyn, 1989. Text on broadcast sales.

Zeigler, Sherilyn K., and Herbert H. Howard. *Broadcast Advertising: A Comprehensive Working Textbook.* 2d ed. Ames: Iowa State UP, 1984. Introductory treatment.

CHAPTER 18

Rates and Ratings

You have probably heard someone say (or even said yourself), "They're canceling my favorite television program! How can they do that? Everybody I know likes it!" Or, "My favorite radio station is changing formats! Why?"

More than likely, in both cases, the answer lies in rates and rating. A *rate* is the amount of money a commercial station, cable system, or network charges to run an announcement or a sponsored program. A *rating* is an estimate of audience size. An advertiser pays a rate for a segment of radio or television time. A rating reports the approximate number who saw or heard that segment. Rate and rating are used to determine advertising formulas, such as CPM (Section 17.2.2).

In this chapter we discuss both rates and ratings. We first look at the rate card and its variables. Then we examine rating terms, methods, and companies.

18.1 THE RATE CARD

An advertising-supported medium publishes a rate card. The card lists the cost to advertise in the medium under various conditions. Conditions include factors such as length or size, frequency, and placement of the ad. The local salesperson or the medium's rep (Section 17.4) uses the rate card to show a potential client exactly what the per-advertisement cost would be in any situation.

18.1.1 Radio Station Rate Cards

A radio station's **base rate** is usually what the station charges to broadcast a one-minute commercial one time, often in a specific daypart (Section 7.1). Most advertisers, however, qualify for discounts of one kind or another, and so few really pay the base rate. The base rate, then, is just that—a base from which to figure the various discounts for which an advertiser may be eligible.

The rate discounts a radio station lists on its rate card (Figure 18.1) are **variables.** One such variable is length; a station's rate varies according to the **lengths of time** the advertiser buys. For example, a 30-second availability (place for a commercial) costs 80 to 90 percent of the one-minute rate; a 10-second availability, 50 to 65 percent; sponsorship of a 5-minute feature or news program, one and a fraction times the 1-minute rate.

Rates also vary by **time of day.** In most

WRUF-FM ROCK 104 100,000 watts 24 hours
COMMISSIONABLE RATES

	Level I		Level II		Level III		Level IV		Level V	
	30s	60s	30s	60s	30s	60s	30s	60s	30s	60s
6 times	$105.00	$110.00	$99.00	$102.00	$91.00	$94.00	$75.00	$78.00	$59.00	$62.00
12 times	$102.00	$107.00	$95.00	$99.00	$87.00	$91.00	$71.00	$75.00	$55.00	$59.00
18 times	$99.00	$103.00	$92.00	$95.00	$84.00	$87.00	$68.00	$71.00	$52.00	$55.00
24 times	$96.00	$100.00	$89.00	$92.00	$81.00	$84.00	$65.00	$68.00	$49.00	$52.00
500 times	$93.00	$97.00	$86.00	$89.00	$78.00	$81.00	$62.00	$65.00	$46.00	$49.00

Combo Rate For WRUF-AM 85 and ROCK 104 Is 150 Percent of Applicable FM Rate

**News, Sports, Remote Broadcasts and Special Program Rates On Request.
NOTE: Two-Week Written Notice Required For Cancellation Of Buy.
Rates Effective July 1, 1988.**

*Maximum Two Spots Per Hour Per Client.
All Commercials Are Preemptable By Higher Rate.*

Figure 18.1 Radio station rate card. (*Source:* WRVF. Used by permission.)

cases the radio station chooses the exact time when commercials run, but the advertiser may specify the daypart. Stations charge the highest rate for dayparts with the largest audience, usually drive times. Rate cards list these as "AAA" time or something similar. Smaller stations may combine all nonpeak time under one rate; others divide remaining hours by audience levels and price them accordingly. Stations in the smallest markets often do not differentiate among dayparts and charge a single rate. Some stations in large markets use a grid rate card, similar to the television rate cards described below.

Radio stations also sell availabilities scattered through different time periods—ROS, BTA, or TAP (Section 9.1.2.3). They usually charge more for specific positions—for example, 4:45 p.m. every weekday afternoon, or immediately after the 6:00 p.m. sports report.

Small- and medium-market radio stations may issue two rate cards—one each for **local** and **spot** (Section 17.4) rates. A station receives national and regional spot sales revenue with 15 percent deducted by advertising agencies (Section 17.2.1) and another 15 percent due out for the rep (Section 17.4). The station raises rates for spot advertising to get a return comparable to that from local advertising. This higher rate structure is the spot rate card. Many stations, however, use one card and charge the same rate for both local and spot sales.

18.1.2 Television Station Rate Cards

Compared with radio, television stations charge more for availabilities and tend to price more by time of day. This results from television's generally higher audience levels and the greater fluctuation of those levels from program to program. Television rate cards typically list specific commerical slots—dayparts and programs—each with

its own price for availabilities (Box 18.1). They have no ROS rate but may offer rotations (Section 9.1.2.3). Most television stations use one card for both local and spot sales.

The 30-second availability is standard in broadcast television. A 60-second availability costs double the 30-second rate; an ID (10-second availability), 50 percent; and stand-alone 15s, around 70 percent. Advertisers can buy program positions at vastly discounted rates.

Television rate cards list prices in a **grid** pattern. The list of commercial slots forms one axis of the grid; grid *positions* form the other axis. Dollar amounts fill the grid field, and the number of grid positions determines the number of prices for each commercial slot. With this arrangement, each slot often has five or six prices, in decreasing amounts down the grid.

A station uses the grid to adjust prices in response to supply and demand. For any given quarter (three-month period), the sales manager (Section 17.3.1) designates a grid position for each commercial slot as the price for availabilities in that slot. Advertisers buy, decreasing the supply of availabilities for the quarter. This makes the remaining availabilities more valuable, and the sales manager designates a higher grid position. Availabilities in high-demand slots cost the most and get the greatest number of upward grid adjustments. Availabilities in low-demand slots cost the least, and their cost rarely or never moves up.

18.1.3 Cable System Rate Cards

As discussed in Section 17.3.2, cable systems often sell on the basis of "television advertising at radio prices." The cable system rate card (Figure 18.2) may even undercut some radio stations in town. As in broadcast television, the 30-second availability is standard.

Box 18.1 Deciphering the Television Station Avails Sheet

Many television stations use a computer-generated avails sheet instead of a traditional rate card. As a station's inventory of availabilities decreases, the station increases prices (Section 18.1.2) and issues another avails sheet.

The multi-page avails sheet lists all programs and time periods that contain local availabilities. Each listing consists of a single price ("COST") and information concerning audience levels. Look, for example, at the second listing on the above avails sheet, "MON–FRI 700A–900A." It gives information on avails for *Good Morning America* (GMA). Check the far right column of the entry, and you see that this hypothetical small-market ABC affiliate sells local availabilities during *GMA* for $90. Check the three middle columns of that entry, and you see rating, share, and cost-per-rating point (CPP; the rating divided into the cost of the avail) figures for a *GMA* avail. The first of those columns is headed "ADI H H (RTG)"; the figures for our entry indicate *GMA* reaches about 8 percent of all households in the ADI (Sections 18.2.1 and 18.2.3), which constitute about 48 percent of all households using television at that time, and that the CPP is $11.25 ($90 ÷ 8). The other two columns contain similar information about persons age 18 years and older ("PRSNS 18+ (RTG)") and women age 25 through 54 years ("WOMEN 25–54 (RTG)"), respectively.

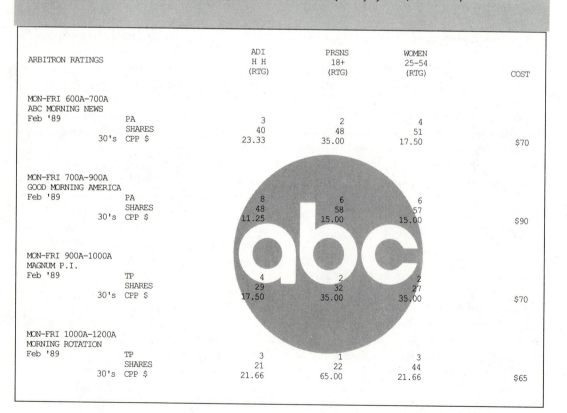

ARBITRON RATINGS		ADI H H (RTG)	PRSNS 18+ (RTG)	WOMEN 25–54 (RTG)	COST
MON–FRI 600A–700A ABC MORNING NEWS					
Feb '89	PA SHARES	3 40	2 48	4 51	
30's	CPP $	23.33	35.00	17.50	$70
MON–FRI 700A–900A GOOD MORNING AMERICA					
Feb '89	PA SHARES	8 48	6 58	6 57	
30's	CPP $	11.25	15.00	15.00	$90
MON–FRI 900A–1000A MAGNUM P.I.					
Feb '89	TP SHARES	4 29	2 32	2 27	
30's	CPP $	17.50	35.00	35.00	$70
MON–FRI 1000A–1200A MORNING ROTATION					
Feb '89	TP SHARES	3 21	1 22	3 44	
30's	CPP $	21.66	65.00	21.66	$65

For internal purposes, the station may utilize an unpublished rate-card-type grid of price differentials. Using our *GMA* example, the $90 price listed on the avails sheet would constitute Section 1 on the station's internally used grid. In bargaining to make a sale, an account executive might be able to let a *GMA* avail go as low as $80 without having to secure approval from management; that would be Section 2. Management might approve a price as low as $70; that would be Section 3. When sold as part of a package—perhaps some type of TAP or impact deal (Section 9.1.2.3)—the cost might be $65; that would be Section 4. And if any *GMA* avails remained unsold, they might be included in an ROS (Section 9.1.2.3) contract at $40; that would be Section 5. When an advertiser buys an avail at a price less than that on the avails sheet, another advertiser may purchase that same avail at a higher price; the station then may give the first advertiser opportunity to pay more and keep the avail or reschedule the commercial for a later date.

As in radio, price variables may include ROS, BTA, TAP (Section 9.1.2.3), and fixed position.

A cable system's rate card typically resembles a radio grid card. The card lays out prices in rows and columns—six rows corresponding to six grid positions, and columns that correspond to dayparts. Other grid columns may list TAP and ROS prices. Where the system affiliates with an interconnect (Section 17.4.1), the card may have multiple grids—one for just the local system and the others for various combinations of systems on the interconnect.

For sales purposes, cable dayparts may not parallel those of either radio or broadcast television. One scheme, for example, divides cable availabilities into the following three dayparts (in ascending order of cost): 6:00 a.m.–noon, noon–6:00 p.m., and prime time, 6:00 p.m.–1:00 a.m.

Unlike their counterparts in radio and broadcast television, cable sales executives deal in multiple channels. These include advertising-supported local origination channels, automated channels, classified-advertising channels, and local windows on national cable networks. Clients can buy availabilities in one or any combination, but the grid position may vary by channel.

18.1.4 Off the Card

Media buyers (Section 17.2.1) routinely attempt to buy both television and radio station time at prices below those on the rate card. And some stations may, indeed, sell below their published rates. The stimulus to sell off the card may come from any of several factors, such as how much the station needs the business, how much management wants that particular account, and how much total money is involved. Sometimes station personnel suggest the lower price. If a local salesperson cannot sell a prospect at rate card prices and the station needs the money, the salesperson may offer the prospect a cut rate.

The simplest way to sell below published prices is to cut rates without publishing a new rate card. But there are other ways, including plugola (Section 9.1.6.7) and payola (Section 9.1.6.9). Per-inquiry advertising (Section 9.1.6.5) and tradeout (Section 9.1.6.6) are both potentially rate-cutting

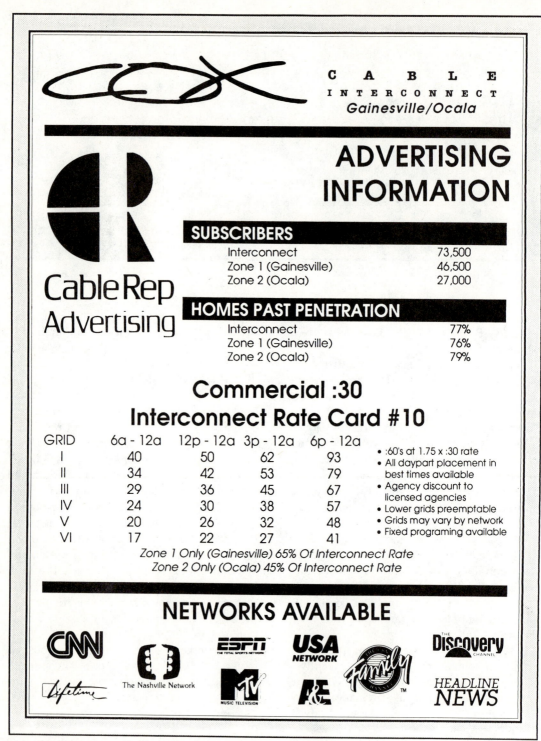

COX

CABLE
INTERCONNECT
Gainesville/Ocala

Cable Rep Advertising

ADVERTISING INFORMATION

SUBSCRIBERS

Interconnect	73,500
Zone 1 (Gainesville)	46,500
Zone 2 (Ocala)	27,000

HOMES PAST PENETRATION

Interconnect	77%
Zone 1 (Gainesville)	76%
Zone 2 (Ocala)	79%

Commercial :30
Interconnect Rate Card #10

GRID	6a - 12a	12p - 12a	3p - 12a	6p - 12a
I	40	50	62	93
II	34	42	53	79
III	29	36	45	67
IV	24	30	38	57
V	20	26	32	48
VI	17	22	27	41

- :60's at 1.75 x :30 rate
- All daypart placement in best times available
- Agency discount to licensed agencies
- Lower grids preemptable
- Grids may vary by network
- Fixed programing available

Zone 1 Only (Gainesville) 65% Of Interconnect Rate
Zone 2 Only (Ocala) 45% Of Interconnect Rate

NETWORKS AVAILABLE

CNN · The Nashville Network · ESPN THE TOTAL SPORTS NETWORK · USA NETWORK · Family · DISCOVERY CHANNEL · Lifetime · MTV MUSIC TELEVISION · A&E · HEADLINE NEWS

Figure 18.2 Cable system rate card. (Courtesy of Cable Rep Advertising. Used by permission.)

transactions. In Chapter 16 we looked at other practices, the result of which was to cut rates, for example, airing commercial promotions as news.

18.1.5 Network Rate Cards

Television broadcast networks usually make public only their program rates. Prices for commercials within network-supplied programs are available on request. Radio networks list charges for 1-minute and for 30-second commercials and, where applicable, price differentials for time of day and quantity discounts.

18.2 RATINGS

Media managers need to know how many individuals are in the audience and who they are in order to set rates and sell to advertisers. Advertisers need the same information to determine first, which outlet, network, or program has the audience they want, and later, whether they reach all the audience for which they pay. Such information is provided by independent organizations—not connected with any radio or television medium, advertiser, or advertising agency. One concept they use to describe an audience is the *rating*.

18.2.1 Basic Concepts

Audience research firms do not count the entire audience of a program or station. Such a count would be prohibitively expensive, would not allow repeats of the count (so that media outlets and advertisers could see trends and changes), and is not even needed to meet accepted standards of accuracy. Instead they use **statistical surveys.** In a statistical survey, the firm selects a relatively small group of individuals and collects data on the group's **tuning activity** (listening or viewing). The firm then **projects** the results, reporting the activity of the group as an **estimate** of tuning for the entire audience.

One important task in the survey is to define **audience.** The audience is a collection of individuals, but individual what? Whatever the answer, that is the **elementary unit,** the basic unit about which a statistical survey gathers information. In audience research, the elementary unit is often the **household.** All households within the survey area make up the **statistical population** (also called *population* or *universe*). Out of the population, the research firm selects the **sample,** the households about whose members it hopes to collect audience tuning data.

18.2.2 The Sample

Many persons do not understand how a sample can represent the entire population of a city, region, or country. But it can. The sample, of course, must meet stringent requirements. The audience research firm must select the sample using a detailed procedure spelled out in advance and published along with the results. The sample must be a **probability sample** (also called a *random sample*), one based on **random selection** procedures. In a random selection, each unit of the population must have an equal chance to be selected for the sample, and each unit in the sample must be selected strictly by chance. This means that when an audience research firm surveys your area, your home has as much chance of being selected for the sample as any other.

The size of the sample determines the accuracy of the survey; as sample size increases, so does accuracy. However, a law of diminishing returns governs sample size. As more units go into the sample, each addition contributes less accuracy. Eventually, an increase in accuracy of just one-tenth of 1 percent requires the addition of hundreds of units. Research firms select a sample size that yields acceptably accurate results without being prohibitively expensive. Sample size may range from several hundred for small markets to 3000 or more for large markets.

The research firm reports tuning activity of household members by categories. They categorize primarily by sex and age (for example, women 25–54), sometimes by race. As the sample is subdivided into these categories, the number of sample persons in each category gets smaller. Smaller numbers reduce accuracy (Section 18.2.5).

With the sample intact, however, surprisingly few units are needed. For example, in its Television Index, Nielsen Media Research uses a national metered sample (Section 18.2.7) of just 4000 households to gauge the number of viewers nationwide who watch national television programs. Since many individual markets need almost that large a sample, you might think that the TV-owning household population of the entire United States would require a much larger sample. But it does not work that way. The size of a sample needed to achieve a certain statistical precision is about as adequate for a nation of more than 90 million households as for a city of 90,000 (Box 18.2).

One caution about the sample—no one person represents you. Many people object to ratings methodology because of the imagined effect of some little old lady in Peoria who turns on the television set in her parlor so that *Golden Girls* reruns can amuse the cat while she makes cookies out in the kitchen. This is a needless worry. This lady's home, if selected for the Nielsen Television Index national sample, would be one of 4000. And it is the viewing activity of the sample as a whole that approximates the viewing activity of the population as a whole. On the other hand, the viewing activity of all persons in the sample who are female and 55 years or older does reflect to a high degree the viewing activity of all persons in the population who are female and 55 years or older. But our little old lady by herself does not represent either all persons in Peoria or all persons 55 years and older.

18.2.3 Market

There are two distinct levels of broadcast audience research surveys—national and local. A **national** survey yields data on audiences for network and syndicated programs. The population is all units in the continental United States, and the sample is drawn randomly from that population.

A survey in a **local market** yields data on audiences for local stations and programs. Usually, a local market consists of an area's largest city and the surrounding countries in which that city's stations are most often heard and watched. The survey report, however, lists not only those stations in the market but all stations to which people listen or view. The population is all units within the market, and the sample is drawn accordingly.

Sometimes a research firm's local report includes two breakdowns—one for the entire market and the other for just the central city. Each research firm has a different concept of what area makes up the market of any given locale.

In audience survey terminology, the urban area that is the heart of the market is the "metro area." The metro area is normally the same as the metropolitan statistical area, as defined by the U.S. Department of Commerce. For the more inclusive geographic concept—metro area plus surrounding counties—Arbitron has developed the concept of the Area of Dominant Influence (ADI). Any market whose TV stations achieve the largest total percentage of the TV audience in a county is the "dominant influence" in that

Box 18.2 How Can a Sample of 1,000 Represent a Population?

Try this interesting experiment—hypothetically (unless you happen to have 100,000 beads handy). Imagine 100,000 beads in a washtub; 30,000 red and 70,000 white. Mix *thoroughly*, then scoop out a sample of 1,000.

Even before counting, you will know that not all beads in your sample are red. Nor would you expect your sample to divide exactly at 300 red and 700 white. As a matter of fact, the mathematical odds are about 20 to 1 that the count of red beads will be between 270 and 330—or 27 percent and 33 percent of the sample. In short, you have now produced a "rating" of 30, plus or minus 3, with a 20-to-1 assurance of statistical reliability.

These basic sampling laws wouldn't change even if you drew your sample of 1,000 from 90 million beads instead of 100,000—assuming that the 90 million beads had the same ratio of red and white. This is a simple demonstration of why a sample of 1,000 is about as adequate for a nation of 90 million households as for a city of 100,000. (*Source:* Nielsen Media Research. Used by permission.)

county; Aribtron then assigns the county to that dominant market's ADI. Arbitron assigns every county to one ADI; there is no overlap. ADIs delineate television markets, but advertisers and agencies have come to use them in dealing with other media, too. Arbitron even includes results for the ADI in some radio reports. The parallel Nielsen delineation is the Designated Market Area (DMA).

Audience research firms survey larger markets more frequently than smaller ones. However, at certain times during the year, they conduct surveys in all markets, small and large, during the same time period. This is a **sweep.** Results from a sweep not only tell individual stations in a market how they are doing but also allow a network to gauge its general effectiveness and that of its affiliates.

18.2.4 Ratings and Shares

A research firm reports the results of its audience survey as ratings and shares. For illustration purposes, assume that a firm conducts a television audience survey in a market of 100,000 households, using a random sample of 1,000 households. The research firm uses the household as the elementary unit and reports results as the number of households tuned to the market's stations. As you follow this illustration, refer to Figure 18.3.

18.2.4.1 Rating Let us look at a specific time—say, 8:30–9:00 p.m. one Wednesday during the survey. The firm's analysis of the data shows the following: 198 sample homes tuned to WAAA, channel 2; 213 to WBBB, channel 5; 227 to WCCC, channel 8; 154 to WDDD, channel 37; and 108 to all other stations. The **rating** for each station is the **percentage of sample households tuned to the station.** For WAAA, figure 198 ÷ 1000 = 0.198. This tells us that WAAA has a rating

of 19.8 (but do not call it 19.8 *percent;* see Section 18.2.5). Similarly, the rating for WBBB is 21.3; WCCC, 22.7; and WDDD, 15.4.

18.2.4.2 HUT and Share Note that television receivers were operating in a total of 900 sample homes (198 + 213 + 227 + 154 + 108 = 900);* in the other 100, the residents were not at home or not watching. These 900 homes, expressed as a percentage of the sample, make up **households using television (HUT).** In our example, figure 900 ÷ 1000 = 0.90. This gives us a 90 HUT rating—which, incidentally, is extraordinarily high! A station's **share** (for *share of the audience*) is the percentage of *audience* (all households in the sample actually *using* television) tuned to that station. For WAAA, figure 198 ÷ 900 = 0.22—a 22 share.

*We are assuming that all receivers in multiset households tune to the same station. If a household contains two or more sets and all tune to the same station, the household counts in that station's audience only once. However, if the various sets tune to different stations, the household counts in the audience of each of those stations.

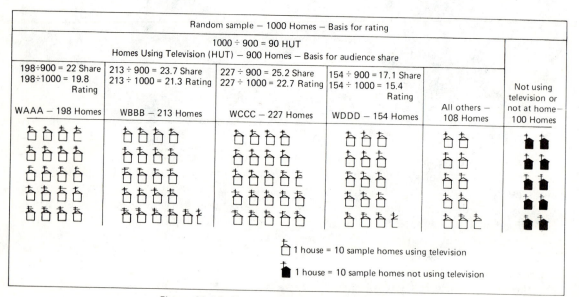

Figure 18.3 Ratings and shares: An illustration.

18.2.4.3 Types of Ratings The WAAA example yielded **program ratings.** A research firm also reports longer-range audience estimates—for example, one week of a radio station's morning drive time, or a television station's 6:00 p.m. local newscast across a four-week period. These are average and cumulative audience ratings.

And here, we must determine what qualifies as listening or viewing. By way of explanation, suppose that an audience research firm includes you in its sample. The firm counts you in the audience of a station or program only if you "tune in" (listen to or view) that station or program for a minimum length of time within a certain period. Typically, firms specify at least 5 minutes in a 15-minute period.

In an average rating, the firm may count you many times; in cumulative ratings, just once. Take the radio station's morning drive time, for example. The relevant period here is the quarter-hour. For one week, the daypart consists of 60 quarter-hours (= 3 [hours] × 4 [quarters] × 5 [weekdays]). For each of those 60 quarter-hours, the firm counts the total number of persons tuned to the station. Then it adds all those totals and divides by 60. The quotient (the result of the division) is, of course, an average. In this example, it is the station's **average quarter-hour rating** for morning drive time. How were you counted more than once? If you listened to the station every morning, Monday through Friday, 6:15–7:00 a.m., you were part of that station's audience for 15 quarter-hours; therefore, you were counted 15 times.

The **cumulative rating** or **cume,** on the other hand, is *not* an average. Cume reflects total *unduplicated* audience. The research firm counts each unit that tuned in at least once during the period under consideration but includes it only once. In our radio station example, the firm includes you in the cume one time, whether you listen to the station for 15 quarter-hours or one 5-minute period.

Advertising sales personnel may refer to reach and circulation. By **reach,** they mean cumulative audience for a program series, while **circulation** is the cume of a station or a network. Both reach and circulation show the number of households or individuals estimated to be in the audience at least once over a length of time.

18.2.5 Projection and Sampling Error

Although based on tuning activity in the sample, ratings purport to describe what the *population* did. The projected figures, therefore, are **statistical estimates,** not exact percentages. If a survey and a census (asking every unit in the population) on viewing activity ran concurrently in a market, we could compare the survey's estimate to the census's actual count. They would probably differ somewhat. This difference is **sampling error,** inherent in the statistical process of sampling.

An audience research firm that follows correct procedures in planning and executing a survey can specify the **confidence level.** The confidence level expresses the probability that the sampling error falls within a certain range. For example, in our survey with a sample of 1000 (Section 18.2.4.1), we may say that the probability is 95 percent (or 19 chances out of 20) that WAAA's 19.8 rating is in error by no more than ±2.6 (plus or minus 2.6 percent). Stated another way, the odds are 20 to 1 that the actual percentage of the TV household population watching WAAA at 8:30–9:00 Thursday evening is somewhere in the range of 17.2 to 22.4 (19.8 − 2.6 = 17.2; 19.8 + 2.6 = 22.4).

The same limitations apply when projecting the rating into *numbers* of units. The population is 100,000 television households, so we multiply the rating times the population (0.198 × 100,000 = 19,800). We can then say that there is a 95 percent probability that

19,800—give or take as much as 2,600—of the market's TV households tuned to WAAA.

When social scientists conduct survey reseach, they often use the 95 percent figure. **Ratings firms generally calculate to a lesser confidence level,** say 68 percent. This lowers the stated sampling error but raises the chance that actual error exceeds stated error.

The range of possible error also varies with audience proportions (the ratings) and sample size (Table 18.1). When programmers in a market draw audiences of nearly equal size, the range of statistical error increases. When rating reports break the sample down by demographic category, the range of error for ratings in each category is greater than for those of the entire sample (Section 18.2.2). For example, one category might be working women 18 years and older, say 200 persons out of a total sample of 1000. The report, then, shows what percentage of those 200 persons tuned to each station. In such breakdowns, each category becomes, in effect, a separate sample. Since the category sample contains fewer units than the total sample, ratings projected from the category sample contain a greater margin of error.

18.2.6 Ratings as History

A rating is history. It reflects a programmer's competitive position *during the time of the survey*—not when the reports were published, or now, or for the next two months. Advertisers accept ratings, however, because broadcast audience patterns are slow to change. They look for trends and changes over several rating periods. When you hear a station promote itself as "number one," that means it *was* number one at the time of the last rating survey. You should also ask at what times and with what audience it was number one.

18.2.7 Data Gathering

Research companies use several methods to gather tuning activity data from the sample. Some of the primary methods include the personal interview, the telephone interview, the diary, the tuning meter, and the peoplemeter.

18.2.7.1 Personal Interview In the personal interview, an interviewer goes to the sample home and questions individuals on listening or viewing within the past 24 hours. This is the **recall method,** and the interviewer often uses a **roster** (list) of outlets and programs to help respondents' memory. Personal interviews can yield detailed information, including data on out-of-home viewing and listening and opinions on programming. On the other hand, respondents may not remember accurately; or they may inadvertently telescope data and report listening or viewing for the past several days as though it occurred on the preceding day. The roster may introduce bias for listed outlets and against unlisted ones.

18.2.7.2 Telephone Interview In a telephone survey, the interviewer uses a list of telephone numbers to contact sample respondents. Telephone surveys usually take one of two forms, recall or coincidental. In **telephone recall** the interviewer asks what listening or viewing the respondent has done within a specified previous time period, often that day plus the previous evening. The **telephone coincidental** gathers data on tuning activity at the time of (coincidental with) the telephone call. The interviewer asks the respondent if there is a receiver turned on in the house and, if so, to what station it is tuned and how many persons are listening or viewing.

The telephone survey is fast and—compared with personal interviews—inexpensive. A telephone interview can yield detailed information, including likes and

Table 18.1 DEVIATION EFFECTS OF SAMPLE SIZE AND RESEARCH RESULTS. Probable Deviation (Plus or Minus) of Results Due to Size of Sample Only (Safety Factor or 20 to 1)

Survey result is:

Size of sample	Probable deviation (plus or minus) of results due to size of sample only (safety factor of 20 to 1)										
	1% or 99%	5% or 95%	10% or 90%	15% or 85%	20% or 80%	25% or 75%	30% or 70%	35% or 65%	40% or 60%	45% or 55%	50%
25	4.0	8.7	12.0	14.3	16.0	17.3	18.3	19.1	19.6	19.8	20.0
50	2.8	6.2	8.5	10.1	11.4	12.3	13.0	13.5	13.9	14.1	14.2
75	2.3	5.0	6.9	8.2	9.2	10.0	10.5	11.0	11.3	11.4	11.5
100	2.0	4.4	6.0	7.1	8.0	8.7	9.2	9.5	9.8	9.9	10.0
150	1.6	3.6	4.9	5.9	6.6	7.1	7.5	7.8	8.0	8.1	8.2
200	1.4	3.1	4.3	5.1	5.7	6.1	6.5	6.8	7.0	7.0	7.1
250	1.2	2.7	3.8	4.5	5.0	5.5	5.8	6.0	6.2	6.2	6.3
300	1.1	2.5	3.5	4.1	4.6	5.0	5.3	5.5	5.7	5.8	5.8
400	0.99	2.2	3.0	3.6	4.0	4.3	4.6	4.8	4.9	5.0	5.0
500	0.89	2.0	2.7	3.2	3.6	3.9	4.1	4.3	4.4	4.5	4.5
600	0.81	1.8	2.5	2.9	3.3	3.6	3.8	3.9	4.0	4.1	4.1
800	0.69	1.5	2.1	2.5	2.8	3.0	3.2	3.3	3.4	3.5	3.5
1,000	0.63	1.4	1.9	2.3	2.6	2.8	2.9	3.1	3.1	3.2	3.2
2,000	0.44	0.96	1.3	1.6	1.8	1.9	2.0	2.1	2.2	2.2	2.2
3,000	0.36	0.79	1.1	1.3	1.5	1.6	1.7	1.7	1.8	1.8	1.8
4,000	0.31	0.69	0.95	1.1	1.3	1.4	1.4	1.5	1.5	1.6	1.6
5,000	0.28	0.62	0.85	1.0	1.1	1.2	1.3	1.4	1.4	1.4	1.4
10,000	0.20	0.44	0.60	0.71	0.80	0.87	0.92	0.95	0.98	0.99	1.0
50,000	0.08	0.17	0.24	0.29	0.32	0.35	0.37	0.38	0.39	0.40	0.40

Table 18.1 Deviation of Sample Size and Research Results. Probable deviation increases as sample size decreases and survey results approach equal proportions. For example, when size of sample is 500 and survey result comes out 25%, you may be reasonably sure (odds 20 to 1) that this result is no more than 3.9 off, plus or minus. Doubling the sample to 1000 reduces this margin to 2.8, percentage points.
Source: Joe Belden, *A Broadcast Research Primer* (Washington, D.C.: National Association of Broadcasters, 1966), p. 19. Used by permission.

dislikes. Procedures exist to overcome problems such as unlisted numbers and new listings not yet in the telephone book. Still, the sample excludes nontelephone homes. Many persons refuse to cooperate with telephone surveys, suspicious that the interview is a sales pitch or a prelude to crime.

Telephone recall is subject to the same memory problems as personal interview recall. Telephone coincidental, by nature, is primarily instantaneous, a problem where average and cumulative data are needed. Research firms must also restrict the hours of coincidental surveys because respondents might resent late-night and early-morning calls.

18.2.7.3 Diary

The diary method relies on self-administration by the respondent. The diary consists of an easy-to-fill-out log of viewing or listening activities. The research firm calls households selected for the sample and asks if household members would consent to participate. In television surveys, the firm sends one diary for each television *receiver* in the household. Instructions tell the sample family to write on the log when the receiver is turned on, to what channel and program it is tuned, and the sex and age of each person watching, including visitors.

In radio, the firm sends one diary for each *person* 12 years and older in the sample household. Individuals take the pocket-sized diaries (Figure 18.4) with them and record time of listening, call letters or dial setting of the station, and whether they listen at home or elsewhere. They fill out age, sex, and address in the back of the diary.

The diaries usually request a record of one week's listening or viewing activities. The instructions ask that respondents, at week's end, put the prestamped and addressed diaries in the mail. Often the firm provides some small payment to encourage completion and return.

As with other methods, the diary has both advantages and disadvantages. It picks up data at all hours, provides information on audience composition, samples both urban and rural audiences, and is fast and economical. On the other hand, diary families may become self-conscious of tuning activity, listen or view more or less than normally, or choose programs they ordinarily would not select. In addition, if respondents do not keep up the diaries as requested—for example, recording a whole week's listening or viewing on the last day—they may make omissions and errors.

18.2.7.4 Tuning Meter

The meter method collects set tuning information automatically (Figure 18.5). Set tuning information consists of whether the receiver is on and, if so, to which channel it is tuned.

As with diary methodology, the audience research firm first contacts each household selected for the sample and asks for participation. If the household agrees, the firm sends personnel to install the meter. The meter connects to each receiver in the sample household and makes a record of tuning. Each meter in the sample has its own telephone line, and the research firm's computer calls periodically to collect stored tuning data. Meter methodology yields results quickly; subscribers may receive household ratings and shares as early as the morning after the program has run. These reports are **overnights.**

The meter method eliminates human error and forgetfulness. It is valuable in making analyses and tabulations of results. Because of the expense involved, the meter remains in and collects data from a sample household longer than other methods; this reduces effects of hypoing (Section 7.7) and self-consciousness. The meter's major disadvantage stems from its inability to collect demographic data; it does not tell who was in the audience.

You count in the radio ratings!

No matter how much or how little you listen, you're important!

You're one of the few people picked in your area to have the chance to tell radio stations what you listen to.

This is *your* ratings diary. Please make sure you fill it out yourself.

Here's what we mean by "listening":

"Listening" is any time you can hear a radio — whether you choose the station or not.

When you hear a radio between Thursday, October 13, and Wednesday, October 19, write it down — whether you're at home, in a car, at work or someplace else.

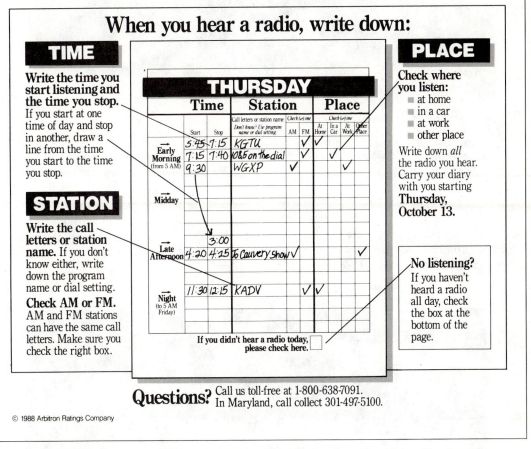

When you hear a radio, write down:

TIME

Write the time you start listening and the time you stop.
If you start at one time of day and stop in another, draw a line from the time you start to the time you stop.

STATION

Write the call letters or station name. If you don't know either, write down the program name or dial setting.

Check AM or FM. AM and FM stations can have the same call letters. Make sure you check the right box.

THURSDAY

	Time		Station	Place					
			Call letters or station name *Check (✓) one*			*Check (✓) one*			
			Don't know? Use program name or dial setting	AM	FM	At Home	In a Car	At Work	Other Place
	Start	Stop							
Early Morning *(from 5 AM)*	5:45	7:15	KGTU		✓	✓			
	7:15	7:40	108.5 on the dial		✓		✓		
	9:30		WGXP	✓				✓	
Midday									
Late Afternoon		3:00							
	4:20	4:25	To Cauvery Show	✓					✓
Night *(to 5 AM Friday)*	11:30	12:15	KADV		✓	✓			

If you didn't hear a radio today, please check here. ☐

PLACE

Check where you listen:
- at home
- in a car
- at work
- other place

Write down *all* the radio you hear. Carry your diary with you starting **Thursday, October 13.**

No listening?
If you haven't heard a radio all day, check the box at the bottom of the page.

Questions? Call us toll-free at 1-800-638-7091. In Maryland, call collect 301-497-5100.

Figure 18.4 Radio diary. Instruction page for an Arbitron radio ratings diary. (Courtesy of The Arbitron Ratings Co. Used by permission.)

Figure 18.5 Tuning meter. Even backyard and patio usage of battery portables can be recorded by the Nielsen Micro-Processor Home Unit through use of a transmitter mounted on the television set and radio-linked to the Home Unit. The Home Unit itself is installed out of sight in a closet, basement, or cabinet. (Photograph courtesy of Nielsen Media Research. Used by permission.)

18.2.7.5 Peoplemeter The peoplemeter (Figure 18.6), on the other hand, *does* yield demographic data. The peoplemeter attempts to combine the best features of the diary and the tuning meter. It records who-watched information, feeds data by telephone lines, and allows overnight reporting. Most versions take the form of electronic diaries. The meter accepts age, sex, and viewing information on individual household

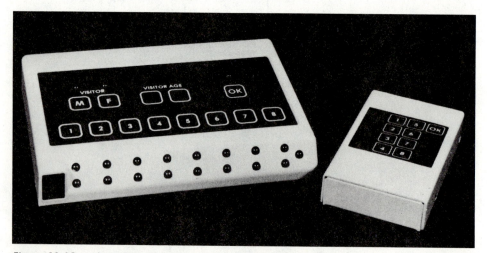

Figure 18.6 Peoplemeter. This is the Nielsen People Meter. (Photograph courtesy of Nielsen Media Research. Used by permission.)

members and visitors. Viewers press buttons on a remote-control device to identify themselves and "log on" and "log off." The meter stores the information, then transmits it when called by the research firm's computer.

During the mid-1980s, AGB Television Research, the U.S. subsidiary of a British firm, played a major role in forcing adoption of peoplemeter technology. The concept was not new. Nielsen, for example, dates its interest from 1957 and began testing in 1978. Nonetheless, AGB caused a stir by announcing a large-scale field test of its peoplemeter in Boston. AGB's ultimate goal was to develop a full-fledged national audience measurement service. Shortly after, both Arbitron and Nielsen also announced peoplemeter field tests. All three companies launched regular peoplemeter service in 1987.

Also in 1987, R. D. Percy & Co. started local peoplemeter service in New York. Percy's system was "passive" (did not require people to punch buttons); an infrared device counted the number of persons in the television room. It also measured audiences to commercials as well as programs. Percy announced plans for a national rating service in 1988.

AGB's service lasted only one year, and Percy did not go national. Of the three major broadcast networks, only CBS had signed on with AGB. ABC and NBC did not, depriving AGB of revenue needed to sustain operations. Deficits mounted. Percy had cash flow problems. In 1988, AGB suspended its national rating service at about the same time that Percy gave up its New York service. Both left legacies, however—use of the peoplemeter in audience research and exploration of "passive" people-counting devices.

Peoplemeters represented a major change in survey technology. They also triggered heated debate and criticism. Nielsen's national peoplemeter sample, it seems, did not deal kindly with broadcast television, partic-

ularly network broadcast television. Compared with Nielsen's diary-based national ratings and local market ratings, peoplemeter reports showed lower HUT figures and lower broadcast network ratings. Network prime-time rating levels, for example, dropped 10 percent. The networks argued that flaws in the service caused at least part of the decline—the sample overrepresented pay cable households, some demographic groups tended to use the meter more conscientiously than others, and many children did not use the meter properly.

The basic criticism seemed to be that some people were not pressing the buttons. On the other hand, the trade had for years accepted diary measurements, a system at least as flawed as peoplemeters. In some diary households, for example, members would conscientiously log their viewing on the first day, then forget about it until time to return the diary, when one person would try to remember what everyone had watched the rest of the week and write in best guesses. These diary flaws *favored* the networks. Ironically, then, peoplemeters may have been criticized—at least in part—not because they were more flawed than diaries but because they were less flawed or flawed in a different manner.

Meanwhile, development proceeded on peoplemeter technology. In 1989, Nielsen and the David Sarnoff Research Center announced a joint agreement to develop a passive system that would identify specific TV viewers in Nielsen homes without requiring any action on the part of those viewers.

18.2.8 Ratings Organizations

Audience research companies syndicate services. A subscriber pays a fee and receives copies of pertinent research reports and permission to use them. Subscribers consist primarily of broadcast stations, cable and broadcast networks, and advertising agencies. The media bear the largest cost of audience research, but agencies specify the information included in the reports. After all, sellers (the media) must package products (advertising time) to appeal to their customers (agencies).

Only subscribers may use a rating report. The report will include ratings of nonsubscribing stations. But a nonsubscriber may not promote its rating to the public or advertisers, even if it has the highest rating in the market.

A number of firms syndicate audience research. During the late 1980s, some of the better-known firms included the following: Statistical Research, Inc.; Birch Radio; The Arbitron Ratings Co.; and Nielsen Media Research.

18.2.8.1 Statistical Research, Inc. (SRI)

SRI conducts **RADAR**—Radio's All-Dimension Audience Research—the only network radio measurement service. RADAR uses telephone recall to collect data. A computer generates random telephone numbers to select a nationwide probability sample of individuals. The respondents, about 250 each week, constitute a panel, and RADAR calls and interviews each one every day for one week about the previous day's listening. RADAR interviews year-round, a total of about 12,000 persons a year. It issues two reports annually, generally in February and July, each covering a sample week. RADAR pertains to national radio usage and network radio only.

18.2.8.2 Birch Radio

Birch Radio, on the other hand, measures radio station audiences. Birch, a division of Birch/Scarborough Research, uses telephone recall methodology. After random selection of the sample, the firm conducts a series of one-person-per-household interviews. The interviewer asks what the sample individual listened to "yesterday." Birch uses the responses to produce average quarter-hour and weekly cume ratings (Figure 18.7). The result is 16 reports per year—12 monthly Trend Reports and 4 Quarterly Summary Reports. The latter contain ratings and qualitative information (such as product, service, and media usage).

Birch entered the radio audience measurement field in 1978. Nine years later, the parent firm merged with a prominent newspaper rating and multimedia research company to form Birch/Scarborough Research. By that time, Birch Radio measured over 250 radio markets and had earned acceptance by advertisers, agency media buyers, and station programmers.

18.2.8.3 The Arbitron Ratings Co.

Arbitron, in business since 1948, measures radio and television audiences in local markets. This company uses both diaries and meters.

Arbitron uses diaries to survey more than 260 radio markets at least once each spring (May through June). It measures larger markets up to three additional times each year. The radio survey period lasts 12 weeks, but the company draws a new sample for each week, and respondents keep diaries for only one week.

Arbitron surveys over 210 television markets (Figure 18.8) each fall, winter, spring, and summer. Major markets are surveyed as many as seven times a year. Arbitron uses two separate samples in large cities. One is its regular diary sample; the other, a sample using a tuning meter, the **Arbitron Television Meter.** Subscribers in these cities receive daily overnight reports, weekly reports, and monthly reports. Since meters report only set usage, the monthly report, published seven times a year, includes data from the market's diary sample to show what type of people were in the audience.

Arbitron introduced its **ScanAmerica** (Figure 18.9) peoplemeter service as a Denver local service in 1987. The ScanAmerica system gives subscribers two types of information. In addition to viewing data, Scan-

Target Demographics
MEN 18-34

BDM
JUNE – NOVEMBER

AVERAGE QUARTER HOUR AND CUME ESTIMATES

	MON – SUN 6:00AM–12:00 MID				MON – FRI 6:00AM–10:00AM				MON – FRI 10:00AM–3:00PM				MON – FRI 3:00PM–7:00PM				MON – FRI 7:00PM–12:00 MID			
	AQH PRS (00)	AQH PRS RTG	AQH PRS SHR	CUME PRS (00)	AQH PRS (00)	AQH PRS RTG	AQH PRS SHR	CUME PRS (00)	AQH PRS (00)	AQH PRS RTG	AQH PRS SHR	CUME PRS (00)	AQH PRS (00)	AQH PRS RTG	AQH PRS SHR	CUME PRS (00)	AQH PRS (00)	AQH PRS RTG	AQH PRS SHR	CUME PRS (00)
WAJD*				16				4				4				4				4
WGGG	3	.7	4.1	29	4	1.0	5.8	14	8	1.9	9.8	14					1	.2	2.1	4
WGGG-FM	10	2.4	13.5	112	8	1.9	11.6	42	15	3.6	18.3	46	11	2.6	14.3	58	2	.5	4.2	15
WKTK-FM																				
WLUS*																				
WRUF	1	.2	1.4	23	2	.5	2.9	16	2	.5	2.4	6	1	.2	1.3	9				81
WRUF-FM	25	6.0	33.8	316	20	4.8	29.0	137	25	6.0	30.5	117	29	6.9	37.7	153	17	4.0	35.4	
WUFT-FM	5	1.2	6.8	112	9	2.1	13.0	53	5	1.2	6.1	16	6	1.4	7.8	37	6	1.4	12.5	44
WYFB-FM				18				4				3				11				3
WYGC-FM	2	.5	2.7	29	4	1.0	5.8	19	4	1.0	4.9	13	3	.7	3.9	15	1	.2	2.1	
WYKS-FM	11	2.6	14.9	167	11	2.6	15.9	89	9	2.1	11.0	57	7	1.7	9.1	58	8	1.9	16.7	43
WYOC-FM	1	.2	1.4	16	1	.2	1.4	4	1	.2	1.2	8								4
WAPE-FM	3	.7	4.1	32	3	.7	4.3	15	3	.7	3.7	11	4	1.0	5.2	16	5	1.2	10.4	16
WJHM-FM	3	.7	4.1	70					2	.5	2.4	3	8	.5	2.6	4	3	.7	6.3	14
WMMZ-FM	4	1.0	5.4	75	2	.5	2.9	9	5	1.2	6.1	35	8	1.9	10.4	31	3	.7	6.3	21
WNFI-FM				13				5				4				13				
WOCL-FM	2	.5	2.7	20									1	.2	1.3	4	2	.5	4.2	4
PUR	74	17.6		411	69	16.4		304	82	19.5		265	77	18.3		308	48	11.4		222

*ESTIMATES ADJUSTED FOR ACTUAL BROADCAST SCHEDULE

BIRCH RADIO

(Used by permission of Birch/Scarborough, Inc.)

Figure 18.7 Birch report.

Time Period Estimates

DAY AND TIME / STATION PROGRAM	ADI TV HH RATINGS BY WEEKS 1 FEB 01 (1)	2 FEB 08 (2)	3 FEB 15 (3)	4 FEB 22 (4)	ADI TV HH RTG (5)	SHR (6)	ADI TV HH SHARE/HUT TRENDS NOV 88 (59)	JUL 88 (60)	MAY 88 (61)	FEB 88 (62)
▲ RELATIVE STD-ERR THRESHOLDS (1σ) 25%					7					
50%					2					
TUESDAY										
7:00P- 7:30P										
WCJB FAMLY TIES-S	•	•	•	•	17	35	36	39	31	39
WOGX WHEEL OF FOR	•	•	•	•	8	18	18	10	18	10
WUFT PTV	•	•	•	•	2	5	6	5	5	5
WESH CURRENT AFFR	•	•	•	•	3	6	3	7	7	5
WJXT INSIDE EDITN	•	•	•	•	2	5	8	15	19	22
H/P/T	•	•	•	•	48		47	40	41	59
7:30P- 8:00P										
WCJB CHEERS-S	•	•	•	•	18	37	39	31	37	39
WOGX JEOPARDY	•	•	•	•	10	20	15	18	11	14
WUFT PTV	•	•	•	•	2	5	5	5	5	4
WESH ENTRTNMT TON	•	•	•	•	4	9	4	7	8	8
WJXT ENTRTNMT TON	•	•	•	•	1	2	5	19	18	17
H/P/T	•	•	•	•	48		49	42	41	60
8:00P- 8:30P										
WCJB WHO THE BOSS	•	•	•	•	23	42	41	37	52	41
WOGX 8 OCLOCK MOV	•	•	•	•	2	5	8	13	3	8
WUFT PTV	•	•	•	•	4	8	5	10	6	7
WESH MATLOCK	•	•	•	•	9	17	14	9	16	21
WJXT TOUR OF DUTY	•	•	•		3	6				
BEST CATCHES				•						
--4 WK AVG--					3	5	3	3	6	6
H/P/T	•	•	•	•	53		51	50	46	61
8:30P- 9:00P										
WCJB ROSEANNE	•	•	•		28	51				
WONDER YEARS				•						
--4 WK AVG--					25	46	37	32	45	41
WOGX 8 OCLOCK MOV	•	•	•	•	3	6	10	13	4	9
WUFT PTV	•	•	•	•	4	8	8	9	6	7
WESH MATLOCK	•	•	•	•	10	18	13	11	17	20
WJXT TOUR OF DUTY	•	•	•		3	6				
BEST CATCHES				•						
--4 WK AVG--					3	5	4	3	8	6
H/P/T	•	•	•	•	54		50	49	45	60
9:00P- 9:30P										
WCJB MOONLIGHTING	•	•			13	27				
ABC MV SP TU			•							
ROSEANNE				•						
--4 WK AVG--					13	26	39	33	38	40
WOGX 8 OCLOCK MOV	•	•	•	•	3	7	10	12	8	9
WUFT PTV	•	•	•	•	2	4	5	6	6	7
WESH HEAT OF NGHT	•	•	•		9	19				
NBC MV WK TU				•						
--4 WK AVG--					8	16	8	10	14	11
WJXT CBS TUE MOV	•	•	•		9	19				
MSS USA PGNT				•						
--4 WK AVG--					8	15	10	8	9	12
H/P/T	•	•	•	•	50		51	53	46	59
9:30P-10:00P										
WCJB MOONLIGHTING	•	•			15	30				
[illegible]										

DAY AND TIME / STATION PROGRAM	ADI RATINGS PERSONS 2+ (11)	18+ (12)	12-24 (13)	12-34 (14)	18-34 (15)	18-49 (16)	21-49 (17)	25-54 (18)	35+ (19)	35-64 (20)	50+ (21)	WOMEN 18+ (22)	12-24 (23)	18-34 (24)	18-49 (25)	21-49 (26)	25-49 (27)	25-54 (28)	W W (29)	MEN 18+ (30)	18-34 (31)	18-49 (32)	21-49 (33)	25-49 (34)	25-54 (35)
▲ RELATIVE STD-ERR THRESHOLDS (1σ) 25%	7	5	18	11	12	8	8	9	7	9	10	8	31	21	13	13	17	15	21	8	20	13	14	17	15
50%	1	1	5	3	3	2	2	2	1	2	2	2	10	6	3	3	4	4	6	2	6	3	4	5	4
TUESDAY																									
7:00P- 7:30P																									
WCJB FAMLY TIES-S	13	11	20	16	15	13	13	10	8	8	8	13	24	16	15	15	13	13	5	10	13	10	11	7	8
WOGX WHEEL OF FOR	5	5	1				1	2	11	6	19	6					1	2	1	4		1	1	1	1
WUFT PTV	2	3	1	2	2	2	2	2	3		5	3	2	2	2	2	1	1	3	3	3	2	3	3	3
WESH CURRENT AFFR	3	3	3	2	1	3	3	3	4	6	3	4	3	3	4	3	4	4	3	2		2	2	3	3
WJXT INSIDE EDITN	1	2	1	1	2	2	2	2	2	3	2	1	1	1	1	2	1	1		2	2	2	3	3	3
H/P/T	37	36	39	33	31	32	31	31	42	39	50	40	41	36	35	33	32	34	26	33	26	28	30	27	28
7:30P- 8:00P																									
WCJB CHEERS-S	12	12	15	15	15	13	13	12	9	10	10	10	14	10	10	12	11	12	5	14	19	15	15	12	13
WOGX JEOPARDY	6	6	2	1		2	2	3	13	8	20	8	2		2	2	3	5	5	5		1	1	2	2
WUFT PTV	2	3	1	2	2	2	2	2	3	1	6	3	2	2	2	2	2	1	3	3	3	2	2	3	3
WESH ENTRTNMT TON	3	3	3	3	3	3	3	3	3	4	2	4	3	5	5	6	5	5	5	2	1	2	1	2	1
WJXT ENTRTNMT TON	1	1				1	1	2	2	2		1			1	1	1	1	1	1	1	2	2	3	2
H/P/T	34	36	32	31	30	31	31	33	42	40	50	39	36	31	33	33	33	35	29	33	29	29	30	31	32
8:00P- 8:30P																									
WCJB WHO THE BOSS	20	17	20	21	18	18	19	20	16	18	14	19	24	21	21	23	25	23	14	15	15	15	16	17	17
WOGX 8 OCLOCK MOV	1	2		1	2	2	2	3	2	2	2	2		2	2	2	3	3	4	2	1	1	2	2	2
WUFT PTV	3	3		2	2	3	3	4	4	4	3	2	1	1	2	2	3	3	3	4	3	4	4	5	5
WESH MATLOCK	6	7				2	2	5	14	13	22	9		1	2	2	3	6	6	6		2	3	4	4
WJXT TOUR OF DUTY	2	2	1	1	1	2	3	3	2	3		1			1	1	1	1	2	3	3	4	5	4	4
BEST CATCHES																									
--4 WK AVG--	1	2	1	1	1	2	2	2	2	3		1			1	1	2	2	2	2	2	3	3	3	3
H/P/T	40	40	27	32	30	36	39	44	51	52	52	42	36	33	37	40	42	42	37	38	27	35	38	45	45
8:30P- 9:00P																									
WCJB ROSEANNE	23	21	21	24	21	22	24	25	20	24	16	23	30	25	26	29	27	26	17	19	18	19	20	24	24
WONDER YEARS																									
--4 WK AVG--	21	18	19	22	20	20	21	23	17	20	14	20	28	23	23	26	25	23	14	17	17	17	18	22	22
WOGX 8 OCLOCK MOV	2	2		1	2	1	2	2	2	2	2	1		2	1	2	2	2	3	2	1	1	2	2	2
WUFT PTV	3	3		2	2	3	3	4	4	4	3	2		1	2	2	3	3	3	4	3	4	4	5	5
WESH MATLOCK	6	7				2	2	5	15	13	23	9		1	2	2	3	6	7	6		2	3	4	4
WJXT TOUR OF DUTY	2	2	1	1	1	2	3	3	2	3		1			1	1	1	1	2	3	3	4	5	4	4
BEST CATCHES																									
--4 WK AVG--	1	2	1	1	1	2	2	2	2	3		1			1	1	2	2	2	2	2	3	3	3	3
H/P/T	40	40	27	32	30	36	39	43	50	51	52	41	36	32	36	38	39	40	34	40	29	36	40	46	46
9:00P- 9:30P																									
WCJB MOONLIGHTING	7	9	7	8	9	7	9	7	9	7	12	11	11	14	11	13	11	10	14	7	4	4	5	4	4
ABC MV SP TU																									
ROSEANNE																									
--4 WK AVG--	9	10	7	9	8	8	9	9	12	10	15	11	11	10	10	12	12	11	9	9	6	6	7	8	8
WOGX 8 OCLOCK MOV	3	2	3	3	3	3	2	2	1	1	1	1		2	1	2	2	2	3	3	5	4	2	2	2
WUFT PTV	1	1		1	1	1	1	1	1		2									2	3	2	2	3	3
WESH HEAT OF NGHT	6	8	2	4	4	7	8	10	11	13	10	8		5	7	8	10	11	10	7	3	7	7	10	10
NBC MV WK TU																									
--4 WK AVG--	6	7	1	3	3	5	6	8	10	12	11	7		4	5	6	8	9	10	6	2	5	6	7	7
WJXT CBS TUE MOV	7	7	4	5	5	6	7	8	10	11	11	10	8	8	8	10	8	10	9	5	2	4	5	7	7
MSS USA PGNT																									
--4 WK AVG--	5	6	3	3	4	5	6	6	9	9	10	8	6	6	6	7	6	8	8	4	1	3	4	5	5
H/P/T	35	37	24	29	30	33	36	39	45	43	49	37	25	29	32	37	38	39	39	37	31	35	35	40	39
9:30P-10:00P																									
WCJB MOONLIGHTING	8	10	7	10	[illegible]	9	10	8	9	7	13	12	11	17	13	15	14	13	18	7	4	4	5	4	4

Figure 18.8 Arbitron local television ratings. (Courtesy of The Arbitron Ratings Co. Used by permission.)

America asks sample households to provide purchasing information by running a scanner wand over the Universal Product Code symbol of each item purchased for the household. Arbitron's computer picks up both viewing and purchasing data. The rating trade refers to simultaneous tracking of two streams of information as *single source.*

By 1990, Arbitron had wired four markets for single-source measurement and had plans for others. Eventually, ScanAmerica meters were to replace the overnight meters (above) in all the company's metered markets, and Arbitron even discussed the possibility of a national service with a sample of 18,000 households.

Arbitron's corporate parent, Control Data Corporation, also owns **Broadcast Advertisers Reports** (BAR). BAR monitors commercials that appear on broadcast and cable television networks, television stations, and radio networks. Stations, advertisers, and advertising agencies use BAR's syndicated reports. These reports provide a variety of in-

(a)

(b)

Figure 18.9 Arbitron's ScanAmerica.   Arbitron calls its peoplemeter system ScanAmerica. (a) When the television receiver operates, the meter prompts for input by inserting a flashing question mark in the upper left corner of the screen. As viewers log in, their names appear briefly on the screen. ScanAmerica includes a removable scanner wand (in holder on top of television receiver). (b) The wand records the Universal Product Code (UPC) symbol of products purchased for the sample household. Instructions direct household members to pass the wand over the UPC symbol on each package as they put away the products. The user returns the wand to its holder, the product codes transfer to the meter, and Arbitron's computer picks up both viewing and purchasing data. (Photographs courtesy of The Arbitron Ratings Co. Used by permission.)

formation on the monitored commercials, such as time, origin (station or network), length, product, brand, advertiser, agency, and average value.

18.2.8.4 Nielsen Media Research Nielsen measures television audiences at both the local and national levels. Nielsen, a subsidiary of Dun & Bradstreet, began in 1934 as a marketing research firm. Several years later the firm bought rights to the first meter (Figure 18.10), a mechanical recorder, and by 1940 Nielsen was in the radio audience measurement business. Nielsen added television research in the late 1940s, adapting its recorder for the visual medium, and got out of radio measurement in 1964.

At the local level, Nielsen competes directly with Arbitron. Nielsen measures some 220 markets in November, February, May, and July of each year. Nielsen uses the diary method for its local-market rating service, the **Nielsen Station Index** (NSI). Nielsen

also uses two separate samples in most of the top-20 markets: the metered sample for overnight information on set tuning and a diary sample for audience demographics. Nielsen calls its tuning meter the **Micro-Processor Home Unit** (Figure 18.5).

Nielsen Television Index (NTI) (Figure 18.11) reports broadcast television network ratings. NTI uses a national sample of 4000 households equipped with **Nielsen People Meters** (Figures 18.6 and 18.12). The People Meters provide information on television viewing throughout the day, year-round. For years, Nielsen offered the only regularly scheduled network rating service. During the 1980s, others entered the business, but programmers and advertisers continued to regard NTI as the standard.

In 1988, Nielsen announced a test of Scantrack Plus Service, its version of single-source data. Aimed at advertisers more than broadcasters, Scantrack Plus would *not* utilize Nielsen's People Meter. The company

Figure 18.10 First Nielsen meter, 1936. (Photograph courtesy of Nielsen Media Research. Used by permission.)

Nielsen NATIONAL TV AUDIENCE ESTIMATES   EVE.TUE. FEB.7

TIME	7:00	7:15	7:30	7:45	8:00	8:15	8:30	8:45	9:00	9:15	9:30	9:45	10:00	10:15	10:30	10:45
HUT	60.4	61.7	63.1	64.8	65.4	67.3	69.2	70.2	69.4	69.3	69.6	69.2	67.1	66.1	64.6	61.5
ABC T.V					WHO'S THE BOSS?		ROSEANNE		←MOONLIGHTING (PAE)→				←THIRTYSOMETHING→			
AVERAGE AUDIENCE (Hhlds (000) & %)					20,160		22,330		12,200				11,390			
					22.3		24.7		13.5	13.8*		13.2*	12.6	12.8*		12.4*
SHARE AUDIENCE %					34		35		19	20*		19*	19	19*		20*
AVG. AUD. BY 1/4 HR %					21.3	23.4	24.5	24.9	14.5	13.1	13.1	13.2	12.8	12.8	12.5	12.3
CBS TV					←TOUR OF DUTY→				←CBS TUESDAY MOVIE LONESOME DOVE PT 3 (PAE)→							
AVERAGE AUDIENCE (Hhlds (000) & %)					9,040				22,420							
					10.0	9.7*		10.4*	24.8	23.6*		24.8*		25.8*		24.8*
SHARE AUDIENCE %					15	15		15*	37	34*		36*		39*		39*
AVG. AUD. BY 1/4 HR %					9.8	9.6	9.7	11.0	23.1	24.2	24.5	25.1	25.6	26.1	25.9	23.7
NBC TV					←MATLOCK→				←IN THE HEAT OF THE NIGHT→				←MIDNIGHT CALLER→			
AVERAGE AUDIENCE (Hhlds (000) & %)					16,360				14,010				11,840			
					18.1	17.7*		18.5*	15.5	15.4*		15.5*	13.1	13.1*		13.2*
SHARE AUDIENCE %					27	27*		27*	22	22*		22*	20	20*		21*
AVG. AUD. BY 1/4 HR %					17.2	18.2	18.8	18.2	15.3	15.5	15.7	15.4	13.2	13.0	13.1	13.2
INDEPENDENTS (INCL. SUPERSTATIONS)																
AVERAGE AUDIENCE	17.0		14.2		11.2		11.2		12.5		12.5		11.6		9.8	
SHARE AUDIENCE %	28		22		17		16		18		18		17		16	
SUPERSTATIONS																
AVERAGE AUDIENCE	4.8		4.1		3.1		3.3		3.4		3.3		2.9		2.4	
SHARE AUDIENCE %	8		6		5		5		5		5		4		4	
PBS																
AVERAGE AUDIENCE	2.1		2.6		3.2		2.9		2.2		2.0		1.6		1.3	
SHARE AUDIENCE %	3		4		5		4		3		3		2		2	
CABLE ORIG.																
AVERAGE AUDIENCE	7.5		7.5		6.4		6.7		7.4		7.1		6.5		5.2	
SHARE AUDIENCE %	12		12		10		10		11		10		10		8	
PAY SERVICES																
AVERAGE AUDIENCE	2.0		2.2		2.5		3.0		3.5		3.4		3.5		3.4	
SHARE AUDIENCE %	3		3		4		4		5		5		5		5	

U.S. TV HOUSEHOLDS: 90,400,000

Figure 18.11 Nielsen Television Index.   (Courtesy Nielsen Media Research. Used by permission.)

planned to maintain a sample for Scantrack Plus separate and distinct from that of the People Meter service. The home device consisted of a wand to record product purchases coupled with a Micro-Processor Home Unit. Nielsen's test involved 1,500 homes, a sample that would gradually expand to 15,000.

In 1980, Nielsen bought out **Cassandra,** a service that reports national ratings on syndicated programs. The company later formed **Nielsen Syndication Service,** a separate operation designed to serve the syndication business.

18.2.9 Computer Access and Delivery

Birch, Arbitron, and Nielsen all offer computer access to ratings or ratings data. Customers obtain the data by telephone line or on floppy diskette. This delivery system has several advantages over printed reports; for example, it gets the information to the customer more quickly and stores it in a form that is more flexible to use. Observers in research, advertising, and programming have predicted that computer delivery would become the primary medium for ratings.

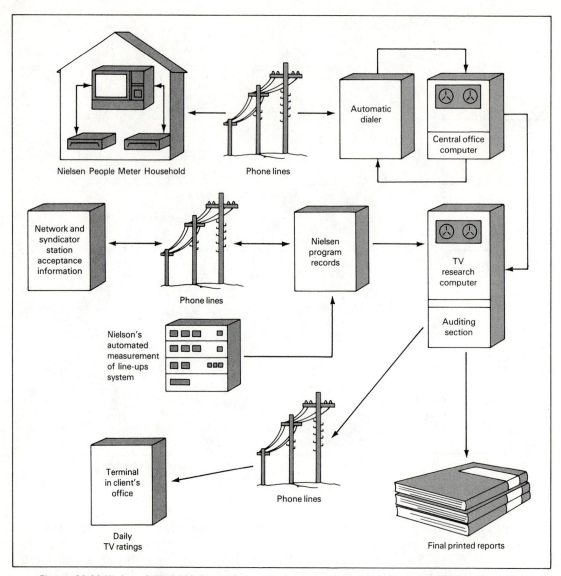

Figure 18.12 Nielsen People Meter system. Each Nielsen People Meter home unit supplies information by telephone line. At least twice a day a Nielsen computer dials each home unit and retrieves the stored viewing information. Nielsen compiles, sorts, and processes this information in aggregated form, then makes it available each morning for clients to call up on terminals in their offices. (*Source:* Nielsen Media Research.)

18.2.10 Cable Ratings

Nielsen set up **Nielsen Home Video Index** (NHVI) as its commitment to measuring new video forms—cable television, pay cable, satellite networks, local cable systems, pay-TV services, and program suppliers. Nielsen measures popular advertising-supported and subscription cable networks, as well as providing services to cable operators in local markets. Companies can also commission Nielsen to do special studies on cable. According to Nielsen, its cable data base is the largest and most complete in the world. Clients number in the thousands for services such as Cable On Line Data Exchange, Cable Audience Profile, and cable coincidentals.

Arbitron measures cable networks on a market-by-market basis. To qualify for Arbitron reporting in any given market, the network had to achieve a 20 percent net weekly circulation; in other words, it had to be watched by at least 20 percent of the market's TV households each week for at least five minutes or more. Arbitron will also do special studies on cable.

However Baldwin and McVoy[1] suggested five reasons why broadcast-style audience measurement is not appropriate for cable. First, the large number of signals available on a cable system fragment the audience much more than the four or five TV stations in a market, so a larger sample is needed. Second, people find it much harder to identify one of the 30 cable channels than one of the four or five local TV stations. Third, certain advertiser-supported pay channels supposedly attract an audience that is higher than average on the socioeconomic scale—the type of person least likely to cooperate with an audience survey. Fourth, the four or five TV stations in town share the high cost of syndicated audience research, while the one cable franchise would have to bear the entire cost. Fifth, cable should be measured in cumes only—for example, the number of different persons who viewed a particular cable channel at least once during a week.

Some cable executives have suggested yet a sixth reason why broadcast-style ratings should not be used for cable. They contend that because a cable channel audience may be small but upscale, the measurement of that audience should yield qualitative data (how much the audience liked the program; how closely they paid attention), as well as quantitative.

18.2.11 Policing and Problems

In the early 1960s, broadcasters began to rely increasingly on ratings in evaluating and making decisions on broadcast programming. Questions were raised about the procedures research firms used and the accuracy of their results. A congressional committee investigation in 1963 and 1964 revealed weaknesses and shortcomings in audience measurement.

18.2.11.1 Electronic Media Rating Council

The National Association of Broadcasters (NAB) led efforts to form a body to ensure that rating services met certain standards. NAB joined with ABC, CBS, NBC, Radio Advertising Bureau, Station Representatives Association, and Television Bureau of Advertising to form the Broadcast Rating Council in January 1964. In 1982, the organization changed its name to Electronic Media Rating Council (EMRC). Various media groups, including both broadcast and cable, have seats on EMRC's board of directors.

EMRC's main objective is to maintain and improve the quality and credibility of syndicated electronic media audience measurement. It works toward this objective in several ways. Perhaps the most important is a voluntary program under which a rating service may apply for accreditation. To be accredited a service must meet Rating Council standards for disclosure ("saying what it does") and must submit to an audit (for which the service pays) to ensure that the service "does what it says." Accredited services may use the EMRC "double check" symbol on all accredited reports. In addition the Rating Council has established committees for television, radio, and cable, which work informally with rating services to act as industry liaison and to make suggestions for improvements.

18.2.11.2 Distortion of Radio Ratings Despite the efforts of EMRC and the research firms, problems do arise. For example, station employees and their families are *not* supposed to be selected for the sample. But occasionally someone will slip through. There have even been cases in which sample families have offered to "sell out" to the highest-bidding station!

Stations occasionally use blatant attempts to influence ratings. Some radio stations, for example, have aired announcements such as "If you're keeping a rating service diary, remember you're listening to WAAA" and "If you have a friend filling out a little book, tell him or her about the new Y-100, KYYY."

18.2.11.3 Distortion of Television Ratings Several incidents during the May 1987 sweeps highlighted problems with television ratings. A Los Angeles station chose this time to broadcast nightly features on Nielsen families during its 11:00–11:30 news. "What better way to boost news ratings," asked *Broadcasting* rhetorically, "than do an eight-part series on Nielsen families in the middle of the May sweeps, promote it heavily and have [the Nielsen families] tune in to find out about themselves?"[2] At the same time, stations in Minneapolis, Orlando, and Atlanta hired a firm to conduct a "survey." The firm sent out thousands of "questionnaires" at the beginning of the rating period, asking recipients to watch the sponsoring station "as often as possible for the next seven days, then tell us your reactions to what you saw."[3]

General managers at competing stations condemned these practices. On the other hand, many stations customarily engaged in contest *hypoing* (Section 7.7) during sweeps, and ratings books would mention such efforts in footnotes. The line, then, between acceptable hypoing and unacceptable distortion was, at best, thin.

EMRC responded to these problems with new guidelines. The council said that hype (hypoing) consists of contests, advertising, special programs, and other promotional efforts. Such activity often "equalizes" (cancels itself out), since most stations do it. Distortion, said the council, encompasses activities aimed directly at the sample that could influence sample respondents to view or report viewing differently than they would normally. EMRC listed examples of distortion and included the types of surveys and programs that had occurred during the May 1987 sweeps. It also included contests run only during sweeps that award prizes more valuable than those awarded during other periods. The council recommended that research firms take one or more of the following measures to deal with distortion: add a footnote that describes the distorting activity, delete the time period during which the distortion occurred, print ratings both with and without the affected programming, and delist (omit the ratings of) the station for the entire period.

18.2.11.4 Other Ratings Problems Some problems arise from the very nature of survey research and ratings. For example, reports from two firms may show different ratings for the same time period. The firms can usually explain disparities, citing differences in elementary units, sampling procedures, statistical treatment of data, and definition of market; in other words, they measure, figure, and report different things in different ways. A survey researcher may see a 23,000 difference in HUT as the logical result of different approaches of two different firms. But a station manager—who must devise a rate card and deal with ratings-conscious media buyers—often does not see it that way.

Another problem with ratings is more subtle, widespread, and long range—their misuse by radio and television programmers. As ratings go up, so do advertising rates. Therefore programmers carefully tune their product to attract maximum audiences. The result is a predominance of inoffensive, middle-of-the-road programming and nearly total absence of minority-taste programming—for example, documentaries; serious music, drama, and dance; and minority racial and ethnic programming. The result is also programming decisions—decisions made on a regular basis but nonetheless preposterous—in which a network cancels a series because "only" 40 million people watch it. Rarely do such programming decisions mean the difference between profit and loss; usually their aim is maximum profit—as much profit as can be squeezed out.

NOTES

1. Thomas F. Baldwin and D. Stevens McVoy, *Cable Communications* (Englewood Cliffs: Prentice, 1983), pp. 285–286.
2. "KABC-TV series on Nielsen draws fire," 8 June 1987: 38.
3. Quoted in "Lines blur between hype and distortion in local sweeps," *Broadcasting* 29 June 1987: 40.

FURTHER READING

Beville, Hugh Malcolm, Jr. *Audience Ratings: Radio, Television, Cable.* Rev. ed. Hillsdale: Erlbaum, 1988. Methodologies, firms, issues. The late author was an NBC research executive and later executive director of EMRC.

Dominick, Joseph, and James Fletcher, eds. *Broadcasting Research Methods.* Boston: Allyn, 1985.

Fletcher, James E., ed. *Handbook of Radio and TV Broadcasting: Research Procedures in Audience, Program and Revenues.* New York: Van Nostrand, 1981. How to read, understand, and do various types of audience research.

————. *Squeezing Profits out of Ratings: A Manual for Radio Managers, Sales Managers and Programmers.* Washington: NAB, 1985. How to use ratings.

Heighton, Elizabeth J., and Don R. Cunningham. *Advertising in the Broadcast and Cable Media.* 2d ed. Belmont: Wadsworth, 1984. Sections on rate cards and ratings.

National Association of Broadcasters. *NAB Research Definitions.* Washington: NAB, 1987. Defines terms used in the arcane language of ratings.

Research Group, The. *MEGARATE$: How to Get Top Dollar for Your Spots.* Washington: NAB, 1986. Pricing and sales policies of successful stations.

Warner, Charles. *Broadcast and Cable Selling.* Belmont: Wadsworth, 1986. Sections on rate cards and ratings.

CHAPTER 19

Local Outlets

The basic unit in American radio and television is the local outlet. Thousands of relatively small radio and television outlets, owned by hundreds of licensees and operators, provide programming for millions of Americans. Despite direct-broadcast satellite, the local outlet is the necessary link in the system. Networks are useless without local stations and cable systems. No matter how elaborate and exciting a network's programming, your community cannot receive it unless there is a station, cable system, or other local outlet that elects to carry it.

Let us consider broadcasting as an example. Many other countries started with more efficient systems—a small number of high-powered transmitters that covered the entire country. A few sources or even a single agency handled all programming. By comparison, American broadcasting's local stations seem redundant and expensive. Yet the American system can serve local needs, a capability largely absent from other nations' systems. The station can function as a member of the community, providing entertainment, information, and opinion. The station is an employer, hiring, firing, and training personnel. It is a mixture of show business and marketing, a meeting ground for commerce and the arts. And most important to

the commercial station owner, the station is a business, an investment from which to expect a profitable return.

In this chapter we concentrate on the local commercial radio or television outlet. We look at station licensees—types of owners, limitations on ownership, and the difficult task of getting, keeping, and transferring a license. We examine station income and expenses. We see what a station is like inside and who works there. We review the organization of a cable system and local outlets in other forms of television. Then we discuss unions in radio and television. Finally, we look at some of the major trade associations pledged to protect the interests of radio and television.

19.1 THE BROADCAST LICENSEE

The **licensee** is the person or corporate entity entrusted with operation of the station by the Federal Communications Commission (FCC). Although the licensee can *own the physical plant*—land, building, equipment, transmitter—the *frequencies on which the station operates are borrowed*, terms of the loan being operation in the public interest. A licensee must sign a waiver disclaiming ownership of frequencies. The license itself is temporary, and the radio licensee must reapply every seven years; the television licensee, every five years. However, if the actual distinction between the two words is understood, "owner" can be used synonymously with "licensee."

19.1.1 Patterns of Ownership

The owner of a broadcast station may be one person, a partnership, or a group of persons. If more than one person, shares of ownership may be equal or varied. The use of *creative financing* (Section 4.5.3.2) brought new concepts of ownership to broadcasting—limited partnerships, for example, in which (1) a *general partner* put up relatively little money, assumed all liability, and ran the business, and (2) *limited partners* invested heavily, assumed no liability, took no part in directing or setting policy for the business, and reaped tax, profit, resale, and other benefits.

Often the official owner is a corporate entity. Even if one individual is sole owner, that owner may incorporate for tax or other purposes. An owner whose sole or main business is one broadcast station is a **single owner.** A **group owner** has two or more stations in different cities. An owner with an AM and an FM radio station in the same city is a **single owner with an AM-FM combination,** even when the stations program independently.

Some licensees also own other media— for example, newspapers, cable systems, or magazines. Broadcasting mixed with other media in the same locale is **cross-media ownership.** Broadcasting mixed with other media in different locations is **media conglomerate ownership,** particularly when the media holdings are large and extensive. Broadcasting mixed with other types of businesses—say, a trucking line, an airline, a kitchen appliance firm, and a tire company— is **conglomerate ownership.**

19.1.2 Limitations on Ownership

The Communications Act and the FCC set up two general types of restrictions on ownership of broadcast stations. One concerns who qualifies for a license; the other, how many licenses an individual (or group or corporate entity) may hold.

19.1.2.1 Licensee Qualifications The Communications Act specifies qualifications that must be met before a license is granted. The applicant must be a citizen of the United States or, if a corporation, must be owned mostly by citizens; must never have had a previous license revoked by a court for violating antitrust laws; and must have filed a written application. In addition, the act directs the FCC to grant a license only after determining that the grant would serve the public interest, convenience, and necessity.

The FCC asks for information about an applicant's **citizenship, character, financial, and "other" qualifications.** The commission frowns on applicants whose records include any of the following: violations of FCC rules and policies or the Communications Act; misrepresentations (lies) or lack of candor before the FCC; fraudulent programming; and certain types of fraud, antitrust, and felony as they bear on the applicant's ability to comply with broadcasting regulation. Every applicant must certify possession of sufficient financial resources; some applicants may be asked for additional financial information. The applicant does not have to be technically qualified personally, but does have to show plans for equipment and staff that reflect adequate technical preparation.

19.1.2.2 Licensee Limitations For years, the FCC had rules to limit the number of stations in which one commercial licensee could hold financial interest. Some of these date back as far as the 1930s. Their purpose is diversification—to prevent broadcast stations from being owned or controlled by relatively few individuals and corporations. The commission reasoned that such monopoly would reduce the number of origins and outlets for different views and ideas, while raising the number of absentee owners unfamiliar with the needs and interests of the communities in which their stations are located.

The oldest of these is the **duopoly rule.** The duopoly rule forbids common ownership of two stations in the same service (AM, FM, or TV) whose signals overlap. In 1988, the FCC relaxed the definitions of *overlap* to allow closer spacing of commonly owned radio stations. Under the new definitions, a broadcaster could own two or more AMs or two or more FMs *not* in the same market but in closer proximity than before. For example, minimum spacing between commonly owned Class A FM stations (Section 11.2.2) was reduced from 30 miles to 17.

The **one-to-a-market** rule prohibits a new licensee from getting both radio and television stations in the same city. When the one-to-a-market rule went into effect, a number of radio-television ownership combinations existed; these were **grandfathered in** (allowed to remain). But later sales were to be arranged to break up the combinations.

The FCC also relaxed the one-to-a-market rule in 1988. The commission announced that it would consider requests for waivers to the rule and would "look favorably" on requests from stations in either of two situations. In the first situation, the requesting stations would be licensed to a top-25 market that had at least 30 separately owned broadcast licenses. A 1989 waiver, for example, allowed Capital Cities/ABC to keep four radio-TV-station combinations (in New York, Chicago, Los Angeles, and San Francisco) that ABC had owned before the net-

work was acquired by Capital Cities (Section 4.5.3.4).

In the second situation, the request would involve stations that had gone dark or were in bankruptcy proceedings. The commission would consider other requests using the following public interest criteria: "the types of facilities involved, the potential benefits of the combination, the number of stations already owned by the applicant, the financial difficulties of the station(s) and the nature of the market, including the degree of cable penetration in [the] light of the commission's continuing diversity and competition concerns."[1]

The **12-station** rule restricts nationwide ownership in each service. This type of limitation dates back to 1940. In 1953, the commission adopted a seven-station rule. Thirty-two years later, the FCC raised the limit to 12 and added a few complications. Under the 12-station (or 12-12-12) rule, one individual may hold ownership interest in

1. no more than 36 stations—12 AM, 12 FM, and 12 TV;
2. an additional two stations in each service (total of six more stations), as long as the additional stations are controlled (more than half owned) by racial minorities;
3. TV stations whose collective market areas encompass no more than 25 percent of the nation's households (even if the stations owned number less than 12);
4. minority-controlled TV stations whose collective market areas encompass no more than 30 percent of the nation's households (even if the stations owned number less than 14);
5. UHF television stations that exceed the 25/30 percent limit, because they are credited with only half the households in their market areas.

The FCC bans certain types of cross-media ownerships and has even required divestiture (breakup) through sales. In 1975, the commission adopted the **newspaper-broadcast cross ownership** rule. This rule forbade broadcast stations to be co-owned with newspapers in the same market. Most existing newspaper-broadcast combinations were grandfathered in; divestiture was ordered only for cases in which the newspaper was the market's only daily (which was the case in 18 small markets).

The **TV-cable cross ownership** rule forbids television stations to be co-owned with cable television systems in the same market. The commission required divestiture only for cases where a cable television system was co-owned with the city's only commercial television station. Congress wrote this rule into law[2] in 1984.

The deregulation movement (Section 4.5.1) affected ownership limitations. In 1979 and 1984, the commission did away with certain types of ownership restrictions that applied to large markets and regional concentrations. And as explained above, the FCC loosened the duopoly and one-to-a-market rules in 1988.

19.1.2.3 WHDH and RKO Cases

Three cases illustrate the problems that applicants can meet with ownership limitations. All involved television stations in Boston. In one, WHDH lost its license for channel 5 at least in part on the issue of diversification of media ownership; the station was owned by the *Boston Herald Traveler* newspaper. A 1971 federal appeals court ruling[3] upheld the FCC's decision, ending a complicated case whose origins went back 17 years.

In a second case, RKO General lost its license for channel 7 for misrepresentation. A 1981 appeals court ruling[4] held that RKO had withheld evidence in its license renewal application regarding certain wrongdoings of its parent, General Tire & Rubber. RKO's troubles continued. In 1987, an FCC administrative law judge denied license renewal for all 14 of RKO's remaining stations, citing fraudulent billing practices and misrepresentation. Had this decision prevailed, RKO would have lost millions of dollars that it had invested in the stations. The next year, however, the full commission finessed the ALJ's decision by ruling that RKO could sell its stations, albeit not at full market value. This ruling failed to resolve the issue of RKO's qualifications as a licensee but did allow—rightly or wrongly—RKO to recover some of its investment.

19.1.2.4 Murdoch's Waivers

An act of Congress prevented the FCC from extending waivers of the newspaper-broadcast cross ownership rule. Rupert Murdoch's News America Publishing Co. owned the *New York Post* and the *Boston Herald*, both in cities where Murdoch wished to buy television stations (Section 4.5.3.4). In 1986, the FCC had granted temporary waivers of the rule to allow him to buy the stations and *then* look for buyers for the newspapers. Murdoch petitioned for an extension of the waivers in 1988. Meanwhile, Congress had enacted legislation that included a one-year prohibition against the FCC changing the newspaper-broadcast cross ownership rule and granting or extending waivers to that rule. The waiver ban aimed specifically at Murdoch. Reportedly, it had been included in the bill by South Carolina Senator Ernest Hollings at the request of Massachusetts Senator Edward Kennedy, often a target of editorial attacks by the *Boston Herald.* A federal appeals court later overturned the ban. By that time, however, Murdoch had sold the *Post.* He kept the *Herald* but put the Boston television station into an irrevocable trust.

19.1.3 The Licensing Process

The process to get a license for a new broadcast station is long and complicated. Many things can go wrong and further complicate the process.

In this section, we trace the steps to license a new broadcast station. We assume that the applicant has done the necessary preliminary work. This includes tasks such as finding a channel, incorporating or otherwise organizing, and raising the money. That being done, the applicant must **file a written application for a construction permit** (CP) on a specific form with the FCC. The application requires technical information and data on the applicant's citizenship, character, and financial qualifications. The applicant must also run a notice about the proposed station in the newspaper.

At the FCC, the staff **receives the application and checks it.** If substantially complete, the application is accepted, and the applicant is notified to supply any missing information. If not substantially complete, the application is returned.

At this point, at least four problems could occur. Anyone could delay grant of the CP and generate additional expense for the applicant. First, someone could file a **petition to deny the application.** The petition must meet several tests before the commission accepts it. If it is accepted, the FCC examines the petition and either rejects it or designates the matter for hearing. Second, others could apply for the same channel. This means the FCC now has **competing applications** and must dispose of them as outlined below (Section 19.1.4). Third, someone may file an **informal objection** to grant of the CP. This is neither as serious nor as formal as the petition to deny or as competing applications, but it could lead to a **hearing on motion by the commission.** The FCC may, of its own volition, hold a hearing any time it has reason to believe that the public interest might not be served by granting the CP.

Let us suppose that the application runs into none of these problems. If the FCC determines that construction of the station would serve the public interest, then the **CP is granted.** Now the applicant is called a permittee and may build the station. The time limit is **24 (for TV) or 18 (for all others) months to complete construction,** although the FCC may grant extensions. Upon completion, the station **runs equipment and program tests and is inspected by the FCC district engineer.** If all goes well, the permittee than **applies for and receives the station license,** changing status from permittee to licensee.

19.1.4 Competing Applications

A 1982 amendment to the Communications Act authorized the FCC to use a **lottery system to select from among mutually exclusive applications** (two or more applicants applying for one channel). At the same time, Congress discouraged the commission from using lotteries to award licenses for radio and full-power television stations. The legislators directed that the FCC had to make a very good case that choice-by-lot was needed before applying it to competing broadcast applicants.

The FCC does, however, take advantage of the lottery option for other services, such as cellular telephone, low-power television, wireless cable (multichannel TV), and the instructional-television fixed service (Section 5.4). In passing the lottery bill, Congress had required that members of certain minority racial groups, then greatly underrepresented in ownership of communications facilities, receive a greater chance in the selection process. Therefore, in setting up a lottery, the FCC gives more weight (more chances to get the license) to applicants that are controlled by minorities. Only after an applicant is chosen by lot does the commission staff examine that applicant's qualifications. If the winning applicant does not meet the minimum qualifications, the commission runs the lottery again among the remaining applicants.

Competing applications for AM, FM, and full-power TV stations, however, still had to go through a cumbersome, time-consuming process that involved hearings before an FCC administrative law judge (ALJ). Considering evidence presented at the hearings, the ALJ evaluated each applicant using **comparative criteria** and then, in the initial decision, awarded the license to the applicant that showed superiority in these criteria. The criteria reflected various stated aims of the commission in licensing. These included local ownership, integration of ownership and management, diversity of ownership of mass media, and furtherance of ownership by women and racial minorities (although the FCC had attempted to eliminate preferences for women and minorities during the 1980s). The criteria were vague at best, and the ALJ often had to base the initial decision on points of difference that most laypersons saw as esoteric at best. Other applicants could (and often did) appeal the decision all the way to the federal courts. By the time all side issues had been cleared and all possibilities of appeal exhausted, years could pass, costing both applicants and taxpayers.

Despite legislative discouragement, the FCC decided, in 1989, to attempt choice-by-lot instead of by comparative hearing. The commissioners voted to show that lotteries should be used to choose among competing applicants for licenses of new radio and full-power TV stations. They labeled the comparative hearing process "unduly burdensome"—slow, and costly to applicants and the FCC. Additionally, in some 80 percent of the hearings, the competing applicants settled among themselves before the ALJs made decisions, so the hearing process often failed to achieve its purpose. Many questioned whether the FCC's bid to use the lottery would pass congressional scrutiny.

19.1.5 Change in Facilities, Ownership, and Control

A licensee may wish to change facilities. Typically, the change might be to raise power, to expand allotted operating time, to move to a different channel or location, to modify an antenna array, or to install improved transmitting equipment. To do so, the licensee must apply for a CP.

The Communications Act stipulates that any change in ownership or control of a broadcast station must be considered by the FCC before that change takes place. If a broadcast licensee wishes to sell the station, application has to be made first to the FCC. On receipt of the application, the commission considers whether the public interest would be served by the transfer. The FCC is prohibited from inviting and considering competing applications, limiting its choice to approval or disapproval of the transfer.

Some applicants do not want to operate a station. They want it just so they can sell it at a profit. This is **trafficking** in station licenses, a practice that was rife after the 1952 end of the freeze on television licensing (Sections 4.1.1–4.1.3). Trafficking negates the concept of licensing a station to serve the public interest. For years the FCC barred a licensee from selling a station within three years of getting it. The commission repealed its antitrafficking rule in 1982, saying that market conditions no longer warranted retention. Two years later, the commission raised the limits on station ownership (Section 19.1.2.2), and the 1980s buy-sell frenzy began in earnest (Section 4.5.3.2). As indicated in Box 19.1, not every broadcaster viewed these developments as positive.

The FCC is interested in other forms of change of control. For example, the trading of major blocks of stock in a corporate licensee could alter control of that licensee. The corporate licensee would still own the

Box 19.1 One Broadcaster's Views on Licensee Responsibility and the Public Interest Requirement

In 1987, the National Association of Broadcasters presented its Distinguished Service Award to Martin Umansky. Over the years, Mr. Umansky earned a national reputation in broadcasting and news at KAKE in Wichita, Kansas. In his acceptance speech,* Mr. Umansky expressed disappointment at the result of at least one aspect of deregulation, the lifting of the antitrafficking rule. He called it an action "that has attracted financially oriented speculators to what they perceive as a cash-cow industry to be milked for all it's worth: the leveraged buyout experts, the fast-buck artists and others who have no real feeling for or understanding of broadcasting. Their bottom-line morality may justify extensive staff firings and wholesale cutting of expenses to satisfy boardroom budget decisions, but they may be seriously damaging the ability of their operations to serve and attract an audience that is already somewhat disenchanted with traditional broadcasting.

"That bottom line may be better served in the long run if investment is made in investigative reporters and public affairs people. Money spent on developing a sound and respected relationship with the community and becoming the trusted, relied-upon communicator; that money will come back many times over."

Contrary to the opinion of marketplace advocates (Sections 4.5.1 and 13.4.2), Mr. Umansky said he felt that the public interest requirement served broadcasting well. "Whoever coined the phrase ' . . . serve the public interest, convenience, and necessity' of the Communications Act deserves five distinguished service awards," he said. "That's what our industry is about. The license requirement never was a burden to good, serious broadcasters who do not live in a vacuum. They ascertain. They see the problems and address them. They know serving the public well is good broadcasting and that's good business. It's the key to success."

*Excerpted in "DSA winner Umansky champions localism," *Broadcasting* 6 Apr. 1987: 76.

station, but a new party or group would control the corporation. A similar situation could occur in a partnership. Such changes require prior written permission of the FCC.

19.1.6 License Renewal

There are two exceptions to the five- and seven-year renewal periods (Section 19.1) for broadcast licenses. One is the short-term renewal (Section 14.1.1.12). The other occurs when a new station gets its first license be-

tween scheduled periods for its state. In the latter case, the station must renew early to get "in phase" with the other stations in the state.

A station files for renewal no later than four months before expiration of its current license. It files on the commission's half-sheet-sized renewal form.

The station must also broadcast public notices of renewal and insert certain material in its public file. This material includes statements that the public notices were broadcast and a copy of the completed renewal application.

19.1.7 Other Requirements

Copies of certain documents—generally, agreements or contracts that affect station management or programming—must be (according to the type of document) either filed with the commission or retained at the station for FCC inspection. Each year, the licensee must either file an Ownership Report or certify the accuracy of the current report on file with the FCC. And each station must maintain a public file (Section 15.3.3.6).

Every station must establish and put into effect a positive, continuing program to afford minorities and women equal opportunity in all areas of employment. It must also submit a Broadcast Equal Employment Opportunity Program Report plan with its license renewal application. Stations with five or more employees complete the program report in detail and also submit an Annual Employment Report. The station bases its EEO program on an FCC "model program." This program works toward including women and minorities in both the general station staff and in the upper-level staff—officials and managers, professionals, technicians, and sales personnel.

19.1.8 Loss of License

In Section 14.1.1.12, we said that two FCC sanctions involved loss of license—denial of renewal and revocation. One study[5] of FCC action during the period 1970–1978 found that the FCC gave seven reasons most often for denial of renewal. They were as follows, in descending order of occurrence: misrepresentation to the commission; failure to apply for or otherwise act on renewal, abandonment (stopped broadcasting), and ignored correspondence from the FCC; departure from promised programming; fraudulent billing practices; unauthorized transfer of control; character qualifications; and technical violations.

Occasionally, one or more parties will challenge the incumbent licensee at renewal time. In some cases, the challenger petitions the FCC to deny renewal of the license. In other cases, the challenger files as a competitor for the license. This competing application is called a strike application. In either situation, the charge is that the incumbent licensee has not done well in serving the public. If the FCC judges that the petition to deny renewal or the strike application has merit, it may designate the matter for hearing.

In a petition to deny renewal, the incumbent may attempt to negotiate with the challenger. If the negotiation is successful and the challenger agrees to withdraw, they seek FCC approval of the settlement. Conditions of the settlement have often required the incumbent to pay the challenger. This gave rise to charges by licensees that most such challenges amount to blackmail. In 1989, the FCC revised its rules to curb such practices, labeling them "abuses" of the renewal process. The commission limited payments and said that it would scrutinize such settlements to ensure that they were in the public interest.

Licensees have also complained about their vulnerability to strike applications. If the matter goes to hearing, the FCC listens to both sides. And in a **comparative renewal** hearing, the challenger would appear to have the advantage. After all, no matter how good the incumbent's *record* in serving the public interest, the challenger could *promise* more. And the challenger's application would certainly be structured to look better than the incumbent in any weighing of comparative criteria (Section 19.1.4) An incumbent who did not wish to go through the expensive and time-consuming hearing process often elected to pay the challenger in return for withdrawing the competing application—which, according to many broadcasters, was exactly why the challenger had filed the strike application in the first place.

A 1982 appeals court decision, however, helped to tilt the process more toward the incumbent in a comparative renewal hearing. That decision affirmed the commission's policy of granting a **renewal expectancy** to deserving incumbents. An incumbent earns a renewal expectancy by demonstrating "meritorious" service to the public—usually a substantial record with respect to ascertainment and programming to meet the problems, needs, and interest of the community (Section 15.3.3.5). The expectancy outweighs any comparative advantage the challenger might have as a result of comparative criteria; the better the incumbent's record, the greater the expectancy to which the incumbent is entitled.

In its 1989 rules revision, the FCC further tilted the process toward the incumbent. The revised rules forbid an incumbent to make any payment if a challenger withdraws a strike application *before* the initial decision in a comparative hearing. The incumbent *may* make a payment for settlement *after* the initial decision, but even then, the commission limits such payments to "legitimate and prudent expenses." Under the changed rules, competing applicants can no longer presume that they can acquire the incumbent's transmitter site (should the incumbent lose), a presumption that previously allowed challengers to avoid completing the engineering portion of their applications and to avoid having to find a new transmitter site. And the FCC revised its construction permit application (Section 19.1.3) to require more detailed financial, ownership, and management–ownership integration information—an instance of *re*-regulation! On the previous form, applicants had only to check a box indicating they were "financially qualified"; on the revised form, they have to estimate the cost of building and operating the station and list their sources of funding.

19.1.9 Distress Sales and Tax Certificates

The FCC has given a break both to licensees faced with renewal or revocation hearings and to members of minority racial groups who wish to get into broadcast ownership. A licensee faced with such a hearing can sell the station to an applicant with significant minority interest at a "distress sale" price, 75 percent of the station's market value, before the hearing begins. In addition, anyone who sells to a minority applicant may apply to the FCC for a certificate that grants a tax break in that it allows the seller to defer capital gains.

The commission attempted to cut out minority preferences. In 1986, the FCC issued a notice of inquiry seeking comment on the constitutionality of its minority preference policies. These policies included preferences awarded to women and minorities in broadcast license proceedings, as well as distress sales and tax certificates. In 1987, however, Congress passed a bill that, among other things, called on the commission to affirm these policies and end the inquiry. The FCC complied. In 1989, a three-judge panel of the U.S. Court of Appeals in Washington declared the distress sale policy unconstitutional. Just three weeks later, however, another panel of the same court affirmed the FCC's policy granting minorities preferences in comparative cases (Section 19.1.4).[6]

19.2 FINANCIAL MANAGEMENT

The primary purpose of any business is to earn a profit. Expenses are deducted from revenues, and the result—the **bottom line**—

determines whether the business has been successful. Since a commercial broadcast station is a business, the owner considers its bottom line to be crucial. Profits make everyone happy; owners get return on investment, employees may get raises, capital improvements may be made to the station, programming and other services to the community may be expanded, and new employees may be hired. Losses can mean layoffs, continued use of poor equipment, and cutbacks in programming. Continued losses can lead to sale of the station or surrender of its license.

19.2.1 Financial Statements

The **balance sheet** (Table 19.1) reflects the general economic condition of the station as a business. The balance sheet sets forth the

Table 19.1 BROADCAST STATION BALANCE SHEET		
(Date)		
	This year	**Last year**
Assets		
Current assets:	$	$
Cash		
Temporary investments		
Receivables, less reserves		
Inventories		
Broadcasting rights		
Prepaid expenses	——	——
Total current assets		
Fixed assets, less depreciation		
Deferred charges		
Broadcasting rights, noncurrent		
Other assets		
Intangibles	——	——
Total assets	$——	$——
Liabilities and capital		
Current liabilities:		
Accounts and notes payable		
Taxes and amounts withheld from employees		
Accrued expenses		
Federal income taxes payable	$——	$——
Total current liabilities		
Deferred income taxes		
Deferred credits		
Long-term debt		
Other liabilities	——	——
Capital stock		
Additional paid-in capital		
Retained earnings		
Treasury stock:		
Common	( )	( )
Preferred	(——)	(——)
Total capital		
Total liabilities and capital	$——	$——

Source: Used by permission of Broadcast Financial Management Association.

value of the station's assets, liabilities, and equity. **Assets** are what the station owns and include the following: land on which the station sits and buildings in which it is housed; equipment; unused rights to program materials; value of a network affiliation contract; and cash on hand, accounts receivable, prepaid expenses, unused inventories, and so forth. **Liabilities** are the station's debts and range from mortgages and dividends declared but not yet paid to employee wages. **Equity** (*capital* or *net worth*) is the amount the licensee actually has invested in the station. The balance sheet is so called because it shows these three elements balanced in this way: assets + liabilities = equity. (Remember, the liabilities value is negative, so adding it to assets results in subtraction.) In other words, if the assets of the station were sold off at face value and all creditors paid from the proceeds, the remainder would go to the licensee. (The station, however, is generally worth more than the sum of its liquidated assets [Section 19.2.3].)

An **income statement** reflects a licensee's economic activity through time. Also called a *profit and loss statement*, the income statement sets forth revenue, subtracts from it expenses incurred in earning that revenue, and derives income after taxes, the "bottom line" mentioned above. A station receives most **revenue** from advertising sales. Other sources include network compensation, talent fees, charges for use of facilities, syndication or sale of programming, merchandising, and return on investment. **Expenses** are frequently divided into four areas—programming, technical, selling, and general and administrative. Salaries, wages, and commissions usually make up the greatest expenditure in each area. Typically, TV stations spend most on programming; radio stations, on general and administrative, with programming as the second largest expense. Table 19.2 shows national averages of reve-

nue and expenses figures for several categories of broadcast stations.

19.2.2 Factors in Profitability

When losses occur or profits drop, some managers panic. They cut advertising rates, program cheaply, accept questionable advertising, fire experienced talent, and drop trade association memberships. Such action may trim losses in the short run but may lead to more serious problems in the long run as audiences notice that quality has dropped.

A good manager builds in reserves that may be cut temporarily to reduce losses. If a station has good programming and acceptable audience levels, the first items cut are waste and inefficiency. Some managers actually raise advertising rates when profits fall or losses are incurred. Assured that they have quality programming that efficiently attracts target audiences, they know advertisers will continue to buy time, even if prices are higher. Some managers spend even more, pumping money into programming, promotion, and sales, sustaining greater losses over a short period to regain the competitive edge that pays off in the long run.

The chances of a station making money vary with the type of station. On the average, full-service TV stations make more than radio stations, VHF television stations more than UHF stations, large-market TV stations more than small-market stations (Table 19.3), and TV network affiliates more than independents. Network-owned television stations—all large-market VHF affiliates—are, on the average, much more profitable than other stations.

In radio, the factors vary somewhat. The edge in earnings and profitability tends to go to stations that are in the FM band and large markets and that have high power. Network affiliation does not have the same value as in

Table 19.2 REVENUE AND EXPENSE OF BROADCAST STATIONS NATIONWIDE (IN THOUSANDS OF DOLLARS)

Revenue and expense items	Radio stations					Television stations		
	Daytime AMs	Full-time AMs	AM/FM combos	FM stand-alones	Affiliates	Independents	All UHFs
Network compensation	8.3	31.6	18.9	21.2	822.9	26.4	252.8
National/regional advertising	41.8	293.8	302.7	334.8	7,749.1	6,820.3	3,821.7
Local advertising	197.6	1,067.8	1,100.9	1,291.0	8,217.1	8,357.7	3,565.6
Total times sales	**229.9**	**1,300.0**	**1,353.0**	**1,614.2**	**16,734.2**	**14,987.8**	**7,559.4**
Agency and rep commissions	12.9	163.0	153.1	210.5	2,751.2	2,509.7	1,354.6
Other revenue	2.4	13.1	18.7	20.1	267.4	267.0	196.3
Total net revenue	**210.0**	**1,071.4**	**1,216.2**	**1,353.2**	**14,239.4**	**12,813.3**	**6,444.9**
Expenses							
Engineering	10.3	48.0	55.6	53.4	760.0	779.6	492.5
Programming	51.1	229.5	241.4	258.2	2,233.7	7,044.9	3,032.5
News	12.1	88.9	39.4	31.3	1,882.1	460.8	314.9
Sales	38.6	183.7	238.7	265.4	892.9	991.7	680.9
Advertising and promotion	7.6	93.7	91.9	166.2	541.1	763.5	391.0
General administrative	91.2	376.3	510.1	539.0	3,287.7	3,268.1	2,253.6
Total expenses	**206.3**	**1,014.8**	**1,175.2**	**1,303.7**	**9,827.8**	**13,040.0**	**7,123.6**
Pretax profit	**16.9**	**(19.5)**	**49.4**	**63.0**	**3,369.1**	**(129.7)**	**(711.5)**
Cash flow	**43.0**	**135.3**	**219.0**	**285.2**	**4,350.2**	**1,182.1**	**223.1**

Table 19.2 Revenue and Expense of Broadcast Stations Nationwide. Responses to a survey of broadcast stations for the National Association of Broadcasters and the Broadcast Financial Management Association yielded these 1987 figures. The greater a station's revenue, the more likely it was to respond to the survey; these figures, therefore, have been weighted to account for resulting over- and under-representation. Totals do not equal their component figures because some stations did not report all information requested.
Source: NAB.

Table 19.3 VARIATION OF TELEVISION STATION REVENUES BY MARKET SIZE.

Markets	Total number of stations in those 10 markets	Average revenue per station	Average pretax profit per station
1–10	72	$53,551,090	$14,849,409
41–50	44	11,629,386	2,061,003
91–100	36	5,693,871	355,471
121–130	37	3,564,486	91,934

Table 19.3 Variation of Television Station Revenues by Market Size. The figures in the second column include all commercial television stations in all indicated markets as of 1989. For example, the ten largest markets (1–10) had a total of 72 stations, while markets 41–50 had 44 stations.
Source: NAB

television. Keep in mind that we are dealing with averages; you can most certainly find exceptions.

19.2.3 Factors in Station Valuation

Buyers and sellers of broadcast properties use various factors to determine the market value of a station. They consider the station itself—management, programming, program inventory, financial obligations, and technical facilities (quality, power, antenna and physical plant, and whether they can be upgraded). They look at the competition—number of stations, types of other stations (AM, FM, VHF, UHF), technical facilities. They look at the market—cost of programming (how much do stations pay in the market?), availability of programming (have the other stations already bought up the best product?), advertising revenue, economic health, and business trends. They also look at the state of the national economy (especially interest rates) and pending legislation (that might affect ability to profit or worth of the station).

One important factor is station revenue. **Cash flow,** for example, reflects the money left after meeting necessary expenses (Section 19.2) to make payments on long-term financial obligations. Since most buyers borrow heavily to buy stations, they figure the worth of a station by the cash it generates to service the buyer's debts. They evaluate a station using cash flow multiples—for example, 6.5 times cash flow. *Leverage* refers to money borrowed on the business itself (rather than on the value of its hard assets), on the business's ability to generate payback cash (Section 4.5.3.2); a station purchased largely on such a basis is said to be **highly leveraged.**

19.3 STATION ORGANIZATION

Two elements, fundamental to any station, are physical facilities and personnel. These are basic tools with which the station builds programming, audience, sales, and profits.

19.3.1 Physical Plant Requirements: Radio Stations

Radio stations come in all sizes. Some fit in small houses (Figure 19.1), office suites, even mobile homes; others, in buildings large enough to house a television station. All radio stations have certain special requirements for which space must be set aside.

19.3.1.1 Transmitter Room Central to the needs of any radio station is space for the transmitter (Figure 19.2). A modern radio

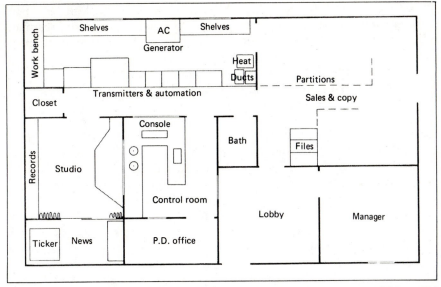

Figure 19.1 Floor plan for small radio station. The building designed for WDDD, a 50-kW FM station in Marion, Illinois, is 26 by 44 feet. Note that from the control room the operator can see the studio, newsroom, automation units, and receptionist in the lobby. (© BM/E Magazine. Used by permission of BM/E and Act III Publishing.)

transmitter is compact, usually housed in the station building itself. Because of FCC requirements, the transmitter is either located where the operator can see it or has a set of remote controls and instruments that the operator can see. A station that automates programming often places its automation units adjacent to the transmitter.

19.3.1.2 Control Rooms and Studios The broadcast operations center is the master control room. Here works the operator, the person on duty who operates the transmitter. Since the operator typically functions as a host/disc jockey (Section 6.1.2), the master control room contains the following: audio control board, turntables, compact disc players, microphones, tape machines, telephone, log and copy book, and bins containing records and tapes. A clock, hot clock charts (Section 7.2.1), a bulletin board full of FCC and station notices, several coffee cups, and assorted chairs, trash cans, and pop music

Figure 19.2 Radio station transmitter room. WRVF Chief Engineer Ed Slimak adjusts the transmitter.

posters complete the usual radio control room. The master control room is built to reduce outside noise and to cut unwanted echoes.

Many stations contain at least one production control room. This is where commercials and special programs are produced. Adjoining the control rooms may be one or more studios. Studios are lined with sound-deadening material and contain microphone outlets. They range from closetlike announce booths to large rooms capable of seating up to 100 persons.

19.3.1.3 Newsroom Most stations have some accommodation for news, the size varying with the complexity of the news operation. Full-time news personnel need work space larger than the usual news-wire-machine closet—at least one office-size room equipped to perform as described in Section 8.2.

19.3.1.4 Office Space The station must contain office space for the general manager, the program director, the sales staff, the copywriter, the traffic director, and the accounting or business staff, as well as a workshop/office for the engineer and a lobby area. A receptionist works in the lobby to greet visitors. In small stations the receptionist may also double in other jobs—manager's secretary, copy writer, traffic manager, or bookkeeper.

19.3.1.5 Storage and Auxiliary Areas A radio station needs closets, storage space, places for files, rest rooms, provision for central heating and air conditioning, and a place for a coffee maker. Although few stations maintain extensive record libraries, larger stations may set aside an entire room for record and tape storage.

Successful stations often have larger quarters. Typically, they use the additional space for conference rooms, snack or vending areas, community meeting rooms, observa-

tion areas, individual offices for news director, chief engineer, and sales manager, and lounges for off-duty air personnel.

19.3.2 Physical Plant Requirements: Television Stations

Television involves more equipment than radio and requires a larger physical plant (Figure 19.3). The television station frequently consists of at least two buildings—the main studio and the transmitter building

19.3.2.1 Transmitter Building The transmitter building is adjacent to the transmitting tower. Since a tower should be located as high as possible and central to the region served by the station, the transmitter building may be in a remote area, even on a mountain.

19.3.2.2 Master Control Room In the television master control room (Figure 19.4), the video signal receives final processing before going to the transmitter. To conserve on personnel, duty or residue directing (Section 6.5.3) may be done from master control, camera control units for all cameras may be in master control, and telecine units and videotape machines may be located in or adjacent to master control.

19.3.2.3 Production Studio and Control Room The station produces local programming in a production studio (Figure 19.5). Studios are, of necessity, large rooms—large enough to hold sets and to allow talent and cameras to move around. A production studio contains cameras, outlets for cameras and microphones, lighting instruments, a grid of pipes near the ceiling from which to suspend lighting instruments, some electrical outlets, and control equipment for the lights.

A production control room contains video monitors, switching panel, video effects generator controls, character generator controls, remote controls for telecine and videotape,

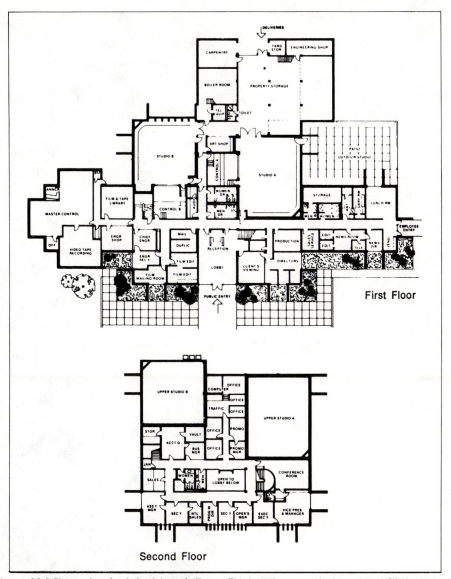

Figure 19.3 Floor plan for television station.   This building was designed for KSTW, channel 11, an independent with strong emphasis on production, serving the Seattle-Tacoma (Washington) market. (© BM/E Magazine. Used by permission of BM/E Magazine and Act III Publishing.)

audio monitor, audio console, audio tape machines, clocks and timers, and communications systems that connect to the studio and master control. The director, assistant director, technical director, and audio technician work from the production control room. Sometimes there is a soundproof announce booth just off production control. Ideally, production control should be situated so that the director can see into the studio through a large observation window.

19.3.2.4 News   The news department in a TV station needs a general newsroom (Figure

Figure 19.4 Television station master control. Central processing and switching point for Orlando's channel 2.

Figure 19.5 Television station production studio. The room must be large enough to accommodate program sets and camera movement. The ceiling must be high enough to accommodate the metal pipe grid from which are suspended many lighting instruments.

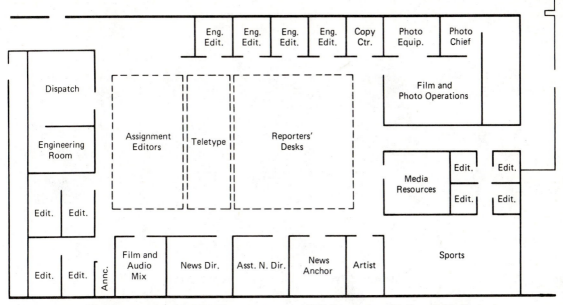

Figure 19.6 Floor plan of television newsroom. KSTP-TV, channel 5, the ABC affiliate for Minneapolis-St. Paul, designed its newsroom for optimum efficiency. (*Source:* KSTP-TV. Used by permission.)

19.6) for staff work space. Other news requirements include space for two-way radio monitoring equipment, wire machines, equipment storage and checkout, film and tape editing, film and slide library, sports, weather, investigative units, and the news director's office.

19.3.2.5 Specialized Areas A television station needs a large, studio-sized area set aside for scenery construction and storage. Engineering personnel need a room outfitted for equipment maintenance and repair. Syndication sources provide much programming, requiring space to ship, receive, and store film and videotape. A station film or tape production unit needs space for equipment and activities. The art department needs a properly equipped area with space for work and storage.

19.3.2.6 Offices and Auxiliary Areas Television stations usually provide separate of-

fices for all major department heads and for traffic, continuity, promotion, sales, and accounting departments. Many stations contain conference rooms and a lounge area or even a snack shop for employees. And, of course, a television station must have the usual complement of rest rooms, file areas, general storage areas, and central heat and air conditioning rooms.

19.3.3 Personnel

There are as many ways in which to classify station personnel as there are stations. We shall use six main categories or departments—management, business, sales, programming, news, and engineering (Figures 19.7 and 19.8). Each of these may be composed of subdepartments, for example, production as part of programming. Larger stations may have more major departments; for example, an increasing number of television

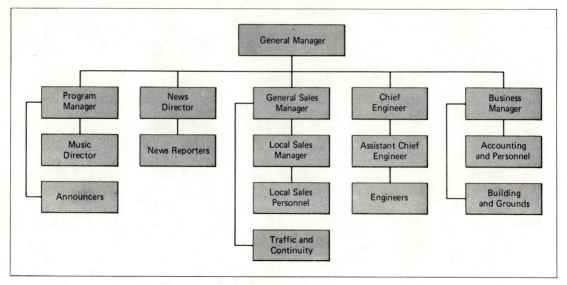

Figure 19.7. Typical radio station organizational chart.

stations have their research directors report directly to the general manager, with research on a level with sales, programming, and news. Smaller stations may have fewer major departments; for example, some news personnel report to program directors, and some station managers head both business and sales areas.

19.3.3.1 Management A broadcast station is headed by a general manager (GM). When the licensee is a corporation, the GM may be a corporate officer, most often a vice president. The licensee sets certain goals for the station, and the GM translates those objectives into station policies. Station department heads report to the GM and implement station policy within their departments. The GM motivates, coordinates, and stimulates. In large operations, separate station managers may carry out day-to-day operations; for example, a radio-television combination may have a radio manager under the GM. Every station also has legal advisers, and some GMs make no move of consequence without first checking with the company's staff law-

yers, its local law firms, its Washington, D.C., communications lawyers, or all three.

19.3.3.2 Business The business department is headed by a business manager, comptroller, or treasurer. This department handles billing, accounting, payroll, budget, and most other fiscal matters. The business department includes personnel functions, also; and a personnel manager accepts applications from prospective employees and maintains records on current employees.

19.3.3.3 Sales The sales manager heads the sales department, which includes local sales staff and liaison with the sales representative firm (Section 17.4). The promotion director (Section 7.7) and the traffic manager (Section 6.5.1) may also report to the sales manager.

19.3.3.4 Programming The program director (PD) has responsibility for all programming, locally produced, syndicated, and network. The PD may also have continuity (script and commercial copywriting) as part

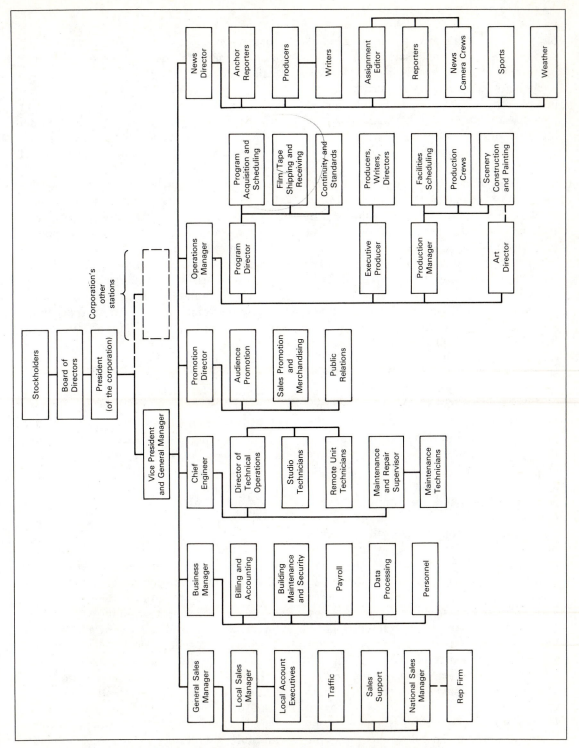

Figure 19.8 Typical television station organization chart.

of the programming area, although in many stations this comes under sales.

In radio stations the PD usually gets directly involved with local production. Duties include scheduling announcers, auditioning records, drawing up play lists, and supervising local program efforts. In larger stations the PD may have assistants—a music director and an assistant PD.

The television PD puts most time and effort into long-range planning and buying of syndicated programming and feature films. At a network-affiliated station the PD also monitors nonbroadcast previews of network programming and advises management of material that should be delayed or even canceled.

The television PD has assistants to supervise local production. An executive producer oversees producers and directors. The production manager manages and schedules studios, production crews, the art department, and the announcing staff.

Some stations have an **operations manager.** This officer typically functions as the program director but also has duties and authority beyond those normally assigned to a chief programmer. The operations manager may, in fact, act as assistant station manager.

Both the sales and programming departments need current research information—information on the market, the station's place in the market, the programming, and the audience. Whether or not the station maintains a central research department to serve these needs, the program director must know how to use research information—and often, how to gather it. For example, a radio station may base its play list in part on results from station-conducted call-out research; a random sample of listeners is called and asked to evaluate new recordings.

19.3.3.5 News The news director is in charge of news and public affairs programming. The news director supervises the regular news, sports, and weather staff, as well as documentary, special projects, and public affairs units.

19.3.3.6 Engineering The chief engineer heads the engineering department. The chief engineer's responsibilities include supervision of transmitter operation, FCC-required checks and reports, maintenance and repair of equipment, purchase of equipment, and long-range technical planning. In small radio stations the chief is the only engineer and does everything personally; some radio stations may operate without a full-time staff engineer, opting instead to contract for technical services. At the other end of the scale, the chief engineer at a large television station rarely performs actual technical procedures, devoting full time to administration and planning.

Under the television chief are supervisors who schedule and oversee technicians and equipment for maintenance, repair, master control, and transmitter operation. Sometimes camera operators, floor personnel, and even building maintenance and custodial services are part of engineering.

19.4 SMALL STATIONS AND LARGE STATIONS

There are still broadcast stations, primarily radio, whose operation is best described by the term **mom-and-pop.** The typical mom-and-pop radio station is relatively low-powered, licensed to a community with a population under 40,000, and run by a family. The husband and wife divide duties—one may manage the station and act as sales manager, while the other may keep books, make out the payroll, pay bills, and send out invoices. One or the other may also take an active hand in programming, auditioning records, or doing a daily special-interest show. Older children pull air shifts or work as office help.

There are four to ten other employees—two or three air personnel who double in news, sales, or engineering; a full-time sales staffer or two; a secretary-receptionist who types logs; an engineer; a program director who works an air shift; and a news reporter who also works a short DJ shift. Licensee and employees know the townspeople, and the townspeople know them. Often the station uses tradeout (Section 9.1.6.6) to get a new car, office furniture, or whatever the station needs.

At the other extreme is the large-market television station. Here the licensee is usually corporate and absentee. A personnel department hires, fires, retires, and keeps track of one hundred or more employees. Workers at such stations may form unions, believing that they stand a better chance as a group than as individuals to get raises, added employee benefits, and improved working conditions.

19.5 CABLE SYSTEM ORGANIZATION

A cable television system is not licensed by the FCC. Instead, it is franchised by the government of the area it serves. A cable system builds, uses, and maintains a physical communication distribution network to deliver its signal. It derives most revenue from subscriber fees. For these reasons, cable system organization differs somewhat from that of a broadcast station.

19.5.1 The System Operator

The franchise holder is called the *operator*. Individual franchisees operate some systems, primarily in small towns and rural areas. A few local governments operate their own cable systems (although the cable trade opposes municipal ownership). Some schools, colleges, and other institutions operate cable systems. For the most part, however, the typical cable system operator is **private and corporate** and is a **multiple system operator** (MSO; operates more than one system).

During the period of cable's greatest growth, the 1970s and 1980s, three restrictions limited system ownership. One was the TV-cable rule (Section 19.1.2.2). A second, the FCC's **network-cable cross ownership rule,** prohibited television networks from owning cable systems. In 1988, the commission launched procedures to eliminate this rule.

The third restriction was the **telco-cable cross ownership rule.** A company could not operate both a telephone system and a cable system in the same area. Most cable companies rent space on telephone poles for trunk and feeder lines (Section 12.9.3). If the local telephone company were allowed to compete with other entities for a cable franchise, the telephone company could set a high pole-use fee, placing its competitors at a disadvantage. Under this rule, however, a telephone company could operate a cable system where it did not provide telephone service. And it could petition the FCC for permission to provide both telephone and cable television service in *areas so sparsely populated that a cable-only operator could not survive financially.*

Congress wrote the FCC's telco-cable rule into law in 1984.[7] Four years later, sources in Congress and the executive branch urged that telephone companies be allowed to get into the cable business, and the FCC was ready to recommend that Congress lift the ban. The telephone companies themselves wanted to get into the business; cable operators wanted the ban to stay in place. Another barrier, however, came from the judicial branch. The modified final judgment issued by U.S. Judge Harold Greene in his supervision of the breakup of AT&T (Section 5.15) prevented the seven Bell operating companies from entering the cable business.

These few restrictions allowed ownership patterns in cable that are barred in broadcasting. Unlike the situation with FM stations discussed in Section 19.1.2.2, for example, you could own cable systems in neighboring communities (which would allow you to enjoy economic advantages from sharing certain facilities among the separate systems). Foreign interests may own cable systems in whole or part; Canadian firms have invested heavily in U.S. cable systems. An entity may own a daily newspaper and a cable system that serve the same area.

19.5.2 The Franchising Process

A cable television franchise grants permission to operate in a particular area. Specifically, the franchise allows the operator to lay cable in rights-of-way controlled by the franchising authority. A large city may divide into several areas, each separately franchised. FCC rules establish minimum standards for franchising, but a local government awards the franchise.

19.5.2.1 Cable Television Ordinance Typically a **city council** draws up and adopts a cable television ordinance (a municipal statute). The ordinance takes into account FCC requirements and spells out terms of the franchise—what a cable system operator may and must do, length of franchise period, time allowed to build the system, franchise fee (percent of gross revenues the cable operator pays the city), and complaint procedure. The ordinance also creates a cable television advisory committee to provide aid and information to the city council on cable matters.

19.5.2.2 Federal Franchise Restrictions Federal law places limitations and requirements on the franchising authority and the franchising process. The authority may re-

quire channel capacity for public, educational, and governmental (PEG; Section 7.4.1.2) use.[8] The authority may make requirements for facilities, equipment, and *broad categories* of video programming or other services but may not require *specific* video programming or services (other than PEG channels). The authority and the cable operator may, however, put an agreement in the franchise to limit or prohibit obscene cable services.[9]

The franchise fee may not exceed 5 percent of the operator's gross revenues from basic service each year.[10] The authority may not regulate the cable system as a common carrier or utility.[11] In awarding a franchise, the authority must ensure that all neighborhoods and groups have cable service, irrespective of income.[12] (Some operators may be tempted to *cream skim*—wire only affluent neighborhoods because they have the potential of high subscribership and low vandalism rates.)

19.5.2.3 Award of the Franchise The city advertises a **request for proposal** (RFP). The RFP invites prospective franchisees to submit applications. These applications describe the system the applicant would build—number and types of channels, tiers, and services; subscriber fees; programming; facilities; ownership; financial support. The city compares the various applications; it may pay a consultant to help in this task, analyzing each proposal to determine which offers the best combination of services balanced with the most realistic financial projection. In a public proceeding, the city council chooses the best proposal and awards the franchise. After the award, there may be negotiation on specific terms of the franchise.

19.5.2.4 System Construction and Operation The franchisee must then build the system, adhering to promises made in the application, to the requirements of the franchise, and to FCC rules. Federal law does provide means, however, for the operator to request changes in requirements for facilities, equipment, or PEG channels.[13] To obtain modification of the franchise agreement, the operator must make either of two cases to the franchising authority. In the first, the operator demonstrates that the requirement is commercially impractical and, therefore, inappropriate. In the second case, the operator shows that the modification would not change the service required by the franchise.

On completion of the system, the operator files with the FCC a registration statement. This statement requires identification, location, and signals carried. At that point, the system begins operation.

The operator wishes to ensure that all who receive cable service in the franchise area pay for it. Federal law helps by prohibiting cable signal piracy. Persons who pirate signals or who manufacture and sell piracy equipment are subject to fines and jail terms.[14]

19.5.2.5 Cable System Competition

Most cable systems set their own subscriber rates. Federal agencies, states, and franchising authorites may regulate charges for basic service only—not for second tiers, pay channels, or any cable service other than the basic tier. Furthermore, they may regulate rates only in the absence of *effective competition*.[15] An appeals court threw out the FCC's first definition of effective competition.[16] Subsequently, the commission decided that a cable system faces competition when three or more off-air signals cover all the system's service area. The three signals do not have to be same ones for all parts of the area.

Most franchises are municipally sanctioned monopolies—one system serves an area. But a series of court decisions beginning in 1985 seemed to end the concept that a franchise *has* to be a monopoly. Even though a city has granted a franchise to an operator,

it must allow others to offer cable service in the franchise area as long as there is space in the right-of-way for additional cables. The cable trade opposes the whole idea of another system competing with the original franchisee and refers to the challenger as an *overbuild*. Several 1987 decisions seemed to undercut provisions of the 1984 Cable Act itself.

19.5.2.6 Franchise Renewal

Toward the end of the franchise period, the operator submits a proposal for renewal. Hearings may be held. If no problems appear, the franchising authority renews the franchise. If, on the other hand, the authority wishes to deny renewal, the denial must "be based on one or more adverse findings"[17] concerning the operator's record with the system. Any of the following on the operator's part might lead to an adverse finding: failed to comply substantially with the existing franchise agreement; provided a quality of service that was unreasonable in the light of community needs; lacks necessary technical, financial, or legal ability to fulfill the promises made in the proposal; presented a proposal that is not reasonable in terms of meeting future needs of the community.

19.5.3 Cable System Physical Plant

The basic physical plant requirements of a cable system are **distribution system, headend,** and **business office.** The distribution system and the headend are explained in Sections 12.9.1 and 12.9.3. The headend and the business office may or may not be in the same location. **Local origination facilities** (if any) may be in yet another location. For example, a large-market cable system may put its tower and receiving antennas on the outskirts of town for better reception, the business office in a centrally located area for convenience, and several production facilities in various neighborhoods for easier access (especially if they feed community access channels; Section 7.4.1.2). Signals of the production facilities feed back to the headend for distribution.

Unlike a broadcast station, a cable system deals directly with its audience. Therefore, it must locate and design its business offices and communications systems to accommodate persons who wish to subscribe, stop or change service, or register complaints about service.

A cable system that does locally produced programming needs facilities similar to that of broadcast stations. Cable studios, however, are generally smaller. Cable video equipment is often more compact, more portable, less expensive, and produces lower-quality pictures (though, in most cases, our eyes cannot tell the difference) than broadcast gear. But there may be more of it (for coverage of outside events and at various community access locations). The physical facilities of a cable radio station parallel those of a comparable broadcast radio station.

19.5.4 Cable System Functional Organization

A **general manager** runs the system for the operator. Typically, five major department heads report to the general manager (Figure 19.9).

The **program services manager** is in charge of local production and production crews. In larger systems, a local origination manager and an access manager may answer to the production manager. The local origination manager supervises all production the system does itself. The access manager coordinates and maintains liaison with the various input sources for the access channels (Section 7.4.1.2).

The **sales and marketing manager** heads

the system's efforts to recruit subscribers. This includes both door-to-door and *telemarketing* (telephone call-out) sales.

Technical areas are headed by the **plant operations manager.** Two key individuals in this department are the chief technician and the installation supervisor. The **chief technician** keeps the signal flowing through the system. Lead technicians, working under the chief technician, supervise teams that maintain, adjust, replace, and repair components of the system from headend to drop lines. The **installation supervisor** does just what the title implies.

While a system is being built, a **construction manager** may be a part of the staff. This individual supervises the actual building of the system—laying lines, installing repeaters, and other construction requirements. Often, the operator contracts with a firm that specializes in building cable systems; in such cases, the construction manager maintains close liaison with the contractor.

A **business manager** oversees billing, accounting, personnel, data processing and other such service. The **customer service manager** supervises both the customer service department and the dispatcher.

Service-connected calls go to the **customer service department.** Customer service representatives take telephone orders for new service and for repairs and handle inquiries and complaints. Requests to downgrade service (for example, drop a pay channel or a premium tier) or to disconnect (drop cable service entirely) are referred to retention specialists. These specialists attempt to resell the customer to prevent the downgrade or the disconnect.

The **dispatcher** plays a key role. New service orders, disconnect orders, localized (not in the system) customer complaints—all go to the dispatcher who, in turn, assigns them to the individual installers. Installers are often contract employees, paid by the job.

The **advertising sales manager** directs

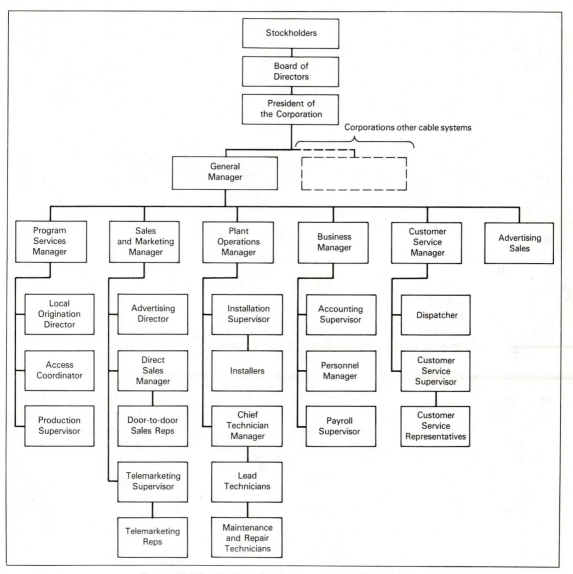

Figure 19.9 Typical cable system organization chart.

the time sales effort. This includes local sales and liaison with the sales representative firm (Section 17.4). The staff consists of a local sales manager, the salespeople, and the traffic department. When an outside firm contracts to handle a system's advertising sales (Section 17.3), the sales staff may locate its headquarters apart from the system's business office. In such cases, the advertising sales department will sometimes have its own creative and technical staff to produce and put commercials on the system's channels. An office manager, who reports to the general sales manager, will supervise this technical staff, as well as clerical, traffic, and other support personnel.

A cable MSO often controls a system more closely than a group broadcast owner does a station. For example, the MSO may maintain a **regional office.** This office, headed by a regional manager, handles several critical functions for the MSO's systems in the area. Typically, these include public relations, promotion, hiring and firing, billing, and accounting. Other functions handled at the regional level could include government relations (lobbying the state legislature) and community relations (often assigned to work with and keep happy the franchising authority).

19.6 OTHER MEDIA

A wireless cable (multichannel TV; Section 5.4) system requires the marketing and customer service functions of a cable system. A satellite master antenna televison (SMATV) system (Section 5.3) has a captive customer base and needs little in the way of marketing and customer support. Wireless cable and SMATV systems rarely do local production, so they need no studios or creative staff. However, many educational licensees of instructional television fixed service systems (ITFS; Section 5.4) do have active local production capabilities. The technical needs of wireless cable and ITFS systems are unique (Section 12.7).

Physical and personnel needs of an LPTV station vary with the purpose of the station. If it operates simply as a translator, an automated repeater of another TV station, it needs space only for its antenna, a small structure to house the electronics, and no full-time staff. At the other end of the spectrum, an LPTV station that functions like a full-service station needs proportionately more space and staff. The typical LPTV station that does local programming has a staff of 10 to 15 persons, each of whom does several different jobs.

The personnel and facilities requirements of national media also vary with purpose. For example, a DBS programmer might lease transponder and ground station facilities, in which case it would need studios, control rooms, business offices, operational staff, and administrative personnel. If the DBS service operated on advertising support, it would also need a sales staff similar to that of a network. A packager that retails satellite networks to TV receive-only (backyard) dish owners would need no studios or sales operations, but it would need staff and facilities for national marketing, subscriber recruitment, sign-up, and billing. A DBS service that operated on a subscription basis would have the same national staff-and-facilities needs.

19.7 UNIONS

Primary unions in radio and television for engineers and technicians (often including camera operators and floor personnel) are the **International Brotherhood of Electrical Workers** (IBEW), **National Association of Broadcast Employees and Technicians** (NABET), and **International Alliance of Theatrical Stage Employees and Moving Picture Machine Operators of the United States and Canada** (IATSE; film industry technical union). For directors, the primary union is **Directors Guild of America;** for writers, **Writers Guild of America.** NABET also has some nontechnical employees, particularly in the news area. For performers, primary unions are **American Federation of Television and Radio Artists** (AFTRA) and **Screen Actors Guild** (SAG). SAG, the film industry performers' union, has jurisdiction in film television; AFTRA, in live and tape-recorded radio and television. However, from the performer's point of view, the differences between film and electronic technologies in radio and television had become all but moot by the 1980s, so SAG and AFTRA considered merging.

Unionization includes few advantages for radio and television outlets. Most managers prefer not to have unions in their shops. For the employee, unions have advantages and disadvantages. Unionization brings the power of collective bargaining, a help to obtain better wages and benefits. Even the existence of unions—perhaps at other outlets in the market—can yield better pay and hours at a nonunion outlet, as management attempts to keep employees happy and the union out. In a union situation an employee with a complaint can go to the union's shop steward, who is generally much more sympathetic than the licensee's personnel manager.

On the other hand, many employees regard radio and television as creative media, the studio and the control room equipment as creative tools. Many disc jockeys, for example, want to run the audio console, spin records, operate the cartridge machine, as well as announce; they "play" the equipment as integral parts of their presentation. Many television reporters like to shoot, edit, and write introductions for their own news tapes. In both cases, unionization makes integration of functions difficult. A disc jockey works with a technician who runs the console and associated equipment. A reporter has a camera operator shoot and an editor put together the tape. The unions argue, however, that such division of labor allows disc jockey and reporter to concentrate on the essence of their jobs—being an air personality and gathering news—without having to worry about the mechanics of equipment operation.

During the 1980s, radio and television unions lost ground, as did unions in other fields. NABET, for example, in a 1987 settlement with NBC, agreed to the elimination of some 200 union jobs. The settlement followed a 17-week strike by 2800 technicians

and others. NBC *immediately* disposed of 35 slots by wiping out two low-level news job categories and let go about 20 news writers. Several weeks later, the network offered ten shares of GE stock to each of the 5000 network employees who had continued to work during the strike. A month after that, NBC announced its conversion to robotics (Section 6.2.1.2), which would cut the need for production crew members and operators.

19.8 TRADE ASSOCIATIONS

As do owners of businesses in other fields, owners of radio and television outlets band together into trade associations. Of all radio/television media, broadcasting is the oldest and has the greatest number of local outlets, so it has the greatest number of trade associations.

19.8.1 Broadcasting Trade Associations

Broadcasting trade associations represent stations in specific geographic areas (for example, Spokane Broadcasters Association, Rocky Mountain Broadcasters Association, and state associations in nearly every state) and with similar special interests (for example, Association of Independent Television Stations, Association of Maximum Service Telecasters [TV stations operating at maximum effective radiated power], Television Operators Caucus [large-market group owners]). Trade associations exist to protect and enhance the ability of members to do business. The National Association of Broadcasters (NAB) is the largest and most comprehensive.

19.8.1.1 National Association of Broadcasters Since its formation in 1922, NAB has grown, broadened in scope, absorbed

several other organizations, and sponsored formation of still others. Through efforts of NAB, Broadcast Music, Inc. (Section 3.1.5.2) was formed in 1939; University Association for Professional Radio Education, ancestor of Broadcast Education Association (Section 21.3.2), in 1947; and Broadcast Advertising Bureau, forerunner of both Radio Advertising Bureau (RAB) and Television Bureau of Advertising (TvB; Sections 17.1 and 17.3.2), in 1949. In 1959, NAB also formed the Television Information Office (TIO), an information service on television to educators, press, government, and others. (TIO dissolved in 1988, at least in part as a result of the three major broadcast networks withdrawing financial support.) NAB absorbed FM Broadcasters Association in 1945 and merged with Television Broadcasters Association in 1951, changing its name to National Association of Radio and Television Broadcasters. In 1958 it changed back to NAB. In 1986, NAB merged with the National Radio Broadcasters Association. And in 1986 it formed the Broadcast Technology Center, a for-profit company founded to develop an improved TV system.

Following are just some of the major tasks of NAB: keep constant watch on and lobby FCC, Congress, and other government agencies; provide members with literature, conferences, and workshops on matters ranging from bookkeeping to dealing with the FCC; formulate engineering standards; fund research. NAB's annual convention brings together all business leaders of broadcasting and includes speeches, seminars, luncheons, receptions, and a giant trade fair of broadcasting equipment. From 1929 to 1982, NAB also encouraged the development of programming and advertising standards through sponsorship of the Radio Code and, later, the Television Code (Section 16.2.1).

Station licensees join NAB. A group owner takes out a separate membership for each station. Annual dues are based on the station's income. Licensees elect members to the board of directors, NAB's governing body. The board has two divisions, the radio board and the television board, each with a chairperson and places for network representatives. The chairperson of the joint board is elected, a working broadcaster; the NAB president is an appointed, salaried, full-time staff member. Both work closely with the executive committee, a small steering group based on the board.

NAB's headquarters and staff are in Washington, D.C. NAB operates through staff divisions and standing member committees. The staff divisions deal with concerns common to all broadcasters and with internal housekeeping and organizational matters. They range from station services to government relations (lobbying). Member committees, on the other hand, are more specialized and deal with matters of current and continuing concern to broadcasting and to specific groups of broadcasters. They vary from the Research Subcommittee on Local TV Audience Measurement and the Daytime Broadcasters Radio Committee to groups with concerns as broad as the First Amendment, copyright, and "radio futures." NAB also maintains the Television and Radio Political Action Committee (TARPAC), which contributes money toward reelection of representatives and senators favorable to NAB's point of view.

In addition to worries from external sources—a sometimes hostile Congress, an occasionally truculent FCC, some activist citizen groups, the threat of new electronic entertainment technologies—NAB has had internal problems. Many spring from its varied constituency. NAB attempts to represent (1) two media (radio broadcasting and television broadcasting) that consist of (2) local outlets in a variety of settings and situations.

For example, what in the world does a large-market, group-owned, network-affiliated VHF TV station have in common with a small-market, mom-and-pop-operated Class II AM radio station? Not much. Each has its own set of problems. The ideal solution to those problems often works to the detriment of some other group of licensees. In which case, the comprehensive trade association finds itself between a rock and a hard place. If it works on behalf of one class of licensees, it antagonizes another. From time to time, licensees ban together to form trade associations that represent their particular situation, groups such as the National UHF Broadcasters Association and the Association of Independent Television Stations. A major drawback of separate organizations, however, is that none has the economic and political clout of the comprehensive NAB.

19.8.1.2 Special Licensee Organizations

Some associations look out for the interests of minority and other special types of licensees. Black licensees may be eligible for membership in the National Association of Black Owned Broadcasters. National Religious Broadcasters, an organization of religious (primarily Christian) licensees, has become increasingly important over the years. The National Association of Farm Broadcasters and the Concert Music Broadcasters Association represent interests of licensees that program in those particular areas.

19.8.1.3 Individual Member Organization

While NAB is an association of station licensees, there are organizations for individuals who work in or with stations. Some of these include National Association of Television Program Executives (television PDs; sponsors a convention every year that has become a major factor in marketing programming to stations), Radio-Television News Directors Association, American Women in Radio and Television, Broadcast Financial Management Association (account-

ing and financial personnel), Federal Communications Bar Association (lawyers who practice before the FCC), Academy of Television Arts and Sciences (sponsor of Emmy awards for prime-time and local Hollywood programs), National Academy of Television Arts and Sciences (sponsor of Emmy awards for all other national and local categories), International Radio and Television Society, Broadcast Designers Association (art direction), Broadcast Promotion and Marketing Executives (promotion directors), Society of Broadcast Engineers, and Society of Motion Picture and Television Engineers.

19.8.2 Cable Trade Associations

As the cable trade has grown, so has the number of trade associations that support and represent it. Cable operators have formed trade associations at the state level to defend their interests in the various legislatures. They have also formed some regional organizations, such as the Southern Cable TV Association.

At the national level, the best-known organization is the **National Cable Television Association** (NCTA). NCTA plays much the same role for cable operators that NAB does for broadcasters. Comparison is almost inevitable; NCTA is the younger organization, with a smaller membership, financial base, and staff. Nonetheless, NCTA has been extremely effective, particularly in dealing with Congress, the FCC, and other organizations. It has proved its effectiveness repeatedly, carefully choosing targets for action. In negotiations over rules and laws that affect cable, NCTA has achieved compromises that allowed its members to grow and thrive. NCTA has a headquarters and full-time staff in Washington, D.C.; members elect the board of directors, which sets policy. In addition to lobbying, NCTA offers membership services, sponsors an annual convention, and maintains its own political action committee. In 1986, NCTA established the **National Academy of Cable Programming** to take charge of its annual ACE (Award for Cable Excellence) awards.

The **Community Antenna Television Association** (CATA) is a second national trade association for cable systems. However, CATA specializes in protecting the interests of small systems.

Cable also has organizations for individuals. One of these is **Cable Television Administration and Marketing Society** (CTAM). CTAM emphasizes the importance of a profitable system, an integral part of which is marketing the cable service to the public. CTAM helped to set up Cable-television Advertising Bureau. Some other cable organizations include the following: National Federation of Local Cable Programmers, Society of Cable Television Engineers, and Women In Cable.

19.8.3 Trade Associations in Other Media

When a new medium opens, the first entrepreneur to enter it has a monopoly. When the second enters, competition begins—and the two form a trade association! Trade associations for some other media include the following: Community Broadcasters Association (low-power television licensees), National Cable Satellite Association (satellite master antenna systems), Satellite Broadcasting and Communications Association (television receive-only and direct-broadcast satellite), Subscription Television Association (STV), and Videotex Industry Association.

The **International Television Association** (ITVA) deserves special attention. This organization serves corporate television—business, industry, and government users of video. Corporate television emphasizes in-

ternal use of video (Section 5.14.2), so the public rarely sees the product of ITVA members. Nonetheless, from the point of view of production and innovative use of television, ITVA members do some of the most interesting and creative things in the field. There are ITVA chapters in most areas that have a high concentration of corporate headquarters and major facilities. Some colleges have ITVA student chapters.

NOTES

1. FCC press release quoted in "FCC to relax one-to-a-market rules," *Broadcasting* 19 Dec. 1988: 41.
2. Communications Act, Section 613(a) (47 U.S.C. §533[a]).
3. *Greater Boston Television Corp.* v. *FCC*, 44 F.2d 841 (1971), *certiorari* denied 403 U.S. 923 (1971).
4. *RKO* v. *FCC*, 670 F.2d 215 (1981).
5. Fredric A. Weiss, David Ostroff, and Charles E. Clift, III, "Station License Revocations and Denial of Renewal, 1970–1978," *Journal of Broadcasting* 24 (1980): 69.
6. "Court muddies minority picture," *Broadcasting* 24 Apr. 1989: 29.
7. Communications Act, Section 613(b) (47 U.S.C. §533[b]).
8. Communications Act, Section 611 (47 U.S.C. §531).
9. Communications Act, Section 624 (47 U.S.C. §544).
10. Communications Act, Section 622(b) (47 U.S.C. §542[b]).
11. Communications Act, Section 621(c) (47 U.S.C. §541[c]).
12. Communications Act, Section 621(a) (3) (47 U.S.C. §541[a][3]).
13. Communications Act, Section 625 (47 U.S.C. §545).
14. Communications Act, Section 633 (47 U.S.C. §553).
15. Communications Act, Section 623 (47 U.S.C. §543).
16. *American Civil Liberties Union* v. *Federal Communications Commission*, 823 F.2d 1554 (1987).
17. Communications Act, Section 626(d) (47 U.S.C. §546[d]).

FURTHER READING

Baldwin, Thomas F., and D. Stevens McVoy. *Cable Communication.* 2d ed. Englewood Cliffs: Prentice, 1988.

Hilliard, Robert L., ed. *Television Station Operations and Management.* Stoneham: Focal, 1989.

Keith, Michael C., and Joseph M. Krause. *The Radio Station.* 2d ed. Stoneham: Focal, 1989. Goals, functions, operations.

Krasnow, Erwin G., J. Geoffrey Bentley, and Robin B. Martin. *Buying or Building a Broadcast Station: Everything You Want—and Need—to Know but Didn't Know Who to Ask.* 2d ed. Washington: NAB, 1988.

Lavine, John M., and Daniel B. Wackman. *Managing Media Organizations: Effective Leadership of the Media.* New York: Longman, 1988. Problems and techniques of various media.

McCavitt, William E., and Peter K. Pringle. *Electronic Media Management.* Stoneham: Focal, 1986. Personnel, programming, sales, promotion of cable and broadcast.

Marcus, Norman. *Broadcast and Cable Management.* Englewood Cliffs: Prentice, 1986. Issues and problems.

National Association of Broadcasters. *The Small Market Television Manager's Guide.* Washington: NAB, 1987. Sales, promotion, engineering, budgeting, personnel, and more.

Quinlan, Sterling. *The Hundred Million Dollar Lunch.* Chicago: O'Hara, 1974. Story of the WHDH case.

Sherman, Barry L. *Telecommunications Management: The Broadcast and Cable Industries.* New York: McGraw, 1987. Planning and leading the local outlet.

CHAPTER 20

Networks

The commercial networks—home of the stars; bright lights; glamour; fame and publicity; big money; large audiences; the Big Time; the ultimate! Broadcast or cable, networks *are* big news and often big business. But what are networks? How and why do they operate? And who are the networks?

In this chapter we seek to answer those questions. We examine the nature of networks, the financial aspects of networks, and then the existing network organizations. Finally, we review criticisms of the network system.

20.1 THE NETWORK CONCEPT

All radio and television networks share several characteristics. Each has two or more interconnected outlets. These outlets receive the same programming simultaneously. The term *network* also refers to the organizations that feed the programs. When most of us talk about "the networks," we usually mean the program distributors, not their affiliated outlets.

20.1.1 Functions and Purposes of Networks

People form networks to make money. On advertising-supported networks, they hope to sell commercial time to regional and national advertisers. At the same time, the network system has certain advantages for both advertisers and affiliates.

Commercial networks offer advertisers convenience, economy, and quality. A firm that buys network time has actually bought time on a group of outlets with one purchase and one bill. The firm pays less for network advertising than it would for comparable spot advertising on the same outlets. The firm's commercials appear within the context of slick, well-produced programming.

Commercial networks offer affiliates programming. An affiliated station or cable system receives contemporary, highly promoted programming that it could not afford to produce on its own. A broadcast television network fills almost two-thirds of a station's schedule, so an affiliate has less to program than an independent. Broadcast network programming increases a TV station's generalized audience-pulling power. An affiliated station, therefore, can usually charge more for advertising than an independent in its market. Advertising-supported cable networks offer cable system affiliates increased variety of programming and local advertising windows (Section 17.5.4).

People put together pay networks, again, to make money. Here, the economic relationship of audience to network is direct. The audience pays to watch uninterrupted, uncut programming. Pay networks offer cable and satellite master antenna systems as added sources of subscriber revenue. They also add to the marketing attractiveness of the systems themselves; some households may subscribe just to get the pay channels.

20.1.2 Network-Affiliate Relationships

Most permanent, full-time, full-service broadcast network organizations have a stable lineup of affiliated stations. In a market with multiple stations, each network tries to get the strongest as its affiliate. A cable franchise area, however, usually has only one cable system. Each cable network tries to get one of a limited number of channels on that system.

An **affiliate contract** ties together the network organization and its outlets. This contract spells out who does what and for how much. Contract terms vary with individual affiliates. Most broadcast network contracts say that the network organization will provide to the affiliate (1) programming, (2) delivery of the programming, and (3) compensation, a share of the advertising revenues from the programming (Section 17.5.4).

This may sound like a one-sided good deal for the affiliate. Remember, however, that a television affiliate gives hours to the network for little cash return. Nationally,

network compensation averages about 8 percent of station revenues. If the station had sold those hours, it could possibly have earned much more money. TV broadcast networks pay out less than 10 percent of gross advertising revenues for compensation. The networks' 90+ percent pays for high-cost overhead, such as the programming, program development, promotion, and time sales expense.

The network economic pinch of the late 1980s (Section 4.5.3.4), however, led ABC, CBS, and NBC to reexamine the very concept of compensation. Certainly, felt network executives, this was one area in which they could save money. They negotiated with their affiliates for new compensation formulas and rates. In the case of a few stations, compensation was eliminated entirely (see, for example, Box 20.1). Some in the trade predicted that the days of compensation to affiliates in all but the largest markets were numbered.

Stations affiliated with a particular network band together into an **affiliate council.** They have greater power as a group. They negotiate with the network much more effectively as a council than as individual stations.

Advertising-supported cable networks usually charge affiliates on a per-subscriber/per-month basis. Section 17.5.4 describes some exceptions. A pay-cable network (premium service) contract requires the affiliated system to pay a fee for each subscriber *to that particular service.*

Ordinarily, a broadcast station affiliates with just one national network. Many stations, however, particularly radio stations, affiliate with a national network and regional or special networks. In markets with only one or two commercial television stations, one station may affiliate with more than one national network. The station has **primary** affiliation with one network and carries most of its programs. Additional affiliations are

Box 20.1 Musical Chairs and Network Muscle in Miami

In 1988, South Florida TV stations played an expensive round of musical chairs with network affiliations. When the music stopped, the networks had grabbed the best seats. But the way they used their financial muscle to win this game may have changed radically the very concept of the network-affiliate relationship.

The stations began with the affiliations shown in the "Before" column. None were network O&Os. They ended with those in the "After" column, two of their number now owned by networks.

The game started when the networks discovered Florida. The state's explosive growth had made it fourth largest in population and showed no sign of slowing. NBC, looking to acquire large-market Florida stations, purchased WTVJ. WSVN still had time to run on its NBC affiliation contract and did not wish to give it up. So for a while, NBC owned and operated a CBS affiliate.

But surely WSVN would get the CBS affiliation.

Well, no. CBS, not to be outdone by NBC, purchased WCIX. When WSVN's NBC affiliation contract ran out, WTVJ would become the NBC affiliate, and WCIX would become the CBS affiliate.

CBS got a bargain. Channel 6 was worth one price as an independent—the price that CBS paid—but would be worth a lot more when it became a CBS affiliate. There was just one problem. WCIX put a relatively weak signal out over the populous area north of Miami. CBS had an affiliate some 60 miles to the north in West Palm Beach, WTVX. But WTVX was a UHF station. That wouldn't do. WPTV was an NBC affiliate and, since NBC was the solid prime-time ratings leader, probably not a candidate to switch networks. So CBS went to work on WPEC. By the time the negotiations ended, CBS had promised WPEC $1 million in capital outlay to upgrade facilities and another $600,000 for promotion—in addition, of course, to whatever compensation the station would get.

So now the West Palm Beach ABC affiliation was up for grabs. Three local stations went after it, one of which was not even on the air yet. And that was the station that got it. WPBF, Channel 25, agreed to *pay* ABC for the privilege of affiliation. Additionally, WPBF would receive no compensation. Between loss of compensation and actual cash payments to ABC, estimates of WPBF's annual cost for affiliation went as high as $1.5 million.

These shenanigans resulted in the following. First, six of the possible eight stations had new affiliation status (apparently the game had neither included nor affected WPLG and WPTV). Second, the value of two stations dropped because they were no longer affiliated with one of "the big three." In the case of WSVN, the loss in value probably amounted to over $100 million. Third, CBS had demonstrated muscle in dealing with affiliates; a network could now come into a lucrative top-25 market, tell an affiliate to do what it wanted, and threaten to buy another station in the market if the affiliate did not go along. CBS, particularly, was in a good position to do this because it did not own its "quota" of TV stations (Section 19.1.2.2). Fourth, network affiliation was apparently no longer a "given" in figuring the worth of a TV station. Fifth, a station had actually volunteered to pay ABC for the same service

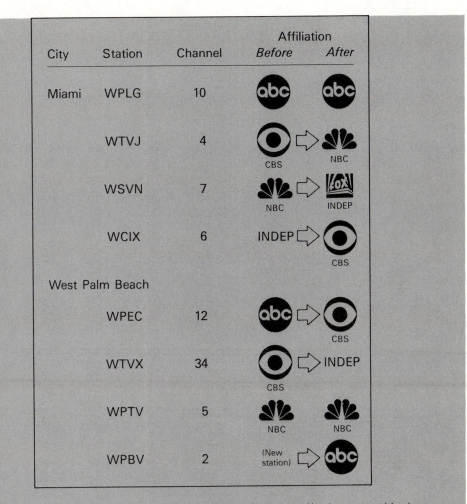

City	Station	Channel	Affiliation *Before*	Affiliation *After*
Miami	WPLG	10	abc	abc
	WTVJ	4	CBS ⇨	NBC
	WSVN	7	NBC ⇨	INDEP (Fox)
	WCIX	6	INDEP ⇨	CBS
West Palm Beach				
	WPEC	12	abc ⇨	CBS
	WTVX	34	CBS ⇨	INDEP
	WPTV	5	NBC	NBC
	WPBV	2	(New station) ⇨	abc

that ABC paid other affiliates to carry. Sixth, and subsequently, in several instances, networks did reduce or eliminate compensation to affiliates in markets that also had strong (usually VHF) independent stations. (See, for example, "In Brief: ABC decided last Friday to renew affiliation of WTVQ-TV Lexington, Ky.," *Broadcasting*, 23 Jan. 1989: 176; and "In Brief: CBS has decided to eliminate annual compensation of roughly $250,000 to its Honolulu affiliate, KGMB-TV, *Broadcasting*, 30 Jan. 1989: 96.)
    Strange things were happening.

secondary, and the station airs those programs as convenience and scheduling allow.

An affiliated station may refuse to carry a network program. The network, in turn, may offer the program to another station in the market. In a three-station market, a TV network with no primary affiliate must give first-call rights on certain programming to the unaffiliated station. The FCC requires the network to offer the independent the first 15 hours of prime-time and weekend programs and sports programs. Then the network may grant the two affiliates access to the remainder of its programming.

Broadcast affiliates usually transmit network programming as they receive it. Sometimes, however, they **delay broadcast** (DB)—tape a program as it comes over the line and transmit it at a later time. They may DB network programs that conflict with valuable local programming or that management feels should air at a later hour. Affiliates receive advance information on content and mechanics of handling programming through network telex and closed-circuit conference calls.

20.1.3 Distribution

Distribution provides the means for interconnection. It gets programs from network organizations to affiliates. Most of the time, the network arranges and pays for distribution costs. In some cases the affiliate must pay.

Most networks use satellite relay to distribute programming. All cable networks use it. Most national radio networks use it. The major television broadcast networks use it. Even state radio networks have begun to use it. Such, however, was not always the case.

20.1.3.1 AT&T For over half a century, American Telephone and Telegraph Co. (AT&T) had a near monopoly on network distribution. This stemmed from AT&T's monopoly on nationwide long-distance telephone lines. AT&T owned the voice-quality lines that tied the nation together, including the high-quality lines needed for broadcast programming. National networks and many state and regional networks had to use AT&T (and had to pay their rates) for distribution.

20.1.3.2 Microwave Relay The development of microwave relay changed that some-

what. In microwave relay, a modulator converts the network signal to microwave frequencies (Section 10.2.1) for long-distance transmission. You have probably seen microwave relay towers, tall metal structures topped by large reflectors. A transmission reflector focuses the microwave signal to a beam aimed at the next tower some 30 miles distant. At the distant tower, another reflector picks up the beam, and a transmitter beams the signal to the next tower. The process repeats until the signal reaches its destination. AT&T replaced its long-distance telephone lines with microwave. Eventually, other companies also built microwave relay systems. These independent carriers offered regional or otherwise limited distribution service.

20.1.3.3 FM Sideband Some state radio networks used FM sideband distribution. The network fed a signal to high-power FM stations. The stations transmitted network programming on subcarriers (Section 11.6.2). Affiliated stations used special receivers to pick up the signal for broadcast.

20.1.3.4 Satellite Relay Development of satellite relay (Figure 20.1) finally broke AT&T's monopoly on network distribution. In the late 1970s, cable and public broadcasting networks began to use satellites, leading a trend away from the telephone company. They found that satellite relay delivered a better-quality signal and was more reliable and flexible than any other method of distribution. Some also found it less expensive than AT&T.

20.1.3.5 Optical Fiber Promoters of fiber optics (Section 5.15), however, planned to bring network distribution back to earth. Optical fiber offered a broader transmission band (Section 12.9) than coaxial cable. It offered secure transmission without scram-

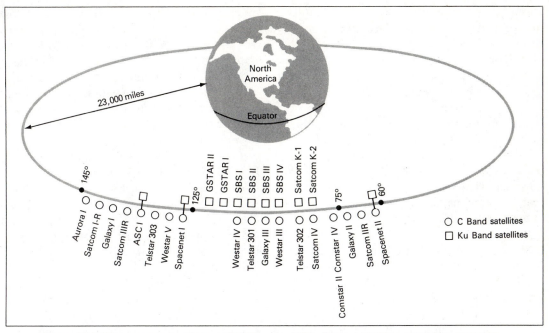

Figure 20.1 U.S. communications satellites. In 1989, these satellites provided domestic communications for the United States and Canada. Four of the satellites most favored by programmers in broadcast, cable, and other media were Hughes' Galaxy I, RCA's Satcom III-R, and Western Union's Westar IV and V. *(Source: Broadcasting Yearbook.)*

bling. NAB executives predicted that, by 1990, some regional radio networks could be the first to adopt fiber optics for distribution.[1] Bell Communications Research organized a trial of fiber-optic cable for delivery of network TV to affiliates in eight cities. ABC, CBS, Fox, NBC, and PBS agreed to participate. The trial began in 1988 and lasted some 15 months.

20.1.3.6 Rebroadcast Occasionally, stations interconnect by rebroadcast. Usually they are radio stations. One station first gets permission to rebroadcast the signal of another. The rebroadcasting station then tunes a regular receiver to, picks up, and retransmits the signal of the originating station. Quality suffers, and interference can be a problem. But it is quick and cheap. A few small-market radio stations have used rebroadcast to get network programming.

20.1.4 Network Variations and Parallels

Our definition of network requires interconnection and simultaneity of reception (Section 20.1). This excludes **tape networks** (or film networks), which send programs to outlets on tape or film. Sometimes, instructions tell the receiving outlet to send the program to yet another after use. The last outlet returns the program to the originating organization. This is a **bicycle network.** Other nonnetworks include broadcasting spot networks (Section 17.4.1) and cable soft interconnects (Section 17.4.2).

By our definition, a direct-broadcast satellite (DBS) does not qualify as a network. Nor does a TVRO program packager (Section 7.4.4). Neither uses intermediate outlets as affiliates. On the other hand, TV superstations do qualify. Satellite relay distributes superstation programming to cable system affiliates beyond the reach of their broadcast signals.

A **temporary network** exists to distribute a one-time event or a finite series of programs. It has no permanent affiliates and does not broadcast a continuous schedule. A temporary network often starts when an organization that is not a network gets radio or TV rights to sports events. The organization arranges for a group of outlets to carry its coverage. Temporary networks based on big-league and major-university sports may change affiliate lineups every season.

An **ad hoc network** is a temporary network set up to carry just one program. An advertiser may bypass the broadcast networks and create an ad hoc network to distribute a one-time entertainment program. A few pay-per-view events are distributed on an ad hoc network of cable systems and sometimes movie theaters.

20.2 PROFIT AND LOSS IN NATIONAL NETWORKING

For years, the big three broadcast network organizations found the national network business to be profitable (Table 20.1). As a group, their radio networks sometimes lost money. Their television networks made so much money that it more than made up for any deficits incurred by their radio network's. By 1988, however, competition for audiences and advertising dollars had network executives worried. For example, Robert Wright, president of ratings leader NBC, said that network advertising sales had been soft for several years. He described network business as getting "worse and worse."[2]

In 1987, *Broadcasting*[3] estimated that the big three network organizations needed just over $2 billion to run themselves. In 1986, their owned TV stations brought in 60 percent of the television profit; TV network operations, 40 percent (just the opposite of the previous year). Their radio networks, however, outperformed their radio stations. As usual, the TV stations reported operating margins (operating income divided by revenue; Section 19.2.1) more than double the margin of the most profitable TV network operation.

Broadcast network operations generate most revenue through sale of time for advertising. Out of gross revenues come affiliate compensation, commissions (advertising agencies, representatives, and others), and any discounts the networks grant for cash payment. As with stations, salaries rank among the highest expense items for both radio and television broadcast networks.

Programming is the most costly single expense category. For radio networks, most of

---

Table 20.1   CORPORATE AND ELECTRONIC MEDIA EARNINGS OF THE THREE MAJOR BROADCAST NETWORK ORGANIZATIONS

	Total revenue (thousands)	Total earnings (thousands)	Earnings per share	Electronic media revenue (thousands)	Media revenue as percent of total
Capital Cities/ABC	$ 4,773.5	$ 387.1	$22.31	$3,749.6	78.60%
CBS, Inc.	2,777.7	1,149.0	11.02	2,777.7	100.00
General Electric	50,089.0	3,386.0	3.75	3,638.0	7.30

Table 20.1 Corporate and Electronic Media Earnings of the Three Major Network Organizations. These figures reflect fiscal year 1988 earnings.
Source: Standard & Poor's; *Broadcasting* 1 May 1989: 35.

their programming consists of news, so most of their programming budget goes for news and public affairs. Television broadcast network programming is so costly that it accounts for about half of all network expenses.

Much of the competition for broadcast television networks has come from cable networks (Section 4.5.2.1). As cable penetration climbed, cable networks gained audience and advertising, often at the expense of the broadcast networks. One forecast predicted that during 1987–1992, national cable advertising expenditures would increase 17 percent; broadcast TV network advertising, just 8.5 percent.[4] Impressive though these percentages are, the actual dollar values put them into perspectives. According to this same forecast, national cable advertising would total $1.9 billion in 1992; broadcast TV network, $13.25 billion—almost 7 times more. And while the broadcast dollars divide just three ways, the cable dollars will be shared by over two dozen entities. (Keep in mind that some advertising-supported cable networks also receive payments from cable system affiliates [Section 17.5.4].)

Overall, cable networks during the 1980s moved toward stability and improvement. An increasing number earned a profit (Section 5.2.3.4). Still, the majority lost money. Several factors contributed to this situation. Many networks were new, and start-up costs were high. They had not become a habit with viewers or advertisers. Most adopted a specialized programming concept, limiting their ability to draw national mass audiences.

Perhaps most important, there were so many of them. Unlike broadcasting, cable gave rise to numerous national networks. Most competed for the already few advertising dollars. And they had difficulty getting on cable systems. Even large-capacity systems could not accommodate every new network that went on the satellite.

20.3 SCOPE OF NETWORKING

At one time, "the networks" popularly meant ABC, CBS, and NBC. Now, we must use modifiers to identify those three entities, " the *three major broadcast* networks." This differentiates them from "fourth networks" such as Fox and from "the cable networks." In addition to national networks, there are regional and state networks.

20.3.1 The Three Major Broadcast Networks

ABC, CBS, and NBC all changed ownership in 1985–1986 (Sections 4.5.3.3 and 4.5.3.4). Their respective parent firms are Capital Cities/ABC, Inc. (CC/ABC); CBS, Inc.; and General Electric Company (GE). You may buy stock in them; their shares are traded on the New York Stock Exchange. CC/ABC and CBS focus on radio and television. GE, one of the country's largest industrial firms, has varied interests, of which broadcasting is but one.

20.3.1.1 Capital Cities/ABC, Inc. CC/ABC consists of broadcasting, publishing activities (Figure 20.2), and cable programming. Both Capital Cities Communications and American Broadcasting Companies brought magazines and newspapers into the 1985 merger. Through its publishing group, CC/ABC puts out trade and consumer periodicals that range from *Iron Age/Metal Producers* to *High Fidelity*. It owns daily and weekly newspapers, shopping guides, specialized data base services (information retrieval services; Section 5.7.4), and a religious communications firm. Some of its publication units also put out books, visuals, directories, and newsletters; conduct meetings and seminars; provide syndication, marketing, and research services; and sell insur-

CAPITAL CITIES/ABC PUBLISHING GROUP

Specialized Publications

In addition to the following, certain operations in this group also publish books, visuals, directories, and newsletters; conduct meetings and seminars; provide syndication, marketing, and research services; and sell insurance products.

ABC Publishing

Consumer and Special Interest Publications

COMPUTE!

COMPUTE!'s Apple Applications (bm)

COMPUTE!'s Gazette

COMPUTE!'s PC Magazine (bm)

High Fidelity

Los Angeles Magazine

McCall's Needlework & Crafts (bm)

Modern Photography

Musical America (bm)

Schwann CD

Schwann Record & Tape Guide (q)

Trade Publications

Assembly Engineering

Automotive Industries

Automotive Marketing

Commercial Carrier Journal

Distribution

Electronic Component News

Food Engineering North America

Food Engineering International (10X)

Hardware Age

IMPO (Industrial Maintenance & Plant Operations)

Industrial Finishing

Industrial Safety & Hygiene News

Infosystems

Instrument & Apparatus News

Instrument & Control Systems

Jewelers Circular Keystone

Machine and Tool Blue Book

Manufacturing Systems

MITE (bm)

Motor Age

Office Products Dealer

Owner Operator (bm)

Personal Publishing

Product Design & Development

Quality

Review of Optometry

ABC Publishing Agricultural Group

Daily Herd Management

Farm Store Merchandising

Feedstuffs (w)

Garden Supply Retailer

Hog Farm Management

Prairie Farmer (16X)

Tack 'n' Togs

Wallaces Farmer (16X)

Wisconsin Agriculturist (16X)

Chilton Company

Fairchild Publications

International Medical News Group

Clinical Psychiatry News

Family Practice News (sm)

Ob. Gyn. News (sm)

Pediatric News

Skin & Allergy News

Magazines

Heat Treating

Home Fashions

M, The Civilized Man

Metal Center News

Scene (bm)

Travel Agent (tw)

Newspapers

American Metal Market (d)

Children's Business

Daily News Record (d)

Electronic News (w)

Energy User News (w)

Entrée

Financial Services Week (bw)

Footwear News (w)

HFD—Retailing Home Furnishings (w)

Metalworking News (w)

MIS Week (w)

Multichannel News (w)

SportStyle (21X)

Supermarket News (w)

W (bm)

Women's Wear Daily (d)

Professional Press Group

Optical Index (sm)

International Eyecare

Hitchcock Publishing Company (includes PEMCO, a trade show operation)

Institutional Investor

Domestic edition

International edition

NILS Publishing Co.

Data base of regulation for insurance industry

National Price Service (loose-leaf price information for electrical & plumbing trades)

Word, Inc. (religious/inspirational communications)

Books and materials

Films

Instructional materials

Sheet music

Song books

Tapes

Daily Newspapers

Albany Democrat-Herald (Albany, OR)

Belleville News Democrat (Belleville, IL)

The Daily Tidings (Ashland, OR)

Fort Worth Star Telegram (Fort Worth, TX)

The Kansas City Star (Kansas City, MO)

The Oakland Press (Pontiac, MI)

The Times Leader (Wilkes-Barre, PA)

Weekly Newspapers

Gresham Outlook (Gresham, OR)

Cottage Grove Sentinal (Cottage Grove, OR)

Highland News Leader (Highland, IL)

Lebanon Express (Lebanon, OR)

Newport News-Times (Newport, OR)

Shore Line Newspapers (Guilford, CT)

26 weekly newspapers from Hartford, CT, to Springfield, MA

Springfield News (Springfield, OR)

Sandy Post (Sandy, OR)

Shopping Guides

Little Nickel Want Ads (Seattle, Tacoma, WA)

Nickel Ads (Portland, OR)

Nickel Nik (Spokane, WA)

Pennypower Shopping News (Wichita, Topeka, KS, Springfield, MO)

Sutton Industries (Orange, San Diego Counties; Sacramento, Stockton, CA)

Figure 20.2 Publishing interests of Capital Cities/ABC. These are *most* of the publications owned by Capital Cities/ABC. The Shopping Guides are weekly publications. All Specialized Publications are monthly unless marked otherwise: 10X = 10 times yearly; 16X = 16 times yearly; 21X = 21 times yearly; bm = bimonthly; d = daily; q = quarterly; sm = semimonthly; w = weekly. Notice that some of these "publication interests" actually involve electronic media. The NILS data base, for example, comes in both electronic and printed form, and Word, Inc., markets films, tapes, and other material. (*Source:* Capital Cities/ABC.)

ance products. Through its broadcast group, CC/ABC participates in ownership of three cable networks. It holds a minority ownership interest in Arts & Entertainment and Lifetime and a controlling interest in ESPN.

20.3.1.2 CBS, Inc.

CBS, Inc., consists of its network and station activities (Figure 20.3). Once a diversified entertainment conglomerate, CBS eliminated most holdings not directly related to its "core business," broadcasting. It had divested some activities before the Tisch takeover (Section 4.5.3.3). Afterward, the company sold off its magazine, book publishing, music publishing, and record divisions. This left the corporation with its broadcast group, some other real estate, half interest in CBS/Fox, a home video partnership with Twentieth Century Fox, and a great deal of cash (Section 4.5.3.3).

20.3.1.3 General Electric Co.

GE divides its diverse activities (Figure 20.4) into four categories. *Technology* businesses include aerospace, defense, aircraft engine, factory automation, medical systems, and plastics. *Core manufacturing* businesses include construction equipment, lighting, major appliance, motor, power systems, and transportation systems. *Support operations* consist of corporate trading, petroleum, semiconductors, and international operations. *Services* include NBC, financial services, and communications and services. Communications and services, in turn, encompasses communications satellites, computer rental and maintenance, business teleprocessing network, design and development of information systems, and assorted communications services for business and the military.

20.3.1.4 Broadcasting Activities

ABC, CBS, and NBC all have headquarters in New York City. They also have production facilities in New York and executive offices and production studios in Los Angeles.

Each network includes (Figure 20.5) owned and operated television stations (O&Os; Table 20.2), O&O spot sales organizations, and the networks' programming activities—news, sports, and TV entertainment. They also have departments of engineering and operations, standards (Section 16.2.2), business affairs, marketing, sales, affiliate relations, and public relations.

ABC and CBS both have radio divisions. The radio division oversees the firm's radio O&Os (Table 20.2), radio networks, and associated activities. NBC sold its radio businesses in the late 1980s (Section 3.4.3).

The entertainment divisions acquire and schedule programs. They divide responsibilities by programming types—for example, prime time, daytime, children's. With network headquarters in New York and production firms in Los Angeles, the network entertainment division normally has personnel in both cities.

ABC and NBC have active cable programming interests. ABC's parent owns three cable networks (Section 20.3.1.1). ABC and NBC share ownership of Arts & Entertainment. NBC also has half interest in and programs Consumer News and Business Channel and, through its investment in Rainbow Program Enterprises, other national and regional cable programmers (Section 4.5.3.4). NBC Productions does programs and series for cable networks. All three networks distribute programming overseas.

20.3.2 "Fourth Networks"

The trade has used the term *fourth network* to mean another ABC/CBS/NBC-style operation. During the three decades following DuMont's demise, the three major networks operated unchallenged. Periodically, speculation arose about a fourth regularly scheduled commercial television broadcast network.

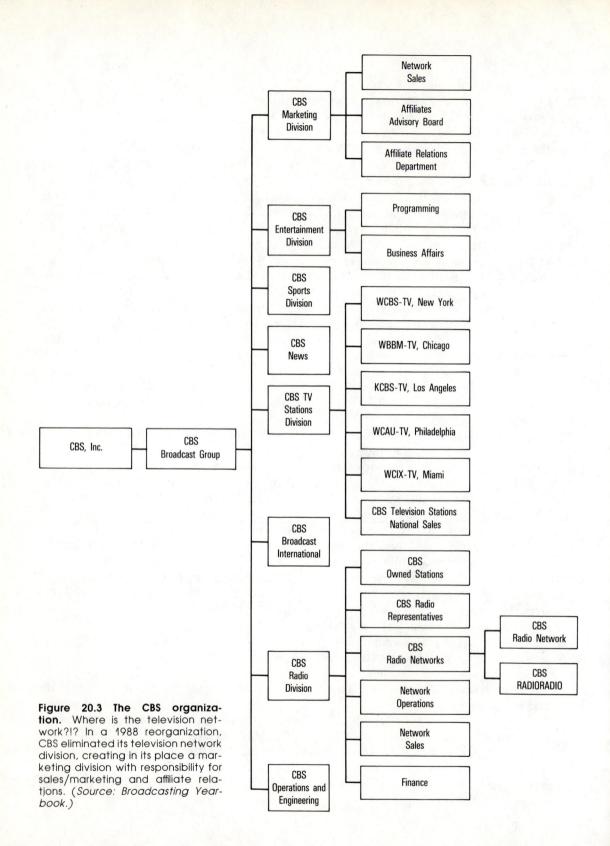

Figure 20.3 The CBS organization. Where is the television network?!? In a 1988 reorganization, CBS eliminated its television network division, creating in its place a marketing division with responsibility for sales/marketing and affiliate relations. (*Source: Broadcasting Yearbook.*)

- **Aerospace Products and Services**

    Electronics and micro electronics

    Avionic systems

    Ordnance systems

    Vehicle equipment

    Automated text systems

    Computer software

    Simulation and control systems

    Spacecraft

    Communication systems

    Radar

    Sonar

    Systems integration

- **Aircraft Engines**

    For military and commercial aircraft

- **Financial Services**

    General Electric Financial Service, Inc.
    (Distribution sales financing, commer-
    cial and industrial financing, real estate
    financing, leveraged buyouts)

        General Electric Capital
        Corporation.

            Time sales financing

            Revolving credit financing

            Inventory financing for retail
            merchants

            Automobile leasing

            Other financial services

        Employers Reinsurance
        Corporation

        Kidder, Peabody Group, Inc.
        (controlling interest)

            Investment banking

    Genelcan Ltd.

        Financial services for Canada

    General Electric Real Estate Corp.

        Equity investment in real estate
        development projects

- **Industrial**

    Factory automation products

    Semiconductors

    Motors

    Electrical equipment

    GE Supply

        Nationwide network of electrical
        supply houses

    Transportation systems

        Locomotives

        Transit propulsion equipment

        Motorized wheels for off-highway
        equipment

- **Consumer Products**

    Lighting products

- **Major Appliances** (General Electric and
Hotpoint brands)

    Kitchen and laundry equipment

        Refrigerators

        Dishwashers

        Ranges

        Washers

        Dryers

        Microwave ovens

        Room air conditioners

    Nationwide service network

- **Materials**

    High performance engineered plastics
    for automobiles, computers, business
    equipment

    Silicones

    Super abrasives

    Laminates

- **National Broadcasting Co.**

- **Power Systems**

    Worldwide products for generation,
    transmission, and distribution of
    electricity

Figure 20.4 Diversity of General Electric. General Electric Company is one of the nation's largest businesses, a true conglomerate. This listing shows most of GE's interests. While NBC was a dominant activity at RCA, at GE the network is but one among many—albeit a glamorous, high-visibility "one among many." (*Source:* GE.)

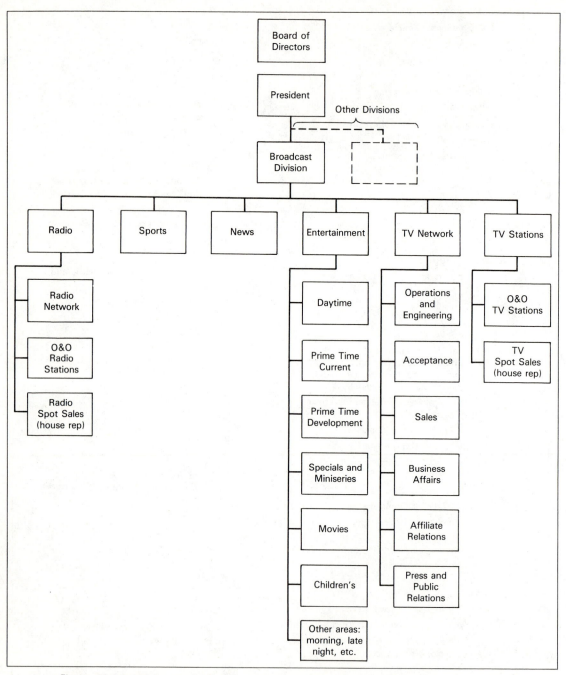

Figure 20.5 Typical organizational chart for national broadcast network. This chart reflects, in broad terms, the operating structure of the broadcast activities of ABC, CBS, and NBC. None, however, are set up exactly like this. NBC, for example, has no radio division, and no cable activities are shown.

Table 20.2 NUMBER AND LOCATIONS OF NETWORK-OWNED AND-OPERATED BROADCAST STATIONS

Market	Market rank	CC/ABC	CBS	NBC
New York	1	AFT	AFT	T
Los Angeles	2	AFT	AFT	T
Chicago	3	AFT	AFT	T
Philadelphia	4	T	AFT	
San Francisco	5	A T	AF	
Boston	6		F	
Detroit	7	AF	AF	
Dallas	8	AF	F	
Washington, DC	9	AF	F	T
Houston	10	T	F	
Cleveland	11			T
Atlanta	12	AF		
Minneapolis	13	AF		
Miami	14		T	T
Tampa–St. Petersburg	17		AF	
Saint Louis	18		AF	
Denver	19	AF		
Providence, RI	44	AF		
Raleigh–Durham	34	T		
Fresno, CA	62	T		
Totals				
AM stations	(19)	11	8	—
FM stations	(22)	10	12	—
TV stations	(19)	8	5	6
Stations	(60)	29	25	6

Table 20.2 Number and Locations of Network-Owned and Operated Broadcast Stations. Sixty stations in 20 markets, 43 of them in the 10 largest markets, all but 4 in the 20 largest markets—this was the combined (and lucrative) O&O lineup for Capital Cities/ABC (CC/ABC), CBS, and NBC by 1990. Trade observers speculated that all three would attempt to purchase or "trade up" for additional top-10 market television stations. In the chart, each A, F, or T represents one broadcast station—AM, FM, or television respectively. All television stations are VHF, except CC/ABC's KFSN, Fresno, which operates on UHF channel 30.

Source: Broadcasting Yearbook.

Such a network operated during 1967. Daniel J. Overmyer, UHF station owner and warehouse operator, originated the idea. After a change in control, the Overmyer Network became the United Network. United actually fed a limited schedule to affiliates. Sales were poor, and the network could not raise enough money for interconnection line charges. Underfunded, United shut down after a month.

The development of satellite relay changed the survival odds for networking (Section 20.1.3.4). Other organizations took advantage of this new distribution technology to start national television broadcast networks.

20.3.2.1 Univision Univision-Spanish International Network feeds a 24-hour schedule of Spanish-language programs. By 1990, Univision's affiliates included some 31 stations (Figure 20.6). Univision schedules a full range of programs. Most news and information programs originate in the United States. Some of the other programming comes from international sources. Protele, an affiliate of

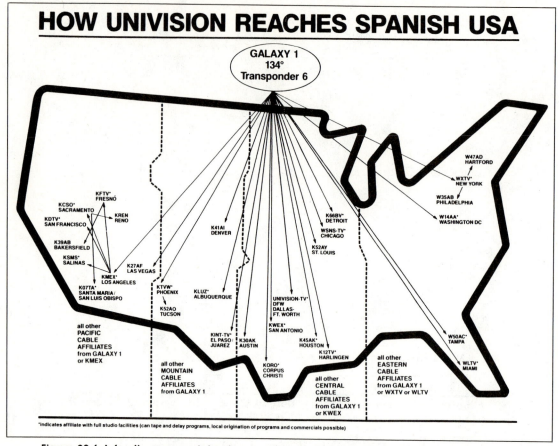

HOW UNIVISION REACHES SPANISH USA

Figure 20.6 A fourth commercial network. Univision-Spanish International Network interconnection for cable, full-power station, and LPTV affiliates. (*Source:* Univision-Spanish International Network. Used by permission.)

Mexico's Televisa network, has a long-term contract to supply programs for Univision. As a rep (Section 17.4), Univision specializes in spot TV sales for Spanish-language stations. Cable systems also carry Univision.

The origins of Univision date from the early 1960s. Formerly Spanish International Network, a 1986 corporate realignment gave the network its present name. In 1988, a division of Hallmark Cards purchased Univision. Hallmark also owns Spanish-language television stations.

20.3.2.2 Fox, Inc. Fox, Inc., encompasses a motion picture studio, a television station group, and a broadcast television network. Fox also produces programming for ABC, CBS, and NBC and distributes through first-run and international syndication, pay cable, and home video. Barry Diller heads Fox, which includes Twentieth Century Fox Film Corporation, Fox Television Stations, and Fox Broadcasting Company. Keith Rupert Murdoch put together the whole group (Section 4.5.3.4) as part of News America Publishing, Inc. News America, a subsidiary of Murdoch's The News Corporation, Ltd., owns newspapers in major U.S. cities. The News Corporation contains over 250 incorporated subsidiaries worldwide and includes media such as newspapers in England and Australia and Sky Channel, Europe's dominant satellite cable network.

20.3.2.3 Home Shopping Network   The advent of Home Shopping Network (HSN) seemed to change the concept of a network (Sections 20.1.1 and 20.1.2). It also changed the conventional medium-advertiser-audience relationship (Section 17.1). First, HSN attracts an audience with continuous advertising, uninterrupted by entertainment or informational programming (Sections 7.4.2.3 and 9.1.3.3). Second, it generates revenue directly from the audience. Third, sales result solely from network messages, a direct measure of advertising effectiveness. Fourth, the network is the advertiser and so does not deal with a third party to generate revenue. Fourth, it bases affiliate compensation on sales.

HSN dates from 1977. A Clearwater, Florida, radio station carried a shopping service that urged listeners to call and order discounted merchandise. Renamed the Home Shopping Channel, the service moved to several Tampa cable systems in 1982. Three years later, the service changed its name to Home Shopping Network and launched national satellite distribution to cable systems. It offered cable systems the chance to tap an additional revenue stream, a commission from every order originating within their franchise areas. In 1986, HSN started a second channel, bought television stations, and announced formation of a broadcast network. HSN's owned stations would, of course, carry HSN programming; so, contrary to normal practice, when HSN bought a station, it did *not* buy rights to syndicated programming for which the station had previously contracted. This meant the syndicators did not get their money.

20.3.2.4 Telemundo Group, Inc.   In 1987, Telemundo Group, Inc., combined its TV sta-

tions with a growing network operation. The network targeted the Hispanic population. Initial offerings included drama, music/variety, movies, and news. Telemundo's Spanish-language television stations formed one of the country's largest TV station groups.

20.3.3 National Satellite/Cable Networks

Satellite or cable networks seemed to proliferate like rabbits in the 1980s. Individuals and organizations saw the continued growth of cable. They looked at the success the major broadcast networks had enjoyed. They wanted to get in on the ground floor of this new video distribution medium (Section 5.2.3.1).

New cable networks encountered many problems. Most took the form of "how-to-gets." How to get sustained financing until the operation could turn the corner and generate a profit. How to get advertisers. How to get a continuing supply of programming. How to get on the right satellite, one that most cable systems could receive.

One important how-to-get involved shelf space. **Shelf space** meant channels on cable systems. Cable systems did not have enough channels to include every new network that went on the satellite. They already carried signals of local TV stations, a premium channel or two, popular satellite basic services, electronic text, and access programming. That did not leave many vacant or discretionary channels. Cable operators tried to avoid duplication, too. After all, a subscriber could watch only one direct-response marketing service at a time (Section 7.4.2.3). Why carry more?

Operator ownership seemed to answer some of the how-to-gets. Multiple system operators (MSOs) wished to encourage the development of *cable* programming (Section 5.2.3.4). They wanted their systems to carry as much programming as possible that was *not* the signals of broadcast TV stations. This would make cable subscription more appealing to consumers. It would also detract from the argument broadcasters made that cable competed with TV stations using the station's own signals.

Programmers found MSOs willing to invest in satellite network operations. MSO investment provided startup and operating funds for the networks. It also meant that the MSOs now had ownership interest in the networks. Given a selection of new networks, a cable system would tend to choose for carriage those in which its operator had invested.

MSOs constitute just one group that invested in satellite networks. Others include broadcasters, broadcast networks (Section 20.3.4), and owners of other media.

During the 1980s, two broad-based media giants, Time Warner, Inc., and Viacom, emerged as the largest, most aggressive satellite network operators.

20.3.3.1 Time Warner, Incorporated Time began in 1923 as a magazine publisher. Nearly 70 years later, however, its media holdings included the following: cable systems (through its subsidiary, American Television and Communications (ATC), one of the country's largest MSOs, and through its half interest in another MSO, Paragon Communications), book publishers (Time-Life Books; Scott, Foresman & Co.; Book-of-the-Month Club; and Little, Brown and Co., among others), and equity in Turner Broadcasting, as well as magazines (*Time, Sports Illustrated, People, Fortune, Money,* and *Life,* among others, plus ownership interest in *McCall's, Parenting, Working Woman,* Whittle Communications, and others). Time's programming activities included Home Box Office, Cinemax, and HBO Video. In 1989, Time's HBO announced that it would start an

advertising-supported all-comedy cable channel (Section 7.4.2.1).

Time also made financial news in 1989 as a result of its merger with Warner Communications which created the giant Time Warner media conglomerate (Section 5.2.5). This merger married the dominant pay-cable service with a major production studio. Warner's dowry also included a large number of cable systems (Time, of course, already owned extensive cable system operations) and significant music and recording businesses. Other Warner interests included TV stations, music and book publishing firms, and *Mad Magazine.*

20.3.3.2 Viacom International, Inc. Viacom originated when the prime-time access rule (Section 14.1.3) put the major broadcast TV networks out of the syndication business. CBS spun off its domestic syndication arm to CBS stockholders, forming the basis for Viacom. In 1987, National Amusements, owner of a large chain of movie theaters, bought out Viacom. Viacom had continued to handle program syndication (*The Cosby Show, All in the Family,* and others) but had also expanded to production of movies, prime-time network TV series, and miniseries; programming and cable ventures overseas; cable systems; and TV and radio broadcast stations. Its satellite cable networks consisted of Showtime, The Movie Channel, MTV, VH-1, Nickelodeon, Nick at Nite, and Viewer's Choice, a pay-per-view service.

Over the years, HBO and Viacom each came to regard the other as its chief competitor. And the competition got fierce at times. Both tried various tactics to get the upper hand, primarily in the areas of marketing and programming. In 1989, Viacom filed a $2.4 billion antitrust suit against Time, Inc. The suit alleged that Time and its cable subsidiaries had engaged in monopolistic practices to prevent carriage and retard the growth of Showtime and The Movie Channel. Time responded that the complaint was "baseless."

20.3.4 Broadcasting and Satellite/Cable

Broadcast and cable do not readily divide into neat, separate cubbyholes. A few examples illustrate.

HSN operates both cable and broadcast networks. It also owns television stations.

Univision and Telemundo are broadcast networks. They also feed cable systems in areas where they have no station affiliates.

The Financial News Network programs primarily for cable systems. However, it is also carried by TV broadcast stations.

CBN runs a cable network. It also operates a radio network and owns broadcast stations. Some CBN Family Channel programs run on television stations. So do the programs of several other cable religious networks.

The Turner Broadcasting operation really blurs the lines between cable and broadcast. The Turner firm operates cable networks. It also owns WTBS, a television station—which programs as a cable network. Turner's CNN makes its news available to TV stations. Turner operates a radio network and a satellite news gathering co-op for television stations.

20.3.5 Television News Networks and Services

Several of the news services mentioned in Section 8.1.4.4 could be classified as networks. For example, Independent Network News (INN), a New York-based service of the Tribune Company, uses satellite to feed complete nightly and weekly newscasts.

Some program syndicators fit in this category. GTG Entertainment launched a satellite-fed version of *USA Today* in fall 1988.

Paramount's *Entertainment Tonight* uses journalistic techniques to assemble a daily satellite feed of soft and show business news.

20.3.6 Special Television Networks

Some firms set up networks on demand. You get TV rights to an event and pay one of these firms to handle production and distribution. Such special or temporary networks range from a one-time station lineup to carry a championship tennis match to seasonal professional sports networks.

Three of the firms that offer turnkey network services are Bonneville, IDB Communications' Hughes Television Network, and Wold Communications. All arrange for production, uplink, and transponder facilities. In addition, syndicators use Wold to distribute program series to stations on a continuing basis.

20.3.7 LPTV Networks

By 1990, several national networks fed programs to low-power television (LPTV) stations. These included The Learning Channel, Country Music Television, Telemundo, ACTS, FamilyNet, Capitol TV Network, Channel America, RFD TV, Video Marketing Network, and most of the religious cable networks. The Fox Network took on its first LPTV affiliates in 1988. A few firms have organized program-service networks designed specifically to serve LPTV stations. Some commonly owned LPTV stations share programming.

20.3.8 Radio Network Organizations

Radio networks provide quality programming to stations. They furnish content the stations might find difficult to produce on their own. They reduce the programming activity that affiliates must do for themselves. They provide a programming product that sounds polished and slick. Yet, they do not dominate an affiliate's schedule and dictate its format, as do TV networks. Instead, they blend with and improve a station's programming. Most radio networks do these things at the cost of a few availabilities. They even pay monetary compensation to some affiliates (Section 17.5.4).

The major national radio network firms include ABC, CBS, Westwood One, United Stations, National Black Network, and Sheridan Broadcasting. The organization of a radio network usually parallels its major functions, with departments of sales, programming, promotion, engineering, and affiliate relations. All use satellite relay for distribution.

Some programming and news services resemble networks. Major services include Satellite Music Network, Transtar Radio Network, Associated Press, United Press International, Turner Broadcasting, and Dow Jones. These firms, too, use satellite distribution.

20.3.8.1 ABC and CBS Radio Networks

ABC Radio Networks includes six full-service radio networks, two talk services, weekly entertainment shows, and concert tour sponsorship. CBS Radio Networks consists of two networks and a program syndication unit. Both firms own radio stations. Both firms' networks target different audiences (Section 7.2.2), continuing the concept of format-specific networks that ABC pioneered (Section 3.4.3). All, however, feature primarily news, information, and sports. ABC also carries network radio's most popular individual programs, the commentaries of Paul Harvey.

During the 1980s, ABC emerged as the radio network company that earned the most in annual advertising sales. In 1987, ABC

contracted to become exclusive sales agent for Satellite Music Network (Section 20.3.8.5).

20.3.8.2 Westwood One

During the mid-1980s, Westwood One, Inc., bought its way into the first rank of radio network firms (Section 3.4.3). Westwood One began as a program distributor. The purchase of Mutual Broadcasting System gave the firm its first 24-hour, full-service network organization. Its NBC purchase brought in the NBC Radio Network, The Source, and Talknet. Westwood One integrated various functions of NBC and Mutual, including their respective news organizations. In the process, management cut out what it perceived as duplication and overlap in the two networks.

Norman J. Pattiz chairs Westwood One. Pattiz, a former TV station account executive, started the firm in 1975 with an initial investment of $10,000. Just 13 years later, Westwood One had grown into the second largest network radio company in annual billings. In 1988, the firm made the first of several planned purchases of large-market radio stations.

20.3.8.3 United Stations

United Stations comprises two network operations and a program distribution arm. US I and US II both deliver primarily news and information but target different audiences (Section 7.2.2). United Stations Programming distributes regularly scheduled entertainment shows.

United Stations formed in 1981. Founders included the firm's president, Nick Verbitsky, and Dick Clark, long-time television personality. United Stations acquired its full-service networks in 1985 (Section 3.4.3). The company distributes regularly scheduled entertainment shows, the majority offered through its United Stations Programming Network. It also broadcasts concerts and specials. In 1987, United Stations principals purchased a minority interest in Transtar (Section 20.3.8.5). United Stations also agreed to handle national advertising for Transtar.

20.3.8.4 National Black Network and Sheridan

National Black Network (NBN) and Sheridan Broadcasting Network both target black and urban contemporary stations. Both provide affiliates with news, features, and daily sports reports. NBN shares ownership with Unity Broadcasting, a radio group station owner and cable operator. Sheridan's parent firm, Sheridan Broadcasting Corp., is also a group radio owner.

20.3.8.5 Satellite Music Network and Transtar

Satellite Music Network (SMN) and Transtar Radio Network are the exceptions to our general introduction (Section 20.3.8). They *do* dominate a station's programming. Their formats *are* the stations' formats. And they *charge* stations a carriage feed. In effect, these two firms seem to represent a cross between a network and a syndicator.

Both SMN and Transtar feature multiple 24-hour music formats. Any one of these satellite-delivered formats provides a station with the better part of each day's programming. The station subscribes by paying a monthly fee. The affiliate also gives up one to three minutes of advertising time per hour that the network sells. For most stations, this loss of advertising time is negligible compared with the savings in program expense they realize.

Most of the firms' revenues come from advertising time sales. Advertisers buy time from the firms; their commercials run on all formats. In large markets where they have no affiliates, SMN and Transtar sometimes pay stations to run their advertising. Transtar shares ownership with Sunbelt Communication, a radio group owner.

20.3.8.6 News Service

The two major news services operate Associated Press Network News and UPI Radio Network. Both operate 24 hours a day, seven days a week, and feed a full schedule of news, sports, features, business and financial news, farm reports, consumer information, and other material. These are *services*; stations subscribe to them. Programs come to a station with no advertising but include slots into which the station may insert commercials. AP also cooperates with WSM, Nashville, to offer the long-form Country Music Overnight on a barter basis, while UPI operates the Spanish Radio Network.

Turner Broadcasting's CNN Radio provides long-form news programming. Dow Jones distributes *The Wall Street Report* designed for AM radio stations and *The Dow Jones Report* for FM stations.

20.4 REGIONAL NETWORKS

Television stations may group together into so-called regional networks to sell national or regional spot advertising time; such networks do little or no interconnected programming. Many of the more than 100 regional radio networks are also really sales groupings with no common programming. But there are exceptions. The Intermountain Network, for example, feeds over 130 stations in 10 western states.

The cable trade has set up regional networks. These include so-called *interconnects* (Section 17.4.2), some of which actually interconnect nearby systems and regional cable sports networks (Section 7.4.2.1).

20.5 STATE NETWORKS

A state network feeds radio stations within a single state. State networks have enjoyed success over the last decade. They have their own trade association, the National Association of State Radio Networks.

Most state networks feed hourly newscasts, sports, and features of state interest. Many also feed farm and commodity news. Network-affiliate arrangements often take the form of barter rather than compensation (Section 17.5.4). Sometimes, the network actually takes the form of a news service for which the affiliate must pay. Increasingly, state networks use satellite relay instead of more traditional forms of distribution.

The North Carolina News Network (NCNN) exemplifies the setup of a state radio network firm. Formerly, NCNN used telephone lines to distribute programming. In 1983, the network completed a transition to satellite relay.

NCNN feeds scheduled daily programming to around 100 affiliates in North Carolina; each uses an earth receive station provided by the network. NCNN programming originates at the studios of WRAL-FM, Raleigh, NC. Programming consists of hourly newscasts that emphasize North Carolina news, several daily sportscasts, and eight weather summaries. Other programming consists of Sunday public affairs material and several daily special-interest topics.

In 1983, NCNN acquired the rights to broadcast football and basketball play-by-play for Duke University and, later, North Carolina State University. Capitol Broadcast Company, which owns NCNN, used these sports rights as the nucleus for creation of the Capitol Sports Network, which operates in tandem with NCNN. Capitol, a group station owner, also operates the Virginia News Network and the University of Virginia Sports Network.

Other regional and state networks include those of college and professional team sports. Sometimes, special networks organize to broadcast a particular event—a gubernatorial inauguration or state capitol reports during a legislative session.

20.6 TVRO AND DBS FIRMS

In Section 20.1.4, we exempted TVRO programmers and direct-broadcast satellites from our definition of a network. Nonetheless, both allow instantaneous distribution of programming over a wide area. Also, activity in these media involves networks. Therefore, the chapter on networks would seem a good place to discuss TVRO and DBS firms.

Some individual programmers *allow* the home TVRO audience to pick them up. Others *set up services specifically for* the TVRO audience. Among the former are the Public Broadcasting System and some of the direct-response marketing and religious networks. Some of the TVRO programmers include K-SAT Broadcasting, a talk-and-call-in radio show run by home-TVRO advocate V. C. Dawson, and Stardust Theater, owned by former NBC programmer Paul Klein, proprietor of the adult Tuxxedo Network. SelecTV, a pay programmer that feeds subscription TV stations, SMATV systems, and LPTV stations, also has TVRO subscribers.

Four of the leading TVRO programming packagers include the National Rural Telecommunications Cooperative (NRTC), Satellite Broadcast Networks, Satellite Direct, Inc., Tempo, and Netlink. NRTC represents more than 300 rural electric and telephone cooperatives (Section 7.4.4). It got into the TVRO packaging business as a service to co-op members who own backyard dishes.

Satellite Broadcast Networks (SBN) originated the idea of network affiliate superstations (Section 7.4.2.2). Formed by former Group W Cable executives, SBN operated under the trade name Primetime 24. SBN picked up one affiliate each of ABC, CBS, and NBC, scrambled the signals, and put them on the satellite. They retailed the package to the TVRO market. Subsequently, the broadcast networks sued SBN for violation of copyright, and others packaged network affiliate signals *with* network approval. However, congressional approval of a 1988 communications bill (Section 15.2.3.3) seemed to clear up copyright uncertainty for SBN and similar firms.

Viacom's Showtime/The Movie Channel created Satellite Direct, Inc. (SDI) in 1986. SDI retails its packages through, among other outlets, home TVRO dish dealers. It even works with an advisory board from the home TVRO trade.

Tele-Communications, Inc. (TCI), the nation's largest cable multiple system operator, controls both Tempo and Netlink. These two firms offer packages directly through a toll-free telephone number and through cable operators. Cooperating cable operators receive a commission. The two TCI firms handle back-office support for authorization (of reception), billing, and collection.

Netlink reached carriage agreements with the major broadcast TV networks. Its package includes signals from affiliates, as well as superstations and basic and pay cable services. Netlink limits distribution of affiliate signals, however, to dish owners who cannot receive a broadcast network signal off the air or from the local cable system. Despite this limitation, broadcast TV affiliates view the Netlink-network agreement with trepidation. They worry that this might be the first step—the opening wedge—to *bypass* stations and deliver network programming directly to viewers.

During the mid-1980s, American business interest in high-power Ku-band direct-broadcast satellite declined. The 1985 demise of the United Satellite Communications venture (Section 5.6.1) had dampened investor enthusiasm for any kind of DBS. Subsequent Japanese and European activity, however, resulted in actual working direct-broadcast satellites. In 1988, TCI's Tempo applied for FCC permission to build and launch high-power satellites. Tempo's satellites would have the capability to beam 32 channels to homes throughout the continental United States. The Tempo application, along with foreign achievements in the field, seemed to rekindle American interest in direct-broadcast satellites.

Some nine other firms already held construction permits for direct-broadcast satellites. All proposed to operate with high power—125–180 watts. Reception would require dishes no larger than 1 foot in diameter. Most of the firms projected launch and operation no earlier than 1991.

Two of those firms had been in on the DBS concept almost since the beginning. United States Satellite Broadcasting Co. (USSB) and Dominion Video Satellite first filed in the initial 1982 round of applications (Section 5.6.1). Hubbard Broadcasting, group station owner and developer of the SNG cooperative (Sections 5.5 and 8.1.4.4), created USSB specifically to establish a foothold in DBS. During the 1985–1988 period, Hubbard and Hughes Communications were almost the only commercial firms still talking about true high-power DBS. Hughes had applied for a DBS construction permit shortly after the first round of applications. Hughes planned a 32-channel satellite that others would lease and program.

The original plans of Dominion, the other pioneer, included religious and family programming. Dominion tried several schemes over the years to secure financing. In 1988, the FCC gave both USSB and Dominion until late December 1992 to build and launch high-power DBS systems.

GE and HBO offered an alternative to both low-power C-band home TVRO and high-power Ku-band DBS. In 1985 they formed Crimson, a joint project that would use GE Americom medium-power Ku-band satellites. The Crimson partners maintained that cable operators and program services should switch to these new satellites. That way, both cable operators and subscribing consumers would need just one 3-foot dish to pick up all services. Crimson could not persuade programmers to join them and gave up the idea in 1988.

20.7 CRITICISMS OF THE NETWORK SYSTEM

When most persons speak of "the networks," they refer not to CNN, HBO, the North Carolina News Network, or Hughes Television Network, but to the three major national commercial television broadcast networks—ABC, CBS, and NBC. Many of the faults critics attribute to networks are faults of the rest of the trade as well. But the rest of the trade is difficult to focus on, consisting, as it does, of scores of networks and programmers and, beyond that, thousands of stations and cable systems in all states and territories. On the other hand, there are the three major TV networks, all headquartered in the same city. And they do exercise much influence. So critics aim for the most obvious targets, "the networks."

Most criticism centers around programming and can be traced to what critics see as the networks' insatiable drive for ever-higher profits. Fred Friendly, a former news executive with CBS, explained that corporate officers run the networks as "profit machines," keeping stock prices high by keeping profits high (Section 16.1.5). Higher ratings translate into higher profits. Therefore ratings determine the worth of a program, not its intrinsic value as entertainment or information. As a result, say critics, light entertainment— and not even very interesting light entertainment—fills network channels. The desire for ratings forces out most thought-provoking programming (Section 7.6.1).

Public interest groups complain that network programs teach values that hinder effective functioning of the individual and society. The programs present untrue pictures of society. These groups contend that networks show too much sex and violence.

They say depictions of women and various racial and ethnic minorities are unfair, untrue, or unbalanced. They say that commercials (and all advertising) condition us to buy for the sake of acquisition and that programming reinforces such conditioning. Critics especially decry programs children watch, particularly for violent content and commercial orientation.

In the past, Congress has investigated the networks for everything from quiz show scandals to bias in news and documentaries. The FCC has investigated and adopted rules to prevent network control of affiliates. The FCC and some production houses said that networks dominated program production, all but curtailing first-run programming; the FCC passed rules designed to correct that situation (Section 14.1.3). The U.S. Department of Justice filed suit against the networks, charging them with monopoly over prime-time television programming.

In the past, creative people have complained of the prudishness of network standards departments (Section 16.2.2). Advertisers and advertising agencies criticize networks for the high prices of advertising time, for commercial clutter (Section 9.5), and even for violence in programming.

Affiliates have criticized the networks. Strong affiliate opposition led the networks to cancel plans to expand early evening newscasts to one hour. Affiliate protests forced the networks to drop plans to ask for repeal of the prime-time access rule. Affiliates objected to the network-Netlink home TVRO packaging agreement (Section 20.6).

The frequency and intensity of criticism increased over the years. They increased as television (and thus the networks) came to occupy more and more of our time and attention. Even as criticism increased, viewing levels rose. The success of cable networks may have changed that. With the increase in cable penetration of U.S. television homes, more persons have gained access to cable networks. They found they had genuine alternatives in popular programming. As broadcast network audience shares dropped, the level of criticism also seemed to drop.

Criticism of cable, on the other hand, increased. Communities took legal action to ban adult programming from local systems. Religious and citizen groups marshaled forces to fight adult channels and sexually explicit material on other channels. Critics denounced the level of violence in music video programming. National Coalition on Television Violence (NCTV) measurements showed that HBO and Showtime/The Movie Channel were twice as violent as broadcast networks. NCTV even found high levels of violence in programming segments on The Disney Channel and CBN. Critics charged that cable operators wielded too much power over programmers. They noted that MSOs had forced the scrambling of signals (Section 5.6.2) and then began buying into the networks.

NOTES

1. "Fiber optics for regional networks, more compact disk and cellular telephone users seen in radio's future," *Broadcasting* 18 Apr. 1988: 84.
2. Quoted in "NBC president tells affiliates that network business is eroding," *Broadcasting* 27 June 1988: 38.
3. "Capcities leads the way," 27 Apr. 1987: 31.
4. "Veronis, Suhler & Associates, Five-Year Forecast," *Broadcasting* 4 July 1988: 48.

FURTHER READING

Bagdikian, Ben H. *The Media Monopoly.* 2d ed. Boston: Beacon, 1987. Twenty-nine firms control most media.

Barnouw, Erik. *Tube of Plenty: The Evolution of American Television.* Rev. ed. New York: Oxford UP, 1982. Analysis and criticism of broadcast networks, primarily programming.

Friendly, Fred W. *Due to Circumstances Beyond Our Control.* New York: Random, 1967. "Profit machine" thesis.

Halberstam, David. *The Powers That Be.* New York: Knopf, 1979. Interwoven history of CBS, Time, Inc., *New York Times*, and *Washington Post.*

Kellner, C. A. "The Rise and Fall of the Overmyer Network." *Journal of Broadcasting* 13 (1969): 125. Story of the 31-day national TV network.

Litman, Barry Russell. *The Vertical Structure of the Television Broadcasting Industry: The Coalescence of Power.* East Lansing: Michigan State UP, 1979. Network programming influence and power over affiliates.

Paper, Lewis J. *Empire: William S. Paley and the Making of CBS News.* New York: St. Martin's, 1987.

CHAPTER 21

Careers in Radio and Television

Now it is time to talk about you. You are reading this book. That means you have at least some interest in radio and television. Chances are good that you may even want to work in the field. That is the subject of this chapter—working, earning a living, making a career in radio and television. We first survey career opportunities—types and availability of jobs, pay, advancement. Next, we look at what you can expect if you stay in the trade, how your career will develop. Then we suggest some ways to prepare for a career in radio and television. Finally, we discuss your first job—how to get it and how to keep it.

21.1 CAREER OPPORTUNITIES

First things first. Yes, you can get a job and make a career in radio and television (Table 21.1). Several assumptions, however, underlie that statement and all that follows. First, you start at the **career entry level**—the place where jobs are (1) available (2) for beginners. That place is *not* the networks, *not* a

major Hollywood program producer, *not* a big market, and *not* a big station.

Second, you are likable and clean. You work hard and have a reasonable amount of intelligence and creativity. You enjoy meeting new people, have confidence in yourself, and respect the feelings of others. You avoid illegal drugs and drink moderately, if at all. You do not have to be a prodigy or a star to get in and stay in the trade. Jerks, drunks, and louts find it almost impossible.

21.1.1 Types of Jobs

By *jobs* we mean a salaried or commission position at a radio or television outlet. *Outlet* includes such organizations as broadcast stations, cable systems, or corporate TV installations.

We exclude radio-TV engineering. Engineering is a highly specialized area. It requires that you understand technical aspects of radio and television. It involves installation, maintenance, and repair of equipment. Often it requires design of circuitry and wir-

Table 21.1 BROADCAST/CABLE EMPLOYMENT

		Women		Minorities	
	Total	Number	Total	Number	Percent of Total
Broadcast					
All positions	177,981	66,534	37.4	28,540	16.0
"Upper four" job categories	147,524	43,072	29.2	20,248	13.7)
Cable					
All positions	80,235	32,379	40.4	14,870	18.5
"Upper four" job categories	38,744	10,613	27.4	5,969	15.4)
Totals	258,216	98,913	38.3	43,410	16.8

Table 21.1 Broadcast/Cable Employment. This was the employment picture in stations and cable systems as reported by the FCC for 1986. The "upper four" job categories consist of "officials and managers, professional, technicians, and sales workers." The "all positions" figures include those for the "upper four"; in other words, broadcast stations had 177,981 employees, of which 147,524 worked in "upper four" positions, while cable systems had 80,235 employees, of which 38,744 worked in "upper four" positions. These figures include only broadcast stations with five or more full-time employees and cable systems with six or more full-time employees. They do not include employment figures for stations and systems with fewer employees nor for other radio-TV facilities, such as broadcast and cable networks, corporate and educational video facilities, and production houses.

Source: Federal Communications Commission.

ing. If you plan to go into radio-TV engineering, you must have an affinity for it.

We exclude business. The business area encompasses jobs found in any business office—secretarial, filing, typing, and billing. It also includes highly specialized skills that require a degree or experience, such as accounting and bookkeeping.

Most people considering radio-TV careers do *not* mean engineering or business. They look for jobs in writing, performance, news, production, sales, or promotion. We assume that you have similar interests and focus the remainder of the chapter on jobs in those areas.

21.1.2 Special Note on Sales

The term *sales* encompasses two areas. In one, the outlet sells time to advertisers. In the other, the outlet sells some programming service to the public, as in cable television.

Often, young persons ignore sales as a radio-TV career area. They fall in love with programming areas, such as production, news, or performance. They see those aspects as the ends of business. Sales—if they think about it at all—they see as some necessary evil. They compare it to hustling encyclopedias door to door or peddling used cars—vaguely dishonest, definitely boring, and noncreative.

Wrong on all counts. This is a good a place to clear up a few misconceptions.

First, most radio-TV managers and owners view sales as a major thrust of the business. They recognize the importance of programming areas *as means to the end of sales.* The sales area provides the lifeblood of the outlet. It generates the money that allows the other areas to exist. Without sales there is no outlet.

Second, sales personnel sell a valid, needed service. Businesses must advertise, and radio and television advertising has proved effective. As for subscriber sales, few other forms of entertainment offer so much for so little. Even a subscription fee as high as $30 a month breaks down to just $1 a day. Figuring in tickets, refreshments, gasoline, and sitter fees, one couple could just barely go to the movies twice for $30.

Third, sales has the greatest potential for

creativity of any area in the outlet. For example, refer to the advertising sales process described in Section 17.3.3. Preparing an effective sales presentation takes much more inventiveness than playing records, pushing a camera, or even directing the six o'clock news.

Fourth, sales personnel have the best chance to get to managerial positions. Look at it from the owner's point of view. Programming areas generate *expenses*. The sales department earns *revenues*. Naturally, the owner selects someone who *makes* money to manage the outlet. Broadcast station managers often come from the area of advertising sales. Cable system managers usually come from the marketing area, for which subscriber sales is the entry-level position.

21.1.3 Other Areas

We leave out areas such as music, dance, and graphic art and design. They have their own career fields. People who do these things in radio-TV settings usually consider themselves in music, dance, or art, not radio or television.

On the other hand, people sometimes overlook certain areas. **Public broadcasting** is one. Public stations often do more local production than commercial stations. This means more opportunity to exercise production skills.

Cable and broadcast television have both fostered the growth of **promotion.** Promotion forms an essential part of a cable system's marketing plan. It serves a TV station as ammunition in the ratings battle. For a large-market station, one additional rating point can yield thousands of dollars. Effective promotion can make the difference.

Corporate television (Sections 5.14.2 and 6.2.1.5) offers excellent career opportunities, particularly for persons interested in production and writing. Some corporate-TV units feature complete state-of-the-art facilities and studios. They turn out highly polished productions. Corporate television often features starting pay, fringe benefits, and advancement opportunities better than those of broadcast or cable.

Believe it or not, some persons do not realize that **cable** offers radio-TV career opportunities. All cable systems need subscriber marketing staffers. Many need advertising sales executives. A system that does local origination may also need personnel with skills in news, writing, production, and performance.

Advertising and public relations firms need people with radio-TV skills. They create, write, supervise, and produce. Some ad agencies have their own production facilities.

21.1.4 Why Radio-TV

The only reason to go into radio and television is because you **want to work** in radio and television. You probably will not make much money in your first job—a living, maybe. Count on no more than the federal minimum wage. Be pleasantly surprised if offered more.

Use this test to determine whether you *really* want to work in radio and television.

- Do you enjoy just being inside a radio or television facility—any facility, *no matter where it is?*
- Do you enjoy doing something in radio-TV—*no matter what?*
- Do you enjoy working in radio or television so much that the possibility of getting paid—no matter how little—would be frosting on the cake, would be *almost secondary in importance?*

If you answered "yes" to *each* question, go for it. Good luck in your radio-TV career.

If you answered "no" to *any* question, choose another field. For your first job, is it important that you live in a large city? Work near home? Make a lot of money? Direct, report sports, or play DJ at an AOR station? Do not go into radio-TV. In first radio-TV jobs, the work is too long, too hard, too low-paid, and too often in the boondocks not to enjoy it for itself.

21.1.5 Attitudes—Theirs and Yours

We have set forth two views on the purpose of a radio-TV outlet. Owners and managers consider the outlet a business, and its purpose is to earn a profit (Chapter 19, introduction and Section 19.2). On the other hand, many people go into their first radio-TV jobs with the idea that the outlet is a creative medium, that its purpose is to provide them a chance to create and experiment. Obviously, these two views clash.

Radio-TV does, indeed, permit creative development. But a beginning employee should keep four points in mind. First, the outlet is a business—an advertising or subscription sales medium. Second, the owner considers all staffers—particularly those who appear before microphone or camera—as salespeople, even though they may not directly service accounts. Third, the owner pays the salaries. Fourth, individual creative development comes within the employment concept developed in points one through three.

21.1.6 Availability of Jobs

If you are a beginner, you begin where beginners begin. *Beginner* refers to a person who has never held a salaried job in radio or television. *Where beginners begin* means small outlets in small markets. Small-market managers would like to hire experienced people. Often, however, they cannot pay enough to attract them. Instead, they must hire and train beginners. After a few years, the employees, no longer beginners, move on to the glamour and higher pay of larger markets. This means that many small-market outlets suffer a continual personnel turnover. It also means small markets are the best places for a beginner to look for a job.

Persons who wish to work in some areas (Sections 21.1.2 and 21.1.3) may be able to start in slightly bigger markets. For example, medium-market stations and cable systems may take on beginning salespeople. Corporate television facilities tend to be in large cities.

The 1980s corporate shenanigans (Section 4.5.3.2) had a negative impact on radio-TV employment. Large businesses went through a period of "slimming down." In the process, they got rid of thousands of jobs and the people who had filled them. Radio-TV firms were no exception (Sections 4.5.3.3–4.5.3.5). This affected few beginner-type jobs directly. However, the decrease in large-market positions could have slowed advancement along the normal career pattern (Section 21.2). In other words, people in radio-TV may not have as much opportunity to move to larger markets and better pay. They may have to stay in one job longer. In that respect, the 1980s layoffs certainly had the potential to make beginner-type jobs more scarce.

The slimming down affected corporate video. Some large businesses decided they could save money by closing down internal video departments. That would eliminate the departments' overhead expense. When the firms needed video production, they would contract for it.

This was just one factor that seemed to increase work for production companies. Another was the plan by cable networks to buy more original programming (Sections 7.4.2.1 and 7.4.3.1). The increase in work, however, would not necessarily translate into an in-

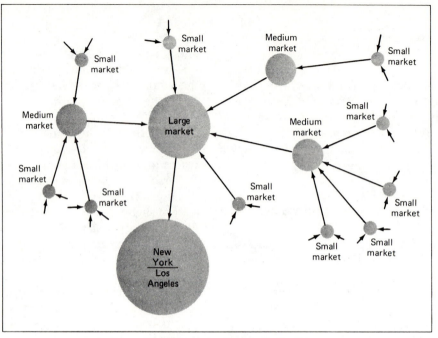

Figure 21.1 Career pattern in Radio-TV.

crease in full-time positions at the production companies themselves. Most production companies are small. They contract for crews, facilities, and studios on an as-needed basis. Larger firms with studios and a permanent staff have their pick of veteran production personnel when they hire for full-time or contract positions. Turnover is slow. Newcomers find the program production field difficult to enter.

21.1.7 Pay and Advancement

If you go into an area other than sales, you will not receive much pay as a beginner. (Sales personnel frequently earn more than others in first jobs.) By your second or third job, however, you will have that important commodity, experience. You should be able to move to a decent salary. As to whether you ever make one of those $100,000-plus big-market salaries, that is up to you. As in any business, you rise as fast and as far as your capabilities and your desire allow. The

intelligent, hardworking, creative individual can advance—to larger outlets, to larger markets, to more responsible positions. At the same time, as jobs get better, competition gets keener.

21.2 CAREER PATTERNS

The usual career pattern in broadcasting and cable starts in a small outlet in a small market and moves to progressively larger markets (Figure 21.1). For example, a typical radio broadcasting career begins in a station serving a city with 25,000 or less population. After two or three years, the individual moves to a medium market of, say, 100,000. After three to five years, the next step may be a large market—500,000 to 1.5 million. From there—with luck, talent, perseverance—one goes to Chicago, Los Angeles, or New York.

Most persons, of course, do not go all the way to the superlarge markets. This does not necessarily mean their careers have stagnated. Some enjoy life in a particular locale and decide to stay. Some work up to larger outlets but not necessarily larger markets. Some advance within an outlet or an ownership firm—a station group or cable multiple system operator. Some go into other work—advertising, public relations, freelance production.

At any rate, you will probably have to change jobs to advance your career. On the other hand, avoid a spotty employment record. Six months at one job, a year at another, four months at a third—this type of record does not reassure a manager that an applicant is dependable and steady. Two years is a good minimum at which to aim for any one job. The longer you are at one place of employment, the better your résumé looks to the prospective employer at the next.

This career pattern helps to explain why beginners have difficulty getting jobs in large markets. The people with whom they compete have *paid their dues*, as it is called. They started in smaller markets and have years of experience. Naturally, managers hire the experienced people.

You will have difficulty breaking into big-time television without experience. News reporters come from local outlets, from wire services, or from newspapers. Sports announcers have worked at local outlets or have previously made names for themselves in other fields. Directors start as script clerks or assistant directors on television commercials, begin at local outlets, or come from other media.

Writers *must* have agents. Production firms usually look at an unsolicited script only when presented by a recognized agent. A fledgling writer must attempt to find an agent who will take on new talent. (Agents often will not represent writers who have no previous credits.)

Performers may have an even harder time breaking into the big time. Actors have usually performed in stage productions before they get their first part in a television commercial or bit part in a dramatic program. Singers and dancers usually have stage, club, or recording credits before they get their first chorus job in television.

Some persons can skip a few dues-paying years. These include the *exceptionally* talented, those whom managers hire because of public pressure or government requirements (Section 19.1.7), and those who have personal ties with management. If you fit one of these categories, take advantage of it. But as a beginner in a big-market outlet you may find yourself at a disadvantage. The small-market outlet serves as a training ground, a learning vehicle, an educational process, a place to make mistakes. The big-market outlet does not. You will have to learn in an organization not prepared to deal with beginners.

21.3 CAREER PREPARATION

You may wish to prepare for your career in radio-TV through a formal educational program. Three popular options include trade school, bachelor's degree program, and associate degree program. You may also wish to consider workplace training.

21.3.1 Trade Schools

Trade schools offer training in radio and television skills. In the past, many became known for their radio-TV electronics courses. But trade schools also teach courses in production areas, such as television camera operation, commercial copywriting, and disc jockey work.

Trade school courses run eight weeks to a year. The exact length varies with subject and school. Every requirement in their curriculum focuses directly on radio-TV. They award no academic degrees but do grant certificates of completion. Many advertise effective placement services to help graduates get that first job. Most operate for profit.

The best trade schools do an unbeatable job of preparing people for first jobs in a short time at low cost. The worst are gyps. If you wish to work in an operational job such as a disc jockey shift, you should consider a trade school. Before you enroll, check the school's placement record. Look at its facilities. Ask for an opinion from three or four graduates and the Better Business Bureau.

21.3.2 Bachelor's Degree Programs

Many colleges offer the opportunity to learn about radio-TV. The required program of study typically takes four years. When a student successfully completes all requirements, the school awards an academic degree, generally a bachelor of arts or bachelor of science.

Of necessity, the college radio-TV program suffers from a split personality. It must provide a liberal education. It must also teach vocationally oriented subjects such as radio-TV writing, production, and law. Many schools add yet a third dimension to their curricula. In these programs, students also study radio and television as powerful informational and cultural forces in society.

You may feel that your career preparation should include a radio-TV degree program. After all, a college degree still commands respect. Many employers require a degree, particularly for promotion to upper-level, decision-making positions. You must, however, bear in mind what the degree program is and what it is not. Its primary purpose is to provide a **broad education.** By definition, a broad education includes elements of English composition, humanities, life sciences, physical sciences, social sciences, and mathematics. Many of the best radio-TV academic programs actually require their students to complete *no more than 25 percent* of their total course work in radio-TV courses. The remaining 75 percent must come from other areas, completely outside mass communica-

tion. The radio-TV degree program is *not* occupational training.

Hundreds of colleges provide degree study in radio-TV. The department that offers radio-TV major courses varies from school to school. Its name typically includes one or more of the following words: broadcasting, communication, journalism, mass communication, radio and television, speech, and telecommunication.

Individual professors may join the Association for Education in Journalism and Mass Communication (AEJMC) and the Broadcast Education Association (BEA). Academic departments may join BEA and an AEJMC affiliate organization. BEA has ties with the National Association of Broadcasters and holds its national convention with that of NAB. BEA and AEJMC publish *Journal of Broadcasting & Electronic Media* and *Journalism Quarterly*, respectively, primary scholarly journals in the field. Some professors join academic organizations in speech, film, and other areas.

A radio-television department may apply for accreditation. Accreditation certifies that the department has been measured against and met a national standard. In its investigation of a department, the accrediting agency evaluates elements such as budget, curriculum, facilities, faculty, and library holdings. The Accrediting Council on Education in Journalism and Mass Communications (ACEJMC) accredits in the area of radio-TV. You can attend an ACEJMC-accredited program with some certainty of getting an excellent education in radio-TV. On the other hand, many fine, respected departments never apply for accreditation.

Do *not* get a graduate degree before your first job. A master's degree does not substitute for experience. It does not make you more attractive to potential employers. It can even be a hindrance. Managers may consider you overeducated for entry-level jobs. Rarely do you need a master's degree to work in radio or television. Primary reasons to get a

Figure 21.2 Junior college training facilities. A student practices at the audio console, College of San Mateo, San Mateo, California. (Photograph courtesy of Jim Threlkeld, College of San Mateo. Used by permission.)

master's degree include the following: desire for advanced, usually theoretical, academic work; preparation for employment in quantitative research, such as with an audience-rating firm; qualification for the few jobs in public broadcasting and at community colleges that require one; and a prelude to doctoral study. Persons headed toward management may find the specialized degree, master of business administration, helpful. In most cases, you should have at least three to five years experience before starting master's study.

The doctorate is a research degree. Doctoral study consists of research and theory, not creative or production courses. Most universities require faculty to have or be well on their way toward completion of a doctorate.

21.3.3 Associate Degree Program

Some community colleges have radio-TV programs. They provide a heavy concentration of skills courses. They also require liberal arts courses such as English, government, and history. They grant an associate in arts degree. Faculty members normally have

at least a master's degree and some experience in the trade. Most of these schools have good facilities (Figure 21.2), maintain a student-operated station or cable channel, and emphasize good teaching. If you want an academic degree, skills course, a minimum of other requirements, and a collegiate setting, look into a community college radio-TV program.

The radio-TV associate degree is a *terminal* program. The curriculum prepares you to work in the trade. Much of the course work does not transfer to a four-year college. If you go to a community college with the intention of transferring, opt for the *general education* program, not the terminal program. Take radio-TV courses *after* you transfer. Many universities, especially those with accredited programs, do not give credit for community college radio-TV courses.

21.3.4 Workplace Training

You can also learn about radio-TV by working in a radio-TV outlet. This is *workplace training*, and its advantages as career preparation are obvious. It puts you directly in the trade. You get experience and learn while doing what you want to do.

These are also its chief disadvantages. In workplace training, you learn "how it's done" at a particular outlet. And that is *not* necessarily "how it's done" at most of the better-run outlets in the trade. Further, you often learn how to do just one particular job. You do not get the global view of radio-TV and their career opportunities that even a trade school course can give.

Nonetheless, workplace training gives you hands-on experience. Take advantage of it, particularly in combination with one of the formal educational programs described above. You are looking for training, experience, eventually a good recommendation, and, in some cases, a chance at employment. Some workplace training situations are really jobs for which you receive pay. You are, however, still a beginner. Paid or not, the workplace is doing you a favor by taking you on. Remember that, and treat the training situation as a *job* that you *need* and *like*. Be reliable, responsible, responsive, on time, thorough, and courteous. Keep at it; don't quit after a month or two. Often, you will draw the menial assignments; do them well and cheerfully, without complaint.

Some of the more popular forms of workplace training include volunteer work, campus outlet positions, internships, and outright employment, part time and full time. Each of these includes elements of on-the-job training.

21.3.4.1 Volunteer Work A few local outlets use unpaid volunteer personnel to augment professional staff. Check, for example, community-licensed public broadcast stations and the access-channel coordinators for cable systems.

21.3.4.2 Campus Outlet Positions Some colleges and trade schools operate their own outlets. These range from campus-limited radio stations (Section 11.8) and cable channels to full-service television stations. These facilities, often student-run, offer opportunity for on-air experience. Some institutions also operate closed-circuit facilities (Section 22.9) to produce video instructional materials. They often use students in the crew positions. When students receive pay for working in an on-campus position, they often have the title *student assistants*. If your school has such positions, make maximum use of them. Get involved early.

21.3.4.3 Internships In an internship, students work at a radio-TV outlet off campus, often for academic credit. Some internships are part time, others full time. The student interns at the installation to learn something new. The installation may or may not pay the intern. The learning aspect should dominate. When a student gets an internship primarily for a paycheck, the nature of the position alters and moves closer to that of a job.

Try for an internship. It can give valuable experience. Sometimes, it leads directly to a job offer. In a *co-op* situation, the student works full time for pay and goes to school alternate terms.

21.3.4.4 Employment Here, the individual works at a radio-TV outlet for pay. In most cases, 40 hours a week constitutes **full-time** employment. Most outlets insist that job applicants have *some* demonstrated competence to qualify for a full-time job, even if only work experience in a related field or a college degree in something. Some of the smallest outlets do, however, have to hire and train rank beginners, people with no qualification other than glimmerings of talent and a willingess to learn.

The typical **part-time** job requires 10–20 hours. Often, these consist of off-time periods—weekends and overnight. Outlets often hire beginners and train them for these positions.

A part-time job allows you to earn and learn in radio-TV while doing something else full time. That "something else" might consist of a 40-hour-a-week job that keeps food on the table while you work at the outlet for peanuts and the chance to learn a radio-TV skill. It might be a full academic schedule, 15 or more semester hours, so you can finish school while earning money and getting experience. In such situations, you must be willing to give up chunks of leisure time and, often, sleep. The part-time job, however, provides an excellent opportunity to gain genuine résumé-building experience.

21.3.4.5 On-the-Job Training Nothing substitutes for experience—not trade school, not a college degree. No matter what your academic preparation, your first job will probably be at the entry level—a small outlet in a small market. As suggested in the previous section, you really need no specific career preparation in some entry-level jobs. Your supervisor and co-workers teach you what you need to know. This is *on-the-job training* (OJT).

Then why bother with academic training? For one thing, it gives a slight competitive edge for that entry-level job. Assume that a job opening calls for a disc jockey. The outlet manager has two applicants—the kid who pumps gas at the service station down the street and a recent college or trade school graduate. All other things being equal, the manager would more likely hire the graduate. Having gone through a radio-TV curriculum, the graduate at least knows concepts, nomenclature, and station operation and may have even worked on the school FM station. The graduate would need less OJT than the gas pump attendant. Later in a career, when the individual is ready to move into a position of increased responsibility, a bachelor's degree may give a competitive edge. Increasingly, the trade requires a college degree for promotion into management.

21.4 THE FIRST JOB

Your first job may be the most important of your career. That is where you get experience. The trick is to get that first job and then keep it.

21.4.1 Finding It

You may hear talk that colleges allow too many students to study radio-TV and that graduates do not find jobs. Indeed, many cannot find jobs—*because they do not know where to look.* And here, the colleges sometimes inadvertently contribute to the problem. Big-market outlets set standards for the trade, so instructors often use them as examples in class. Rarely do students hear about entry-level positions, the advantages of starting in a small market, or the necessity of experience as a prerequisite for big-market employment. Naturally, when students graduate, they go to big markets to look for a job. Just as naturally, the big-market outlets, which have their pick of experienced people, do not hire these beginner/graduates. The graduates then say there are no jobs available. The big-market managers complain that the colleges graduate too many people in radio-TV. To further confuse matters, talk show hosts, game show emcees, network news anchors, and others who *seem* to know what they are talking about (but don't) tell young people that jobs are scarce and to stay out of radio-TV. Meanwhile, entry-level jobs go begging.

In addition, some people restrict the geographic area in which they will work. In doing so, they also restrict their chances of getting a first job. If you insist on working near home, then you may have a long wait. If you live in a large city, you may wait even longer. Even though you *live* there, to the stations you are still a beginner. Meanwhile, jobs open in other parts of the country—in towns that could even be nicer than your own, in areas about which you have only heard, full of people who could become your closest friends.

You must apply in person. Most managers have file drawers full of résumés. But when they have openings, they hire someone who walks through the door and applies. Résumés, tapes, letters of reference, sample copy—these support, but do not take the place of, a personal visit. Letters and telephone calls rarely yield job offers. Mass mailings of résumés benefit no one but printers and the U.S. Postal Service.

Plan your visits. Use *Broadcasting Yearbook*, road maps, and other reference material. Call and set up appointments about a week before your visits. Be on time.

At the same time, check other sources of job leads. These include trade press classified ads, state trade association job bulletins, and school placement center listings. Follow up such a lead immediately. Otherwise the job will be gone.

You may have difficulty finding corporate television facilities. Most of the usual reference sources do not list them. One long-range job-hunting strategy involves attending meetings of the nearest chapter of International Television Association (Section 19.8.3). Take advantage of the lower rate and join as a student member, if eligible. Volunteer to run registration tables, straighten chairs, hand out name tags. This gives you a chance to get to know and impress the members. If you have anything on the ball, they will remember you when they have openings.

21.4.2 Keeping It

Attitude has a lot to do with keeping a first job. Here are a few hints on attitude. First, remember that the owner of the outlet pays your salary. Do what management says, in the way management says to do it. Above all, be dependable!

Second, consider your job a continuation of your education (Figure 21.3). Even if you have been graduated from a top urban uni-

Figure 21.3 First jobs: a continuation of your education. (*Source: Feedback,* 2/77: 15. Used by permission.)

Figure 21.4 First jobs: expect the worst job assignments. (*Source: Feedback*, 11/76: 17. Used by permission.)

versity and work with a bunch of high school dropouts in a coffeepot radio station at a wide spot in the road, you can learn from them. Those station people have worked in the trade longer than you. They know more than you. Learn from them. Here, you begin to develop what "marketable skills" you really have to offer.

Third, be friendly and courteous. Avoid office politics. Stay away from the malcontents. Do your part. Be responsible.

Lastly, expect the worst shifts, the longest hours, the weekend assignments, the dog client list (Figure 21.4). You are the new employee. But those things should really not matter. After all, you are working in radio or television. That is what counts.

FURTHER READING

Becker, Lee B., et al. *The Training and Hiring of Journalists.* Norwood: Ablex, 1987. Impact of education.

Bone, Jan. *Opportunities in Cable Television.* Lincolnwood: NTC, 1984. Guide to getting the first job.

Costello, Marjorie, and Cynthia Katz. *Breaking into Video: A Guide to Career and Business Opportunities.* New York: Simon, 1985. Production companies, broadcasting, cable corporate video.

Mogel, Leonard. *Making It in the Media Professions: A Realistic Guide to Career Opportunities in Newspapers, Magazines, Books, Television, Radio, the Movies, and Advertising.* Chester: Globe, 1987. Subtitle says it.

National Association of Broadcasters. *Careers in Radio.* Washington: NAB, 1986.

———. *Careers in Television.* Washington: NAB, 1986.

Reed, Maxine, and Robert M. Reed. *Career Opportunities in Television.* 2d ed. New York: Facts, 1986.

Weinstein, Bob. *Breaking into Communications.* New York: Arco, 1984. Covers broadcasting, cable, newspapers.

SIX

COMPARATIVE PERSPECTIVE

So far, we have concentrated on profit-seeking radio and television in the United States. Now we examine alternative forms of electronic mass media—noncommercial in Chapter 22 and foreign systems in Chapter 23. These alternatives provide us with bases for comparison and, as such, help us to understand better the American commercial system. We shall also learn that these alternatives have taken on some of the characteristics of the American commercial system.

CHAPTER 22

NONCOMMERCIAL RADIO AND TELEVISION

Unlike the situation in some other industrialized countries of the world, the commercial system dominates radio and television in the United States. Nonetheless, the United States does have a noncommercial system. The noncommercial system offers the public alternative programming, something it lacked for years. And despite setbacks and myriad problems, that system gains audience and adherents as it matures.

In this chapter we focus on public broadcasting. But we look at other forms of noncommercial radio and television, also.

22.1 HISTORY

Some of the very first AM broadcast stations were started by educational institutions, often the physical sciences departments of colleges and universities (Figure 22.1). Soon, however, the technical novelty of broadcasting wore off, and the financial reality of operating expenses set in. Some educational licensees began selling advertising. Many more gave up their licenses.

22.1.1 The Struggle for Reserved Channels

At times, it seemed as though the government connived with commercial interests to wrest frequencies from educational licensees

Figure 22.1 9XM, Forerunner of WHA. The origins of WHA, the University of Wisconsin's radio station, date back to 1915 and the university's physics department. Here, Malcolm Hanson "broadcasts" radiotelegraphic messages via 9XM in 1920. It was about this time that the station launched its first experiments in voice transmission. (Photograph courtesy of State Historical Society of Wisconsin. Used by permission.)

so that they could be used to sell products. Educational licensees would find their frequencies changed, their power reduced, and their status changed from full-time to share-time operations.

22.1.1.1 NAEB In 1925, educational licensees organized to fight such treatment and to urge that radio channels be reserved for education. They called their ogranization the Association of College and University Broadcasting Stations. Nine years later, the group reorganized as the **National Association of Educational Broadcasters** (NAEB).

22.1.1.2 Radio During the period 1921–1936, 202 licenses were issued to educational institutions. Out of this total, only 38 stations were on the air at the beginning of 1937, and some of these operated on a commercial basis. Educators tried to have some AM channels reserved for education when Congress was about to pass the Communications Act of 1934. Commercial broadcasters convinced Congress and the FCC that they were already carrying educational material, and Congress made no educational reservations. Shortly thereafter, the commercial broadcasters' educational programs began to disappear.

Through efforts of the NAEB and other organizations, the FCC realized that channel reservations were, indeed, needed if education was to have a broadcast voice. In 1940, when the FCC established the first FM band at 42–50 MHz (Section 3.3), it set aside 5 of the 40 channels for noncommercial educational use. Five years later, the commission moved FM to its present position and **reserved the first 20 channels** for noncommercial educational stations.

In 1948, the FCC authorized **low-power** operation for stations in the reserved band. This way, an educational institution could go on the air with a 10-watt transmitter for little initial investment, gain experience and ex-

pertise, and later improve facilities and power.

22.1.1.3 Television By this time, television had begun to grow, and the FCC imposed the freeze (Section 4.1.1). The commission had reserved no channels for education in its 1941 authorization of television. Now, during this period of reconsideration, commercial broadcasters argued against the idea of educational reservations. Educational broadcasters responded. The NAEB played a key role, serving as coordinating and rallying point for their efforts. They found a sympathetic audience in **Frieda Hennock** (see Figure 22.2), first female member of the FCC. Commissioner Hennock worked hard to persuade her colleagues to the idea of educational reservations.

In 1950, the NAEB and several other elements of the educational community formed the **Joint Committee on Educational Television** (JCET). JCET coordinated the effort to convince the FCC of the need for reserved channels.

Figure 22.2 Commissioner Hennock and the first educational television station. KUHT, the first station to operate on a reserved educational television channel, signed on the air May 25, 1953. Attending the June 8 dedication ceremony were (left to right) Dr. W. W. Kemmerer, president of the University of Houston (the licensee); Federal Communications Commissioner Frieda Hennock; and Hugh Roy Cullen, benefactor of the establishment of the station. (Photograph courtesy of KUHT. Used by permission.)

The FCC's 1952 *Sixth Report and Order* (Section 4.1.2) provided for educational television. Among other things, it established an expanded table of assignments, reserved nearly 12 percent of those assignments for noncommercial educational television (ETV) stations, and opened the UHF band. Many of the new ETV reservations were on UHF channels.

22.1.2 Federal Funding: Facilities

Now the educational community had its own television channels. However, the problem of where to get money to build and operate staions still remained. By the end of 1953, Houston's KUHT (Figure 22.2) and Los Angeles' KTHE were the only educational stations on the air, and KTHE signed off the following September. The **Ford Foundation,** through its **Fund for Adult Education** (FAE), subsidized the initiation and operation of a number of stations. But the stations' minuscule operating budgets came mostly from the institutions to which they were licensed—communities, state universities, school systems, state educational television authories.

Congress passed the **Educational Television Facilities Act of 1962** to provide federal matching funds for construction of noncommercial television stations. The ETV Facilities Act directed the secretary of health, education and welfare (HEW) to work with state agencies to award a total of $32 million over a five-year period for construction, purchase, and improvement of the physical facilities of educational television stations. The act specified awards be made on a 50–50 matching basis—HEW would match every dollar the local station could raise. (Congress later moved responsibility for facilities funding to the National Telecommunications and Information Agency [Section 22.4].)

The 1962 act helped put new stations on the air and expand the facilities of others. The year before its enactment, there were 60 ETV stations on the air. By the end of 1966, the number had more than doubled to 121. Many of the new stations operated on UHF channels, having received additional encouragement when Congress adopted all-channel receiver legislation in 1962 (Section 4.1.4). Now it was time to upgrade programming.

22.1.3 Federal Funding: Programming

The NAEB had been active in program exchange among educational radio stations as early as 1935. In 1949, the NAEB started a bicycle network (Section 20.1.4)—taped program series, circulated by mail among radio stations.

The Ford Foundation financed and encouraged the most ambitious television program exchange of the early years. Ford's FAE organized the Educational Television and Radio Center in 1952. The next year, the center found a home in Ann Arbor, Michigan. In 1956, the Ford Foundation assumed direct financial responsibility for the center. In 1959, the center moved its administrative offices to New York City and added "National" to its name. Later, the name was shortened to **National Educational Television** (NET). Using the bicycle network concept to ship its films and tapes to stations, NET was educational television's first and primary source of national programming—its network—until 1970.

Despite NET and other programming efforts, educational broadcasting failed to achieve the critical mass needed to fund and distribute high-quality programming. Even at this seminal stage, a local-versus-national resentment had begun. Some ETV station managers carped about what they felt were high-handed programming decisions made by NET in New York.

A 1964 conference of ETV station personnel recommended formation of a commission to suggest national policy on ETV. In 1965, the Carnegie Corporation provided funds, members were appointed, and a staff was hired. Endorsed by President Lyndon Johnson, this blue-ribbon panel was the **Carnegie Commission on Educational Television.** In its February 1967 report,[1] the commission urged creation of a Corporation for Public Television. This corporation would receive and disburse government and private funds and improve programming. President Johnson presented a legislative proposal to establish a congressionally chartered nonprofit **Corporation for Public Broadcasting** (CPB) to encompass both radio and television. Congress passed the **Public Broadcasting Act of 1967,** extended the ETV Facilities Act for three more years, and authorized funds.

The act renamed the noncommercial service from *educational* to *public* broadcasting. It aimed to strengthen programming by providing for a higher level of funding. However, national programming did not begin on a regular basis right away. The Ford Foundation funded a weekly *Public Broadcasting Laboratory*, distributed by live interconnection. But most programming was locally produced or came to stations on tape or film from NET.

The Public Broadcasting Act prohibited CPB from owning or operating a network service, so in 1969 the corporation created the **Public Broadcasting Service** (PBS) to provide the interconnection for television programming. PBS did not create programming; it distributed programming funded and created by others. PBS began live interconnected program distribution in October 1970. In 1973, PBS was reconstituted. No longer a creature of CPB, it was now a station-owned membership organization.

CPB created **National Public Radio** (NPR) in 1970. NPR was to provide programming, as well as interconnection service. NPR began live network operations in May 1971.

Through increased funding and interconnected networking, programming improved (Figure 22.3) and audiences increased. Public television programs such as *America, The Forsyte Saga, The Ascent of Man, Civilisation, The Incredible Machine,* and *Masterpiece Theatre: Upstairs/Downstairs* drew both critical notice and measurable audiences. Public broadcasters paid more attention to ratings, and they offered evening programming that held broader appeal than before 1967.

Viewing patterns for public programming did not parallel those of commercial programming (Section 7.3). Most public television audience members viewed *selectively.* They tuned in for specific programs, then tuned out. Nonetheless, public television picked up enough selective attendance that, by the end of the 1980s, more than 100 million viewers watched public television in an average week. The average PBS household watched public television over $3\frac{1}{2}$ hours a week.

22.1.4 Problems

Serious problems persisted for public broadcasting. One such problem involved internecine **struggles among various components of the public broadcasting establishment.** Public television stations transferred their resentment from NET to CPB. The stations jealously guarded their own programming power and felt that CPB was trying to wrest that away by forcing a lockstep commercial network-style program schedule. CPB and PBS fought over control of programming and the interconnection. Since the PBS board consisted primarily of station representatives, the stations sided with PBS. Some noncommercial broadcasters felt that their medium should devote it-

(a)

(b)

Figure 22.3 Public television programming. Two of public television's most popular series were (a) *Ascent of Man* with Jacob Bronowski and (b) the *Masterpiece Theater* series *Upstairs, Downstairs*. Rose (left) was played by Jean Marsh, while Hudson was played by Gordon Jackson. (*Source:* AP/Wide World.)

self primarily to formal instruction and resented the move toward general-interest public broadcasting.

A second problem stemmed from **political meddling.** The Carnegie Commission had recommended that the corporation be trust-funded by a dedicated federal excise tax on television sets. This would provide revenue without having to depend entirely on congressional appropriations, thereby insulating the Corporation for Public Broadcasting from political interference in programming. To avoid controversy and to get the Public Broadcasting Act passed, this trust fund tax was not made part of the legislative package. As the commission foresaw, there was political interference in programming policies both from members of Congress and from the executive branch, particularly during the administration of President Richard M. Nixon.

Nixon fought PBS efforts to build up its news and public affairs programming. He viewed such programming as too liberal and critical of his administration and policies. Clay Whitehead, head of Nixon's Office of Telecommunications Policy, gave a speech at the 1971 NAEB convention and accused public broadcasting of turning into a fourth network, contrary to the principle of localism. In addition, Sander Vanocur and Robert MacNeil had just been hired away from commercial broadcasting at salaries higher than the government paid members of Congress. Vanocur and MacNeil were also known for stating their opinions, opinions which frequently ran counter to those of the Nixon administration. In 1972, Nixon vetoed a two-year funding bill for public broadcasting, saying that PBS and CPB both undermined localism. All this helped drive the wedge of disagreement deeper between the stations and CPB.

A third problem involved **money.** Public broadcasting needed funding that would continue for longer than one year. This would allow long-range planning and operational stability. Congress began multiyear appropriations for CPB in 1975. However, the national legislature attached conditions to the appropriations. One bill, for example, established salary ceilings for CPB, PBS, and NPR employees (thereby ending the possibility that a public broadcasting commentator would make more than a member of Congress!). And, of course, the appropriations came in the form of matching funds.

Other problems emerged—constant interruption of broadcasts to raise funds, leading to complaints from viewers; continual reliance on corporate underwriting of programming, leading to complaints from commercial broadcasters; inadequate programming for attracting large national audiences or meeting special-audience and strictly instructional needs. In response, the Carnegie Corporation announced formation and funding of a new commission in 1977.

The Carnegie Commission on the Future of Public Broadcasting released its report in January 1979. **Carnegie II**[2] called for funding to increase some 300 percent to $1.16 billion by 1985. The money was to be derived at least in part from a spectrum-use fee to be paid by commercial licensees. The report recommended replacing CPB with two new organizations, one to guide and maintain public broadcasting, the other to concentrate on programming. Carnegie II called for further controls to insulate public broadcasting from government control. Congress put some of the proposals into the various attempts to rewrite the Communications Act (Section 13.4.1). But, since these rewrite attempts failed, none of the Carnegie II revisions was carried out.

In 1973, CPB and PBS reached a compromise agreement on program control. The CPB programming department would make final decisions on CPB-funded programs, but PBS could dissent from such decisions. A complicated system of joint CPB-PBS committees would referee scheduling of the interconnection and running of programs not funded by CPB that either organization felt were not balanced or objective. An increased portion of CPB funds would flow directly to the stations. This agreement eased the problem of internal feuding, at least for the time being. The problems of lack of money and political meddling intensified.

22.1.5 The Scramble for Survival

In his campaign for election to the presidency of the United States, Ronald Reagan vowed to cut "government spending" and reduce the federal deficit. After the election, President Reagan made clear that one area in which he would reduce spending was public broadcasting. In fiscal year (FY) 1983, CPB's appropriation dropped $35 million, a 20 percent decrease from FY 1982. Public broadcasting stations and organizations scrambled to accommodate the cut in funds. Personnel were released, programs cut. All possible alternative funding sources were explored—even commercials!

22.1.5.1 Noncommercial Commercials Historically, federal regulation had prohibited public stations from airing advertising of any kind. Corporate underwriting credits could contain only visual and aural identification of the donor, no reference to the business or product. The FCC loosened restrictions somewhat in 1981, permitting use of logos and identification of product lines. That same year, responding to the probability of reduced government funding, Congress passed a bill to allow a few public stations to experiment with limited advertising. The law established a **Temporary Commission on Alternative Financing for Public Telecommunications** (which public broadcasters abbreviated as TCAF). TCAF, in turn, set up the experiment whereby selected public television stations ran advertising between programs.

The experiment began in early 1982 and ended in June 1983. Of the stations that completed the experiment, six ran actual commercials; another two ran enhanced underwriting—clustered underwriting credits. At the end of the experiment, the stations reported overall that they made money and that they had received little or no negative reaction from their viewers. Several said that pledge drives conducted during the experiment made more money than before.

Nonetheless, TCAF's final report said that public television should *not* carry advertising. The commission feared the negative impact it might have on subscribers, legislators, and underwriters. TCAF said that public stations should be allowed to run regular commercial-style advertising only if it could be shown that stations that did not carry advertising would not share the risks associated with advertising. Such risks included possible increases in copyright and union costs.

Instead, TCAF recommended that public broadcasters be permitted to air enhanced underwriting announcements. Such announcements could identify program supporters by use of brand names, trade names, slogans, brief institutional-type messages, and public service announcements.

The FCC subsequently revised its guidelines for underwriter identification. Under the revised guidelines, public broadcasters could air the following information about the donor: logo or slogans that identify but do not promote; locations; value-neutral descriptions of product line or service; and trade names, product, or service listings that aid in identifying the contributor.

Public broadcasters could *not* air paid announcements for profit-making entities. By 1986, however, some station licensees felt they *could* broadcast general service announcements (GSA). GSAs were local enhanced underwriting announcements that *looked like* commercials. National underwriters worried that GSAs might obscure national program credits. In response, PBS drafted guidlines to separate GSAs from some fully underwritten national programs.

22.1.5.2 Other Funding Alternatives The funding problem remained. Public broadcasting explored myriad ways to generate revenue. Even commercial broadcasting organizations offered suggestions. (The NAB, for example, did not relish the prospect of noncommercial stations competing for advertising dollars.) Despite the plethora of attempts and suggestions, TCAF reported to Congress in 1982 that, for the short run, there was no reasonable alternative to continued federal funding. For the long term, the temporary commission recommended a national tax credit and an excise tax on new television sets and, possibly, radio sets. The National Telecommunications and Information Agency, official voice of the Reagan administration for domestic telecommunications matters, criticized TCAF's report for assuming that the existing public broadcasting organization should be maintained.

22.1.6 NPR's Year of Tribulation

Of all major elements in public broadcasting, NPR seemed to be in the best shape to generate its own funding. NPR had entered into a number of agreements with communications firms to supply its satellite relay system and the subcarriers of its affiliates for various types of revenue-producing service. In 1983, NPR formed Ventures, a subsidiary to pull together its several joint technological enterprises.

Just a few weeks later, word went out that NPR was deeply in debt and that the debt was growing larger. NPR's president, Frank Mankiewicz, stepped down, soon followed by other officers. An audit revealed that NPR had not used adequate financial procedures and controls. Soon, it became clear that NPR would have a $9.1 million deficit by the end of the fiscal year. Various rescue plans were put into effect, but none could produce enough money to guarantee the majority of the debt.

The end of July was almost the end of NPR. The network had a $500,000 payroll due and no money to meet it. Finally, at almost the last minute, CPB agreed to guarantee a loan. NPR's member stations repaid the loan. NPR survived and instituted fiscal policies and accounting procedures designed to prevent similar problems in the future.

22.1.7 The Same and More

The problems remained. Internecine squabbles, political meddling, and lack of funding—all continued into the 1990s in one form or another.

Money was probably the basic problem. The Reagan administration continued to resist federal support for public broadcasting. Nonetheless, by FY 1988, Congress had managed to restore CPB appropriations.

Over the years, individual members of Congress tried to establish a permanent trust fund. During the trading frenzy of the mid-1980s (Sections 4.5.3.2 and 5.2.5), for example, Senator Ernest Hollings proposed a transfer tax on the sale of telecommunications properties. Most of the money would have gone for a trust fund to support public broadcasting. In 1987, the Hollings bill met the same fate as all other such proposals—defeat.

The apportioning of federal appropriations shifted. More money went to local stations, less to the national level. This trend had begun earlier but accelerated in the latter part of the 1980s. In 1986, for example, CPB and NPR agreed on *the business plan*, a restructuring of public radio budgeting and op-

erating procedures. Under this plan, programming funds previously allocated to NPR now went to the stations. The stations, in turn, chose whether to pay NPR membership fees for the entire "bundle" of NPR programming. The plan seemed to work well. The stations, however, always arguing for more "local control," urged further revision. Two years later, NPR responded by adopting an *unbundling plan*. Under this plan, stations bought separate packages of programming from NPR. The plan also provided for purchase of NPR programming by nonmember stations. In the meantime, Congress worked on proposals to restructure public television along the lines of radio's business plan, and CPB looked toward the possibility of having to narrow the number of activities for which it provided financial support.

Other problems involved cable and independent producers. In the wake of must-carry's demise (Section 4.5.2.1), some cable systems cut second and third public stations from their channel lineups. Some system operators shifted public stations from their original cable channels to other, often less desirable, cable channels. Cable networks competed for programming and audiences ("Special interest," Section 7.4.2.1) that public television had once considered its exclusive franchise. Independent producers felt that CPB and PBS had denied them the opportunity to make and air programs. They lobbied Congress for a share of CPB's funding without CPB control.

22.2 PUBLIC BROADCAST PROGRAMMING

Despite the litany of woes just recited, the progress made by noncommercial broadcasting must be recognized. Public (as they were now called) radio and television had improved immeasurably since 1960. Their programming was often just as slick and professional as that of commercial television—more so, in the case of the consistently fine dramas from the Public Broadcasting Service. They demonstrated that high-quality programming could succeed, could attract audiences seeking alternatives to existing commercial programming. And in doing so, they earned the ultimate (and probably unwanted) compliment that commercial programmers could bestow—immitation and competition.

22.2.1 National Public Programming

Programming for public broadcasting at the national level is largely the responsibility of PBS and NPR. The federally funded CPB provides funds to PBS for network interconnection, to individual production organizations for program production, and to individual stations for programming and other operations. The PBS network program schedule consists of those programs whose productions CPB has funded directly, those selected and paid for in large part by the stations as a group, those financed by corporate underwriting or by foundations, those produced by individual stations for local audiences and then selected for national exposure, and those that have been aired previously on the network and have been selected to repeat.

The PBS **National Program Service** includes prime-time, general audience, and children's programs. PBS produces no program itself but does distribute programming on the public television satellite system (Figure 22.4). And it provides the vehicle by which member stations select programs to finance and include in the National Program Service.

The affiliated stations themselves select and pay for a large portion of the programs on the PBS schedule. They do this primarily through the **Station Program Cooperative** (SPC). Under the SPC, PBS solicits program proposals for its upcoming season schedule. Affiliates indicate which programs on the list they would be willing to broadcast and help finance with the money provided for that purpose by CPB. Examples of the programs that have made this first cut are screened at an annual Program Meeting to allow station personnel to see and discuss the choices. Several more selection rounds follow. When a program has drawn enough station commitments to finance its creation, it is put on the PBS schedule.

Sources of programming include PBS member stations, organizations set up especially to produce for PBS, and production organizations from outside the public broadcasting pale. Major producing stations include WGBH, Boston; WNET, New York City; KQED, San Francisco; KCET, Los Angeles; WETA, Washington, D.C.; WTTW, Chicago; and WQED, Pittsburgh. Probably the best-known special public television production agency is Children's Television Workshop (CTW), producer of *Sesame Street* (Figure 22.5), *Electric Company,* and the 1977 miniseries *The Best of Families.* Long a major source of programming outside the U.S. public broadcasting establishment British television has contributed programming ranging from *Upstairs/Downstairs* (Figure 22.6), and *Civilisation* to *Monty Python's Flying Circus* and *Fawlty Towers.*

PBS actually offers stations two sources of programming—the interconnect and Encore. The interconnect carries the National Program Service, the programs selected through the station selection procedures, plus programs funded through other sources—CPB, foundations, or some combination. Encore, a program library service, includes many programs that have already run on PBS.

National Public Radio provides programming and technical operations for member stations. For a yearly membership fee, qualified stations receive extensive programming and support services, such as marketing assistance, a computerized satellite-delivered communications system, and engineering training and advice. NPR also works with stations to represent their interests before the Federal Communications Commission and Congress. NPR broadcasts many events that are economically unfeasible for commercial networks to carry, for example, congressional committee hearings and broadcasts of National Press Club speakers. Some of the better-known regular NPR offerings include the weekday news magazines *Morning Edition, All Things Considered* (Figure 22.7), and *Weekend Edition* and the daily arts program *Performance Today.*

In 1982, representatives of four public radio stations and one regional public radio organization formed **American Public Radio.** The new network was to complement, not compete with, NPR by providing additional access to qualtiy radio programming. For years, American Public Radio's best-known offering was the Saturday afternoon variety show *A Prairie Home Companion* (Box 22.1), produced by Minnesota Public Radio. Other major APR-distributed programs include *Good Evening, Monitoradio, St. Paul Sunday Morning, The Thistle and Shamrock,* and the Los Angeles Philharmonic Orchestra concerts.

22.2.2 Local Public Programming

Public television stations often display symptoms of a split personality. During daytime, a station may broadcast instructional material for in-school use or for-credit home study. Quality of instructional material varies with the amount of money, time, and creativity put into it.

During afternoon and evening hours, the station typically airs general-interest programming. Most will come from PBS, but the station will get some from other sources and produce some itself. Other sources might include free or low-cost programming from regional networks, other public television stations, government agencies, or educational institutions. A public television station may buy programming from commercial syndication sources to put together its own classic film festival or to air documentaries, specials, or even old entertainment series produced for and first broadcast by commercial television.

The quality also varies for locally produced general-interest programming. Some public television stations maintain near-network quality levels in all local production. Too often, however, local productions are poorly produced and boring. Lack of funding is a primary cause.

Many public radio stations program a fine arts/classical music format. Others program jazz, talk, public affairs, even black and progressive rock music. Still others program a little bit for everybody and opt for an eclectic format, attempting to mix blocks of various programming types into an integrated whole. A dual format focuses on two different program forms, say jazz and classical music. The station might program for classical music listeners during the day, then appeal to jazz fans in the evening.

Religious stations that operate in the reserved portion of the FM band program their messages in a variety of ways. Such programming ranges from the subtle approach, featuring classical music and discussion programs, to 24 hours of hard-driving preaching, hymns, "Jesus rock," and "beautiful inspirational music."

Many noncommercial radio stations are neither NPR affiliates nor religious stations. Their programming is so diverse as to defy

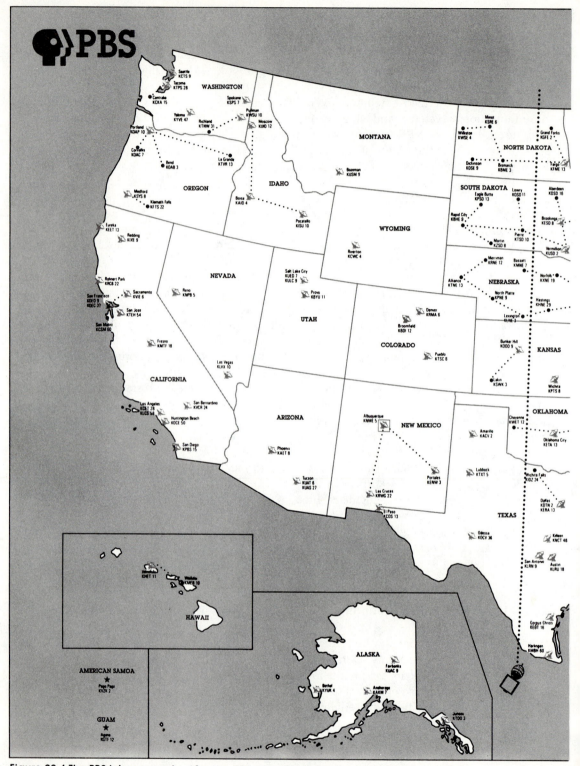

Figure 22.4 The PBS interconnect. (*Source:* PBS. Used by permission.)

PUBLIC TELEVISION
INTERCONNECTION SATELLITE SYSTEM

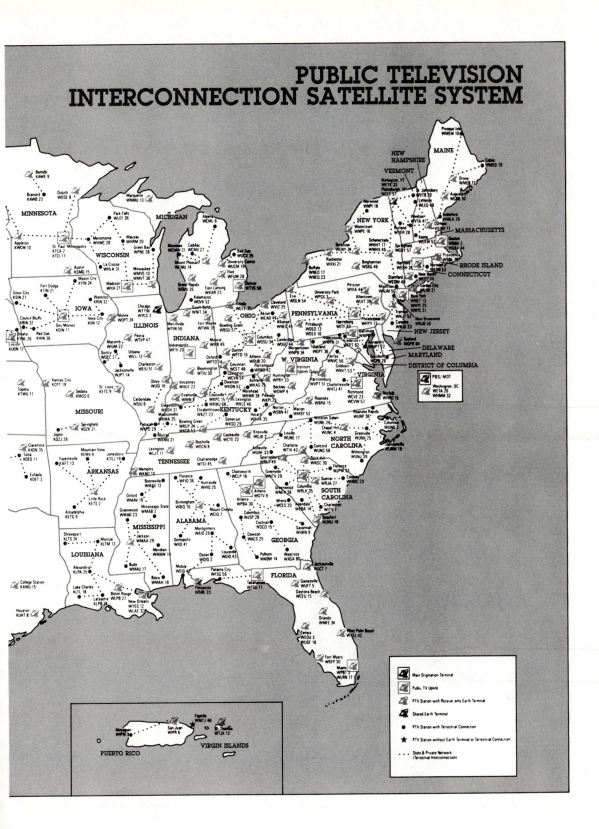

MAINE
Presque Isle WMEM 10

NEW HAMPSHIRE
Colsa WMED 13
Orono WMEB 12

VERMONT
Burlington, VT WETK 33
Portsmouth WCFE 57
Windsor WVER 28
Rutland WVTA 41

St. Johnsbury WVTB 20
Littleton WLED 49
Augusta WCBB 10

MASSACHUSETTS
Biddeford WMEA 26
Durham WENH 11
Boston WGBH 2 / WGBX 44
Keene WEKW 52
New Bedford WLNE 6

RHODE ISLAND
Providence WSBE 36

CONNECTICUT
Springfield WGBY 57
Hartford WEDN 24
New Haven WEDY 65
Bridgeport WEDW 49
Stamford WEDW 49

NEW YORK
Norwood WNPI 18
Watertown WNPE 16
Syracuse WCNY 24
Rochester WXXI 21
Binghamton WSKG 46
Buffalo WNED 17 / WNEQ 23
Pittston WVIA 44
University Park WPSX 3
Erie WQLN 54
Elmira WSTM
Watkins Glen WSKG

NEW JERSEY
New Brunswick WNJB 58
Camden WNJS 23
Trenton WNJT 52

PENNSYLVANIA
Cleveland WEAO 49
Akron WNEO 45
Alliance WNEO 45
Pittsburgh WQED 13 / WQEX 16
Johnstown WWCP
Harrisburg WITF 33
Scranton WVIA

DELAWARE

MARYLAND
Frederick WFPB 31
Oakland WGPT 36
Annapolis WMPT 22
Salisbury WCPB 28
Hagerstown WWPB 31
Owings Mills WMPB 67 / WMPT 22

DISTRICT OF COLUMBIA
Washington, DC WETA 26 / WHMM 32

VIRGINIA
Harrisonburg WVPT 51
Charlottesville WHTJ 41
Richmond WCVE 23 / WCVW 57
Norfolk WHRO 15
Roanoke WBRA 15
Goldvein WNVT 53
Goldvein WNVC 56
Fairfax WNVC 56

W. VIRGINIA
Institute Uplink WSWP
Huntington WPBY 33
Morgantown WNPB 24

OHIO
Bowling Green WBGU 57
Columbus WOSU 34
Cincinnati WCET 48
Portsmouth WPBO 42
Oxford WPTO 14
Dayton WPTD 16
Athens WOUB 20
Toledo WGTE 30

INDIANA
Merrillville WYIN 56
Fort Wayne WFWA 39
Gary WYIN
Muncie WIPB 49
Indianapolis WFYI 20
Bloomington WTIU 30
Vincennes WVUT 22
Evansville WNIN 9

MICHIGAN
Alpena WCML 6
Cadillac WCMV 27
Mount Pleasant WCMU 14
Bad Axe WUCX 35
University Center WUCM 19
Flint WFUM 28
Detroit WTVS 56
Grand Rapids WGVU 35
East Lansing WKAR 23
Kalamazoo WGVK 52
South Bend WNIT 34
Marquette WNMU 13
Menominee WPNE 38

WISCONSIN
Park Falls WLEF 36
Wausau WHRM 20
Green Bay WPNE 38
La Crosse WHLA 31
Milwaukee WMVS 10 / WMVT 36
Madison WHA 21
Menomonie WHWC 28

MINNESOTA
Bemidji KAWE 9
Brainerd KAWB 22
Duluth WDSE 8
St. Paul-Minneapolis KTCA 2 / KTCI 17
Appleton KWCM 10
Austin KSMQ 15

IOWA
Fort Dodge KTIN 21
Sioux City KSIN 27
Council Bluffs KBIN 32
Waterloo KRIN 32
Des Moines KDIN 11
Iowa City KIIN 12
Mason City KYIN 24

NEBRASKA
Lincoln KUON 12
Omaha KYNE 26

ILLINOIS
Moline WQPT 24
Chicago WTTW 11 / WYCC 20
Peoria WTVP 47
Macomb WIUM 22
Urbana WILL 12
Quincy WQEC 27
Jacksonville WSEC
Charleston WEIU 51
Olney WUSI 16
Carbondale WSIU 8

MISSOURI
Kansas City KCPT 19
St. Louis KETC 9
Sedalia KMOS 6
Springfield KOZK 21
Joplin KOZJ 26

KANSAS
Topeka KTWU 11

OKLAHOMA
Claremore KOED 35
Tulsa KOED 11
Eufaula KOET 3

ARKANSAS
Mountain View KEMV 6
Jonesboro KTEJ 19
Fayetteville KAFT 13
Little Rock KETS 2
Arkadelphia KETG 9

KENTUCKY
Owensboro WKOH 31
Madisonville WKMA 35
Paducah WKPD 29
Murray WKMU 21
Bowling Green WKGB 53
Elizabethtown WKZT 23
Somerset WKSO 29
Covington WCVN 54
Louisville WKPC 15 / WKMJ 68
Lexington WKLE 46
Ashland WKAS 25
Morehead WKMR 38
Pikeville WKPI 22
Hazard WKHA 35
Pikeville WKPI 22

TENNESSEE
Memphis WKNO 10
Lexington WLJT 11
Nashville WDCN 8
Cookeville WCTE 22
Knoxville WSJK
Sneedville WSJK
Chattanooga WTCI 45

INDIANA
Clarksville

NORTH CAROLINA
Winston Salem WUNL 26
Chapel Hill WUNC 4
Greenville WUNK 25
Asheville WUNF 33
Charlotte WTVI 42
Concord WUNG 58
Linville WUNE 17
Roanoke Rapids WUNP 36
Columbia WUNJ 2
Jacksonville WUNM 19
Wilmington WUNJ 6

SOUTH CAROLINA
Greenville WNTV 29
Greenwood WNEH 38
Rock Hill WNSC 30
Sumter WRJA 27
Florence WJWJ 33
Conway WHMC 23
Columbia WRLK 35
Allendale WEBA 14
Charleston WITV 7
Beaufort WJWJ 16

GEORGIA
Chatsworth WCLP 18
Athens WGTV 8
Atlanta WPBA 30
Columbus WJSP 28
Cochran WDCO 15
Dawson WACS 25
Pelham WABW 14
Waycross WXGA 80
Savannah WVAN 9

ALABAMA
Florence WFIQ 36
Huntsville WHIQ 25
Louisville WGIQ 43
Dozier WABW 14
Birmingham WBIQ 10
Mount Cheaha WCIQ 7
Montgomery WAIQ 26
Demopolis WIIQ 41

MISSISSIPPI
Booneville WMAE 12
Oxford WMAV 18
Greenwood WMAO 23
Mississippi State WMAB 2
Jackson WMAA 29
Meridian WMAW 14
Bude WMAU 17
Biloxi WMAH 19

LOUISIANA
Shreveport KLTS 24
Monroe KLTM 13
Alexandria KLPA 25
Lake Charles KLTL 18
Lafayette KLPB 24
Baton Rouge WLPB 27
New Orleans WYES 12 / WLAE 32

TEXAS
College Station KAMU 15
Houston KUHT 8

FLORIDA
Pensacola WSRE 23
Panama City WFSG 56
Tallahassee WFSU 11
Gainesville WUFT 5
Jacksonville WJCT 7
Daytona Beach WCEU 15
Orlando WMFE 24
Tampa WEDU 3 / WUSF 16
West Palm Beach WXEL 42
Fort Myers WSFP 30
Miami WPBT 2 / WLRN 17

PUERTO RICO
Mayaguez WIPM 3
San Juan WIPR 6
Fajardo WMTJ 40

VIRGIN ISLANDS
St. Thomas WTJX 12

Legend:
- Main Origination Terminal
- Public TV Uplink
- PTV Station with Receive only Earth Terminal
- Shared Earth Terminal
- PTV Station with Terrestrial Connection
- PTV Station without Earth Terminal or Terrestrial Connection
- State & Private Network (Terrestrial Interconnection)

PBS/MOT

Figure 22.5 Sesame Street. (*Source:* AP/Wide World.)

Figure 22.6 Home-grown public television programming. Public television has been criticized for using too much programming made outside the United States. Nonetheless, a number of indigenous programming efforts have become national favorites—for example, *Mister Rogers' Neighborhood* with Fred Rogers. (Photograph used by permission of Family Communication.)

Figure 22.7 NPR Informational Programming. Robert Siegel, co-host of NPR's *All Things Considered,* ready to go on the air.

Box 22.1 "Gives Shy People the Courage to Get Up and Do What Needs to Be Done"

A Prairie Home Companion, one of radio's most popular programs, aired on American Public Radio from 1980 through 1987. During the program, host Garrison Keillor (in light suit) extolled the virtues of a number of "sponsors" from "Lake Wobegon," Minnesota, one of which was Powdermilk Biscuits—tasty, expeditious, and (allegedly) good for the reticent. In this picture, Robin and Linda Williams, two of the show's regulars, are behind Keillor. The house band was the Butch Thompson Trio. Performed before a theater audience, the program broadcast live every Saturday evening. *A Prairie Home Companion* was produced by Minnesota Public Radio and distributed by American Public Radio. Keillor ended the program after 13 years (he actually began it as a Minnesota-only broadcast in 1974), citing a desire to "resume the life of a shy person." Tapes of the program continued on public radio stations, and in 1989, Keillor announced that he would return with a new live series, *American Radio Company.* (Photograph courtesy of American Public Radio Network. Used by permission.)

classification, ranging from wall-to-wall classical or progressive rock to straight variety formats; from university student-government playgrounds to radio-television production laboratories. A few actually air courses for credit.

Colleges and high schools have found campus-limited stations (Section 11.8) particularly useful. These stations allow students to practice and experiment with programming. Some even sell advertising and air commercials.

22.2.3 Community Stations

One novel programming form is that of *community stations*. Community station programming represents a radical departure from standard radio fare. Each and all can have access to the airwaves. This brings unpopular causes, antiestablishment ideas, and strong language before the microphones. Community station proponent Lorenzo Milam has described it as "free-form noninstitutional radio."

Milam played a major role in spreading the community station concept. In late 1962, Milam put his first community station on the air for $7000. This was KRAB (FM), Seattle. Later, he helped develop seven other FM stations and turned them over to local groups. Some of the best-known examples of community station programming come from stations of the Pacifica Foundation (Section 15.3.5.1). It's first station, KPFA, in Berkeley, California, went on the air in 1949.

When the first community stations signed on, the public did not know what to make of them. Their programming was unlike anything they had heard before. Community stations depended solely on listener support. Since much of the community felt alienated by their programming, the stations seemed to lurch from financial crisis to financial crisis.

"Odd" and "antiestablishment" as these stations are, they embody a principle on which was founded the political structure of the United States—freedom of expression. Despite the supposed universality of this principle, many ideas receive their only chance for broadcast on community stations. Sadly, threats and even bombings target these stations, revealing that there are citizens who either do not understand or do not agree with the First Amendment to their own Constitution.

22.3 PUBLIC STATION LICENSEES

Most noncommercial stations are owned by nonprofit organizations. Beyond this generalization, it is difficult to categorize types of ownership. PBS and NPR affiliates tend to be owned by state educational broadcasting commissions, by colleges and universities, by broad-based nonprofit community corporations (Figure 22.8), and by school boards and systems. The ownership of noncommercial radio stations that are not affiliated with NPR is even more diverse—universities, community corporations, school boards, churches, religious groups, seminaries, high schools, college student government associations, cities, counties, and boys' clubs.

Most noncommercial radio stations are in the reserved portion of the FM band. Some licensees, however, operate noncommercial broadcast stations in the AM band. For example, Ohio University operates WOUB, Athens, at 1340 kHz, and the University of Illinois operates WILL, Urbana, at 580 kHz. (Some nonprofit institutions also operate commercial stations, for example, University of Missouri's KOMU-TV, channel 8, Columbia; Loyola University of the South's WWL, 870 kHz, New Orleans; and University of Florida's WRUF, 850 kHz, and WRUF-FM, 103.7 MHz, Gainesville.)

Limitations on the number of licensees do not apply to noncommercial broadcasting. Twin Cities Public TV, for exmaple, operates two television stations in St. Paul: KTCA-TV, channel 2, and WTCI-TV, channel 17.

22.4 FUNDING SOURCES

Overall, **public broadcasting gets about half its money from taxes** (Figure 22.9a). But less than 20 percent of its money comes from the federal government. Sources of public broadcasting's tax revenues include

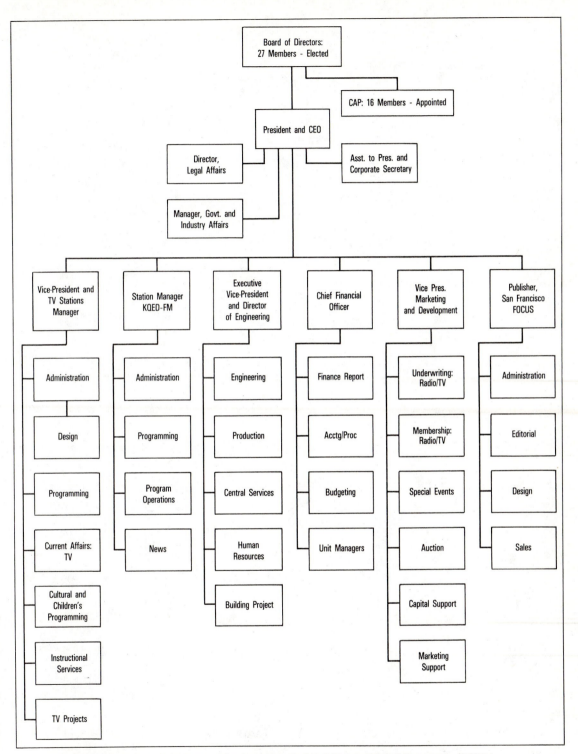

Figure 22.8 Organizational chart for large-market public broadcast licensee. KQED Inc., the licensee, is a nonprofit community corporation. It controls three San Francisco public stations—KQED, channel 9; KQEC, channel 32; and KQED-FM, 88.5 MHz. (*Source:* KQED, Inc. Used by permission.)

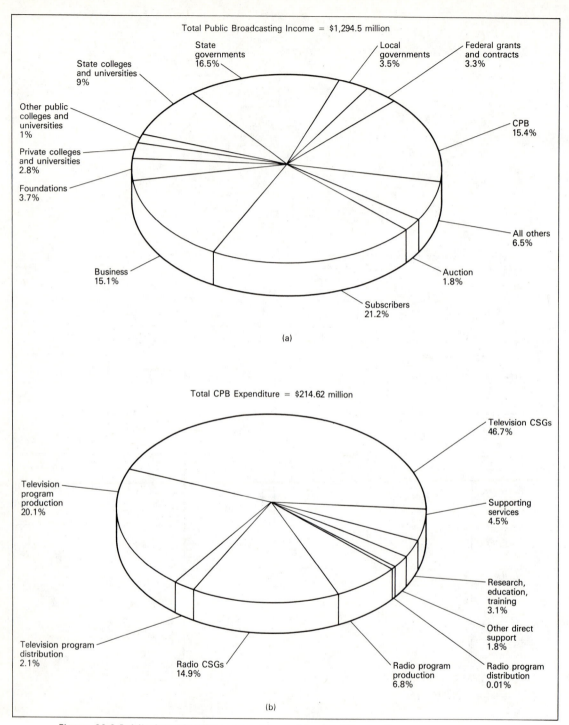

Figure 22.9 Public broadcasting revenues and expenditures. These were the percentages for (a) sources of funding for all public broadcasting and (b) expenditures of the Corporation for Public Broadcasting in 1987. The letters CSG stand for *community service grant,* CPB money given directly to stations. (*Source:* CPB, NAPTS.)

state governments, CPB, tax-supported colleges and universities, local governments, and federal government grants and contracts. The other half comes from subscribers, businesses, foundations, auction participants, private colleges and universities, and other sources.

In actual dollars, public broadcasting operates on a relatively minuscule budget. In FY 1987, for example, Congress appropriated CPB a record $200 million. This figure represented a 46 percent increase over FY 1983's Reagan-induced low (Section 22.1.5). During the same period, the three commercial networks paid an average fee of $800,000 for each hour of prime-time programming (Section 7.3.1.1). CPB's total annual congressional funding for one year would not quite cover expenses for three hours of programming per day for three months on one commercial television network.

Congress specifies how CPB should spend its federal appropriation (Figure 22.9b). Only a small portion may go to CPB's operating expense. The majority goes to television and radio at a ratio of about three to one. For each medium, most of the money has to go for **community service grants** (CSG), the remainder for national programming. A station must apply and meet certain criteria to qualify for a CSG. CPB gives CSGs on a matching basis; the exact amount for each station varies according to a formula. The station may spend the money almost any way it wishes. It uses a portion for programming; for example, a public television station must pay for the programs it obtains through the SPC.

The National Endowment for the Arts (NEA), the National Endowment for the Humanities (NEH), and the U.S. Department of Education provide additional federal funds for programming at both national and local levels. The National Telecommunications and Information Agency (Section 14.3.1.2) administers the Public Telecommunications Facilities Program, which makes facilities grants for local stations.

PBS derives about a quarter of its funding from CPB. This pays for management and operation of the satellite relay interconnection. The other three-quarters comes from the dues PBS charges its member stations, from interest income, and from its program library and other services.

NPR's member stations provide more than 60 percent of NPR's operating budget with their membership dues. Stations derive funds from their listeners, businesses in their communities, and grants from the Corporation for Public Broadcasting. To make up the difference in its operating budget, NPR also seeks grants and underwriting from corporations, foundations, associations, and individuals.

22.5 THE COMMERCIAL ACTIVITIES OF NONCOMMERCIAL BROADCASTING

The matching-funds concept has led public broadcasting to a continual search for nonfederal money. Public stations have engaged in a number of activities to raise money, several of which parallel, or at least bear a resemblance to, advertising.

Many public broadcast stations, as well as a number of commercial classical music and fine arts stations, publish and distribute **program guides** to their audiences. These guides often contain advertising. Revenue from program guide advertising helps defray the publication expense and, perhaps, even contributes toward station operating expenses.

Public stations also broadcast announcements somewhat analogous to the advertising of commercial broadcast stations. These include underwriting announcements, general service announcements, pleas for money, and auctions.

The **underwriting announcement** is probably most familiar. Many public broadcasting programs are supported by grants from various organizations, including major companies. Local businesses and even individuals support programming on stations. Announcements notify the audience that the program or programming has been underwritten or supported or made possible by a grant from Mobil, Goerings' Book Center, or whomever. These announcements fulfill federal requirements for sponsorship identification (Section 14.1.1.3).

Some public television stations' **general service announcements** (GSAs) bear a striking resemblance to commercials. GSAs air between programs, ostensibly to recognize businesses that donate money to the station. In reality, local advertisers pay for them, and they look like advertising spots.

Another type of announcement, peculiar to public broadcasting, is the **plea for money.** Stations usually air these pleas during membership drives. Individuals go on the air to ask for donations or subscriptions for the station, often promising gifts or premiums in return. Some public television stations have periodic **auctions** to raise money. Showing and describing the items to be auctioned, together with the names of merchants or manufacturers donating them, would seem to parallel the promotional announcements of commercial broadcasting.

In considering these announcement types, the case could be made that public broadcast stations seem to sell time, much as commercial stations do. They sell foundations and businesses on underwriting programs, then mention the underwriters by name before and after the programs. They sell merchants and other retailers on donating goods and services for auctions, then name the businesses and extol the products over the air. Some GSAs look suspiciously like outright commercials.

Many complain about public broadcasting's fund-raising efforts. Stations conduct what seem like almost continual pleas for donations and subscribers, and audiences compare them unfavorably to advertising on commercial broadcasting. *Broadcasting* magazine has editorialized against commercial-like practices of noncommercial stations on several occasions. Commercial broadcasters generally object to any semblance of advertising in noncommercial broadcasting.

The problem, however, is not that public stations engage in commercial practices or siphon off a few potential advertising dollars. The basic problem is funding. Given that public broadcasting is to continue to provide a high-quality, audience-drawing service, then unless and until some means are found to provide continuing, adequate, full funding—*not* tied to matching funds and not tied to the appropriations process—public broadcasting will be forced to continue to engage in money-raising schemes. And no amount of trade group objections or trade press harassment will change that.

22.6 PUBLIC BROADCASTING ORGANIZATIONS

Perhaps more than any other segment of radio and television, public broadcasting seems to be a sea of alphabet soup, thick with the initials of constituent organizations. We have already discussed several of these. The Corporation for Public Broadcasting is an important source of funding for stations, programming, and the public television interconnection. CPB is a congressionally chartered, nonprofit corporation, not a branch of the federal government; however, Congress provides its funding.

The primary national noncommercial networks are PBS and NPR. Both were organized by CPB. Both have headquarters in

Washington, D.C. Stations must meet certain minimum criteria to become member stations of either organization.

Neither PBS nor NPR parallels exactly its commercial counterparts. While PBS arranges for, manages, and sends programs to affiliated stations, it does not exercise absolute control over its own programming. It must share that control with CPB and, through the Station Program Cooperative, with the stations it serves. NPR does produce and control its own programming. Member stations, however, pick and choose the programming they wish to pay for and air.

NPR also acts as a station membership and representation organization. Stations join, and NPR uses station dues to provide membership and professional services and to represent the stations' interests before CPB, Congress, the executive branch, and the general public. In other words, NPR functions as a network, as an affiliate association, and as a public broadcasting equivalent of NAB.

Public television stations, however, have split the lobbying and programming functions between two organizations. PBS provides programming and membership services (such as promotion, engineering, and advertising assistance). Lobbying, planning, and research were spun off into a separate organization in 1979, the **National Association of Public Television Stations.**

Stations may join NPR and PBS only if they meet certain professional, staffing, technical, and operational standards. This excludes many high school and college FM radio stations.

American Public Radio is a private, nonprofit network of public radio stations. APR produces no programming itself. However, the network nurtures development of radio productions from all over the country and the world. It also provides promotion and marketing services.

The **National Federation of Community Broadcasters** (NFCB) is an organization for non-NPR public radio stations licensed to community organizations. It distributes programs, provides training, and assists groups seeking to develop new stations. NFCB looks out for the interests of its constituent licensees in dealing with Congress, the executive branch, the FCC, and other agencies in Washington, D.C.

The National Association of Educational Broadcasters (NAEB) was an influential organization for over four decades. Originally, its membership consisted of noncommercial broadcast stations. In 1956, it started admitting individuals. In 1973, the stations pulled out since they now had lobbying organizations outside NAEB. NAEB converted to an organization of individuals who worked or were interested in education and broadcasting. Without station dues, however, NAEB could not support the broad array of services and publications it had established. In 1981 it declared bankruptcy and went out of business.

On the other hand, a descendant of National Educational Television still exits. Until 1963, most production of NET programs was done by other organizations. That year, NET reorganized and began to build up its own production crews. NET was instrumental in assisting New York City's VHF educational television station WNDT, channel 13, to get on the air in 1962. NET continued as a major producer of programs for noncommercial television until 1969, when it merged with WNDT. The television station changed its call letters to WNET and assumed a role as one of the primary sources of national programming for PBS.

There are a number of regional and state organizations. Regional groups include the following: Central Educational Network, Eastern Educational Network (which also operates the Interregional Program Service), Eastern Public Radio, Pacific Mountain Network, Public Radio in Mid-America, Rocky Mountain Corporation for Public Broadcasting, Rocky Mountain Public Radio, Southern Educational Communications Association, and West Coast Public Radio.

One of the earliest noncommercial networks was the Wisconsin Public Radio Network (WPRN). It began in 1945 as the State Radio Network. Twenty-six years later, the radio network became part of the newly created Educational Communications Board (ECB). ECB's activities now include three interconnected networks (Figure 22.10)—WPRN, the Wisconsin Public Television Network, and the Wisconsin Narrowcast Service.

Many states have set up central governmental bodies to operate public television stations. Some of these state systems are interconnected. Among the more elaborate networks are those of Alabama, Georgia, Kentucky, Mississippi, Nebraska, North Carolina, and South Carolina. In most states a specially created state agency operates the system; in others a state university or the state department of education runs the network.

22.7 PUBLIC BROADCASTING, DEREGULATION, AND NEW TECHNOLOGIES

Generally, public broadcasting organizations at all levels have welcomed the coming of new forms and new uses of radio and television. They see these new media not only as alternative delivery systems but also as possible sources of sorely needed funding.

The FCC has also helped by removing some regulations that blocked public stations from generating revenues. For example, the FCC eased restrictions on underwriting announcements, allowed noncommercial FM stations to use their subcarriers for money-making ventures, and permitted educational entities to lease unused time on their ITFS channels to MDS programmers.

Public broadcasting organizations now lease programming for use on videocassettes and video discs, provide teleconferencing services, rent out unused time on their satellite systems, and cooperate in various schemes to make profitable use of their satellite interconnection and their subcarriers—for example, paging and data distribution. Some stations have experimented with electronic text and with cable television. The phrase "public broadcasting" may already be dated; we may be witnessing a metamorphosis—a change from stations and station organizations to a group of self-sustaining, nonprofit telecommunications programmers.

22.8 INSTRUCTIONAL BROADCASTING

Noncommercial educational broadcasting takes two basic forms. We have discussed one of these, public broadcasting, in some detail. However, we have done little more than mention the other, instructional broadcasting. *Instructional broadcasting* refers to the use of public airwaves for formal academic instruction.

22.8.1 The McMurrin Report

The Public Broadcasting Act of 1967 provided money for a comprehensive study of instructional radio and television. The study was to help Congress determine whether to provide federal funding for instructional use of broadcast media. It was to do for instructional broadcasting what the Carnegie Commission's report did for public broadcasting.

A **Commission on Instructional Technology** (CIT) was formed. Sterling McMurrin, graduate dean of the University of Utah and fomer head of the U.S. Office of Education, headed the commission. The task

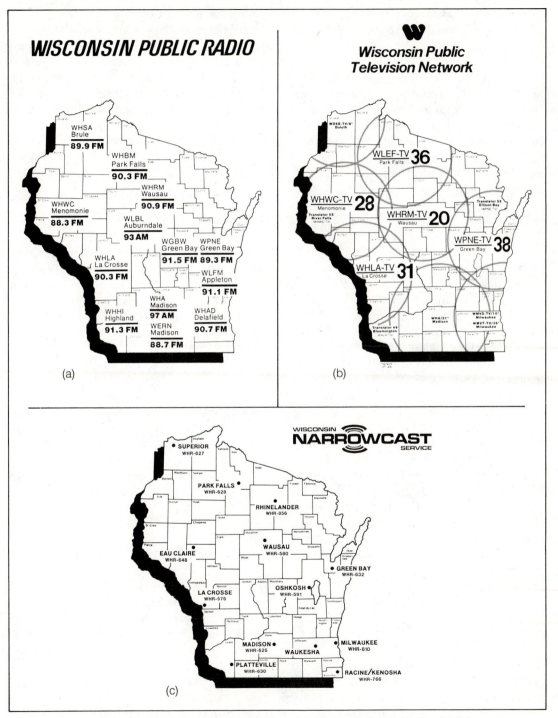

Figure 22.10 Noncommercial state networks. (a) Wisconsin Public Radio. (b) Wisconsin Public Television Network. (c) Wisconsin Narrowcast Service utilizes ITFS technology. (*Source:* Wisconsin Educational Communications Board. Used by permission.)

of the CIT was expanded, and the commission made a comprehensive study of the status of instructional media in the United States.

In 1970, the McCurrin commission submitted to Congress its report and recommendations.[3] Thorough and well done as it was, this report did not get the public notice or the congressional action that the Carnegie report had. The McMurrin report would remain an excellent but unused evaluation of instructional technology.

22.8.2 Mostly Television

Instructional broadcasting is done primarily by television. Radio could be used to teach many different things, many of the same things for which television is now used, and at a fraction of the cost. However, instructional radio is not widely used in the United States, so our discussion deals mainly with instructional television.

Public television stations often broadcast instructional materials weekdays (Section 22.2.2). Sometimes the organization that initiates or uses the instructional programming is the station's licensee, as in the case of a station owned by a public school system. Usually, however, instructional programming involves second parties, often school districts. School districts contract with a station to air instructional material, each district paying a share based at least in part on the number of students in that district who use the programming.

22.8.3 Uses

Some instructional broadcasts are designed for use **in the classroom.** Instructional broadcasting can be used at any and every level of schooling, from kindergarten through college postgraduate. It has come into increasing use to offer freshman/sophomore-level college courses in the general education area. Instructional broadcasting may be used **to teach an entire subject, to teach part of a subject,** or **to provide supplementary material.** Instructional broadcasting may also be used **to allow study at home.** Community colleges, particularly, use television to offer credit courses in American history, government, English, life and physical sciences, and other basic requirements.

22.8.4 Program Sources

Sources of instructional programming include institutions that sponsor or give credit for the broadcast courses, stations themselves, state and regional organizations, and national production centers and libraries.

During the 1980s, both PBS and CPB took on educational responsibilities. PBS's Adult Learning Service works with public TV stations and local colleges to make television courses available to adult learners nationwide. Its Elementary/Secondary Services provides leadership in the development and distribution of quality instructional TV series and services to stations and school agencies. The PBS National Narrowcast Service delivers video-based training and educational programming to business, industry, and colleges by satellite, ITFS (below), and addressable cable.

A special grant funds CPB development of college-level instructional materials, primarily audio and video courses. Some of the courses have included *Planet Earth, The Africans,* and *Economics USA.* Each academic year, more than 150,000 students enroll in courses offered by over 1,000 colleges. Named for the donating and administering agencies, this Annenberg/CPB Project also funds applications that demonstrate how communications technologies can increase opportunities for higher education.

22.8.5 ITFS and Satellite

Some school districts, community colleges, and other educational instututions utilize **instructional television fixed service** (ITFS; Section 12.7) for wireless distribution of instructional programming. ITFS is not broadcasting; however, it has characteristics that parallel both broadcast and closed-circuit distribution.

An institution uses ITFS when it wishes to distribute video educational materials to a number of physically separated units. An ITFS licensee may operate multiple channels, a distinct advantage over broadcast television. ITFS does not cost as much to build and operate as broadcast television, nor does it require a continuous broadcast-style schedule of programming. On the other hand, its line-of-sight transmission characteristic means that distance and transmission paths are critical in setting up an ITFS system. Also, few homes are equipped to receive ITFS, negating its use for home study. In some cases this can be overcome if a cable system agrees to carry the ITFS programming.

By 1988, a regional consortium made plans to serve rural high schools with satellite delivered instructional programming. The 18-state Satellite Educational Resources Consortium selected four schools for initial tests and followed with a full-scale effort in the fall of 1989. A U.S. Department of Education grant helped with financing. The plan targeted rural schools with scarce resources.

22.9 CLOSED-CIRCUIT RADIO AND TELEVISION

Closed circuit means that signals are distributed in a way that limits access to reception (Figure 22.11). The uses of closed-circuit television (CCTV) are almost endless. They range from video observation systems used in banks, retail stores, and other places to the cameras and monitors used in space, atomic, medical, and biological research; from taping and playback of dating service clients to recording trials so that deliberating jurors may review testimony. And it is used to teach.

Like instructional broadcasting, CCTV may be used to teach an entire subject, to teach part of a subject, or to provide supplementary material. It can be used to teach almost any number of persons, from one to as many as viewing facilities permit (Figure 22.12). It is used by public and private schools, colleges, and universities; by industry; by the military; and by every level of government.

22.10 AUTOTUTORIAL TECHNOLOGY

Autotutorial is a coined term that combines the concept of self-teaching with that of individualized instruction. Some educators have adapted technology to programmed learning to create highly sophisticated autotutorial situations.

Programmed learning requires that educational goals be carefully set forth in advance. Those goals are broken down into the smallest possible units of instruction, precisely defined teaching points. Methods are selected to present, reinforce, and test for the learning of those points. Often, this involves **branching**—if the student successfully learns the first teaching point, the next one is presented; if not, additional material is presented to help the student understand and learn the first point. If this learning program (the software) can be applied to some medium (hardware—say a book, slide/tape, or videotape), the student can operate it and go as fast or as slow as individual capabilities permit. This is the autotutorial aspect.

Some instructional technology developers have extended this concept to **interactive video instruction.** In one configuration, a

Figure 22.11 Large-screen instructional televison.   (Photograph courtesy of Ed Cenedella, St. Petersburg Junior College.)

personal computer is linked with a videodisc player. The videodisc's frames and motion sequences contain teaching points and testing material. The computer receives and processes student responses and tells the videodisc player what frame or motion sequence to play. In use, the videodisc displays a motion sequence that illustrates a teaching point and then shows a frame containing a question (on the sequence) along with five answer choices. The student responds by entering an answer choice into the computer. If the answer is correct, the computer directs the videodisc player to display sequences and frames that congratulate the student for giving the right answer and then go on to ex-

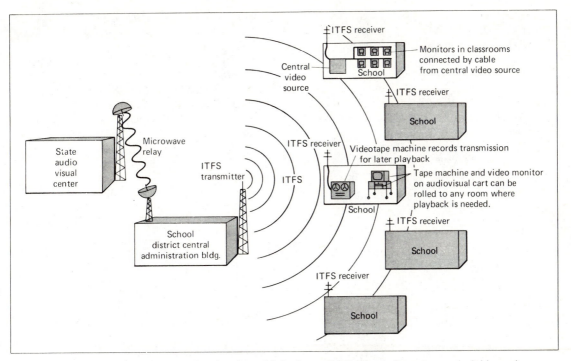

Figure 22.12 Closed-circuit instructional televison distribution. Program material is sent by microwave relay from state audiovisual center to the headquarters of a school district. The school district transmits the material to each of its schools via the instructional television fixed service. One school feeds it directly by coaxial cable to each video monitor in the building. In another school, a videotape machine records the material for later playback, perhaps using a portable videotape machine and monitor to deliver it to rooms where needed.

plain the next teaching point. If wrong, the display so informs the student, shows why and how the answer was incorrect, and re-explains the previous point.

NOTES

1. Carnegie Commission on Educational Television, *Public Television: A Program for Action* (New York: Harper, 1967).
2. Carnegie Commission on the Future of Public Broadcasting, *A Public Trust* (New York: Bantam, 1979).
3. Commission on Instructional Technology, *To Improve Learning: A Report to the President and Congress of the United States* (Washington: GPO, 1970).

FURTHER READING

Avery, Robert K., and Robert Pepper. *The Politics of Interconnection: A History of Public Television at the National Level.* Washington: NAEB, 1979. Development of public broadcasting from the creation of PBS to 1977.

Blakely, Robert J. *To Serve the Public Interest: Educational Broadcasting in the United States.* Syracuse: Syracuse UP, 1979. History and federal regulation of noncommercial broadcasting. Author was an officer with the Fund for Adult Education in 1951–1961.

Corporation for Public Broadcasting. *A Report to the People: 20 Years of Your National Commitment to Public Broadcasting 1967–1987.* Washington DC: CPB, 1987. Each CPB annual report gives trends and financial statistics. This one was a special edition.

Educational Media and Technology Yearbook. Littleton: Libraries Unlimited. Annual compilation of information on instructional technology and media.

Gibson, George H. *Public Broadcasting: The Role of the Federal Government, 1912–1976.* New York: Praeger, 1977.

Hudspeth, DeLayne R., and Ronald G. Brey. *Instructional Telecommunications: Principles and Applications.* New York: Praeger, 1986.

Milam, Lorenzo. *The Radio Papers: From KRAB to KCHU.* San Diego: Mho, 1986. His views on free-form radio.

Romixzowski, A. J. *Developing Auto-Instructional Materials: From Programmed Texts to CAI and Interactive Video.* London: Kogan, 1986.

Thomas, Thomas J., and Theresa R. Clifford. *The Public Radio Legal Handbook: A Guide to FCC Rules and Regulations.* Washington: NFCB, 1987.

CHAPTER 23

Foreign National and International Radio and Television

Now we examine radio and television outside the United States. Our examination includes electronic mass media, first, as systems within the boundaries of other countries and, second, as informational products that cross national boundaries. We begin with an analytical model that summarizes operational characteristics of national systems of mass communication. We examine the electronic mass media of four nations. We discuss the growing use of new technologies by other countries, major international organizations related to radio and television, the flow of programs in the world market, and the phenomenon of foreign media ownership. Finally, we review U.S. international radio-TV efforts.

23.1 WELLS'S ANALYSIS

Alan Wells[1] noted five key requirements, which he called *dimensions*, that are shared by all national systems of mass communica-

tion. For each dimension he listed several *options*. The options represent methods that he found nations employ to meet these requirements. If we look at Wells's key dimensions and the options for each, we should have an idea of the variety of national broadcasting systems and the alternatives countries employ to deal with radio and television. Wells's analysis is diagrammed in Table 23.1 and explained below.

Wells's dimensions are control, finance, programming goals, target audiences, and feedback mechanisms. Options for **control** include the following: direct operation by the government; operation by a private corporation in which the government has stock interest; operation by private companies, with government regulation in varying degrees; and operation by sponsoring institutions such as churches, political parties, or listener organizations.

Wells listed five options for **finance** of systems. Finance options include a tax or license fee paid by owners of receivers, subsidiza-

Table 23.1   KEY DIMENSIONS OF MEDIA SYSTEMS

Dimensions	Options
Control	State-operated, public corporation, partnership, private enterprise (with varying degrees of government regulation), institutionally sponsored
Finance	License fees, general taxation, advertising and taxation combination, advertising, private subsidy
Programming goals	Entertainment, education, sales, culture, political ideology, cheapest possible operation (utilizing foreign material)
Target audience	Elite, mass, specialized
Feedback mechanism	Reports from field workers, audience participation, polls and ratings, reports from critics and sponsors

Source: Alan Wells, *Mass Communications: A World View* (Palo Alto: Mayfield, 1974). Used by permission.

tion from general tax revenues, sale of advertising time, subsidization by private organizations or individuals, and subsidization through a combination of advertising and taxation.

Programming goals include one or any combination of six options. These options are as follows: entertainment, education, sales, culture, political ideology, or operation as cheaply as possible.

There are three **audience options.** These include elite, mass, and specialized. *Elite* refers to the wealthy, the educated, the literate. An example of a specialized audience could be workers in a particular factory.

Feedback mechanism refers to the means by which audience response to programming is determined. Wells listed four feedback mechanism options: reports from field workers, audience participation and local control, polls and ratings, and evaluation by critics and sponsors.

23.2 NATIONAL SYSTEMS: FOUR EXAMPLES

At this point we go from theory to practice and find how some of these options translate into actual operation. As examples, we examine the electronic mass media systems of four countries—the United Kingdom, Union of Soviet Socialist Republics, India, and the Netherlands. These systems do not represent the total spectrum of options across each dimension. They do, however, show how four quite different countries use electronic media to serve specific needs.

As in all national systems of mass communication, each of these four is dependent on the money available for operation. Relatively, India has a much more limited system than the other three. Nations in Third World countries do not have money to provide more extensive radio-TV service.

23.2.1 The United Kingdom

The United Kingdom (UK) is a highly industrialized nation with which the United States shares a common heritage of language and democratic political institutions. In the UK, broadcast licenses are issued by the Home Secretary for ten-year periods. Two organizations hold licenses—the British Broadcasting Corporation (BBC) and the Independent Broadcasting Authority (IBA).

Under the goverment of Prime Minister Margaret Thatcher, the United Kingdom accelerated the privatization of industry. *Privatization* refers to the transfer of formerly government-run industries and services to private, profit-seeking companies. England's trend toward privatization included the electronic media. In 1988, for example, Parliament considered a proposal that would allow an auction of three new national radio channels to compete with the BBC. The proposal would also authorize hundreds of local, commercially supported radio stations and a new national television network. In a television proposal for 1992, two program services—one BBC and one IBA—would move from the regular broadcast band to direct-broadcast satellite. The newly available terrestrial frequencies would then be used for additional national and regional program services.

Although the BBC and IBA are independent of direct, day-to-day government control, they do have certain obligations in their programming. For example, programs must be impartial in controversial matters and display balance and a range of subject matter. Codes restrict the violence in television programs, especially during hours when children are likely to be viewing.

Both organizations are required to be informed about public opinion toward programs and, for IBA, advertising. In the case of television, for example, the BBC and IBA jointly own the **Broadcaster's Audience Research Board.** Information is gathered through meters attached to television receivers in about 3000 private homes. Surveys are also regularly conducted by both organizations.

23.2.1.1 BBC The BBC was established in 1927 by royal charter. The crown appoints its board of governors. The board sets policy and appoints a director-general to carry out that policy and to run the corporation.

For years, the BBC had a monopoly. Its noncommercial programming largely reflected the taste of the upper-class British in-dividuals who set its policy. There was little audience research, the BBC purposely programmed slightly above the perceived level of the public in an effort to raise taste. However, a number of factors militated against the status quo—a carefully organized campaign to introduce commercial television, offshore radio competition, demand for local service, and sociopolitical activism in Scotland, Wales, and Northern Ireland. As a result, British broadcasting underwent sweeping changes in the 1950s and 1960s, beginning with the Television Act of 1954. This legislation created the BBC's first domestic competition in 27 years, the organization now known as the IBA.

The BBC operates local radio stations, four national radio channels, and two national television channels. The local radio stations work with local radio councils to produce a full range of programming by and for their communities. The national radio channels broadcast from a series of high-powered transmitters. Each radio channel carries a different type of programming—popular music, light entertainment (music, serials, sports), cultural programming (primarily classical music), and news and speech programs. In Scotland, Wales, and Northern Ireland, there are separate radio services.

The combined programming on the BBC's two television channels is designed to serve the range of viewer interests. BBC 1 presents more programs of general interest, such as light entertainment and sports. BBC 2 emphasizes minority interests and includes programs such as documentaries, serious drama, and international films. Across both channels, about 30 percent of all programming consists of documentary and information programs. Feature films and light entertainment account for another 30 percent; remotes and education, 25 percent; and drama, religion, music, and other programming, the remainder.

The BBC runs **no commercials.** Owners of television sets pay **license fees,** from which Parliament makes grants to the BBC. **Parliament exercises no direct control** over programming.

23.2.1.2 Independent Broadcasting Authority

The Home Secretary appoints members to the IBA. The authority, in turn, chooses a director-general, approves program plans, and controls advertising. Like the BBC, the IBA has two television channels, ITV and Channel 4, and a number of local radio stations. The IBA owns and operates its radio and television transmitters but does no broadcasting itself. Instead, it chooses **independent companies** to do the programming. These companies support operations and earn profits through the **sale of advertising time.** They may broadcast an average of seven minutes of commercial messages per hour; however these messages must be carried **at the beginning, the end, or natural breaks** of programs. Each company pays a rental fee to the IBA and a levy, based on net advertising revenues, to the Exchequer, the UK treasury.

In the case of ITV, the IBA divides the country into regions, each serviced by an independent program company. Several companies share the contract for London. The companies exchange programs among themselves, with most such exchange network programming coming from the largest companies. The companies have set up Independent Television News, a nonprofit company that produces news programming which they all may use. All together, IBA companies devote about 60 percent of broadcast time to plays, drama, serials, entertainment, music, sports, and feature films, and about 20 percent to news and documentaries.

IBA has created Channel 4 as a subsidiary company. Channel 4 has special responsibility to program for national and ethnic minorities. It also broadcasts a higher proportion of serious, factual programs. About 25 percent of Channel 4's programming consists of news and documentaries.

In radio, a different contractor operates each independent local radio station (ILR). The ILRs emphasize local programming. They also feature a good deal of call-in programming. London Broadcasting Company runs an all-news ILR and serves as the headquarters for Independent Radio News (IRN). Local stations may use IRN for their national news.

23.2.1.3 British Educational Broadcasting

Both BBC and IBA transmit educational programming. This programming includes in-school and continuing education material. An individual can earn a degree entirely by television through Open University courses. British broadcasting provides educational radio programming, as well as television.

23.2.1.4 British Use of Other Electronic Media

The UK pioneered teletext and videotex. In 1974, the BBC introduced CEEFAX, a teletext news and information service (Section 5.7.3). Shortly thereafter, independent television started its own teletext service, ORACLE. Some of the content of these services comes from traditional news agencies, but much of the material is generated by the broadcast organizations that operate them. In 1979, the Post Office launched Prestel, an interactive videotex service (Section 5.7.4). In 1983 cable television was introduced, although growth has been slow (see Section 23.3). By 1990, one British DBS venture had been launched, and others were planned (Section 23.3).

23.2.1.5 Proposals for Change in British Radio and Television

In 1988, the Conservative Party government of Prime Minister Margaret Thatcher proposed broad reforms for electronic mass media. The program went to the House of Commons in the form of a white paper for shaping into a bill. Most immediate changes would affect commercial radio-TV. For example, ITV would lose its monopoly on television advertising, and its separate regional franchises would be auctioned to the highest bidder and opened to takeovers.

Other proposed changes would inaugurate the following: a fifth terrestrial TV channel, starting in 1993 and covering 65 to 70 percent of the country, with programming supplied by different companies for each daypart; commercial nighttime TV services, with one using nighttime hours on one of the BBC channels; new local TV franchises, possibly by 1991, using either cable or microwave transmission or both; two additional satellite channels on the direct-to-home British Satellite Broadcasting Service (Section 23.3) for operation several years earlier than expected; three new national commercial radio stations and as many as several hundred local stations on the air in the early 1990s; an Independent Television Commission to replace the existing broadcasting and cable authorities, with the handing over of controlled transmission services to the private sector; a new Radio Authority for all independent radio; a Broadcasting Standards Council to reinforce standards on sex and violence on TV; a requirement that 25 percent of original programming on BBC and independent terrestrial channels comes from independent producers; and freedom of all TV services to raise money through subscription, sponsorship, and (except for the BBC) advertising.

The BBC would experience long-term changes in its license fee-funding mechanism. After 1991, the government would no longer guarantee inflation-adjusted annual increases in revenue. It would urge the corporation to experiment with subscription in-

come, with an eye toward ultimately making it the channel's only revenue source.

23.2.2 Union of Soviet Socialist Republics

The Union of Soviet Socialist Republics (USSR) covers more territory than any other country. It encompasses varied peoples, sundry cultural groups, and disparate languages and dialects. In the USSR, as in many Communist nations, the mass media have played a far different role from those in Western nations.

23.2.2.1 Goals and Purposes of Soviet Media In the Western world, mass media entertain, inform, and, in many cases, advertise. According to one Soviet official, the media in the USSR inform the people about developments at home and abroad, advance political and aesthetic education, mold public opinion, and organize cultural leisure.[2]

Soviet media must **interpret general government policy** in terms of what that policy means and how it applies to their particular audiences. Specialized media serve that interpretation function for every level and sphere of Soviet life.

Soviet media also serve as **vehicles for criticism.** This includes criticism from the top, especially from the party. It also includes criticism from the bottom, from individuals, collectives, and unions. The criticism aims not at the system or the policies but at the way individuals, government agencies, factories, districts, and so on fail to reinforce the system and carry out the policies.

Beginning with Leonid Brezhnev, in the mid-1960s, Soviet leaders grew increasingly aware of the ways in which the media could be used to advance party and government objectives. Surveys were conducted to learn what programs people liked and did not like.

Under Mikhail Gorbachev's *Glasnost* (openness) policies of the late 1980s, Soviet media showed incresing agressiveness in criticism of corruption and coverage of domestic events such as the disaster at the Chernobyl nuclear plant. Reflecting changing policies toward the United States, Soviet television provided extensive coverage of U.S. President Ronald Reagan's visit to the Soviet Union in 1988.

The **Communist party** plays a dominant role in Soviet media, ensuring that key media personnel are also loyal party members. A **state censorship agency** exists to check all media but rarely has to act, since beliefs and practices of the individuals who work in the media are usually consonant with government and party policies and aims. For example, shortly after becoming General Secretary of the party, Gorbachev met with leaders of the Soviet media to encourage them to be bolder in their criticisms and to explore previously forbidden subjects. With the leader of their nation directly communicating his wishes, there was little doubt among the media as to the direction they should take.

23.2.2.2 Soviet Radio Broadcasting in the USSR is **state operated.** Radio and television are guided by the **State Television and Radio Committee,** the head of which is a member of the USSR Council of Ministers.

The National Moscow Radio Network broadcasts five national program services on eight channels, all in Russian. Because there are ten time zones in the Soviet Union, programs are often repeated so that they will be accessible at convenient times for listeners. Program emphases vary, but overall they focus on news, sociopolitical subjects, talks, and culture and fine arts, especially music.

There are also radio services and stations in all political units that make up the USSR, as well as in factories and on collectives and state farms. Each station is the responsibility of a **local radio and television committee.** These regional and local operations both relay programming from Moscow and originate their own programming in one of the USSR's 69 languages.

Many local operations use a **wired distribution network.** Such a network feeds programming to individual receivers by wire, rather than over the air. These wired systems both relay broadcasts and originate local programming.

23.2.2.3 Soviet Television Moscow's Central Television broadcasts four program services. The First Channel covers the entire country. The Second Channel serves the Moscow area. The Third and Fourth Channels reach various parts of the rest of the country. The Third Channel carries educational programming, both for students and for teachers and other professionals.

Official surveys have found that television viewers in the USSR, like those in the United States, watch television **primarily for relaxation and entertainment.** Probably for educational and financial reasons, viewers in rural areas rely on television, rather than newspapers, for much of their news and information. Favorite types of programs include those on literature, the arts (especially dance and music), and sports. The nightly news program *Vremya* (Time) has an estimated audience of 150 million people. For some 30 percent of viewers, *Vremya* is the main or only source of news each day.[3] Examples of other popular programs include *The Experts Investigate*, a detective program supposedly based on police records, and a science program, *Incredible But True.*[4]

With Gorbachev's rise to power, relations between the United States and the USSR improved. American programs appeared on Soviet televison. For example, ABC sold program rights to the made-for-television movie

The Day After to the Soviets, and commentaries by Jean Enersen, of Seattle's KING-TV, were presented live on Soviet television. During President Reagan's 1988 trip to the USSR, the Discovery Channel telecast Soviet news programs to U.S. viewers.

The Soviet Union has over 115 program origination points or "television centers." It also has some 660 transmitters and 2000 relay centers. Satellite relay is used extensively to distribute programming to stations in the various regions of the vast country. Local and regional programming, especially news and sports, originates at the local studios.

23.2.2.4 Financial Support of Soviet Broadcasting

The USSR does not tax receivers; however, those using the wired system must pay a small monthly fee. Both radio and television are **subsidized by the state** and, to a much lesser degree, by **income from the sale of announcements.**

Moscow's Second Channel carries advertising for one hour per week. The regional services also accept advertising. Radio advertising is broadcast at selected times throughout the day.

In 1988, Pepsi-Cola became the first American company to run commercials on Soviet televison. Pepsi-Cola, Visa, and Sony Corporation bought time during a series of news documentaries, *Pozner in America*, produced by Seattle's King Broadcasting and Soviet Gostelradio.

23.2.3 India

An influential member of the Third World, India is an Asian country—vast, with 750 million people, and 16 official languages. Much of the population is poor by Western standards, illiterate, and tradition-bound. One of the goals of broadcasting, especially television, is to help create a sense of unity among India's many ethnic and language groups.

India has one of the largest film production industries in the world and exports programs to other countries, especially in Africa. India has two broadcasting organizations, All-India Radio and Doordarshan. Broadcasting is **controlled by the government** Ministry of Information and Broadcasting and is financed by **parliamentary grants and by advertising.** Until 1984, license fees on receivers were also collected. Although there have been efforts to persuade the government to give control of broadcasting to a separate agency, the government has refused, apparently fearing that the mix of programs would become too heavily dominated by entertainment, at the expense of educational programs.

23.2.3.1 All-India Radio

All-India Radio (AIR) broadcasts a national radio program service from transmitters around the country. The national service features popular music, light features, and some commercial advertising.

AIR also maintains regional services. Each carries the national program service, produces its own programs, and runs programs produced by the individual stations within the region. These regional services broadcast in a number of national or regional languages, 23 local languages, and 146 tribal and other dialects. India has also accepted suggestions to inaugurate local stations to be run primarily by the people of the communities they serve. Four local stations have been commissioned.

From Delhi, the News Services Division of All-India Radio broadcasts 81 news bulletins daily in its Home Services in 19 languages, including English. The regional services broadcast 124 news bulletins daily, in 61 languages and dialects, from 42 stations. Commentaries on the proceedings of Parliament are broadcast from Dehli in English and Hindi. Similar commentaries are broadcast from the state capitals when the legislatures are in session.

23.2.3.2 Doordarshan Doordarshan (DDI) handles television broadcasting for India. It uses about 200 transmitters and extensive satellite distribution to reach more than 70 percent of the population. DDI has 19 television centers, including Television Centre in New Delhi. DDI also accepts advertising.

DDI provides three types of program services. Regional programs, in local languages are telecast from respective centers between 6:00 and 8:40 p.m. Common national programs are carried by all transmitters between 8:40 and 11:15 p.m. Area-specific and development-oriented programs are telecast in rural areas in six Indian states between 5:00 and 8:40 p.m. A second channel broadcasts between 6:30 and 8:30 p.m. in Delhi, Bombay, Calcutta, and Madras.

Two 20-minute news programs, one in English and one in Hindi, are telecast each night as part of the national program. Regional centers also telecast news programs. News about parliament is telecast from Delhi when it is in session.

23.2.3.3 Indian Educational Broadcasting India has enlisted the broadcast media in the **fight agianst ignorance and illiteracy.** In line with this, AIR issues broad programming guidelines to radio stations. For example, 6 to 10 percent of the programs must be "development" broadcasts, such as family planning, cultivation, and health care. Television programs are intended to support developmental activities and the educational system. One example is the use of "prodevelopment" soap operas, which entertain and, at the same time, subtly attempt to convey educational and development themes.

Radio is used extensively in schools and for adult and continuing education.

For a number of years, India encouraged supervised group attendance to radio and television programming. Thousands of villages had community radio receivers for collective listening. Delhi television also transmitted programs especially for farmers' teleclubs. Troubles, however, plagued these projects, and the government eliminated them.

23.2.3.4 Indian Use of Other Electronic Media India has begun use of various new technologies. In fact, it was the first country to make extensive use of direct-broadcast satellites to reach rural populations. In the 1975 SITE Project experiment, the United States lent a communications satellite to the government of India to transmit educational television programs to 5000 villages. In 1983, India launched its own Insat satellite for direct broadcast of educational television. Thanks to Insat, some 90 percent of India's population could receive television by 1990.

A teletext service was introduced in Delhi in 1985. The service, known as INTEXT, is transmitted over the city's second television channel. It carries information such as news, weather, and rail and airline schedules.

23.2.4 The Netherlands

The Netherlands is a small, prosperous European democratic monarchy. The **Ministry of Welfare, Health and Culture has overall responsibility and broad supervisory authority** over broadcasting. However, the ministry rarely has to exercise these powers, due to the high caliber of the organizations licensed to program.

23.2.4.1 Pillarization The shape of Dutch broadcasting is deeply rooted in the very fabric of Dutch society. The origins of its structure actually predate the development of broadcasting. At the end of the nineteenth century, Catholics and Protestants rebelled against the dominance of the Conservative Liberals. The religious groups were successful in winning subsidization for their schools equal to that of the state schools. This success led to *pillarization* of Dutch society—a separate institutional framework for each denomination. Each had its own political party, church, trade union, schools, newspapers, even leisure clubs.

As broadcasting developed in the 1920s, it was set up to conform to this pillarization concept. Four denominational groups and one neutral group divided radio broadcasting time and facilities. With the coming of television in the 1960s, the boundaries between the pillars started to soften. The Broadcasting Act of 1969 provided for access to broadcasting by new groups, and three more organizations emerged. The **Media Act,** which took effect in 1988, brought significant changes to Dutch broadcasting.

23.2.4.2 The Broadcasting Groups The broadcasting groups are **associations** that represent cultural, religious, or political mainstreams in Dutch society. One association is Catholic; two are Protestant; one is Socialist; three are neutral; and one is neutral/progressive. To gain regular time on the schedule, an association must have at least 150,000 dues-paying members. Broadcast time is then divided among the groups in a 5:3:1 ratio, with groups in the largest membership category getting the most time. Some time, however, is reserved for groups with at least 60,000 members to help them attain the required 150,000 needed for full participation. To gain access to the reserved time, however, these smaller groups must propose content significantly different from existing programming. In addition, time is reserved for some 30 "minibroadcasters"—churches, political parties, and cultural and educational institutions.

23.2.4.3 NOS The groups work together through NOS, the Nederlandse Omroep Stichting (Netherlands Broadcasting Foundation). In 1988, the Media Act made significant changes in the role NOS played in Dutch broadcasting. Previously, organizations were required to use NOS facilities for all productions. This was changed to 75 percent, breaking the monopoly NOS had on production and allowing other producers to provide programs.

The NOS Program Foundation coordinates services and such joint programming as news, sports, and cultural presentations. Eight members of the Board of Govenors are appointed by the broadcasting organizations, and five, including the chair, are appointed by the Crown.

Transmitters are owned by NOREM, a company created by the post office. NOS, representing the broadcasting organizations, owns 40 percent of the shares.

23.2.4.4 Financial Support of Dutch Broadcasting Advertising provides about one-quarter of the operational funds for broadcasting; license fees, the remainder. Stichting Ether Reclame (**STER;** Foundation for Advertising over the Air), a government body, produces and sells all **broadcast advertising.** Commercial announcements are allowed just before and after scheduled news programs and in blocks between programs. All STER profits go back into broadcasting.

The government collects **receiver license fees** and allots them to the broadcasting organizations. The broadcasting groups also receive income from membership dues and the sale of advertising in their program guides.

23.2.4.5 Dutch Programming Radio in the Netherlands consists of five national program services, ten regional services, and a growing number of services in the larger cities. The national services program separate offerings—information, family, popular music, classical music, and educational and specially targeted programs.

Television consists of three program services. The first two operate 3:00 p.m. to midnight. One is operated by the Catholic, Protestant, and Socialist groups; the second, by the neutral organizations. The third, programmed by NOS, educational broadcasters, and "minibroadcasters," operates from 6:00 to 11:00 p.m. Joint television programming accounts for around one-fourth of all programming. A portion of each week is devoted to educational programming, primarily on the third channel.

23.2.4.6 Continuing Evolution Radio and television continue to evolve in the Netherlands, especially under the influence of broadcasting services from neighboring countries. During the 1980s, cable penetration exceeded 70 percent. Subscription television was permitted, and the first satellite pay-television services appeared on major cable networks. Parliament and the Ministry of Welfare, Health and Culture agreed to permit commercial television broadcasting if at least two of the existing organizations voluntarily withdrew from the existing structure and from government support and subsidies.

23.3 NEW TECHNOLOGIES: A GLOBAL VIEW

During the 1980s, new technologies became increasingly important throughout the world, just as they did in the United States. The Canadians and the Japanese, for example, produced television programs in high-definition televison. The French government established **Minitel,** a national videotex service, which provides a variety of news, bulletin boards, and telephone listings. All homes receive a Minitel terminal at no cost. Even in corporate television, ITVA, the professional video organization, established affiliate chapters in 11 countries outside the United States.

Perhaps the most significant changes have occurred in Europe as a result of communication satellites. While cable television has been used in some countries, growth has been slower elsewhere. In Britain, for example, initial enthusiasm about cable, spurred by the Thatcher government, was dashed by the costs of constructing systems in the major cities. Even in the late 1980s, England had only about 250,000 subscribers, most of whom were served by four-channel systems.

Into this breach came communication satellites. By 1990, satellites delivered more than 20 program services to owners of satellite dishes, as well as cable subscribers in Europe. These included basic services, such as Rupert Murdoch's Sky Channel, and pay services such as Premiere, owned by a consortium of American movie and pay cable companies.

Many felt DBS would compete successfully with cable and even supplant the land-based medium. In the free world, DBS came first to Japan. Much of Japan's population lived in remote mountainous regions or in cities in which high-rise buildings blocked television signals, and satellites proved the most efficient means of delivering television programs.

In 1989, Murdoch launched Sky Television, a direct-broadcast satellite (DBS) service. Sky Channel utilized transponders on the Luxembourg Astra satellite to offer a mix of advertising-supported and subscription channels. Competing DBS services were to include other Astra satellite programmers and the separate British Satellite Broadcasting satellite.

By 1990, investors were trying to determine which distribution system would become dominant in Europe, cable or DBS. Recent international decisions had opened the way for DBS. There were many who believed it would develop quickly. If DBS did, indeed, develop quickly, it could offer multichannel programming across wide distances, including areas to which cable had not yet spread. Thus DBS could "leapfrog" and obviate the need for cable television.

An important consequence of the new technologies has been an opening of channel space to private, commercial program services. Previously, where a country had only a small number of channels, government-owned or -subsidized services could easily fill programming needs. Satellites and cable allowed greater numbers of channels and created an opportunity that commercial services exploited.

Faced with competition from these services, many government-owned broadcsting systems became partly or entirely privatized. The American government supported the moves on ideological grounds but also for economic reasons. The commercialization of media in other countries created an opportunity for American companies to buy commercial time to advertise their products overseas, a move that could help to reduce the U.S. trade deficit.

23.4 INTERNATIONAL BROADCASTING ORGANIZATIONS

A number of organizations promote cooperation among broadcasters across national boundaries. Most are regional. One of the most important, however, goes beyond both broadcasting and regionalism. This is the International Telecommunications Union.

23.4.1 International Telecommunications Union

Attached to the United Nations, the International Telecommunications Union (ITU) (Figure 23.1) deals with all uses of radio waves and includes over 150 nations in its membership. Within the framework of this organization, the member nations decide **how the various frequency bands are to be used and who gets to use which frequencies.** ITU works with nations to eliminate interference, make the best use of radio frequencies, and foster cooperation among members to keep common-carrier rates reasonable. ITU also helps Third World countries to build and improve communications facilities. ITU's **International Frequency Registration Board** (IFRB) maintains records on frequency use.

At ITU's headquarters in Geneva, Switzerland, a secretary-general heads a permanent staff that deals with day-to-day operations. Member nations meet periodically in a **Plenipotentiary Conference** to make ITU policy. Regulations covering radio, telephone, and telegraph are made in **World Administrative Radio Conferences** (WARCs). At the 1979 WARC, for example, agreements were reached concerning frequencies allotted to and uses of AM radio, shortwave radio, UHF television, and direct-broadcast satellites.

WARC 1979 also revealed that ITU was undergoing a basic change in character. In past conferences, the United States and other industrialized nations had successfully drawn on their technical expertise in dealing with the ITU membership. Thus, frequency allocations and uses were arranged to the best advantage of the industrialized nations.

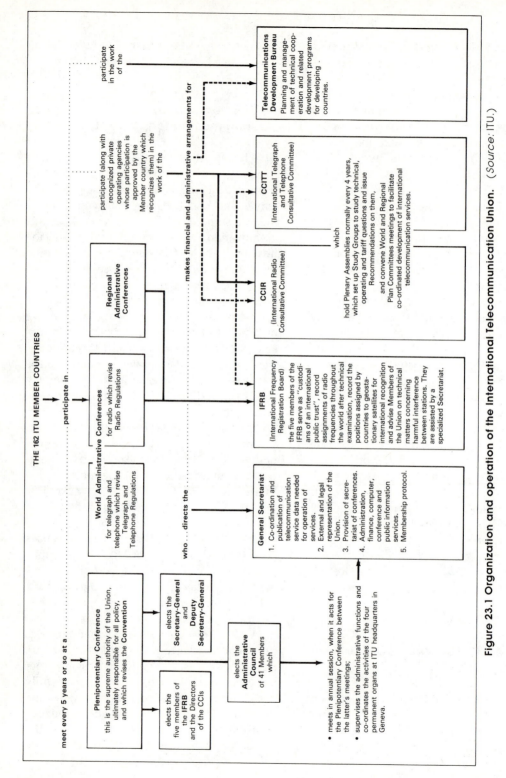

Figure 23.1 Organization and operation of the International Telecommunication Union. (*Source*: ITU.)

After all, these were the nations that could make the most efficient and immediate use of the frequencies. However, during the two decades since the previous WARC, ITU had doubled its membership to 155. Two-thirds of the total were Third World countries. Most could not take immediate advantage of new technologies and uses of radio frequencies, but they wished to reserve the opportunity to do so. And in ITU's one-nation/one-vote forum, they had the strength to do so.

The focus of ITU was seen to be changing from an arena where strictly technical considerations prevailed to one in which political and cultural interests had to be recognized. This trend became more obvious in 1985. WARC representatives, including the United States, agreed to allow developing nations access to geostationary satellite orbital slots, even though they were currently unable to use them.

23.4.2 Regional Broadcasting Organizations

In addition to ITU, Geneva hosts headquarters for the **European Broadcasting Union** (EBU). EBU consists of active member broadcasting organizations in countries within ITU's European Broadcasting Area. There are also associate (nonvoting) members from other countries. EBU promotes study of common problems and exchange of information, assists in development of broadcasting, and fosters cooperative production and exchange of news and programs among members. EBU operates full-time facilities for exchanges. EBU's technical center serves as master control for incoming and outgoing news material and programs.

The **International Radio and Television Organization** (OIRT) is basically the Communist bloc version of EBU. Member broadcasting organizations must be either state owned or state operated or under control of the state. OIRT membership includes European Communist countries, independent republics in the USSR, the USSR itself, various other Communist countries around the world, and some non-Communist countries, such as Finland, and Japan, which is an associate member. OIRT's purposes and technical facilities are similar to those of EBU. Headquarters and technical center are in Prague, Czechoslovakia.

EBU and OIRT cooperate with each other and with other regional broadcasting unions. EBU's Eurovision network and OIRT's Intervision network provide technical facilities for exchange of television news and programming not only among their respective member countries but also with each other's member countries. They also exchange with Nordivision, a separate television network formed by EBU members in Scandinavian countries. On both Eurovision and Intervision, most of the program exchanges involve news and sports.

Regional broadcasting associations exist for Asia, North and South America, the Caribbean, the Middle East, and Africa. Some include very poor countries. Some include countries separated by vast distances. For these and other reasons, none has the scope of facilities and operations of EBU and OIRT. Nonetheless, all work toward cooperative international program sharing.

Nearby countries make individual agreements among themselves concerning use of frequencies. They also band together to make multicountry, regional agreements. Normally, such agreements comply with overall parameters set by the ITU.

The **European Community,** while not a regional broadcasting organization, does exemplify cross-national cooperation that extends to radio and television. The European Community (EC) consists of twelve nations that resolved to eliminate tariff barriers for the purpose of creating a single market. They include Belgium, Denmark, France, the Federal Republic of Germany, Greece, Ireland, Italy, Luxembourg, the Netherlands, Portugal, Spain, and the United Kingdom. Scheduled to unify by the end of 1992, these nations would form the greatest economic power in the world, producing more than the United States and twice as much as Japan. In effect, the EC would resemble an international government, complete with parliament, executive, and court.

One of many building blocks for the EC was the "TV Without Frontiers" directive. This directive would ease barriers to satellite and other TV channels crossing from one European country into others. It included loosely construed quotas on non-European programming, various program and advertising content guidelines, and limits on total ad time. In 1989, ministers of the EC countries met and passed the directive. That move sparked angry comments from the group most likely to feel its economic conse-

quences—the American production community.

23.4.3 International Satellite Communication

The use of satellites for international communication has led to the creation of a number of organizations. The largest is **Intelsat,** the International Telecommunications Satellite Organization (Figure 23.2). The purpose of Intelsat is to develop, build, and operate a worldwide commercial satellite system for telecommunications. Intelsat membership is open to any nation that belongs to ITU and agrees to follow the organization's rules. Members contribute financially but also receive shares of the organization's revenues.

On a regional level, other organizations exist to coordinate communications satellites. Examples include Eutelsat, a consortium of Western European nations, Intercos-

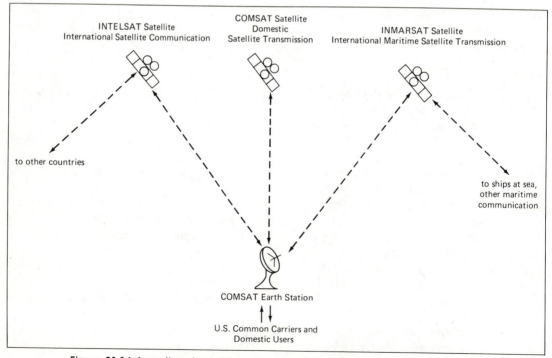

Figure 23.2 International satellite communications organizational relationships.

mos/Intersputnik, composed of Soviet-bloc nations, and Arabsat in the Middle East.

Private firms began to compete with Intelsat in the 1980s. Early in the decade, the U.S. Federal Communications Commission had received applications from companies who wished to offer international communications satellite service. Intelsat consisted of member *nations*, yet these applications came from *private enterprise*. This situation raised questions such as how the proposed private systems would fit in with the existing Intelsat system. Intelsat and most of its members opposed private competition. The United States took an official stand on the matter late in 1984 when President Reagan stated that international communications satellite systems that would operate outside the Intelsat organization "are required in the national interest."[5] Diplomatic and organizational maneuvering on the part of the United States managed to remove Intelsat objections. As a result, Intelsat approved Pan American Satellite Corporation (PanAmSat) to offer separate satellite service between the United States and Peru in late 1986. Other competitors followed.

In the meantime, Intelsat had suffered a scandal. Intelsat officials, including its director-general and deputy director-general, were fired, accused of defrauding the organization of millions of dollars. As the new director-general, the United States was able to secure the election of Dean Burch, who had chaired the FCC during the administration of President Nixon. This placed a strong believer in private enterprise at the head of the international organization.

23.5 THE INTERNATIONAL PROGRAM MARKET

World trade. Most of us—if we think of it at all—conceive of world trade as the flow across national borders of commodities such as coal, wheat, automobiles, and iron ore. It also includes canned programming, such as sound recordings, motion pictures, television programs, news packages, even entire programming services. Entering the last decade of the twentieth century, programming was one of the few product categories in which the United States exported far more than it imported.

23.5.1 American Programs Sold Overseas

The United States serves as an important source of programs for many foreign broadcasting services. Almost since the beginning of television, American programs have appeared in other countries. This has been an important source of income for producers—so important, in fact, that payment for programs sold overseas was one of the major issues in a strike of television writers that delayed the start of the fall 1988 network season. The widespread use of American programs has also been controversial, leading to charges of "media imperialism" (Section 23.5.3.1).

23.5.1.1 Syndication Rights Just as American fast-food restaurants and soft-drink companies have spread throughout the world, so have popular American television and radio programs. Off-network and first-run episodes of everything from *I Love Lucy* to *Sesame Street* to the nightly newscasts of the three major broadcast networks are seen by viewers throughout the world.

Sale of these programs can be an important source of income to producers and syndicators. According to an official of one company, the exporting of U.S. programs brings in about $1.5 billion each year.[6] The three major broadcast networks, prohibited from most domestic syndication by federal regulation, face no such restriction in the international market (Section 14.1.3).

Generally, the most popular American

programs shown overseas have been action/adventure, soap operas, and sports. Situation comedies have not done as well, largely because humor seems to be related to culture and language. On the other hand, car chases or seductions seem to have universal appeal, and sports such as basketball and even American-style football have fans in all countries.

23.5.1.2 Program Services The availability of technologies allowing multichannel programming, such as cable and satellites, has produced a new trend in the spread of American programs overseas. Entire program services are now available in some countries. For example, the United Kingdom's Premiere, a pay cable channel, is owned by a consortiun of 20th Century-Fox, Columbia Pictures, HBO, and Showtime. Cable News Network is seen in many countries. In 1987 cable and satellite subscribers in 14 European nations began receiving MTV Europe, joining viewers of MTV Japan and MTV Australia. In 1988, NBC signed Australia's Seven Network to a five-year affiliation agreement, acquired an option to buy into Qintex Entertainment (Seven's parent firm), reached an agreement for Visnews to syndicate NBC News materials worldwide, and bought a 38 percent interest in Visnews, a British firm.

23.5.2 Foreign Program Suppliers to American Media

For the most part, the flow of programs has been largely from the United States to foreign countries. Few programs have made their way to commercial broadcast stations and even fewer to the networks. Perhaps because of language, Canadian and British productions have been the rare exception. For example, ITC, a British company, syndicated a number of programs, including the highly successful *The Muppet Show*. Thames Tele-

vision's *The Benny Hill Show* has been a staple of late-night programming on many stations for years.

In some cases foreign programs have served as models for successful American shows. In the 1970s, for example, such American hits as *All in the Family, Three's Company,* and *Sanford and Son* were directly based on British situation comedies.

There are two notable exceptions to the absence of foreign programs on American broadcast televison. One is PBS. Programs from Britain, ranging from *Masterpiece Theatre: Upstairs/Downstairs,* to the complete series of plays of William Shakespeare, to *Monty Python's Flying Circus,* have been among the most successful in public television history.

The second exception is the programming on the growing number of Spanish-language stations. Latin American and, to a lesser extent, Caribbean and Spanish productions fill much of the air time of these stations. Especially popular are the *novelas,* which combine elements of soap operas and miniseries. Univision and Telemundo provide their affiliates with hours of programming produced in Hispanic countries.

In recent years, the rise of cable-delivered services has created a demand for additional programming. Cable networks that have made significant use of foreign productions include Arts & Entertainment, The Discovery Channel, and even ESPN, which has scheduled sports such as Australian football and Grand Prix auto racing. Foreign motion pictures have been shown on both basic and pay cable services.

23.5.3 Consequences

The spread of American programming and media has not been without controversy. Many observers have complained of American media imperialism. Other critics, especially in the Third World, argue that news media in America and other Western countries present a distorted view of world events.

23.5.3.1 Media Imperialism

Some critics argue that many U.S. television and radio programs promote unhealthy values. When these programs are broadcast in other countries this argument becomes even more important. Third World countries battle ignorance, poverty, disease, tribal animosities, illiteracy, overpopulation. At the same time, they attempt to use radio and television programs to promote a sense of national unity and preserve their cultural heritage. American programs, produced more slickly and with higher budgets than most nations can afford, often promote such values as sexual attractiveness, wealth, and dominance by any means. Even in industrialized nations, the cultural values of American programs may conflict with indigenous values.

Many countries attempt to limit the influence of American programs. In most cases, they restrict the number of imported programs. In Canada, for example, a certain proportion of broadcast programs must be produced by Canadians.

Some individual American programs are prohibited. For example, many Moslem countries do not allow programs which conflict with their religious beliefs. The United Kingdom has established a board with the authority to ban foreign television programs on the basis of "sex, violence, taste and decency."[7] The attitude of the British toward American programs was expressed by a former vice chairman of the BBC who said, "The U.S. is a violent country with a violent TV culture, and their TV reflects it."[8]

The European Community's "TV Without Barriers" directive (Section 23.4.2) also contained quotas and limitations. It would reserve for European productions a majority of each nation's transmission time, thus limiting the amount of American programming that could be telecast. U.S. interests believed the directive's advertising regulations to be overly restrictive. They felt the directive would hamper growth of private broadcasting and would adversely affect American plans to tap a market they see as increasingly lucrative.

The spread of communication satellites has complicated the issue of media imperialism. A single satellite signal, or footprint, can cover as much as one-third of the earth, crossing numerous borders. While authoritarian governments can successfully prevent citizens from owning receiving dishes, this is more difficult in democracies. In Western Europe, for example, many countries have been forced to give up efforts to maintain a media service free of foreign cultural influence. Even in the United States, some have worried that Americans may become susceptible to persuasion from programs transmitted by satellite from the Soviet Union or other unfriendly sources.

23.5.3.2 New World Information Order

Another concern of many, especially in the Third World, has been the flow of information from their countries to the industrialized world. They complain that Western news media often present negative images of their countries, concentrating on failures, upheavals, or natural disasters.

The developing countries led a fight to allow governments to control information flow both within and across their borders. They wished to overcome what they called the West's "colonialist domination" of international news, to have some control over news reports originating within their countries. Controls would include measures such as licensing of journalists, a government-written code of conduct for journalists, and even censorship.

This desire to control communication ran counter to the Western ideal of a free flow of information. The United States, of course, supports the free-flow concept. And both the United Nations and the UN Educational, Scientific and Cultural Organization (UNESCO) supported the free flow of information. But the developing countries used UNESCO as a forum to discuss their problems and, over a period of years during the 1970s, succeeded in winning some ground in their fight for information sovereignty. To complicate matters (at least for the United States), the USSR and other Communist-bloc nations supported the developing countries in their efforts. After all, they had been restricting information flow for years!

In 1978, UNESCO commissioned a report by an international committee on what became known as the *new world information order*. Sean McBride, former Irish foreign minister, headed this Commission on International News. In 1980, the McBride commission released its report. The report supported the concept of open information flow. It condemned press censorship and urged that journalists everywhere be allowed to talk with political dissidents. But it also attempted to respond to Third-World concerns, and Western media interests viewed a number of its recommendations as encouragement of government censorship.

Nonetheless, the United States supported the report at UNECSCO's 1980 biennial general meeting in Belgrade. At the same time, the United States successfully sponsored a proposal for the agency to help Third World countries upgrade their own media efforts as a means to divert UNESCO from efforts to regulate the world press. The International Program for Development of Communications was created as an independent agency of UNESCO to help Third World countries obtain communications equipment—printing presses and radio-TV gear—and training for journalists. The administration of U.S. President Ronald Reagan, however, had

other complaints concerning UNESCO. As a result, at the end of 1984, the United States withdrew from the agency it had helped found 38 years before, the United Nations Educational, Scientific and Cultural Organization.

23.6 FOREIGN OWNERSHIP OF AMERICAN MEDIA

As we have seen, the growth of new technologies has led some American program suppliers to develop into multinational organizations (Section 23.3). As more national communication systems head toward privatization, American firms may well increase their ownership or program control of foreign media. The reverse—foreign ownership of American electronic media—has also occurred.

U.S. law limits the extent to which foreign nationals can own American broadcast stations. However, no such limits exist regarding cable television systems, other electronic media, and program suppliers. Rogers Communications, for example, one of the largest multiple-system operators in the U.S. cable industry during the 1980s, operated from Toronto headquarters. Australian-born Rupert Murdoch built most of his communications empire *before* he took out American citizenship (Section 4.5.3.4). Most of his media holdings are still outside the United States.

Similarly, some foreign companies view American production firms as profitable investments. Among the late-1980s foreign purchases of American media firms were the following: the 1985 purchase of 20th Century-Fox Film by Rupert Murdoch's Australia-based News Corporation (Section 4.5.3.4); the 1988 purchase by Television South, holder of England's south and southeast ITV franchises (Section 23.2.1.2) of MTM Enterprises, producer of such hits as

Hill Street Blues and *L.A. Law;* and the 1989 purchases of Filmation Studios by France's L'Oreal, of 24.4% interest in Barris Industries by the Australian firm Westfield (Network Ten), and of Columbia Pictures by Sony Corp. for $3.4 billion. Some in the financial community predicted that all U.S. movie studios would eventually be purchased by foreign interests.

23.7 INTERNATIONAL BROADCASTS

As early as World War I, nations made use of radio to transmit propaganda to other countries. Today, most countries have **external services** that beam programming to areas beyond their own national boundaries. External-service broadcasts often have two aims. First, they provide a way for their own citizens living on foreign soil to keep up with events at home. Second, they present the broadcasting nation's views on the news and the world situation directly to citizens of other countries. The BBC World Service has been particularly successful in achieving this latter aim. Over the years, the United Kingdom's external voice has earned a reputation for comprehensive and objective coverage of international events. As a result, the BBC World Service has built up what may be the largest external-voice audience in the world.

There is also a small number of private stations that broadcast religious or advertising-supported entertainment programs. For example, WRNO, in New Orleans, broadcasts a format of top-40 music, sports, and commercials to a worldwide audience. Like most international broadcasters, WRNO uses shortwave frequencies.

The United States government operates the **Voice of America** (VOA), Radio Free Europe/Radio Liberty, and the American Forces Radio and Television Services. VOA is operated by the United States Information Agency (USIA). VOA is the U.S. government's official broadcast voice to the people of other nations. It attempts to gain listeners and credibility with accurate, objective news reporting, presentation of a broad range of American thought and institutions, and presentation of, and discussion and opinion on, U.S. policies. VOA is also a source of American music and entertainment, especially for young people. VOA has more than 100 transmitters, two-thirds of which are located overseas. It broadcasts in some 40 languages, operating on short- and medium-wave frequencies, and has an estimated worldwide audience of 130 million.

A special service of VOA is **Radio Martí,** established in 1984 to transmit programs from Florida to Cuba. Radio Martí operates independently of direct VOA supervision, with its own advisory board. The initial proposal for Radio Martí drew opposition from U.S. broadcasters. They feared that Cuba would retaliate by interfering with American domestic stations. Cuba had, in the past, occasionally turned up the power on its radio transmitter and purposely interfered with American stations. The Cuban government, however, chose not to retaliate for Radio Martí.

In 1988, The U.S. government announced plans for a television version of Radio Martí. This **TV Martí** would transmit using an antenna on a high-altitude balloon anchored in Key West to enable its signal to reach Cuba. Opponents of TV Martí argued that the signals of existing South Florida televison stations already reached Cuba, allowing residents to see American news and information. In 1989, the Cuban TV network said that it would shift programming from Havana channel 6 to channel 13—the same channel planned for TV Martí.

The USIA also operates **Worldnet,** an international television service. Originally, the purpose of Worldnet was to allow journalists in other countries to conduct video interviews with American officials. It has since taken on other functions. Available by satellite throughout the world, Worldnet distributes news and information about the United States. Stations in other countries pick up and use its material. Foreign home-dish owners can pick up Worldnet directly.

The Board for International Broadcasting, to which members are appointed by the president of the United States, operates **Radio Free Europe/Radio Liberty** (RFE/RL). While VOA strives for respect as an unbiased and unimpeachable source of information, RFE/RL's programming reflects the foreign policy objectives of the U.S. government, especially with reference to the Soviet-bloc countries of its target audience. At one time, Radio Free Europe and Radio Liberty masqueraded as privately funded organizations when, in fact, they were created and operated by the U.S. Central Intelligence Agency. The Soviet Union, which had jammed transmissions of RFE/RL and even VOA, stopped most such efforts in 1987 and 1988. So did other Soviet bloc countries.

American Forces Radio and Television Service (AFRTS) provides programs of information, education, and entertainment to U.S. military personnel overseas. The 1988 film *Good Morning Vietnam* told the story of a disc jockey who worked at an AFRTS station in Saigon during the early days of the Vietnam War.

A Los Angeles AFRTS center produces some material and selects some from syndication sources. Selected material includes music, drama, variety, religious, and talk shows. These are distributed by satellite to certain overseas AFRTS stations. For others, the material is recorded and mailed.

AFRTS operates more than 800 radio and television outlets—some closed-circuit and others broadcast—in a number of countries. The broadcast stations operate at low power

to limit coverage to American bases but can often be received and enjoyed by nationals who live near the bases. In this respect, AFRTS also qualifies as international broadcasting.

NOTES

1. Alan Wells, ed., *Mass Communications: A World View* (Palo Alto: National, 1974) 7–9.
2. Vladimir P. Panov, "The Supreme Goal of Social Production," *Soviet Economy Today* (Moscow: Nosi; Westport: Greenwood, 1981) 214.
3. Angus Roxburgh, *Pravda: Inside the Soviet News Machine* (New York: Braziller, 1987) 57.
4. Ellen Propper Mickiewicz, *Media and the Russian Public* (New York: Praeger, 1981) 20.
5. Quoted in "President extends free-market doctrine to space," *Broadcasting* 3 Dec. 1984: 37.
6. "Programing the World: Shifting Tides of International TV Production," *Broadcasting* 18 Apr. 1988: 74.
7. Richard Mahler, "U.S. Producers May Face British Censorship Hurdles," *Electronic Media* 23 May 1988: 37.
8. Mahler 37.

FURTHER READING

Briggs, Asa. *The History of Broadcasting in the United Kingdom.* New York: Oxford UP. Published in four volumes—*The Birth of Broadcasting,* 1961; *The Golden Age of Wireless,* 1965; *The War of Words,* 1970; *Sound and Vision,* 1979. History of the BBC and the IBA.

Browne, Donald R. *Comparing Broadcast Systems: The Experience of Six Industrialized Nations.* Ames: Iowa State UP, 1989. France, the Netherlands, East and West Germany, USSR, and Japan.

————. *International Radio Broadcasting: The Limits of a Limitless Medium.* New York: Praeger, 1982. Uses of various international broadcast operations from 1920.

Chang, Won Ho. *Mass Media in China: The History and the Future.* Ames: Iowa State UP, 1989. Focuses on reforms of Deng Xiaoping.

Head, Sydney W. *World Broadcasting Systems: A*

Comparative Analysis. Belmont: Wadsworth, 1985. Comparision of structures, programming, and regulation of foreign broadcast systems.

Many Voices, One World: Communication and Society, Today and Tomorrow. New York: Unipub, 1980. Final report of the McBride Commission.

McPhail, Thomas L. *Electronic Colonialism: The Future of International Broadcasting and Communication.* 2d ed. Newburyport: Sage, 1987.

Mickelson, Sig. *America's Other Voice: The Story of Radio Free Europe and Radio Liberty.* New York: Praeger, 1983. Includes RFE/RL's intelligence community background.

Noam, Eli M., ed. *Video Media Competition: Regulation, Economics, and Technology.* New York: Columbia UP, 1985. Issues arising from international programming and new technologies.

Powell, Jon T. *International Broadcasting by Satellite: Issues of Regulations, Barriers to Communications.* Westport: Quorum, 1985. History, international organizations, and policy questions.

Rosen, Philip T., ed. *International Handbook of Broadcasting Systems.* Westport: Greenwood, 1987.

Roxburgh, Angus. *Pravda: Inside the Soviet News Machine.* New York: Braziller, 1987. Role of news and workings of the press.

World Radio & TV Handbook. New York: Billboard, annual. Hours, frequencies, and programs of international stations.

SEVEN

SOCIOPSYCHOLOGICAL PERSPECTIVE

We now look at the interplay between radio-television and human behavior, the impact of one on the other. In Chapter 24, we define factors that determine impact. In Chapter 25, we examine the nature of that impact. And in Chapter 26, we review some of the theoretical structures that attempt to explain the impact. We take into account not only the media and their messages but also the individual, the group, and the society. As we shall see, these elements all consist of systems within systems within systems, and each affects the other.

We have left this topic until last to emphasize its importance. Chances are, you welcome radio and television into your life for hours most days. Now it is time to find out what that means to you and to the society of which you are part. More than the last entry on the profit and loss statement of any radio or television facility, *this* is the bottom line.

CHAPTER 24

Factors in Degree of Impact

You have probably read or heard that television is a near-omnipotent vehicle of persuasion. Yet researchers have found it difficult to establish a direct cause-effect relationship between mass-media messages and human behavior. Historically, they have had better luck in controlled experiments (Section 26.1.2). They would lead subjects into the laboratory, hold constant all factors except those under study, and presto—yes, a mass-media message does have the power to persuade. However, many experiments and most field studies fail to show such a direct relationship. Field studies examine mass communication where the audience normally receives it—in homes, automobiles, or wherever. Since researchers cannot control the situation in field studies, other factors mitigate the impact of the message.

You live in the real world, not in a laboratory. These other variables are present and affect the way you react to a televised message. Let us say, for example, that you are watching television, and a commercial comes on for a particular brand of beer. Do you inevitably and immediately get up, leave the room, open a can of beer, and begin to swig

it down? Perhaps—if you (1) are thirsty, (2) like beer, and (3) happen to have that brand available. But you probably do not. You may be diabetic, on a diet, allergic to beer, or have some other health condition that would proscribe imbibing. You may own stock in a rival beer company. Your religious or moral convictions may prevent use of alcoholic beverages. Your family or friends may frown on it. You may react negatively to that particular commercial or to commercials in general, to that beer company or to big business in general. There may be none of that brand immediately available, and you do not feel like taking the trouble to get any. Or, you may not even have noticed the commercial; you may be so inured to the almost continual flow of televison advertising that you automatically tune out most commercials.

The lesson here is that television—or any mass medium—does not work in isolation. It is part of an environment of factors that affects your behavior. Television must usually interplay with these other factors. That interplay determines whether there will be an impact and, if so, what it will be. Some of the more important of these factors include the following: your mental makeup, other persons, conditions of reception, medium, message, and communicator.

24.1 YOU

You, the audience, bring as much to the television viewing situation as does the material you view. Perhaps more. Your attitudes, your predispositions, your personality, your degree of involvement—all figure in your reception of a mass-communicated message and what you do with it.

24.1.1 Attitude Formation

You have certain attitudes about things, people, and places. You may feel that belief in a Supreme Deity is preferable to atheism. You may think that dark bread is better than white bread, or you may feel that police are underpaid in most communities. But attitudes are more complex than just feelings or beliefs about things. Attitude theorists tell us that at least four dimensions—social, cognitive, behavioral, emotional—must be considered to understand attitudes.

24.1.1.1 Socialization   You did not adopt attitudes. You acquired them. You acquired them unconsciously and gradually as a result of experience. You are, in large part, the product of all that you have ever experienced.

You learn from experiences, and the learning is called socialization. Formal agents of socialization include parents, teachers, and religious leaders. Friends and other peers are also agents of socialization. Even places, things, and strangers with which you come in contact play a part in attitude formation.

Your experiences have been different from anyone else's. This means that what you have learned is also different from anyone else. This is **differential learning.** As a result of differential learning, you have a particular and special-to-you way of making sense of the world, of mentally dealing with the objects, things, persons, messages, and situations that you encounter.

24.1.1.2 Cognition   This making sense/dealing with is called *cognition*. Cognition includes the many processes of assimilating experiences and relating them to previous experiences, of attaching meaning and value to them, and of ordering them into organized patterns of knowledge and feeling.

You are not a passive receptacle for a television commercial or any other persuasive message. You do things to it. You receive the message and put it through the cognitive processes—trim it down, add to it here and there, reshape it to make it fit into your particular system of order, your own individual set of beliefs, values, and attitudes.

Your very **need for cognition** differs from that of anyone else. In other words, you are different from others regarding the extent to which you *need* to learn, think, and deal with your environment. This, too, affects the way you deal with a message.

24.1.1.3 Behavior   Behavior, something that you do, can directly contribute to your attitudes. You may, for example, prefer sweetened tea because you always drank sweetened tea. You may prefer Democratic political candidates because you have previously voted Democratic. A change in behavior can result in a change in attitude. Research experiments have shown that people who are forced to perform a behavior that is contrary to a stated attitude—such as advocate eating a food for which they have expressed a distaste—will actually change their attitude to be more consistent with the behavior. They may even begin to eat the food on their own!

24.1.1.4 Emotion Attitudes have an emotional component. You may oppose depictions of violence in movies and television, for example, because you fear being a victim of violence yourself. In experimental research, appeals to emotions such as fear did, indeed, change attitudes. Rational/logical appeals, however, proved more effective in bringing about long-lasting changes in attitudes.

24.1.2 Predisposition

The behavior-attitude relationship (Section 24.1.1.3) works both ways. Not only does behavior affect attitudes, attitudes also affect behavior. They make you susceptible to acting in certain ways. These susceptibilities are predispositions, and they include selective exposure, selective perception, and selective retention.

24.1.2.1 Selective Exposure Your predispositions determine in part what you do with a televised message, whether you even expose yourself to it in the first place. You tend to watch or notice those messages that correspond with your opinions and interests. This message-interests correspondence is **congruence;** your tendency to pay attention is selective exposure.

Suppose, for example, you watch television one evening during the political season. A campaign program comes on featuring the Republican candidate for some office. You are more likely to watch the program if you are a Republican than if you are a Democrat.

Some research studies have suggested that you may tend to avoid messages that run counter to your opinions and interests. This tendency, however, has not been as consistently demonstrated as other implications of predispositions.

24.1.2.2 Selective Perception The cognition process makes you hear, see, and mentally emphasize some elements of a message and ignore or de-emphasize others. This is selective perception, and it helps to explain why two people perceive and interpret the same message in different ways.

In our campaign program example, a Republican is likely to perceive the Republican candidate's television speech as reasoned, logical, and eloquent. A Democrat might view the same speech as distorted, inconsistent, and flatulent.

Semanticists, scholars who study meaning, help to explain this. Words, they say, contain no meaning in and of themselves. Any meaning comes from within the people who use and understand those words. This is basic to the process of selective perception. Someone speaks the word "republican." On hearing that word, you assign a *personal* meaning to the word, a meaning that does not necessarily correspond to that intended by the speaker. The meaning that we hold for words evolves, again, through differential learning, so people often assign different meanings for the same words.

Perception can be so selective that an individual may actually interpret a message in a way that is exactly the opposite from its intent. This is the **boomerang effect.** If, for example, during that televised speech, the candidate tells a joke to illustrate the absurdity of bigotry, a racially prejudiced supporter might actually interpret the story as advocating bigotry.

24.1.2.3 Selective Retention In selective retention, you tend to remember messages that jibe with your opinions and interests and to forget those that do not. You are much more likely to remember the name of that Republican candidate who spoke on television if you are a Republican than if you are a Democrat.

Selective exposure, selective perception, and selective retention (sometimes referred to collectively as *selective perception*) are not inevitable; they are tendenceis. So, yes, you may find yourself paying attention to messages that deal with matters outside your interests or that run counter to your opinions.

24.1.3 Personality

Some persons are more persuadable than others, irrespective of issue or type of influence. If you are one of these persons, it is likely that television could affect you more than someone who is not so persuadable. Among the factors that affect persuadability are **self-esteem, intelligence,** and **age.**

If you have a high level of self-esteem and regard for your own abilities, you tend to resist persuasion and propaganda. Intelligence seems to affect not so much the degree of persuadability as the kinds of persuasive appeals that are most effective. If you are highly intelligent, inconsistent and illogical arguments probably do not work as well on you as on persons of lower intelligence, whereas complex, difficult arguments usually do not work as well on persons of lower intelligence. And the younger you are, the more persuadable you are.

24.1.4 Involvement

Degree of involvement also affects persuadability. You become interested in a particular topic—read about it, search out information on it, work on it, spend time on it. As your involvement grows, your susceptibility to being persuaded *on this topic* decreases.

24.2 OTHERS

The impact any given televised message has on you is determined in part by your relations with other persons, persons whose acquaintance and opinions you value. In social psychological terms, these persons serve as your **psychological reference group.** A reference group is any group of persons with whom you share a very personal and defensive sense of belonging. These groups are not necessarily formal organizations, although they can be. You probably have a number of different reference groups, perhaps even one for each major facet of your life.

The particular reference group that comes into play in any given situation depends on the nature of the situation and on you as an individual. The group can be large, small, inclusive, exclusive, formal, or informal. It can be your family, your social club, your religious group, people who live in your neighborhood, your political organization, members of your racial or ethnic group, people in your occupation, your Friday afternoon drinking buddies, or people you meet in the laundromat. You adopt the group's norms—its behaviors, values, priorities—as your own. The group, in turn, reinforces and validates your adopted opinions.

The content of a televised message may be perceived, discussed, and approved by the group as meeting its norms—usually informally, of course. It may be as simple as a discussion among friends after Sunday mass, a discussion condemning the pro-abortion stand taken by a political candidate in a recent televised campaign speech, condemning the candidate for advocating the murder of unborn children. Or it may be as elaborate as members of your civil rights organization at a meeting one evening favorably discussing that same stand because the candidate defended the individual woman's right to freedom of choice. Group approval and interaction increase the chances that your attitude or behavior will change toward the direction of the televised message. Disapproval lessens that chance.

Even if the group does not discuss the message, you may be familiar enough with group norms to know what the group *would* say, and that can influence you, just as though the group had actually discussed it. For example, if you were a member of the National Rifle Association (NRA) and you saw that political candidate speak on television in favor of gun control legislation, you might resolve right then to vote against the candidate, no matter how sound the arguments for gun control. You would assume from past experience the NRA's opposition to the candidate.

So far in this chapter we have used examples primarily from the area of political programming. But the same principles apply in all areas—news, information, entertainment, and advertising. Product advertisers make positive efforts to take advantage of the various factors involved in impact. Many commercials, for example, attempt to provide surrogate reference groups. Thus you see commercials that feature one young mother telling a slightly younger mother which disposable diaper to use, or one laun-dromat patron telling another which detergent to use, or a manicurist telling a customer which dishwashing liquid to use.

The young mother, the laundromat patron, the manicurist—these represent advertisers' attempts to depict opinion leaders. As originally conceived, the relationship between mass media and interpersonal communication consisted of a **two-step flow of communication** (Figure 24.1). Within the group, certain individuals were thought to be more sensitive to media messages. These individuals, the **opinion leaders,** would bring up the messages for discussion by the group. Thus the flow of information and influence went from media to opinion leaders in one step, and from opinion leaders to the group in a second step. In reality, this two-step model is probably too simple to describe the actual flow of communication. There are many steps and many opinion leaders involved at all levels. Nonetheless, interpersonal communication and influence do affect television's impact.

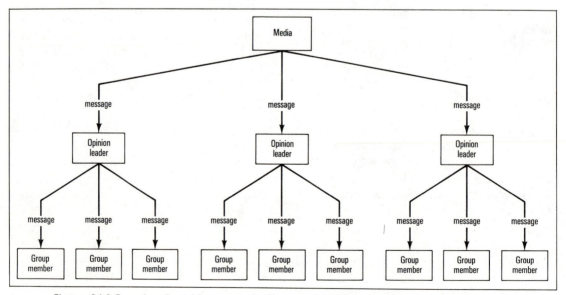

Figure 24.1 Two-step flow of communication. Although the actual process is probably more complex, this early model does illustrate that interpersonal communication and influence affect television's impact.

24.3 CONDITIONS OF RECEPTION

Where and how you view affect television's impact. Consider a scary movie on television. It will have much more impact on you if you watch it at home by yourself late at night than if you watch it while others are present, while carrying on a conversation, or during the daylight hours.

24.4 MEDIUM

The medium of television helps determine impact. You probably watch televison primarily for relaxation and entertainment. You switch off your critical faculties. Yet precisely because you do not have your guard of critical awareness up, you may be more vulnerable to messages than at other times. You may be more vulnerable to intended messages, such as commercials. You may also be more vulnerable to unintended messages, such as the themes, values, and depictions of society emphasized in programs and commercials.

Your own experience with the medium also bears on television's impact. You know, for example, the difference between commercials, entertainment, and information programs. From the first you expect puffery; from the second, fantasy; from the third, fact. And that is how you judge messages in each of those categories.

If you are like many persons, you tend to hold television news in high regard, relative to other news media. As mentioned at the beginning of Chapter 8, polls over the years have shown that people feel television to be the most believable news medium.

24.5 MESSAGE

The message itself is a factor in television's impact. Any or all of the following aspects of a message may affect your reaction to it: amount of discrepancy between your opinion and that advocated in the message, whether the message presents one side or all sides of an argument, whether the conclusion to a particular line of argument is stated, novelty of information contained in the message, whether the message arouses fear, and the style of presentation of the message.

24.6 COMMUNICATOR

The nature of the individual who delivers the message affects your reaction to it. This is, in large part, a function of the communicator's prestige, what you perceive as the communicator's intent (to sell, to entertain, to report, and so forth), how much you like the communicator, and the degree to which you empathize with or perceive yourself as similar to the communicator.

Television advertisers attempt to take advantage of this factor. They make commercials that feature persons who are well known, who appear to be members of the professions, who radiate sincerity, who look like or may actually have been newscasters, who look like what ad agencies think you look like, and who look like what ad agencies think you want to look like.

FURTHER READING

Bem, Daryl J. *Beliefs, Attitudes, and Human Affairs.* Monterey: Brooks/Cole, 1970. Components of attitudes; relationship between attitudes and behavior.

Comstock, George, et al. *Television and Human Behavior.* New York: Columbia UP, 1978. Chapter 3 reviews and summarizes research on who watches how much of what on television and what they think of it.

Katz, Elihu, and Paul F. Lazarsfeld. *Personal Influence: The Part Played by People in the Flow of Mass Communication.* Glencoe: Free, 1955. Sets forth the idea of the two-step flow.

Kiesler, Charles A., Barry E. Collins, and Norman Miller. *Attitude Change: A Critical Analysis of Theoretical Approaches.* New York: Wiley, 1969. Reviews literature on attitude formation and change.

Klapper, Joseph T. *The Effects of Mass Communication.* New York: Free, 1960. Chapters 2–5 in this classic review and summarize pioneer studies in persuasion.

Larsen, Charles U. *Persuasion: Reception and Responsibility.* 3d ed. Belmont: Wadsworth, 1983. Surveys persuasion in all forms.

CHAPTER 25

Impact

In the previous chapter we examined major factors in television's impact. Here we concentrate on the impact itself. We look first at impact on individuals, then on society. We conclude by considering long-range impact.

25.1 IMPACT ON INDIVIDUALS

Public concern and research have focused on several areas of television's impact on us as individuals. These include attitudes and values, behavior, and the special case of children, the subject of so much research on television's "effects."

25.1.1 Attitudes and Values

In Section 24.1.1 we found that attitudes affect our perception of televised messages. These messages, on the other hand, can also affect our attitudes. Types of impact include reinforcement, creation, and conversion. They may also try to canalize existing attitudes. And they work best in influencing attitudes when they function in a monopolistic communications environment.

25.1.1.1 Reinforcement   Television's role in changing attitudes and values is governed in large part by the audience's predispositions (Section 24.1.2). As a result, television is more successful at reinforcing existing attitudes. Reinforcement is by far the most common type of impact. After all, since you continually expose yourself to messages congruent with your existing interests and opinions, you continually affirm those interests and opinions.

25.1.1.2 Creation   Creation of new opinions is the next most frequent effect, although not nearly as frequent as reinforcement. If you have formed no opinion on a subject, a televised message may be able to win you to its point of view.

25.1.1.3 Conversion   Television's rarest effect is conversion. If you believe one way, television alone will usually not convince you otherwise. If you change your mind about a subject after exposure to a televised message, other factors have probably worked in favor of the change as well. These other factors "softened you up," so to speak, for the conversion over a period of time. Yes, the television message triggered your change, but you were ready to change. The message by itself probably could not have caused the change.

25.1.1.4 Canalization

Most product advertising therefore does not aim for conversion. Television commercials do not attempt to convince you to use a particular product. What they try to do is—if you already use a product—convince you to use their brand.

The key here is that you probably do not make meaningful, deep-seated cognitive commitments to specific brands of laundry detergent, toothpaste, bath soap, and shaving cream. But you do have certain attitudes, values, and opinions concerning personal cleanliness, appearance, and health that lead you to wash clothes, brush teeth, and bathe. Commercials attempt to canalize these attitudes, that is, channel them toward a particular brand. Canalization seems to work best on decisions that are not really important, and for most of us the choice of a particular brand is not important.

25.1.1.5 Monopolization

An advertiser would stand a much better chance of achieving conversion if that advertiser could dominate the mass media. All media (not just television) would feed commercial messages only about that advertiser's product. Those messages would be the only advertising you receive. You would have no alternatives to consider. This would be monopolization.

Monopolization is economically unfeasible in most capitalistic countries. In the United States, law and regulation forbid monopolization (Sections 19.1.2.2). However, the term "monopolization" was actually developed within the context of political propaganda. If a political regime controls all media of mass communication in a country, it can program the media to carry only its propaganda and to modify the attitudes in the population.

Consider, for example, the situation in the People's Republic of China. For years, all mass media in China carried the same ideological themes. The Chinese reinforced those themes at the interpersonal level. The people had to meet in groups to discuss ideology. The Chinese attempted to condition the minds of their people so that they would not just accept but actively support the dictates of the Communist Party.

25.1.2 Behavior

Discussion, concern, and research that focus on television's impact on individual behavior can be divided into four general areas. These include violence, sexual material, life patterns, and inactivity, withdrawal and escape.

25.1.2.1 Violence

Violence in television has been a major public issue since the 1950s. Organizations have protested it, and politicians have investigated it. The assumption is that televised violence causes aggressive behavior in viewers and leads them to commit violent acts.

There are at least four approaches to explain the impact of televised violence. These approaches, though not fully developed and in some cases not supported by research, are referred to as theories in most social science literature.

The **catharsis theory** suggests that when you watch televised violence, you drain off aggression-causing frustrations. The drain-off decreases the probability that you will act violently. This approach has received little support from research.

The **aggressive cues theory** (also called *stimulating effects theory*) assumes that exposure to televised violence increases your level of physiological and emotional arousal. This arousal increases the probability that you will act violently or aggressively.

The **observational learning theory** assumes that you can learn aggressive behavior by watching it on television. Under certain conditions, you copy aggressive behavior of television characters.

Reinforcement theory posits that exposure to televised violence reinforces existing patterns of behavior. If you are normally a nonviolent person, you selectively perceive a program so that it reinforces your nonviolent norms and attitudes; if a violent person, you selectively perceive a program to support that inclination.

In 1972, the surgeon general of the United States released the report of a year-long program of federally funded research into the effects of television violence on children. The report noted that the bulk of studies indicated no catharsis effect. Instead, they seemed to point to a "preliminary and tentative" conclusion that viewing of televised violence **can lead to aggressive behavior.** However, any such violence-aggression relationship operates **only on some children who are already predisposed to be aggressive.** In addition, such a relationship operates **only in some contexts.** Various elements seem to alter impact, elements such as parental advice and guidance in viewing, whether the outcome of the violence is favorable or unfavorable, and whether it is perceived as fantasy or reality.

Six years later, a landmark review of the literature was published that further implicated television violence. A team headed by George Comstock reviewed some 2500 reports and comments on research into the impact of television. Based on this evidence, the team concluded that **television may increase aggressive behavior** in three ways. First, it can **teach viewers hostile acts** with which they were previously unfamiliar. Second, it can generally **encourage various ways of using aggression.** Third, it can set off or **"trigger" aggressive behavior**—behavior that imitates television or behavior that is different from that depicted on television. Comstock's team noted that effects are never certain. Someone could view televised violence, acquire aggressive tendencies, but not commit an aggressive act because the situation would not allow it. However, that individual might commit an aggressive act later, when the situation would allow it.

The research of George Gerbner led to the development of what he called **Cultivation Theory.**[1] This theory asserts that the verbal and nonverbal messages of mass media contain certain symbols. As mass-media audiences, we are exposed to these symbols on a continuing, long-range basis. The media thus create for us a *symbolic world.* This symbolic world is not real, but these media messages or symbols continually affect or *cultivate* our perceptions of reality.

Television is most efficient at cultivation because it exposes millions of us nationwide, even worldwide, to the same messages. Therefore, we have a common symbolic experience. As television shows violence, we come to accept violence as a reality of our environment, even to the extent of overestimating the amount of actual violence that occurs. Gerbner has acknowledged that light viewers are less likely to be influenced or cultivated. Heavy viewers, meanwhile, may be *mainstreamed* with other heavy viewers into a common view of the world.

25.1.2.2 Sexual Material By and large, radio and television have stayed free of obscenity, a result of federal law and trade self-regulation. Yet, times and programming concepts have changed. In the 1950s, we watched Lucy and Desi retire to separate beds. Forty years later, we could watch programs based on sexual comedy. We could choose from "adult" pay cable and satellite channels. We could watch uncut R-rated motion pictures on HBO and its clones. We could view motion pictures and programs on advertising-supported television that dealt with subjects such as rape, homosexuality, and incest. We could hear records such as "Can't Get Enough," "Get It On," "Love to Love You Baby," "Sister" (dealing with incest), and "Tonight's the Night." We could tune in to radio stations that featured sexual conversation—from so-called "therapists" who offered callers advice on their love life to raunch-radio hosts who attempted to make up for lack of originality by using juvenile rest-room humor.

Certainly you could object to the increase in sexual openness—just as to any other aspect of radio and television programming—on the basis of taste. But what about impact? Segments of the American public believe that sexual materials in general lead to moral breakdown, to rape, and to loss of respect for women. There is little evidence specifically on the effects of televised sexual material. However, some research has been done on the effects of erotic stimuli in other media, for example, textual material, photographic slides, and motion picture film.

In 1967, Congress established a commission to investigate the effects of pornography and obscenity on the people of the United States. The commission released its report in 1970. According to the report, yes, **erotic stimuli produce sexual arousal** in most men and women. But when men and women follow up stimulation with sexual activity, they do so **within the framework of individual preexisting patterns of sexual behavior.** In other words, if a man's normal sexual behavior patterns do not include rape, exposure to a skin-flick movie will not be sufficient by itself to make him commit rape.

In addition, the report pointed out that exposure to erotic stimuli appears to have **little or no effect on existing attitudes** concerning sexuality or sexual morality. This means that you do not become a dirty old man or woman simply by looking at dirty pictures.

Finally, exposure to explicit sexual mate-

rials seems to bear **no relationship to delinquent behavior.** If these findings can be generalized to television, they meant that while televised sexual material may lead to sexual arousal, the material by itself does not produce antisocial attitudes or deviant behavior.

Research has raised concern, however, about some more subtle types of effects. For example, one study found that men, after viewing pornographic pictures of women, advocated lighter sentences for convicted rapists.[2] Such results pointed to the need for continuing research.

As pointed out in Section 15.2.7, the limits of pornography are difficult to draw. Most persons, however, felt that these limits had been crossed in the case of two types of pornography that attained notoriety in the 1970s and 1980s—so called "snuff films" and "kiddie porn." The first—if they really existed—included the actual killing on-camera of one of the performers; the second, use of children to make pornographic visual material. The taking of human life and the corruption of children aroused universal disgust and revulsion. Irrespective of what such material might or might not do to the sick individuals who purchased it, such activities caused damage or even death to the persons who "performed."

25.1.2.3 Life Patterns Television, by its very existence, affects the way you live. When television first appeared in the American home, people adjusted their lives to it. They reduced time spent with magazines, radio, books, movies, and other media. They also reduced nonleisure activities and coordinated viewing routine with household duties.

If you are like most persons, you **spend more time watching television than any other activity,** except sleeping and working. Television **brings your family together physically, but you interact or converse**

little with each other because you are all watching the program. If you live in a multiset household, however, television may actually help to separate family members as each watches a different program on a different set.

Television **does not make you passive unless you are already predisposed toward passivity.** How-to programs such as *This Old House, Frugal Gourmet,* and *Victory Garden* may pique your interest, but not beyond viewing; that is, you watch the program, but do not put to rights old houses, fix inexpensive gourmet meals, or start a garden. On the other hand, a televised movie or program based on a novel may inspire you to read the novel.

25.1.2.4 Inactivity, Withdrawal, and Escape Some social scientists have contended that television and other media may *cause* you to be inactive, to withdraw attention from contemporary affairs, and to escape from reality. Mass communication researchers refer to these negative implications of media use as **media dysfunctions.** For example, if you watch television news and information programs, you may feel that you are interested and informed. You may even discuss public issues with acquaintances. Yet, you may also take no action to affect the issues—a result, perhaps, of your assumption that, since you know about the issues, "they" must be "doing something." In this case, television works as a narcotic, lulling you into a false sense of security. This effect, if it exists, is **dysfunctional** since one of the prerequisites for a democratic society is a politically active and alert electorate.

Another dysfunction is **privatization.** We used this term in Chapter 23, but in the present context it has a quite different meaning— a psychological retreat from public to private concerns. News, by definition, features primarily aberrant behavior, that is, events that deviate from the norm or from what most people believe to be right and true. In privatization, you feel overwhelmed by all the bad news television and other media feed and frustrated by your inability to deal with it. You therefore turn away from these public affairs over which you have no control to focus completely on matters in your own life over which you do have a degree of control. You concern yourself with personal appearance, family, interpersonal relations, homemaking, or whatever to the exclusion of social, political, and economic reality.

On the other hand, some social scientists say that you use television for the very purpose of escape. You use it to get away from daily problems and worries. You may also use it to relax, to stimulate imagination, to be able to discuss programming with others, for emotional release and vicarious interaction, or just to kill time. If you **overuse television for escape, it is a dysfunction.** However, **in most cases television's escape function probably serves you in a positive fashion,** giving your critical and creative processes a rest, allowing your mind to lie fallow, helping recharge your mental batteries.

25.1.3 Children

Despite the disturbing nature of the material reported concerning violence above, the news is not all bad. In fact, the bulk of research shows that **an emotionally balanced child suffers little, if any, long-lasting negative effects** from television.

A number of factors influence what programs and how much television the child watches. A few of the more important ones include age, intelligence, social level, personality, level of self-esteem, and example of parents. Most children are selective viewers, and television does not dominate their existence. A child's taste in television reflects taste in other areas. For example, interest in monster movies, monster toys, and monster magazines will show up as a preference for television programs featuring monsters. The child's cultural tastes are determined much more by parental example and home environment than by television. And the emotionally healthy child normally probably develops no antisocial behavior from viewing adult programs.

On the other hand, **an emotionally disturbed child or one who is predisposed toward antisocial or aggressive behavior patterns may suffer negative effects** from television. Some children are more likely to believe that what they see on television is the norm and that what they see in real life (that which does not jibe with television depictions) is the exception.

Very young children often cannot distinguish between fiction and nonfiction on television. However, even children as young as six years recognize commercials for what they are, and by eight or nine they are skeptical about advertising claims. Nonetheless, repeated exposure to a television commercial can move the child from skepticism toward persuasion. And children in homes where television is on constantly tend to suffer more negative effects, even when the television is on largely as background with no one viewing.

Parental interaction with the child concerning television content can counter most such effects. Therefore, in the matter of your child and television, factors of **the child's own mental and emotional state, your example and interaction with the child, and the home environment you provide seem to outweigh television as an influence.**

Television viewing does not necessarily adversely affect schoolwork. It may even help young viewers get a head start before they begin school. This was found to be particularly true with viewers of *Sesame Street*, although differences between viewers and nonviewers seemed to even out after a few years. Television has not had much effect on children's bedtime.

25.2 IMPACT ON SOCIETY

Society is more than an aggregate of individuals. It is also the customs, morals, values, standards, and institutions shared by those individuals. We now look at the impact of television on society in the United States, impact that involves culture, politics, and social change.

25.2.1 Culture, Style, and Taste

At various times, critics have charged that television degrades public taste by pandering to the lowest common denominator. They contend that television could be used to raise the cultural level of the population. However, **taste is much more influenced by social, personal, educational, and family determinants** than by television. You probably come to television with your tastes already formed and seek programming congruent with them. Therefore, if *Jake and the Fatman* or *Married . . . With Children* plays opposite *Masterpiece Theatre* or *Great Performances*, you watch the program that best reflects your customary taste.

As for television's ability to raise the general cultural level, there are doubts about that. Despite the BBC's years of monopoly and its attempt to raise taste (Section 23.2.1.1), large percentages of the population in the United Kingdom switched over when other programming sources—foreign, pirate, and indigenous commercial stations—became available. On the other hand, concentrated use of appropriate programming in emerging nations has led many of their citizens to show increased interest in their cultural heritage.

Television can also **bestow prestige and enhance authority.** This comes close to being a tautological situation—what you see on television must be important or famous *because* it is on television; the very fact that it appears on television makes it important. Examples abound. Merchandisers take advantage of television-granted prestige by paying performers to endorse products. The name of television performer Johnny Carson appears on a line of men's clothing.

This phenomenon of bestowed prestige occurs in other media. In many cases, successful contemporary radio stations and MTV can make a music recording popular by playing it as though it were popular. Newspapers and magazines have long spread the word on style, taste, and manners.

Motion pictures have a history of influencing style and manners. Jean Harlow's popularity started the bleached blond fad that exists to this day. A scene in *It Happened One Night* (1934) showed that Clark Gable wore no undershirt, and the sale of men's undershirts dropped nationwide. The roles played by Marlon Brando in *The Wild One* (1953) and James Dean in *Rebel Without a Cause* (1955) spawned a whole cult of thin-skinned, inarticulate young men. Brigitte Bardot's film portrayals inspired thousands of young women to affect bee-stung lips and tight dresses.

Recording artists can have the same effect. During the 1960s, the Beatles influenced the hair style and fashions of millions of young people. Twenty years later, performers such as Michael Jackson, Prince, and Madonna influence fad followers.

Television programs tell us what to like and how to dress. The television series *Miami Vice* (Figure 25.1) convinced what appeared to be an entire nation that hot pink

Figure 25.1 Media fad starter. *Miami Vice:* Maybe dry-cleaners and barbers were on strike. (*Source:* AP/Wide World.)

and neon green formed an attractive color combination and that men looked attractive when they needed a shave, a shirt, a tie, and a good pressing of their jackets.

25.2.2 Politics

Politicians have known instinctively for years that television alone will not change anyone's mind. A good political campaigner writes off voters who favor the opposition. No amount of media persuasion will change their minds. So the campaigner "goes where the ducks are" and **concentrates much advertising on voters who favor the candidate.** The campaigner seeks to reinforce the voters' positive feelings to the point where they go to the polls and vote.

Increasingly, the modern election campaign features two opposing candidates who have nearly equal support among the active, politically aware portion of the electorate, both party members and independent voters. The balance of power then lies with the third group—the uncommitted nonvoters who neither know nor care about the campaign. These persons are characterized by high use of one medium above all others—television. If you wish to arouse these people, to get their vote, you use television advertising. But television time is expensive. Therefore, the candidate must either have great personal wealth or make the compromises necessary to attract large contributors.

Because nonvoters usually do not respond to issues, the campaigner attempts to short-circuit reasoning processes, to harness the existing prejudices and opinions of nonvoters long enough to get them to the polls. Heavy use is made of slogans and catch phrases. Advertising aims for name recognition, irrespective of evaluative judgment. Expensive political advertising specialists are hired to research public preferences and to create an image of the candidate to meet those preferences.

All this presents a rather chilling spectacle—public office available only to those of great personal wealth or beholden to large contributors, who run on slogans and catch phrases, who are packaged and merchandised like soap and dog food, and who owe election to a constituency that does not know and does not care. Luckily, elections do not always work that way. Some of the most expensive campaigns have failed. And the overall record of success for professional political image makers is about 50 percent—the same percentage you get on a chance basis.

Politics are also affected by television's **ability to confer status and prestige.** It can transform someone like Michael Dukakis, the governor of Massachusetts, into a national political figure. Veteran television performers, particularly news and weather reporters, have used television-granted fame and prestige to make successful bids for elective office. Former film stars, such as Ronald Reagan, George Murphy, and Shirley Temple Black, have entered politics after gaining fame first through motion pictures, then through subsequent television exposure of those pictures.

Social scientists suggest that the greatest **impact of television on voter preference comes between campaigns,** not during them. As discussed in Section 8.1.5, television news, by its very nature, must select, edit, and order. Even live and on-the-scene, a camera operator must select specific portions of the scene to send on to us. Therefore television does not merely transmit messages. It structures what you perceive to be reality by selecting, emphasizing, and interpreting events. Television does this all the time, so small but cumulative changes may take place between campaigns. Your political party or candidate preference may change, or you may acquire a new perspective within which you perceive, interpret, and respond to the campaign. In the 1964 U.S. presidential campaign, for example, the war in Southeast Asia was not an issue. By 1968, television and other media coverage had made it *the* issue. The media had not told us what to think, but they had told us what to think about. Social scientists call this the **agenda-setting function** of the media.

Television campaign coverage and candidate advertising seem to **help turn out the vote.** However, researchers have found some evidence that **national television coverage of voter returns influences those who have not yet voted.** Critics had expressed concern that televised reports of presidential returns from early time zones, along with computer-generated projections of who would probably win, might influence people in later time zones who had yet to cast ballots. Studies of the 1964 and 1968 elections failed to find any such effect. But research on subsequent presidential elections seemed to show a definite decline in voter turnout. For example, estimates of the number of Californians who were discouraged from voting because of early network projections range from 280,000 for the 1982 election to 800,000 in 1980.

25.2.3 Social Change

Radio and television outlets and networks try for the largest possible audiences. Therefore they program material that they hope will not offend you so that you will not turn away from the programming. They program material that tends to reflect and promote universal values and attitudes so that they have a better chance—on the average—of attracting you in the first place.

Television exposes deviations from established and normal behaviors. By bringing deviation to public attention, television forces people to take a stand on it. The net effect is to force some kind of public action against what may previously have been privately tolerated. Thus, television programming **both enforces and exposes deviations from normal attitudes and behavior patterns in society.**

It would be logical to assume that such impact obstructs social change, promotes conformity, weakens individualism, and decreases tolerance of differences. Yet television has played a significant role in, for example, publicizing the problems and complaints of women, blacks, and other minorities. For years, however, it has also played a significant role in reinforcing ethnic and sexual stereotypes.

On the other hand, television and other media seem to help new ideas and products gain acceptance. In adopting a new concept, you probably go through five overlapping stages—(1) you become **aware** of the concept; (2) you become **interested;** (3) you **evaluate** information; (4) you **try or test** the concept; and (5) you **adopt** it, that is make a decision on continued use. During this process, you talk to other people about the concept, but you also get much information from the media.

This five-part adoption model also helps to explain how new ideas and concepts spread. A few persons are quick to adopt a new concept; others are slower in varying degrees. This means that as the concept spreads, various groups of persons are going through the five phases of our adoption model. For example, you, as one of the few early adopters, may have been one of the very first to get a videocassette recorder or a home computer. On the other hand, it may take years before the few laggards—the very slowest adopters—decide to buy one of these machines. Between the few at either end of the scale are the majority of persons who buy VCRs or computers.

25.2.4 The Knowledge Gap Hypothesis

Mass media disseminate information to broad segments of society. One effect of this, however, may be to increase the disparity in knowledge levels among various social classes. This potential media dysfunction is called the **knowledge gap hypothesis**.[3] According to this hypothesis, all social classes learn from the media, but over a period of time persons in higher socioeconomic classes will likely accumulate more knowledge concerning public affairs, science, and current events. Thus, the knowledge gap may grow ever wider.

Researchers have offered several reasons for the knowledge gap phenomenon. First, certain media, including multichannel cable and magazine subscriptions, are more affordable to higher-income households. Second, the mass media may target higher-income consumers who are more likely to have greater interest in and more ability to understand certain topics. And persons of higher social status are more likely to communicate with others of similar status, thus allowing the multistep flow of communication (Section 24.2) to contribute to the knowledge gap.

25.3 LONG-RANGE IMPACT

Most of the types of impact we have discussed so far are short range. For example, by itself, exposure to a violent television program normally will not lead you to commit a violent act. Or, by itself, a televised persuasive message will not change your mind. Where we dealt with long-range impact, we used hedge words such as "seems to," "likely to," and "probably." This is because researchers find it difficult to test for long-range impact. The research studies themselves must be long range and cover a span of months, even years. Therefore, we have little research concerning the overall long-range impact of American commercial television on the general public.

We do know, however, that commercial television does not depict what most perceive as the true nature of the world. It emphasizes certain themes and values, those which draw the largest audiences and sell products—violence; sexual innuendo; conformity; high adventure; absurd situations; sharp demarcation between good and evil; absolute resolution of all problems within a time frame of 30 to 60 minutes; the glamour of a life of crime and the ease with which laws are broken; stereotyped roles and behavior for men, women, and various racial groups; beauty, youth, and sexual desirability as important goals; acquisition for the sake of acquisition; one-upmanship, showing off, "flaunting it"; getting more and getting it easier than everyone else; the importance of winning; being "cool" and uncaring; and worship of the Cult of Number One. Critics contend that these themes and values are dysfunctional, that is, undesirable from the point of view of the welfare of society.

We learned in Sections 25.1.2.1, 25.1.2.2, and 25.1.3 that certain other factors usually militate against television having a negative effect on "normal" people. Foremost among these other factors were agents of socialization and interpersonal contact. But there are situations in which other factors are largely absent. For example, in many families parents use the television set as a combination sitter, companion, and opiate for their young children. The children watch anything they want, as long as they keep quiet and out of the way. The parents take little time to interact with their children. The children have no religious training. They do not attend school. In effect, **a high percentage of their total sensory input**—their experiences that help form attitudes for life—**comes from television, unchecked, in the most critical, formative years of their lives.** Television has become their principal means of socialization, the process by which they learn the norms, values, and behavior patterns of society.

Of course, that cannot happen to you or to your children. You care, and television viewing is monitored and regulated in your home.

Maybe. But there are a few facts you should keep in mind. First, one of the conditions that determine the impact of television is **exposure pattern.** This means that the more a message (such as a particular set of themes and values) is repeated, the greater is its chance to be effective.

Second, as discussed above, American commercial television (including subscription cable services) continually **stresses certain themes and values, and we expose ourselves to them for long periods of time.** Each of our homes averages over 40 hours per week of viewing activity, the majority of which is commercial and subscription television. That means the TV set runs over one-third of our waking hours, over 2000 hours per year, exposing us to these themes and values.

Third, **other media stress the same themes and values.** In fact, many of the different types of impact we have attributed to television alone actually apply to that whole group of institutions and products we call "mass media."

Fourth, social scientists tell us that the **mass media represent a new force in the socialization process.** As such, the media supplant at least partially parents, teachers, and other direct authority figures.

True, television and the other media do not mirror society. Contrary to what some prominent reporters contend, not even television news mirrors society; it focuses on the deviant, the aberrant, the exception. But, of course, neither did *Hamlet* mirror early seventeenth-century English or Danish society. And it, too, is full of violence, greed, immorality, and all that other stuff critics say television carries. Yet *Hamlet* is held up to us as "good literature." Is that fair?

Perhaps not. On the other hand, *Hamlet* is not available in your living room at the flick of a switch 24 hours a day.

NOTES

1. G. Gerbner, L. Gross, M. Morgan, and N. Signorielli, "The Mainstreaming of America," *Journal of Communication* 30 (1980): 10–29.
2. D. Zillman and J. Bryant, "Pornography, Sexual Callousness, and the Trivialization of Rape," *Journal of Communication* 32 (1982): 10–21.
3. P. J. Tichenor, G. A. Donohue, and C. N. Olien, "Mass Media Flow and Differentiated Growth in Knowledge," *Public Opinion Quarterly* 34 (1980): 159–170.

FURTHER READING

Adler, Richard P., et al. *The Effects of Television and Advertising on Children.* Lexington: Lexington, 1980.

Davison, W. Phillips, James Boylan, and Frederick T. C. Yu. *Mass Media: Systems and Effects.* 2d ed. New York: Holt, 1982. Complexities of media systems; effects theory.

Dorr, Aimée. *Television and Children: A Special Medium for a Special Audience.* Newbury Park: Sage, 1987. Children as a specific audience subgroup.

Frank, Ronald E., and Marshall G. Greenberg. *The Public's Use of Television: Who Watches and Why.* Beverly Hills, CA: Sage, 1980. Profiles viewer types.

Gordon, George. *Erotic Communications: Studies in Sex, Sin, and Censorship.* New York: Hastings, 1980. History and state of the "art."

Graber, Doris A. *Media Power in Politics.* 2d ed. Washington: CQ, 1989.

Harris, Richard Jackson. *A Comparative Psychology of Mass Communication.* Hillsdale: Erlbaum, 1989.

Hiebert, Ray Eldon, and Carol Reuss, eds. *Impact of Mass Media: Current Issues.* White Plains:

Longman, 1988. Impact of media on our social and political lives.

Liebert, Robert M., Joyce N. Sprafkin, and Emily S. Davidson. *The Early Window: Effects of Television on Children and Youth.* 3d ed. New York: Pergamon, 1988. Comprehensive review.

Nimmo, Dan, and James E. Combs. *Mediated Political Realities.* 2d ed. White Plains: Longman, 1990. Transformation into fantasy by media.

Rogers, Everett M. *Diffusion of Innovations.* 3d ed. New York: Free, 1983. Spread and adoption of the new.

Television and Behavior: Ten Years of Scientific Progress and Implications for the Eighties. Washington: GPO, 1982. Posits a stronger cause-effect relationship between televised violence and aggressive behavior in children than an earlier (1972) report.

CHAPTER 26

Research and Theory

Mass communication research is the field within which radio and television research is conducted. Mass communication also includes research into advertising, newspapers, magazines, sound recordings, motion pictures, and other media. Note that the singular form is used—mass *communication*. Scholars study the social, historical, and psychological *process*, not the technical aspects of equipment. They believe the plural form "communications" connotes the latter, so they use the singular to describe their field.

26.1 RESEARCH

Research begins with a question. Usually, it asks what causes some particular phenomenon.

26.1.1 Notion of Science

Scientific research is **empirical, objective, systematic, and in most cases quantitative.** The empirical researcher gathers data by di-rect experience or direct observation. The researcher strives for objectivity by using certain methods designed to minimize personal bias. The researcher ensures that the work will be systematic by specifying procedures—the design and methodology—in advance, then following them to the letter. During actual execution of the research, the researcher methodically observes and records previously selected categories of information, called **primary data.** In quantitative research, the researcher uses statistical techniques to deal with and analyze the data.

We said that research begins with a question. When that question is formally stated, it is often in the form of a **hypothesis.** The research tests that hypothesis, and the results allow the researcher to accept or reject the hypothesis and, thus, answer the question. The question often asked is, What, if any, relationship exists between two entities? The entities are **variables.** If alteration in one causes a corresponding change in the other, they are **independent** and **dependent** variables, respectively. A researcher might, for example, want to test whether a radio station's news programming affects overall station ratings. The data might indicate that a professional news operation actually **causes** ratings to go up. Here, the independent variable is the quality of the news operation, and the dependent variable is the station's ratings.

We must be very careful, however, before concluding that any variable *causes* a change in another. In fact, three elements of proof must be present. First, the variables must be statistically related. In other words, as one increases, the other increases or decreases to some extent. In this example, ratings would be higher when the quality of news programming was higher. Second, the independent variable (the quality of the news operation) must precede the dependent variable (high ratings) in time.

Third, there must be no other variables that can account for the relationship, variables that we are not considering or have not thought about that might explain the higher ratings. In this case, our ratings may have gone up because we changed our music format at the same time we upgraded our news. If so, we cannot assume a cause-and-effect relationship between our original two variables.

Hypothesis-testing research may be **based on theory.** The researcher examines a general principle or theory, then derives a hypothesis from that theory. The primary goals of theory-based research are to evaluate the theory—to determine whether it makes accurate predictions, whether it has limitations, and whether it is correct—and to expand the theory. Much hypothesis-testing research in mass communication is *not* theory based, one reason being that we still do not have adequate theories addressing many practical concerns of media professionals. However, in formulating a hypothesis or research question, the mass communication researcher does review and take into account previous and related research.

26.1.2 Research Methodologies

Mass communication scholars use a variety of methods to find answers. In the **historical-critical method,** the researcher examines documents and firsthand reports contemporary with the era, event, or phenomenon under investigation. For example, a scholar who wished to find the root causes of the 1970s controversy over the NBC News documentary *Pensions: The Broken Promise* (Section 8.4) would certainly wish to study a copy of the documentary itself, its script, and the records and decisions of the FCC and the courts, as well as to interview the complainant, the program's producer, and other individuals involved.

In the **case study method,** the researcher examines in detail a mass communication situation or a series of such situations for underlying principles. Two classic case studies are those by Warren Breed on social control in the newsroom[1] and David Manning White on the gatekeeper functions (selection of news items) of a newspaper wire editor.[2] Examples of case studies in radio and television include those by Lynch[3] and Ravage[4] on the production of two specific weekly network television series.

Most scholars who investigate impact use some form of **quantitative** research. They literally count things—things such as hours of television viewing, degree of interest in a particular radio format, or aggressive acts. After counting, the researcher attempts to determine whether the number counted is significant. For example, results of a study might suggest that people tend to exhibit more aggressive behavior as they watch more television. The researcher would run statistical tests on the numbers involved to determine whether relationships were strong enough to indicate some connection between the two variables or so weak that they could have occurred strictly by chance.

Historical-critical and case study research

may utilize quantitative methodology. Suppose, for example, that a study posits some relationship between network television prime-time program development effort and series longevity. In this case, the researcher might determine the number of program development projects the three major television networks had supported each year over a period of time and then count the total number of episodes of each series that started in the same years. If the long-running series tended to be those that made their debut during years of high spending on program development, some relationship could be said to exist between those two variables. Quantitative methodology, however, does not have to be used to do historical-critical or case study research.

Two types of research that almost inevitably involve numbers are the field study and the experiment. In the **field study,** the researcher does not alter conditions but studies the mass communication process as it occurs in real life. The researcher goes into the environment and asks questions, observes behaviors, and administers tests. The data are then examined for relationships between variables, for example, between prolonged television viewing and social isolation among children.

Some field study researchers observe and record. They might watch, for example, workers such as news gatherers, or families viewing television and interacting in the home. They take extensive notes to be analyzed to form the basis of conclusions. The important distinction of field research is that observations are made, as unobtrusively as possible, in the natural working or viewing environment.

The **experimental method,** on the other hand, is used most often in the laboratory. In one of its simpler forms, the researcher exposes two groups of subjects to conditions that are identical in all respects save one. The researcher then tests both groups to see if any differences show up in the expected areas.

For example, a researcher might expose each of two similar groups of children to different versions of a television program. The two versions would be identical except that one contained violence and the other contained no violence. After exposure, the children of each group would be allowed to play, and the researcher could watch and count the number of aggressive acts—for example, one child pushing another. If children in the violent-action-exposure group commit a significantly greater number of aggressive acts than those in the other group, the researcher could tentatively attribute the increase (the dependent variable) to the televised violence (independent variable).

Experimental laboratory research has the advantage over field study research with respect to control. In the laboratory, the researcher can use a carefully constructed research design to hold constant—ensure the sameness of—all variables except those under study. Given positive results and assurance of no significant threats to the validity of the study, our laboratory researcher could conclude, with a fair degree of assurance, that exposure to televised violence increases the number of aggressive acts children commit during play. But our field researcher—even with results that show a positive relationship—cannot draw such an unqualified cause-effect conclusion. There was no control; thus there were probably multiple other variables at work in addition to television—parents, peers, other media, and so on.

Yet the field study has an advantage precisely because of these multiple other variables. After all, they are present in real life. Besides, the laboratory study is a contrived situation. Subjects are taken out of the real world and know that something is expected of them. Much laboratory research is done on college campuses, and the subjects are often college sophomores, hardly a representative sample of the actual population.

Still another method combines aspects of both experimental and field studies. In the **field experimental method,** the researcher uses laboratory controls but conducts research in the real world. As you can imagine, the ideal of control over mass communication content is difficult to coordinate and put into effect. Relatively few large-scale field experiments have been conducted.

The **survey method** is used extensively in mass communication research. Social scientists, professional media researchers, and the ratings firms use data collected from samples of a population to draw conclusions about the entire population (Sections 18.2.1, 18.2.2, 18.2.5, 18.2.7).

We live in the age of the computer, and it has become easy for a researcher to utilize these electric aids as nets in "fishing expeditions," seining data in the hope of catching results. Here, the researcher is interested in a particular variable but has no clear hypothesis about the effect of the variable. In these cases the research question is a broad one, for example, "What other factors **correlate** with increased aggressiveness following exposure to televised violence?" In this context, *correlate* means *have mutual relationships.* So, in addition to numbers of aggressive acts committed, other data are collected—perhaps a personality test is administered, demographic information is gathered, and estimates of weekly hours of TV viewing are recorded—and entered into the computer. The computer is programmed to sift through the data using various statistical tools. And the researcher examines the results to see if any relationships appear.

26.1.3 History of Mass Communication Research

The origins of mass communication as a field for research go back to World War I. Governments of the combatant nations used propaganda to mobilize their populations. They described the enemy as subhumans whose primary aims were to rape, pillage, and kill. These were the first formal, widespread government uses of propaganda in modern times, and they worked. Whole countries threw themselves into the war effort.

After the war, reaction set in. The public learned of the techniques by which they had been manipulated. They began to fear propaganda as some omnipotent force against which they were powerless to resist. As a result, psychologists became interested and were the first to analyze propaganda and to research the process of persuasion by mass media.

Mass communication research soon spread beyond inquiry into propaganda. Social scientists from sociology, social psychology, political science, and other disciplines conducted research in mass communication. They left behind a residue of results from the perspectives of, and based on the principles and theories in, their respective disciplines.

Faculty members in university schools of journalism adopted methodologies from the social sciences and launched their own research. Here, for the first time, were scholars who considered their primary research interests to be mass communication. University speech departments added the word "communication" to their titles. They, too, adopted social science research methodologies. During the 1950s, journalism and speech areas graduated from their doctoral programs a new generation of scholars who considered themselves to be social scientists and their research field to be mass communication.

26.2 THEORY

In our discussion of research we slipped in the term *theory* and brushed by it with a few remarks about usefulness and scarcity. However, theory is a rather important subject. So at this point we need to backtrack and take a close look at theory—what it is, what it does, and what forms it takes in mass communication.

26.2.1 Definition and Characteristics of Theory

A simplified definition of theory is **a set of interrelated statements that explains and predicts a phenomenon.** Note that theories must go beyond mere explanation or description. They must **predict** phenomena and explain not only what happens but **why and how** the process occurs as well.

For example, information-processing theory has challenged mass communication scholars for several decades to explain how and why media messages are received, decoded, and processed by individuals. This theory, like most others in social and behavioral science, is incomplete. But we do know more about the process and research continues because of the basic formulations.

Theories must also be **testable.** If we cannot evaluate the validity and accuracy of theoretical statements, we can never fully accept the explanations. In other words, a theory **must be capable of being proved false.** On the other hand, theory-based research normally does not and cannot prove a theory to be true with full certainty. That is not necessarily a fault of the research; it is simply the nature of theory. Researchers can, however, offer support for theoretical holdings through research and, to some extent, through practical application of the theory.

26.2.2 Intervening Variables

Theory has a special meaning in research. In the natural sciences a proposition must meet rigorous criteria and serve specific functions before it can be labeled a theory. However, it is difficult for theories in the social and be-

havioral sciences to meet these criteria. In most natural sciences—physics, for example—a scientist can *see* the variables. The scientist can observe what goes on, can measure precisely the values and quantities involved, and so can account for all occurrences. Not so in the behavioral and social sciences.

For example, two people react to the same stimulus in different ways. How do we account for the difference? There being no obvious explanation anyone can see, psychologists suggest the existence of **intervening variables.** Two classes of intervening variables seem to play large roles in the effect of message stimuli on people—**psychological makeup** (such as attitudes, beliefs, and values; Section 24.1) and **interpersonal relationships** (influence of other persons; Section 24.2).

Let us use an example involving psychological makeup to illustrate the difficulty of dealing with intervening variables. A communication stimulus encounters a different set of attitudes in each person. These different attitudes result in different perceptions of the stimulus. And different perceptions lead to different reactive behaviors.

Of course, no one can *see* an attitude. It is not an organ, a gland, a particular part of the brain. It is something psychologists have posited to explain differential behavior. Since an attitude cannot be seen or located, there is no way to measure it directly. Instead, psychologists measure **overt behavior,** under the assumption that the attitude (*if* it exists) underlies behavior and therefore behavior reflects attitude. They use all kinds of measurements, from pencil-and-paper personality tests to counting the number of times a button is pushed. But these are all *indirect.* They measure behavior, not attitude, and so are at best only indicators of what *might* be going on in what they *believe* to exist.

So it goes with social and behavioral sciences. Any time you deal with human beings, you deal with variables that cannot be measured with the precision achieved in the natural sciences. A theory in physics or chemistry yields hypotheses that predict exact results that can be measured in number of foot-pounds, molecules, degrees of temperature, atoms, electrons. A theory in psychology or sociology can yield hypotheses, but it cannot, for example, predict that attitude A will move X degrees in direction Y.

26.2.3 Theories of Mass Communication

For years, mass communication study and research had no central, unifying thematic structure, no central theories or general principles. The little bits of research results scattered about by the psychologists, sociologists, political scientists, and others who first opened the field were too disparate for successful integration.

26.2.3.1 Borrowed Theories Some mass communication researchers borrowed theories from other fields. The information processing theories, which were developed in psychology, have proved especially interesting to communication researchers. Other borrowed theories used extensively by mass communication researchers have included those that focused on persuasion, attitude change, and reference groups.

26.2.3.2 Effects Theories *Theories of Mass Communication* (see Further Reading) is a widely read book in the field. In its first two editions, the various research results on impact of mass communication were pulled together into several coherent formulations called, for convenience, "theories." These formulations also served to illustrate developments and changes in the way researchers regarded mass communication and its relationship to individuals.

The first of the formulations—and one that has been discarded by social scientists—was the **bullet theory.** The bullet theory was the earliest conception of mass communication, and it grew out of the World War I propaganda successes discussed in Section 26.1.3. According to this theory, the individual was thought to be socially isolated. Thanks to sociological and geographic moves to what was called the *mass society*, people had no meaningful social ties. Traditional values had been abandoned. Ties of clan, tribe, even family and friendship were disappearing. People were moving from the country and small towns, where everybody knew everybody else's business, to the large cities, where nobody knew and nobody cared.

From a psychological point of view, the theories of Darwin and Freud were cited to show that humans had certain instincts over which they had no control. They had inherited these instincts from their common animal ancestors. A powerful communications stimulus, such as a propaganda message, could reach these instincts, and humans would respond. They would respond because they had no control over these instincts, and they would all respond the same way because they all shared a common instinctual inheritance. A given stimulus yielded a given response. To get a different response, the stimulus was changed so that it touched off a different instinct.

In other words, the individual was cognitively passive—helpless in the face of a strong communications stimulus. Since meaningful interpersonal, organizational, or societal ties were missing, they could not influence behavior or otherwise interfere with a stimulus. Mass communication messages were compared with bullets, each finding its mark and getting its reaction.

As we shall see, this bullet theory was eventually discounted. Nonetheless, it influenced thinking for years. Many people sincerely believed that we were helpless, passive receptacles at the mercy of mass media messages. This view guided public policy as set by our representatives in government. Advertising experts based their copy and campaigns on it. Even the very terminology used by researchers seemed to be influenced by this viewpoint. Social scientists investigated the *effects* of mass communication, the implication being that the messages did everything. We as individuals brought nothing to the communication act.

However, studies and experiments in psychology soon led to the startling conclusion that people are different—the **individual differences** theory. We discussed many of the concepts encompassed by the individual differences theory in Section 24.1.

Pioneer individual-differences researchers, however, based their work on faulty assumptions about how and why we respond to messages. True, they recognized that individuals differ. But they did not recognize that individuals are cognitively active, that individuals interpret and utilize media messages according to their own needs and interests. These researchers still assumed that people were essentially passive and responded only to external stimuli, such as media messages. As a result, research in the area of individual differences was unproductive, and it was virtually abandoned during the 1960s.

Social categories theory added a sociological component to the individual-differences (psychological) perspective. This theory, too, acknowledged that individuals differ. But it added the notion that people from a particular religious, ethnic, work, and neighborhood environment would tend to think like other people from the same environment. In other words, similar environments produce similar cognitive structures, which, in turn, yield similar responses to a media stimulus. A Palm Beach teenager would, therefore, have concerns and interests which would be similar to those of other Palm Beach teenagers but dissimilar (for the most part) to those of middle-aged Minnesota farmers.

The discovery that people, after receiving information from mass media, talked with and influenced one another led to formulation of the **social relationships** theory. During the 1940 presidential campaign, three researchers[5] studied a panel of some 600 residents of Erie County, Ohio. They wanted to determine how and why people vote as they do. They wanted to find out the impact of the campaign itself, including its mass media aspects, on voting intentions. But when they asked their panelists to describe recent exposure to campaign communications of all kinds, the medium the panelists named most often was not radio, newspapers, magazines, billboards, direct mail, or any other mass medium. It was conversation—talking to other people. Out of this and other studies that attested to the effectiveness of personal contact developed the whole idea of the role of interpersonal relations in mass communication, including the opinion leader process and the two-step flow hypothesis, discussed in Section 24.2.

The last of this group is the **cultural norms** theory. This is the term used to describe the concerns we discussed in Section 25.3. The assumption here is that mass media, through selective emphasis on certain themes and values, create the impression in their audiences that what they see on television is what "the real world" is really like. The impact on the norms of society can be conscious or unconscious and can either reinforce existing norms or institute new ones. Research seems to indicate that mass media actually have little power to change norms in the short run but more likely reflect and reinforce trends that already exist. At least some researchers, however, believe that, over the long run, the mass media do act to create and change social norms. See, for example, the discussion of cultivation theory in Section 25.1.2.1.

These "effects theories" were never fully developed. Perhaps this was because the research was motivated more by fear of the potential power of the media than by objective scientific curiosity. Or it may have been due to the faulty assumptions about human behavior. Still, research was never able to establish that the media were all-powerful.

Eventually, researchers began using a **limited effects** model in their theoretical approaches. They realized that human behavior could not be explained by simplistic, passive, stimulus-response "effects" models. So they turned to the uses and gratifications approach.

26.2.3.3 Uses and Gratifications

The uses and gratifications approach posits a cognitively active individual. It asks what *we use communication* for, rather than what are communication's effects on (that is, what is communication doing to) us. Somewhat similar to a theoretical framework called *functionalism*, the uses and gratifications approach includes **utility theory.**

Utility theory suggests yet another explanation for selective perception. According to utility theory, you attend, perceive, and remember communication that is pleasurable or that helps you in some way. The communication itself does not have to be in accord with your existing ideas. If you think the communication will be useful or will give you satisfaction, you will expose yourself to it; if not, you will try not to expose yourself to it, or you will disregard or forget it.

Charles R. Wright[6] suggested that the media serve four basic functions for society. These include surveillance, correlation, transmission of culture, and entertainment. In performing the **surveillance** function, mass media provide information for society. This corresponds roughly to handling the

news, but we get information from all media content, not just formal news. For example, MTV and contemporary hit radio tell us what recordings are popular.

The **correlation** function includes interpretations of information and suggestions on how we should respond. Editorial and propaganda messages attempt correlation most directly, but again, we take cues for behavior from all types of content.

In the **cultural transmission** function, audience members pick up cultural cues and indices from mass media messages. This is "education" in the broadest sense of the term. Just as *Sesame Street* can teach us the alphabet, so can soft-drink commercials teach us that it is "in" to be slim.

The **entertainment** function refers to mass communication messages intended for amusement, irrespective of what other impact they may have. Any one mass media message may serve all four functions for us. For example, we watch television news programs to get information. But the treatment of news at many television stations has made the entertainment function a very important factor in its presentation (Section 8.1.5). At the same time, we receive cues concerning correlation (what the president says, what people are doing and saying, editorial comment) and cultural transmission (this is what happens to people who disobey the laws of society, this is how the very wealthy or powerful or popular behave, this is what the in-crowd is doing or wearing).

Wright has proposed that the role of mass communication in society be analyzed by asking the 12-element question shown in Figure 26.1.

26.2.3.4 Other Theories

Some other theoretical frameworks include various short-range theories, play theory, and the frame theory. Researchers have developed short-range theories to account for specific types of

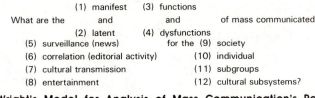

Figure 26.1 Wright's Model for Analysis of Mass Communication's Role in Society.
Manifest means that they are there, we are aware of them, and they are intended. *Latent* means that they are hidden, we are not aware of them, and they are unintended. *Functions* work to maintain harmony or progress. *Dysfunctions* work against smooth functioning.

mass media impact. Examples of these are the four theories concerning impact of televised violence described in Section 25.1.2.1

Play theory distinguishes between work (reality, earning a living) and play (largely unproductive, except for self-satisfaction). According to play theory, the central concern of mass media is to allow people to throw off social control and withdraw into play. Like utility theory, play theory avoids the helpless audience/all-powerful media situation that the word "effects" seems to imply. Both posit a psychologically active audience.

The **frame analysis theory,** developed by Dennis K. Davis and Stanley J. Baran,[7] is based in turn on the frame analysis perspec-

tive.[8] This perspective is phenomenological; that is, it has to do with the way things seem to us on the basis of our perception of them. On the one hand, mass communication messages have influenced our cognitive processes—the way we perceive and make sense of things. On the other hand, our cognitive processes influence our comprehension and interpretation of mass communication messages. The relationship between these two influences is reflexive; that is, each affects the other (Figure 26.2).

26.2.3.5 Dependency Theory
While the first two editions of *Theories of Mass Com-*

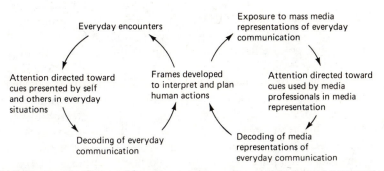

Figure 26.2 Communication and framing process.   (From MASS COMMUNICATION AND EVERYDAY LIFE, A PERSPECTIVE ON THEORY AND EFFECTS by Dennis K. Davis and Stanley J. Baran. © by Wadsworth, Inc. Reprinted by permission of Wadsworth Publishing Company, Belmont, California 94002.)

munication set forth the formulations cited above as "effects theories," they were not really theories in the formal sense. In subsequent editions, however, authors Melvin De Fleur and Sandra Ball-Rokeach integrated these formulations with other major factors, variables, and relationships into a general theory of the impact of mass communication on individuals and society.

De Fleur and Ball-Rokeach call theirs a **dependency theory of audience-media-society relations.** They posit that when informal communications channels outside the immediate group begin to be disrupted, people start to depend on mass media for information. The degree of dependency varies. As the media serve more information-delivery functions and as social change and conflict increase, people become more dependent on the media. Under these conditions, the mass media achieve a broad range of cognitive (how we perceive things), affective (how we feel about things), and behavioral (what we do about things) effects.

These effects, however, are not entirely one way. The relationship among audience, society, and media is actually tripartite. The alteration of audience cognitive, affective, and behavioral conditions feeds back and, in turn, alters both society and the media.

26.2.3.6 The Spiral of Silence The last theory we will discuss suggests that the mass media are actually quite powerful—more powerful than we are able to ascertain through available methods of research. Elizabeth Noelle-Neumann argues that when individuals perceive their opinions and ideas to be in the minority, they remain silent.[9] The media, by helping create dominant opinions, help form impressions that public opinion is either contrary to or moving away from individual minority positions. Thus, the individuals remain silent, resulting in a *spiral of silence.* As this process continues, minority viewpoints disappear.

Several factors increase media influence on public opinion. First, the media are ubiquitous and readily available to the masses. Also, the mass media have a sort of "cumulative" effect on individuals in that certain messages or ideas may be heard and seen repeatedly on radio and television and in magazines and newspapers. These messages become dominant over those that are less emphasized or not presented by the media. Finally, Noelle-Neumann suggests that the shared perceptions of major television networks, newspapers, and magazines help shape majority opinion and contribute to the spiral of silence.

26.3 RESEARCH AND THE COMMUNICATION PROCESS

Historically, the bulk of empirical research has dealt with effects—what the mass media *do to* people. However, there are other ways to study mass communication.

Claude E. Shannon's 1948 paper "The Mathematical Theory of Communication"[10] opened important new insights on the subject of human communication. In the article, he dealt with communication by analogy. Shannon identified a few key elements and relationships present in every communications system—a **model** of the communication process (Figure 26.3). He focused on mechanical and electronic systems such as telegraphy and telephony. But scholars in the social sciences also found the idea of using models useful to illustrate and study the process of human communication. Scholars have constructed a number of interesting models that depict their concepts of the process of mass communication.

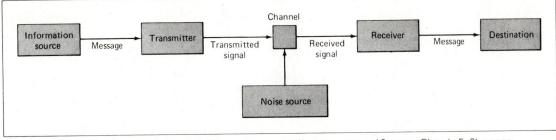

Figure 26.3 Shannon's model of the communication process. (*Source:* Claude E. Shannon and Warren Weaver, *The Mathematical Theory of Communication*, 11th printing, 1967 (Urbana: University of Illinois Press, 1964. Used by permission.)

26.3.1 Decoder and Receiver

One of the simpler, more universal models appears in Figure 26.4. Note that it applies equally well to either interpersonal or mass communication.

As noted above, most research in mass communication has focused on the decoder and receiver, that is, effects on the audience. During the 1980s, however, researchers seemed to rediscover the individual-differences approach in their study of audience members. Discarding outdated notions of a simplistic stimulus-response bullet theory, researchers again focused on how individuals attend to, process, and utilize media messages.

26.3.2 Message

A second line of research has concentrated on the message (Figure 26.5). Here scholars use **content analysis,** a research technique

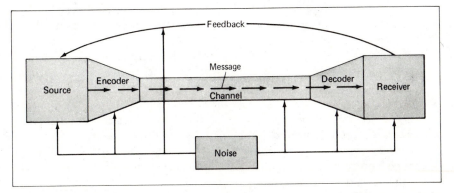

Figure 26.4 Communication model. A model such as this can be used to represent almost any level of human communication—for example, the present discussion. My mind is the source, and I have a message about communication models to get to your mind, the receiver. I encode my message by committing it to writing. It travels through the channels of this book and the light rays that enter your eyes as reflected from the printed symbols on this page. You decode the message by readingt it, and your mind assimilates it. Feedback could be as direct and specific as a letter from you or as general as sales of this book. Noise may enter at any point in the model; my inability to explain, your watching television while trying to read, a poor printing job on this page, and so on.

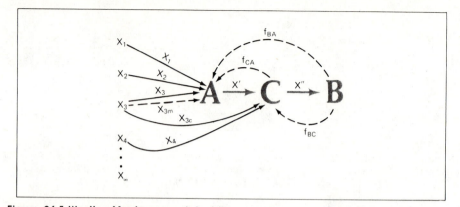

Figure 26.5 Westley-MacLean model of the mass communication process. This model depicts the gatekeeper functions (i.e., culling and selection of messages and themes for presentation). Westley and MacLean explain it as follows:

> The messages C transmits to B (X″) represent his selections from both messages to him from A's (X′) and C's selections and abstractions from Xs in his own sensory field (X_{3C}, X_4), which may or may not be Xs in A's field. Feedback not only moves from B to A (f_{BA}) and from B to C (f_{BC}) but also from C to A (f_{CA}). Clearly, in the mass communication situation, a large number of Cs receive from a very large number of As and transmit to a vastly larger number of Bs, who simultaneously receive from other Cs.

(*Source:* Bruce H. Westley and Malcolm S. MacLean, Jr., "A Conceptual Model for Communication Research," *Journalism Quarterly*, 34 (Winter 1957): 35. Reprinted by permission.)

that employs scientific methodology (orderly procedures) to describe the message—for example, number of violent acts in a television program, or number and type of portrayals of ethnic minorities in television commercials.

26.3.3 Encoder

A third line of research centers around the encoder, for example, media organizations and their personnel. The narrative-style case study has been used most often in describing encoding activities, but researchers now also use quantitative methodology. The role of the gatekeeper (person[s] that decides which encoded media messages will be sent through the channel for ultimate reception; Section 26.1.2) has been the focus of considerable media research.

26.3.4 Feedback

One type of feedback research is part and parcel of the very system of commercial radio and television—the ratings. But feedback also includes consumer behavior in response to advertising and telephone calls resulting from per-inquiry and direct-response marketing formats. It encompasses unsolicited letters, telegrams, and telephone calls to networks, outlets, and individual performers. Some content analysis has been done on certain types of feedback to the mass media as well.

26.3.5 Channel

Researchers have studied channels, that is, the media themselves. Often these studies take the form of surveys designed to determine public attitudes toward a particular medium. Another form of channel study occurred with great frequency during the 1950s and 1960s. That was the period during which considerable laboratory research was carried out to determine television's suitability as a channel for education.

26.3.5.1 Marshall McLuhan Quite a different approach gained popularity in the 1960s. In a number of books and articles, the late Herbert Marshall McLuhan, a Canadian scholar of English literature, advanced the theory that media content really does not matter. The structure of information (the way it is presented) on the dominant medium (the one from which most people get most information) of a culture affects the way members of that culture perceive reality. If you lived when print was the dominant medium, you viewed the world in terms of the printed page—that is, linearly, with the cold logic of the eye, each part in its right place at the right time.

Now, television is the dominant medium. According to McLuhan, since the television picture is a mosaic (bits of information; Section 12.2.2) rather than a solid visual ground, you must fill in the spaces between the bits (you do this unconsciously), and—a big jump in logic here!—in the process you become involved in the medium with *all* your senses. So you view the world in all-sensory terms.

McLuhan's thesis that **the medium is the message** proved popular with two disparate groups—commercial television and advertising people and the so-called "counterculture" young people of the 1960s. Although McLuhan's theory had to do with effects, social scientists found it difficult to test empirically. Therefore, it failed to meet one important criterion of a good theory—testability. As a result, it could not be proved or disproved with numbers, and most academics

and researchers tended to reject it out of hand. By the 1990s, the popularity of McLuhan's approach had all but disappeared.

NOTES

1. Warren Breed, "Social Control in the News Room? A Functional Analysis," *Social Forces* 33 (1955): 326.
2. Reported as "The Gatekeeper: A Case Study in the Selection of News," *Journalism Quarterly*, 27 (1950): 383.
3. James E. Lynch, "Seven Days with 'All in the Family'," *Journal of Broadcasting* 17 (1973): 259.
4. J. W. Ravage, "' . . . Not in the Quality Business.' A Case Study of Contemporary Television Production," *Journal of Broadcasting* 21 (1977): 47.
5. Paul F. Lazarsfeld, Bernard Berelson, and Hazel Gaudet, *The People's Choice* (New York: Columbia UP, 1948).
6. Charles R. Wright, *Mass Communication: A Sociological Perspective*, 2d ed. (New York: Random, 1975), pp. 8–22.
7. Dennis K. Davis and Stanley J. Baran, *Mass Communication and Everyday Life: A Perspective on Theory and Effects* (Belmont: Wadsworth, 1981).
8. Erving Goffman, *Frame Analysis: An Essay on the Organization of Experience* (Cambridge: Harvard UP, 1974).
9. "Mass Media and Social Change in Developed Societies," *Mass Communication Review Yearbook* (Beverly Hills: Sage, 1980) 1: 657–678; and "The Spiral of Silence: A Theory of Public Opinion," *Journal of Communication* 24 (1974): 43–51.
10. Reprinted along with exposition and comment by Warren Weaver in book form as *The Mathematical Theory of Communication* (Urbana: U of Illinois P, 1949).

FURTHER READING

De Fleur, Melvin, and Sandra Ball-Rokeach. *Theories of Mass Communication*. 5th ed. New York: Longman, 1989. Reports history and development of mass communication theory, including dependency theory.

Hsia, M. J. *Mass Communication Research Methods: A Step-By-Step Approach.* Hillsdale: Erlbaum, 1988.

Lowery, Shearon A., and Melvin L. De Fleur. *Milestones in Mass Communication Research.* 2d ed. New York: Longman, 1988. Series of essays on major media events and phenomena.

McCombs, Maxwell E., and Lee Becker. *Using Mass Communication Theory.* Englewood Cliffs: Prentice, 1979. Discusses practical applications of media theory.

McLuhan, [Herbert] Marshall. *Understanding Media: The Extensions of Man.* New York: McGraw, 1966. Expounds "the medium is the message."

McQuail, Denis. *Mass Communication Theory: An Introduction,* 2d ed. Newbury Park: Sage, 1987. Excellent review of theoretical approaches.

Severin, Warner, and James Tankard, Jr. *Communication Theories: Origins, Methods, Uses.* 2d ed. New York: Hastings, 1988. Includes media theory.

Singletary, Michael W., and Gerald Stone. *Communication Theory and Research.* Ames: Iowa State UP, 1988. Includes both explanations and exercises.

Startt, James D., and William David Sloan. *Historical Methods in Mass Communication.* Hillsdale: Erlbaum, 1989.

Tan, Alexis S. *Mass Communication Theories and Research.* Columbus: Grid, 1981. Also a good review of theoretical approaches.

Wimmer, Roger D., and Joseph R. Dominick. *Mass Media Research: An Introduction.* Belmont: Wadsworth, 1983. Basic introduction to quantitative research.

INDEX